QuarkXPress 4–Keyboard Shortcuts

Navigation

Command	Mac	Windows
Fit in Window	⌘+0	Ctrl+0
Fit largest spread in window	⌘+Option+0	Ctrl+Alt+0
Actual Size	⌘+1	Ctrl+1
Thumbnails	Shift+F6	Shift+F6
Show/Hide Guides	F7	F7
Show/Hide Baseline Grid	Option+F7	Ctrl+F7
Snap to Guides	Shift+F7	Shift+F7
Show/Hide Rulers	⌘+R	Ctrl+R
Show/Hide Invisibles	⌘+I	Ctrl+I
Go to Page	⌘+J	Ctrl+J
Display master pages	Shift+F10	Shift+F4
Display next master page	Option+F10	Ctrl+Shift+F4
Display previous master page	Option+Shift+F10	Ctrl+Shift+F3
Display document pages	Shift+F10	Shift+F4
Display next page	Shift+Page Down	Shift+Page Down
Display previous page	Shift+Page Up	Shift+Page Up

Special Characters

Command	Mac	Windows
Indent here	⌘+\	Ctrl+\
Discretionary new line	⌘+Return	Ctrl+Enter
New paragraph	Return	Enter
New line	Shift+Return	Shift+Enter
New column	Enter	Enter
New box	Shift+Enter	Shift+Enter
Right-indent tab	Option+Tab	Shift+Tab
Nonbreaking standard hyphen	⌘+=	Ctrl+=
Discretionary (soft) hyphen	⌘+-	Ctrl+-
Nonbreaking en dash	Option+-	Ctrl+Alt+Shift+-
Breaking em dash	Option+Shift+-	Ctrl+Shift+-
Nonbreaking em dash	⌘+Option+=	Ctrl+Alt+Shift+=
Nonbreaking standard space	⌘+Spacebar	Ctrl+5
Breaking en space	Option+Spacebar	Ctrl+Shift+6
Nonbreaking en space	⌘+Option+Spacebar	Ctrl+Alt+Shift+6
Breaking flex space	Option+Shift+Spacebar	Ctrl+Shift+5
Nonbreaking flex space	⌘+Option+Shift+Spacebar	Ctrl+Alt+Shift+5

Special Characters

Command	Mac	Windows
Get Picture	⌘+E	Ctrl+E
Increase scale 5%	⌘+Option+Shift+>	Ctrl+Alt+Shift+>
Decrease scale 5%	⌘+Option+Shift+<	Ctrl+Alt+Shift+<
Resize box constraining box shape	Shift+drag	Shift+drag
Resize box maintaining aspect ratio	Option+Shift+drag	Alt+Shift+drag
Resize box and scale picture	⌘+drag	Ctrl+drag
Resize box and scale picture constraining box shape	⌘+Shift+drag	Ctrl+Shift+drag
Resize box and scale picture maintaining proportions	⌘+Option+Shift+drag	Ctrl+Alt+Shift+drag
Center picture	⌘+Shift+M	Ctrl+Shift+M
Fit picture to box	⌘+Shift+F	Ctrl+Shift+F
Fit picture to box maintaining proportions	⌘+Option+Shift+F	Ctrl+Option+Shift+F
Make picture negative	⌘+Shift+-	Ctrl+Shift+-

Palettes

Command	Mac	Windows
Show/Hide Tools	F8	F8
Show/Hide Measurements	F9	F9
Show/Hide Document Layout	F10	F10
Show/Hide Style Sheets	F11	F11
Show/Hide Colors	F12	F12
Show/Hide Trap Information	Option+F12	Ctrl+F12
Show/Hide Lists	Option+F11	Ctrl+F11

Using
QuarkXPress
4

Kelly Kordes Anton

Rochelle Barnhart

Kate Binder

David B. Gray

Joe Millay

A Division of Macmillan Computer Publishing, USA
201 W. 103rd Street
Indianapolis, Indiana 46290

Contents at a Glance

Using QuarkXPress 4

International Standard Book Number: 0-7897-1659-3

Library of Congress Catalog Card Number: 98-84535

Printed in the United States of America

First Printing: *May 1998*

00   99   98   4   3   2   1

Trademarks

Publisher
Jordan Gold

Executive Editor
Beth Millett

Managing Editor
Brice Gosnell

Credits

Acquisitions Editor
Rachel Byers

Development Editor
Robyn Holtzman

Project Editor
Kevin Laseau

Copy Editors
San Dee Phillips
Michael Brumitt
Cheri Clark

Technical Editors
Kate Binder
Joe Millay

Cover Designers
Dan Armstrong
Ruth Harvey

Book Designers
Nathan Clement
Ruth Harvey

Indexer
Bruce Clingaman

Production
Marcia Deboy
Michael Dietsch
Jennifer Earhart
Cynthia Fields
Maureen West

Contents

About the Authors

Kelly Kordes Anton is a freelance technical and marketing writer specializing in publishing, while also dabbling in everything from accounting systems to local newsletters. Kelly recently completed five years of employment at Quark, Inc. where she started out writing about Apple Events scripting and eventually led the development of the QuarkXPress 4.0 documentation. As a home-based freelancer, Kelly now has the opportunity to spend more time with her 18-month-old son, Robert.

Rochelle Barnhart has been a freelance desktop production artist since 1985 (d/b/a Type & More). Rochelle has also done Quark training and seminars for companies across the U.S. and Canada. She teaches regular QuarkXPress classes at the Electronic Imaging Center in Minneapolis, and maintains an active desktop production business.

Kate Binder is a freelance writer and production artist living on Boston's North Shore. The author of *Teach Yourself QuarkXPress 4 in 14 Days* and coauthor of *Photoshop 4 Complete*, she also writes articles on desktop production tools and techniques for Desktop Publishers Journal. Her three favorite things (this month) are her Power Mac, cable modems, and continuous electrical power. She can be reached at UrsaDesign@aol.com, and her Web page is at http://members.aol.com/ursadesign.

David B. Gray is the executive director of the Society for News Design, a 2500-plus member organization in 51 countries, made up of people involved in the design of news and information for newspapers, magazines, and the new media. A graduate of the Rhode Island School of Design, he had a 28-year career at the *Providence Journal-Bulletin* newspaper as a designer, photo editor, and managing editor in the news operation of the papers.

His design work has appeared in *Graphics Annual* and he has edited and designed many books and special reports. He has written for *DESIGN*, The Journal of SND; *News Photographer* magazine; *Editor* and *Publisher* and other magazines. He is a past president of the New England Associated Press News Executives Association (NEAPNEA). He is currently an adjunct faculty member at RISD and is an authorized Quark trainer.

Joe Millay is employed at Americolor, the prepress divison of The Printing Company in Indianapolis. He is a graduate of Northern Kentucky University.

Dedication

To my mother, Kathleen Kordes, an outstanding grandmother.

> *— Kelly*

To Reggie White the Younger, for all her help and support.

> *— Kate*

To my wife, Janet, for enduring the long nights while I worked in front of the computer, thinking all the while it was like watching TV; and to Lindsey, the first grandchild, who will probably grow up thinking computers are just another tool like a toaster, and not the frustrating complication in our lives that they have been so far.

> *— David*

For Linus

> *— Joe*

Acknowledgments

From Kelly Kordes Anton: Thank you to Elizabeth Jones, Steve Gray, Trevor Alyn, Dan Murphy, and Shawn McLaughlin of Quark for their friendship and constant supply of information. Also, thanks to Dan Brogan, Kimberlee Lynch, and Amanda Faison at *5280 Magazine* for advice and publishing samples, and to Patrick Kanouff for legal advice. Kelly also thanks her very supportive family and friends: John Anton, Robert Anton, Dennis Kordes, Jean Cantey, and Ralph Risch.

From Rochelle Barnhardt: Thanks to Heidi Waldmann, Eureka! Design in St. Paul Minnesota for assistance with questions related to using QXP in the Windows operating system and to Harry Brindley, Intelligent Ideas, Johannesbury, Gauteng (RSA) for help with scripting for QXP.

From Joe Millay: To my Dad, for allowing me to spend so much time on his computer.

To my wife, Denise, for never complaining about the amount of time I spend on my computer.

To Bob Knight, for providing me with a great leisure time activity and for running a big time college sports program the way it should be run.

To the production department at Macmillan, I can certainly appreciate your work.

Introduction

Since its 1986 release, QuarkXPress has come to rule the design world. It's the top page layout application among design professionals, and for good reason. Its strong feature set allows users to work like artists, placing elements on a page "by eye" and rearranging them at will, and like draftspeople, precisely positioning and linking elements in iron-clad grids. As a QuarkXPress user, you can choose either way of working or combine the two to come up with the way that works best for you.

Power is what QuarkXPress is all about today. In addition to its basic page layout framework and excellent text formatting tools, it contains a huge number of advanced features that are always available but never intrusive, like automatic trapping and the ability to create Be[as]zier objects and multi-ink colors. Whether you're designing and producing 1/8-page newspaper ads or 200-page coffee table books, QuarkXPress is the best tool available.

With the release of QuarkXPress 4, Quark added features in three major areas:

- *Drawing.* Version 4 incorporates Be[as]zier drawing tools similar to those found in illustration programs like Adobe Illustrator, Macromedia FreeHand, and CorelDraw. Be[as]zier boxes can hold imported pictures or text, or be used simply as free-standing graphic elements. Perhaps most fun of all, text can be bound to a Be[as]zier shape[md]now it's easy to flow text in a circle, around corners, or along curving or angled freeform lines.

- *Color.* Support for Pantone Hexachrome and multi-ink colors has been added. Hexachrome's six printing ink colors (the standard four process colors plus orange and green) increase the gamut of printable colors enormously and add vibrancy to existing process colors. Now, if your printing company supports six-color printing, you can take full advantage of its possibilities. Meanwhile, it's now possible to mix spot and process inks within QuarkXPress documents just as you can in real life. Need a darker version of that spot purple ink? Just add black!

- *Long document production.* The new Book, Index, and Lists features allow you to assemble individual files into a long document, automate indexing of that document, and then create automatic tables of contents, lists of tables, and other lists. Smoothly integrated into QuarkXPress's existing feature set, these features expand the program's usefulness by an order of magnitude for long document publishers.

Learning to use these new features to their fullest can be time-consuming—which is why you're holding this book. The goal of *Using QuarkXPress 4* is to teach you what you need to know about QuarkXPress at any given time to accomplish your own goals.

Why This Book?

Have you ever purchased a *Using* book from Que? The *Using* books have proven invaluable to readers as both learning guides and as references for many years. The *Using* series is an industry leader and has practically become an industry standard. We encourage and receive feedback from readers all the time and we consider and implement their suggestions whenever possible.

Using QuarkXPress 4 incorporates fresh new ideas and approaches to the *Using* series. This book is not a compiled authority on all features of QuarkXPress. Instead, it is a streamlined, conversational approach for using QuarkXPress productively and efficiently. New features include:

- *Improved Index. To help you find information the first time you look!* What do you call tasks and features? As we wrote, we anticipated every possible name or description of a task that we've heard people call it. For example, if you wanted to know how to include artwork in your letterhead, where do you look? Should you check the index for artwork, clip art, scanned images, graphics, letterhead, or pictures? The answer is **yes**-check the index for any of those terms and you will find your answer on the first pass.
- *Real-life answers.* Throughout the book you will find *our* real life examples and experiences. After all, we've been there and done that! We understand that *how* to perform a task is only one question you may have, and perhaps the bigger question is *why* and *what for*?
- *Relevant information written just for you!* We have carefully scrutinized which features and tasks to include in this book and have included that that apply to your everyday use of QuarkXPress.

We realize that very few people use as much as 50% of QuarkXPress' capabilities. Our experience tells us that there are two reasons for this:

- *Time*. You can spare the time from work to attend classes on QuarkXPress. You don't have time to explore every nook and cranny of the software. And, when you do need to perform a task that is new to you, you need to get it done quickly.

- *Need*. Why invest in material that teaches you how to perform tasks you never need to perform? QuarkXPress is a powerful (and complex) software program. But does your work include powerful, complex document layout tasks? Will it ever? Why spend time on features you don't need?

- *Reference or Tutorial*. You can learn to quickly perform a task using step-by-step instructions, or you can investigate the why and wherefore of a task with our discussions preceding each task.

- *Wise Investment*. Pay the right price for the right book. We won't waste your valuable bookshelf real estate with redundant or irrelevant material, nor do we assume you "know it all" or need to "know it all." Here is what you need, when you need it, how you need it, with an appropriate price tag.

- *Easy to find procedures*. Every numbered step-by-step procedure in the book has a short title explaining exactly what it does. This saves you time by making it easier to find the exact steps you need to accomplish a task.

- *Cross referencing, to give additional, related information*. We've looked for all the tasks and topics that are related to a topic at hand and referenced those for you. So, if you need to look for coverage that leads up to what you are working on, or if you want to build on the new skill you just mastered, you have the references to easily find the right coverage in the book.

- *Sidebar elements with quick-read headlines save you time*. Often times, we'll want to give you a little tip or note about how to make something work best. Or we'll need to give you a caution or warning about a problem you may encounter. By giving these SideNotes precise titles that explain their topic and by placing them in the margins, we make each one easy to skim while still preserving the flow of text around it.

Who Should Use This Book

Anyone who uses QuarkXPress and needs to accomplish a specific task, solve a problem, or wants to learn a technique that applies to something they need to get done. Basically, anyone who:

- Has basic computer skills but is new to QuarkXPress.
- Uses QuarkXPress, but wants to become more proficient in QuarkXPress.
- Uses QuarkXPress at work.
- Uses QuarkXPress at home.
- Needs to create special documents, such as posters, magazine layouts, or newsletters.

How This Book is Organized

Using QuarkXPress 4 has task-oriented, easy-to-navigate tutorials and reference information presented in a logical progression from simple to complex tasks. It covers features of the program you use in your daily work. Features are explained thoroughly. Examples are real life. You can work through the book lesson by lesson or you can find specific information when you need to perform a job quickly.

Using QuarkXPress 4 is divided into six parts.

Part I: Getting Started

This section introduces new features in QuarkXPress 4, explains how to set preferences and defaults, and gets you started creating and saving QuarkXPress documents. With this information, you'll be able to set up QuarkXPress to match the way you work, maximizing your efficiency, and you'll learn about the capabilities and best uses of each tool in QuarkXPress.

Part II: Page Layout

QuarkXPress Documents are built from pages, and pages are built from text, pictures, and graphic elements—each of these kinds of object has its own characteristics. These chapters explain the different kinds of objects that can be created in QuarkXPress, cover different ways of using styles and objects in more than one document, and go through the document-building process step-by-step.

Part III: Adding and Formatting Text

Although QuarkXPress is not a word processor, text is the reason for the program's existence. At some point in almost every document you create, you'll need to import or create text and edit it. Part III starts with creating a multi-page text flow, then moves on to editing and formatting text. The chapters cover the fine points of typographical excellence, as well as creating and applying style sheets.

Part IV: Adding Graphics

Supporting most common graphic file formats, QuarkXPress lets you bring imported pictures into the mix, as well as graphic elements created within the program. Here you'll learn how to illustrate with complex Bézier objects, how to modify images, and how to combine type and graphics for myriad effects.

Part V: Color and Output

Color is a complex subject, and getting documents from the screen of your computer onto paper or film is only slightly less complicated. With QuarkXPress's advanced color and output features, however, you only need to delve as far into these subjects as you have time for. Here you can learn some color theory, some printing technology and terms, and ways to get the most for your money when using color or sending documents for output. If you're in a hurry, you can start with the basics of creating, altering, and applying colors and printing documents and move on to the advanced stuff later. Also covered in this section are ways of turning a print project into a multimedia one, destined for the World Wide Web or a desktop presentation.

Part VI: Advanced Features

These days, working in QuarkXPress often means more than laying out a page or two. Fortunately, QuarkXPress's XTension architecture allows third-party vendors (along with Quark itself) to supply new features in the form of add-on software that can be installed when you need it and uninstalled when you don't. This section covers the care and feeding of XTensions, along with ways to use XPress Tags, QuarkXPress's text tagging language, to automate text formatting. Here you'll also discover version 4's new long document features, which allow you to automate the creation of indexes and tables of contents and collect individual files together into multi-file books.

Conventions Used in This Book

Commands, directions, and explanations in this book are presented in the clearest format possible. The following items are some of the features that will make this book easier for you to use:

- *Menu and dialog box commands and options.* You can easily find the onscreen menu and dialog box commands by looking for bold text like you see in this direction: Open the **File** menu and click **<u>S</u>ave**.

- *Hotkeys for commands.* The underlined keys onscreen that activate commands and options are also underlined in the book as shown in the previous example.

- *Combination and shortcut keystrokes.* Text that directs you to hold down several keys simultaneously is connected with a plus sign (+), such as Ctrl+P.

- *Graphical icons with the commands they execute.* Look for icons like this ⊕ in text and steps. These indicate buttons onscreen that you can click to accomplish the procedure.

- *Cross references.* If there's a related topic that is prerequisite to the section or steps you are reading, or a topic that builds further on what you are reading, you'll find the cross reference to it after the steps or at the end of the section like this:

SEE ALSO

➤ *To see how to create newspaper columns, see page xx*

- *Glossary terms.* For all the terms that appear in the glossary, you'll find the first appearance of that term in the text in *italic* along with its definition.

- *Sidebars.* Information related to the task at hand, or "inside" information from the author is offset in sidebars as not to interfere with the task at hand and to make it easy to find this valuable information. Each of these sidebars has a short title to help you quickly identify the information you'll find there. You'll find the same kind of information in these that you might find in notes, tips, or warnings in other books but here, the titles should be more informative.

Your screen may look slightly different from some of the examples in this book. This is due to various options during installation and because of hardware setup.

Getting Started

Introducing QuarkXPress 4

Before getting into hundreds of pages of specifics about QuarkXPress 4, this text will spend a little time reviewing the basics of the program. The days of drafting boards, type galleys, layout boards, waxers, and X-Acto knives for making keylines are almost gone. The electronic keyline has captured the graphics industry, and that is where this discussion starts.

QuarkXPress is page layout software; its sole purpose is to help you design and lay out documents for printing. XPress will not make you a good graphic designer, a good writer, or a good typesetter. However, it does give you all the tools you need to become any or all of those things. You can use it to design and lay out documents as simple as a one-color sign for posting on a telephone pole announcing that you have lost your pet gerbil, to multicolor, multipage catalogs with varnishes, die cuts, and more. As your QuarkXPress skills improve, so will the quality and reliability of your printed materials. That's what this book is here for, and that's why you've picked up this book.

Everything Goes in a Box

Learn to love them; QuarkXPress depends on them—they're called boxes. The first and main idea you need to understand is that everything you do in QuarkXPress goes in a box of some sort. QuarkXPress 4 has taken the concept of boxes to some new and exciting heights, so set aside the idea of a box as a square or rectangular form. You'll work with four types of boxes (if you count lines); they are the basic building blocks for your document. These are the four types:

- *Text boxes* in various shapes
- *Picture boxes* in various shapes
- *No-content boxes* in various shapes
- *Lines* (which are actually very narrow boxes)

Text, Pictures, and Color in Boxes

Text boxes (no matter what their shape) are the place to type in text or import text from a word processor or the Clipboard.

Picture boxes are the place to put pictures or other graphic images you have created in a drawing, paint, or photo-editing program.

New in QuarkXPress 4 is the no-content box. It too can take any shape, but it accepts neither type nor pictures. It is used only for blocks of color. If you used an earlier version of QuarkXPress, you'll appreciate this little box. No longer will you have to worry about the problems sometimes created by empty text or picture boxes when you send your work to an *imagesetter* (a high-resolution, high-quality film or paper output device).

Lines and Text Paths (They're Really Boxes)

Think of lines as very thin boxes. You can't put anything inside them, but you can color them. QuarkXPress 4 offers the same default lines present in earlier versions and lets you create custom line styles.

Text aligned along a path (new to version 4) is also a type of box. You don't have to start with a box, though; the text and its path just become a box, the boundaries of which are determined by the shape of the line and text together. It might be stretching the idea a bit to call this a box, especially if you're new to QuarkXPress, but put aside your high-school geometry ideas about boxes. Just remember that boxes are the basic building blocks and this is one of them.

SEE ALSO

➤ *To create and modify boxes, see page 104*

Frames on Boxes

With one exception, all text and picture boxes can have frames, which are styled similarly to lines. You can create new frames beyond the 11 *PostScript* (scalable) and 9 *bitmapped* (nonscalable) frames offered as defaults. Frames or lines can be any color you have defined, but you cannot use the color None (which is one of the default colors). The one exception is the "box" formed by text on a path because there really is nothing to frame, unlike with a regular text box.

SEE ALSO

➤ *To apply frames (borders) to boxes, see page 114*

Boxes Go on Pages

Well, you have all these boxes; where are you going to put them? You're going to put them on pages. Think of your project as a pyramid: the boxes are the top section of the pyramid, and the pages are the middle. Boxes of all types can go on one page. You might have three or four text boxes, a couple of picture boxes, some type running along a path, and a few lines all on the same page.

You can position your boxes on a page by just moving them around to where you think they look good (a practice that is not uncommon among many graphic designers), or you can position them to within 1/1000 of an inch of a precise spot on the page. The location of a box is determined by the x,y coordinate of the box's upper-left corner. This location is displayed in QuarkXPress's Measurements palette and in the Modify dialog box. At either of these locations, you can type new x,y coordinates and move a box.

One other basic concept about boxes is that they stack on top of each other even if they are not touching or overlapping. This is known as layering. Every time you put a new box on a QuarkXPress page, it goes in its own layer. If you have 15 boxes on a page, you have 15 layers on a page. You can't see the layers, and there is no place in QuarkXPress where the layer number of a box is displayed. However, you can "feel" them.

Sometimes when you move a box that looks as though it is in front, it goes behind another box. This is because the box you're moving has a lower layer number than the one you're trying to put it in front of. Understanding the idea of stacking boxes and layering is important because often you will need to place boxes entirely or partially on top of each other. You can change the order of boxes sitting on top of each other through the **Item** menu's **Bring to Front** and **Send to Back** commands.

SEE ALSO

➤ *To place boxes where you want them on a page, see page 123*

Pages Make Up Documents

The bottom part, the foundation, of the pyramid is the document. Your document can have many pages, but all the pages need to be exactly the same size and orientation (*landscape* or *portrait*). Pages in a document can, however, have different margins and different numbers of columns.

Actually, building the document foundation is the first thing you do when starting a new project in QuarkXPress. When you select **New** from the **File** menu, and then **Document** from the submenu, you are asked to determine the size of your page, the orientation of the page, the number of columns, whether you want to use an automatic text box, and whether you want to have facing pages (like those in a magazine or book) or single pages (as in an advertising flyer).

As you create a new QuarkXPress document, you automatically create a *master page*, which is like an internal template. Every document has at least one master page. What it looks like (until you start working with it) depends on the choices you make in the New Document dialog box.

After you've chosen among all the options in the New Document dialog box and clicked **OK**, your document unfolds on the screen before you, complete with one built-in master page; at this point, you can create more than 200 additional master pages. A document can contain up to 2,000 body pages, depending on the amount of RAM you have available.

While working with your document, you can add more pages (based on either one of the master pages or a blank page), move pages around, delete pages and everything on them, or copy entire pages to another document.

SEE ALSO

➤ *To create a new document, see page 84*

➤ *To create and edit master pages, see page 153*

New Boxes and More

QuarkXPress 4 comes packed full of new features, some of which you'll use every day, others of which are designed for some very specific purposes. Here is a brief introduction to these features, all of which are explained in more detail in appropriate sections of this book.

Beyond Polygons: Bézier Boxes and Lines

In QuarkXPress 3, you could create polygon-shaped text and picture boxes. QuarkXPress 4 adds *Bézier* tools, which let you draw true curves. This means your boxes and lines can take on free-form shapes and have natural-looking curves.

You can create highly complex shapes in QuarkXPress without leaving the program in favor of a drawing program or an illustration program. In the long run, this means fewer files generated outside of QuarkXPress for you to keep track of when the time comes for final output. It also means fewer points that need to be sent through the RIP of those finicky PostScript imagesetters.

SEE ALSO

➤ *To create Bézier objects, see page 314*

Clipping Path and Alpha Channel Support

QuarkXPress 4 reads *clipping path* and *alpha channel* information contained in both imported *TIFF* and *EPS* files. This information is used to isolate an image from its background. Earlier versions of QuarkXPress read clipping paths only in EPS files. Those who prefer to work with TIFF images will appreciate this addition.

Completely new in QuarkXPress 4 is the capability to generate a clipping path while in QuarkXPress for either TIFF or EPS files. You can use this feature to isolate an image from its background or use it to create several different views of the same image. Now you don't have to go back to an image-editing application to make these kinds of decisions.

SEE ALSO

➤ *To create and edit clipping paths, see page 373*

Text Wrap Enhancements

To the delight of many people, QuarkXPress 4 allows you to run text around all sides of an imported graphic (rather than around just one side or the other) and even inside part of an imported image (see Figure 1.1). In addition, the interface for this feature has been improved with a graphical representation of how your text wrap choices will appear in the document.

FIGURE 1.1

QuarkXPress 4 features improved text wrap capabilities.

SEE ALSO

➤ *To wrap text around graphics, see page 384*

Merge and Split Commands for Complex Box Shapes

To simplify creating complex shapes for either picture or text boxes, QuarkXPress allows you to merge a group of boxes into a single box. In many instances, merging shapes is more efficient than trying to draw a complicated shape with a Bézier tool. For example, you can create a heart-shaped box by merging two circles and a triangle, or create an L shape by merging two rectangles. You can also split some complex shapes. There are seven choices under the **Item** menu's **Merge** submenu to help you finesse your merges and splits.

SEE ALSO

➤ *To merge and split boxes, see page 320*

Improved Item Handling

A new command under the **Item** menu is the option to change a box from one type to another. After you have carefully placed and sized a picture box only to remember that you really wanted a text box, all you have to do is change it through the **Content** menu command, and the box is ready to accept your typing or imported text. You also have the choice of having a box with no content at all (you start with either a picture or a text box first). This is for the times when you want neither picture nor text box, just a spot of color somewhere on your page.

You can resize several boxes and lines at the same time if they have been grouped together. There is no menu command for this action; you simply select a corner or side point on the group defined by the dotted marquee and move it. To keep your resizing proportional, hold down the Shift key.

A feature that will be appreciated by anyone who ever has to design any kind of form is the capability to anchor lines within text. This is an improvement on the feature that, in earlier versions, allowed you to anchor either picture or text boxes within another text box. After the line is anchored, it will always move with, and stay attached to, the word immediately preceding it. A line so anchored can still be edited for size, length, style, endpoints, color, and so on.

Another improvement is the capability to anchor nonrectangular boxes within a text box. You can even anchor a piece of text on a path to a point within another text chain.

SEE ALSO

➤ *To change the content of boxes, see page 111*

➤ *To resize objects and groups, see page 106*

➤ *To anchor objects in text, see page 406*

Flexible Item and Content Mode

The Item and Content tools are a bit more forgiving than they used to be. You now can place a graphics in a picture box even if you have the Item tool active, and you can select multiple items even if you have the Content tool active. However, you cannot place text in a box if the Item tool is active. Users of earlier versions will be surprised at how much difference this makes in how you work.

SEE ALSO

➤ *To place graphics in a picture box, see page 338*

➤ *To place text in a text box, see page 204*

Additional Tools and Customizable Tool Palette

At first glance, the Tool palette looks a lot like it did in earlier versions, but on closer inspection you will see some big differences.

First, pop-out choices have been added to the palette. They are available any time you see a small triangle in the upper corner of the tool's box. If you want to use something other than a rectangular text box, you no longer have to go through the hassle of going to the **Item** menu and changing the box there. Instead, you click and hold, and a whole range of choices pops out to the side. There are similar pop-out choices for the Picture Box tools, the Line tool, and the Text-Path tool.

Second, new tools are available, the most significant ones being those related to Bézier paths, whether they're text boxes, picture boxes, or text on a path.

Third, you can customize the Tool palette. If you have a tool you use often that is generally one of the pop-out selections, you can make it part of the main Tool palette by holding down the Control key before you select it. The Tool palette expands to accommodate this addition.

Custom Line and Frame Styles

If you don't like the selection of lines and box frames QuarkXPress 4 gives you, you can create your own. Check near the bottom of the **Edit** menu, where you will find a command called **Dashes & Stripes**. This opens a new dialog box where you can create as many line styles as you like.

SEE ALSO

➤ *To create custom box frames, see page 114*

Character-Based Style Sheets

A welcome feature for anyone doing anything but the most simple documents is the addition of character styles. Earlier versions of QuarkXPress allowed only entire paragraphs to be formatted using *style sheets*. With this version you can create styles and apply them only to a single character or word and use them without losing the overall formatting of the paragraph.

SEE ALSO

➤ *To create and apply character-based style sheets, see page 299*

Find/Change Style Sheets

QuarkXPress 4 has added a search element in the Find/Change dialog box. You can look for particular style sheets and change any or all occurrences to a different style sheet. In this way you can Find/Change all the attributes of a text selection at one time, such as tabs and rules, rather than simply changing font and character information.

SEE ALSO

➤ *To use the Find/Change command, see page 211*

Flow Text on a Curved Path

Another new feature designed to save you the trouble of bouncing back and forth between a drawing/illustration program and QuarkXPress is the capability to flow text along a curved *path*. This, of course, is made possible with the addition of the various Bézier tools. You can place your text along paths created with four different tools: a freehand Bézier line, a point-to-point Bézier line, an angled line, or an orthogonal line. The text is completely editable and can be styled using any of the style sheets available in your document.

SEE ALSO

➤ *To create text paths, see page 396*

Convert Text to a Box

Ever want to put text in text? Ever want to put a picture in your words? Ever want to make your headlines textured? The capability of QuarkXPress 4 to convert text to a box lets you do all of these and much more (see Figure 1.2). Check under the **Style** menu for the **Text to Box** command. This is another new feature that will save you time by letting you stay in QuarkXPress to do something instead of using a different software application.

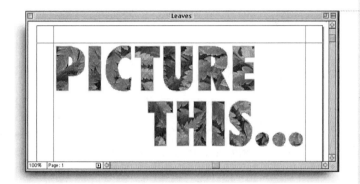

FIGURE 1.2
Converting text to a box allows you to fill it with a photograph texture, among other fun effects.

SEE ALSO

➤ *To convert text to boxes, see page 403*

Book Files for Multidocument Publishing

With version 4.0, QuarkXPress takes a big step toward efficiency in long-document publishing by offering under the **File** menu's **New** submenu the choice of **Book**. This powerful new feature gives you the tools to organize long documents, such as this book, into multiple linked files. Changes made in one of the files can be automatically applied to all the files. If the color palette changes in the *master document*, it will change in all the linked files. If a style sheet changes, it will change in all the files. If you add pages to the third section of the book, all the page numbers in the following sections are updated. If you publish long documents, you'll be more than appreciative of this feature and its related table-of-contents and indexing features.

SEE ALSO

➤ *To create and use book files, see page 577*

Style Sheet-Generated Lists for Tables of Contents

Tables of contents for long (or even short) documents are easily generated through this feature, found under the **Edit** menu's **Lists** command. By creating style sheets used exclusively by document paragraphs such as chapter headings and chapter sub-headings, you can use a few simple steps to automatically generate a table of contents with all the correct page numbers. No more digging around through hard copy or worrying that an extra page somewhere has negated all that hard work.

SEE ALSO

➤ *To create lists, see page 592*

Indexing XTension

Tucked away at the bottom of the **View** menu is a command called **Show Index**. This is your starting point to at least partially automate the indexing process for long documents. Unfortunately, you still need to manually select the words or phrases you want indexed.

SEE ALSO

➤ *To create indexes, see page 600*

Multi-Ink and Hexachrome Colors

Blending spot colors has become a reality with QuarkXPress 4. The Edit Color dialog box gives you the option of combining two or more previously created *spot colors*, or a tint of them, into a new color.

Hexachrome color (also called *High Fidelity color*) allows you to print a wider, more vibrant range of colors. Instead of using just four ink colors for process color, the Pantone Hexachrome color system uses six, orange and green being the additional colors. Your print shop also needs to be able to work with Hexachrome color for you to use this color system.

SEE ALSO

➤ *To create colors that use more than one ink color, see page 466*

➤ *To use colors from the Pantone Hexachrome color matching system, see page 465*

Color Management XTension

International Color Consortium (ICC) *color management* has been added to give your documents more consistent color fidelity. ICC developed a standardized format for creating profiles for each separate input or output device you might use. This industry-wide standard has eliminated the earlier problem of proprietary color device profiles. You will need to have the Quark CMS XTension installed to take advantage of color management.

SEE ALSO

➤ *To use Quark's color management system, see page 467*

Enhanced Printing Controls

A whole range of printing controls, which used to be available only to users who purchased the QuarkPrint XTension, has been folded into this version. You can select which color plates you want to print and select noncontiguous page ranges. You can set up an allowance for *bleed*—especially important when you're exporting a page or an element as an EPS file. You also can select a Fit to Page option and get a thumbnail preview of how your document will print on the paper size you have selected.

SEE ALSO

➤ *To print documents, see page 495*

Print Styles for Saving Print Settings

If you find yourself changing your print settings every time you output a file, you'll appreciate the capability to create, name, save, and instantly apply print settings by using the **Edit** menu's Print Styles command. Create settings for your color proofing device, for film negative, film positive, different paper sizes—the list could go on. After you have saved your print styles, a quick trip to the **Print Style** pop-up menu in the Print dialog box is all you'll need the next time you want to use identical settings.

SEE ALSO

➤ *To create and use print styles, see page 515*

Selective Append of Style Sheets, H&Js, Colors, and Such

Reusing a style you created for a previous document saves time and often adds the consistency you seek. Significantly improved in QuarkXPress 4 is the activity known as *appending*. A new command called **Append** has been added to the **File** menu. Using it lets you append all sorts of things at the same time, yet be selective about your choices (see Figure 1.3). You can pick just one or two paragraph styles, a couple of colors, and perhaps one H&J from very long lists. You can also directly append style sheets, colors, H&J settings, list settings, and Dashes & Stripes settings from the **Edit** menu.

FIGURE 1.3

The new Append dialog box allows you to choose which styles to import.

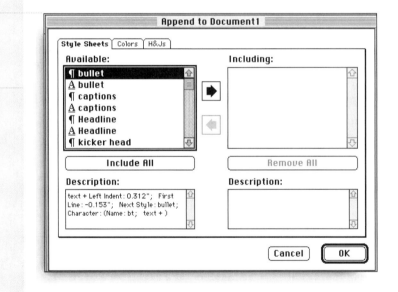

The dialog box gives you a description of the item you have selected. If there is a conflict with something already existing in the target document, you will see a complete description of the conflict and be presented with four choices. If you want to rename the item you are bringing into the document, you can do it then and there.

If you append style sheets that contain colors, *H&Js*, or other items not available in the target document, the Append command will bring in all the necessary features to make the style work. In previous versions, you had to append colors and H&Js (hyphenation and justification settings) before you appended style sheets.

When you append style sheets from a document created in QuarkXPress 3, *character styles* are automatically created to accompany every *paragraph style*. This means you can have several new character styles added to your document that are actually the same but have different names based on the paragraph style to which they are attached. For example, you might find a Text character style and a Bullet character style that are exactly the same.

SEE ALSO

➤ *To append items from other documents, see page 146*

XTensions Manager and PPD Manager

A built-in XTensions Manager gives you control over which *XTensions* load when you open QuarkXPress (see Figure 1.4). You can create sets of XTensions for specific types of work or even for a specific document, if you want. However, the XTensions Manager does not change active XTensions on the fly. You must quit and reopen QuarkXPress before a new set is activated. Although you cannot disable the XTensions Manager, you do have control over when it appears—when there has been a change in the content of the XTension folder, when there is a conflict between XTensions, or every time you open QuarkXPress. When QuarkXPress is open, you can make changes, or create new sets, by choosing **XTensions Manager** from the **Utilities** menu to display the XTensions Manager dialog box. Changes will take effect the next time you open the application.

The PPD Manager (choose **PPD Manager** from the **Utilities** menu) allows you to select which printer descriptions are available in the Print dialog box (see Figure 1.5). Activating *PPDs* only for printers you actually use will streamline your work.

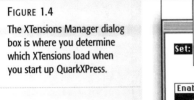

FIGURE 1.4

The XTensions Manager dialog
box is where you determine
which XTensions load when
you start up QuarkXPress.

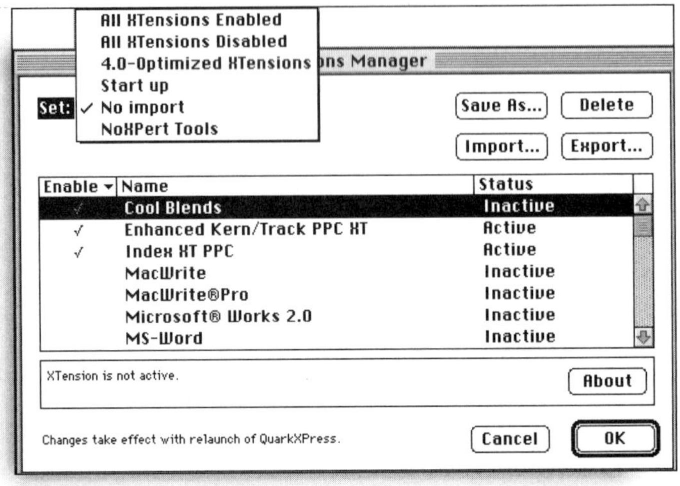

FIGURE 1.5

The PPD Manager dialog box
lists all available printer
descriptions and shows which
will be available in the Print
dialog box.

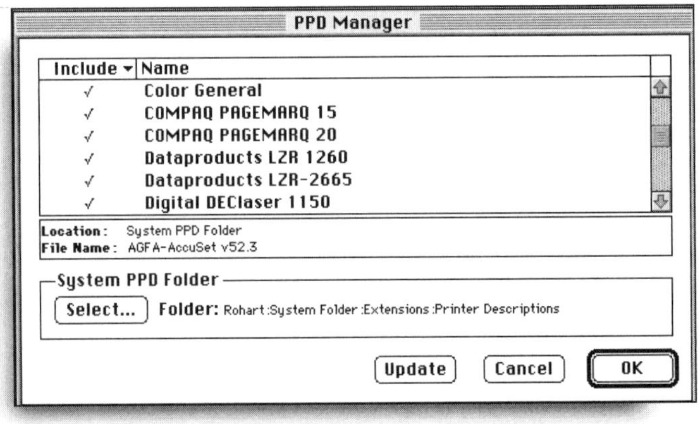

SEE ALSO

➤ *To use the XTensions Manager, see page 555*

➤ *To use the PPD Manager, see page 492*

The New Interface

At first glance, QuarkXPress 4 will look quite familiar to users of earlier versions. Yet there are some major changes in the design of the interface, all created to make your work easier and faster.

Tool Palette

The Tool palette retains its previous look. The order of tools is exactly the same. After you start working with this palette, however, you will find some significant changes (see Figure 1.6).

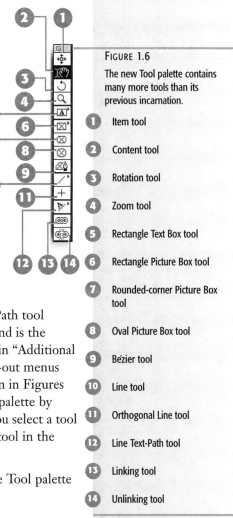

FIGURE 1.6

The new Tool palette contains many more tools than its previous incarnation.

1. Item tool
2. Content tool
3. Rotation tool
4. Zoom tool
5. Rectangle Text Box tool
6. Rectangle Picture Box tool
7. Rounded-corner Picture Box tool
8. Oval Picture Box tool
9. Bézier tool
10. Line tool
11. Orthogonal Line tool
12. Line Text-Path tool
13. Linking tool
14. Unlinking tool

The first change is the addition of the Line Text-Path tool located directly above the Linking tools. The second is the presence of the pop-out menus mentioned earlier in "Additional Tools and Customizable Tool Palette." These pop-out menus are where the other new tools are hidden, as shown in Figures 1.7 through 1.10. You select a tool in the pop-out palette by dragging and releasing your cursor on it. When you select a tool from the pop-out window, it replaces the original tool in the main palette.

The third change is the capability to customize the Tool palette for the tools you use most often.

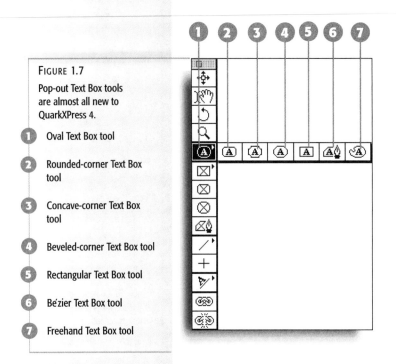

FIGURE 1.7

Pop-out Text Box tools are almost all new to QuarkXPress 4.

1 Oval Text Box tool

2 Rounded-corner Text Box tool

3 Concave-corner Text Box tool

4 Beveled-corner Text Box tool

5 Rectangular Text Box tool

6 Bézier Text Box tool

7 Freehand Text Box tool

SEE ALSO

➤ *To customize the Tool palette, see page* 79

This feature is explained in detail in Chapter 2, "Setting Up Shop."

Tabbed Dialog Boxes

Though new to QuarkXPress, the tabbed dialog boxes will be familiar to many users because other software programs also use this type of interface. You can move to a new tab by clicking on a tab or with ⌘+Tab (Ctrl+Tab). Move through any dialog box which requires you to enter numbers using the Tab key alone to jump from one field to the next.

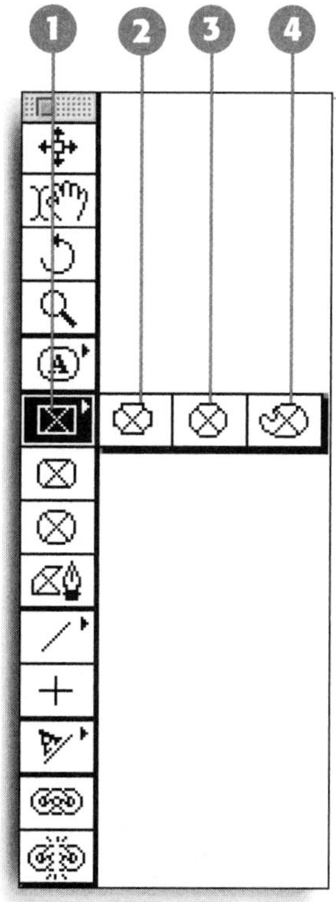

FIGURE 1.8

Pop-out Picture Box tools don't include the Rounded-corner and Oval Picture Box tools because they're found in the main Tool palette.

1 Rectangular Picture Box tool

2 Concave-corner Picture Box tool

3 Beveled-corner Picture Box tool

4 Freehand Picture Box tool

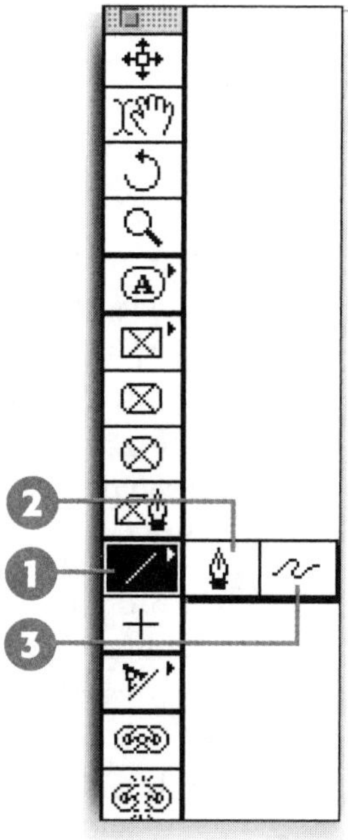

FIGURE 1.9

Pop-out Line tools include a Bézier and Freehand Line tool.

1 Line tool

2 Bézier Line tool

3 Freehand Line tool

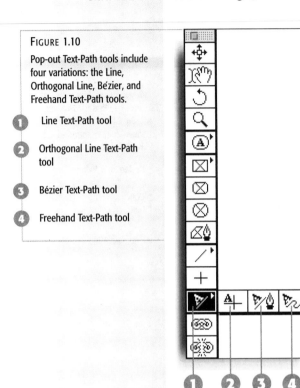

FIGURE 1.10

Pop-out Text-Path tools include four variations: the Line, Orthogonal Line, Bézier, and Freehand Text-Path tools.

1 Line Text-Path tool

2 Orthogonal Line Text-Path tool

3 Bézier Text-Path tool

4 Freehand Text-Path tool

Tabbed dialog boxes are used for the Application Preferences (see Figure 1.11), Document Preferences, Paragraph Formats, Modify, Usage, and Print dialog boxes. In each of these instances, you'll see selections in the tabs that used to require you to go to a separate dialog box.

Previous users will find the most changes in the Document Preferences dialog box, shown in Figure 1.12. Trapping, Typographic, and Tool Preferences, which used to be accessed separately, are now grouped under Document Preferences. **Trapping** and **Tool** have their own tabs, and items that used to appear under Typographic Preferences have been split into two separate tabs, **Paragraph** and **Character**.

The Print tabbed dialog box, shown in Figure 1.13, contains all the commands you need for printing. Those items that in earlier versions were under the Page Setup dialog box have been combined into this one location. Users who regularly reset print controls will be pleased with this enhancement.

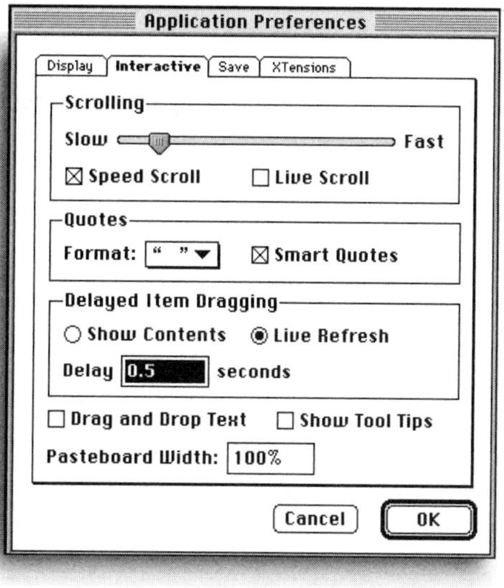

Application Preferences

Display | **Interactive** | Save | XTensions

┌─Scrolling───────────────────────────
│ Slow ──●──────────────── Fast
│ ☒ Speed Scroll   ☐ Live Scroll

┌─Quotes──────────────────────────────
│ Format: " " ▼   ☒ Smart Quotes

┌─Delayed Item Dragging───────────────
│ ○ Show Contents ⦿ Live Refresh
│ Delay 0.5 seconds

☐ Drag and Drop Text   ☐ Show Tool Tips
Pasteboard Width: 100%

[Cancel] [OK]

FIGURE 1.11

The Application Preferences tabbed dialog box includes controls that affect the entire QuarkXPress application.

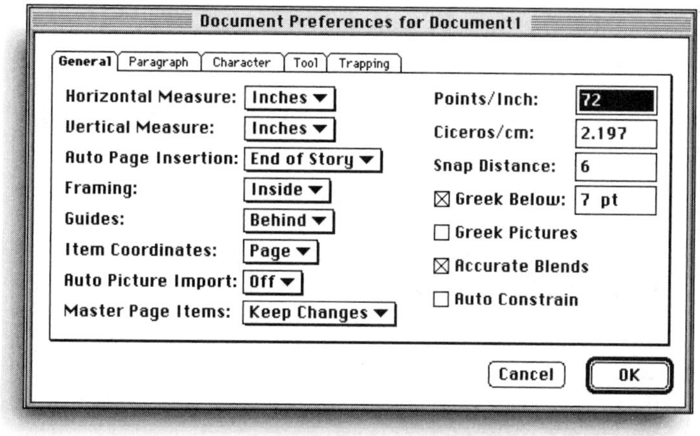

Document Preferences for Document1

General | Paragraph | Character | Tool | Trapping

Horizontal Measure: Inches ▼
Vertical Measure: Inches ▼
Auto Page Insertion: End of Story ▼
Framing: Inside ▼
Guides: Behind ▼
Item Coordinates: Page ▼
Auto Picture Import: Off ▼
Master Page Items: Keep Changes ▼

Points/Inch: 72
Ciceros/cm: 2.197
Snap Distance: 6
☒ Greek Below: 7 pt
☐ Greek Pictures
☒ Accurate Blends
☐ Auto Constrain

[Cancel] [OK]

FIGURE 1.12

The Document Preferences tabbed dialog box includes controls that affect only the current document.

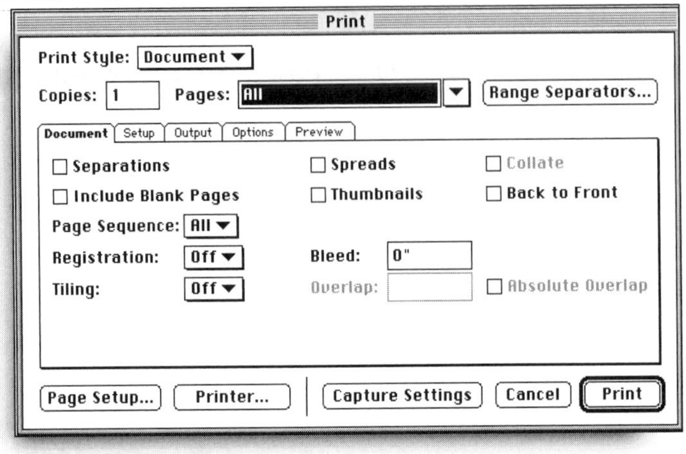

FIGURE 1.13

The Print tabbed dialog box
has many more options than
its former incarnation.

FIGURE 1.13

The Print tabbed dialog box
has many more options than
its former incarnation.

The new Usage tabbed dialog box (choose **Usage** from the
Utilities menu), shown in Figure 1.14, gives you access to both
font and picture usage at the same time, as well as providing
more complete information.

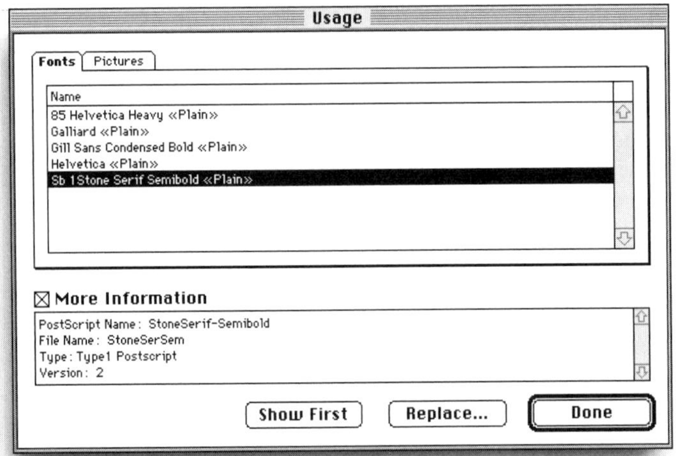

FIGURE 1.14

The Usage tabbed dialog box
shows both picture and font
use information.

It is important to point out that when you either make a menu selection or use a keyboard command, you will go to these same tabbed dialog boxes, with the appropriate tab already open. For example, if you want to change leading and you use either the **Leading** command in the **Style** menu or ⌘+Shift+E (Ctrl+Shift+E), you get the Paragraph Attributes tabbed dialog box, shown in Figure 1.15, opened to the **Format** tab with the entry field for **Leading** already highlighted. If you want to change the runaround on an item and you use the **Item** menu's **Runaround** command or ⌘+T (Ctrl+T), you are taken to the Modify tabbed dialog box opened to the **Runaround** tab.

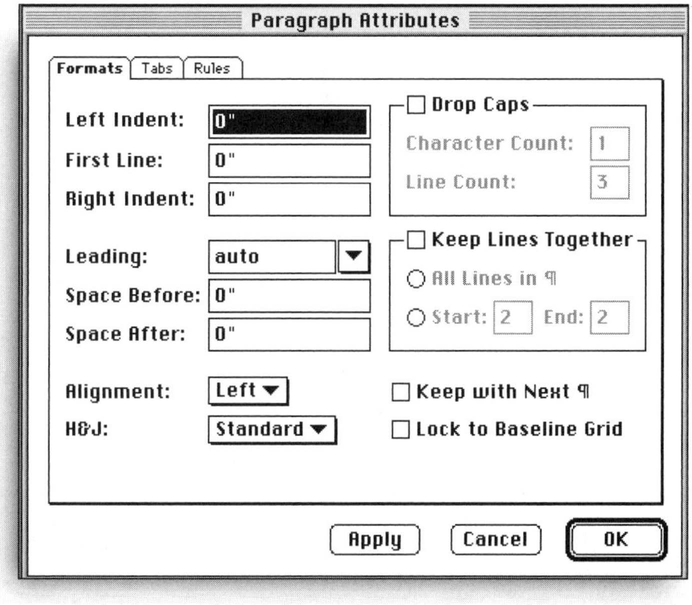

FIGURE 1.15

The Paragraph Attributes tabbed dialog box incorporates controls for rules and tabs.

The Modify tabbed dialog box, shown in Figure 1.16, contains everything that used to be in the Modify dialog box, plus access to frames and runarounds, as well as an **Apply** button.

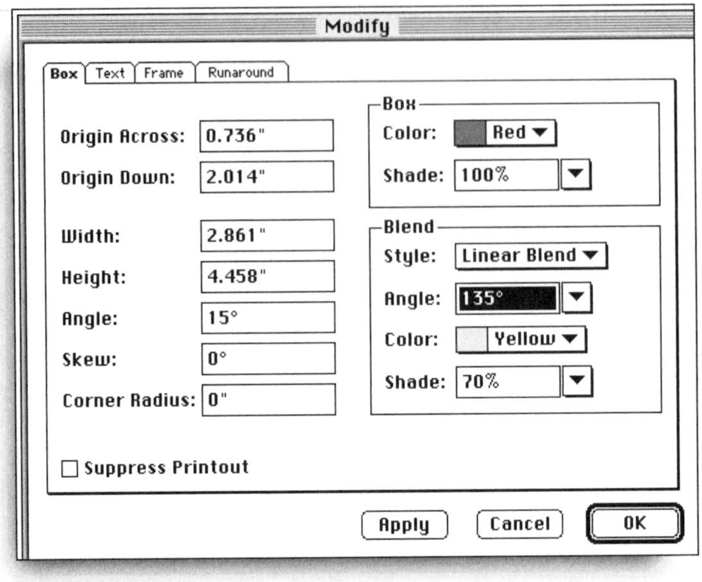

FIGURE 1.16

The Modify tabbed dialog box shows different controls depending on the item selected.

Additional Keyboard Commands in Menus

Drop-down menus contain all the function key alternatives (see Figure 1.17) and an expanded selection of keyboard command alternatives. These replace the keyboard templates that were used as visual clues in some earlier versions.

Edit Dialog Boxes: Select and Display Options

Dialog boxes that are accessed via the **Edit** menu (such as Edit Style Sheets and Edit Colors) have been enhanced to give you additional information and ways of viewing and selecting information. Generally, you can ask to see all available items in the dialog box, only those that are used in the document, those that are not used, and other specifics, depending on the particular dialog box you are viewing (see Figure 1.18). You can select multiple noncontiguous items in the dialog box by holding the ⌘ (Ctrl) key and clicking (see Figure 1.19). This group of items can be deleted or appended to another document.

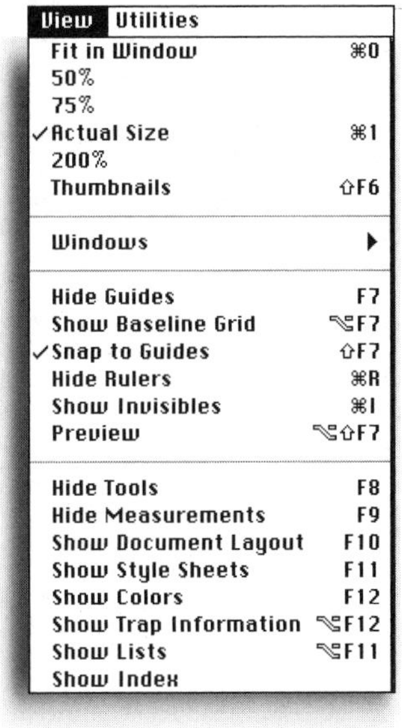

View	Utilities	
Fit in Window	⌘0
50%	
75%	
✓ Actual Size	⌘1
200%	
Thumbnails	⇧F6
Windows	▶
Hide Guides	F7
Show Baseline Grid	⌥F7
✓ Snap to Guides	⇧F7
Hide Rulers	⌘R
Show Invisibles	⌘I
Preview	⌥⇧F7
Hide Tools	F8
Hide Measurements	F9
Show Document Layout	F10
Show Style Sheets	F11
Show Colors	F12
Show Trap Information	⌥F12
Show Lists	⌥F11
Show Index	

FIGURE 1.17

Expanded drop-down menus finally show all the available keyboard shortcuts.

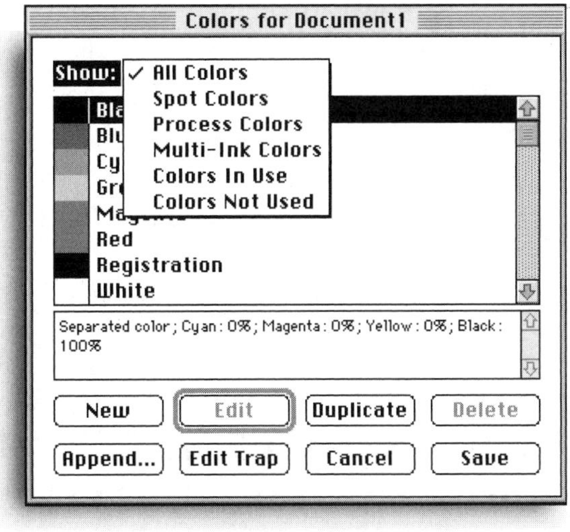

Colors for Document1

Show:
✓ All Colors
  Spot Colors
  Process Colors
  Multi-Ink Colors
  Colors In Use
  Colors Not Used

Bla
Blu
Cy
Gr
Magenta
Red
Registration
White

Separated color; Cyan: 0%; Magenta: 0%; Yellow: 0%; Black: 100%

New   Edit   Duplicate   Delete

Append...   Edit Trap   Cancel   Save

FIGURE 1.18

Display options in the Edit Colors dialog box let you see the colors you've used, the ones you haven't used, or other groups of colors.

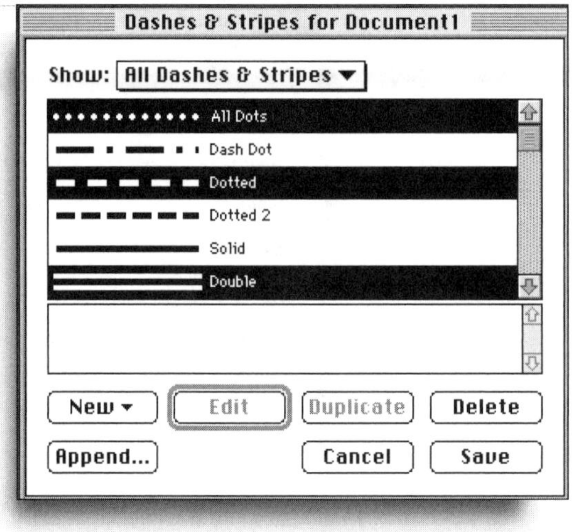

FIGURE **1.19**

Multiple selections in the Edit
Dashes & Stripes dialog box let
you work with more than one
Dashes & Stripes setting at a
time.

FIGURE **1.19**

Multiple selections in the Edit
Dashes & Stripes dialog box let
you work with more than one
Dashes & Stripes setting at a
time.

Increased View Scale

On the Macintosh side, you will be able to view your documents
on your monitor at up to 800 percent of their original size. On
the Windows side, the percentage of enlargement will depend on
the resolution of your monitor.

System Requirements

Generally, you will find that QuarkXPress 4 would like a little
more RAM and a bit more hard disk space than earlier versions.
Following are platform-specific minimum requirements.

Mac OS: Business as Usual

You'll need to make sure that you're using System 7, but then
hardly anyone doing desktop publishing is using System 6, right?

68K Macintosh

- A 68020 or greater processor
- System 7.1 or later
- 5MB of free RAM (8MB or more recommended)
- 13MB of free hard disk space for full installation
- Adobe Type Manager 3.8.2 or above recommended

Power Macintosh (or Compatible)

- PowerPC processor
- System 7.1.2 or later
- 8MB of free RAM (10MB recommended)
- 14MB of free hard disk space for full installation
- Adobe Type Manager 3.8.2 or above recommended

Windows: 386s Not Allowed

If you've been looking for an excuse to unload that old computer, here it is. QuarkXPress 4 is a 32-bit application requiring at least a 486 with Windows. If you are upgrading from an earlier version of QuarkXPress, be alerted that you will need to update all of your XTensions.

- 486 or greater processor
- Windows 95, Windows NT 4.0, or Windows NT 3.51
- 12MB of free RAM (more recommended)
- 12MB of free hard disk space for full installation
- VGA or higher resolution display adapter and monitor supported by Windows 95 or Windows NT
- Adobe Type Manager 3.0 or above recommended (required to view and print Type 1 fonts)

Setting Up Shop

Set default values for objects you create

Set default style sheets, colors, and other attributes for documents you create

Set preferences to fit your work requirements

Choose the right option in the Nonmatching Preferences alert

Customize the Tool palette

You can sit down and start using QuarkXPress without ever changing a preference or default setting—and that's probably exactly how you work. Until you've worked with QuarkXPress for a few months, you probably won't even recognize repetitive tasks and opportunities to streamline your work. But once you start to get proficient in the program, take an hour to go through QuarkXPress and customize it. You'll save hours in the long run—by not creating the same *PANTONE color* over and over, by not changing inches to picas every time you open a document, and more.

Once you get in the customizing groove, take a step further and start looking at *XTensions*. XTensions are add-ons to QuarkXPress designed to meet specific publishing needs.

SEE ALSO

➤ *To buy XTensions, see page 554*

➤ *To determine which XTensions load when you start QuarkXPress, see page 555*

Setting Defaults

Defaults are settings that all new documents are based on. When you create a new document, it contains a default set of *style sheets* for text formatting, colors, *H&Js* for hyphenating and/or justifying text, *lists* (which let you create tables of contents), and *Dashes & Stripes* (custom line and frame styles). If an auxiliary dictionary is open, new documents include a link to it. New documents also reflect the current settings in the Document Preferences dialog box (**Edit** menu).

New documents can carry a lot of baggage, so it's definitely worth checking out these defaults. Unfortunately, most people skip this step. Sure, they'll set up the colors in each document one-by-one. They'll create style sheets when they need them. But who goes in and cleans up the default colors and style sheets for the entire application? A few simple steps can save time every time you start working in a new document.

When no documents are open, you can customize the default list of style sheets, colors, H&Js, lists, and Dashes & Stripes.

Editing the Default Style Sheets

Maybe you never use the Normal style sheets, so the plainness of Helvetica/Arial doesn't bother you. But if you do use Normal, by all means give it your favorite or most commonly used font. You can further customize both the Normal paragraph style sheet and the Normal character style sheet to suit your general needs. You use QuarkXPress to make things look beautiful, so don't settle for typewriter fonts. To edit Normal, simply choose **Style Sheets** from the **Edit** menu when no documents are open.

If you always use the same set of style sheets, append them from the template to the default style sheet list. If your work is indeed this repetitive, you'll get the correct style sheets with all new documents.

SEE ALSO

➤ *To create and edit style sheets, see page 297*

➤ *To append style sheets, see page 146*

Editing the Default Colors

By default, QuarkXPress puts red, green, and blue in all new documents. Unless you work at Target, it's unlikely that all your new documents need red in them. (Okay, even if you work at Target, you probably aren't publishing in *RGB*.)

Cleaning up the default colors list has the twin benefits of decreasing file size by removing unnecessary information (albeit minimally) and preventing misuse of colors. At the very least, get rid of the default RGB colors.

To delete red, green, and blue from a document:

1. When no documents are open, choose **Colors** from the **Edit** menu or press Shift+F12.

2. ⌘+click (Ctrl+click) to select **Blue**, **Green**, and **Red**.

3. Click **Delete**.

4. Click **Save**.

That's about all you can do with the default colors—the rest can't be edited or deleted with the exception of *Registration*, which looks black but will show up on all color plates if you print color separations. If you have a need to customize the color of Registration, go ahead—you'll be changing the way it looks onscreen, but you can't affect which color plates it prints on. Now add the colors you use in most documents (see Figure 2.1). For example, you can add the PANTONE color used for your corporate logo.

All new documents will no longer contain red, green, and blue, but they will contain the new colors you added.

SEE ALSO

➤ *To create new colors, see page 428*

➤ *To edit existing colors, see page 431*

Editing the Default Hyphenation and Justification Settings

Although you can customize the default list of H&Js, it's not as useful as customizing the style sheets and colors lists. For one thing, hyphenation and justification settings usually rely on the type of document, the text, the font size, and the column width. If you hate hyphenation entirely though, turn off hyphenation in the Standard H&J. You might also make one default H&J that allows hyphenation and one that does not. To edit the default

H&Js, choose **H&Js** from the **Edit** menu when no documents are open. First, edit Standard, the H&J included with the Normal paragraph style sheet. Then create any other H&Js you consistently use.

SEE ALSO

➤ *To create and edit H&J settings, see page 268*

➤ *To apply H&J settings to paragraphs of text, see page 258*

➤ *To specify H&J settings in style sheets, see page 298*

Creating Default Lists and Line Patterns

The Lists feature works by finding text tagged with certain paragraph style sheets (heads, subheads, and so on), pulling that text out of a document, compiling it according to the hierarchy you specify, and then applying new styles. This is how you make tables of contents. Because lists are style-sheet dependent, it's hard to make default lists. If you do make the same lists over and over, *append* them from the same source you append the style sheets from. You can append style sheets and lists simultaneously in the Append dialog box (**File** menu).

Dashes and stripes are design elements. Unless you design a coupon border you love and use daily, it's unlikely that you need to edit the default dashes and stripes. But you can. Choose **Dashes & Stripes** from the **Edit** menu when no documents are open to customize the default line and frame patterns.

SEE ALSO

➤ *To create lists, see page 593*

➤ *To generate lists within a document, see page 597*

➤ *To create Dashes & Stripes, see page 117*

➤ *To apply Dashes & Stripes to objects, see page 114*

Setting Preferences

What do preferences do? They let you work the way you prefer. The problem is, QuarkXPress has so many preferences that it's hard to figure out what they do, much less decide how they

Print styles aren't document-specific

There's no need to make a point of editing the default list of *print styles*. Print styles are not document-specific—if you make one, you can use it with any document any time. That's why a little line in the **Edit** menu separates **Print Styles** from the other default commands such as **Colors**, **Style Sheets**, and so on.

should do it. If you just leave the preferences completely alone, it might not cause you too much heartache. You won't be taking advantage of all the customization and productivity features in the software, but you won't suffer too much either.

I have to admit, many preferences in the software are kind of silly. They enable you to emulate the way QuarkXPress worked in previous versions. By default, these types of backward-compatible preferences are set to reflect improved ways of working in newer versions. This section describes every preference in QuarkXPress and gives advice on when to set it.

Understanding Application Versus Document Preferences

QuarkXPress has two types of preferences: Application and Document. Both are accessed through the Preferences submenu of the Edit menu. The Application Preferences dialog box controls the mechanics of QuarkXPress—how documents display, save, and so on. The Document Preferences dialog box combines the General, Typographic, Tools, and Trapping Preferences from 3.x into one tabbed dialog box.

Application Preferences apply to QuarkXPress; therefore, they affect the way all documents are handled. None of the controls in Application Preferences affect the way documents print, so their settings have no effect on individual documents. Document Preferences affect only the active document. However, if you change Document Preferences with no documents open, the new preferences become defaults for all new documents. The controls in Document Preferences affect fundamental attributes of a document: the way text is hyphenated, the way colors are *trapped*, the type of items the tools create, and so on.

Setting XTension preferences

If you have the Index XTension and the Quark CMS XTension enabled, you can set preferences for those as well. Some third-party XTensions have preferences settings as well.

Setting Application Preferences

To open the Application Preferences dialog box, select **Application** from the **Preferences** submenu of the **Edit** menu or press ⌘+Option+Shift+Y (Ctrl+Alt+Shift+Y). Click the four tabs—**Display**, **Interactive**, **Save**, and **XTensions**—to see the types of controls in Application Preferences. When you open Application Preferences, the last tab you worked in displays by default.

Display Tab

There's nothing earth-shattering in the **Display** tab of Application Preferences (see Figure 2.2). If you never looked at it or changed the settings, you'd probably never know. Things worth looking at include **Full-screen Documents** and the **TIFF** settings.

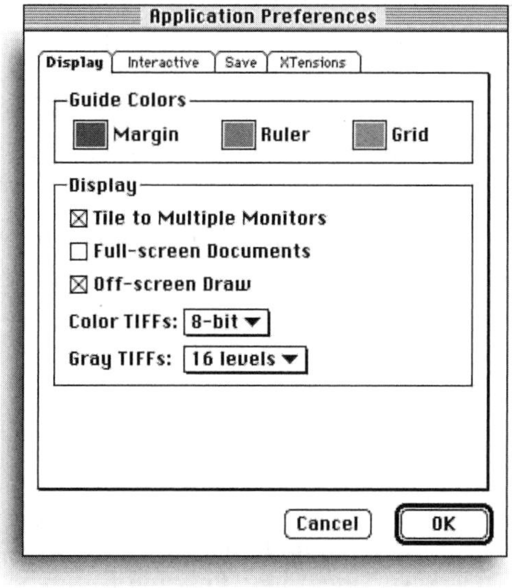

FIGURE 2.2

The **Display** tab provides options for customizing the color of margin guides, ruler guides, and gridlines.

Guide Colors

If you hate the default colors for *margin guides* (blue), *ruler guides* (green), and the *baseline grid* (hot pink), this is the place to go. When you create *clipping* and *runaround paths*, QuarkXPress uses these colors again. The margin guides color outlines the item, the ruler guide color indicates the runaround path, and the baseline grid color shows the clipping path.

To change one of the colors, click the color box to access your system's standard color wheel. If you have a grayscale monitor, you can alter the shades of gray.

Changing the guide colors is partly personal preference and partly pragmatic. Sometimes, it won't make sense to use particular colors; if all your documents (oddly enough) have a green background, you'll have a hard time seeing green guides. And the hot pink baseline grid is truly frightening. Try out a few color schemes with sample documents and see what works best for you.

Tile to Multiple Monitors

Only the Mac-heads get this one. If you have more than one monitor hooked up, and if you turn this setting on, the **Tile to Multiple Monitors** command (**Windows** submenu of **View** menu) distributes documents on all your monitors rather than crowding them on your main monitor.

If you don't have two monitors, forget this exists. If you tile a lot to prepare for *thumbnail drag* (to share pages between documents), dragging across monitors can be a little annoying. If it bugs you, don't check it.

Full-Screen Documents

Full-screen Documents spreads documents out over the whole screen. A little strip is left along the right so you can click on your desktop. **Full-screen Documents** is overridden by the new **Save Document Position** feature in the **Save** tab. If both are checked, QuarkXPress full-screens only new documents and 3.x documents that haven't been saved in version 4 yet.

The default is not checked, but there's no reason not to check it. You should get to see as much of your document as your monitor can display. In fact, I would turn off **Save Document Position** and use only **Full-screen Documents**. Any odd window resizing I've done is usually for a one-time purpose such as dragging in an item from another document, so I don't want to save that position.

Off-Screen Draw

This one's tough to see—maybe it's my zippy machine, or maybe I just don't get it. When you're scrolling and **Off-Screen Draw** is on, QuarkXPress redraws the entire screen rather than redrawing a little bit at a time.

The only reason I've seen to check this is when trainers demo the software. Jerky redraw in large files can detract from the demo. Unless you have a painfully slow machine, don't check this feature.

Color TIFFs and Gray TIFFs

When you import a color *TIFF* file into a *picture box*, QuarkXPress makes a screen preview for you. The *color depth* or *gray levels* used in the preview is based on your selection in the **Color TIFFs** and **Gray TIFFs** menus.

In **Color TIFFs**, select **8 bit** for 256 possible colors, **16 bit** for thousands of possible colors, and **32 bit** for millions of possible colors. In **Gray TIFFs**, select **16** or **256** possible levels of gray. What's all this "possible" stuff? Well, obviously if you scan a picture at 16 levels of gray, QuarkXPress isn't going to magically create a preview with 256 levels of gray. This feature doesn't even touch picture files; it's for display and proofing only, not for final printed output.

Are you printing 32-bit color TIFFs with PICT previews to a QuickDraw printer? If so, you have to choose **32 bit** for **Color TIFFs**. Now that you have that information, how should everyone else set it? The higher settings create previews with more data, which result in larger QuarkXPress files and slower redraw. If file size and speed are an issue for you, set these low. If accurate screen representation is more important to you, set these high.

SEE ALSO

➤ *To import images into picture boxes, see page 338*

Display DPI Value (Windows Only)

The **Display DPI Value**, a Windows only option, is how you tell QuarkXPress how many *dots per inch* your monitor displays. This allows QuarkXPress to provide a more accurate representation of your document onscreen. You can check the accuracy of your **Display DPI Value** setting by holding a ruler up to the horizontal ruler onscreen and comparing. You have to set it or what you see won't be what you get.

Interactive Tab

The **Interactive** tab of Application Preferences has a variety of information that didn't fit anywhere else (see Figure 2.3). (I would have put the scrolling information under the **Display** tab, but either the engineers were being too literal or they ran out of room. I think they ran out of room.) Controls of interest in this tab are **Speed Scroll**, **Quotes**, and **Delayed Item Dragging**.

FIGURE 2.3

If you have a slower machine, the **Interactive** tab has options for speeding up scrolling.

Scrolling

Unless you work with huge pictures, you probably don't think about scrolling too much. But you can customize your pictures in a few ways:

- The slider specifies how fast documents scroll when you click the scroll arrows in the window.

- **Speed Scroll** *greeks* pictures (shows lines or bars instead of text) and blends while you scroll, which can radically increase scroll speed.

- **Live Scroll** updates the document view as you drag the boxes in the scroll bars. Otherwise, the view updates when you stop scrolling. (On a Mac, you can toggle Live Scroll by pressing the Option key when you drag a scroll box. Toggling Live Scroll is not available for Windows users.)

The importance of the scroll speed set in the slider depends on how much you use the scroll arrows. (I never use the arrows because I like to jump around to specific pages and then use the Grabber Hand to position the page.) If you use the scroll arrows a lot, you might want to set a relatively slow speed so you can control it. If you set the speed to the max and click the down arrow, it can be scary. **Speed Scroll** is interesting—you should check it. **Live Scroll** is sort of like **Off-screen Draw**. If you can figure out what it does that's so different, maybe you can figure out which setting you prefer.

Quotes

Checking **Smart Quotes** makes QuarkXPress smart enough to enter typographers' or "curly" quotes instead of "straight" quotes while you type (this includes 'single' quotes and apostrophes). The **Format** pop-up menu provides the typographers' quotes used in different languages; if the menu options confuse you, don't worry about it. Just choose the familiar English quotation marks. When you check **Convert Quotes** in the Get Text dialog box, QuarkXPress looks at the **Format** you selected here to decide how to convert the quotes.

QuarkXPress provides a key command to override **Smart Quotes** when you need foot and inch marks. Type Ctrl+ ' (Mac or Windows) for foot marks and Ctrl+Shift+ " (Ctrl+Alt+ ") for inch marks.

Unless you type a basketball program, leave **Smart Quotes** checked. And when you type in English, obviously you want the English quotation marks. The good thing about these settings is that you can change them temporarily any time you want. If you do need to import some French text, you can choose « » from the Format menu, import the text, and then change the setting back.

Delayed Item Dragging

QuarkXPress always had a subtle feature called *live drag*. If you selected an item and held the mouse button for a second before dragging, you could see the contents of the item while you moved it. If you were impatient and just grabbed an item and started moving it, you saw only the outlines.

This built-in feature has become a button called **Show Contents**. If you click this button, item dragging works just like 3.x. The other option, **Live Refresh**, is an enhanced version of live drag. When you select an item, pause, then start dragging and you see the actual layering of the item and any *text reflow* that occurs. This is great for experimenting with text runarounds.

Basically, you can decide whether you want live drag (**Show Contents**) or better live drag (**Live Refresh**). Using the **Delay** field, you can now specify how long you have to hold the mouse button to activate **Show Contents** or **Live Refresh**.

If your machine is slow, don't worry about this setting because you shouldn't attempt to live drag at all. Just grab things and drag so the redraw occurs at the end. If you were into live drag before, at least give **Live Refresh** a try. You'll quickly find out whether your machine and documents can handle it. If it's too slow, switch to **Show Contents**. As for that **Delay** field, right before shipping, Quark upped the default from half a second to three quarters. This causes you to wait an entire .75 of a second before live drag occurs. Personally, having a Power Mac, I prefer knocking it down to a quarter second for almost instantaneous live drag.

Drag and Drop Text

Drag and Drop Text lets you use the mouse to cut, copy, and paste text within the same *story*. (Notice the word "story." You can't drag and drop between *text chains*.) To cut and paste text, you highlight it, hold the mouse button for a second, and then drag it to a new location. To copy and paste text, do the same thing with the Shift key held down. Most word processors have done this for years.

Unless you do a lot of text editing, leave this one off. If you drag and drop accidentally (and you will), you can make a huge mess. On Mac OS, you have a compromise—activate it temporarily with keyboard commands. Select some text and then press ⌘+Ctrl to cut and ⌘+Ctrl+Shift to copy while you drag.

SEE ALSO

➤ *To edit text, see page 204*

Show Tool Tips

This Windows-standard feature is implemented on the Mac OS as well. Tool Tips are square balloons that give you the name of each tool in the Tool palette and some icons in the Measurements palette.

On the one hand, the 28 tools in the new Tool palette can be bewildering. A little help figuring out what they are can't hurt. On the other hand, all you get from Tool Tips is the name of a tool or icon. If Orthogonal Line tool means nothing to you, receiving that information in a balloon is not likely to help you. Because **Show Tool Tips** is on by default, you might want to quickly look at the new tools and palette icons to become familiar with them; then turn it off.

Pasteboard Width

The *pasteboard* is the blank work area surrounding each document page or spread. You always have .5 inch above and below each page. You can decide how large the pasteboard is on either side of a page or spread. **Pasteboard Width** is specified as a percentage of page width. For example, an 8.5- × 11-inch document with the default 100% **Pasteboard Width** setting, has 8.5" to the left of the page and 8.5" to the right.

Because the width of a document and its pasteboard must be within the 48" limit, QuarkXPress shrinks the pasteboard as necessary in wider documents. In addition, QuarkXPress always puts at least .5" of pasteboard around each document page regardless of your **Pasteboard Width** setting.

The pasteboard is usually handy for drawing items, editing items separately from their backgrounds, and temporarily storing items. 100%, the maximum and the default, seems to work well, so leave this setting alone. Keep in mind that leaving extra items on the pasteboard can increase file size and confuse *service bureaus*. If you need a place to store something, put it in a library.

SEE ALSO

➤ *To use the pasteboard to store items, see page 125*

Save Tab

The **Save** tab of Application Preferences has preferences for how QuarkXPress saves files (see Figure 2.4). All the controls in this tab are worth consideration.

FIGURE 2.4

Use the **Save** tab to specify how QuarkXPress automatically saves your files.

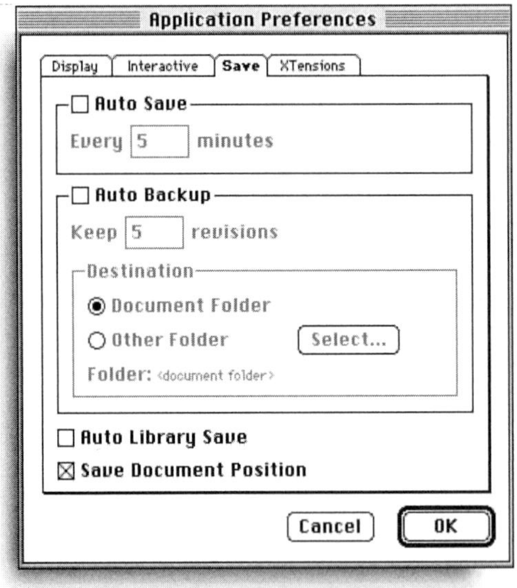

Auto Save

Auto Save saves your documents for you while you work. If the power goes out or (more likely) your application or system crashes, you lose only a minimal amount of work with **Auto Save** on. The **Every __ minutes** field enables you to specify how often QuarkXPress saves automatically. The Auto Save feature tries to work its saves in when you're not doing anything, but if you're working frantically, it might interrupt you for a couple of seconds. **Auto Save** doesn't kick in on brand new documents because the new file doesn't have a name or location; it wouldn't know where to save to.

Auto Save doesn't save over your original document. It makes a new file and stores changes there until you actually save by yourself. When you open an auto-saved document after a crash, you see two files: the regular one and the auto-saved one. Select either one; the documents are smart enough to know that they're one and the same. An incredibly long alert dialog lets you know that you're opening an auto-saved document, but it gives you no option but to click **OK**. Once you acknowledge the alert, you can start working in the document (hopefully, close to where you left off), or you can use the **Revert to Saved** command to lose all the auto-saved information.

Any time you work with **Auto Save** on, you can revert a document to either the last manual save or the last auto save. To revert to the last manual save, just select **Revert to Saved**; to revert to the last auto save, press the Option (Alt) key while choosing **Revert to Saved**.

Should you use **Auto Save**? I say yes. But don't make the saves more frequent than five minutes; the interruptions can drive you crazy. Unless you work in spurts of genius, you can even change the interval to ten minutes. The only time you might want to turn Auto Save off is when you work on large documents over a file server. You'll get some lengthy, rude interruptions when auto save kicks in with the laborious process of saving over a network.

Auto Backup

Auto Backup automatically creates up to 100 revisions of a document. Whenever you save (that means you, not auto save), QuarkXPress places the previous copy of the document in your specified Auto Backup folder. There, the revisions are numbered sequentially, with the highest number representing the latest version. Older revisions are deleted as necessary to make room for newer revisions. Enter how many revisions you want of each document in the **Keep __ revisions** field.

To specify where the revisions are stored, click **Document Folder** or **Other Folder**. Whenever you need one of these revisions, simply go to this folder and open it.

The thing to consider with **Auto Backup** is space. These revisions are full copies of QuarkXPress documents and they can consume a lot of hard drive space. The backups aren't automatically deleted, so they add up. Plus, if you're in the habit of saving all the time, all your auto backups will be only minutes apart from each other.

However, it's worth saving at least one revision of a document, especially if you have no other backup system. And how can I put this clearly? Never, never, never store auto backups in the document folder. You will get the backups mixed up with the original because the filenames are so similar. Create a folder that contains nothing but auto backups; this makes it easy to locate the backups and gives you an easy target when you need to make some room on your hard drive.

Auto Library Save

Auto Library Save saves each change you make to a *library* as you make it. If it's not checked, libraries are only saved when you close them or quit QuarkXPress.

Check it. The only reason I've heard to have it not checked (which is mysteriously the default) is that if you add a lot of things to a library, all that saving can be slow. Excuse me, but if you're doing that much work on a library, wouldn't that be the worst possible time to risk not having your changes saved?

SEE ALSO

➤ *To create libraries, see page 143*

➤ *To use items from a library, see page 144*

Getting the most from Auto Save and Auto Backup

If you want to save a true revision of a document from each work session, use **Auto Save** and **Auto Backup** together. To make this work, you have to let Auto Save do its job. Don't choose **Save** or press ⌘+S (Ctrl+S) until you want to update the auto backup file. For example, say you work on a brochure on Monday. On Tuesday, you open the brochure again and edit it for an hour. You don't save while you're working because Auto Save is protecting you. When you close the document, your Tuesday changes are saved. Auto Backup kicks the Monday version of the document into your auto backup folder. When you come in Wednesday, you have Monday's document and Tuesday's document available. To get out of the painstaking habit of saving all the time, make a mental note each time Auto Save runs. Let this satisfy your craving to save.

Save Document Position

Save Document Position remembers the position, size, and proportion of document windows for the next time they're opened. If you shrink up a document window to 2" square and put it in the upper-left corner of the screen, that's where it will be the next time you open it.

Save Document Position is a perfect example of why you need preferences. Some people love it (which is why it was added to version 4), and other people hate it. I hate it because any time I'm doing weird things such as making document windows 2" square, it's usually to get the window out of the way for a minute. The next time I open the document, I don't want it all squished and hidden. Anyway, it's up to you. Think about why you resize and move windows—for a one-time use or permanently—and set the preference accordingly.

XTensions Tab

QuarkXPress 4 includes an XTensions Manager so you can specify which XTensions load using a dialog box rather than manually dragging **XTensions** around between folders, as shown in Figure 2.5. The XTensions tab controls if and when the XTensions Manager displays when you launch QuarkXPress.

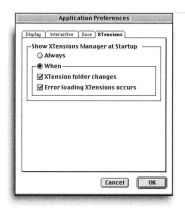

FIGURE 2.5

The **XTensions** tab enables you to control whether the XTensions Manager displays when you launch QuarkXPress.

Show XTensions Manager at Startup

Displaying the XTensions Manager at startup gives you the power to change which XTensions are going to load. Click **Always** to have it display every time you launch QuarkXPress. Click **When** to have it display only under certain circumstances, for example, when you change the contents of the XTension folder (by adding or removing XTensions) or when an error loading an XTension occurs.

Even if you specify that the XTensions Manager never displays at startup (by clicking **When** and not checking both boxes), you can invoke it by pressing the Spacebar when you launch QuarkXPress.

The default settings are pretty good; the XTensions Manager displays only when an error occurs. The only reason to display the XTensions Manager when the XTension folder changes is if you're still manually moving XTensions around. Even when you install a new XTension, thereby changing the folder, you'll still find out if an error happened because **Error loading** is checked. Service bureaus might consider clicking **Always** so they always know which XTensions are running.

SEE ALSO

➤ *To use the XTensions Manager, see page 555*

Setting Document Preferences

To open the Document Preferences dialog box, select **Document** from the **Preferences** submenu of the **Edit** menu or press ⌘+Y (Ctrl+Y). Click the five tabs—**General**, **Paragraph**, **Character**, **Tools**, and **Trapping**—to see the types of controls in Document Preferences. In 3.x, these controls were in separate preferences dialog boxes (General, Typographic, Trapping, and Tools). When you open Document Preferences, the last tab you were working in displays by default.

Because of space issues, the Typographic Preferences were split into two tabs: **Paragraph** and **Character**. (If you had the keyboard commands memorized for opening the General and Typographic Preferences dialog boxes, they still work. ⌘+Y (Ctrl+Y) takes you to the General tab and ⌘+Option+Y (Ctrl+Alt+Y) takes you to the Paragraph tab.)

Remember that changes to Document Preferences affect the active document. If no documents are open, changes affect all new documents.

General Tab

The **General** tab of Document Preferences is about mechanics (see Figure 2.6). You tell certain features how to work—for example, the measurement system the ruler should display, whether pages are added automatically, and where guides are displayed. None of the settings in this dialog box cause reflow in your document, so you can feel free to change them while you work as necessary.

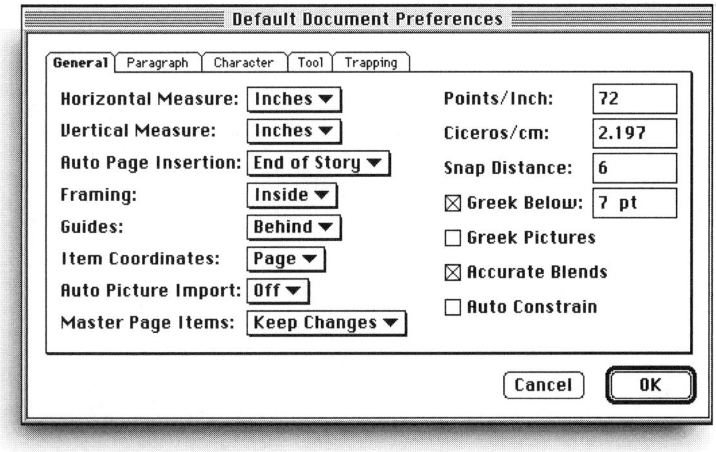

FIGURE 2.6

The **General** tab lets you control how various layout features in QuarkXPress work.

Horizontal Measure, Vertical Measure

By default, all new documents display a ruler across the top and down the left side. You control the ruler display by selecting **Show/Hide Rulers** from the **View** menu or pressing ⌘+R (Ctrl+R). The default measurement system for the rulers and inches is used in most palettes and dialog boxes for item placement, indents, tabs, and so on.

You can control the measurement system for the horizontal ruler (*x coordinates*) and the vertical ruler (*y coordinates*) separately. Once you select an option, you no longer need to enter the abbreviation for that measurement system when you enter values in fields. For example, if your rulers are set to inches and you enter 1 in a **Width** field, QuarkXPress knows you mean 1 inch. And if you don't want to specify a value in inches, you can still use any other measurement system's abbreviation. QuarkXPress converts the value to your preferred measurement system (except font size, leading, frame width, and line width, which are always converted to points).

The **Horizontal** and **Vertical Measure** options and their abbreviations are shown in Table 2.1. It's a good thing these are document specific because the measurement system you choose often depends on the type of document. I worked on some advertisements for the *Wall Street Journal* a few years ago and they gave us the dimensions in *agates*. Agates are new to QuarkXPress 4, so back in the 3.x days, we had to do some hideous math to work it out.

TABLE 2.1   **Measurement systems and their abbreviations**

System	Abbreviation
Inches (inches in eighths)	in or "
Inches Decimal (inches in tenths)	in or "
Picas	p
Points	pt
Millimeters	mm
Centimeters	cm
Ciceros	c
Agates	ag

You'll probably want to use inches for items that are traditionally measured in inches—letters, envelopes, and so on—and use *points* or *picas* for everything else. The measurement system you choose also depends on your training. The typographers I work with wouldn't ever use inches; meanwhile I can't make sense of those little p's you have to insert in picas.

Auto Page Insertion

If you want QuarkXPress to automatically insert pages to contain text that you're importing or typing, you need to use **Auto Page Insertion**. You can decide whether pages are inserted at the end of a story (which might be in the middle of a document), the end of a section (which, again, might be anywhere), or at the end of a document. You can also turn it off all together.

This setting depends on the type of publication. In a magazine, you might want **End of Document** if you put all the story continuations in the end of the magazine. In a book, you'd probably want **End of Section** so that when you add text it stays with its chapter. On a one-page advertisement, you might never notice how this is set. If it's on, though, and your text is in an *automatic text box*, it might irritate you that QuarkXPress drops in a blank page to contain your overflow. In that case, turn it off.

SEE ALSO

➤ *To add pages to a document, see page 161*

➤ *To delete pages in a document, see page 163*

Framing

Framing determines whether box frames are placed inside or outside boxes. Frames inside boxes obscure parts of pictures or backgrounds, but they don't obscure text. QuarkXPress uses the **Text Inset** value (set in the **Text** tab of the Modify dialog box) for the space between frames and text. Frames outside boxes increase the width and height of boxes; the new boundaries are reflected in the boxes' x and y coordinates.

Changes to the **Framing** setting affect only new boxes. If you already have boxes with frames in a document, and you change this setting, the existing frames will not change. Therefore, changing this setting cannot cause text reflow or change the look of a document.

Leave it at the default, **Inside**, so your box width and height isn't changed. If a frame is hiding too much of a picture, don't move the frame, just make a bigger box.

SEE ALSO

➤ *To apply frames to boxes, see page 114*

➤ *To resize boxes, see page 106*

Guides

When you select **Show Guides** from the **View** menu or press F7, QuarkXPress displays margin guides and page guides according to this setting. If you select **Behind**, page guides are placed behind all items on a page. If you select **In Front**, guides are placed in front of all items on a page. The **Guides** setting also applies when you select **Baseline Grid** from the **View** menu or press Option+F7 (Ctrl+F7).

Placing guides behind items makes your guides essentially useless. If you can't see them, you can't use them. Leave the setting at the default, **In Front**.

SEE ALSO

➤ *To use ruler guides, see page 123*

Item Coordinates

The **Item Coordinates** pop-up menu controls how the horizontal ruler displays measurements for pages in a spread. The default setting, **Page**, has the ruler start at 0 at the beginning of each page. The alternate setting, **Spread**, has the ruler count all the way across both pages. For example, if you choose **Spread** for an 8 1/2 × 11-inch *facing-page document*, the horizontal ruler starts at 0 on the left edge of the left-facing page and ends at 17 inches on the right edge of the right-facing page. This setting alters the x and y coordinates of items in the second, third, and other pages in a spread.

Page is usually a good choice. If page elements are habitually crossing the line while you work on *spreads*, you might give the **Spread** option a try. Don't set the **Item Coordinates** to **Spread** to fake a wide document. If you want a 17-inch wide document, make one in the New Document dialog box. Don't change the coordinates and pretend you have a 17-inch wide document. Your printer won't know that's what you want.

SEE ALSO

➤ *To use the rulers to position objects on a page or spread, see page 123*

Auto Picture Import

When you import a picture into a document, QuarkXPress builds a preview of the picture for you, and then it remembers where the original file is. You might edit those original files, and QuarkXPress will never show it until you print the document.

That is, unless you use **Auto Picture Import**. Then when you open a document, QuarkXPress looks at those files for you to see if they've been edited.

Auto Picture Import has three options:

- **Off**, which means, "don't even look—just leave my picture files alone."

- **On**, which means, "go find my pictures and update them, and don't make any noise about it." QuarkXPress updates only pictures it can find; if you move pictures, they're not updated.

- **On (verify)**, which is a tentative sort of on. It means, "if there's anything to update, show me an alert and I'll decide what to update." QuarkXPress displays the Missing/ Modified Pictures alert (the same one that's displayed when you try to print missing pictures).

If you want to use **Auto Picture Import**, use **On (verify)**. The problem with **On** is that it's not reliable. You can throw out a picture file and it won't tell you. It quietly updates the pictures it can find and leaves everything else alone. Rather than be misled that all your pictures are fine, put up with the alert.

Turn **Auto Picture Import** off when you work with *FPOs* (For Position Only images) or if you're in a situation where people are constantly updating, renaming, and moving files. The alert will drive you crazy if you get it every time you open a document.

SEE ALSO
➤ *To import an image into a picture box, see page 338*
➤ *To update imported pictures, see page 356*

Master Page Items

Master page items are items on document pages that were placed by *master pages*. QuarkXPress lets you edit master items on document pages—but it assumes that you mean it. If you edit a master item on a *document page* and then edit that item on the master page, the item in the document is not updated.

Say, for example, that your master page has a .25-point rule. You shortened that rule on all the document pages to accommodate other design elements. Then your production department finds out the rule is too thin to print clearly. So they tell you to move it up to 5 pt. To make the change, you might think you can edit the rule on your master pages and the change will be reflected on the document pages. This is not true. When you edited the rules on the document pages, you changed them to *local items*.

When you apply a new master page to a document page (or re-apply the current master page), QuarkXPress can either keep the modified master items on the page (**Keep Changes**), or change them back to the way they are on the master page (**Delete Changes**). The unmodified items (the "clean" ones) are changed to match the master page, regardless of this setting. The **Master Page Items** setting is not retroactive; if you change it while you work, it doesn't go back and look at previous master page changes and start restoring or deleting items.

Unless you apply a master page to a blank page, changing a page's master page is a messy proposition. If you say **Keep Changes**, the new master page items are plopped on top of the old items. You have to figure out which items are which and paste any content you need into the new master items. If you say **Delete Changes**, you run the risk of losing content in the existing master items. Don't worry about the setting. If you need to reformat a page, stick its content over on the pasteboard, delete everything else, and then apply a new master page.

SEE ALSO

➤ *To create and edit master pages, see page 155*

➤ *To apply a master page to document pages, see page 159*

Points/Inch

On traditional metal typographic rulers, there are approximately 72.27 or 72.307 points per inch. Desktop publishers, however, simplified the number of points in an inch to 72. You can override the 72 points-per-inch standard for more precise (traditional) point and pica measurements. QuarkXPress gives you a broad range—you can specify anywhere between 60 and 80 points per inch.

Changing the **Points/Inch** value in midstream won't change the size of items or reflow text. It just updates measurements to reflect the new value.

Don't change this unless you actually own and use a traditional typographic ruler.

Ciceros/cm

Ciceros/cm is a lot like **Points/Inch**. Desktop publishers rounded off the cicero to centimeter conversion, slightly altering the size of the cicero. To use traditional *ciceros*, you can enter a new value between 2 and 3.

Unless you use ciceros, don't worry about this one. Even then, make sure you understand why you're changing it.

Snap Distance

When you drag items around in QuarkXPress, it might seem like the guides are magnetic; items automatically jump over to them and latch on. It doesn't always work this way—only when **Snap to Guides** is checked (**View** menu). When it is on, QuarkXPress looks at the **Snap Distance** field to determine the size of the guide's magnetic field. The default, 6 *pixels*, means that when you drag an item within 6 pixels of a guide, it will automatically align with the guide.

Snap to Guides is a blessing and a curse. It helps you align items quickly, but it won't let you drag items and place them too close to a guide. It grabs the item (whether you like it or not). This is all a personal problem of **Snap to Guides** and has little to do with **Snap Distance**. The **Snap Distance** default is fine; if you're having snap troubles, press Shift+F7 to turn **Snap to Guides** off. (Actually, I do use a larger **Snap Distance** on my PowerBook. I can't control item dragging too well with the trackpad, so I like it when items jump right to the guides.)

Greek Below

Greek Below displays text as gray bars to speed up screen redraw. If **Greek Below** is checked, greeking affects text below the point size you enter in the field. View size is also factored in, for example, at the 7 point default, all text below 7 points is greeked in Actual Size view. Meanwhile, at 200% view, text below 3.5 points is greeked. At 50% view, text below 14 points is greeked.

If you edit text, it's probably best to turn off Greek Below so you can see all the text. If you take an overall look at the design of a text-heavy document, you might want to use **Greek Below**. Change the point size to the most logical for the document; if all the body text is 11 point, make the **Greek Below** setting 12 point. You usually want to set the threshold so headlines display but body text doesn't.

Greek Pictures

Greek Pictures displays imported pictures as gray boxes to speed up screen redraw. If you select a picture, it displays normally.

Just as designers don't always care about text, editors don't always care about pictures. Plus, editors are usually at the end of the food chain when it comes to computing power so displaying pictures can be painful. If you're primarily concerned with text, check **Greek Pictures**. If you need to write a caption or check picture placement, you can always select a picture to display it.

Designers probably want to look at pictures most of the time and should not check **Greek Pictures**. There are times when you might want to turn it on, edit the document, and then turn it off (for example, if all you need to do is look at the *folios* in a brochure full of color TIFFs).

Accurate Blends

Blends are box backgrounds consisting of two colors that phase into each other in a certain pattern. The **Accurate Blends** preference controls the display of blends on 8-bit (256-color) monitors. When **Accurate Blends** is checked, blends display without *banding* and with more accurate color.

If your monitor uses a *16-bit* or *24-bit* video board and you take advantage of it in your system settings, blends always display as accurately as possible and this setting is moot. **Accurate Blends** is strictly *8-bit*. Don't check it if speed is an issue because more accuracy takes longer to draw. Check **Accurate Blends** for accurate screen representation.

SEE ALSO

➤ *To create blends, see page 445*

Back in the old days (the late '80s), all items in QuarkXPress had a parent-child relationship. Big boxes actually contained the small boxes you drew within them. You couldn't drag the child boxes outside the boundaries of the parent boxes. Not to sever the family relationship, but the parent boxes are called *constraining* boxes in Quark-speak.

Auto Constrain

Auto Constrain is a walk down memory lane. You can still work like you did years ago by checking it. All the items you draw will automatically constrain the items you draw inside them. Remember that constrained items automatically become part of *groups*, and as such the items are moved, resized, or deleted along with the rest of the group.

You can still ungroup and unconstrain items resulting from **Auto Constrain**. If you change this preference while you work, it doesn't work backward. New items become constraining items, but existing items won't.

Leave it unchecked! Constraining is an odd way to work. If you have the need for a constraining box, use the **Constrain** command in the **Item** menu.

Paragraph Tab

The **Paragraph** tab of Document Preferences provides control over leading calculations, baseline grid increments, and *hyphenation* algorithms, as shown in Figure 2.7. If you're going to change these settings, it's a good idea to do it with no documents open or before you start flowing text into a document. Changing these preferences is about guaranteed to cause text reflow.

These settings should be familiar to 3.x users—they were jammed into Typographic Preferences along with what is now Character Preferences. You can use the old 3.x keyboard command for opening Typographic Preferences, ⌘+Option+Y (Ctrl+Alt+Y), to jump directly to the **Paragraph** tab of Document Preferences.

FIGURE 2.7

The **Paragraph** tab lets you set up a baseline grid and control automatic leading.

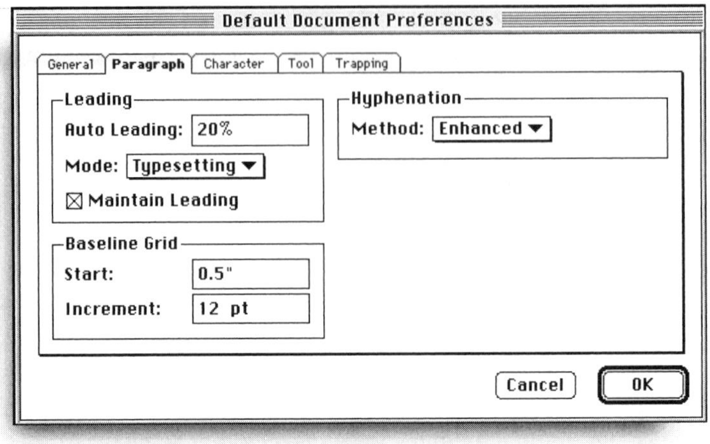

Auto Leading

When you use *auto leading* to space lines of text, QuarkXPress uses the value in the **Auto Leading** field to calculate the leading. **Auto Leading** comes in two flavors: percentage-based and incremental.

- Percentage-based auto leading looks for the largest font size on each line, takes a percent of its size, and then adds that to the font size. For example, when **Auto Leading** is set to the default 20%, 10-point type is leaded 12 points. To specify percentage-based auto leading, enter a value followed by a percent sign.

- Incremental auto leading looks for the largest font size on the line and then adds or subtracts a specific number of points. For example, if **Auto Leading** is set to 6, 24-point type is leading 30 points. To specify incremental auto leading, enter an absolute value preceded by a plus or minus sign.

The most common thing you'll hear about auto leading in QuarkXPress is: Don't use it. If you're not using auto leading, the **Auto Leading** value is moot. However, if you do choose to use auto leading, you might want to change the default from percentage-based to incremental. Why does everyone hate auto leading so much? Because paragraphs that contain mixed font sizes end up with mixed leading values, which makes for uneven (and usually ugly) line spacing.

Leading Mode

Leading Mode is the method QuarkXPress uses to measure the amount of space between lines of text. **Typesetting** measures from *baseline* to baseline, whereas **Word Processing** measures from *ascent* to ascent.

If anyone knows the value of this feature, speak up. If you wanted to use a word processor, you wouldn't use QuarkXPress. Select **Typesetting** and forget about it.

Maintain Leading

Maintain Leading comes into play only in a specific situation. You need to have an obstructing item (an item with *runaround* set for it) in a box or column with text flowing above and below it. When the text gets past the obstruction, it needs to know where to go. It can be placed according to its leading value (**Maintain Leading** checked), or it can be "stuck" to the bottom of the obstruction (**Maintain Leading** unchecked). When you don't check **Maintain Leading**, the ascent of the line touches the obstructing item within any runaround value applied to it.

You might have to set this one on a template-by-template basis. You see the situation often when *pull quotes* jut into a column of text. But whether or not to turn on **Maintain Leading** is up to the designer.

SEE ALSO

➤ *To change the leading amount for a text selection, see page 253*

Baseline Grid

A baseline grid is a form of design-by-numbers, where the leading and space between paragraphs is calculated mathematically. Using a baseline grid in paragraphs throughout a document ensures that text in columns aligns horizontally. The **Start** field specifies where the baseline grid starts in relation to the top of a page. The **Increment** field specifies the amount of space between baselines in the grid. Text locked to the grid always snap to the next available line in the grid.

There's more to the baseline grid, though. To display it, select **Show Baseline Grid** from the **View** menu. To lock paragraphs to the baseline grid, check **Lock to Baseline Grid** in the **Formats** tab of Paragraph Attributes (**Style** menu). In the hierarchy of vertical text spacing, **Lock to Baseline Grid** is most important. It overrides leading, space before/after, and the vertical alignment set for the *text box*.

If you're not locking paragraphs to the baseline grid, there's no reason to change it. But if you are, you almost need to customize the grid. In fact, you should plan templates and style sheets from the ground up with the baseline grid in mind. Set the **Start** and **Increment** to work well with the design of the document. Changing the baseline grid—or deciding to lock paragraphs to it—isn't the kind of thing to decide on-the-fly. It will cause radical reflow in your documents.

SEE ALSO

➤ *To set up a design that uses the baseline grid, see page 237*

➤ *To lock paragraphs to the baseline grid, see page 260*

Hyphenation Method

When QuarkXPress hyphenates text automatically, it looks to the **Hyphenation Method** for rules. The three methods are associated with sequential releases of QuarkXPress. **Standard** is the hyphenation algorithm used in versions of QuarkXPress prior to 3.1. **Enhanced**, used with versions 3.1–3.3, represents an improved algorithm. **Expanded** combines the improved algorithm with a built-in hyphenation dictionary.

The hyphenation dictionary serves as a helper to the algorithm, providing correct hyphenation options for words that often suffered incorrect hyphenation under algorithm-based methods. The list is not entirely comprehensive, and because "correct" hyphenation is somewhat subjective, wordsmiths might or might not be happy with the results.

Documents remember their **Hyphenation Method** from version to version of QuarkXPress. However, if you change the **Hyphenation Method** in an existing document, chances are your document will reflow. In fact, if you're not concerned about text reflow in 3.x documents, update their **Hyphenation Method** to **Expanded** as well. The only reason to choose **Standard** or **Enhanced** is if you try to mimic text flow from a previous version of QuarkXPress. (Or if you find that the hyphenation provided in the new hyphenation dictionary is not to your liking, go back to **Enhanced**.) The hyphenation in the dictionary appears to be more modern than traditional.

SEE ALSO

➤ *To create and edit H&J settings, see page 268*

➤ *To apply H&J settings to paragraphs of text, see page 258*

➤ *To create and edit hyphenation exceptions, see page 277*

Character Tab

The **Character** tab of Document Preferences enables you to customize type styles, activate automatic *kerning*, and specify the width of *flex spaces* and *em spaces* (see Figure 2.8). Character preferences are fairly subtle, so although changing them can cause reflow, it shouldn't be too dramatic.

If you're a 3.x user, you remember the character controls from the old Typographic Preferences dialog box. If you were accustomed to adjusting a certain character preference by jumping into Typographic Preferences using the keyboard command, you need to add a keystroke. ⌘+Option+Y (Ctrl+Alt+Y) will jump you to the **Paragraph** tab of Document Preferences; then press ⌘+Tab (Ctrl+Tab) to jump to the **Character** tab.

Superscript

Superscript type style is used for things such as footnote numbers. You can specify the size and placement of superscript characters on a document-wide basis. The **Offset**, measured as a percentage of font size, specifies how high above the baseline QuarkXPress places superscript characters. The **Vscale** and **Hscale** control the height and width of the characters.

Do any of your type specs call for superscript style? If not, don't worry about customizing it. If so, set up some sample text with the appropriate font, size, and leading; then experiment with different **Offset**, **VScale**, and **HScale** values. You'll probably find that superscript characters look a little better if you adjust the 100% defaults downward. It's a good idea to do this before you start using superscript style throughout your text.

SEE ALSO

➤ To apply superscript style to a text selection, see page 243

Subscript

Subscript type style is used for things like the "2" in H_2O. You can specify the size and placement of subscript characters on a document-wide basis. The **Offset**, measured as a percentage of font size, specifies how far below the baseline QuarkXPress places subscript characters. The **Vscale** and **Hscale** control the height and width of the characters.

As with superscript, the preferences for subscript characters are only a concern if you actually use subscript. You'll probably want to make subscript characters smaller than the 100% default settings. Experiment with sample text to see how subscript characters look best. As always with Character preferences, it's a good idea to set them before you've completely formatted a document.

SEE ALSO

➤ *To apply subscript style to a text selection, see page 243*

Small Caps

Small caps are   little versions of capital letters, shrunk down according to the values in the **VScale** and **HScale** fields. This preference is used when you apply the small caps type style to text, but not when you select the small caps version of a font. **VScale**, measured as a percentage of font size, specifies the height of characters. **HScale**, measured as a percentage of the font's width as specified by the designer, specifies the width of characters.

First ask yourself, "Do I use the small caps type style?" If the answer is "no," move on. Even if you just use it occasionally, it might not be worth playing around with. But if you use them all the time, you should absolutely take a look at the **Small Caps** preference.

I worked on a manual that listed all Windows keyboard commands in small caps. The keyboard commands consisted of combinations of letters and numbers, and because numbers are not affected by small caps, the commands tended to look fairly ugly. (In fact, CTRL+F7 was so ugly that we compromised and used CTRL+F7.) We still wanted to use small caps because all caps is so intimidating (and IT TAKES UP SO MUCH SPACE). It didn't occur to us until later that if we boosted the small caps size up from 75% to 85%, the transition between letters and numbers would be more subtle. We made the change late, which required us to change multiple documents based on the same template and suffer the reflow consequences.

SEE ALSO

➤ *To apply small caps style to a text selection, see page 243*

Superior

Superior type style is often used on trademark% symbols so they don't interfere too much with text. **VScale**, measured as a percentage of font size, specifies the height of characters. **HScale**, measured as a percentage of the font's width as specified by the designer, specifies the width of characters.

If you do use superior on trademark symbols, the 50% defaults seem to work nicely with all different typefaces. If the look of superior characters is bothering you though, experiment with the settings. You're unlikely to get reflow unless your whole document is in superior. Eek.

SEE ALSO

➤ *To apply superior style to a text selection, see page 243*

Auto Kern Above

The space between characters is controlled by kerning tables that are built into most fonts. To use these kerning tables, or kerning tables you create using the QuarkXPress Kern/Track Editor, you need to check **Auto Kern Above**. Then enter a value in the field to specify the point size above which automatic kerning should occur. (If you want automatic kerning on most of the time, enter 2 in the field. You can't enter 1, so if you have 2-point type in a document it's not going to get kerned automatically.)

Check **Auto Kern Above** and enter 2 in the field, and do it with no documents open so it becomes the new default setting. Kern with abandon. It doesn't cost anything and it looks better. You use QuarkXPress to get professional results, so use it right. Some people tell you that excessive kerning slows down the application. But if you can perceive the difference in redraw between kerned and unkerned text, you need a new hobby.

SEE ALSO

➤ *To kern type manually, see page 290*

➤ *To edit kerning tables with the Kern/Track Editor, see page 280*

Flex Space Width

The flex space in QuarkXPress is your opportunity to set up a space of any width that you consistently use in a document. The advantage to a flex space is that not only is it the size you specify, but it maintains its width, even in the midst of justified text. The default setting, 50%, is a percentage of the *en space* width specified by the font designer. You can enter a value from 0 to 400% in the **Flex Space Width** field.

If you use flex spaces in the first place, you might want to adjust the size. For example, I know a typographer who uses a flex space between the state abbreviation and zip code in addresses. One standard space was too small and two was too big. So he uses a flex spaces with the Flex Space Width set to 150%. In some cases, the default 50% works fine. If you use the term "Mac OS" all over the place, you need a little space between "Mac" and "OS," but not too much. And you want the space to be like part of the word, so it doesn't get distorted. The 50% **Flex Space Width** works well there (and, of course, you enter a nonbreaking flex space so "OS" doesn't get abandoned).

Standard Em Space

When **Standard Em Space** is not checked, QuarkXPress thinks an em space is the width of two zeroes in any given font. Check it, and you get an em space that's the same width as the point size of the text (29-point type gets a 29-point em space).

Before QuarkXPress 3.2 (Mac OS) and 3.3 (Mac OS and Windows), there was a furor in the QuarkXPress world about the woefully nonstandard em space. Not being a big em spacer, I was untouched by the furor. However, the ability to change the definition of an em space at the document level has its merits. For example, if you have a job that specifies one em space after a *run-in head*, you'd check **Standard Em Space** so those spaces will be the same size as the point size of the text. If you use en spaces to line up columns of numbers (such as when you make numbered lists allow for two digits), don't check it.

Accents for All Caps

Accents for all caps does what it says: it allows accents to show on characters with All Caps type style applied.

This is a matter of editorial style and typography. Set it according to your publication's standards.

To enter a flex space in text

Press Option+Shift+Space (Ctrl+Shift+5). For a non-breaking flex space, press [cmd]+Option+Shift+Space (Ctrl+Alt+Shift+5).

To enter an em space in text

To enter an em space in text, you actually enter two en spaces: Option+Space (Ctrl+Shift+6) gives you a breaking en space and ⌘+Option+Space (Ctrl+Alt+Shift+6) gives you a nonbreaking en space.

Ligatures (Mac OS Only)

A *ligature* is two characters in one. Some characters sit so closely to each other, and look so natural together, that typographers combine them into one character. Most Mac OS fonts provide ligatures for "fi" and "fl." That's what you get when you check Ligatures—automatic "fi" and "fl" combinations that you can spell check and find/change with no problems.

You might not want ligatures in loosely tracked or kerned text. The **Break Above** field enables you to specify a tracking or kerning value above which QuarkXPress stops inserting ligature characters. And because Mac OS fonts don't usually provide the traditional three-character ligatures for "ffi" and "ffl," you can turn ligatures off in those instances by checking **Not "ffi" or "ffl."** (Although the difference would be subtle, it can look funny to have a standard "f" followed by an "f" that's married to an "i" or "l."

What's with the Mac OS only? Windows fonts don't usually contain ligatures. Some do, and you can enter them manually with keyboard commands. Unfortunately, those "hard" ligatures cause problems when you try to spell check or use Find/Change.

If you share documents between Mac OS and Windows, you should probably turn ligatures off. As much as you might like them, the text reflow problems that can occur will not be worth it. If you're a single-platform Mac fanatic, absolutely use ligatures. If you track out headlines or other display type, set the **Break Above** to divorce the ligatures or you won't get even letter spacing. Go ahead and check **Not "ffi" or "ffl."**

Tool Tab

There are two different things going on in the **Tool** tab (see Figure 2.9). You can select the **Zoom** tool and customize how it works. Not a huge deal. Then there's the item creation tools. You can customize the default attributes of every type of box or line you create in QuarkXPress. You definitely want to take a look at the preferences for simple text boxes and picture boxes. To open the **Tool** tab of Document Preferences quickly, double-click an item creation tool or the **Zoom** tool.

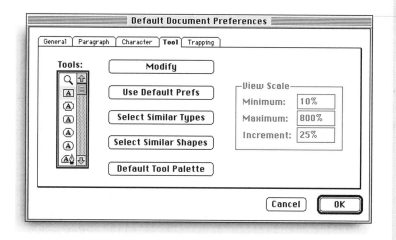

FIGURE 2.9

The **Tool** tab lets you customize multiple item creation tools simultaneously.

Tools and Modify

The **Tools** list shows the **Zoom** tool and all the item creation tools in QuarkXPress. You can select the **Zoom** tool and modify the way it works, or you can select as many item creation tools as you want and modify their common attributes. Shift+click to select a range of item creation tools; ⌘+click (Ctrl+click) to select noncontiguous tools. Once you select some tools, you can modify them.

Clicking **Modify** opens the Modify dialog box with options for the selected tool. For example, if you select the **Text Box** tool, the Modify dialog box contains the standard **Box**, **Text**, **Frame**, and **Runaround** tabs. Fields or options that cannot be set as defaults are grayed out (such as **Width** and **Height**).

If you have multiple tools selected, the Modify dialog box provides options that are common to all the selected tools. For example, if you select two text box tools, you get almost all the same options; however, if you select several box tools and a line tool, you'll only get to choose a default color.

There are a few default preferences to consider changing. It's a good idea to change the default **Text Inset** for the **Rectangle Text Box** tool from 1 point to 0. That 1 point default can throw off all your indent measurements. Other preferences are more subjective. Do you always put frames on certain shaped boxes? Do you always apply the same background color? These are the types of changes to make through Tool Preferences.

Use Default Prefs

The **Use Default Prefs** button reverts the preferences for the selected tools to the original preferences that QuarkXPress ships with. To revert all the tools, select the **Zoom** tool, scroll down to the bottom of the list, and Shift+click the last tool. Then click **Use Default Prefs**.

If you take over someone else's copy of QuarkXPress, and that person had a penchant for hot pink text boxes, you might want to reset tool preferences. Otherwise, if you're going to be looking at preferences, you might as well look at each setting and make sure you like it rather than blindly using the defaults.

Select Similar Types

The **Select Similar Types** button looks at the tool you have selected, and then selects tools that create items of the same type so you can modify them all at once. If you have a picture box tool selected, it selects all the picture box tools. If you have the text path tool selected, it selects all the text path tools. And so on. Very few options are grayed out in the Modify dialog box because the items are essentially the same.

Use the **Select Similar Types** button every time you want to make a global change to text boxes, picture boxes, text paths, or lines. For example, if you hate the default **Text Inset** of 1 point (and you should), you might want to change it for all the text box tools. Or if all the lines you draw are hairlines rather than 1 point, you can select all the line tools and change the default **Width**.

Select Similar Shapes

The **Select Similar Shapes** button looks at the tool you have selected and then selects the other box or line tool of the same shape so you can edit them together. If you have the **Rectangle Picture Box** tool selected, it selects the **Rectangle Text Box** tool. If you have the **Orthogonal Line** tool selected, it selects the **Orthogonal Text-Path** tool. The Modify dialog box contains item attributes only; you can't modify content attributes because they differ.

I'm not sure when this situation would come up. Maybe all your oval text boxes and picture boxes have the same frame? I don't see a big need for this.

Default Tool Palette

You can add, remove, and rearrange the item creation tools in the QuarkXPress 4 Tool palette. If you want to revert to the original Tool palette that ships with version 4, you can click **Default Tool Palette**. Even though this button is within Document Preferences, it changes the Tool palette for the application. Click with care.

The default Tool palette isn't necessarily the best assortment of tools—it's designed to be the least threatening assortment of tools for the 3.x user. If you're new to version 4, or if you're taking over someone else's copy of QuarkXPress, you might want to click **Default Tool Palette** to start editing the Tool palette from scratch. But don't click it thinking it's going to give you the ideal Tool palette. It's far from it.

View Scale

If, and only if, the **Zoom** tool is selected, the **View Scale** area is available. You can use this area to specify the minimum document view (to as low as **10%**) and the maximum view (as high as **800%**) that you can get with the Zoom tool. The **Minimum** and **Maximum** fields control only the Zoom tool. If you enter **400%** in the **Maximum** field, you can still enter **800%** in the view percent field all day long—you just can't use the Zoom tool to get to **800%**. (The **Maximum** view scale allowed varies on Windows according to the **Display DPI Value** specified in the Display tab of Application Preferences.)

The **Increment** field specifies how much the view scale increases or decreases when you click with the Zoom tool. (To decrease the view scale, press the Option (Alt) key when the Zoom tool is selected.)

Because I just memorize the keyboard commands for my favorite views—Thumbnails, Fit in Window, Actual Size, and the toggle to 200%—I rarely use the Zoom tool. But when I do, it's to get up close. Of course, I wouldn't drop the **Maximum** view down. I do occasionally work in 10% view because the little pages are like thumbnails except you can edit them. If you were going to change anything, I'd pick the **Increment**. Who wants to sit there and click to jump up 25%? I'd go for at least a **50%** increase, maybe even **100%**. If you find an **Increment** you really like, go back and set it with no documents open so it becomes the default for all new documents.

SEE ALSO

➤ *To change the view percentage, see page 93*

Trapping Tab

Most people are terrified by *trapping*, and rightly so (see Figure 2.10). If you don't know what you're doing, stay away from it. Not to say that you can't get professional results from QuarkXPress—you just need to know what you're doing. If you're unsure, let the printer or service bureau handle it, or at least have them tell you what to do in QuarkXPress.

Trapping Method

To determine the trapping relationship between object and background colors, QuarkXPress looks at the **Trapping Method**.

- The default method, **Absolute**, uses the values in the **Auto Amount** and **Indeterminate** fields to create traps according to object and background colors. If the object color is darker, the background *chokes* the object color by the **Auto Amount** value. If the object color is lighter, the object is *spread* into the background by the **Auto Amount** value.

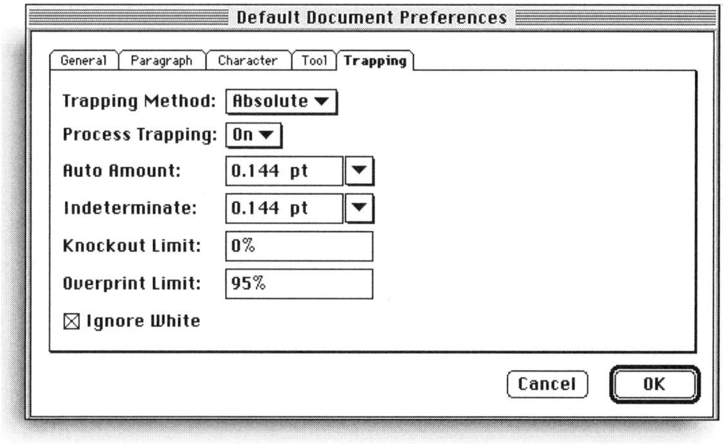

Default Document Preferences

| General | Paragraph | Character | Tool | **Trapping** |

Trapping Method: [Absolute ▼]

Process Trapping: [On ▼]

Auto Amount: [0.144 pt] [▼]

Indeterminate: [0.144 pt] [▼]

Knockout Limit: [0%]

Overprint Limit: [95%]

☒ Ignore White

[Cancel]   [OK]

FIGURE 2.10

The **Trapping** tab controls the default method QuarkXPress uses for trapping colors.

- The **Proportional** method uses the value in the **Auto Amount** field multiplied by the difference between the *luminosity* of the object color and background color to create traps. Proportional trapping compares the luminosity of the object color and background color to determine how different they are, and applies trapping accordingly.

- **Knockout All** turns trapping off.

Process Trapping

Seems like this should be a check box because the only options are **On** and **Off**. When **Process Trapping** is on, QuarkXPress compares the darkness of process components in object colors to the darkness of process components in background colors and traps appropriately. When **Process Trapping** is off, QuarkXPress uses the trapping relationship between the object color and the background color to trap all process components the same way.

Auto Amount

You can specify a positive and negative amount of automatic trapping for individual colors in the Trap Specifications dialog box (accessed by selecting a color in the Colors dialog box and clicking **Edit Trap**). When you do this, the value you enter in this field is used for trapping those colors. You can also choose to *overprint* all colors with **Auto Amount** specified by selecting **Overprint** from the menu attached to the field.

Indeterminate

An **indeterminate** background consists of an imported picture or multiple colors with conflicting trapping relationships. This field specifies the amount of trapping applied to object colors on top of indeterminate backgrounds. Rather than entering a value in the field, you can select **Overprint** from the menu.

Knockout Limit

The **Knockout Limit** specifies when an object color *knocks out* a background color. The value is a percentage of the object color's luminosity compared to the background color's luminosity.

Overprint Limit

Colors that are set to overprint don't always get to. If you use a shade of black or another color that is set to overprint, that object only overprints if its shade percentage is above the **Overprint Limit**. The **Overprint Limit** also applies to the black component of a *rich black*; if the component is lower than the **Overprint Limit**, the rich black won't overprint.

Ignore White

Ignore White does what it sounds like; when it's checked, QuarkXPress doesn't consider white when trapping object colors to background colors. When not checked, all objects overprint white backgrounds. If the background includes white and other colors, the objects trap according to indeterminate.

SEE ALSO

➤ *To use QuarkXPress's trapping controls, see page 479*

Setting Index Preferences

When the Index XTension is running, the **Index** option is added to the **Preferences** submenu of the **Edit** menu. Oddly enough, Index Preferences is where you specify the punctuation added to an index when it's built (see Figure 2.11). It seems logical that this information would be in the Build Index dialog box. Maybe it's in preferences so the one actual preference, **Index Marker Color**, wouldn't get lonely. If you never index your publications, don't worry about these preferences, and disable the Index XTension as well (choose **XTensions Manager** from the **Utilities** menu).

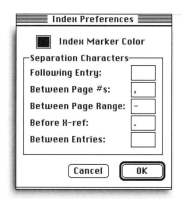

FIGURE 2.11

The Index Preferences dialog box enables you to specify the punctuation to be inserted into your index.

Index Marker Color

Index markers are brackets and flags that signify indexed text. The Index markers display when the Index XTension is running and the Index palette is open. You can customize the color of the markers by clicking the **Index Marker Color** box. This displays your system's default color picker so you can select a color.

This is the one and only preference that can be set by someone who is not a professional indexer. The color simply does not matter. You want something bright enough to see but not too bright to be distracting. Something like, say, blue—the default.

SEE ALSO

➤ *To insert index markers, see page 610*

Following Entry

This is the punctuation or text following each index entry. For example, in "Computer technology, 295–312," a comma and a space are following the entry. Don't forget to enter the punctuation and any spaces in the Following Entry field. You can even enter text such as "on" and special spaces such as *nonbreaking spaces* or flex spaces. If an index entry is followed by a cross-reference, the **Before X-ref** punctuation is used instead of the **Following Entry** punctuation.

This is not something to set on a whim. Find a finished, formatted index that you find easy to read and then see what is following each index entry. Your organization might already have a style for this; if so, follow it. Indexing is serious business. Just because there's now an indexing feature in QuarkXPress doesn't mean amateurs should start indexing.

Between Page #s

This is the punctuation or text between the page numbers listed for each index entry. For example, in "Computer technology, 295, 303–304, 309–310," a comma and space is used between page numbers. It doesn't have to be punctuation; you can use the word "and" between page numbers. You need to enter the punctuation (or text) and space in the field.

Set this the same way as **Following Entry**; follow the style of a professional index.

Between Page Range

This is the punctuation or text used to indicate a range of page. You'll probably press Option+hyphen (Ctrl+Alt+Shift+hyphen) to enter a nice *en dash*, but you can enter words such as "through." If you do enter a word, make sure to precede and follow it with a space in the field.

Set this the same way as **Following Entry**; follow the style of a professional index.

Before X-ref

When a *cross-reference*, or "see also," follows an index entry, or the page numbers listed for an entry, it's usually set off by punctuation. Most often, it's a period, but it can be anything including text.

Set this the same way as **Following Entry**; follow the style of a professional index.

Between Entries

Between Entries is different for run-in and nested indexes.

- A *run-in index* is a two-level index that resembles a paragraph rather than a hierarchical list. Each index entry is followed by a series of subentries and their page numbers and cross-references. (Part of a run-in index might look like this: "Computers, 236–240; In education, 237; Training teachers to use, 239.") The subentries are separated by the punctuation you enter in the **Between Entries** field. In the example, it's a semicolon and a space.

- A *nested index* is your standard hierarchical index. If you enter a character in the **Between Entries** field, it's used as the ending punctuation for each line (or paragraph) in an index.

If you create a nested index, stay away from this. Trust me: You don't want punctuation at the end of each line. Otherwise, take the same advice as for **Following Entry**; follow the style of a professional index.

SEE ALSO

➤ *To generate an index in a document, see page 622*

Setting Color Management Preferences

When the Quark CMS XTension is running, the **Color Management** option is added to the **Preferences** submenu of the **Edit** menu. Before you can do anything, check **Color Management Active** to turn on *color management*. The requisite system software must be installed and active as well (ColorSync or Kodak on Mac OS and Kodak on Windows). Use this dialog box to specify default *profiles* for imported pictures, monitors, and printers. If you never use color management, don't worry about these preferences, and disable the Quark CMS XTension (choose **XTensions Manager** from the **Utilities** menu).

Destination Profiles

Basically, what you're doing here is telling Quark CMS what kind of equipment you generally use. Choose the profile for your monitor from the **Monitor** pop-up menu. Choose the profile for the printer you use for *color proofs* from the **Composite Printer** pop-up menu. Finally, choose the imagesetter you use for printing *color separations* from the **Separation Printer** pop-up menu.

The way to set this is obvious; pick what you have or are plan to use. If your equipment is not listed, contact the manufacturer about obtaining a profile.

Default Source Profiles

Colors in imported pictures and colors defined in QuarkXPress all have to come from somewhere. RGB pictures, for example, probably came from a scanner; RGB colors came from your monitor. The tabs in the **Default Source Profile** section enable you to specify default color and image source profiles for *RGB*, *CMYK*, and *Hexachrome* colors.

Choose the input equipment you use (scanners, monitors, and so on) and the output equipment you intend to use (printing methods).

Display Correction

The Quark CMS XTension can attempt to simulate a different color space on your monitor. For example, it can display what it thinks a document will look like printed in CMYK. If you choose **Off**, it doesn't attempt anything. If you choose **Monitor Color Space**, it makes the document look as good as possible according to the profile selected for your monitor. Choosing **Composite Printer Color Space** or **Separation Printer Color Space** is the scary thing. Your monitor tries to display colors according to the profiles selected for the composite printer and separation printer.

The **Correction/Color Model** list at the bottom of the dialog box is tied to the **Display Correction**. When **Display Correction** is on, it only attempts to simulate colors created in the color models you check. For example, if **Display Correction** is set to **Separation Printer Color Space**, and you check **CMYK**, then CMYK colors in the document will be corrected to simulate the color space of the separation printer you specified in **Destination Profiles**

For this to work, your monitor must be set to display at least thousands of colors. Results vary according to the quality of your monitor and the viewing conditions. In all honesty, it's a simulation. Monitors can't show what will come off a printing press. You might want to check out a composite or separation printer simulation for a minute, but as a general rule, let your monitor do its work and display RGB.

SEE ALSO

➤ *To use QuarkXPress's color management feature, see page 467*

What's in the XPress Preferences File?

What do you think is in the XPress Preferences file? Probably the things that QuarkXPress actually calls Preferences: Application Preferences and Document Preferences. Although Application Preferences are always saved in this file, and Document Preferences are saved here when no documents are open, there's a bunch of other information in XPress Preferences as well.

Why do you care what's in there? Because that's how you know what triggers the *Nonmatching Preferences alert* when you open a document, and that's how you know how to share information among documents. First, look at the list of what's in the XPress Preferences file:

- Application Preferences
- XTensions Manager settings
- PPD Manager settings
- Print styles
- Default Document Preferences
- Default style sheets, colors, H&Js, lists, and Dashes & Stripes
- Path to the default *auxiliary dictionary*
- *Kerning tables* created with the Kern/Track Editor

- *Tracking tables* created with the Kern/Track Editor
- Hyphenation exceptions
- *Bitmap frames* created with Frame Editor on Mac OS

The items in the XPress Preferences file can be divided into three categories according to the way QuarkXPress automatically saves them with your document.

Saving in XPress Preferences

Application Preferences, print styles, XTensions Manager settings, and PPD Manager settings are easy to understand. When you change them, the changes have no effect on the current document. The changes affect QuarkXPress and are saved in the XPress Preferences file. You will never see the Nonmatching Preferences alert as a result of changing these settings.

Saving in XPress Preferences or the Document

Document Preferences, default styles (style sheets, colors, H&Js, lists, and Dashes & Stripes), and the path to the default auxiliary dictionary are not too hard to understand. If you change them with no documents open, the changes affect new documents and are saved in the XPress Preferences file. If you change these settings when a document is open, the changes affect that document. You will never see the Nonmatching Preferences box as a result of changing these settings.

Saving in XPress Preferences and/or the Document

These are the troublemakers: kerning tables, tracking tables, hyphenation exceptions, and bitmap frames created with Frame Editor. So why are these preferences so annoying? It's the way they are saved: If no documents are open when you change them, the changes are saved in the XPress Preferences file and affect all new documents. Easy enough? If a document is open, as you'd expect, changes are saved only with that document. Here's the catch—changes are saved only with the document unless you clicked **Use XPress Preferences** when you opened the document. In that case, changes you make to these preferences settings are saved in both the document and the XPress Preferences file. (Therefore, the updated preferences will be used for all new documents.) Here's where Nonmatching Preferences rears its ugly box.

Dealing with Nonmatching Preferences

The next time you get the Nonmatching Preferences box, take a second to actually read it. It lists the information that doesn't match the current preferences: hyphenation exceptions, kerning/tracking information, and so on. Keep in mind that this means the preferences saved with the document don't match your own XPress Preferences, not some standard XPress Preferences.

Now's your chance to figure out what's going on. Did the person that created this document add new kerning/tracking information? And should they have? If you're sure that whatever changes were made to the preferences should not have been made, click **Use XPress Preferences**.

What if you're not sure about the changes? You can always click **Keep Document Settings** and take a quick look at the document—even print it out for reference. Then, close the document and reopen. This time, click **Use XPress Preferences**. Look through the document to see if anything has changed. If the document has changed dramatically, choose **Revert to Saved** from the **File** menu. This gives you a chance to change your mind about the Nonmatching Preferences button you choose.

Customizing the Tool Palette

Never make round text boxes? Hate that crosshair line tool? In QuarkXPress 4, it's now you see it, now you don't. You can customize the Tool palette, to a certain degree, to show the tools you use most in the order you prefer. If you're one of those people that needs to lay all your options out on the table, you can display all 28 tools in all their glory. If you're a minimalist, you can pare the palette down to a few squares reminiscent of Mondrian.

Displaying the Tool Palette

QuarkXPress has many ways to open and close the Tool palette. You wouldn't think this is necessary because most people keep their tools up all the time. But still, if you want to open and close them on-the-fly to maximize screen space, here's how you can do it.

- If you like your mouse, select **Show Tools** or **Hide Tools** from the **View** menu.
- If you have an extended keyboard—and you're not using the function keys for QuicKeys or something else—press F8.
- All other keyboarders, press ⌘+Tab or ⌘+Shift+Tab (Ctrl+Alt+Tab or Ctrl+Alt+Shift+Tab).

Windows users have the option to display the Tool palette vertically or horizontally. To change the direction, press the Ctrl key while you double-click the Tool palette's title bar. If you're accustomed to using a word processor, you might prefer the horizontal orientation.

Selecting Tools

Put the Tool palette where it works for you

The Tool palette remembers where you put it onscreen. If you're right-handed, there's no reason to have the tools in their default location on the left. Place the tools in the most convenient location for you, and each time you launch, they'll show up in that location.

Selecting a tool is easy; just click on it. QuarkXPress also provides some keyboard commands for temporarily switching tools. If you want to use the Item tool for a second, just press ⌘ (Ctrl). To zoom in, press Ctrl (Ctrl+Spacebar); to zoom out, press Ctrl+Option (Ctrl+Alt+Spacebar). To use the Grabber Hand for scrolling, press Option (Alt).

If the Tool palette is already open, pressing ⌘+Tab (Ctrl+Alt+Tab) selects the next tool in the palette for you. Pressing ⌘+Shift+Tab (Ctrl+Alt+Shift+Tab) selects the previous tool. If you're switching between two sequential drawing tools in the palette, these commands can be helpful.

The concept of the "selected" tool is slightly different from version 3.x to version 4. In 3.x, the selected tool is document-specific; each active document remembers which tool you used on it last. In version 4, the selected tool is application-specific; the same tool is selected regardless of the active document.

Adding and Removing Tools

QuarkXPress 3.x had 13 tools that showed up all the time whether you liked it or not. QuarkXPress 4 has 28 tools! Most of them are hiding inside pop-outs indicated by little triangles next to tools. In the version 4 palette, you get some control over which item creation tools display, but you're still stuck with all the manipulation tools. So you can hide the odd and useless Orthogonal Line tool (the big plus sign), but whether you're a rotater or not, the Rotate tool is there to stay. You're also stuck with the Item tool, the Content tool, the Zoom tool, the Linking tool, and the Unlinking tool. You can't hide all the item creation tools either. You're forced to keep one for each type of item: text box, picture box, line, and text path. Quark's Tool palette programmer refers to these as the "big daddy" tools.

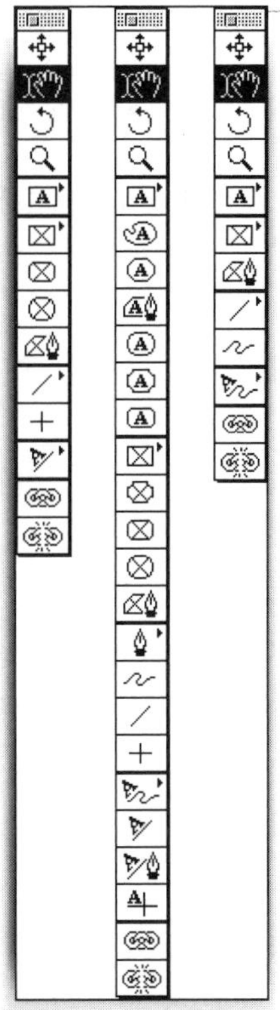

FIGURE 2.12

The default Tool palette (left) is designed not to frighten 3.x users; we prefer the configuration on the far right. The Tool palette in the center is the madness resulting from displaying all the tools.

Showing tool names

If you're not sure what all those tools are for, try the neat new Tool Tips feature. To use it, open the Application Preferences dialog box and click the **Interactive** tab. Check **Show Tool Tips** and click **OK**. When you point at a tool with your mouse, a little pop-up gives you a descriptive tool name.

The default QuarkXPress 4 Tool palette is designed not to frighten the 3.x user. All your familiar tools are there, plus a few new ones. Quark wouldn't want anyone to think their favorite tool is gone! However, this collection of tools is fairly inefficient and you should consider changing it. If you're afraid to mess with the palette, don't worry. A big button in Tool Preferences lets you revert the palette to its default state.

- To display the pop-out tools, click and hold on one of the tools with a triangle next to it.
- To replace the tool in the palette with a pop-out tool, drag to select it.
- To add a tool to the palette, press the Ctrl key while you display a pop-out and select a tool.
- To hide a tool inside a pop-out, press the Ctrl key and click on it.

You might need to work with QuarkXPress for a while to figure out which tools you use most. As a starting point, consider hiding the Rounded-corner Picture Box tool, the Oval Picture Box tool, and the Orthogonal Line tool. If you think you'll be creating Bézier text boxes, add the Bézier Text Box tool to the palette.

Working with QuarkXPress Files

You've taken a quick tour of new features and a general look at the basic interface of QuarkXPress; now it's time to find out how those features are used in the everyday world of page layout and design. QuarkXPress has become a more complete design tool package, and many of the new features will make your work more efficient in even those very basic tasks of creating, opening, and saving documents.

Creating Documents

As with most projects worth doing, creating a document is also worth planning. Before you create a new document in QuarkXPress, take some time to think through all of its elements. What size will it be, will you need to do multiple (three or more) page spreads? Do you want to use a *facing page* format? Should you use *automatic text boxes*? What elements need to be on a *master page*, and how many master pages will you need? *Spot color*, *process color*, both? Having a clear understanding of where you're headed before you take the first step will make the trip easier and require less backtracking.

Start with the Right Page Size

The first thing you need to do is start with the correct page size. After you have set up a page size in a new document, it is difficult to change it. You can make it bigger, but, of course, you probably will need to rearrange all the elements on all your pages. Making a page smaller, however, leads to real problems. When you try to make pages smaller, QuarkXPress is likely to give you an error message saying that it can't place elements off the *pasteboard*. That means your boxes are too big for the new page size. If you err in this direction when setting up a document, it's probably best to start fresh with another document and the correct page size.

The correct page size is usually the *trim size* of your document. The exception would be if you are creating something small, such as business cards or name tags or tickets, and plan to print several on a single sheet.

SEE ALSO
➤ *To change the width of the pasteboard, see page 43*
➤ *To use the pasteboard to store items, see page 125*

Filling Out the New Document Dialog Box

The New Document dialog box, shown in Figure 3.1, is accessed from the **File** menu (choose **New Document**). It is divided into four sections, each reflecting a different choice you need to make when creating a new document.

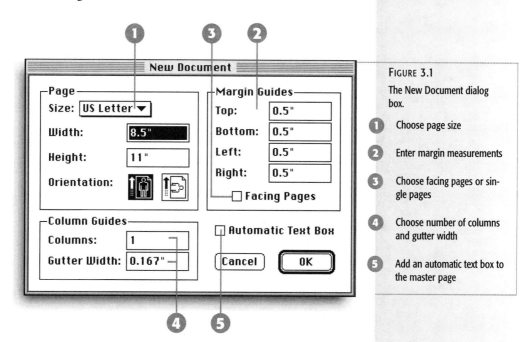

FIGURE 3.1

The New Document dialog box.

1. Choose page size
2. Enter margin measurements
3. Choose facing pages or single pages
4. Choose number of columns and gutter width
5. Add an automatic text box to the master page

Page Section

The **Page** section is where you will select your page size. Remember that your page size is usually the same as the trim size of your final printed piece. QuarkXPress contains some built-in common page sizes (**US Letter, US Legal, A4 Letter,**

B5 Letter, and Tabloid), or you can enter your special size numbers in the **Width** and **Height** boxes. Clicking on the **Orientation** icons changes your pages from *portrait* (tall) to *landscape* (wide).

Margin Guides

In the **Margin Guides** section, you type the amount of margin you want on each page. The default value is 1/2 inch (or its equivalent if you are using a different measurement system). You can enter any value you want in the **Top, Bottom, Left**, and **Right** fields, using any measurement system you want. These are the values that QuarkXPress uses to determine the "live" area on your page. Nonprinting guidelines will appear on each page at these measurements in from the outside edges of the page. These are guidelines only; you can place elements that you want to print outside of them if you want. They simply provide you a visual clue to the white space around the edge of your page.

The **Margin Guide** choices change if you decide to make your document use a facing-page format by clicking the button next to **Facing Pages**. In a facing-page document, page 1 is always on the right side (as are all odd-numbered pages), and the left side contains even-numbered pages. Instead of **Top, Bottom, Left**, and **Right**, you see **Top, Bottom, Inside**, and **Outside**, with **Inside** representing the measurement applied to the *gutter* area where the pages meet in the middle. Each master page consists of a two-page spread.

SEE ALSO

➤ *To change master guide settings after a document is created, see page 157*

Column Guides

To set up the number of columns on your page, place a number in the **Columns** box. If you are new to QuarkXPress, know that every page has at least one column—it might be the entire width of the page, but QuarkXPress considers that a column. This box does not accept the number zero. The **Gutter Width** is the space allowed between columns. The default is .167 inches or 1 pica.

If you select **Automatic Text Box**, the choices you make for **Column Guides** will appear in the automatic text box. If you selected to have three columns, the automatic text box will be divided into three columns. However, if you decide not to use **Automatic Text Box**, you can draw your own boxes based on the nonprinting guidelines on your page, or another size.

SEE ALSO

➤ *To change column and gutter settings after a document is created, see page 157*

Automatic Text Box

When you select the **Automatic Text Box** option, a linked text box appears on your master page and on every new page in the document based on that master. The size of the automatic text box is determined by the margins you selected; the automatic text box fills the area inside the margins.

When text is imported (or typed) into an automatic text box and you have **Auto Page Insertion** turned on in the General Preferences, QuarkXPress automatically creates a new page whenever you get to the end of a page until all the text has been imported. It's fast and you don't have to know how many pages you need before you start importing the text. Each of the newly created pages is identical to the one where you started the text flow.

The best use for an automatic text box is for long documents in which you will import large text files, such as books and manuals. If text is simply going to flow in a straight continuous line, from column to column or from page to page, your document is a candidate for an automatic text box. It's also a candidate if you really don't know how many pages you'll need to accommodate your text. Allowing QuarkXPress to automatically create enough pages to place all your text is a true time-saver. If, however, you are doing newsletters or newspapers, even though they might have several pages, you'll find it easier to work by creating your own boxes and linking them manually.

SEE ALSO

➤ *To create an automatic text box on an existing master page, see page 190*

Opening Documents and Templates

Opening an already-existing QuarkXPress document is as easy as choosing **Open** from the **File** menu (see Figure 3.2). Select the file you want to open, and click on the **Open** button. The dialog box displays the last date and time modified, version, and size of any file highlighted in the list. A preview window shows a miniaturized version of the document's first page if the **Preview** check box was selected when the document was saved.

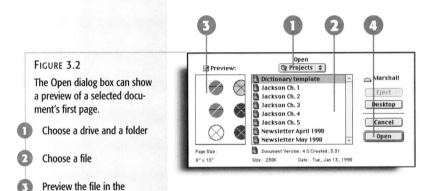

FIGURE 3.2

The Open dialog box can show a preview of a selected document's first page.

1 Choose a drive and a folder

2 Choose a file

3 Preview the file in the window

4 Click to open the file

An existing document opens with the name of the document displayed across the top of the menu bar. *Templates*, on the other hand, open with no name; like any new document, they are called Document #, in which # is a real number depending on how many templates you've opened or new documents you've created during any work session with QuarkXPress.

SEE ALSO

➤ *To save a document as a template, see page 90*

➤ *To design an efficient template, see page 200*

Saving Documents

Documents don't have a very long shelf life, unless you save them. There are many saving options in QuarkXPress, so take the time to familiarize yourself with all of them and how they might help you. The best hint about saving a document? Always save your document before you print even one page!

When you do a hard, or manual, save of a document for the first time, you see the Save As dialog box, shown in Figure 3.3. Users of earlier versions will notice a couple of minor changes, but the command to save is the same: choose **Save** from the **File** menu, or press ⌘+S (Ctrl+S).

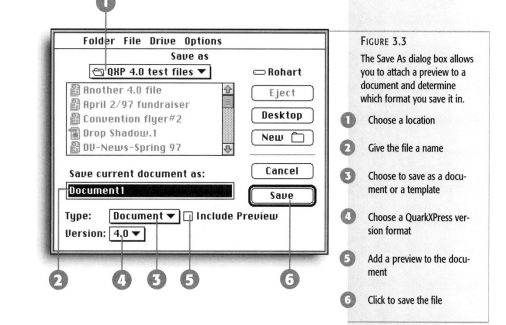

FIGURE 3.3

The Save As dialog box allows you to attach a preview to a document and determine which format you save it in.

1. Choose a location

2. Give the file a name

3. Choose to save as a document or a template

4. Choose a QuarkXPress version format

5. Add a preview to the document

6. Click to save the file

To save a document, select the location for the file in the list window, and type a name in the **Save Current Document As** field. Before you click on the **Save** button, you must make three other choices: type, version, and preview. The pop-up menu called **Type** allows you to choose between saving as a document and saving as a template (the default is **Document**). The pop-up menu called **Version** allows you to save QuarkXPress 4 documents so that they can be read by version 3.3. (the default is **4.0**). The **Include preview** box creates a thumbnail of the first page of your document or template in the window to the left. After you've made all your choices, click on the **Save** button and you're done.

The Auto Backup and Auto Save features also save your document for you. Auto Backup creates a backup copy each time you save, and Auto Save remembers to save at specified intervals so you don't have to.

SEE ALSO

➤ *To set Auto Save and Auto Backup preferences, see page 44*

Saving a Copy of a File

The Save As menu choice also is used to give an existing document a new name or save it in a new location. Select **Save As** from the **File** menu, choose a location to save in, and type a new name (if you want) in the **Save Current Document As** field. You then have a new version of your existing document without overwriting the first version. From this point on, you're working in the new document, so if you want to return to working in the original document, choose **Close** from the **File** menu (or press ⌘+W (Ctrl+W)) and re-open the original document.

Saving Documents as Templates

A template is a pseudo-document that provides a pattern for other documents. You can use it over and over to create similar-looking documents. If you have a document you want to turn into a template or are specifically creating a template, you must use the **Save As** menu choice. Select **Template** as the **Type**. It's handy to include a preview of your template. Templates always open as unnamed documents. If you are doing intermediate saves of work on a template, you need to use **Save As**, select **Template**, and keep giving it the same name. This action overwrites any earlier versions of your template.

Downsaving: 4.0 Documents in 3.3 Format

You can save QuarkXPress 4 documents so that someone using version 3 can open them and work on them. However, any of the features specific to version 4 will be lost. Bézier boxes will turn into polygon boxes; text aligned along a line of any type will be turned into text in a text box. If you have anchored lines, they will disappear. If you have anchored a nonrectangular box in a text box, it will become rectangular. Character style sheets are lost, but the style remains applied to the text. Believe it or not, no-content boxes stay no-content boxes, even though that feature didn't exist in QuarkXPress 3.

Using Book and Library File Types

Besides documents, QuarkXPress 4 lets you create *library* files and *book* files. There are some specifics you should know about these formats.

When you create a new book or library, you are asked to name it immediately. The dialog box is identical for both choices except for the title at the top (see Figure 3.4). After you name it, a new floating palette appears on your screen where you will keep the contents of either a library or a book.

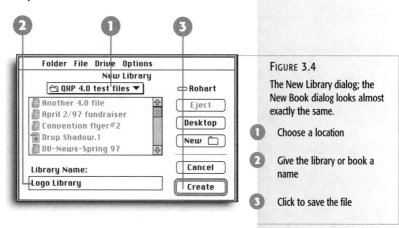

FIGURE 3.4

The New Library dialog; the New Book dialog looks almost exactly the same.

1. Choose a location

2. Give the library or book a name

3. Click to save the file

Libraries and books have icons distinctive from document icons (see Figures 3.5 and 3.6). This difference helps you spot them in folders or in the Open dialog box. They are opened in the same way you open a document, by choosing **Open** from the **File** menu. In Mac versions of QuarkXPress, you'll see that the information at the bottom of the dialog box labels libraries as XLIB documents and books as XBOK documents.

FIGURE 3.5
The Library icon.

Logo Library

FIGURE 3.6
The Book icon.

Great American Novel

Book and Library floating palettes are automatically saved when you close the palette window. Libraries can also be saved every time you add a new element by selecting **Auto Library Save** in the Application Preferences **Save** tab.

SEE ALSO

➤ *To store items in libraries, see page 143*

➤ *To organize multi-file projects with book files, see page 578*

Navigating Documents

QuarkXPress provides many ways to move through your document and view it onscreen. Navigating means moving to different pages, to different locations on the same page, or to a different view size. Become adept at all these methods. You'll find that you develop your own style of doing things; but take the time to learn the shortcuts, and you'll save a lot of time.

Changing Views

QuarkXPress gives you several ways to change the view of documents on your monitor. You can make them larger or smaller, depending on the size of your monitor and how much of the document you want to see. Macintosh users can view a page at up to 800% of its original size; for Windows users the amount of enlargement depends on the resolution of the monitor. On either platform, you can reduce the view size to 10%.

Zoom Tool

The Zoom tool $\boxed{Q}$, located on the Tool palette, is the one that looks like a magnifying glass (that makes sense, doesn't it?). Select it and click on a spot on your page, and it keeps enlarging by increments you set in the Tool Preferences. The area you click on moves to the center of your screen. Hold down the Option (Alt) key while using the Zoom tool, and the view size decreases.

The Zoom tool is also used to *marquee* (select by dragging the cursor) a specific spot on your page for enlargement. With the tool selected, click and drag around your target area. When you release the mouse button, the marqueed area expands to fill your screen (within the limits of QuarkXPress and your monitor).

You also can access the Zoom tool while using the Content tool by holding down Control (Ctrl+Alt). The Content tool temporarily turns into the Zoom tool, reverting to the Content tool when you release Control (Ctrl+Alt).

View Menu

The drop-down **View** menu, shown in Figure 3.7, gives you some built-in choices for document display size. Hold down the Option (Alt) key while selecting **Fit in Window**, and your entire spread and pasteboard are displayed.

Customize the Zoom increment

You can set the increment of enlargement or reduction in Document Preferences. A fast way to get there is by double-clicking on the Zoom tool (this works for setting preferences for any tool).

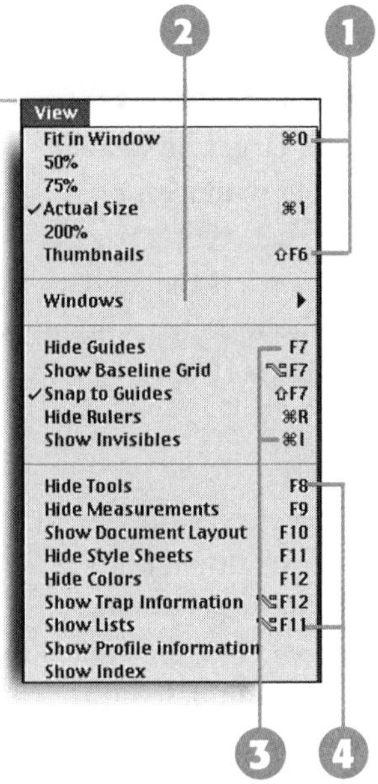

FIGURE 3.7

The **View** menu lets you determine which document you're looking at, at what size, and what palettes are shown.

1 Use these commands to change the view magnification

2 Choose an open document from the Windows submenu

3 Use these commands to hide and display rulers, guides, and text formatting characters

4 Use these commands to hide and display QuarkXPress's palettes

View	
Fit in Window	⌘0
50%	
75%	
✓Actual Size	⌘1
200%	
Thumbnails	⇧F6
Windows	▶
Hide Guides	F7
Show Baseline Grid	⌥⇧F7
✓Snap to Guides	⇧F7
Hide Rulers	⌘R
Show Invisibles	⌘I
Hide Tools	F8
Hide Measurements	F9
Show Document Layout	F10
Hide Style Sheets	F11
Hide Colors	F12
Show Trap Information	⌥⇧F12
Show Lists	⌥⇧F11
Show Profile information	
Show Index	

Keyboard Commands

Table 3.1 contains some of the keyboard shortcuts for changing the view size of your document.

TABLE 3.1   Shortcuts for changing the view size

Action	Mac OS	Windows
Fit in Window	⌘+0 (zero)	Ctrl+0 (zero)
100%	⌘+1	Ctrl+1
Thumbnail	Control+V, T, Enter	
Go to View Percent Field	Control+V	Ctrl+Alt+V
Toggle between 100% & 200%	⌘+Option+click	Ctrl+Alt+click
Fit Spread and Pasteboard in Window	⌘+Option+0	Ctrl+Alt+0 (zero)
Grabber hand	Option+drag	Alt+drag

Switching Pages

There are also several ways of moving to a different page in your document.

Page Menu

The drop-down **Page** menu, shown in Figure 3.8, has several built-in options.

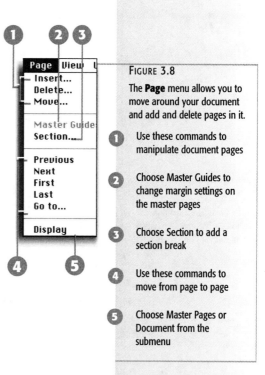

FIGURE 3.8

The **Page** menu allows you to move around your document and add and delete pages in it.

1 Use these commands to manipulate document pages

2 Choose Master Guides to change margin settings on the master pages

3 Choose Section to add a section break

4 Use these commands to move from page to page

5 Choose Master Pages or Document from the submenu

Keyboard Commands

You also can move between pages by using keyboard commands. Table 3.2 lists these shortcuts.

TABLE 3.2   Shortcuts for moving between pages

Action	Mac OS	Windows
Go to Page ?	⌘+J	Ctrl+J
Next Page	⌘+Page Down	Page Down
Previous Page	⌘+Page Up	Page Up
Page 1	⌘+Home	Ctrl+Page Up
Last Page	⌘+End	Ctrl+Page Down

Page Icons

The Document Layout palette (accessible by choosing **Show Document Layout** from the **View** menu) provides a visual way of moving around in your document (see Figure 3.9). Double-click on any page icon and move immediately to that page. You can move to master pages displayed on this palette in the same manner.

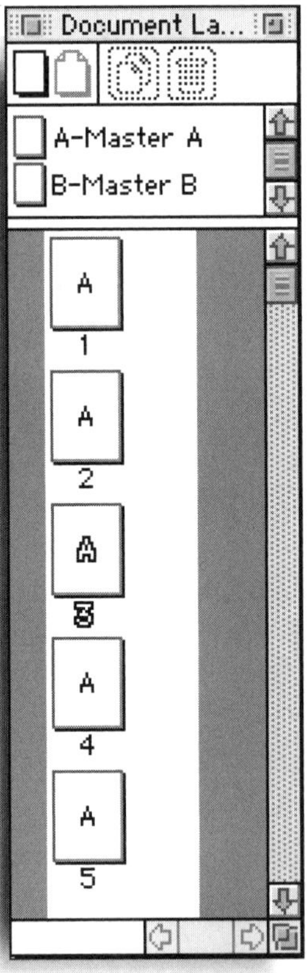

FIGURE 3.9

The Document Layout palette shows a document's master pages and its document pages.

Hold down the triangular button at the bottom of a document window by the page number, and page icons pop out (see Figure 3.10). Move to a page by dragging the arrow until the desired page has a dark border on it and then releasing. You can distinguish master pages from document pages by the margin guides that appear only on master page icons. Earlier versions of QuarkXPress used an *XTension* called Bobzilla to add this function. With QuarkXPress 4, you no longer need Bobzilla.

Stacking and Tiling Documents

Stacking/cascading and *tiling* refer to the way in which multiple open documents are displayed on your monitor. Stack is a term used with the Mac OS, and cascade is used with Windows. If you stack/cascade the documents, they sit on top of each other, and only the frontmost is visible. If you tile them, the window containing each document is made smaller, and each open document is visible on the monitor at the same time. Users with two or more monitors can opt to have documents tile to multiple monitors by altering the Application Preferences. If you are using the Windows operating system, stacking, tiling, and a list of open documents all turn up under the **Windows** drop-down menu that is part of the Windows operating environment.

Mac OS users can find **Stack** and **Tile** under the **Windows** submenu in the **View** menu, as shown in Figure 3.11. You can move through multiple open documents by using the submenu or (and much quicker) by holding down the Shift key and clicking on the document title bar, as shown in Figure 3.12. Immediately, a list drops down, showing all currently open documents (as well as the **Stack Documents** and **Tile Documents** commands), and you can highlight the one you want to move to the front.

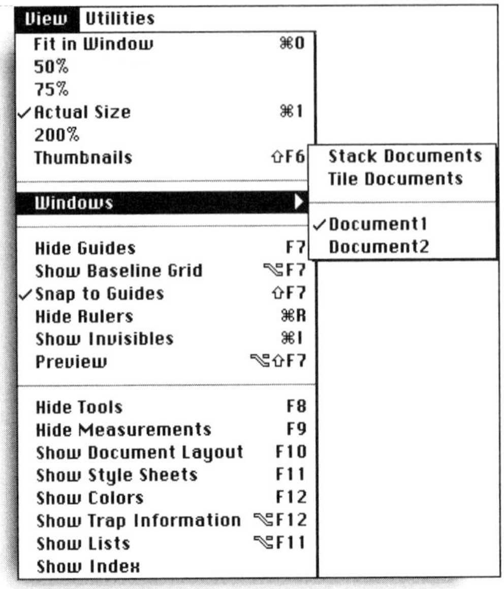

FIGURE 3.11

The **Windows** submenu lists all the open documents.

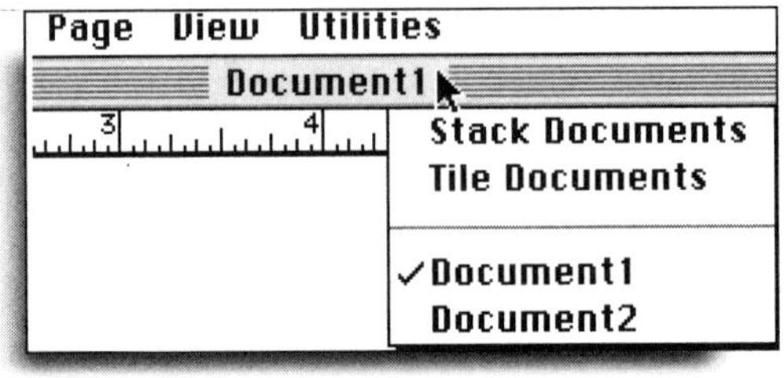

FIGURE 3.12

Clicking on the title bar shows a drop-down menu of open documents, with stacking and tiling options also available.

Stacking and Tiling to Specific Sizes

There are some convenient keyboard commands that let Mac OS users change the view size of a document while either tiling or stacking the display through the **Windows** submenu in the **View** menu. Table 3.3 lists these commands.

TABLE 3.3   Changing the view size

Action	Command
100% of size	Control+Tile/Stack
Fit in window	⌘+Tile/Stack
Thumbnails	Option+Tile/Stack

To access these options from the document title bar, use the commands shown in Table 3.4.

TABLE 3.4   Changing the view size from the title bar

Action	Command
100% of size	Control+Shift+Tile/Stack
Fit in window	⌘+Shift+Tile/Stack
Thumbnails	Option+Shift+Tile/Stack

Windows users will find that when they right-click on the title of the document, a drop-down menu appears. In this menu you can select **Restore**, **Move**, **Size**, **Minimize**, **Maximize**, or **Close**.

Page Layout

Laying Out Pages

Create boxes and lines

Resize and reshape boxes and lines

Add text or pictures

Change an item's content type

Apply frames to boxes

Create custom frame styles

Use rulers and guides to position items on a page

Align and distribute items evenly

Group items

Skew boxes

We started out by saying that everything in QuarkXPress uses a box and you should learn to love them. Now you'll begin to understand why. This chapter introduces you to boxes, how to make them, how to put things into them, how to arrange them, how to dress them up a bit, how to move them around —within a document and between documents—and how to save them for future use. This chapter discusses mostly basic box shapes.

Standard Boxes and Lines

You create both text and *picture boxes* by using the appropriate tool. For basic rectangular *text boxes*, select the fifth tool down in the Tool palette that looks like a box with the letter A in it 🄰. You create picture boxes using any of the next three tools 🄰 🄰 🄰 , each of which gives you a different shape of box.

To create a box:

1. Move your cursor over the Tool palette.
2. Click on the box type you want to use.
3. Your cursor turns into a tiny crosshair.
4. Move the cursor back to your page and drag to create a box in the shape you want.

If you want a perfectly square box, hold the Shift key down while using a rectangular box tool. For a perfectly round box, hold the Shift key down while using one of the oval box tools.

QuarkXPress has a collection of built-in corner types for rectangular or square boxes: concave corners, round corners, beveled corners. To use these, select the version of the text or picture box tool that looks like it has one of these corner styles. You can change the corner style of an existing box by choosing **Shape** from the **Item** menu and then choosing an option from the submenu.

You can also edit rounded corner styles in the **Box** tab of the Modify dialog box.

SEE ALSO
➤ *To change a rounded-corner box's corner radius, see page 108*

Drawing Text Boxes

Text boxes, of course, contain all the text in your document that you either type in QuarkXPress or import from a word processing document. Although you might have set up your document to use an automatic text box, you probably still need additional text boxes in your document.

Drawing Picture Boxes

Picture boxes have an X drawn through them until you fill them with some sort of graphic element *imported* from another application. This helps you distinguish between empty text boxes and picture boxes as you lay out your document; the X only shows on screen—it doesn't print. If all you do is fill a picture box with a background color, it will still have an X drawn through it.

Inputting Text

To fill your text box with text, you must have the Content tool
[ ] selected. Click on your text box after selecting the Content tool and a blinking text cursor called a *text insertion bar* appears. All that's left for you to do is to start typing.

Perhaps you need to import text already prepared in a word processing application. Choose **Get Text** from the **File** menu or press ⌘+E (Ctrl+E). Select the text file you want to import and click on **OK**.

You can paste text into a text box by selecting the box with the Content tool and choosing **Paste** from the **Edit** menu or pressing ⌘+V (Ctrl+V). Use this if you have just copied a block of text to the *Clipboard* from either another application or another box in QuarkXPress.

SEE ALSO

➤ *To include document styles when importing text, see page 186*

➤ *To convert quotation marks and em dashes when importing text, see page 183*

Importing or Pasting Pictures

Using either the Content [⌖] or Item [✥] tool, pictures are *placed* in much the same way as text. Select your target picture box and choose **Get Picture** from the **File** menu, or press ⌘+E (Ctrl+E). In the Get Picture dialog box, highlight the graphic file you want to put in the box and click **OK**.

Similarly to text, you also can paste a picture into a box by choosing **Paste** from the **Edit** menu or pressing ⌘+V (Ctrl+V).

SEE ALSO

➤ *To learn more about importing pictures, see page 338*

Drawing Straight Lines

Although boxes are used as containers for either text or graphic images, lines (often called rules) might be used on pages to define or set off certain spaces. They might serve an artistic, design or organizational purpose.

To draw a line:

1. Move the cursor over the Tool palette.
2. Click on the Line [╱] or Orthogonal Line [+] tool.
3. The cursor turns into a tiny crosshair.
4. Move the cursor back over the page and drag to create a line.

The Line tools do just what they look like they should do. The one that looks like a crosshair draws only horizontal or vertical lines. It's known as the Orthogonal Line tool (which I've always thought sounds like something painful in the dentist's office). The tool that looks like an angled line draws lines that can be rotated 360 degrees.

Resizing and Reshaping Boxes and Lines

You'll be glad to know that you don't have to get everything right the first time around. QuarkXPress lets you resize and reshape boxes and lines at will, and even offers several different ways to do it.

Dragging Handles

Notice that all text and picture boxes have eight handles on them, one in each corner and another in the middle of each side. While using either the Content [icon] or Item [icon] tool, dragging on any of these handles reshapes your boxes (see Figure 4.1). The cursor turns into a pointing finger and the original size and shape of your box remains visible (while the adjusted size and shape appear as well in a shadowy gray form) until you release the mouse (see Table 4.1).

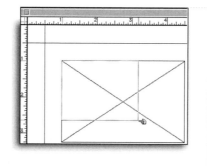

FIGURE 4.1

Drag any handle to resize a box.

TABLE 4.1   Resizing text and picture boxes

Action	Command
Change width only	Drag middle handle on right or left.
Change height only	Drag middle handle on top or bottom.
Change width & height	Drag corner handle.
Change width & height and maintain aspect ratio	Option+Shift+drag (Alt+Shift+drag) any handle.
Change to square or circle	Shift+click any handle.

It's worth experimenting with the last two commands to see what happens when you use them with different handles. The position of your resized box depends on which handle you use. The point opposite the one you move remains stable. All the other points move.

Straight lines, however, have only two handles, one at each end. Dragging either handle changes the length of any line and can change the angle, depending on which direction you drag. There are ways, however, to *constrain* the movement of angled lines when you resize them (see Table 3.2).

TABLE 3.2   Resizing angled lines

Action	Command
Constrain the angle	Option+Shift+drag (Alt+Shift+drag) handle.
Constrain angle to 45 degree increments	Shift+drag handle

SEE ALSO

➤ *To resize more than one object at a time, see page 134*

Entering Values

A less visual but more precise way of changing the size of boxes and lines is through the Modify dialog box or the Measurements palette.

For text and picture boxes you can enter precise dimensions in the **Height** and **Width** fields (see Figure 4.2). Note that even round or oval boxes are bound by an imaginary square or rectangle that determines their size.

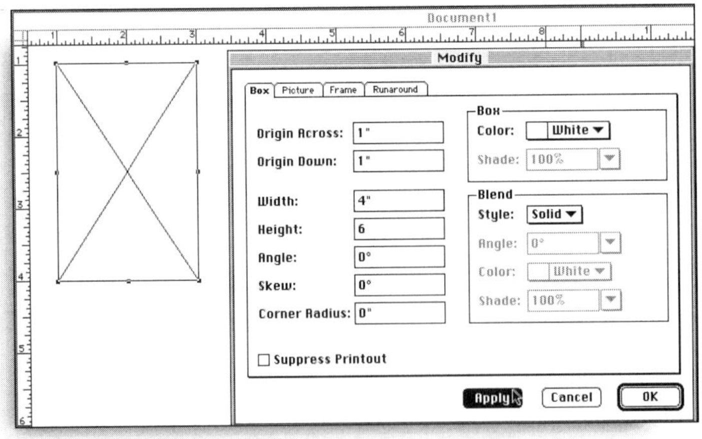

FIGURE 4.2

The Modify dialog box's **Box** tab contains numerical controls for a box's attributes.

The **Box** tab also allows you to change a rectangular box to a rounded-corner one and adjust how rounded the corners are. In the **Corner Radius** field, you can enter any measurement between .001 inch and 2.0 inches. The default measurement for all these styles is .25 inch. (See Figures 4.3 and 4.4.)

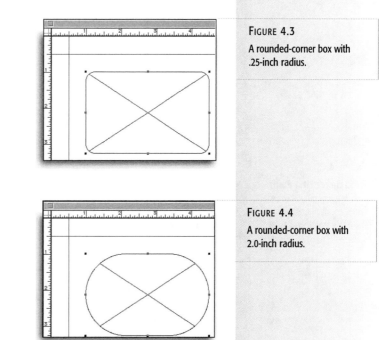

FIGURE 4.3

A rounded-corner box with .25-inch radius.

FIGURE 4.4

A rounded-corner box with 2.0-inch radius.

Similar options are available in the Modify dialog box's **Line** tab (see Figures 4.5 and 4.6). But you need to pay attention to the **Mode** pop-up menu that lets you pick how you want the measurements for your line displayed. If you choose **Endpoints** (which is the default), you see the *x,y coordinates* for both ends of your line. If you select any of the other options, you get only one set of x,y coordinates, but you see the precise length of your line and any rotation angle. Enter a measurement for the new length of your line or the new position of its *endpoints* in the appropriate fields.

FIGURE 4.5

If you choose **Endpoints**, the coordinates for both ends of the line are shown.

FIGURE 4.6

If you choose **First Point**, only the first point's coordinates are displayed, along with the line's length and angle.

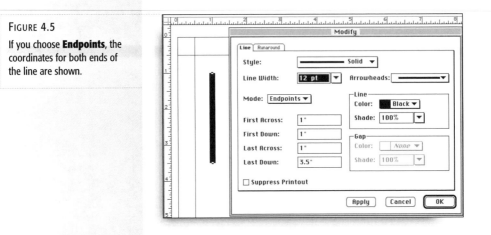

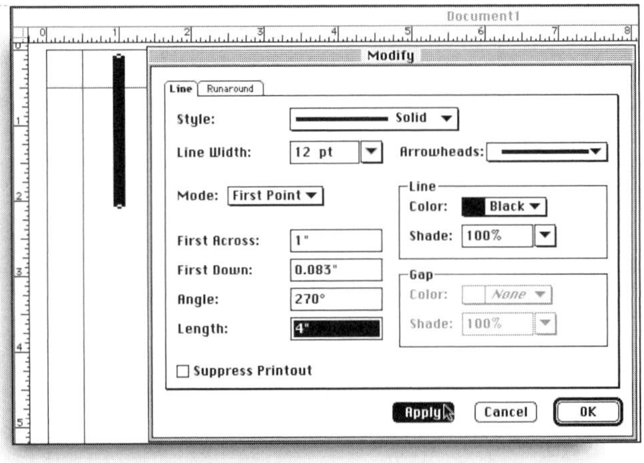

The left side of the Measurements palette (see Figures 4.7 and 4.8), which you usually find at the bottom of your display, also gives you size information on boxes or lines. Move your cursor to this palette and you can type in the precise dimensions you need for either a box or line. As far as item dimensions go, the Measurements palette gives you exactly the same choices as the Modify dialog box. Many users think it's easier and quicker to use the palette for this type of change. ⌘+Option+M (Ctrl+Alt+M) takes you directly to the Measurements palette, and pressing the Tab key moves you through the values you can change.

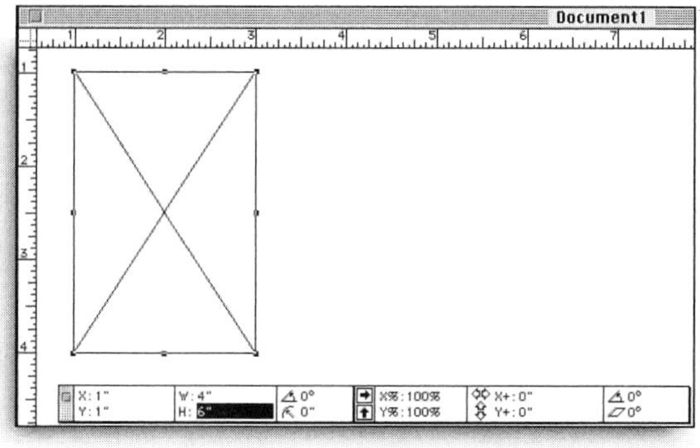

FIGURE 4.7
The Measurements palette shows box information.

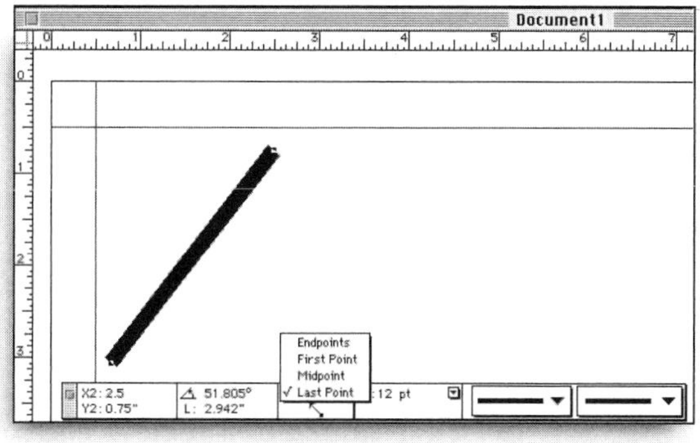

FIGURE 4.8
The Measurements palette changes to display line information.

Item Types

The **Item** menu in QuarkXPress 4 has some choices not available in earlier versions that allow changing items after you have drawn them.

Converting Content Type: Text, Picture, or None

One of those choices is to change the type of content your item box accepts. When you draw a text box, all you can put in it is text; a picture box accepts only graphic file formats such as *TIFF*, *EPS*, *PICT*, *JPEG*, and so on. There is no way to put both text and graphics in the same box, but you can change what goes in an individual box.

The **Content** submenu in the **Item** menu (see Figure 4.9) lets you change a text box into a picture box and vice versa. Although this might sound like an unnecessary feature, you'll be surprised how many times you carefully draw, size, and position a box only to find it's the wrong type. Quickly changing its content type is much easier than going through the process all over again. This is a new feature in QuarkXPress 4.

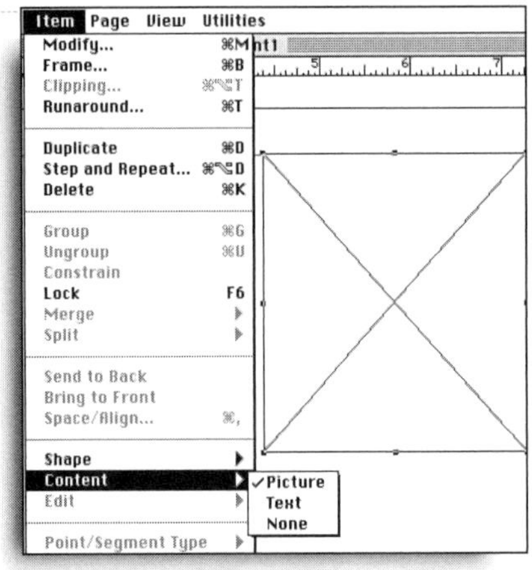

FIGURE **4.9**

The **Content** submenu lets you alter the type of content a box can accept.

There are two points to remember about changing content type:

- You can change only one box at a time.
- Any previous content is lost when you change the type.

The third option in the **Content** submenu is the new-to-QuarkXPress-4 *no-content box*. This box accepts neither text nor graphics but is a place for blocks of color. One advantage of the no-content box is that you don't accidentally have even non-printing characters in extraneous fonts sitting in boxes that do no more than provide a spot of color on a page.

A bit higher on the **Item** menu is a command that lets you change the actual shape of an item (see Figure 4.10). This is different than changing the size discussed earlier. When you have drawn a rectangular box and decide it would look better as a circle, or you want to change the corner type, choosing **Shape** from the **Item** menu is the only way to make that change. You also can change the shape of lines by selecting one of the bottom three options.

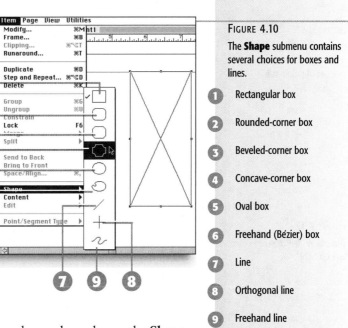

When you need to manually reshape a box, choose the **Shape** submenu from the **Item** menu and select the freeform shape. Your box is now defined by points wherever there is an angle change (see Figure 4.11). You can move any of these individual points without moving the others and reshape your box at will. In the case of a circular or oval box, you have eight points at 45-degree increments around the shape. Hold down the Option (Alt) key as you move your cursor over the line now defining the shape of your box, and click wherever you want another point added. To delete points, hold down the Option (Alt) key and click on any existing point. This type of conversion does not affect the content of the box, although text *reflows* and pictures *crop* in a new way.

You can also turn a box into a single line by selecting one of the bottom three choices in the **Shape** submenu. This is a new feature in QuarkXPress 4. Picture boxes lose their content, but you at least get a warning before this happens. Text boxes, how-ever, keep their content and the text flows along the line (see Figure 4.12).

FIGURE 4.11

Changing a box to a polygon replaces its handles with a new set of points at its corners.

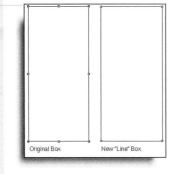

FIGURE 4.12

Text box on left changed into a line on right.

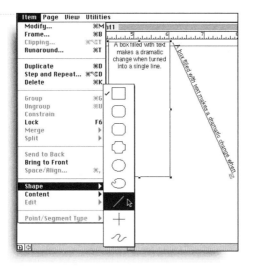

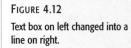

SEE ALSO

➤ *To set type along a path, see page 396*

Applying Frames to Boxes

Frames are added to boxes through the **Frame** tab in the Modify dialog box (choose **Modify** from the **Item** menu and click on the **Frame** tab), or by pressing ⌘+B (Ctrl+B), which takes you directly to the **Frame** tab (see Figure 4.13).

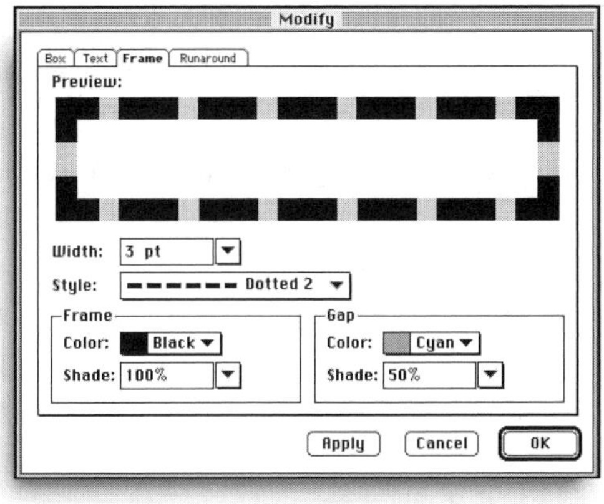

FIGURE 4.13

In the **Frame** tab, you can choose a width and style for the box frame, as well as colors.

The **Frame** tab includes several components to help you make your choice about picking a frame. Many components are actually pop-up menus and clicking on them displays a variety of pre-built choices.

- **Preview** shows what your selected frame looks like applied to a box.

- **Width** is a pop-up menu with predefined sizes, or you can type in your own choice. This is where you find the preferred size for *bitmapped* frames in outlined type.

- **Style** is another pop-up menu that displays all the frame styles defined for the open document. Highlight the one you want to use.

- **Frame** is where you define the color of the dark segments of the frame through the **Color** pop-up menu and then determine the shade of the color through the **Shade** pop-up menu or by typing in a percentage.

- **Gap** gives you the same choices as **Frame**, but this time the color and shade are applied to the white segments of your dash or stripe. This is most useful when your dash or stripe is around a box that has a color in it. This is a new feature in QuarkXPress 4. You can use it with a white or transparent box to create a dash or stripe of alternating colors, or you can have alternating colors in your dash that contrast with the box color.

- The **Apply** button applies your selection to any selected boxes in your document so you can see how the choice looks in context.

- **Cancel** lets you exit without making any changes; **OK** lets you exit and applies the frame style to the active boxes in your document.

You can add a frame to more than one box at a time; all you have to do is make a multiple selection before going to the Frame tab. Both picture and text boxes can be selected and have a frame added to them at the same time.

Applying Styles to Lines

There are three different ways to apply a style to a line: the **Style** drop-down menu, the Measurements palette, and the Modify dialog box's **Line** tab.

When you use the **Style** menu, you can modify a single attribute of a single line (see Figure 4.14). With repeated trips to the **Style** menu you can change all the attributes of your line. If you just want to change the color of a line, this might be the quickest path to follow. If you need to change several attributes at once, check out the other two methods.

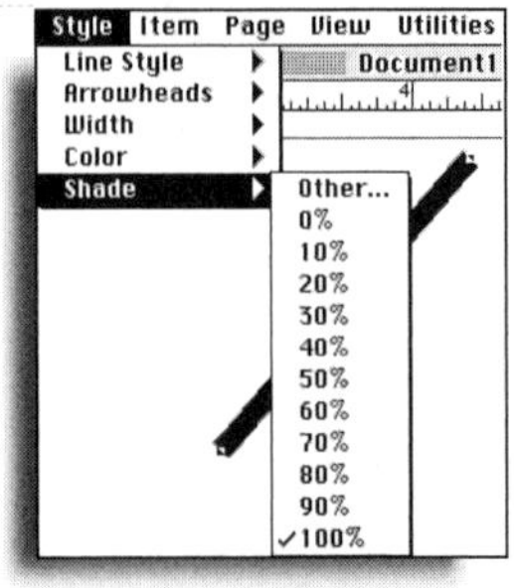

FIGURE 4.14

Style drop-down menu.

Using the Measurements palette, you can select the line style, arrowheads (if you need arrows), and weight. These changes can be applied to one line at a time (refer to Figure 4.8).

When using the Modify dialog box's **Line** tab (refer to Figure 4.5), you can make many more changes at once, and you can apply the changes to more than one line at a time. You can alter the style, width, arrowheads, mode, line color, and gap color through pop-up menus. If necessary, you can also move the line, change its rotation, and suppress its printout through the same menu.

If you have several lines selected at once, you see something a bit different when you select **Modify** from the **Item** menu; you see the **Group** tab (see Figure 4.15). Although similar to the Line tab, remember that **Origin Across** and **Origin Down** apply to the entire group of lines you have selected, not just one line. If you select **Suppress Printout**, none of the selected lines prints.

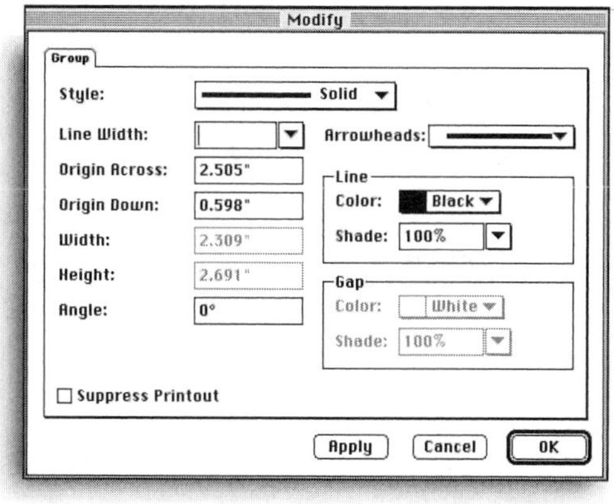

FIGURE 4.15
The Modify dialog box's **Group** tab appears when more than one object is selected.

Creating Custom Dashes & Stripes

A new feature in QuarkXPress 4 is the ability to create unique solid and dashed line styles to use with either lines or frames. This capability is found by choosing **Dashes & Stripes** from the **Edit** menu. Dash and stripe styles created while a document is open are active only in that document. If you want to have new styles available in all your documents, create them after starting QuarkXPress and before you open any documents.

The first dialog box you see (see Figure 4.16) lets you pick the styles you want displayed. There is also a small window that shows how a particular style of dash or stripe is defined. Study these as guides to creating your own stripes and dashes. The remaining buttons in the box are very similar to the actions you see when creating a type *style sheet*.

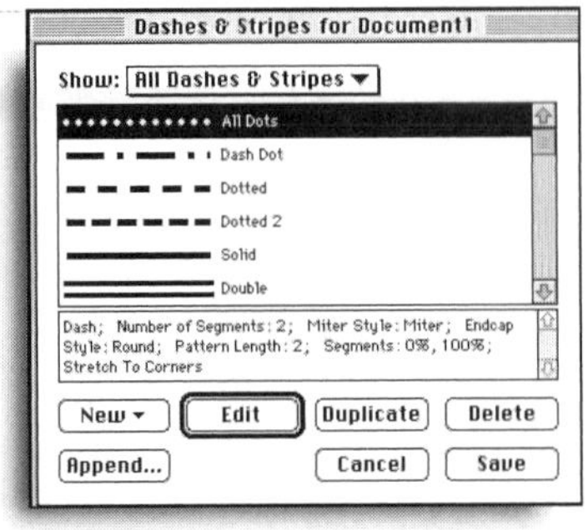

FIGURE 4.16

The Dashes & Stripes dialog
box lets you create custom
styles for box frames and lines.

FIGURE 4.16

The Dashes & Stripes dialog
box lets you create custom
styles for box frames and lines.

- The **New** button reveals a pop-up menu that gives you a choice between creating a new stripe or a new dash.

- **Append** allows you to import styles for other documents.

- **Duplicate** creates a copy of the highlighted stripe or dash.

- **Delete** lets you remove items from the list and your document.

- **Cancel** negates any actions you might have taken and returns you to the document leaving Dashes & Stripes styles untouched.

- **Save** makes any changes you have made permanent.

- **Edit** allows you to make changes to an existing style.

As with other types of styles created in a document, editing a Dash or Stripe style will be retroactive throughout your document. Any existing line using the edited style changed to the new style. This is actually a quick way to make changes document-wide. If you want to keep existing lines in the current style, make a copy of the style, do your editing on the copy, and save it to a new name.

SEE ALSO

➤ *To append Dashes & Stripes from another document, see page 146*

Dash Styles

The Edit Dash dialog box has several controls within five different windows (see Figure 4.17). Some of the items reveal pop-up menus.

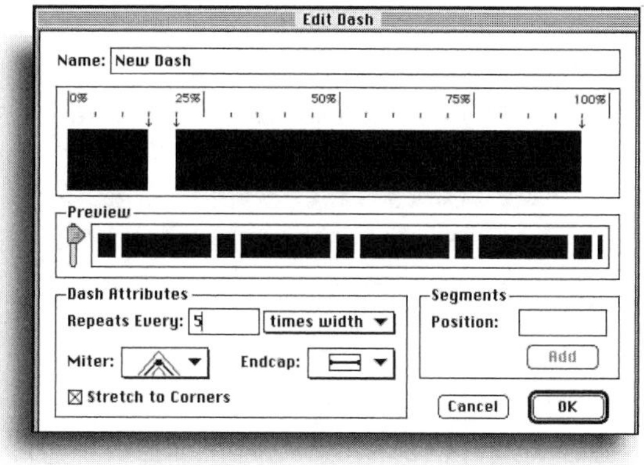

FIGURE 4.17
The Edit Dash dialog box lets you set how long and wide dashes are and how far apart they fall.

- The **Name** field gives you a place to name your new style.

- The box with the long line and percentage numbers is where you actually build your dash style. The heavy black line is like a slider that you can move around to define the length of your dash.

- The **Preview** box gives you an interactive example of what your style looks like when repeated on a line. The arrow on the left slides up and down to change the size of the preview.

- **Dash Attributes** is where you refine your style. You set up how often and based on what size your style repeats, select how corners will look and determine endcap appearance if your dash is applied to a line rather than a frame. Turn on **Stretch to Corners** to make sure there are no ugly gaps in your dash at the corners of frames.

- The **Segments** window is where you add additional segments to your dash style if you want more than a simple dash.

- **Cancel** takes you out of this dialog box without making any changes. **OK** takes you back to the Dashes & Stripes dialog box where you save your changes.

Stripe Styles

The Edit Stripe dialog box is very similar to the Edit Dash dialog box (see Figure 4.18).

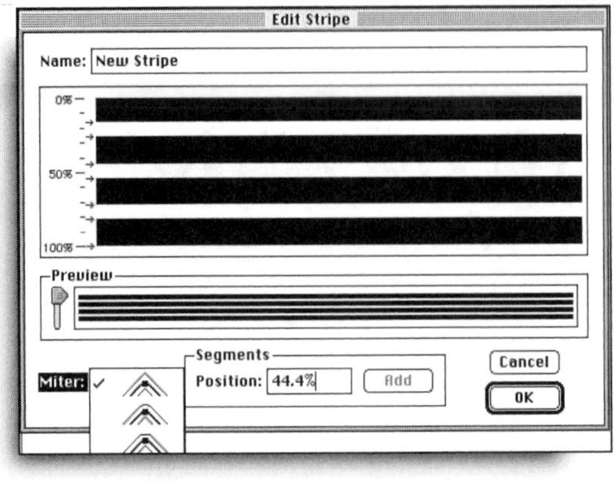

FIGURE **4.18**

The Edit Stripe dialog box lets you set widths for the stripes and the gaps between them.

- The **Name** field is where you name the new line.
- The box with percentages in it is where you edit or create your new stripe. The heavy black line works like a vertical slider, moving up and down.
- The **Preview** box shows you what your creation looks like. The arrow on the side increases the size of the preview.
- The **Miter** box is a pop-up menu that lets you choose how your stripe will join at corners.
- The **Segments** box is where you choose a location for an additional segment in your line. Once you add it, you can move it around with the slider.
- **Cancel** takes you out of this dialog box without making any changes. **OK** takes you back to the Dashes & Stripes dialog box where you save your changes.

One quick warning about creating a new stripe. You must have a segment of the stripe at the very top of the editing window. Although the preview leads you to believe you can just put a stripe between 45% and 50%, for example, when you use the stripe in your document, you find another segment added to it. That segment will be at the top of the stripe.

Creating Custom Bitmapped Frames

Mac users can create their own more complex custom frames using the Frame Editor, a separate application found in the

QuarkXPress folder on your hard drive. When you do this, you're really only creating *pixels* to be *RIPed* at the time of printing, rather than creating a truly scalable frame. By editing all four corners, and all four straight portions that connect the edges, you can create more complicated frames than the Dashes & Stripes dialog box allows. The editing is done like the old MacPaint program: with a "pencil," one pixel at a time (see Figures 4.19 and 4.20).

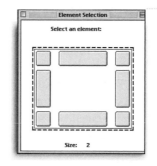

FIGURE 4.19

Editing a frame takes eight different windows that have to be edited, pixel-by-pixel.

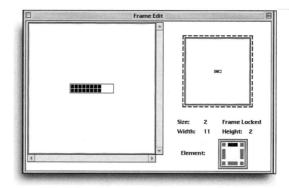

FIGURE 4.20

Each corner and side segment of a frame must be created.

Special frames can add print time to your job. We created a special frame for a picture border at the newspaper where I worked: a one-pixel frame top, left and right, with a four-pixel piece for the bottom edge of the frame. Then we couldn't figure out why it took 5 to 10 times longer to RIP (print) a page. The culprit turned out to be the frame. So use the Frame Editor with this caveat.

Frame Editor can't find XPress Preferences?

If you get a message that says "Can't find XPress Preferences," try launching Frame Editor without QuarkXPress running. Frame Editor is a standalone application, but it does alter the XPress Preferences file in your QuarkXPress folder by adding the frame styles.

Deleting and Replacing Line Styles

As was true in earlier versions of QuarkXPress for paragraph styles and colors, you also can delete Dash & Stripe styles and choose to replace them with a different style. Styles are deleted by selecting **Dashes & Stripes** from the **Edit** menu, highlighting the style you want to remove, and clicking the **Delete** button. If the style is used in the document, you will be asked if you want to replace it with something else, and you see a pop-up menu from which to choose.

One reason to delete line styles is to slim down the size of your document. After all, why lug all this information and data around if you are not going to use it? Choose Dashes & Stripes from the Edit menu, scroll through the **Show** pop-up menu, and highlight **Show Dashes & Stripes Not Used**. You can delete them singly, or hold down the Shift key, highlight all of them and delete them in a single stroke.

Comparing Line Styles

You can compare different line styles in the same document. In the Dashes & Stripes dialog box, highlight any two lines you want to compare, then hold down Option (Alt); the **Append** button turns into a **Compare** button. When you click on this, a new window appears containing all the information about the two styles you have selected (see Figure 4.21). Use this to compare styles that, although they look a lot alike on your monitor, might print out very differently.

FIGURE 4.21

The Compare dialog box shows you the specs for the selected Dashes & Stripes styles.

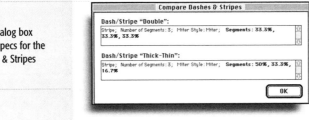

Positioning Items on the Page

As with most tasks in QuarkXPress, there are several different methods you can use to position items on your pages. No one method is better than another. At one time or another you will use them all, depending on what you are doing, where your cursor is on the page (what's closest), and how comfortable you are with keyboard commands.

Using Rulers and Guides

Rulers are a visual tool to help you find your way around a page. Appearing across the top and left side of your screen, they do not print with your document. In the same way, *guides* are nonprinting horizontal or vertical lines that you can use to help position items accurately, or to create a *"snap to"* place on your page. *Margin guides*, which you define when creating a new document, are another type of nonprinting guide, but you cannot move them around at will.

You have a choice of whether to display guides and rulers. There are times when you will want to turn them off. Viewing controls are found under the **View** menu. The selections in the **View** menu act as toggle switches. Drop-down the menu and highlight your choice. If guides and rulers are currently visible, the choice will be to **Hide**. If you cannot see guides or rulers on your monitor, the choice will be to **Show**. You can also show/hide these elements using command and function key shortcuts. Notice that there are several other options besides guides and rulers for Show/Hide in the **View** menu that also use keyboard shortcuts (see Table 4.3).

SEE ALSO

➤ *To change the colors for ruler and margin guides, see page 37*

➤ *To change the units displayed on the rulers, see page 49*

➤ *To determine whether guides fall in front of or behind objects in a document, see page 52*

➤ *To determine whether the horizontal ruler continues across a page spread or starts over at zero on the righthand page, see page 52*

No Compare button?

The **Compare** button only appears if you have just two styles selected. With more styles selected, it stubbornly stays an **Append** button.

TABLE 4.3   Keyboard shortcuts to View/Hide

Action	Mac OS	Windows
View/Hide Guides	F7	F7
View/Hide Rulers	⌘+R	Ctrl+R

Creating Guides

You must have rulers visible in order to place guides on your *document page*, *spread*, or *master page*. To make a guide, move your cursor over the horizontal or vertical ruler and then click and drag. A guide moves out from the ruler and continues to follow your cursor until you release it. Watch the Measurements palette while you do this and you will see the x,y coordinates change as you move the guide, so you know where you are placing it.

There are two different types of guides: *page guides* and *spread guides*. A page guide appears only within the boundaries of your page. To create a page guide, make sure your cursor is over your page when you position the guide. Spread guides extend off the edges of your page onto the area of the *pasteboard*. To create a spread guide, your cursor needs to be over the pasteboard area when you position the guide. The guide then appears on all the pages comprising that spread. Spread guides are distinguishable by the fact that they extend over the pasteboard area.

You can convert page guides to spread guides (and the other way around, of course) by clicking on the guide and moving the cursor to the necessary location either on the page or on the pasteboard. You do not need to move the guide. Its original location remains visible until you release the cursor.

The distinction between page and spread guides is important when using them on master pages. If you want the guide to show up on every document page based on a particular master page, you must use a page guide. If you want the guides to be visible only on the master page, you must use a spread guide.

You can reposition guides after you create them by dragging on the guide.

Deleting Guides

Guides can be removed from a page or spread by dragging them off the nearest edge of your screen. It is not necessary to drag vertical guides to a vertical edge, or horizontal guides to a horizontal edge.

There are also keyboard commands to help you get rid of several guides at the same time (see Table 4.4).

TABLE 4.4   Keyboard commands for deleting guides

Action	Command
Delete all vertical page guides*	Option+click (Alt+click) in vertical ruler
Delete all horizontal page guides*	Option+click (Alt+click) in horizontal ruler
Delete all vertical spread guides	Option+click (Alt+click) in vertical ruler
Delete all horizontal spread guides	Option+click (Alt+click) in horizontal ruler

*Edge of page must be touching the designated ruler.

Using the Pasteboard

Every page or spread in QuarkXPress has extra work space known as the pasteboard. It is the area you see on your monitor surrounding the page you defined. There is quite a bit of room to either side, but just a small space above and below (approximately 1/2 inch). Pasteboard width, left and right, is by default the same as the width of your page up to a maximum of 46 inches. The pasteboard is associated with the page or spread it surrounds. You get a fresh pasteboard with each page or spread. Consider it a work table, a place to temporarily store bits and pieces of text or graphics.

There are some technical things about the pasteboard of which you should be aware. When QuarkXPress saves your document, the pasteboard and everything on it are also saved. The bigger your pasteboard and the more information you have sitting there, the bigger your file size will be. If you are transporting a document file either on disk or electronically, you can make the file size smaller by deleting items on the pasteboard because

Showing guides only at specified magnifications

Hold down the Shift key while dragging a guide from the ruler and it will be visible only in the current view percentage or larger. If your view is set at 200% when you Shift+drag a guide, it will not appear on the screen when the view percentage is 199% or less. You pick the numbers that work for you. I find that this eliminates a lot of clutter when I work in smaller views or when I want to get the big picture.

there is less information for QuarkXPress to keep track of. By the same token, you can make the file size smaller by actually reducing the physical size of the pasteboard. This is particularly helpful if your document page size is quite wide.

SEE ALSO

➤ *To change the width of the pasteboard, see page 43*

Although generally QuarkXPress does not print anything sitting on the pasteboard, it will print, up to 1/4 inch outside the page edge, anything sitting there that accidentally or purposely touches the page. Be careful not to let pasteboard items touch your page unless you want them to print.

You can use the pasteboard to leave instructions to your print or prepress shop. For example, if you included special *trim lines*, *fold lines*, or *perforation lines* in your document, you can leave a short note about them on the pasteboard, even with an arrow pointing to the line. Create a text box on the pasteboard within 1/4 inch of the edge of a page that just overlaps onto the document page. Type any notes you need in the box but make sure all the text is outside the trim edge of the page. The notes will be *imageset* right on the film or paper you give to the print shop. If you use an arrow, anchor it in the text box that contains your instructions or notes; otherwise it won't print (see Figure 4.22).

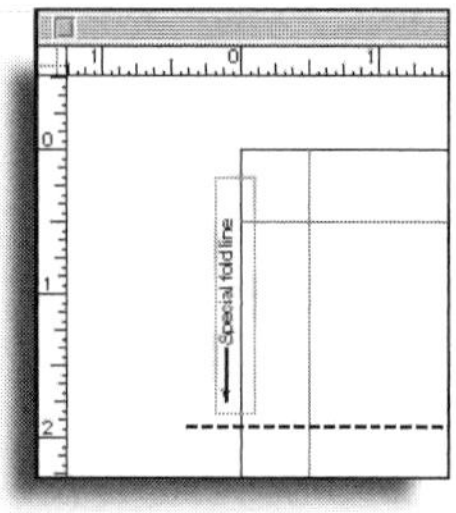

FIGURE 4.22
Pasteboard notes and arrows.

Moving Items

Yet again, QuarkXPress offers a variety of ways to move items in your document. We are talking about items here, so be sure the Item tool ⊕ is selected.

Item Tool

The easiest and quickest way to move an item (box or line) is to drag with the Item tool. You can drag an item around a page, move it to the pasteboard, or even move it to a different page.

You also can nudge items a bit by using the arrow keys on your keyboard. An item moves in one point increments in the direction of the arrow you use.

Hold down the Shift key as you select an item, and you can select several items at the same time—just continue clicking on all the items you want to select. The Item tool also works as a *marquee* to select multiple items. Select the tool, then click on an empty spot on your page and drag. Everything the marquee touches will be selected, even if it touches only a small corner of an item. These multiple selections can be dragged or nudged to another location.

Values in X,Y Fields

If all this heavy lifting and dragging is too much for you, or if you know precisely where an item needs to sit on a page, you can type in the coordinates in either the Measurements palette (refer to Figure 4.7) or in the Modify dialog box's **Box/Line** tab (refer to Figures 4.5 and 4.6). The coordinate you need to know for boxes is the upper-left corner. Depending on the mode you select for a line, you might need the center, right, or left points, or you might need to know where each end of the line is located. You can use this method for multiple selected items, also.

To tweak the location of an item, use the Measurements palette or the Modify dialog box's **Box/Line** tab and add or subtract values from the current location. Adding numbers will move an item to the right and/or down. Subtracting numbers moves an item left and/or up. In Figure 4.23, an item moves 6 picas to the right and 1.5 inches higher (up) on the page. You also can divide (/) and multiply (*) in these boxes, and you can enter numbers in any measurement system you want—QuarkXPress does the necessary conversions and the appropriate math automatically. This method also works with multiple selected items.

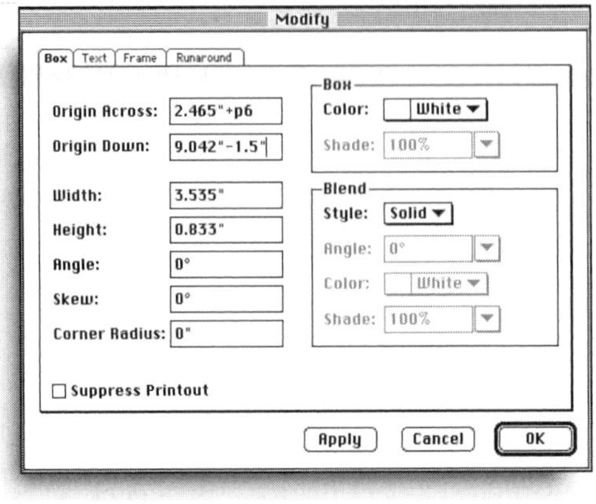

FIGURE 4.23

Adding and subtracting in the Modify dialog box's **Box** tab.

Locking Items

You can prevent items from accidentally moving around the page. Select an item, and choose **Lock** from the **Item** menu or press F6 to make it impossible to move it with the cursor when the Item tool is active. Items on both master and document pages can be locked in this fashion. You can select several items at the same time. Once an item is locked, your cursor turns into a padlock when you try to select the item (see Figure 4.24).

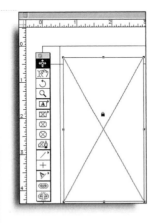

FIGURE 4.24

A special cursor shows that you're trying to move a locked item.

This is especially handy if you have carefully placed a lot of lines or small text boxes on your page. You also might think about locking items if you are sending your files off for someone else to look at or work with.

A word of caution, however. The **Lock** command is not like hardened cement. Items can still be moved, but it must be done more deliberately by typing in coordinates in the Measurements palette or the Modify dialog box's **Box/Line** tab. The locking feature is really designed to prevent accidental moves.

Copying Items

Often you don't want to move an item, but you do want a duplicate of it located in another place in your document.

There are two ways to make a single copy of an item or group of items that has been selected with the Item tool. The first is to choose **Copy** from the **Edit** menu or pressing ⌘+C (Ctrl+C), then move to the new location in the document and choose **Paste** from the **Edit** menu or press ⌘+V (Ctrl+V). The copy appears on whatever part of the document page is in the center of your monitor.

The second way to make a single copy is to duplicate an item by choosing **Duplicate** from the **Item** menu or pressing ⌘+D (Ctrl+D). This places an exact duplicate of the item very close to the original. Then you can move it wherever you want.

When you need several duplicates of an item, choose **Step and Repeat** from the **Item** menu or press ⌘+Option+D (Ctrl+Alt+D). This method allows you to set the relationship of the multiple duplications to each other (see Figure 4.25).

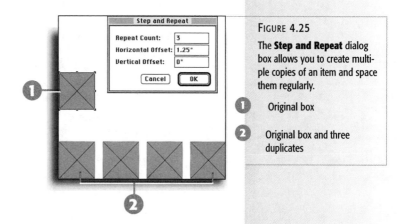

FIGURE 4.25

The **Step and Repeat** dialog box allows you to create multiple copies of an item and space them regularly.

1 Original box

2 Original box and three duplicates

Type in the **Repeat Count**, which is the number of duplicates
you want. Then determine how they need to be offset from each
other. If you don't want items sitting on top of each other, make
sure you include the height and width of the item in addition to
the space between them in the **Horizontal Offset** and **Vertical
Offset** fields. In Figure 4.25, three duplicates are being made of
a box that is 1 inch square. There will be .25 inches of space
between the boxes and the top edges will line up.

A couple of cautions are in order here. The default values for
Step and Repeat are .25 inches for both **Horizontal** and
Vertical offset. This value is what is applied if you use the
Duplicate command to make a single copy. As soon as you
change these offsets, however, the new values remain intact until
you close the document. The next time you press ⌘+D (Ctrl+D)
to make a single copy, that single duplicate will be offset from
the original by whatever values you typed in earlier. But the next
time you open the document, the offset values in **Step and
Repeat** revert to .25 inches.

Layering Items

Chapter 1 mentions that everything in QuarkXPress sits on its
own layer. You can't see the layers, you can't see the numbers of
the layers, and you can't turn layers on and off. If there are 19
items on a page, the page has 19 layers. The first item you place
on a page is on the bottom layer, the next item sits one layer
higher, and the next item sits one layer above that. This is not a
concern as long as no items on a page overlap. As soon as some
overlap starts, though, you need to pay attention to how items
are stacking up.

When you have overlapping items, you obviously want some to
be in front of others. Unfortunately, most of us do not build our
pages in such an organized fashion that every item naturally falls
on the right layer.

Two commands move items from layer to layer. Choose **Bring
to Front** from the **Item** menu to move an object to the front
layer, or choose **Send to Back** to bring an item to the back
layer. Hold down the ⌘+Option (Ctrl+Alt) keys before you

choose **Bring to Front/Send to Back**, and the item moves one layer higher or lower. Be patient. Because you can't see what layer an item is on, you might have to do this several times to get it to the layer you want. There are also function keys that accomplish the same task and are quicker if you have to move an item through several layers (see Table 4.5).

TABLE 4.5   Moving through layers

Action	Mac OS	Windows
Bring to front layer	F5	F5
Send to back layer	Shift+F5	Shift+F5
Move one layer forward	Option+F5	Alt+F5
Move one layer back	Option+Shift+F5	Alt+Shift+F5

Spacing Items Evenly

Although you can use the Modify dialog box or the Measurements palette to type in measurements and align items on your page, the quickest way is to choose **Space/Align** from the **Item** menu or press ⌘+, (Ctrl+,). **Space/Align** offers two different methods for positioning items, each with several variations. To use this command you must have more than one item selected.

Positioning Items with Absolute Values

To position items on a page according to a specific value:

1. First, pick whether you want **Horizontal** alignment, **Vertical** alignment, or both.

2. Type the value you select in the **Space** field. Enter **0** to align the objects' edges or centers.

3. Then make a selection from the **Between** pop-up menu that gives four choices for each type of alignment: **Horizontal** offers **Items**, **Left Edges**, **Right Edges**, and **Center**; **Vertical** has **Items**, **Top Edges**, **Bottom Edges**, and **Center**. The **Apply** button shows you the effect of your choice.

4. Click **OK** to apply the changes.

Selecting buried items

When you have items stacked directly on top of each other, or completely buried behind another item, you can cycle through the layers to get to the one you want without changing the stacking order. Use the Item tool to select the topmost item, and then hold down ⌘+Option+Shift (Ctrl+Alt+Shift) and keep clicking the mouse until the item you need becomes active. After editing the active item in any way you need, it returns to its layer. Cycling through items in this manner avoids constantly moving items to the front to edit and then working to get them in their proper layer again.

For example (see Figure 4.26), to position all the items you have selected across your page with 1/2 inch between them, select **Horizontal**; type .5 " in the field by **Space**; and choose **Items** from the **Between** pop-up menu. To stair-step items down a page, select **Vertical** and put a measurement in the field by **Space** and select **Top Edges** from the **Between** pop-up menu. You can do both vertical and horizontal positioning at the same time.

FIGURE 4.26

The Space/Align dialog box allows you to distribute items evenly or align them with each other.

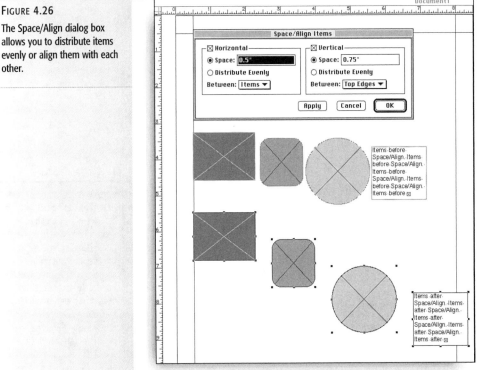

When aligning items to the left or top edge, QuarkXPress aligns all the selected items to the leftmost or highest edge. When positioning items to the right or bottom edge, all the items align to the rightmost or lowest edge of the group. Two or more items center based on the location of the topmost or leftmost item.

Distributing Items Evenly

The second radio button in **Space/Align** lets you space items equally by automatically computing the space that needs to be placed between each of them. The horizontal or vertical space the items will arrange themselves across is determined by the left and right or top and bottom edges of the selected items (see Figure 4.27). The same options are available in the Between pop-up menu as positioning by absolute values.

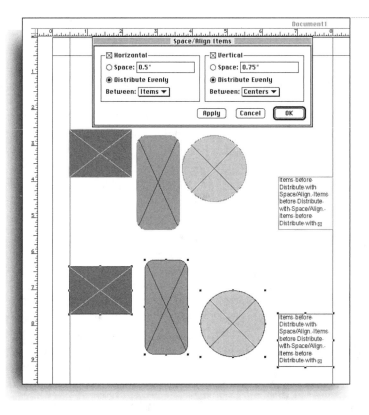

FIGURE 4.27

Distributed items have an equal amount of space between them, or between their edges or centers.

Grouping and Ungrouping Items

Grouping items together is a convenient way of maintaining spatial relationships between many items. Groups selected with the Item tool can be copied, pasted, cut, moved, and resized. Individual items within a group can always be edited or resized by using the Content tool.

Make any selection of two or more items and group them by choosing **Group** from the **Item** menu command or pressing ⌘+G (Ctrl+G.) To break a group back into its original components, choose **Ungroup** from the **Item** menu or press ⌘+U (Ctrl+U). Two or more groups might be combined into a single group using the same commands. However, the subgroups remain intact as a group, so what you have is a group of groups, not a group of individual items. Ungrouping a group of groups uses the same **Ungroup** command but only ungroups one level of groups at a time. If you have combined three groups into a single group, you will have to invoke the command twice to ungroup all the items.

Resizing Groups and Items within Groups

Groups can be resized as a group by clicking and dragging on any of the handles surrounding the group. Dragging on a corner handle allows horizontal and vertical resizing at the same time (see Figure 4.28). To maintain the aspect ratio of items within a group, hold down the Option+Shift (Alt+Shift) keys as you drag from any of the handles. Using only the Shift key as you resize turns the group into a square. Resizing in this manner, however, does not resize the content of any of the items within a group. Hold down the ⌘ (Ctrl) key after you select a corner handle, and the contents of the boxes also will be resized as you drag.

You can also resize groups by specific percentages by selecting the group and using the Measurements palette. The second set of numbers in the Measurements palette are the dimensions of your group. You can multiply, divide, add, or subtract from these numbers to resize a group. For example, if you want to double the size of a group, multiply (using the * sign) both width and height by 2. Strike the Enter or Return key and the group resizes automatically.

You can resize individual items in a group by selecting them with the Content tool and dragging on any of the handles. You can edit the content of boxes within a group the same way you edit if they were not part of a group.

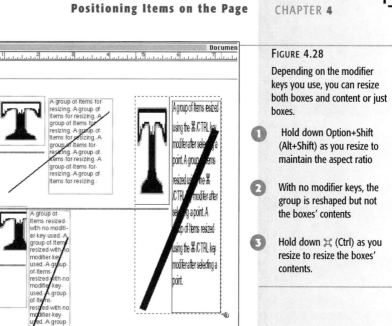

FIGURE 4.28

Depending on the modifier keys you use, you can resize both boxes and content or just boxes.

1 Hold down Option+Shift (Alt+Shift) as you resize to maintain the aspect ratio

2 With no modifier keys, the group is reshaped but not the boxes' contents

3 Hold down ⌘ (Ctrl) as you resize to resize the boxes' contents.

Rotating Items

QuarkXPress gives you two different ways to rotate items; each way produces the same result but arrives at the result by a different means.

Rotation Tool

The Rotation tool ⟳ is the third from the top in the Tool palette. With it, you can rotate any unlocked item or group. Select an item to be rotated, using either the Item or Content tool, and then select the Rotation tool. The selected item rotates on an axis determined by the location of the Rotation tool. You do not have to rotate by selecting a handle on a box. After selecting the Rotation tool, drag from any spot on the page and the item rotates around that point (see Figure 4.29). You can pull a handle out from the Rotation tool much like a lever. The longer the handle, the finer you can adjust the rotation angle.

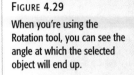

FIGURE 4.29

When you're using the
Rotation tool, you can see the
angle at which the selected
object will end up.

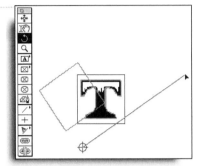

Values in Angle of Rotation Field

You can also enter a specific angle of rotation in the
Measurements palette or the Modify dialog box (see Figure
4.30). Items rotated this way always rotate from the center of the
item. This is an important distinction to make between using the
Rotation tool and the absolute value method. QuarkXPress cannot rotate an item if it must take it off the pasteboard to accomplish the task. This usually happens when an item is very large
or located near the top or bottom of a page. If you get an error
message when entering an absolute value, it is often easier to
switch to the Rotation tool.

FIGURE 4.30

Rotating with the
Measurements palette always
rotates objects around their
centers.

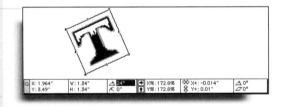

Skewing Boxes

Picture and text boxes can be *skewed*, or slanted, through the
Modify dialog box's Box tab. A positive value skews a box to
the right and a negative value skews to the left. This also skews

the content of the box (see Figure 4.31). Unlike most actions in QuarkXPress, the Modify dialog box's Box tab is the only way you can skew a box and its contents—there's no alternative tool or field in the Measurements palette.

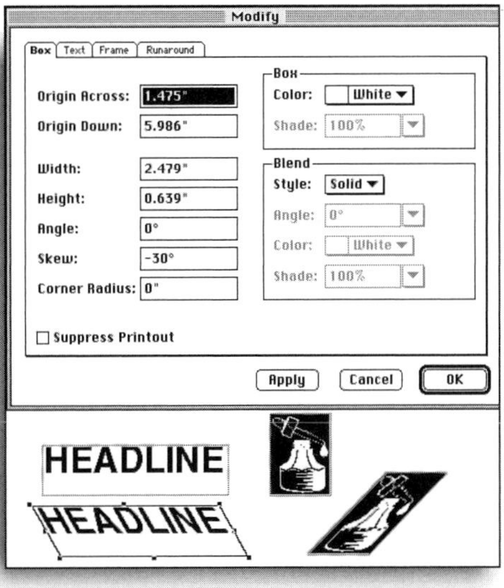

FIGURE 4.31

Using the Modify dialog box's Box tab, you can skew picture and text boxes, and their contents, to the right or left.

SEE ALSO

➤ *To skew the contents of a picture box without skewing the box, see page 344*

Reusing Elements

Copy and paste items between documents

Drag pages between documents

Use the "thumbnail drag" technique to repair documents

Store items in libraries for easy access

Label library items for sorting

Append style sheets, H&Js, Dashes & Stripes, Lists, and colors from other documents

One of the best things about desktop publishing is the ability to easily reuse documents or pieces of documents. You don't have to tear apart a keyline carefully waxed down on a layout board to use something; you just electronically copy it without destroying the original.

Sharing Items between Documents

Sharing items between documents is as easy as using an item more than once in the same document. Using the Item tool ⊕ , select any item or *group* in a document and choose **Copy** from the **Edit** menu or press ⌘+C (Ctrl+C). Open a new or existing document and choose **Paste** from the **Edit** menu or press ⌘+V (Ctrl+V). There is no magic here—simply copy and paste.

An even easier method is to have an originating and destination document open at the same time. Arrange them on your monitor so both are visible. Now, using the Item tool, click on an item and drag it to the destination document. Don't panic—it stays in the originating document and a copy is automatically created in the destination document. When you do this, notice that the originating document remains the active document, even as you are dragging an item to another document. To make your destination document active so you can edit it in some way, you need to select the document by actually clicking on it someplace.

You can drag all the elements on a page to a destination document in one operation by choosing **Select All** from the **Edit** menu or press ⌘+A (Ctrl+A) when the Item tool ⊕ is active. (An alternative would be to use the Item tool as a *marquee* to select everything on a page.) After everything is selected, simply drag it on to a page (probably an empty one) in the destination document. When you move an entire page this way, you do not add a copy of the master page to the destination document.

SEE ALSO

➤ *To create new documents, see page 84*

➤ *To open existing documents, see page 88*

Sharing Pages between Documents

When you have large number of pages to move between documents, it is usually easiest to copy the entire page, rather than just the Items on the page. There are a couple of caveats to consider here:

- Both documents must be in *Thumbnail view*.
- The target document page size must be at least as large as the originating document.

There are five simple steps (see Figure 5.1).

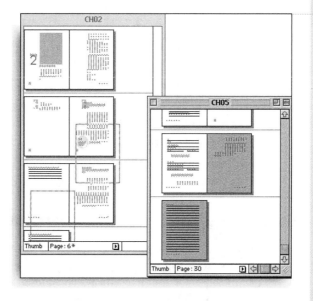

FIGURE 5.1

Thumbnail drag is the way to move entire pages to a new document.

To drag pages from one document to another:

1. Set the view on both documents to Thumbnail.
2. Use the Item tool [⊕] to select a page.
3. Shift+click to select more than one page.
4. The pages will become dark, indicating selection.
5. Drag the pages to any location in the target document.

SEE ALSO

➤ *To change the view percentage, see page 93*

Dragging Pages and the Results

When you use what QuarkXPress veterans affectionately call *thumbnail drag* to put pages into another document, several things will happen to your target document. Many of these are not of concern if you drag pages to a new document.

- For every page you thumbnail-drag, an accompanying master page will be created in the target document.

- Colors used on the page in the originating document will be added to the target document. If they have the same name, they will be redefined to match the color in the target document.

- Character and paragraph *style sheets* used on the page in the originating document will be added to the target document. If they have the same name, the text from the originating document will retain its formatting.

- If you are using automatic page numbering in the target document, page numbers will change.

- *H&Js* and *hyphenation exceptions* do not transfer to the target document. This might cause text reflow in your moved pages.

Using Thumbnail Drag to Repair Documents

QuarkXPress veterans have long used thumbnail drag for one very specific purpose: to repair damaged documents. I'm not a technical person and have always considered this to be something akin to white magic, but it does work. (I think it actually has something to do with creating a new header in the *PostScript* language that describes the document, if you are into that sort of thing.)

If you encounter a document that is acting a bit strange—perhaps it won't print, perhaps it doesn't display properly on the monitor, perhaps you get a lot of error messages while working with it—thumbnail drag might be your relatively quick and simple answer.

Create a brand new document, exactly the same size as the troublesome one. Make sure H&Js are set exactly the same in both documents. Although you can move several pages at a time, I find that moving them one at a time is more effective. Save the target document to a different name, and save it after every page you move. After you move all the pages, save, close, and then reopen the new document. Most, but not all, of the time, your troubles will have disappeared.

Thumbnail drag is not a guaranteed way to fix corrupted documents, but a lot of anecdotal evidence over the years indicates it is reliable.

Using Libraries

Libraries are great places—there is just so much information! The best part is that it's all organized so you can find it quickly and go back to it again and again. QuarkXPress *libraries* are a bit like that, only better, because in a QuarkXPress library, nothing is ever checked out (the shelf is never empty); what you need is always there for you.

SEE ALSO
➤ *To create a new library, see page 91*

Putting Items in Libraries

Chapter 1 talked about how to create a library by using choosing **New** from the **File** menu and then **Library** from the submenu. Now it is time to put some items on the shelves, or in the library document to be more precise. Items are moved into a library either by the copy/paste method or by simply dragging an item onto the Library palette (see Figure 5.2). When you drag an item from a open document into a library, it remains in the document as well, so don't worry about losing items from the document.

No matter what size item you place in a library, all you see in the palette is a small representation of the item. Single items might go in a library and even the entire contents of one or more pages can be stored for future reference in a library, but they all will be represented in a space approximately two inches square.

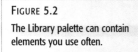

FIGURE 5.2

The Library palette can contain elements you use often.

Retrieving Library Items

Library items are moved into a document as easily as they are moved into the library. Select an item and use copy and paste or drag the item into your document. It appears in its original size on your document page. Items can be permanently removed from a library by choosing **Cut** from the **Edit** menu or by clicking on a library item and pressing Delete.

Labeling Library Items

Small items placed in libraries are sometimes difficult to see clearly. Other times, libraries grow so large that it is hard to remember what is in them, let alone retrieve it. That's why you label items. Double-click on any library item and a small dialog box appears so you can name it (see Figure 5.3).

Once items in a library are labeled, you can get to them quickly by using the pop-up menu in the upper-left corner of the Library palette. Highlighting an item name displays only that item in the palette and places a small check mark by its name. Be careful here. If you have too many highlighted items, you still might have difficulty finding them. You can toggle the display of checked items off by highlighting them again or select **All** in the pop-up menu to redisplay all the library items. Libraries generally open as a long narrow palette; you can resize that palette and set the display anyway you desire.

So, what happens to all these wonderful reusable elements you save to a library when you start placing them in different documents?

FIGURE 5.3
Naming items in the Library palette makes it easier to keep track of them.

- *Picture boxes* retain *path* information for the content of the box.
- Colors used in a library item will be added to the document.
- There will be no warning about conflicts in names of style sheets or colors.
- *Character style sheets* will be added to the document, but beware of library item character style sheets that have the same name as the target document style sheets. The character styling of the library item remains the same, but the actual style sheet definition remains as defined in the document.
- *Paragraph style sheets* also follow a library item, but again, if they have the same name as a paragraph style in the target document, the target document style remains intact while the library item still looks like it does in the library.
- H&Js follow a library item, unless an H&J of the same name exists in the target document. In that instance, the H&J of the target document overrides the library item and *text reflow* might occur in the library item.
- Hyphenation exceptions do not follow a library item. These exceptions will be overridden by the target document and text might reflow.

Appending from Other Documents

Once you've gone to all the trouble of creating Dashes & Stripes, style sheets, or *spot colors* in one document, there's no need to recreate those items in other documents. You can append them instead, along with H&J settings and lists. Each of these items can be appended from its own dialog box (click **Append** in the Edit Lists dialog box, for example), or you can append all of them at once by choosing **Append** from the **File** menu. Either way, you first see an Open dialog box (see Figure 5.4) where you choose the file to append from, then you see the Append dialog box.

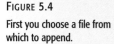

FIGURE 5.4

First you choose a file from which to append.

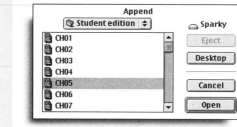

If you use the main Append command, the dialog box has tabs for each item you can append; in each tab, you can choose some, all, or none of the available items in that category (see Figure 5.5). The individual Append commands, found in the Edit dialog boxes, bring up a dialog that looks like the corresponding tab from the main Append dialog box.

To append items:

1. In the main Append dialog box, click the tab for the kind of item you want to append. In the individual Append dialog boxes, go directly to step 2.

2. Select a single item by clicking on it. Select a range of items by holding down the Shift key and clicking again at the end of the range. Select noncontiguous choices by holding down the ⌘ (Ctrl) key as you click on them. Notice that windows in the bottom of the dialog box give you a description of the selected items, whether they're colors, style sheets, or other kinds of items. To speed things up, click **Include All**. To clear out the Including list if you mess up, click **Remove All**.

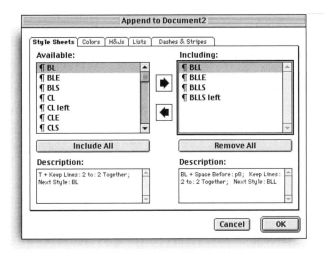

FIGURE 5.5
Then you choose which items to append.

3. To add selected items to the current document, move them into the **Including** box by clicking on the right-pointing arrow.

4. When all the lines you want are in the **Including** box, click **OK**. QuarkXPress warns you if there are conflicts and lets you decide how you want to resolve them (see Figure 5.6).

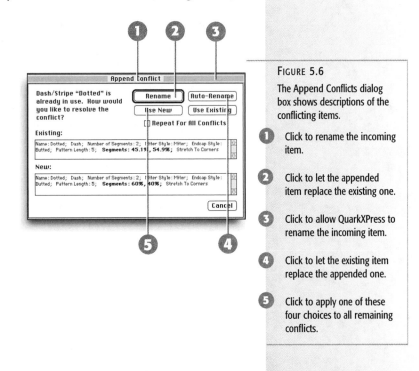

FIGURE 5.6
The Append Conflicts dialog box shows descriptions of the conflicting items.

1 Click to rename the incoming item.

2 Click to let the appended item replace the existing one.

3 Click to allow QuarkXPress to rename the incoming item.

4 Click to let the existing item replace the appended one.

5 Click to apply one of these four choices to all remaining conflicts.

What causes Append conflicts? They happen when the current document already contains an item with the same name as one you're appending. And because some items bring others along with them, you can append items you don't even know about. When you append style sheets, for example, they bring along all their baggage of colors, embedded style sheets (those used for Based On and character style sheets embedded in paragraph style sheets), H&Js, and Dashes & Stripes. All this baggage often leads to naming and definition conflicts.

A bunch of wordy alerts tell you when these conflicts occur. The sheer amount of text in the alerts is frightening, but they're actually helpful. You can see the differences between the two elements and choose whether to use the element as it exists in the document or go ahead and append it as is with a new name.

SEE ALSO

➤ *To create new style sheets, see page 297*

➤ *To create new colors, see page 426*

➤ *To create new H&Js, see page 268*

➤ *To create new lists, see page 593*

➤ *To create new Dashes & Stripes, see page 120*

Comparing Appended Items

You can't see the **Compare** button, but it's there. ⌘+click (Control+click) to select two paragraph style sheets or two character style sheets in the list. Then, press the Option key (Alt key) to change the **Append** button to **Compare** and click it. The Compare dialog box shows you both style sheet definitions with the differences in bold. Use **Compare** any time you need to know the difference between two similar style sheets—especially if the difference is something subtle like different tab settings.

Building Documents

In Chapter 1 you were invited to consider your QuarkXPress project as a pyramid—the top part being boxes; the middle, pages; and the base of the pyramid, the document. So far you've reviewed the topics of tools in QuarkXPress, the items that go on pages, and even building a page. The time has come to consider the foundation of our structure, a complete document, probably containing more than one page.

Using the Document Layout Palette

The Document Layout palette is underused by many people, ignored by many others, and maximized by the really clever and efficient users of QuarkXPress.

Displaying the Palette

The palette, shown in Figure 6.1, is displayed by choosing **Show Document Layout** from the **View** menu or by pressing F10. There are three separate, but related, areas of the palette: the button area at the top, the *master page* area in the middle, and the *document page* area at the bottom.

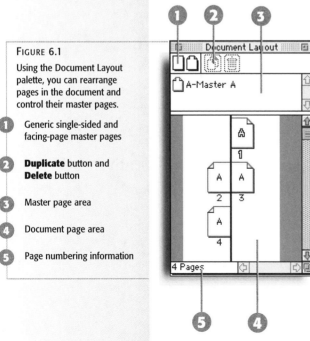

FIGURE 6.1

Using the Document Layout palette, you can rearrange pages in the document and control their master pages.

1 Generic single-sided and facing-page master pages

2 **Duplicate** button and **Delete** button

3 Master page area

4 Document page area

5 Page numbering information

Using the Buttons

There are four separate buttons across the very top of the Document Layout palette. Sometimes they are grayed out, meaning they are not available. When they are black, you can use them for various actions.

The first two buttons add a new blank (not associated with any master) page in either the document page section or the master page section, depending on which area you drag them to. The first button is a blank single page; the second (which looks like it has dog-eared corners) is for adding a blank facing page and is available only if you selected **Facing Pages** in the New Document dialog.

The third button, which looks like two pages stacked together, is for making an exact duplicate of a master page. Select one of the master page icons immediately below; click on the **Duplicate** button; and a new master page, based on an already existing master page, appears in the master page section of the palette.

The final button looks like a trash can, and that is exactly what it is. Highlight either document or master page icons in the Document Layout palette, click on this little trash can, and the master pages disappear from the document.

Displaying the Master Page Area

The next area, the master page area, contains icons representing each of the master pages you create for a document. Remember that every document has at least one master page, which is defined by the choices you made in the New Document dialog box.

Master page icons are always arranged down the left side of the palette, so if you have several of these, you'll have to do lots of scrolling to get to them; or you could make that section of the palette larger. Place your cursor over the bar that runs along the bottom of this section. Your cursor turns into an arrow, as shown in Figure 6.2. Click and hold, and you get a new cursor that, when you drag the mouse, resizes the master page area.

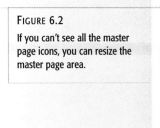

FIGURE 6.2

If you can't see all the master page icons, you can resize the master page area.

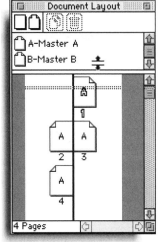

Displaying the Document Page Area

The document page area gives you a complete bird's-eye view of your document's organization. Every page in your document is represented in this section of the palette, arranged exactly the way you have arranged it in the document.

The letter in the center of each page icon tells you which master page is associated with the document page. Under each page icon is a number that indicates the page number in your document. If you have set up your document to have different *section starts*, or to start numbering pages with something other than 1, that is reflected here. This has changed from earlier versions of QuarkXPress.

The master page letter and document page number of whichever page is touching the upper-left corner of your monitor window are displayed in outline type.

You can resize this area of the palette by clicking and dragging on the lower-right corner of the palette. You can change both the width and the depth.

At the bottom of the document page area, two types of page information are displayed. While you work in the Document

Layout palette, the palette displays the number of the page you selected as an active page (by clicking on it), even if that page is not displayed in the active area of the palette. If several pages are selected, this area of the palette is blank. When you are not working with the palette, this area displays the total number of pages in your document.

SEE ALSO

➤ *To add pages to a document with the Document Layout palette, see page 161*

➤ *To create new master pages, see page 155*

➤ *To rearrange document pages with the Document Layout palette, see page 165*

➤ *To rearrange master pages with the Document Layout palette, see page 164*

Working with Master Pages

Consider master pages as a basic building block for your document. They are like internal *templates*, or *style sheets* if you will, that arrange items on a page for use again and again in a document. Master pages can contain text boxes, with or without text in them; picture boxes, with or without pictures; lines; or any combination thereof.

Perhaps the easiest way to explain master pages is by example. Think about a simple eight-page newsletter. It probably has a front page with a *banner* of some sort, date and issue information, and perhaps a *rule* or some other design element at the bottom of a page. The back page might be completely different. It might have only half a page of regular copy because the newsletter is folded for mailing. So that page always contains return-address information, and maybe a *mailing indicia*. It might contain a page number. The remaining six interior pages probably all have a somewhat similar format. Each has a page number, there might be a unifying graphic across the top of the page (a *header*), and there might be another graphic or text along the bottom of the page (a *footer*).

All the elements mentioned in the preceding paragraph are candidates for items on a master page. Our hypothetical newsletter would have at least four master pages, two if the document used *facing pages*—two master pages or one *spread* for the front and back, and two pages or a spread for the inside pages. There could be more masters, depending on the design of the internal pages.

If you were designing a book, you might have many master pages, but two basic ones would be a chapter opener page and a facing-page master for right and left pages. Then you might add additional masters for the table of contents, prefaces, introductions, indexes, appendices, and so forth.

Before creating a new document, take some time to think all the way through the process. Although it would be foolish to suggest a checklist here that applies to every type of document you might want to create, the general topic of master pages leads to at least a few starter questions:

1. How many pages will there be in your document?

2. Will the number of columns vary from page to page?

3. Are you going to import very long strings of text (such as an entire book chapter)?

4. Do you need various column *guides* (with or without *automatic text boxes*)?

5. Will you be using page numbers on every page (or most pages)?

6. Will you have a header, a footer, or both on every page (or most pages)?

7. Will you have a logo or some other graphic that appears on the same place on many different pages?

8. Will you have two or more pages on which the page geometry will be pretty much (or exactly) the same?

A little time spent thinking through these and similar questions before you start work will save you a lot of time over the course of working on a document. With a little planning, you will avoid doing some tasks over and over and over (and trying to remember how you did it two days ago) by creating master pages to use throughout a document.

Using the Default Master Page

A default master page, shown in the Document Layout palette as A-Master A, is created when you fill out the New Document dialog box. It will have the margins you selected, the number of columns you selected, and an automatic text box if you selected that option. If you opted to have your document use facing pages, your A-Master A will actually be a spread—two pages, side-by-side.

Don't worry too much if you make a mistake when setting up a document in the New Document dialog box. You can always go to this A-Master A and make changes in the margins, change the columns, delete an automatic text box, or even add one if you need to do so. You can add items (such as page numbers, headers, and footers) to this default page just as you would for any other master page.

Creating a New Master Page

New or additional master pages are created from the Document Layout palette. There are two choices: drag a blank page from the top of the palette into the master page area, or duplicate an existing master page by highlighting it in the palette and clicking on the duplicate button. Because it already contains some needed items, a duplicated master page not only helps preserve consistency, but also saves time. Once you've duplicated a master page, delete any unnecessary items on the duplicate and add or change others to complete the new master.

Renaming Master Pages

Each master page is given a default name, alphabetically in the order created. These names are not very exciting or intuitive, so you might want to change them, particularly if you have several master pages in your document.

The master page name must consist of two parts, a letter followed by a hyphen and then the name of the page. The designation before the hyphen can be up to three characters long. The portion after the hyphen can be up to 64 characters long. To edit the names of your master pages, simply use your cursor to high-light the page name in the master page area, and type a new name (see Figure 6.3). Most of the time, the letter and hyphen will remain even after you type over them with your own name; the only way to avoid this is to add your own letters or numbers and a hyphen before the master page's name. Make names for your master pages that help you distinguish them from each other and give you a hint about when to use them. Name them in a way that will make sense to others who might have to work with your document somewhere along the line.

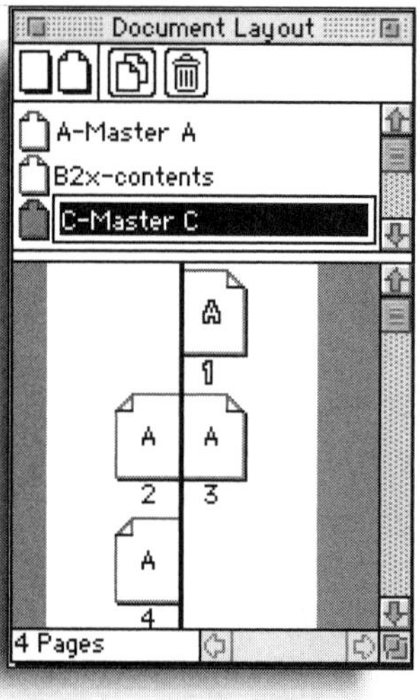

FIGURE 6.3

Renaming master pages makes them easier for you—and others—to use.

Rearranging Master Pages in the Document Layout Palette

Although you can resize the area in the Document Layout palette that displays master pages, if you are working on a document with several master pages, you might want to move the ones you use most often to the top of the display. Highlight the master page icon, and click and drag it to a new location in the palette. This might save you from scrolling through the palette for frequently used master pages.

Editing Master Page Items on Document Pages

It's nice to know that you can always edit master page items. If you edit them on the master page (change the size, move, change color, and so on), the change applies everywhere in the document that the master page is used. One edit, multiple changes. Now you are beginning to understand the value of master pages!

On the other hand, you also can edit master page items on regular document pages. Don't do this without pausing first, however. When you edit a master page item on a document page, that item loses its connection with the master page. So if you then go back to the master page and edit the item, the edit is not applied on the document page on which you previously edited the item. It's very important to remember this—mess with master page items on document pages and they are no longer master page items! There is nothing wrong with doing this. Just make sure you understand what you are doing.

Formatting Master Pages

There are standard items to place on master pages, the most obvious of which is a text box containing page numbers. Other items you might consider are headers and footers and any graphics (either lines or imported graphics) that are part of the page geometry. Consider creating a master page for any page design that is going to be used more than once in your document. When creating a template, think about a master page for a page design that might be used only once in a document, but because the template will be used again and again in multiple documents, it will be handy to have that master page available.

Master pages are built exactly the same way as document pages. There are some actions you might want to consider for master pages that you might not take on a regular document page, however.

Empty text boxes placed on a master page can be "prestyled" so that when you type in them, or import text into them, on the document page, the type is formatted exactly like you want.

Place your cursor in a text box, and then select all the attributes you want the type to have. Pick the font, size, leading, alignment, and so on. You don't actually need to place any type in the box to accomplish this task. Style sheets also can be applied to empty text boxes on master pages. Simply place the cursor in an empty text box and apply any style you have already defined in your document.

Naturally, only one style or set of attributes can be applied to any master page text box. While you're working on a document that has text boxes created on a master page, placing text in the box does not destroy the link with the master page.

The margin guides on a master page are created based on the settings in the New Document dialog box, but you can change their positions while working in the document.

To change master page guides:

1. Display the master page or spread by double-clicking its icon on the Document Layout palette.

2. Choose **Master Guides** from the **Page** menu.

3. To change the number or width of columns, enter new values in the **Columns** and **Gutter Width** fields.

4. To change the width of the page margins, enter new values in the **Top**, **Bottom**, **Left**, and **Right** fields. The field names will be different if the document uses facing pages: **Top**, **Bottom**, **Inside**, and **Outside**.

5. Click **OK** to apply the changes. Master guides can only be changed for one master page or spread at a time.

SEE ALSO

➤ *To place automatic page number characters on a master page, see page 172*

➤ *To create an automatic text box on a master page, see page 190*

➤ *To apply style sheets, see page 303*

➤ *To draw boxes and lines on a master page (or any page), see page 104*

➤ *To design an efficient template, see page 200*

Applying Master Pages to Existing Pages

Applying a master page to a document page is a single-step
process that can be accomplished only through the Document
Layout palette. Click on a master page icon in the master page
area, and drag it directly on top of a document page icon (see
Figure 6.4). Don't release the icon too soon, or you will actually
add a page to the document instead of changing a page format.
When the icon is released, the letter in the center of the document page icon changes to be the same as the master page icon
you just used. In the case of applying a master page to a blank
document page, the master page letter should be added to the
document page icon. Returning to the window where your work
is displayed, you see that the page you changed contains all the
master page items just added.

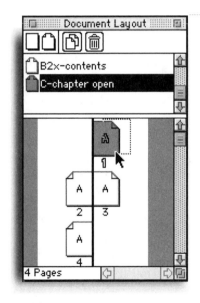

FIGURE 6.4

Once the mouse button is
released, the page 1 icon will
have a C instead of an A.

You can alter several document pages at the same time. First,
either Shift+click on a range of icons, or ⌘+click (Ctrl+click) to
select non-adjacent pages. Then Option+click (Alt+click) on the
master page icon you want to apply. All the selected document
page icons change to reflect the new master, and the document
pages themselves are updated.

Reapplying or Applying Different Master Pages

Even though you might have already applied a master page to a document page, you can continue to make changes as you work. Perhaps you have made several changes on a document page and want to get back to the original master page layout. In this instance, you would reapply the same master page. If you want to change a document page to a different master page, click and drag the desired master page icon directly on top of the document page icon.

There is a preference setting that affects how master page items edited or changed on a document page are handled when you reapply a master or apply a new master to that page. This preference gives you the choice of deleting or keeping master page items that were edited on document pages. Here are your choices:

- **Delete Changes:** All previous master page items on a document page will be removed from the page when you reapply the master page or apply a different master.

- **Keep Changes:** If you changed a master page item on a document page, it will remain on the page when you reapply the master page or apply a different master. For instance, if you changed the background color of a text box and reapplied the master, the document page would contain both text boxes with the new one sitting on top of the edited one.

Whether you opt to delete or keep changes depends on what those changes have been and your reasons for reapplying a master or applying a new master.

SEE ALSO
➤ *To set preferences for master page items, see page 49*

Adding, Deleting, and Rearranging Pages

There are three ways to add new pages to a document. Two of the methods involve adding pages manually, and the third method adds pages automatically.

Inserting Pages Based on Master Pages

The first method of adding pages is done through the Document Layout palette. Click and drag an icon from the master page section of the palette to a location in the document section of the palette. While you're doing this, the cursor changes to a bar with an arrow. This little arrow points down, left, or right, indicating how the existing pages in a document will shift to accommodate the new page (see Figure 6.5). If the arrow is not visible, that means you cannot place the page at that location. If you see a page icon, instead of an arrow, that means no shifting will occur (such as along the right edge of a spread) if you place the page at that location.

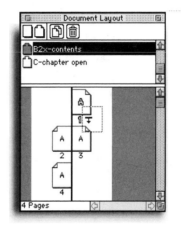

FIGURE 6.5

The arrow indicates where the new page will be placed with respect to existing pages.

You also can add a blank page (not based on any master page) with this method by clicking and dragging a blank page icon from the button section of the palette.

Use this first method to add a single page at a time. When you need to add several pages at once, choose **Insert Pages** from the **Page** menu to bring up the Insert Pages dialog box (see Figure 6.6). All the pages added using this method will be placed together in the same location and based on the same master page.

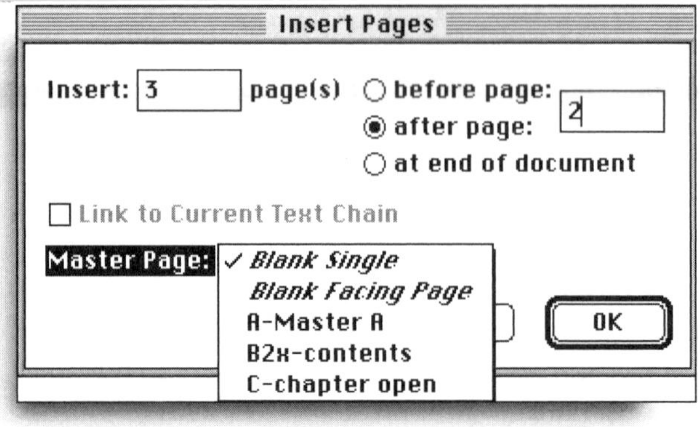

FIGURE 6.6

The Insert Pages dialog box lets you insert several pages at once.

FIGURE 6.6

The Insert Pages dialog box lets you insert several pages at once.

The Insert Pages dialog box allows you to make several choices:

- **Insert ## page(s):** This is where you indicate how many pages you need to add.

- **Before page ##, after page ##:** These buttons let you pick the location in your document.

- **At end of document:** This option does not require a page number. Click on the button and all new pages will come at the end of your document.

- **Master Page:** This is a pop-up menu where you determine what master page you want to use, or you can opt for blank pages.

- **Link to Current Text Chain:** This option is available for selection when you are inserting a master page that contains an automatic text box and a text box is active on a document page.

When you have made all your choices, click **OK**. The new pages are then added to your document.

Inserting Pages Automatically

When you are importing text files into QuarkXPress that are many pages long, you might want to use automatic page insertion, which allows QuarkXPress to add as many pages as necessary to accommodate the text. A couple of conditions must be met for you to accomplish this task:

Insert multiple pages in the Document Layout palette

Hold down the Option (Alt) key when you drag a master page icon into the document page section of the palette, and the Insert Pages dialog box automatically opens. The dialog box opens with some of the choices already made based on the master page icon you were dragging.

- Auto Page Insertion must be turned on in Document Preferences.

- The master page must contain an automatic text box.

Automatic text boxes are created either when you first set up your new document or later when you designate a text box on a master page to be automatic.

SEE ALSO

➤ *To turn on* **Auto Page Insertion** *in the Document Preferences, see page 49*

➤ *To create a new document with a default automatic text box, see page 84*

➤ *To create a automatic text box on an existing master page, see page 190*

➤ *To determine how automatic page insertion will affect your document, see page 188*

Deleting Pages

One way to delete pages is through the Document Layout palette (see Figure 6.7):

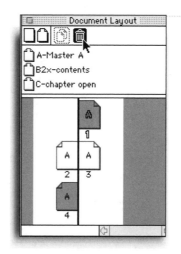

FIGURE 6.7

One or more pages can be deleted using the Document Layout palette.

- To remove just one page, highlight it by clicking on it; then click on the trash can in the button area of the palette.

- To delete several adjacent pages at once, click on the first page you want to remove and then Shift+click on the last page you want to remove. All the intervening pages will be highlighted. Then click on the trash can.

- To delete several non-adjacent pages, ⌘+click (Ctrl+click) each page you want to remove. When they are all highlighted, click the trash can.

A second way to delete pages is by choosing **Delete** from the **Page** menu (see Figure 6.8). You can remove a single page or a range of pages through this menu, but you cannot delete non-adjacent pages. You can delete every page from a particular page to the end of the document by typing end in the **thru** box. If you have sectioned your document, you need to enter the section page numbers in the window, or enter *absolute page numbers* with a + sign in front of them.

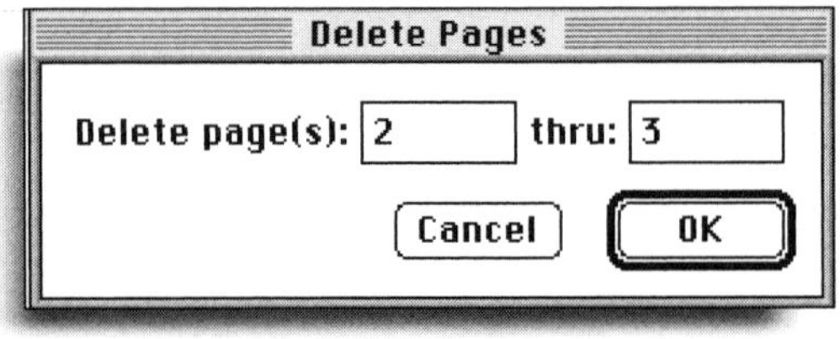

FIGURE 6.8
The Delete Pages dialog box.

Delete Pages

Delete page(s): 2   thru: 3

Cancel   OK

One caution about deleting pages: If Auto Page Insertion is turned on and you try to delete pages containing a chain of text in an automatic text box, QuarkXPress deletes the pages and then automatically creates new ones. They will never disappear! The solution is to turn off Auto Page Insertion before deleting the pages, or to delete some of the text. Often extra carriage return characters at the end of a story are responsible for this phenomenon.

SEE ALSO
➤ *To create sections within a document, see page 173*
➤ *To use absolute page numbers, see page 176*

Rearranging Pages

You will find three ways to rearrange pages in a document. A couple of tips and warnings are in order before you start moving pages around, however:

- If you are using automatic page numbering, page numbers will change when you move the pages.

- If you have sectioned your document, you will also find that page numbers will be revised and updated. Be careful unless you are moving an entire section, or pages within a section, or really do want a page to be part of a different section.

- *Text chains* will remain in the same order. If you have text starting on page 2 continuing to page 3 and you move page 2 to become page 25, the text will flow from page 25 back to wherever page 3 now sits.

Icons in the Document Layout Palette

One quick way of moving pages around is to use the Document Layout palette. Just click on a page icon (it will turn gray) and drag it to a new location in the palette. You can move multiple pages this way also, by using the Shift key to select a range of adjacent pages, or by using ⌘+click (Ctrl+click) to select non-adjacent pages. However, if you move pages in a document that's set up in a *single-sided* format, even if the pages were originally arranged in spreads, they will move back to a single-sided arrangement. You will need to move them again, one at a time, to restore the spreads.

Pages in Thumbnail View

You can also move pages when your document is in Thumbnail view. It works much the same as using the Document Layout palette. Click on the page in the document window (it turns black) and drag it to the new location (see Figure 6.9). The advantage over using the Document Layout palette is that, even though it might be just a small representation of the page geometry, you do have some idea of what each page looks like. This view is helpful if you are rearranging several pages. Since you can see what the pages look like, you don't have to worry so much about keeping track of which page had which number before you started to move them around.

FIGURE 6.9

Rearranging pages in Thumbnail view works similarly to using the Document Layout palette.

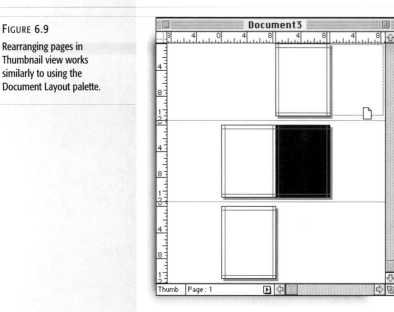

If you are rearranging a lot of pages (for instance, setting up simple *imposition* for your print shop), you might want to consider moving them into a new document while in Thumbnail view. This way the page numbering in the original document does not keep shifting with each move you make, which sometimes can get a bit confusing. Another advantage is that the target document also has stable page numbering.

The same rules apply here as when using the Document Layout palette. Shift+click selects a range of adjacent pages, and ⌘+click (Ctrl+click) selects non-adjacent pages. You might find that spreads (if you're using a single-sided setup) do not reappear just the way you want if you move multiple pages at the same time.

SEE ALSO

➤ *To change the view magnification, see page 93*

➤ *To drag pages into a new document, see page 141*

The Move Pages Dialog Box

The third way to move pages is through the Move Pages dialog box; choose **Move** from the **Page** menu (see Figure 6.10). You need to know page numbers to do this because there is no visual representation of what you are doing. The dialog box for moving pages is very much the same as for inserting or deleting pages.

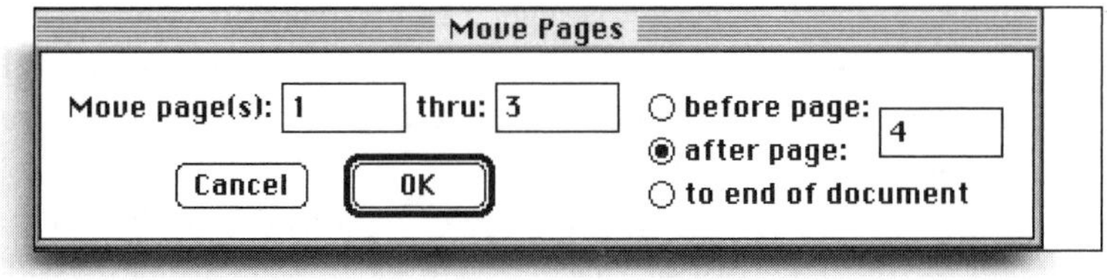

Move Pages

Move page(s): 1   thru: 3   ○ before page:
                                  ⦿ after page: 4
Cancel   OK   ○ to end of document

FIGURE 6.10
The Move Pages dialog box gives you three choices of where to move pages.

The Move Pages dialog box allows you to make several choices:

- **Move page(s):** This is where you enter the page number or the range of numbers you want to move. If you have sectioned your document, you can enter absolute page numbers by typing a + sign in front of the number.

- **Before page ##, after page ##:** These let you pick the location in your document.

- **To end of document:** This option does not require a page number. Click on the button and the pages will move to the end of your document.

Creating Facing-Page Documents and Spreads

Whether or not you need a facing-page document will change from project to project. It is another one of those decisions you should make before you start working. Facing-page masters contain two pages, one for the right side of the spine and the other for the left. In a facing-page document, odd-numbered pages are, by default, always on the right side of the spine, and even-numbered pages are on the left. QuarkXPress tries to force pages into this format. If you set up a section start on a right page and give it an even number, QuarkXPress shuffles the following pages to move it to the left side. Although there are ways to force QuarkXPress to do something different, a little time spent planning ahead can save you a lot of time as you work on your project. Another reason for planning is that it is not particularly easy (or efficient) to turn a facing-page document into a single-sided one.

Starting with Facing Pages

The most obvious way to create a facing-page document is to start with one right up front. In the New Document dialog, click on Facing Pages. The fields that were labeled Right and Left margins become Inside and Outside, the inside margin being where the two pages meet (the *spine* or *gutter*). Your default master page will consist of a facing page, or two pages side-by-side (see Figure 6.11). Don't be confused by this. You still can add pages to your document one at a time, if you want. QuarkXPress will determine whether you need to add the right or left side of a master page depending on where you are inserting the new page.

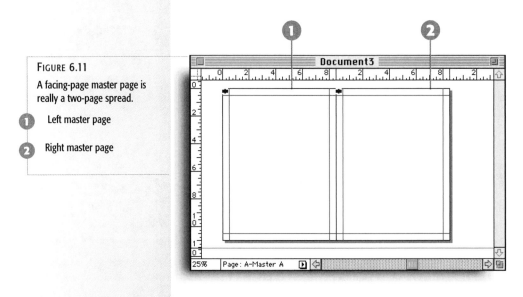

FIGURE 6.11

A facing-page master page is really a two-page spread.

1   Left master page

2   Right master page

In the Document Layout palette, the blank facing-page icon (the one with the dog-eared corners) will be available for use along with the single-page icon.

Starting with Single Pages

You also can build a facing-page document by using single pages. It is a little more work, but some people prefer to work this way. This technique does let you start a book section on a left page and take advantage of continuous page number updating. Using this system requires separate master pages for right-side and left-side pages. Right and left margins need to be set with the gutter in mind; they might be different for the two masters.

When adding pages to a single-sided document, you must manually move them side-by-side if you need spreads. If you add many pages at once, you will probably also need to apply the appropriate master page to either the right or left page.

You can never access the facing-page icon in the Document Layout palette if you set up your document for single-sided pages.

Creating Multipage Spreads

Documents easily can have more than two pages in a spread. QuarkXPress allows a total width of a document up to 48 inches. Use the Document Layout palette (see Figure 6.12) to add pages to your extended spread by clicking and dragging either a master page icon or a blank page icon into the document section of the palette.

In a facing-page document, QuarkXPress adds the correct side of the master (or blank) page depending on which side of the spine in the Document Layout palette you drag the new page to. In a single-sided document, all the pages line up along the left side of the Document Layout palette (see Figure 6.13).

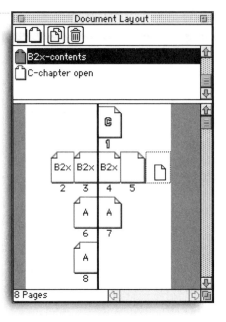

FIGURE 6.12

Multipage spreads in the Document Layout palette can have "extra" pages on either side.

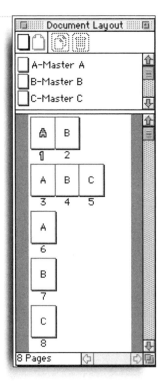

FIGURE 6.13

Multipage spreads in a single-sided document, with all the "extra" pages on the left.

Avoiding Size Changes

Although it is possible to change the page size and setup and orientation of a QuarkXPress document through the Document Setup dialog (choose **Document Setup** from the **File** menu—see Figure 6.14) after you have started working, it is not advisable. You also can change facing-page documents into single-sided documents (and the other way around), but it might not be worth the effort.

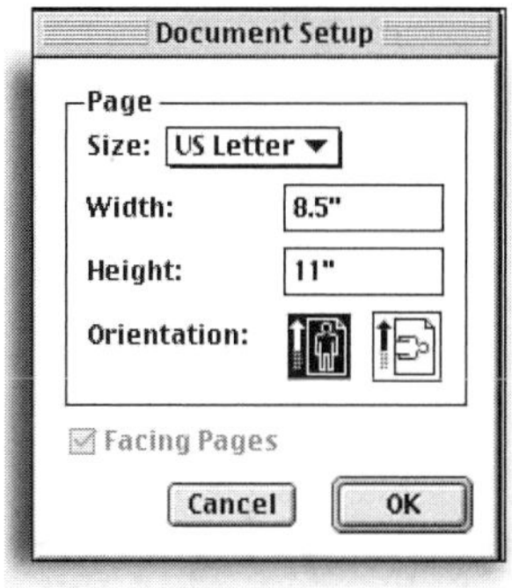

FIGURE 6.14

The Document Setup dialog box lets you change your mind about document attributes after creating a document.

Making a page smaller often results in a message from QuarkXPress saying that this will cause items to be positioned off the pasteboard, something that QuarkXPress simply cannot do. If the change isn't big enough to invoke that message, you still will find that items have not readjusted their positions to accommodate the new page size. Enlarging pages will not invoke a warning message from QuarkXPress, but you still will need to rearrange items to take the larger page size into account.

Changing the *orientation* is also likely to produce the "The item cannot be positioned off the pasteboard" warning, particularly if you switch from *portrait* (tall) to *landscape* (wide). Just as with changing page sizes, you will need to reposition items on your pages by hand.

Switching from a single-sided document to a facing-page document is not a disaster, but it probably won't be worth the effort. Existing master pages will remain single-sided masters. If you have used them, and now want them to be facing-page masters, you'll have to create new facing-page masters and copy and paste to these from the single-sided masters. Original document pages remain related to a single-sided master page; you'll have to decide whether you want to keep them related to the single-sided master or reapply the new facing-page masters to all of them.

Turning a facing-page document into a single-sided document is more complicated. If you have used any master page, QuarkXPress will not allow you to change the setup until you get rid of the master pages. Of course, if you used them, you'll want to re-create them as single-sided masters first. Then delete the old facing-page masters, and QuarkXPress allows you to change the setup. The next step would be to apply the single-sided masters throughout your document, since you lost all the master page items when you deleted the original facing-page masters.

Automatic Page Numbering

You have two choices for numbering pages in your documents. You can create a text box on each page, type in a number, and style it, or you can use automatic page numbers. These automatic numbers will number your pages consecutively throughout the document. If you move a page, the numbers will rearrange themselves, taking into account the new page order.

Placing the Automatic Page Number Character

Typing ⌘+3 (Ctrl+3) in a text box generates automatic page numbers. If you type this code into a text box on a master page, it appears as <#> on the master page and the correct page number on the document page. If you type it in a text box on a document page, it immediately shows the correct page number. Most often, automatic numbers are placed on master pages, avoiding the necessity of remembering to put them on every page. The text box containing the automatic number might contain other text such as part of a header or a footer (see Figure 6.15). Remember, if you use facing pages, put a number on both sides of the master spread. These numbers can be styled the same way you would style any text element.

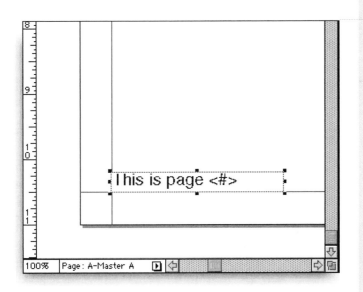

FIGURE 6.15
Automatic page numbers on a master page.

SEE ALSO

➤ *To apply formatting to text on master pages, see page 238*

Sectioning a Document

Documents are usually sectioned because you need to start new or different page-numbering schemes within the same document. For instance, you might have table of contents pages that need to be numbered one way, while the remaining pages in the document need to start numbering with page 1. This is where sections are essential.

To create a section, activate what will be the first page of the section (make sure that the page number is in outline type on the Document Layout palette), and choose **Section** from the **Page** menu (see Figure 6.16). You can also Option+click (Alt+click) on the area at the lower-left of the Document Layout palette.

FIGURE 6.16

The Section dialog box allows you to determine what page number a section or document begins with.

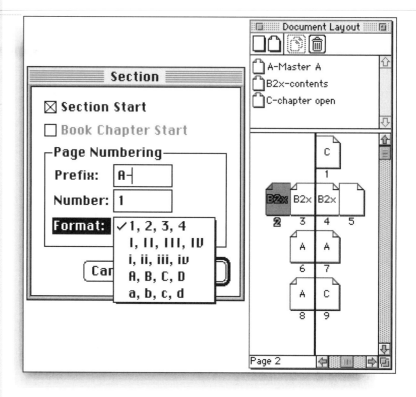

If your document is set up to use the QuarkXPress *Book* feature, then you'll need to deal with the option **Book Chapter Start**. This discussion assumes just a single document that needs to be divided into sections. Here are the options:

- **Section Start** needs to be selected. Click on it and an X appears in the box.
- **Prefix** allows you to add one or more identifying characters before the page number.
- **Number** gives you control over which page number starts the new section. It might be that a section starts on page 26, so enter that number. It might be that the section starts renumbering the pages from 1, so enter 1.
- **Format** gives you a choice of five ways to display the actual page numbers in the section: Arabic numerals, upper- and lowercase Roman numerals, upper- and lowercase letters.

The page number generated from this dialog and any prefix you selected will appear in the text box where you typed the command for an automatic page number. The section start page, and all the following pages, will be renumbered using the selected format. This will continue to the end of the document unless you set up another section start page. Every time you start a new section, the first page of the section has an asterisk (*) after the number, providing a visual clue to your document's organization.

The numbers generated from the Section dialog box will appear in the Document Layout palette, in the window at the lower-left of your display showing the current active page number, and in the pop-out window at the bottom of your display showing all the pages in the document (see Figure 6.17). You are now using *section page numbers* in your document instead of absolute page numbers.

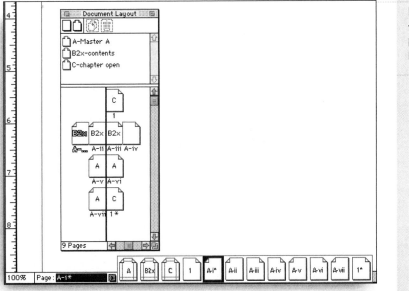

FIGURE 6.17

The document shown actually has two page 1s, the first and last pages in the document.

To change or eliminate a section start, activate the page where the section starts, return to the Section dialog, and click again on the Section Start box. The X disappears and so does any special numbering scheme you set up for that section. All the pages that had been contained in the section are renumbered consecutively from the beginning of the document or from a previous section, if one was set up.

After creating sections in a document, you still can rearrange pages using any of the techniques described earlier. However, if you move a page from one section into another, it will take on the numbering attributes of its new section. Moving pages within a section affects only the number; any associated attributes, such as prefix or format, remain the same.

Absolute Page Numbers

Even if you decide to use section page numbers, QuarkXPress can always recognize and find a page based on its absolute number—and so can you, by placing a + in front of the number. You can enter absolute page numbers in any dialog box asking for a page number or range of numbers by inserting the + sign first. So +1 to +5 would print the first five pages of your document even if you have four different section start pages there. To see the absolute page number of a page in the Document Layout palette, Option+click (Alt+click) on a page in the Document Layout palette. The absolute page number appears in the area at the lower-left of the palette.

Creating "Continued" References

Keeping track of stories that *jump* to a new page can be a real hazard as far as the continued to/from references, or *jumplines*, are concerned. QuarkXPress has a nice feature that solves this problem and automatically updates any continued to/from page numbers if pages are rearranged.

The first part of the solution is the code for displaying the numbers in a continued to/from reference:

- ⌘+4 (Ctrl+4) places a character that QuarkXPress reads as the number on the page where the story is continued to.
- ⌘+2 (Ctrl+2) places a character that QuarkXPress reads as the number on the page where the story is continued from.

You could place these characters in a line of text at the bottom or top of a column or text box at the point where the jump occurs. You could, but you shouldn't. They then become part of the text flow, and if you do any editing on the story, the line of text containing the continued to/from code might no longer be where you want it to be.

Instead, put these jumpline codes in a separate text box that overlaps the jump point (see Figure 6.18). It takes two boxes— one where the continued-to notation needs to be made and another where the continued-from notation needs to be seen. These boxes must overlap and be in front of the box containing the actual story that is jumping to or from a different page.

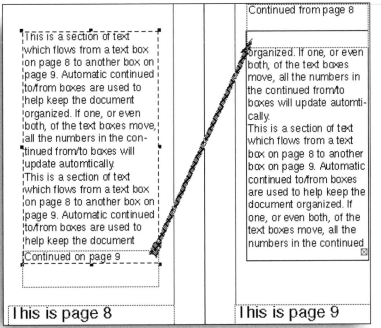

Continued on page 9

Continued from page 8

This is page 8

This is page 9

FIGURE **6.18**

Special Continued to/Continued from characters make jumplines easy.

You can put whatever notation you want in these overlapping boxes along with the continued to/from keystroke code. For example, you might use "Story continued on page ⌘+4 (Ctrl+4)" or "Story continued from ⌘+2 (Ctrl+2)." Since these references are in boxes separate from the main story, they will not move if you do any editing on the story. If you rearrange pages, the numbers will automatically change. If you move just the box containing the story, make sure that you move the continued to/from box with it. You might consider grouping these boxes so that they are not accidentally separated from each other.

SEE ALSO

➤ *To group boxes, see page 133*

➤ *To edit text, see page 204*

PART

Adding and Formatting Text

Flowing Text Throughout a Document

Import text files

Export text for use in other applications

Transfer text formatting from word processing documents

Link and unlink text boxes

Create automatically linking text boxes on master pages

Format multiple columns of text

Design efficient templates

Most, but certainly not all, documents contain text that flows from box to box and even page to page. QuarkXPress provides two ways of getting text to go where you want: a manual method and an automatic method. Both methods work whether you import text or type it in XPress.

Importing Text Files

In most workflows, a layout artist working in QuarkXPress imports copy from a professional writer who's working in a word processor. The text file may be produced on either Mac OS or Windows, and it might or might not be formatted. QuarkXPress accommodates all these scenarios. You can import plain old *ASCII text* from anywhere, or you can import preformatted text in Quark's proprietary tagging language called *XPress Tags*. On the Windows side, you can import *RTF* files. Finally, you can import text from any word processor for which Quark provides a filter.

Using Import/Export Filters

QuarkXPress ships with a variety of filters that enable you to import formatted text from word processors. If you chose to install the filters when you installed QuarkXPress, they are placed in the XTension folder inside your QuarkXPress folder. If they're not there, check your XTension (Disabled) (XTension.off) folder. If you didn't install the filters, you need to run the installer again to get them off the QuarkXPress CD-ROM.

Import/Export Filters Available

In general, QuarkXPress provides filters for the following applications: Microsoft Word, WordPerfect, AmiPro, MacWrite, MacWrite Pro, Windows Write, Microsoft Works, and WriteNow. However, these word processing filters are always in varying states of disrepair depending on the platform and word processor upgrades, and not all these filters are supplied for both platforms. (Mac users don't get AmiPro or XyWrite filters, and Windows users don't get MacWrite filters.) And there's a catch to the way the filters are named. The ones that are actually called *filter* go both ways (you can import and export text in that format), while the ones called *import* only let text in.

Quark puts periodic updates to these filters online at http://www.quark.com. The updated filters include ReadMes that explain their limitations in full.

Enabling Filters

Word processing filters are actually *XTensions*. To use one, you need to enable it using the XTensions Manager (choose **XTensions Manager** from the **Utilities** menu). The XTensions Manager lists all the XTensions in your XTension and XTension (Disabled) (XTension.off) folders. The Enable column displays a check mark for all XTensions that are currently running. If a filter you need is not enabled, select it and click in the Enable column to add a check mark. You need to restart QuarkXPress to have the change take effect.

Getting Text

Once the word processing filters you need are running, you're ready to "get text."

To import text into a box or text path:

1. Text is considered box contents, so select the Content tool 🖑.

2. Click to select a *text box*. (Text can be imported onto a *text path* as well—click to select the text path.)

3. If the box already contains text, click to position the text insertion point where the text should be inserted. If any text is selected, the imported text will replace it.

4. Select **Get Text** from the **File** menu or press ⌘+E (Ctrl+E). (If the command says **Get Picture**, a picture box is selected.) The Get Text dialog box opens (see Figure 7.1).

Slimming down memory requirements

As with other XTensions, word processing filters consume memory that would otherwise be available to QuarkXPress. If you aren't likely to receive text in one of the formats—or if you've never even heard of some of the word processors—disable those filters. If you do need them, you can always enable them later.

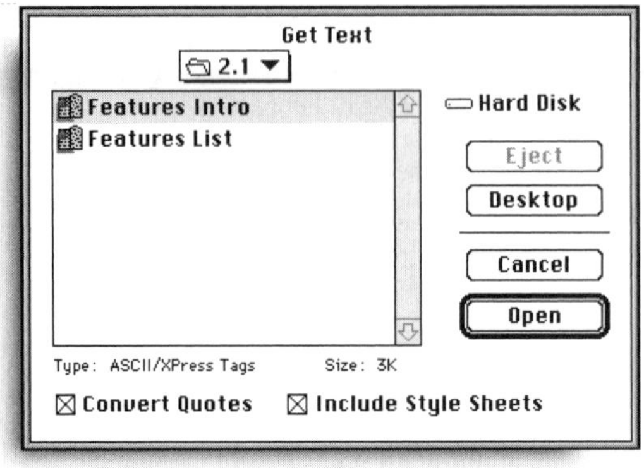

FIGURE **7.1**

The Get Text dialog box lets you import any type of text file into the active text box.

Get Text

📁 2.1 ▼

📄 Features Intro
📄 Features List

⊖ Hard Disk

Eject

Desktop

Cancel

Open

Type: ASCII/XPress Tags   Size: 3K

☒ Convert Quotes   ☒ Include Style Sheets

Can't import a Word file?

Don't try to import a fast-saved Word file. Consult your Word documentation for how to turn off Fast Save.

---

5. Find the text file and select it.

6. To import style sheets in a Word, WordPerfect, or XPress Tags file, check **Include Style Sheets**. If the text is not in one of these formats, or the appropriate filter is not running, **Include Style Sheets** is grayed out.

7. To convert straight quotes to *typographers' quotes* and double hyphens to *em dashes* when the text is imported, check **Convert Quotes**. The quote format used depends on the preference settings.

8. Click **Open** or double-click.

The text flows into the selected text box. If there is too much text for the box, QuarkXPress adds pages to contain it or displays the red text overflow symbol ☒ in the lower corner of the box. QuarkXPress adds pages when you import text into an *automatic text box* and the Auto Page Insertion preference is on.

SEE ALSO

➤ *To turn on Auto Page Insertion in the preferences, see page 49*

Exporting Text

If you need to take text out of QuarkXPress for editing, translation, archiving, or whatever, you can export it. Without a third-party XTension such as TeXTractor, you can't export all the text in a document at once though—you need to do it a story at a time. And if you want to export the text with formatting for a specific word processor, you need to be sure both that the filter isn't named "Import" (because that means it can't export) and that the appropriate filter is currently running.

To export text:

1. Text is considered box contents, so select the Content tool 🖐.

2. Click to select a text box or text path.

3. To export only part of a story, select that part. Otherwise, the entire story will be exported.

4. Select **Save Text** from the **File** menu or press ⌘+Option+E (Ctrl+Alt+E). The Save Text dialog box opens (see Figure 7.2).

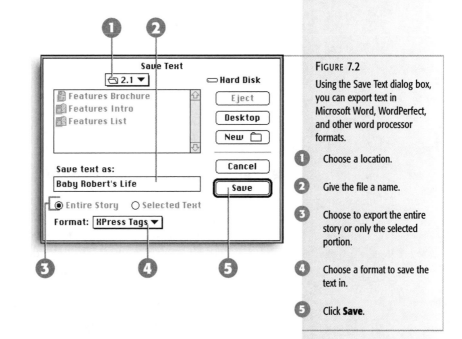

FIGURE 7.2

Using the Save Text dialog box, you can export text in Microsoft Word, WordPerfect, and other word processor formats.

1 Choose a location.

2 Give the file a name.

3 Choose to export the entire story or only the selected portion.

4 Choose a format to save the text in.

5 Click **Save**.

5. Specify a location for the text file and type a name in the **Save Text As** field.

6. If no text is selected in the active story, the **Entire Story** and **Selected Text** buttons are grayed out. However, if text is selected, export just the selected text or click **Entire Story** to export all of it.

7. Use the **Format** pop-up menu to select the word processor or other format for the text. The list varies according to which filters are running, and the amount of formatting information saved with the text depends on the filter.

- **ASCII** preserves no formatting at all, but it can be used by any application anywhere.

- **RTF** (Windows only) is Rich Text Format, for use with most word processors.

- **XPress Tags**, available when the filter is running, embeds XPress Tags codes that are converted to formatting when the text is imported back into QuarkXPress.

8. Click **Save**.

QuarkXPress creates a text file in the specified location. You can use this text in any application that supports the designated format, and you can import it back into QuarkXPress.

SEE ALSO

➤ *To purchase XTensions, see page 554*

➤ *To enable and disable XTensions, see page 555*

➤ *To use XPress Tags for text formatting, see page 565*

Retaining Formats When Getting/Saving Text

The reliability of importing and exporting formatted text depends on the word processing filter, the word processor, and the type of formatting applied to the text. Because the filters and the word processors are periodically updated, it's difficult to provide a set list of what is and isn't imported or exported with text. This problem is aggravated because updates to filters and word processors are not always simultaneous on Mac OS and Windows. However, in general, you can expect the following:

- If you use Word or WordPerfect, QuarkXPress enables you to import the *style sheets* applied to the text. You can apply and edit those style sheets in QuarkXPress. You can also export QuarkXPress style sheets for use in Word or WordPerfect.

- QuarkXPress imports and exports most simple character formatting from most word processors. This means, you'll usually retain bold, italics, and underline, but you may not retain superior, subscript, and superscript. At the paragraph level, you'll get paragraph alignment, indents, and space before/after. You'll almost never retain QuarkXPress formatting such as horizontal scaling, tracking, kerning, leading, H&Js, and so on.

- Document formatting such as *headers*, *footers*, and page numbers do not import or export with text. (Nor should they—text is rarely on the same page in QuarkXPress as in a word processor.)

- Word processing features such as tables, automatic bulleting, and automatic numbering are not imported. Footnote text imports but is placed at the end of a *text chain*.

- *Embedded* pictures travel well between QuarkXPress and Word, as long as you stick to square picture boxes. *Anchored* lines and text boxes will not travel. With other word processors, transferring anchored items is an unlikely scenario.

If your writers are using one of the less popular word processors, they should stick to the general rule of less is better. They should apply type styles for emphasis only. If your writers are using Word or WordPerfect, you can really set them up. You can create basic style sheets for headlines, subheads, body copy, and captions for the writers to use in their word processor. Then you can import the text into QuarkXPress with style sheets. Since the style sheets are already applied, you can spend your time jazzing up the text by simply editing the style sheets.

The trick to transferring style sheets back and forth between word processors and QuarkXPress is testing. Use sample text to experiment with importing and exporting, and you'll quickly discover the danger zones.

SEE ALSO
➤ *To create and edit style sheets, see page 297*

Picking Up New Styles

An easy way to transfer text between QuarkXPress and Word or WordPerfect is to name style sheets the same, but define them differently. Just be sure the names are exactly the same, including capitalization, and remember to turn on Include Styles when you import the text files into QuarkXPress. Your QuarkXPress style sheets will be applied to the appropriate paragraphs as the text is imported.

Using an Automatic Text Box

Here's another plan-ahead topic: do you need automatic text boxes to flow text you are importing from a word processing application into QuarkXPress? It depends. Ask yourself a few questions before you set up your document:

- How long is the text being imported each time—one page? Twenty-five pages?

- How is the text flow organized? Will the text simply stream from page to page (like a book), or will it start on a page and then skip a couple of pages (like a magazine or newspaper)?

- Do you want QuarkXPress to generate enough pages to accommodate your imported text, or do you want to add the pages yourself?

If the answer to the first question is "really long," the answer to the second is "like a book," and the answer to the third is "let QuarkXPress do the tedious work," then you should consider using an automatic text box along with automatic page insertion.

Creating a Default Automatic Text Box

You can create an automatic text box on your default *master page* by selecting **Automatic Text Box** in the New Document dialog box. A new document will be created with a text box on the default master page. It will fill the area of the page defined by the margins you selected and will have as many columns as you requested. If you have a facing-page document, there will be an automatic text box on each side of the two-page master spread. Any new master pages you create based on this default page (by selecting the page and clicking on the **Duplicate** button in the Document Layout palette button area) also will have an automatic text box.

To really take advantage of automatic text boxes, you also need to use Auto Page Insertion; otherwise, all you have done is saved yourself the couple of seconds it takes to put a box on a master page. So the next step is to make certain that **Auto Page Insertion** is turned on in the **General** tab of Document

Preferences. Do not immediately create a whole slew of *document pages* based on this master and then flow a huge string of imported text into your document. QuarkXPress will simply ignore all the pages you added to the document, create new ones, and put them wherever you asked in the Preferences dialog.

Think about these guidelines for using automatic text boxes and automatic page insertion:

- The master page QuarkXPress uses to generate new pages depends on the parameters you establish for auto page insertion in the preferences. If you specify **End of Story**, new pages will be based on the same master as the page where you started importing the text. If you specify **End of Section**, new pages will look like the last page in the section (which might or might not be what you want). If you select **End of Document**, the pages will look like whichever master page was originally the last document page before you imported the new text.

- If you apply a different master page to a document page that contains part of a text flow, QuarkXPress will reflow the text through that page's text box only if it's an automatic text box. This is true even if the pages containing the text flow were linked manually rather than by Auto Page Insertion.

- QuarkXPress will not reflow text through a different master page if it does not contain an automatic text box.

- QuarkXPress will not reflow text if a master page with an automatic text box is reapplied to a page that originally did not contain an automatic text box, even if the text boxes were manually linked. To reestablish the text flow, you'll have to link the text boxes yourself.

SEE ALSO

➤ *To create a new document, see page 84*

➤ *To duplicate a master page, see page 155*

➤ *To turn on Auto Page Insertion in the preferences, see page 49*

➤ *To apply a new master page to a document page, see page 159*

Adding an Automatic Text Box to a Master Page

You do not need to start with automatic text boxes in a document; you can easily add them to master pages after you get started. Select a master page and draw a text box. There will be a broken chain link icon in the upper-left corner of the page. Select the Linking tool ⟦⟧, click on the broken chain icon ⟦⟧, and then click on the text box (see Figure 7.3). It is now an automatic text box, and it will function in exactly the same way as those created with a new document or those created via duplication of a default master page containing an automatic text box.

FIGURE 7.3
To create an automatic text box, link the chain icon in the corner of the master page to a text box.

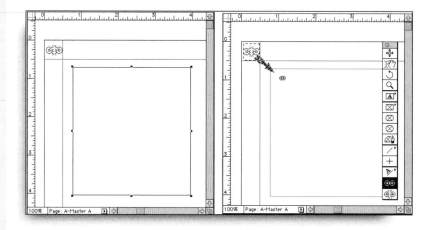

Also, you can have more than one text box on a master page with automatic text boxes. Simply continue linking all the text boxes you create on the master page in the order in which you want the text to flow through them. Just remember, the chain of boxes must start with the chain icon (see Figure 7.4).

If necessary, you can change an automatic text box into a plain vanilla text box by selecting the Unlinking tool ⟦⟧ and clicking on the feather part of the arrow indicating the chain.

SEE ALSO

➤ *To view a document's master pages, see page 151*

➤ *To draw a text box, see page 105*

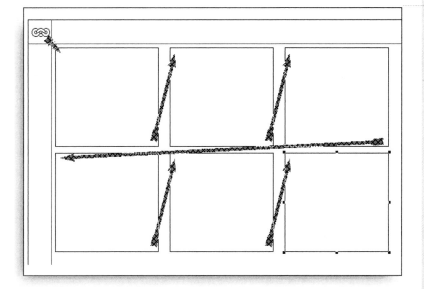

FIGURE 7.4

A master page can contain several linked automatic text boxes.

Linking and Unlinking Boxes

There will be times when you neither want nor need automatic text boxes or automatic page insertion. You can always link boxes on document or master pages manually.

Linking a Series of Boxes

Click on the Linking tool and then click on the text box where your text chain will start. The outside of the box turns into a moving dashed line (some people call this the marching ants!), indicating that it is ready to be linked to another box. Then click on another text box and the two are linked (see Figure 7.5). Any text placed in the first box overflows into the second. You see an arrow on the screen showing the direction of the link.

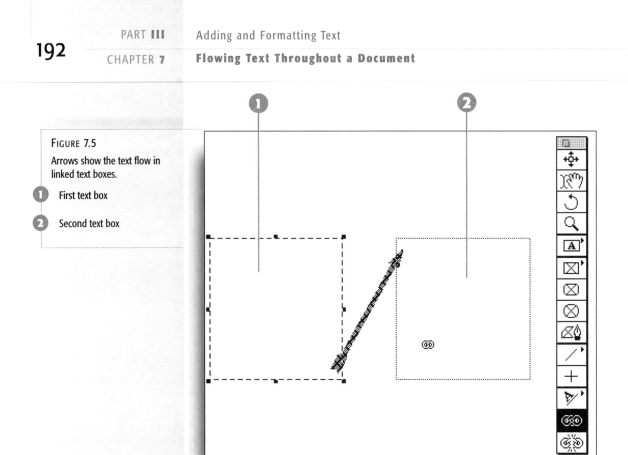

FIGURE 7.5

Arrows show the text flow in linked text boxes.

1 First text box

2 Second text box

You can link several boxes, making a chain that flows throughout your document or through several boxes on the same page. To speed up this process, hold down the Option (Alt) key when you select the Linking tool. The tool remains active until you decide you are done creating a chain and select another tool. You also need to exit from the Linking tool before starting a new text chain by selecting a different tool.

When you're linking multiple boxes, either on the same page or on different pages in a document, it helps to work in smaller views. This allows you to see several spreads at the same time and link boxes without having to scroll through a lot of pages in the document.

If Auto Page Insertion is turned on and there is a master page with an automatic text box, QuarkXPress automatically adds additional pages to your document when there is text overflow in your linked boxes.

SEE ALSO

➤ *To change the view magnification, see page 93*

➤ *To turn on Auto Page Insertion, see page 49*

Rerouting Box Links

If you need to reorganize a text chain, simply redo the links using the Linking tool 🔗 . The text will reflow according to the new links (see Figure 7.6). Notice that when you select the Linking tool and click on a linked box, arrows appear on the screen showing all the links in that particular text chain. This helps you keep track of your text chain even if you are working in a small view and might not be able to read the text onscreen.

FIGURE 7.6

To reroute links, just start over again, linking the boxes in the new order.

It can be difficult to add a box to the beginning of the chain. There are probably production artists who have lost countless hours of sleep trying to push a text chain around to get it to start in a different place. The easiest way is to add a new text box to the chain immediately after the first box. Reroute your chain through this new box by clicking on the first box in the chain and then on the new box. The text will reflow through the new box while all the other boxes remain in the same order. Then, using the Item tool ⊕ , delete the first box in the chain, and the newly created second box is now the first.

Delete any box or boxes from any point in the text chain, and the chain rearranges itself and reflows just as if the box or boxes were never there. To do that, use the Item tool, click on the box, and cut or press Delete. However, if you still need the box and simply no longer want the text chain to flow through it, select the Unlinking tool 🔗 and hold down the Shift key while clicking on the target box. The box remains, but the text chain no longer flows through it (see Figure 7.7).

FIGURE 7.7

Unlinking a text box from a chain with the Shift key removes that box from the flow without deleting it.

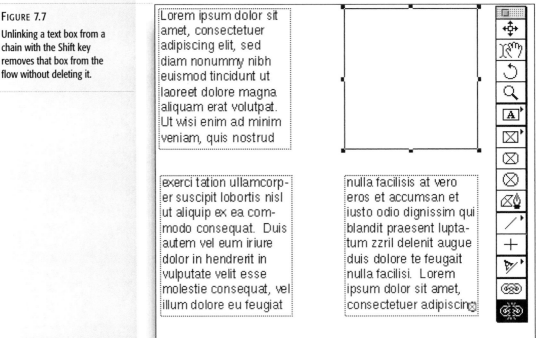

Unlinking Boxes

Text chains can be unlinked as easily as they are linked. Use the Unlinking tool (the broken chain at the bottom of the Tool palette) and select a box at the point where you want to break the chain. Again, the arrows showing the direction of the chain appear. Click on the "feather" in this target box, and all links from it are broken (see Figure 7.8). Click on the "arrow head" in the target box, and the link into the box is broken.

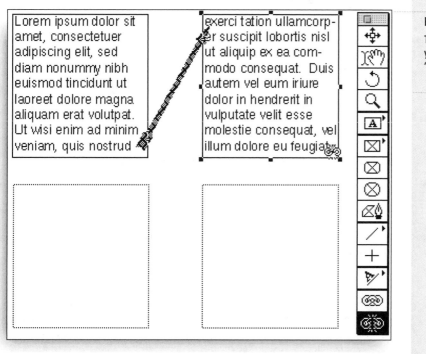

FIGURE 7.8

To unlink text boxes, make sure you're clicking directly on the "feathers."

Usually when you do this you get a text overflow symbol ☒ at the end of the remaining chain, indicating that there is unplaced text. But if you have Auto Page Insertion turned on, QuarkXPress solves that problem for you by creating new pages in your document to accommodate the overflow text. You might, or might not, be happy about that. If you had Auto Page Insertion turned on because you had a long piece of text to import, and you need to break the automatic text chain, take the time to go back to the preferences and turn off Auto Page Insertion. As with most preferences, there is no problem with changing this setting back and forth during the course of working on a document.

SEE ALSO

➤ *To turn Auto Page Insertion on or off, see page 49*

Using Columns

Suppose a layout calls for two or more columns. In QuarkXPress, there's no need to draw multiple boxes to accommodate these multiple columns; each text box can be divided into as many as 30 columns. You can specify the width of the *gutters*—the space between the columns—and the column width is a function of the text box width, the gutter width, and the number of columns.

Specifying Columns in Automatic Text Boxes

When using automatic text boxes, you can set up columns in them when you create a new document (see Figure 7.9). One of the choices in the New Document dialog box asks how many columns you want on a page and the gutter width, which is the space between the columns (note that you are not asked how wide you want the columns to be). QuarkXPress then calculates the width of the columns based on the width of the automatic text box (which is the width of the page minus the amount of space used for margins), minus the amount of space used for the gutters. Your default master page will have an automatic text box with columns ready to flow text.

SEE ALSO

➤ *To create a new document, see page 84*

Specifying Columns for Any Selected Text Box

You don't need to make a decision regarding columns when you set up your document, nor do all of your pages need to have the same number of columns on them. Individual text boxes on document pages can have columns, text boxes on master pages can have columns, and automatic text boxes can have columns. The number of columns in any of these text boxes can be changed whenever you want, and text will reflow accordingly.

Use either of these methods to change or add columns to any type of text box:

- Select any text box, and choose **Modify** from the **Item** menu, then go to the **Text** tab, shown in Figure 7.10, to add or change the number of columns. You can also set the space between the columns in the same tab.

- Select any text box, and use the Measurements palette, shown in Figure 7.11, to add or change the number of columns. However, the gutter width will default to one pica.

Column Guides without Column

If you want column guides, but you don't want the default automatic text box to be divided into columns, you can change the master page guides. While on a master page, choose **Master Guides** from the **Page** menu (see Figure 7.12) and fill in the choices regarding number of columns and gutter space. Nonprinting guidelines, the same color as your margin guides, are placed on the master page.

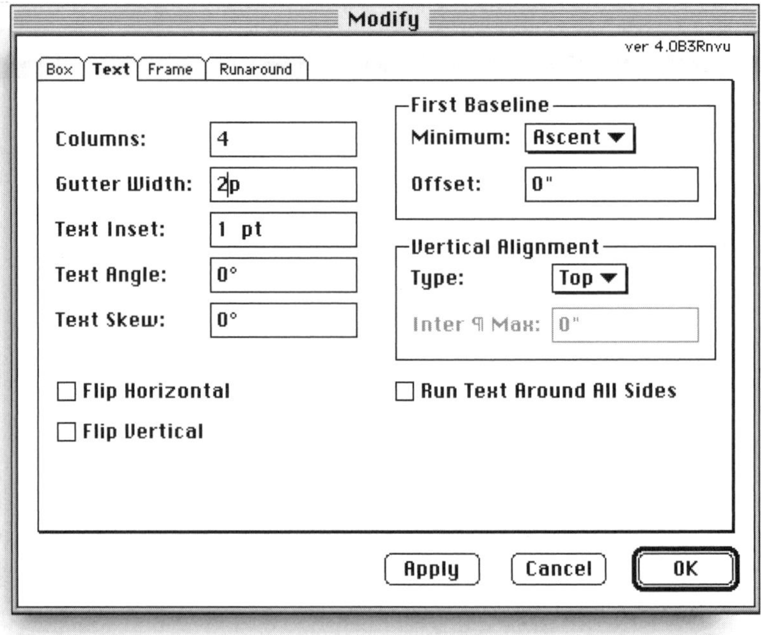

FIGURE 7.10

You can specify column numbers and gutter width in the Modify dialog box's **Text** tab.

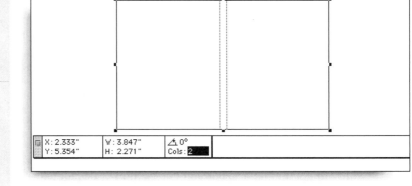

FIGURE 7.11

The Measurements palette lets you specify the number of columns but not the gutter width.

Because the columns QuarkXPress makes in a text box are all the same width, you can use column guides to help create pages with non-uniform column widths. If you create column guides for a three-column setup, you can manually draw a text box two columns wide, and draw another that is a single column wide. These can be converted to automatic text boxes and the two columns can be linked; or they can remain separate.

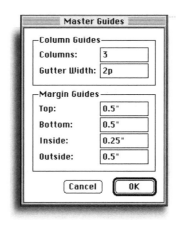

FIGURE 7.12
The Master Guides dialog box lets you add and change column guides.

To create only column guides when setting up a document, fill in all the required information in the New Document dialog box, but do not select Automatic Text Box. The default master page will then contain guides for you to work with.

Forcing Text to the Next Column

When working with columns, you'll find times when you want to push, or force, text into the next column before it gets to the bottom of its current column. The Enter key on the numeric keypad part of your keyboard forces any text after the cursor location into the next column. If there is only one column in a box, the text is forced into the next box in the chain. To force text in a multicolumned box into a new text box while ignoring any other columns in the first box, insert your cursor at the appropriate point and press Shift+Enter.

Columns versus tabs

Should there be a debate about using columns or tabs? Probably not. Columns are for flowing strings of text. Tabs, on the other hand, are used for horizontal spacing within a column of text. Don't try to use columns to set up tabbed information like that found in charts—you'll be much happier and have much better control of your chart information by using tabs. QuarkXPress 4 allows an unlimited number of tabs in a text box, so you should be able to create charts with as many "columns" as you need without feeling the need to resort to text boxes with a whole lot of narrow columns in them just to mimic tabs.

Do not attempt to mimic this action by typing a whole string of carriage returns, or even one or two extra ones. The return character actually takes up a line, even though you can't see it. If you edit your text, change column width, change the box size, or do anything that causes your text to reflow, you could find yourself with blank space at the top of the column (occupied, of course, by that nasty invisible return character).

Creating a Perfect Template

Templates are those designs you use over and over. They can be very simple, or complex, consisting of many elements, but using them is no different from creating a document. When templates are done correctly, you might find them useful for months or even years, saving countless hours in setup and recreation of work done previously. They provide consistency on a document-wide basis in the same way that master pages and style sheets provide consistency within a document. In fact, master pages and styles are the key elements of a perfect template.

Starting with Final Master Pages

The first building block in a perfect template is the master page or pages. Build your page geometry on master pages, not document pages. Set up text boxes, decide whether you need automatic text boxes, determine how columns will be arranged (perhaps the document will have several arrangements). Put in headers, footers, and page numbers if you need them. Add any repeating imported graphics. If you are unsure about whether you need a particular layout for a master page, include it anyway; you don't have to use it.

For example, if you are producing a book, include all the sections of the book in your template, including front matter (table of contents, prefaces, introductions, and such) and back matter (index, appendices, glossaries, and so forth), all of which might have slightly different page layouts. Whether you have 2 or 20 master pages, name them in a way that will mean something to you six months later, or to a different user two days later. Stay away from generic names like Master Page One, Master Page Two.

Templates usually don't need to contain more than the single obligatory document page. On the other hand, some layouts may work better if you create document pages and apply the correct master pages in the template. When you're asking QuarkXPress to use an automatic text box and automatic page insertion, it is probably best not to arrange a lot of document pages. When the document based on the template consists of a lot of different master pages, perhaps with manually linked text boxes, it makes sense to arrange the corresponding document pages and set up the links as part of the template.

SEE ALSO

➤ *To create new master pages, see page 155*

➤ *To duplicate master pages, see page 155*

➤ *To format master pages, see page 157*

Confirming All Document Components

After building the master pages, think about all the other elements of your document. Create all the style sheets, colors, *H&Js*, *lists*, *Dashes & Stripes*, and so on that you will need when you utilize this template. Then, delete everything you won't need. Delete colors you won't use and Dashes & Stripes you won't use. Set Document, Tool, and Trapping preferences to work most efficiently on this particular template. Don't worry about what you might do or need on another job; this template is meant to do just one thing.

SEE ALSO

➤ *To create style sheets, see page 297*

➤ *To define colors, see page 426*

➤ *To create hyphenation and justification settings (H&Js), see page 268*

➤ *To define table of contents and other lists, see page 593*

➤ *To create Dashes & Stripes, see page 593*

Saving the Document as a Template

When all the components are present to your satisfaction, save this document as template. Use Save As and be sure to check the Template setting. When you open the template, it will open

Save often to save time

As is true in anything you do on a computer, save your work often. Even while building master pages, you should be saving. After all, one reason for templates is for saving time. You won't be saving any time at all if you have to keep starting from scratch because of a system crash or power outage. Save templates incrementally by giving them different names, or use Save As to overwrite a previous file.

as an unnamed document. This eliminates the danger of accidentally overwriting the template. Your template is now ready to work for you.

One shortcut to making templates is to create one out of an existing document. Open a document in which styles, colors, master pages, and so on have already been completed. Delete all the pages in the document, and rebuild the layout using empty master pages. Reestablish any needed links between text boxes. Choose Save As from the **File** menu and check **Template**. Pick a name and you have a new template.

SEE ALSO

➤ *To save documents as templates, see page 90*

Editing Text

The hallmark of QuarkXPress is typography, which obviously requires text. QuarkXPress offers a straightforward environment for entering, importing, and editing text, along with a few sophisticated word processing features such as search and replace and spell check. Most of the commands for manipulating text are the same as those in word processors and other applications, so you'll immediately feel comfortable working with text. However, due to its emphasis on page layout, QuarkXPress does not supply word processing tools such as a thesaurus, revision control, or sorting. As a result, most publications rely on copywriters using word processors to produce initial drafts, which are then flowed into QuarkXPress and fine-tuned.

SEE ALSO

➤ *To import text into a QuarkXPress document, see page 182[*

Working with Text

Editing text in QuarkXPress is like the good old days of word processing. You get to cut and paste, spell check, search and replace, and apply type styles. What more do you want? Apparently a lot—the toolbar alone in Microsoft Word is enough to frighten seasoned page layout devotees. I know writers who compose text in QuickMail to dodge the rampant featuritis of popular word processors.

But if your needs are basic—no need for sorting or tables, for example—you can use QuarkXPress as a word processor. Better yet, you can start with text from a word processor and edit it in QuarkXPress to accommodate the layout. In QuarkXPress there's no story editor or galley view, so what you see is what you get. Plus, what you type is what you get; the software won't presume to alter your well-considered spelling and punctuation.

Entering Text

To enter text into QuarkXPress, you need a *text box* or *text path*. (Other page layout applications let you start typing anywhere you click. If you're used to that method, keep reminding yourself that everything in QuarkXPress goes in a box). You can have an automatic text box, which you specify in the New Document dialog box or on a master page. Or you can draw a text box or text path with any of the tools that have an "A" on them.

To enter text, select a box or path with the Content tool 🖑 and start typing. If you can't type for some reason, it's probably because the wrong tool is selected. Just remember that text is content, so you need the Content tool. (The fact that even professional QuarkXPress trainers call the Content tool the "hand tool" doesn't help. But if you look closely, there's a little text insertion bar to the left of the hand.)

After you start typing, you can type all you want. If you use an *automatic text box* and *Auto Page Insertion* is on, QuarkXPress automatically gives you a new page with a new text box so you never run out of space. If you use a standard text box or path, you can type until it's full and then resize it or link it to another box or path.

In addition to entering text in an empty box or path, you can insert text within any other text. All you have to do is click the mouse to position the text insertion point. You can also reposition the text insertion point using the following keyboard commands.

TABLE 8.1 Moving around within text

Move insertion point	Mac OS	Windows
Character		
Previous	Left arrow	Left arrow
Next	Right arrow	Right arrow
Word		
Previous	⌘+left arrow	Ctrl+left arrow
Next	⌘+right arrow	Ctrl+right arrow
Line		
Previous	Up arrow	Up arrow
Next	Down arrow	Down arrow

continues…

TABLE 8.1 Continued

Move insertion point	Mac OS	Windows
Line		
Start	⌘+Option+left arrow	Ctrl+Alt+left arrow or Home
End	⌘+Option+right arrow or End	Ctrl+Alt+right arrow
Paragraph		
Previous	⌘+up arrow	Ctrl+up arrow
Story		
Start	⌘+Option+up arrow	Ctrl+Alt+up arrow or Ctrl+Home
End	⌘+Option+down arrow or Control+End	Ctrl+Alt+down arrow

SEE ALSO

➤ *To create a text box, see page 104*

➤ *To create a text path, see page 375*

➤ *To flow text through a document with automatic text boxes, see page 188*

Selecting Text

Once you have text, you can start moving it around and formatting it. As with all things in QuarkXPress, there are myriad options. First, you have to select some text. One thing to keep in mind is the difference between selected paragraphs, selected characters, and the text insertion point.

- Any time a portion of a paragraph is highlighted or the text insertion point is in a paragraph, that entire paragraph is selected for the purpose of formatting. You can apply paragraph attributes and paragraph *style sheets* to that text.

- Characters are selected only when they are highlighted.

- The text insertion point can absorb character attributes. If you click in text, specify character attributes or a character style sheet, and start typing, the text you type will reflect that formatting.

Drag

The most intuitive method for selecting text, dragging, is also the slowest. Not only is it physically slow, but it depends on your dexterity with the mouse. It can be difficult to see exactly which characters and spaces you are selecting; and that can be important, especially when it comes to applying *character style sheets*.

Dragging is useful for quickly selecting a chunk of paragraphs you want to format the same way. Because you don't have to select the whole paragraph, you can be pretty messy about this (see Figure 8.1).

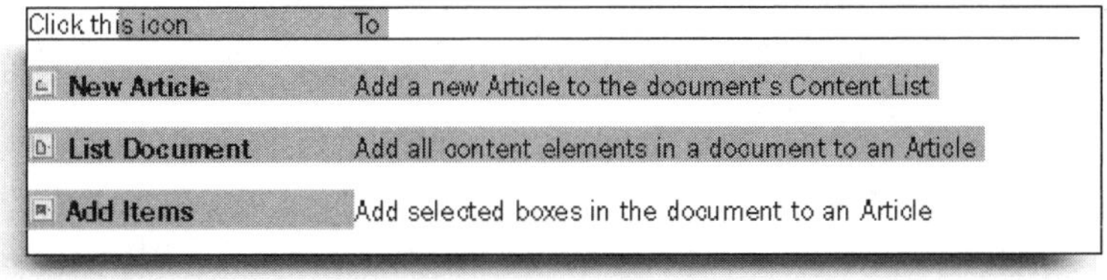

Click this icon	To
New Article	Add a new Article to the document's Content List
List Document	Add all content elements in a document to an Article
Add Items	Add selected boxes in the document to an Article

FIGURE 8.1

When selecting paragraphs, you only need to highlight a portion of each line.

Clicking the Mouse

Most people use multiple mouse clicks: two for a word, three for a line, four for a paragraph, and five for the active story. It's precise and easy. Of course, if you're going to be clicking the mouse five times, you might consider just pressing ⌘+A (Ctrl+A) for Select All. The good thing about using five clicks or Select All is that you can select all the text in a story even if it's on another page or overflowing a box. Table 8.2 provides a quick mouse-click reference.

TABLE 8.2   Selecting text with mouse clicks

To Select A	Click
Word	Twice in word
Word and period, comma, and so on	Twice between word and punctuation
Line	Three times
Paragraph	Four times
Story	Five times

Extending a selection

Once you have a little text selected via clicking the mouse, you can extend the selection by holding the mouse button down and dragging.

There's a catch to the double-click. When you double-click a word to select it, all you get is the word. If you cut the word, it brings its space with it even though it wasn't selected. However, if the word was followed by a period or other punctuation, it leaves that alone. Then, when you paste that word in text, a space is inserted for you. Quark calls this *smart space*.

"Smart" is the last word typesetters will be thinking. If they want to bold a word that is followed by a comma, they want to select the comma with the word. Seems impossible in QuarkXPress 4, but it's not. All you do is double-click between the word and the punctuation rather than in the middle of the word. In Figure 8.2, the only one-step method for selecting the word "Note" and the colon following it is to double-click between the "e" and the colon.

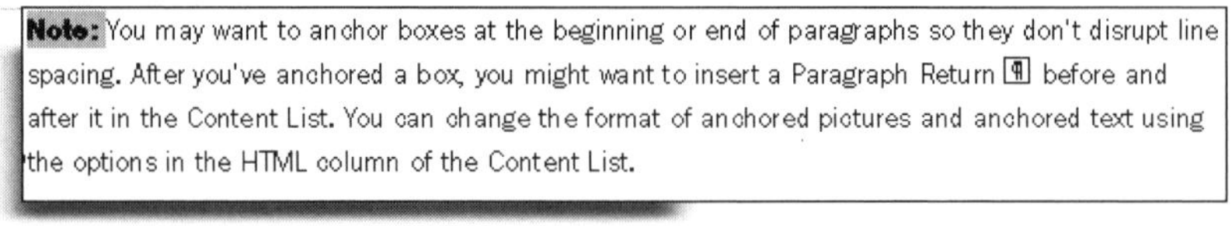

FIGURE 8.2

To select the word "Note" along with the colon after it, you need to double-click between the word and its punctuation.

Note: You may want to anchor boxes at the beginning or end of paragraphs so they don't disrupt line spacing. After you've anchored a box, you might want to insert a Paragraph Return ¶ before and after it in the Content List. You can change the format of anchored pictures and anchored text using the options in the HTML column of the Content List.

Keyboard Commands

More sophisticated users select text with the arrow keys on the extended keyboard. You might want to give these a try, but, for whatever reason, these commands don't get a lot of press (see Table 8.3).

TABLE 8.3   Selecting text with the arrow keys

Selecting Text	Mac OS	Windows
Character		
Previous	Shift+7	Shift+7
Next	Shift+8	Shift+8
Word		
Previous	⌘+Shift+7	Ctrl+Shift+7
Next	⌘+Shift+8	Ctrl+Shift+8

Selecting Text	Mac OS	Windows
Line		
Previous	Shift+9	Shift+9
Next	Shift+0	Shift+0
To start	⌘+Option+Shift+7	Ctrl+Alt+Shift+7 or Shift+Home
To end	⌘+Option+Shift+8	Ctrl+Alt+Shift+8 or Shift+End
Paragraph		
Previous	⌘+Shift+9	Ctrl+Shift+9
Next	⌘+Shift+0	Ctrl+Shift+0
Story		
To start	⌘+Option+Shift+9	Ctrl+Alt+Shift+9 or Control+Shift+Home
To end	⌘+Option+Shift+0	Ctrl+Alt+Shift+0 or Control+Shift+End

Rearranging Text

Moving text from one place to the next in QuarkXPress is no groundbreaking task: It's cut and paste, drag and drop, or plain old delete and retype. The method you prefer is likely to match the method you prefer in your email and word processing applications. The best thing you can say about QuarkXPress in this arena is that it's standard. Everything works exactly the way you expect it to, so you don't need to learn anything new.

Cutting, Copying, and Pasting Text

When you have selected text, you can start moving it around. To cut or copy text, just use the standard Edit menu commands or keyboard commands from Mac OS (⌘+X for cut, ⌘+C for copy) or Windows (Ctrl+X for cut, Ctrl+C for copy). Click the text insertion bar to indicate where you want to insert the text—even in a different text box. To insert the text, use the standard paste commands: ⌘+V (Ctrl+V). If you get interrupted in the middle of a cut and paste, you can make sure your text is still on the Clipboard by choosing **Show Clipboard** from the **Edit** menu.

If you're serious about editing text...

Serious keyboarders can edit text without ever touching the mouse. Using the keyboard commands listed in the previous sections for selecting text and moving the text insertion point, along with the keyboard commands for cut, copy, and paste, editors can work quickly.

Dragging and Dropping Text

Drag-and-drop is the mouser's method for editing text. You select blocks of text, click and hold with the mouse for a second, and then drag the text to a new location. If you're not accustomed to using it, drag-and-drop can be fairly annoying. It's so easy to do that you end up dragging and dropping text all over the place accidentally. Plus, it doesn't really save much time. Fortunately, drag-and-drop is a preference that is turned off by default.

If you are a tried and true drag-and-dropper, here's how to use it. First, turn it on by checking **Drag and Drop Text** in the **Interactive** tab of Application Preferences. Then, select some text and release the mouse button. Click and hold the mouse button, and the selected text becomes sort of an item that you can move around. As you drag the mouse around, you see a little text insertion point floating in a box. Release the mouse button when the insertion point is in the proper location. By default, drag-and-drop cuts and pastes text. To copy and paste text, press the Shift key while you drag the text.

On Mac OS, you can drag and drop text even when the preference is off. To temporarily activate it, press ⌘+Control (to cut) and ⌘+Ctrl+Shift (to paste) while you drag text. Using these keyboard commands is a nice compromise to the tedious prospect of having drag-and-drop on all the time.

SEE ALSO

➤ *To turn* **Drag and Drop Text** *on and off, see page 142*

Deleting Text

Getting rid of text is not too hard. Select the text and press Delete (Backspace) or type over it. If you're sorry you did it, choose **Undo** from the **Edit** menu or ⌘+Z (Ctrl+Z) right away because it's not stored on the Clipboard. You can use keyboard commands to delete text that is not selected (see Table 8.4).

Drag-and-drop limitation

The drag-and-drop implementation in QuarkXPress has a small limitation; it only works within the active story. Say you want to drag a headline from one text box to another—sorry, but you can't.

TABLE 8.4   Deleting text

Delete	Mac OS	Windows
Character		
Previous	Delete	Backspace
Next	Shift+Delete	Delete or Shift+Backspace
Word		
Previous ⌘+Delete	Ctrl+Backspace	
Next	⌘+Shift+Delete	Ctrl+Delete or Ctrl+Shift+Backspace

Searching and Replacing

In QuarkXPress, Find/Change goes way beyond the simple search and replace of a word. You can find any combination of text, character formatting, and style sheets and replace it with entirely new text and formatting. The Find/Change controls are contained in a palette, giving you the flexibility to stop, edit text, and start the search again with little interruption.

Using the Find/Change Palette

If you need to make a global change to a document—whether it's to a word, a type style, style sheet, punctuation, whatever—it's worth using Find/Change. Although the sheer volume of Find/Change controls make the feature intimidating, it's definitely worth learning. For one thing, it saves you time. For another, it's always right. It will absolutely find every instance of the find criteria and it will change it as requested. No matter how good your proofreaders and copy editors are, they might miss subtle changes that Find/Change can't possibly miss.

Find/Change is now a palette, which means it stays open and in front of all open windows all the time. If you need to edit text during a Find/Change, you can hop in and out of the palette without losing sight of it. To start, open the Find/Change palette. You might ceremoniously pull down the **Edit** menu and select **Find/Change** if you're setting up a complex search on a long document. But even then it's wasted effort. Get used to the keyboard commands so you can find text on-the-fly. Press ⌘+F (Ctrl+F) to open the palette and ⌘+Option+F (Ctrl+Alt+F) to close it.

In the lower-right corner, there's a check box called **Ignore Attributes**. Remove the check mark and all attributes break loose. The palette doubles in size and goes icon crazy (see Figure 8.3.) You will grow to love the features in the expansive palette. However, if you just want to replace some text, by all means click again to hide the attribute controls.

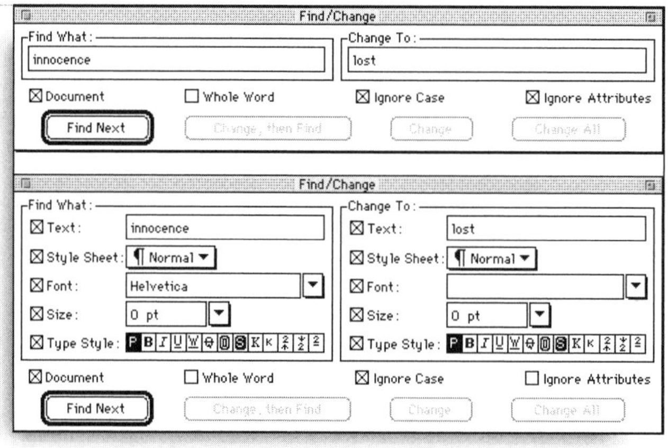

FIGURE 8.3

When **Ignore Attributes** is unchecked, the Find/Change palette expands to provide options for specifying style sheets, fonts, sizes, and type styles.

SEE ALSO

➤ *To create and use style sheets, see page 297*

Finding and Changing Text

The beauty of the expandable/collapsible Find/Change palette becomes apparent when you need to search for a simple word or phrase. You can hide most of the palette and concentrate on the controls you need: the **Text** fields and the **Whole Word** and **Ignore Case** check boxes. The **Text** fields let you enter more than text; you can search for and replace special characters such as tabs and paragraph returns, and you can use wildcard characters to search for variations of text.

Searching for Text

A simple Find/Change operation is usually for editing purposes such as replacing a super-secret code name with a final product name, seeking out politically incorrect terms, and so on. Save first, since **Undo** doesn't work with Find/Change operations.

To find and change text:

1. Enter the search text in the **Find What** field on the left.

2. Enter the replacement text in the **Change To** field on the right.

3. To search a story, click in it to select it and make sure **Document** is not checked. To search an entire document, check **Document**. (When a master page is displayed, the **Document** check box changes to **Masters**.)

4. Decide whether to find only the word or the word embedded inside other words. For example, in a search for "Rob," should QuarkXPress find only instances of "Rob," or also instances of "Robert?" To find only the word (no embedded cases), check **Whole Word** (see Figure 8.4).

FIGURE 8.4

To find all instances of Rob and change them to Robert, you probably want to check **Whole Word**. Otherwise, QuarkXPress will find instances of "Rob" inside other words such as "Robin" and change those to new "words" such as "Robertin."

5. Decide whether capitalization is a consideration. To find only text that is capitalized exactly like the text in the **Find What** field, remove the check mark from **Ignore Case**. For example, in a search for the name "Rob," to avoid finding the verb "rob," remove the check mark from **Ignore Case**.

6. Decide where to start the search. A **Document** search begins on the active page; a story search begins at the

location of the text insertion point. To search only that much of a document, go ahead and click **Find Next**. To search an entire story or document, press the Option (Alt) key to change **Find Next** to **Find First** and click that (see Figure 8.5).

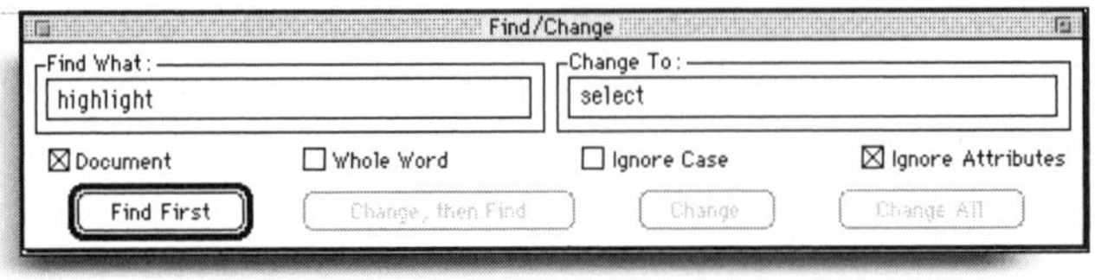

FIGURE 8.5

To ensure that you're checking a document or story from the very beginning, press the Option (Alt) key to change the **Find Next** button to **Find First**.

7. When QuarkXPress finds the first instance of the **Find What** text, it highlights it in the document. There are four choices:

   - Click **Find Next** to skip over the found text and continue the search. If Find Next is grayed out, then **Document** is not checked and no story is selected (or a story is selected with the Item tool). QuarkXPress doesn't know what text to search. Either click in a story with the Content tool or check **Document**.

   - Click **Change and then Find** to change the found text and continue the search.

   - Click **Change** to change the found text, but stay right there to check out the results; then click **Find Next** to get the search going again.

   - Click **Change All** to change all instances of the found text without stopping; a count of the changes is displayed when the replacement operation is finished (for example, "126 instances changed").

If you're going to use **Change All**, it's almost imperative that you click **Change** first and check the results. You don't want to make a global, erroneous change.

When QuarkXPress has found all instances of the **Find What** text, it beeps to indicate that the search is over. If you accidentally skipped over some instances of found text, you can start the search again from the beginning. Otherwise, close the palette or move it out of your way and continue working.

Searching for Special Characters

To prepare text for high-end publishing, you may need Find/Change to strip out extraneous characters. For example, if you import text from a typewriter fanatic who faithfully placed two spaces after each period and colon, you can use Find/Change to strip out the extra spaces. Find/Change is also handy for removing paragraph returns used for space between paragraphs and double tabs used in place of one big tab.

The hardest part about searching and replacing special characters is entering them in the **Find What** and **Change To** fields. You can copy invisible characters in text and paste them in the field. And you can enter many invisible characters using keyboard commands. Essentially, all you do is press ⌘ (Ctrl) while you enter the character. The characters show up in the fields as abbreviations preceded by a backslash (/p for paragraph return, /t for tab, and so on.). Because the backslash is used in this shorthand, you also need to press ⌘ (Ctrl) when you actually want to search for a backslash. See Figure 8.6 for how to search two paragraph returns and replace them with one.

> **How Ignore Case really works**
>
> When **Ignore Case** is not checked, QuarkXPress replaces text according to the capitalization entered in the **Change To** field. When **Ignore Case** is checked, QuarkXPress does its best to replace words but maintain the appropriate capitalization for the context of the text. If a found word has an initial cap, the replaced word will get an initial cap; the same occurs with all lowercase or all caps. However, when **Ignore Case** is checked, QuarkXPress can't mimic the popular intercapping in words such as "QuarkXPress." It can't figure out how to cap the "X" and "P."

FIGURE 8.6

You can search and replace most special characters by entering codes into the **Text** fields. This Find/Change operation finds two paragraph returns in a row and replaces them with one.

Text and special characters are not mutually exclusive. If you need to search for a tab followed by a bullet, you can enter that in the **Find What** field. If you remove the check mark from **Ignore Attributes**, you can search for text, special characters, and attributes. Table 8.5 provides a quick reference to keyboard equivalents for commonly used special characters.

TABLE 8.5   Keyboard equivalents for special characters

Character	Mac OS	Windows
Next box	⌘+Shift+Enter	\b
Next column	⌘+Enter	\c
New line	⌘+Shift+Return	Ctrl+Shift+Enter
Paragraph return	⌘+Return	Ctrl+Enter
Tab	⌘+Tab	Ctrl+Tab
Punctuation space	⌘+. (period)	Ctrl+. (period)
Flex space	⌘+Shift+f	Ctrl+Shift+f
Backslash	⌘+\	Ctrl+\
Previous box page number	⌘+2	Ctrl+2
Current box page number	⌘+3	Ctrl+3
Next box page number	⌘+4	Ctrl+4

Find/Change and the wild card character

You can only find the wild card character. Because it's an unspecified placeholder, you can't use it as replacement text.

Searching for Unknown Terms

In the wild, wild world of Find/Change, you may not be sure what you're trying to find. Maybe you know the writer didn't know the difference between "capitol" and "capital," so you want to look at every case of each. To search two words in one step, you use the wild card character. In the **Find What** field, press ⌘+? (Ctrl+?) to enter the wild card symbol /? in the field. So to search "capitol" and "capital," you'd enter "capit/?l" in **Find What**. QuarkXPress will be happy to find all instances of "capital," "capitol," and even "capitil" or "capitsl" if you haven't spell checked yet. You can combine searches for text, special characters, and the wildcard character with attributes for sophisticated search and replace functions.

Finding and Changing Attributes

After you discover the power of finding and changing attributes, you'll do it all the time. And half the time you might not even be changing text. You might just be changing everything in

Futura with Bold type style to Futura Extra Bold regardless of the words. Or you might change combinations of text and attributes, such as finding all the bullets in your document and applying a certain character style sheet to them. And you still have all the power of Find/Change for text—Whole Word, Ignore Case, special characters, and wildcard characters.

Setting Up Find Criteria

First, make sure Ignore Attributes isn't checked. Then use the Find What side of Find/Change to specify the search criteria. Check the box for each category you want to search, and then specify its criteria. By default, the information in each category reflects the attributes at the location of the text insertion point.

- **Text**—Enter the text you want to find. Remember, you don't have to change the words. You can find specific text and change only its attributes. The Text field accepts an almost unlimited amount of characters.

- **Style Sheet**—Select the paragraph or character style sheet you want to find. The list shows only style sheets used in the document.

- **Font**—Select a font you want to find. The list shows only fonts used in the document.

- **Size**—Enter a size in the field or select one from the list to specify the size text to find.

- **Type Style**—The type style icons have three states: on (reversed) for "find me," off (plain) for "don't find me," and indeterminate (gray) for "find text regardless of me." To toggle between the three states, click the icons.

Setting Up Change Criteria

The controls on the **Change To** side of the expanded Find/Change palette are exactly the same as the controls on the **Find What** side. However, you don't have to use the same categories. You can check **Text** on the **Find What** side to search for a specific word and then check only **Type Style** on the **Change To** side. The **Type Style** icons have the same three states: on (reversed) means "apply me," off (plain) means "remove me," and indeterminate (gray) means "leave me alone."

Gray icons in Find/Change

The tricky **Style** icon state is gray. For example, if the **Italic** icon is gray, Find/Change would search for text that met all the other find criteria whether or not it was italic. If you wanted to find only italic text, click to reverse out the **Italic** icon. If you wanted to find text that is absolutely not italic, click until the icon is plain.

Finding a Combination of Text and Attributes

Once you set up the **Find What** and **Change To** criteria, use the buttons at the bottom of the Find/Change palette to start the search. Keep in mind how the buttons work:

- You can change the **Find Next** button to **Find First** by pressing the Option (Alt) key.
- Click **Find Next** when you want to skip.
- Click **Change and then Find** to keep a search moving.
- Click **Change** to confirm that a Find/Change is doing what you want it to do.
- Click **Change All** only after you confirmed the results by clicking **Change**.

Using Find/Change Efficiently

So exactly what do you do with all this search and replace power? For one thing, you can use it as a replacement for specifying local attributes while you type. The numbered lists in one of the templates you work with is set up like this: tab; number set in bold, Universe 55, purple; tab; Stone Serif. Most users cut-and-paste the whole paragraph and type over the text (this explains why a lot of lists have repeat numbers).

For maximum efficiency, you group the color, font, and type style into a character style sheet. But rather than waste the keystrokes applying the character style sheet as you type, you just enter a tab, the number, and then a tab. Then you use Find/Change to apply the correct formatting. On the **Find What** side, you enter "/t/?/t" to represent a tab, a wildcard character for the numbers, and another tab. You know that all your numbered lists use this pattern and that no other text in the template does, so remove the check mark from **Style Sheet**, **Font**, **Size**, and **Type Style**. On the **Change To** side, remove the check mark from everything except **Style Sheet**. There, pick the character style sheet for the numbers (see Figure 8.7). After a quick check to make sure you set it up right, you **Change All**.

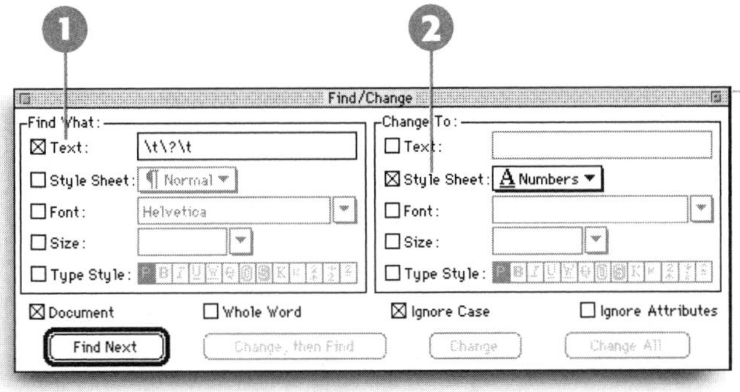

FIGURE 8.7

This Find/Change operation locates a tab, followed by a character (any character signified by the wild card), and another tab. When the text is found, a character style sheet is applied to it.

❶ Search for special text characters

❷ Change the style sheet without replacing the text

Checking Spelling

QuarkXPress may not be the greatest spell checker in the world, but it's definitely worth using. And you can customize it all you want with *auxiliary dictionaries*. To use the **Check Spelling** commands, the XPress Dictionary (xpress.dct) file must be in your QuarkXPress folder when you launch the application.

Unless you're working on a really long file, you might want to get in the habit of spell checking every time you open and edit a document. Nothing makes you look worse—and nothing is more preventable—than a spelling error. (But beware: If you're not familiar with the text and you start making changes prompted by spell check, you might make things worse.)

QuarkXPress enables you to check the selected word, the selected story, or the entire document.

Checking a Word

To check a word, select **Check Spelling** from the **Utilities** menu and then choose **Word** from the submenu, or press ⌘+L (Ctrl+L). This compares the word containing the text insertion bar to the XPress Dictionary and the open auxiliary dictionary. QuarkXPress immediately displays a dialog box with your word listed at the top as "Suspect." It's not because your word is necessarily spelled wrong. It's just offering a list of similar words that you might have been trying to type.

If the suspect word matches a word in the list, it's considered "correct." The match is highlighted in the word list. If you agree that the spelling of the word is correct, click **Done/Close**. If you don't like the spelling of the word, you can select a word from the list or enter text in the field. Click **Replace** to change the word and jump back to the document (see Figure 8.8).

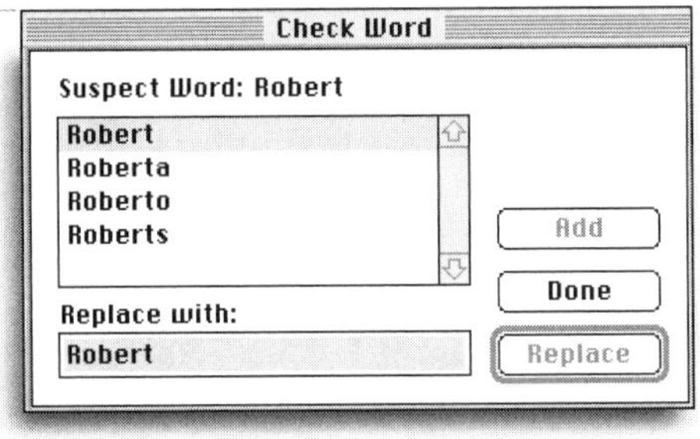

FIGURE 8.8

When you check the spelling of a word, QuarkXPress doesn't give a yes or no answer. If a match is found for the word you're checking, it's highlighted within a list of similar words you might have been going for.

Checking a word is the best way to check spelling on-the-fly. If you spot a word you're not sure about, press ⌘+L (Ctrl+L) and check it. If you're typing and you get stuck on spelling, use the **Check Word** command and solve the mystery. It only takes a second and it doesn't affect the rest of the document.

Checking a Story or Document

QuarkXPress enables you to check an individual story or all the text in a document. The controls work essentially the same for both. The thing to remember with QuarkXPress is that it wants you to spell the same word the same way all the time. There's no concept of "skip this instance" and "skip all." If you make a change to a word spelling, it gets made everywhere. Also, QuarkXPress doesn't restrict repeated spell checks to recently edited text. It checks all the text in the story or document every time. This can be time-consuming, so decide carefully whether you want to check a word, story, or document.

To check a story, click in it to select it. Select **Check Spelling** from the **Utilities** menu, then choose **Story** from the submenu. To check a document, select **Document** from the submenu. (Neither of these commands checks text on master pages. When master pages are displayed, the **Word** and **Story** options are grayed out and **Document** changes to **Masters**.) Whether you're checking a story, document, or master pages, the same things happen.

The first thing QuarkXPress does is give you a word count (see Figure 8.9). This is a good workaround for finding out the length of a story, but it's not that helpful when it comes to spell check—unless the number is incredibly huge so you know you can relax and do nothing but spell check for a while. QuarkXPress also tells you how many different words are in the story (**Unique**) and how many of those might be spelled wrong (**Suspect**).

FIGURE 8.9

After you select **Check Story** or **Check Document**, QuarkXPress skims through the document. The Word Count dialog box displays the results: the total number of words, the number of unique words, and the number of suspect words.

After you look at the word count, click OK. If you don't find the information helpful, get in the habit of starting spell check and pressing Return (Enter) right away to bypass this dialog box.

Replacing Misspelled Words

Now you're in the Check Story, Check Document, or Check Masters dialog box. The dialog box lists the first suspect word it encounters, starting at the beginning of the document or story, as shown in Figure 8.10. QuarkXPress jumps to the page containing the word and highlights it so you can see it in context. Now you must make a decision.

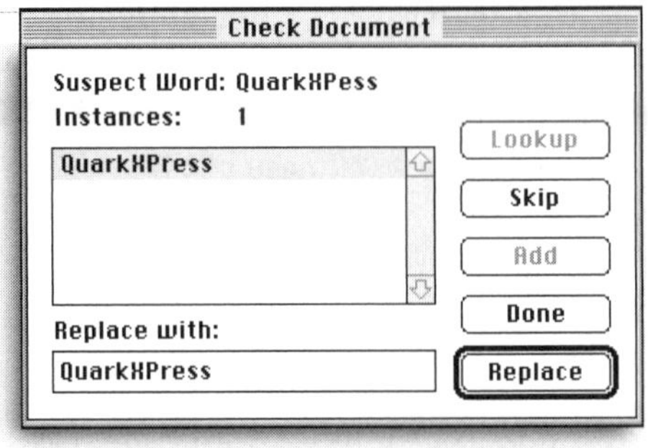

FIGURE **8.10**

Clicking **Lookup** in the Check Story or Check Document dialog box displays a list of alternate spellings for the current Suspect Word.

- If you think the spelling is wrong, but you're not sure what's right, click **Lookup**. QuarkXPress gives you a list of reasonable alternatives. If none of these work, don't guess. Grab a real dictionary and look up the word.

- If you like the word as it's spelled, click **Skip**. The **Instances** area shows how many times the word appears in the document; the spell checker will skip all those instances.

- If you know a word is spelled correctly (such as a last name), and you're tired of hearing about it from Check Spelling, click **Add** to add the word to the open auxiliary dictionary. If **Add** is grayed out, then there's no auxiliary dictionary open—see the next section to create and open one.

- To correct the word, select a word in the list or edit the word in the field and click **Replace**. If you want to use a word in the list as a starting point, click it to enter it in the field, change it, and click **Replace**.

After you deal with all the suspect words, QuarkXPress closes the dialog box for you automatically. If you get tired of spell checking before that, click **Done/Close**. **Done/Close** is not like **Cancel**; the changes you've already made are maintained. You can do an entire spell check without touching the mouse using keyboard commands (see Table 8.6).

Table 8.6   Checking spelling with keyboard commands

Check Spelling	Mac OS	Windows
Check Word	⌘+L	⌘+W
Check Story	⌘+Option+L	⌘+Option+W

Check Spelling	Mac OS	Windows
Check Document	⌘+Option+Shift+L	⌘+Alt+Shift+W
Lookup button	⌘+L	Alt+L
Skip button	⌘+S	Alt+S
Add button	⌘+A	Alt+A
Add all button	Option+Shift+Done	Alt+Shift+Close
Done button	⌘+period	Ctrl+period

Working with Auxiliary Dictionaries

An auxiliary dictionary is a list of words that you compile to use with the XPress Dictionary. Auxiliary dictionaries make your spell check life easier. You can add names and words specific to your business to an auxiliary dictionary, and you can make different auxiliary dictionaries for different documents and clients.

Creating, Opening, and Closing Auxiliary Dictionaries

To create an auxiliary dictionary, select **Auxiliary Dictionary** from the **Utilities** menu. Click **New**. Name and select a location for the dictionary, and then click **Create**. Now you have one, but it's empty. To add words to the dictionary, use the **Edit Auxiliary** command in the **Utilities** menu.

To open an existing dictionary, select **Auxiliary Dictionary** from the **Utilities** menu. Select an auxiliary dictionary file and click **Open**. To close an auxiliary dictionary, select **Auxiliary Dictionary** from the Utilities menu and click **Close**.

Adding Words to an Auxiliary Dictionary

To add words to an auxiliary dictionary, the dictionary must be open. First, select Edit Auxiliary from the Utilities menu. Now you can start entering words. You can pretty much add all the words you want (see Figure 8.10). Don't bother trying to capitalize words though; spell checking is not case-sensitive so the cap will just drop right back down to lowercase.

Make sure whoever is editing your auxiliary dictionaries is detail-oriented. An auxiliary dictionary with mistakes in it is worse than not having one at all.

Linking auxiliary dictionaries to documents

When you create or open an auxiliary dictionary, it becomes associated with the open document. If no documents are open, the new/open auxiliary dictionary becomes associated with all new documents. Documents can use only one auxiliary dictionary at a time.

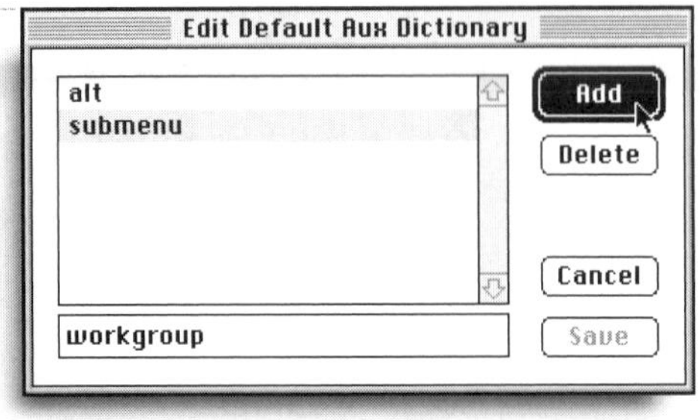

FIGURE **8.11**

You can add industry-specific terms and proper names to an auxiliary dictionary to customize the spell check of your documents.

The Edit Auxiliary dialog box is convenient for adding a few words or looking over the list. But for serious dictionary building, open a document containing a lot of custom words and spell check it. If you're not sure you want to add all the suspect words in the document, click Add when you find one you want to keep. If you are sure, Option+Shift+click (Alt+Shift+click) the **Done/Close** button and you're finished. For example, if you have a corporate style guide, open it or import it into QuarkXPress. Spell check the text and add all its unique words to the auxiliary dictionary. Do the same with a corporate directory; add all the name spellings in an instance.

Editing the Auxiliary Dictionary

In addition to adding words, you can change spellings and remove words through the Edit Auxiliary dialog box. Use the **Auxiliary Dictionary** command in the Utilities menu to open the dictionary you want to edit. Then, select **Edit Auxiliary** from the **Utilities** menu.

To remove or change a word, first you need to select it. You can scroll through the list to find it or enter the first few characters so QuarkXPress will jump to it. To remove a word, select it and click **Delete**. To change a word's spelling, you actually add a new word and delete the original: First, select the word in the list so it's entered in the field. Edit the word and click **Add**. Then delete the original word.

Managing Auxiliary Dictionaries

When you open an auxiliary dictionary for a document, the document knows it needs that dictionary for spell checking and it remembers the location of the auxiliary dictionary file. But auxiliary dictionaries are not saved with documents. If you try to spell check a document that's hooked to an auxiliary dictionary, and you don't have the dictionary, you have several options:

- Rebel. Close the dictionary; then go ahead and spell check. The owner of the document probably won't appreciate it, but it's better than giving up and deciding not to spell check at all. You might even open your own auxiliary dictionary.

- Submit. Contact the document originator and get a copy of the dictionary. A lot of times it's not too hard to find out who owns the dictionary because she named it something such as "Susie's Dictionary."

- Solve the problem once and for all. Require that people in your workgroup store auxiliary dictionaries on a server so they are accessible to all. No matter how many times you move a document, it remembers where its dictionary lives and goes to find it.

Basic Typography

QuarkXPress is known for its typographic power and precision. You have precision down to .001 of even the smallest units of measure. You have control over the space between lines, paragraphs, words, and characters. You have special characters for a quick *hanging indent*, a *nonbreaking space*, a *right-indent tab*, a *discretionary hyphen*, and more. And you have tons of fine-tuning options from automatic *kerning* and *ligatures* to *drop caps* and *tab leaders*.

QuarkXPress gives you the power to accomplish just about any effect you want and then automate the effect with keyboard commands, *style sheets*, or *XPress Tags*. What you don't get with QuarkXPress is a typographer, or even a typesetter. You can do it all in QuarkXPress, but it's open to you, the professional, to know what to do.

Fonts

Without fonts, there is no text, and without text, no typography. So, let's start out with a discussion of fonts.

The word "font" has undergone a metamorphosis since software began to replace metal type. The term used to refer to one style and one size of a particular typeface. Type designers did not create fonts; they created typefaces, which were designs that could be molded into differently sized sets of metal characters called fonts. Nowadays, though, typefaces are scaleable, so "font" has come to mean the software that contains a typeface design. Fonts are not part of, nor do they come packaged with, QuarkXPress. They can be used within QuarkXPress, but they exist as separate files.

Fonts fall into one of three major categories: *PostScript* Type 1, Multiple Master, and TrueType. In case you're wondering, Type 2 fonts do not exist.

PostScript Fonts

By far the most common font type among graphic arts professionals is PostScript Type 1, developed by Adobe Systems. A Type 1 font consists of two pieces: the printer font and the screen font. The first is defined by mathematical curves and is used to print the font; the second is a *bitmap* used to render the font onscreen. Most Type 1 fonts come with more than one screen font, each of which is used to render a specific size. These different sizes normally come in a font suitcase. There is also a font metrics file or AFM file on some font disks. This file is unnecessary and should not be installed.

Adobe Type Manager (ATM) automatically renders all Type 1 fonts smoothly onscreen no matter how they are scaled, and no matter which size is selected. That's because ATM uses the curve data stored in the printer font file to render the font onscreen. (In QuarkXPress' font **Size** menu, the outlined numbers represent installed screen sizes, which render accurately without ATM as long as the document is viewed at actual size.) When printing to a PostScript-compatible printer, Type 1 fonts print smoothly regardless of ATM's presence. When printing to a non-PostScript printer, ATM is needed for smooth output of Type 1 fonts.

We strongly recommend using ATM with Type 1 fonts. Users working with Type 1 fonts on a system without ATM have major difficulty in visualizing the spacing and typographical characteristics of onscreen text.

SEE ALSO

➤ *To print documents, see page 495*

Multiple Master Fonts

Multiple Master fonts, developed by Adobe, are a special kind of Type 1 font. Theoretically, a typeface's design should undergo subtle alterations as the font size changes; otherwise, its aesthetics and readability suffer. Fuddy-duddies of traditional typesetting used to say that old type technology was better than desktop type because the design of nonelectronic typefaces changed according to the size chosen.

Multiple Master fonts solve this problem. Users buy one typeface that has eight "master designs" built in. You can then use the Font Creator *XTension* packaged with QuarkXPress to create different "instances" of the typeface (Mac OS only). The user creates each instance with a specific size, weight, and width in mind. For example, if you want a font designed especially for 72-point sizes, you can create such a font instantly. There's only one catch: Once you're ready to design your document, in addition to selecting 72 in the **Size** field of QuarkXPress' Measurements palette, you also need to go through the added chore of selecting the 72-point instance in the **Font** field.

SEE ALSO

➤   *To install XTensions, see page 557*

TrueType Fonts

TrueType is a scalable font technology developed by Apple, and it is available for both Mac OS and Windows. All the screen rendering and printing data that the font needs is stored in one TrueType font file. Also, TrueType fonts are less expensive than Type 1. However, incompatibilities between fonts and applications are more common with TrueType fonts than with Type 1 fonts. Many graphics professionals use a combination of TrueType fonts and Type 1 fonts, but most will tell you not to stake your life on TrueType.

Choosing Typographic Specifications

Beyond the basic size and name of a typeface you want to use in your document, QuarkXPress lets you set up relationships between your text, your page, and design elements on your page, as shown in Figure 9.1. These relationships can be specified and applied to pages automatically to turn one good-looking page into thousands of good-looking pages in a reasonable amount of time. As soon as you determine what you want the text on your page "to do," you can specify settings in QuarkXPress to get the same results over and over again with speed and consistency. All it takes is a well-defined set of typographic specifications and good knowledge of all the typographic features of QuarkXPress.

Five Denver Brides Share Their Worst Wedding Horror Stories

Are you thinking your wedding is going to go over without a hitch? Think again. A few snags are likely to spring up somewhere along the line. So be realistic in your expectations. Take a deep breath. Keep your eyes open. Cross your fingers. And if anything does veer off track, just remember that – someday – even the worst of disasters will likely turn into chuckles.

WENDIE OF WESTMINSTER (left) is our honorary poster child of bad bridal karma. Wendie's traumas began with her bridesmaids' dresses, which she ordered from a popular Denver bridal salon. When the supposedly higher-end dresses arrived, the seams were crooked, the hems were uneven, and one sleeve was tighter than the other. Each dress had to be ripped apart and remade, and each bridesmaid was reimbursed with a paltry $10.

Although Wendie and her bridesmaids ended up looking fine walking down the aisle, Wendie's fiancé had no such luck. He made the mistake of not trying on his tuxedo before leaving the shop and therefore had to squeeze himself into a pair of too-snug pants. "They were so tight he looked like he was wearing tights," Wendie says.

But at least the groom made it to the altar, which is more than Wendie can say for her flower girl. The three-year-old, probably too young to cooperate, stood in one spot and screamed. "I almost picked her up and carried her," says Wendie. The flower girl was relieved of duty.

After the ceremony as the bridal party waited for their limo, several people decided to have a smoke – right behind Wendie. Some of their ashes fell onto her veil and burned holes right through it. When Wendie's new mother-

$300 for alterations, at the final fitting the dress was way too tight. The salespeople accused her of gaining weight and wouldn't back down until Connie insisted they retake her measurements to prove she hadn't gained weight. She hadn't, and finally got the dress the day before the wedding.

Despite the fact that only half the expected guests showed because the other half "made other plans" for the Labor Day weekend, the wedding went smoothly until Connie discovered she had hired the DJ from hell. That he wasn't ready on time because he was out smoking was just the beginning of the fiasco. He later swiped a cherished bottle of champagne Connie's father had bought for her the day she was born, drank it, and left the empty bottle in the parking lot. The DJ also stole the groom's wallet and charged $700 on his credit card, for which he was arrested. As a result, the groom had no photo identification to use on their honeymoon. Unfortunately, the DJ's employer still refuses to even reimburse the couple for the cost of the DJ.

LIGAYA OF LAKEWOOD fumes at the thought of videotapes featuring an alternate perspective to the one she had in mind when she hired a videographer to capture her wedding on film. "She was short so she only got the top of people's heads," Ligaya says in amazement. She couldn't believe the blurry images of the top of her brother-in-law's head as his voice rang out from behind the piano while he sang. "My sister's friend's video is better than that!" Ligaya had no way to send a letter of complaint as the videographer had printed only her phone number on her business card and in the phone book. "I had to get a friend to pretend she was interested to sneak the address to send a letter of complaint," she says. Then Ligaya cancelled the check.

FIGURE 9.1

Complementary typographic specifications create well-balanced, interesting pages. In this example, the Spilt Milk typeface in the headline communicates the humor and distress of the article topic while still blending in with the otherwise conservative page.

Relating Type and the Page

The most important relationship your words have with their page is the layout or *grid* of the page, which consists of the margins at the edges of the page, the number of columns on the page, the division of the page into different sections for specific information, miscellaneous indicia such as page numbers, page *headers*, page *footers*, mastheads, icons or logos, bar codes, whatever (see Figures 9.2). Establishing effective type sizes and spacing can be simplified when you have detailed specifications for your grid. Consider the following issues while deciding on your typographic specifications.

How Type Interacts with Your Grid

QuarkXPress offers many features to control the way your text interacts with your page, including the linking tools that control the "flow" of your text from one position on your page to another place on your page (or to another page), the **Lock to Baseline Grid** paragraph attribute that "snaps" lines of text to a grid of horizontal lines that you specify on your page, and the capability to split text boxes into multiple columns of type across your page. You can anchor items other than words and characters into the "text flow" of your QuarkXPress text box. Anchored items can include horizontal lines (called *paragraph rules* in QuarkXPress) that sit above, below, or in the middle of your words and change in length and position as your text changes in length and position; boxes that flow with your text and can contain pictures or text; drop caps (large letters used at the beginning of a paragraph of type) that automatically appear at the beginning of paragraphs and flow with the rest of your text; and empty space.

FIGURE 9.2

The template for this magazine has a strict three-column grid. The headline always spans three columns and the introductory picture always spans the first two.

In QuarkXPress, horizontally oriented space that flows with your text takes the form of tab stops and left and right indents from the edges of a text box. Vertically oriented blank, empty spaces that flow with text include the blank space between lines of text called *leading*, and space between paragraphs.

SEE ALSO

➤ *To link text boxes, see page 191*

➤ *To create multiple columns in a text box, see page 196*

➤ *To anchor boxes in text, see page 406*

➤ *To create a drop cap, see page 258*

Position of Words Related to Lines, Shapes, Pictures, and Spaces

If your page specifications call for certain rules, shapes, pictures, or spaces to remain statically placed on your page but still have a relationship to the placement of your type, QuarkXPress lets you specify that text will flow around the object, or partially through the object, or completely over the object. QuarkXPress calls this relationship a *runaround*. The creative possibilities for specifying relationships between pictures, lines, and box objects and the edges of your type wait for you in the **Runaround** tab of the Modify dialog box (**Item** menu) in QuarkXPress. Go ahead, give 'em the runaround.

SEE ALSO

➤ *To force text to run around a box, see page 384*

Organization of Text

You can often determine how many different typographic specifications will be necessary for the text on your page by examining the different uses of text on your page. Text that contains a complex structure of titles, subtitles, articles, subarticles, points, notes, quotations, excerpts, tables, lists, equations, and miscellany can demand a long list of typographic specifications. However, some text can function well with a small set of typographic specifications for all the text on the page. Specifying the hierarchy and function of different groups of text on your page can direct and focus your work of choosing typographic specifications.

Designing Type for the Grid

There are many, many typefaces. Besides magic eight balls, dartboards, and dice, how do you choose a typeface that works for your page and your text? As mentioned previously, start with a specified grid of columns and areas on your page that will be filled with type. From the grid, determine what the type in each area needs to do. Does a certain area of type on your page need to stand out? In addition to choosing a distinctive, eye-catching typeface, you can use the Space Before and Space After features in QuarkXPress to surround this text with white space, or the Paragraph Rules feature to surround this text with lines or bars.

In addition to choosing a typeface that lends itself to comfortable reading, in QuarkXPress, you can change the size of the typeface with great precision to fit more or fewer words on each line of the big block of type. You can adjust the leading to fit more or fewer lines of type in a given area on the page or to lead the reader's eye comfortably from one line of type to the next line of type. For legibility, you can adjust the amount of blank space between each character and each word, and the amount of blank space left at the end of each line of type using the Hyphenation and Justification (H&J) settings. As soon as you have areas on your page to fill with type, you can concentrate on the specifics of the type.

SEE ALSO

➤ *To specify hyphenation and justification (H&J) settings, see page 270*

Letterforms

When choosing typefaces for a specific QuarkXPress grid, the first and most obvious consideration is the shape of the characters, or the *letterform*. The shape of the letterforms that you choose for your page can enhance the desired effect of your page and make it useful and valuable to your reader. Do you have a large number of words per page that you want to be presented as simple and straightforward? Maybe choose a traditional, Roman, *serifed* letterform. Do you have a few words for each page you want to imply an idea or quality that the words don't express by themselves? Maybe use a decorative letterform that conforms to your intended genre. Typefaces are collections of letterforms or characters that have common characteristics, including strokes, distances, and empty spaces.

Word Spacing

When the distance between words is too great, you can get "rivers" of white space that run vertically through paragraphs of type. Rivers are generally inconsistent with your intended typographic "weave" and distracting to the reader. In QuarkXPress, you can both decrease the space between words and increase the space between characters (using the H&J control features) to visually compensate for the rivers that giant word spaces leave in your type. Individual troublesome lines and paragraphs of type can be adjusted using the tracking controls. If the space around certain letterforms in a font doesn't work for your page, you can adjust spacing between pairs of letterforms using the Kern/Track Editor XTension with QuarkXPress.

SEE ALSO

➤ *To create custom kerning and tracking tables, see page 280*

Characters and Character Spacing

The strokes and shapes that compose letterforms usually have consistent qualities within a typeface. The character of the strokes in a typeface can lend a certain feel to the words on your page; some strokes look spontaneous and urgent, some strokes look precise and methodical. Some are light, some are heavy; some combine to make discrete and legible letterforms, some combine to make a mess; some lead the eye at a steady pace to the next word in a line of type, some stop and stagger the eye across each line. Subtle differences in the character of the strokes in different typefaces can have dramatic influences on your page and can demand different spacing specifications within QuarkXPress.

Know the demand for different types of letterforms before you choose typefaces for your page. Some typefaces don't contain ligatures (see Figure 9.3); some use *old-style numerals*; some, while having terrific upper- and lowercase letterforms, have punctuation marks from Mars; some are great for typesetting short equations and tables, but are hard to read for long lines of type. If you know what characters you need, you can find a single typeface that will accommodate all the typographic demands of your text.

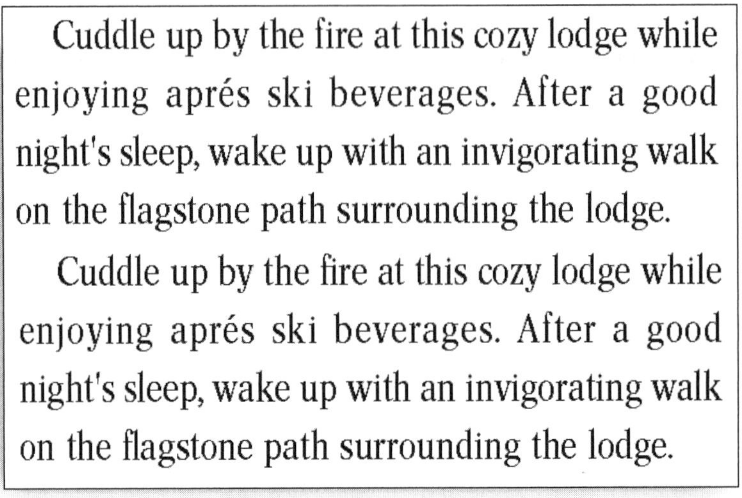

FIGURE 9.3

In the first paragraph of this text, ligatures are not used. Notice the word "fire" in the first line and "flagstone" in the fourth line. In the second paragraph, ligatures are in use; notice the difference in the same words.

Cuddle up by the fire at this cozy lodge while enjoying aprés ski beverages. After a good night's sleep, wake up with an invigorating walk on the flagstone path surrounding the lodge.

Cuddle up by the fire at this cozy lodge while enjoying aprés ski beverages. After a good night's sleep, wake up with an invigorating walk on the flagstone path surrounding the lodge.

QuarkXPress has many features that automatically make use of specific letterforms in a typeface and adjust the letterforms for specific typographic situations on specific pages. The ligatures feature (Mac OS only) automatically replaces combinations of the f letterform and the i letterform with the fi ligature and replaces combinations of the f letterform and the l letterform with the fl ligature. With certain typefaces, the dot in the i and the top of the l letterforms bump into the top of the f letterform and make a mess of your typographic pattern—using ligatures avoids dark spots in your type. Some typefaces have all sorts of custom ligatures, including "st" and "ct" ligatures.

Although QuarkXPress automatically accommodates the common "fi" and "fl" ligatures without screwing up your spell checker, the land-of-a-thousand-ligatures (available with many expert fonts) is full of many mysterious keyboard combinations and many suspect words flagged in your spell checker. The Smart Quotes feature in QuarkXPress automatically replaces straight foot and inch letterforms with curly apostrophe and quotation mark letterforms. The Flex Space feature lets you create a custom-width space that you can insert in lieu of a standard space.

SEE ALSO

➤ *To use flex spaces, see page 64*

➤ *To spell check text, see page 219*

➤ *To turn on ligatures in the preferences, see page 96*

Interlinear Spacing and Column Width

The space between lines in paragraphs and the width of columns you set type in must complement the typeface and character spacing. In fact, the space between lines is often the strongest predictor of legibility, and the space between lines is heavily influenced by the column width.

You can call the amount of space between lines any number of things—the most descriptive yet bulky term being *interlinear spacing*. Most people, and desktop publishing applications, hark back to the days of lead presses and use the term "leading." Leading is measured in points from the baseline of one line of text to the baseline of the next line. Since leading is not merely a measurement of the little bit of white space between two lines of text, but of the entire space including that filled by text, leading is usually expressed in relation to the point size of the type. For example, you'll often hear that text is set 10 on 12 (abbreviated as 10/12), which means the type is 10 points and the leading is 12 points.

Typesetters often use 20% of the current point size as a starting point—for example, 10-point type often uses 12 points of leading. For smaller text, sometimes you can just add 2 points to the current point size, so you might have 9-point type with 11 points of leading. When you're setting leading, consider the type of information. Is it eye-catching display type, intro fluff, or hard-hitting news copy? While striving for legibility, choose leading that reflects the content.

Column width is part layout determination and part typesetting determination. The key to a comfortable line length is making sure the readers can find the next line reliably. Do they have to literally turn their head to finish reading one line? Can the readers feel their eyes moving horizontally across a line? If so, those lines are probably too long. However, very narrow columns make the readers work for their comprehension—the readers' eyes are in constant motion jumping back and forth and up and down between lines.

Baseline Grid for Interlinear Spacing

A *baseline grid* is a set of non-printing horizontal lines that runs across your QuarkXPress page. You can specify an offset from the top of the page for the placement of the first line of the baseline grid and a uniform distance between each subsequent line of the grid. QuarkXPress starts with the first line based on your offset and draws gridlines all the way down your page based on the separating distance that you specify.

When **Lock to Baseline Grid** is checked in the **Formats** tab of Paragraph Attributes, QuarkXPress repositions each line of type in the paragraph so the baseline of each line sits on one of the lines of the baseline grid. QuarkXPress looks at the leading distance you specified for the paragraph and bumps it up to the next multiple of grid spaces. For example, if you specify the increment for the lines in your baseline grid to be, say, 5 points, and the original leading of your paragraph before was, say, 12 points, when you check **Lock to Baseline Grid**, QuarkXPress increases the distance between lines to the next multiple of grid spaces (which in this case is 15 points, or 3 grid spaces). However, QuarkXPress still shows the original leading distance after you check **Lock to Baseline Grid**.

It's not until you bump the leading to be greater than 15 points that QuarkXPress increases the space between lines to the next multiple of gridlines, which with a 5-point baseline grid increment would be 20 points. If you use a baseline grid, it helps to think of your leading (or space between lines) as multiples of the grid spaces. If you use a 12-point grid increment, the space between your lines of type can only be 12, 24, 36, 48, 60, 72, or another multiple of 12.

SEE ALSO

➤ *To specify baseline grid settings in the preferences, see page 81*

Implementing Typographic Specifications

QuarkXPress has four interacting ways to specify formatting for text: Document Preferences, text box attributes, paragraph attributes, and character attributes. Document Preferences control global typographic options such as the size of a flex space and the meaning of auto leading. Text box attributes cover how many columns are in a box and how the text is positioned in the box. It's when you get to paragraph attributes and character attributes that you actually apply styles to text. Paragraph attributes, such as alignment and leading, affect all the lines in a paragraph. Hyphenation and justification settings, which can have a dramatic impact on type, are implemented as paragraph attributes. Character attributes, such as size, type style, or scaling, affect selected characters.

Checking Typographic Preferences

Before you start formatting text or creating style sheets, look over all the typography-related options in Document Preferences. Character Preferences include options for customizing the superscript, subscript, small caps, and superior type styles; **Auto Kern Above**; **Flex Space Width**; **Standard Em Space**; **Accents for All Caps**; and **Ligatures** (Mac OS only). Paragraph Preferences provide **Leading**, **Baseline Grid**, and **Hyphenation** controls. Changing Character or Paragraph preferences later can severely reflow a document, especially if you decide to change things such as the **Hyphenation Method** or **Standard Em Space** settings.

SEE ALSO

➤ *To set Character and Paragraph preferences, see page 48*

Reviewing Text Box Attributes

A few typographic effects can occur at the text box level. These controls are in the **Text** tab of the Modify dialog box (choose **Modify** from the **Item** menu). Part of the options control how the text is positioned in the box, including **Columns, Gutter Width, Text Inset, First Baseline**, and **Vertical Alignment**. The remaining controls actually work on the text in the box—**Text Angle, Text Skew, Flip Horizontal, Flip Vertical**, and **Run Text Around All Sides** (see Figure 9.4).

SEE ALSO

➤ *To create a text box, see page 105*

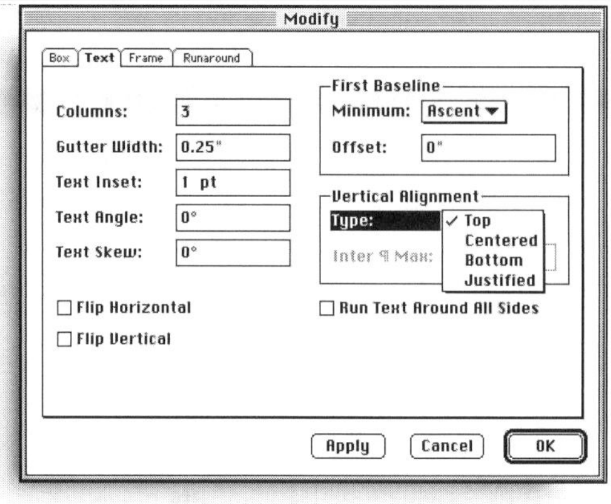

FIGURE 9.4

The **Text** tab of the **Modify** dialog box controls text box attributes.

Setting Character Attributes

Character attributes are easy to set; just use the **Style** menu, the Measurement palette, or keyboard commands. Using the Content tool [image], select the text you want to style or click to place the *text insertion bar* where you want to insert text. When you start typing, the new attributes are applied.

The top portion of the **Style** menu provides submenus and commands for applying character attributes. This is the definitive list—every way you can manipulate a character in QuarkXPress. The Character Attributes dialog box, which displays when you choose **Character** from the **Style** menu, summarizes all these attributes (with the exception of **Text to Box**). See Figures 9.5 and 9.6.

The right side of the Measurements palette provides menus and buttons for applying fonts, type sizes, and type styles. In the middle of the Measurements palette, two horizontal arrows allow you to change kerning/*tracking* (see Figure 9.7). The [A] at the top of the Colors palette allows you to apply a color to selected text.

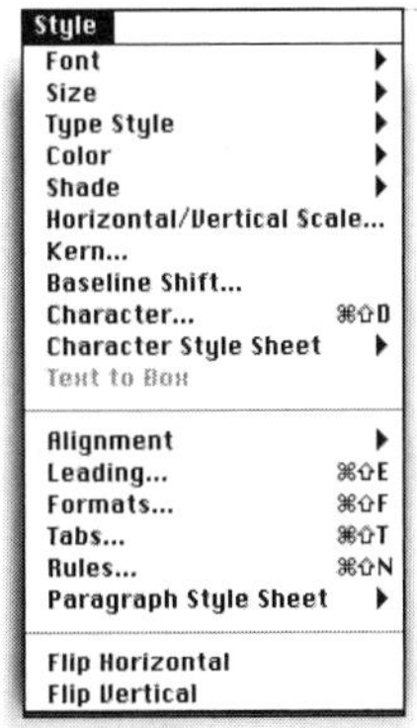

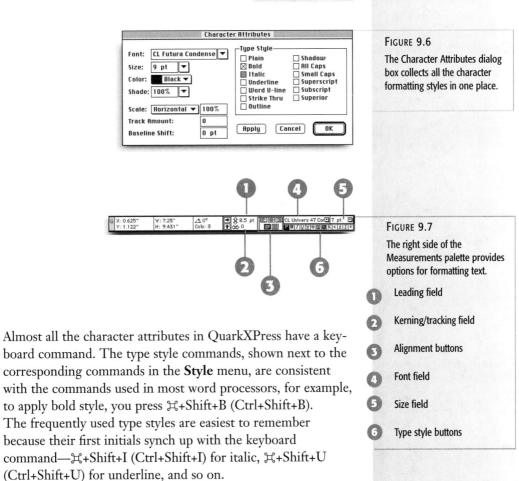

FIGURE 9.5

All character formatting styles are available via the **Style** menu.

FIGURE 9.6

The Character Attributes dialog box collects all the character formatting styles in one place.

FIGURE 9.7

The right side of the Measurements palette provides options for formatting text.

1 Leading field

2 Kerning/tracking field

3 Alignment buttons

4 Font field

5 Size field

6 Type style buttons

Almost all the character attributes in QuarkXPress have a keyboard command. The type style commands, shown next to the corresponding commands in the **Style** menu, are consistent with the commands used in most word processors, for example, to apply bold style, you press ⌘+Shift+B (Ctrl+Shift+B). The frequently used type styles are easiest to remember because their first initials synch up with the keyboard command—⌘+Shift+I (Ctrl+Shift+I) for italic, ⌘+Shift+U (Ctrl+Shift+U) for underline, and so on.

Style options may change

The **Style** menu, the Measurements palette, and the Colors palette are context-sensitive, meaning that they offer different options depending on the selected tool and item. You must have the Content tool selected and a text box or text path selected to access text formatting options.

Using the submenus and commands in the **Style** menu is generally the most inefficient method for formatting text. The Character Attributes dialog box is a good choice for setting up overall specifications such as font, size, color, and so on. You might do a few touch-ups with the Measurements palette, changing the tracking here and there, for example, or formatting a headline differently. The Colors palette works far better than the **Color** submenu of the **Style** menu for experimenting with different colors. When you format text as you type it, keyboard commands work great.

SEE ALSO

➤ To define colors, see page 426

➤ To apply colors to text, see page 432

Font

The **Font** submenu of the **Style** menu shows you all the fonts currently available to QuarkXPress. Depending on the font management software you use, you may need to relaunch QuarkXPress when you add new fonts or change the active fonts.

From the **Style** menu, you have to drag down and choose a font from the submenu, but in the Measurements palette or Character Attributes dialog boxes, you can type the first few letters of the font name in the **Font** field until it's recognized. Keyboard commands for changing fonts are shown in Table 9.1.

TABLE 9.1   Keyboard shortcuts for changing fonts

To do this...	...press this
Jump to the **Font** field	⌘+Option+Shift+M (Ctrl+Alt+Shift+M).
Choose the next font	Option+F9 (Ctrl+F9).
Choose the previous font	Option+Shift+F9 (Ctrl+Shift+F9).
Enter one character in Symbol	⌘+Shift+Q (Ctrl+Shift+Q).
Enter one character in Zapf Dingbats	⌘+Shift+Z (Ctrl+Shift+Z).

Size

The **Size** submenu of the **Style** menu shows the most commonly used *point sizes*; this same list shows in the Character Attributes and Measurements palette **Size** menus. The **Other** option allows you to enter a value from 2–720 points in increments as fine as .001.

Keyboard commands let you bump the size up and down one point or according to a preset range: 7, 9, 10, 12, 14, 18, 24, 36, 48, 60, 72, 96, 120, 144, 168, and 192 points. You can also use keyboard commands to resize text as you resize its text box (see Table 9.2).

TABLE 9.2   Keyboard shortcuts for resizing text

To do this...	...press this
Highlight the Size field in the Character Attributes dialog box	⌘+Shift+\ (Ctrl+Shift+\)
Jump to the Size field in the Measurements palette	⌘+Option+Shift+M, then Tab (Ctrl+Alt+Shift+M, then Tab)
Increase the size one point	⌘+Option+Shift+> (Ctrl+Alt+Shift+>)
Increase the size within the preset range	⌘+Shift+> (Ctrl+Shift+>)
Decrease the size one point	⌘+Option+Shift+< (Ctrl+Alt+Shift+<)
Decrease the size within the preset range	⌘+Shift+< (Ctrl+Shift+<)
Change the point size, auto leading, and scaling	⌘ (Ctrl) while resizing a text box
Change the point size, auto leading, and scaling proportionally	⌘+Option+Shift (Ctrl+Alt+Shift) while resizing a text box

Resizing drop caps

When you highlight an automatic drop cap, the size is reported as 100%; you can resize the drop cap from 10–400% in .1% increments.

Type Style

QuarkXPress has three different ways of showing type style options: the **Type Style** submenu of the **Style** menu spells them out, the Character Attributes dialog box provides a check box for each option in the **Type Style** area, and the Measurements palette provides a string of icons.

When possible, QuarkXPress likes to let you know which type styles are "on." When you highlight a range of bold text, for example, the **Type Style** submenu has a check mark next to bold, the **Bold** icon on the Measurements palette is highlighted, and the **Bold** check box in Character Attributes is checked. However, when mixed type styles are applied to highlighted text, QuarkXPress can't tell you precisely what is applied. For example, if all the highlighted text is bold, and a few words are italic, the **Type Style** submenu has a check mark next to **Bold** but nothing next to **Italic**. The **Bold** icon on the Measurements palette is highlighted, but the **Italic** icon is gray. Similarly, in Character Attributes, **Bold** is checked, but **Italic** is gray.

You can apply almost as many type styles as you want to the same text—not that you probably should. Combining too many type styles can confuse your message. It doesn't make sense to combine some type styles, so QuarkXPress has made those mutually exclusive. That's why turning **Underline** on turns **Word Underline** off; the same thing happens with **All Caps** and **Small Caps** and **Superscript** and **Subscript**.

Because applying styles through the **Type Style** submenu is fairly tedious, the following definitions include Measurements palette icons and keyboard commands.

Plain

Plain removes all other type styles. Click $\boxed{\text{P}}$ on the Measurements palette or press ⌘+Shift+P (Ctrl+Shift+P).

Bold

Bold changes the text to the bold font in the font family; if it's not available, QuarkXPress simulates bold. Click $\boxed{\textbf{B}}$ on the Measurements palette or press ⌘+Shift+B (Ctrl+Shift+B).

Italic

Italic changes the text to the italic (or oblique) font in the font family; if it's not available, QuarkXPress simulates italics. Click $\boxed{\textit{I}}$ on the Measurements palette or press ⌘+Shift+I (Ctrl+Shift+I).

Underline

Underline underscores characters and spaces, but not tabs. Click ⊔ on the Measurements palette or press ⌘+Shift+U (Ctrl+Shift+U).

Word Underline underscores characters, but not tabs or spaces (including en space, half-en space, and punctuation space). Click ⊎ on the Measurements palette or press ⌘+Shift+W (Ctrl+Shift+W).

Strike Thru

Strike Thru places a one-point line through characters, but not through tabs. To position the strike-thru line, QuarkXPress first looks in the font to see if the font designer specified a position. If so, that position is used. If not, QuarkXPress finds the largest character on the line and positions the strike-thru line one third of the way up its ascent height. Click ⊟ on the Measurements palette or press ⌘+Shift+/ (Ctrl+Shift+/).

Outline

Outline draws a line around the inner and outer contours of characters, converting the center of the character to white. Click ⊚ on the Measurements palette or press ⌘+Shift+O (Ctrl+Shift+O).

Shadow

Shadow creates drop shadows the same size as the type, offsets them slightly, and places them behind the characters. Click ⊠ on the Measurements palette or press ⌘+Shift+S (Ctrl+Shift+S).

All Caps

All Caps displays lowercase letters as the uppercase letters in the font. Applying **All Caps** should not be confused with typing with the Caps Lock key down. When you remove the all caps type style, you have upper/lowercase text again. But when you type with Caps Lock on, there's no built-in way to convert the text to upper/lowercase. Click ⊠ on the Measurements palette or press ⌘+Shift+K (Ctrl+Shift+K).

Small Caps

Small Caps displays lowercase letters as reduced-size uppercase letters. You specify the size reduction in the **Character** tab of Document Preferences; the default is 75%. QuarkXPress always creates its own *small caps*, even if a small caps version of the font is available. If you have a small caps font, you need to apply it via the **Font** controls. Click ⬚ on the Measurements palette or press ⌘+Shift+H (Ctrl+Shift+H).

Superscript

Superscript raises characters above the baseline and scales them down according to your specifications. You specify the placement and scale in the **Character** tab of Document Preferences; the default offset is 33% and the default horizontal and vertical scale is 100%. Click ⬚ on the Measurements palette or press ⌘+Shift++ (Ctrl+Shift++).

Subscript

Subscript drops characters below the baseline and scales them down according to your specifications. You specify the placement and scale in the **Character** tab of Document Preferences; the default offset is 33% and the default horizontal and vertical scale is 100%. Click ⬚ on the Measurements palette or press ⌘+Shift+hyphen (Ctrl+Shift+hyphen).

Superior

Superior raises characters to the cap height of the font and scales them down. You specify the scale in the **Character** tab of Document Preferences; the default horizontal and vertical scale is 50%. Click ⬚ on the Measurements palette or press ⌘+Shift+V (Ctrl+Shift+V).

Color

The **Color** submenu of the **Style** menu, the **Color** menu in Character Attributes, and the Colors palette all show you the full list of colors created for the document.

Applying a color to text can be irritating; there are no keyboard commands and you can't type in the Character Attributes **Color** field to specify a color. No doubt, you'll forget to click ⟦A⟧ on the Colors palette and end up coloring a box background a few times (or every time). Once you click ⟦A⟧, it's pretty easy to experiment with text colors. But if you know the color you want, it may be just as easy to leave the Colors palette alone and stick with the **Color** submenu of the **Style** menu.

SEE ALSO
➤ *To define colors, see page 426*
➤ *To apply colors to text, see page 432*

Shade

The **Shade** submenu of the **Style** menu, the **Shade** field in Character Attributes, and the **Shade** menu/field on the Colors palette all show you a list of color saturation values in 10% increments. The **Other** option in the Shade submenu jumps you right into the **Shade** field of Character Attributes. You can enter a custom saturation value in .1% increments in this field, or in the field on the Colors palette.

Horizontal/Vertical Scale

Horizontal scaling makes characters shorter and fatter, while **Vertical** scaling makes them thinner and taller. Scaling allows you to modify a font slightly or completely distort a font for effect.

The **Scale** field in Character Attributes is preceded by a menu that lets you choose **Horizontal** or **Vertical**. Once you choose a direction to scale, enter a value between 25 and 400% in the field. To experiment with scaling, use keyboard commands:

- Increase the horizontal scale of characters 5% by pressing ⌘+] (Ctrl+]). To increase horizontal scale 1%, add the Option (Alt) key.

- Decrease the horizontal scale of characters 5% by pressing ⌘+[(Ctrl+[). To decrease horizontal scale 1% add the Option (Alt) key.

- You can experiment with the scale and size of text at once by pressing the ⌘ (Ctrl) key while dragging a text box handle. This technique, called interactive text resizing, works on all the text in a box. Therefore, it's best for display copy (see Figure 9.8).

FIGURE 9.8

The titles in this publication masthead are usually in 6-point Universe Bold. As you can see, even small amounts of scaling–90–110% horizontally or vertically–have a significant impact on the integrity of the font.

Editor & Publisher: Normal
Daniel Brogan

Art Director: 90% Horizontal
Kimberlee Lynch

Assistant Editor: 110% Horizontal
Amanda M. Faison

Copy Editor: 90% Vertical
Kelly Kordes Anton

Circulation Manager: 110% Vertical
Eve Leinweber Brogan

Kerning and Tracking

Kerning adds or removes space between the two characters separated by the text insertion bar. If text is highlighted, QuarkXPress switches you over to the tracking controls. Tracking adds or removes space to the right of highlighted characters. See Figures 9.9 and 9.10. Kerning and tracking are measured the same way and applied using the same fields and keyboard commands.

One kerning or tracking unit is equal to 1/200 of an *em space*. Therefore, if you kern +3 between two characters, you are kerning 3/200 of an em space. The width of the em space used for kerning/tracking depends on whether you have **Standard Em Space** checked in the **Character** tab of Document Preferences. If it's not checked, the em space is equal to the width of two zeros in the font. If it's checked, the em space is equal to the current point size.

FIGURE 9.9

Text in a headline size such as 52 points generally needs tighter tracking. This headline is highlighted and tracked –7.

FIGURE 9.10

Because some characters ended up too close together, the designer had to manually touch up the text. The space between the "e" in "Clue" and the question mark is kerned out +5.

To apply kerning/tracking, you can use the **Kern/Track** field in Character Attributes, which helpfully changes its name depending on whether text is highlighted or not. You can also use the kern/track field and the kerning arrows on the Measurements palette.

- Enter kerning/tracking values in the fields in increments as small as .001.

- Click the arrows on the Measurements palette to change kerning/tracking in increments of 10. Press the Option (Alt) key while clicking to change kerning/tracking in increments of 1.

- Increase kerning/tracking in increments of 10 by pressing ⌘+Shift+} (Ctrl+Shift+}). Add the Option (Alt) key to change the increment to 1.

- Change the direction of the bracket from out } to in { to decrease kerning/tracking: ⌘+Shift+{ (Ctrl+Shift+{) decreases kerning/tracking by 10; throw in the Option (Alt) key to decrease by 1.

Any kerning you apply this way is added to automatic kerning (if you have **Auto Kern Above** checked in the **Character** tab of Document Preferences) and to any kerning specified for the font through the Kern/Track Editor. Any tracking you apply is added to any tracking specified for the font through the Kern/Track Editor.

SEE ALSO

➤ *To set the width of an em space, see page 65*

➤ *To turn on automatic kerning, see page 64*

➤ *To edit kerning tables, see page 283*

➤ *To edit tracking tables, see page 281*

Baseline Shift

Baseline shift allows you to nudge characters up or down slightly. It's useful for individual characters that need to rise above or fall below the baseline, but it should not be used on whole lines or paragraphs as a replacement for effective **Leading**, **Space Before**, and **Space After** values (see Figure 9.11). You may need to use baseline shift to place text within a paragraph rule. Baseline shifting doesn't change character size, nor does it cause uneven line spacing when auto or incremental leading is in use.

FIGURE 9.11

These two lines are almost touching—an effect achieved by baseline shifting the word "Weddings" until it almost touched the descending "g" in "Mile High." Although designers often use this method, changing the leading would be a cleaner way to go.

The range you can baseline shift a character is three times its font size, so you can shift 12-point type up 36 points or down 36 points. You can enter values in increments as fine as .001 in the **Baseline Shift** field of Character Attributes, or you can experiment using keyboard commands.

- Shift text up one point by pressing ⌘+Option+Shift++ (Ctrl+Alt+Shift++).

- Shift text down one point by pressing ⌘+Option+Shift+hyphen (Ctrl+Alt+Shift+hyphen).

SEE ALSO

➤ *To create paragraph rules, see page 411*

Setting Paragraph Attributes

The one thing to remember about paragraph attributes is that they affect the entire paragraph. You cannot, for example, have different tab stops or different leading specified for lines in the same paragraph. All the formatting you can apply to a paragraph is consolidated in the Paragraph Attributes dialog box, which you open by choosing **Formats** from the **Style** menu (see Figure 9.12).

The one-stop shopping offered by Paragraph Attributes is the best method for setting up paragraphs, so get used to pressing ⌘+Shift+F (Ctrl+Shift+F) to open it. The old keyboard commands you remember for opening the Tabs dialog box, ⌘+Shift+T (Ctrl+Shift+T), and the Rules dialog box, ⌘+Shift+N (Ctrl+Shift+N), now open Paragraph Attributes with the **Tabs** or **Rules** tab displayed. You'll probably save most of your paragraph attributes in paragraph style sheets, but you may find yourself jumping into this dialog box often to touch up tabs, spacing, and so on. You can access a few of these paragraph attributes through the **Style** menu, the Measurements palette, and keyboard commands as well.

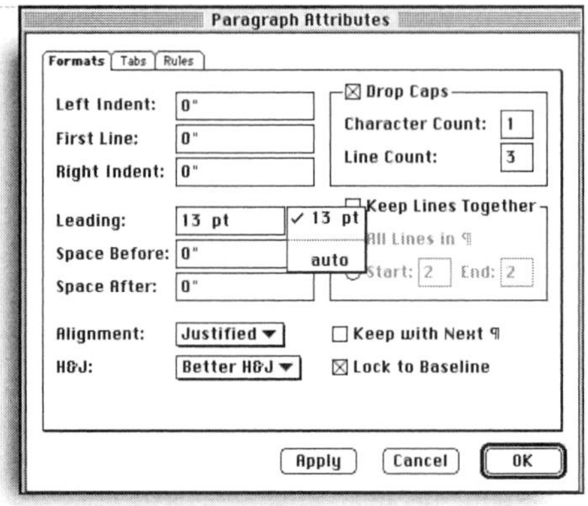

FIGURE 9.12
The Paragraph Attributes dialog box consolidates all the paragraph formatting possibilities.

Alignment

Alignment controls how the lines in a paragraph are positioned within a column: left, right, centered, and so on. Paragraphs are aligned within the text boundaries established by any **First Line**, **Left**, and **Right Indent** set for the paragraph and any **Text Inset** set for the text box. **Text Inset**, which is specified in the Text tab of the Modify dialog box, affects the top, bottom, left, and right edges of a box. **Text Inset** does not affect the left and right edges of the inner columns in a box.

QuarkXPress has alignment options all over the place: the **Alignment** submenu of the **Style** menu, the **Alignment** menu in Character Attributes, the **Alignment** icons on the Measurements palette, and keyboard commands. The alignment options are fairly obvious: **Left**, **Centered**, **Right**, **Justified**, and **Forced**. The only difference between **Justified** and **Forced** is that **Forced** always justifies the last line in the paragraph (see Figure 9.13). To change a paragraph's alignment with keyboard commands, see Table 9.3.

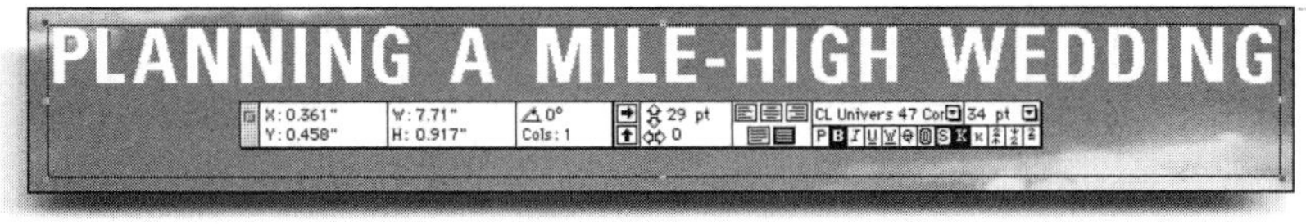

PLANNING A MILE-HIGH WEDDING

| X: 0.361" | Y: 7.71" | △ 0° | ⊞ ✗ 29 pt | CL Univers 47 Cor | 34 pt |
| Y: 0.458" | H: 0.917" | Cols: 1 | ↕ ◇◇ 0 | P B I U V Q O S K | |

FIGURE 9.13

To quickly spread a one-line paragraph across its box, use forced alignment.

TABLE 9.3 Keyboard shortcuts for aligning paragraphs

Alignment	Keyboard Shortcut
Left	⌘+Shift+L (Ctrl+Shift+L)
Centered	⌘+Shift+C (Ctrl+Shift+C)
Right	⌘+Shift+R (Ctrl+Shift+R)
Justified	⌘+Shift+J (Ctrl+Shift+J)
Forced	⌘+Option+Shift+J (Ctrl+Alt+Shift+J)

Leading

Leading can be measured two different ways: from baseline to baseline or ascender to ascender. There's a preference in the **Paragraph** tab of Document Preferences called **Mode**—just make sure you have **Typesetting** selected.

The second thing to know about leading is that there are three types in QuarkXPress: absolute leading, auto leading, and incremental leading. The three types of leading are specified differently and result in different line spacing.

Absolute Leading

Absolute leading is simple: You give QuarkXPress a number in points and that's the amount of space used between baselines of text. For example, you might enter 12 points of leading for 10-point text. The good thing about absolute leading is that it guarantees you the same amount of space between all the lines in a paragraph. Unless your design calls for varying line spacing, you should use absolute leading.

Auto Leading

Auto leading uses a percentage of the largest character on a line to calculate the leading value. Here's how it works:

- First, QuarkXPress finds the "largest" character in a line. It's not looking for the tallest character or the character in the highest point size. It's looking inside each font at a built-in spacing value. QuarkXPress uses that value as the starting point for calculating auto leading. (Usually, that number is similar to the point size of the character.)

- Next, QuarkXPress multiplies that spacing value by the **Auto Leading** percentage. The **Auto Leading** percentage is 20% by default, but it can be changed in the **Paragraph** tab of Document Preferences.

- QuarkXPress takes the result of the multiplication, adds it to the spacing value of the largest character, and uses that number for leading.

Many people will tell you that auto leading is calculated like this: 10-point type multiplied by 20% results in 2 points; the 10 and 2 are added to come up with 12 points of leading. Although that's the simplest way to explain it—and it's close to the actual results —it's just not true. If you've ever popped a character of Zapf Dingbats into an auto-leaded paragraph, you probably got a tiny bit more space above that line. It's because, even at the same point size, Zapf Dingbats has a larger spacing value in the font (see Figure 9.14).

FIGURE 9.14

Auto leading wreaks havoc on the leading in the last paragraph because, although the Dingbats are in the same point size as the rest of the paragraph, the spacing value in the font is obviously much larger.

Augusta, Westin Hotel, 1672 Lawrence St. (Downtown) *Contemporary.* Not your typical hotel restaurant, Augusta serves light Mediterranean fare using fresh ingredients and pastas. Art deco-style dining room. Excellent but pricey Sunday brunch. Reservations accepted. Mon-Sun 6 a.m.-

11 p.m. AmEx, DC, MC, V. ♿♥ 572-7222. $$$$

Therein lies the problem with auto leading. It calculates leading line-by-line. If there are mixed fonts or mixed point sizes in a paragraph, the lines end up spaced differently. That's why most people don't use auto leading beyond the experimentation phase of designing a document.

Incremental Leading

Incremental leading is just another form of auto leading. However, rather than working with the **Auto Leading** percentage, you simply specify how many points to add to the largest character on a line. For example, you might add two points of leading to the largest character on a line to come up with the leading value. Incremental leading has all the same spacing problems as auto leading.

Specified Leading

To specify leading, you can use the **Leading** field in Character Attributes, the **Leading** field and arrows on the Measurements palette, and keyboard commands. For absolute leading, just enter a plain old number in the field. For auto leading, enter the word auto or a zero (0) in the field. The **Leading** field in Character Attributes also includes a little menu so you can choose **Auto**. For incremental leading, enter a plus sign before the value in the field (such as +2). You can enter leading values from –1,080 to +1,080 in increments as fine as .001.

To increase or decrease leading by 1 point, click the vertical arrows on the Measurements palette. To increase or decrease leading by a tenth of a point, press the Option (Alt) key while you click the arrows. If you change leading using keyboard commands or the arrows on the Measurements palette, auto leading is converted to absolute leading. For keyboard commands that control leading, see Table 9.4.

TABLE 9.4   Keyboard shortcuts for changing leading

To do this...	...press this
Increase leading by 1 point	⌘+Shift+' (Ctrl+Shift+')
Increase leading by 1/10 point	⌘+Option+Shift+' (Ctrl+Alt+Shift+')
Decrease leading by 1 point	⌘+Shift+; (Ctrl+Shift+;)
Decrease leading by 1/10 point	⌘+Option+Shift+; (Ctrl+Alt+Shift+;)

Maintain Leading

There's one more mention of leading in the software, and we can't help but bring it up here. It's a check box called **Maintain**

Leading in the **Paragraph** tab of Document Preferences. **Maintain Leading** applies to a line of text that falls right below an item with runaround set for it. When **Maintain Leading** is checked, the line is placed according to its applied leading value. When **Maintain Leading** is not checked, the ascent of the line touches the item (or any runaround outset).

SEE ALSO

➤ *To change leading mode, see page 59*

➤ *To change the value for auto leading, see page 58*

➤ *To turn on **Maintain Leading** in the preferences, see page 59*

Indents

Indents position paragraphs horizontally within columns. QuarkXPress allows you to indent paragraphs from the left and right, and it allows you to specify an additional indent for the first line. Any text inset affecting the edges of a box is added to the indents. Text inset, which is specified in the **Text** tab of the Modify dialog box, affects the top, bottom, left, and right edges of a box. Text inset does not affect the left and right edges of the inner columns in a box.

Paragraph Attributes offers two methods for specifying indents, numerical and visual:

- If you're the numeric type, enter values in the **Left Indent**, **First Line**, and **Right Indent** fields. You can enter values in any measurement system in increments as fine as .001; the range of values you can enter depends on the column width.

- If you're the visual type, use the little triangles on the ruler above the column containing the selected paragraph. When you drag the triangles, the values in the **Left Indent**, **First Line**, and **Right Indent** fields update so you can see precisely where the indent will be set. The triangle on the right represents the **Right Indent**. On the left, the top half of the split triangle represents the **First Line** indent and the bottom half represents the **Left Indent**. When you drag the Left Indent triangle, the **First Line** indent comes along because it's measured from the **Left Indent**. You can also modify indents using the ruler when the **Tabs** tab of Paragraph Attributes is displayed.

To create a *hanging indent*, which you usually see following a bullet, you use a combination of **Left Indent**, a negative **First Line** indent, and a tab. For example, to hang the text to the right of a bullet, you might enter .25 in the **Left Indent** field and –.25 in the **First Line** field. Then set a tab at .25. When you enter a bullet and then a tab, all the text aligns to the right of the tab.

You can create hanging indents on-the-fly using the Indent Here character. Just press ⌘+\ (Ctrl+\) to align the remaining lines in a paragraph to the right of the text insertion bar. See Figure 9.15.

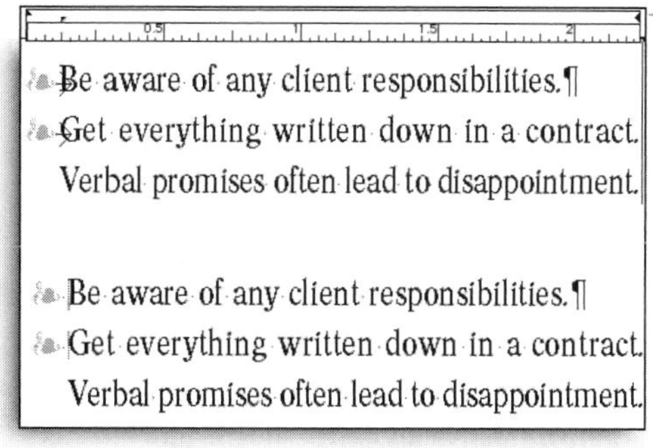

FIGURE 9.15

The first two paragraphs use negative **First Line** indent combined with a positive **Left Indent** to create a hanging indent. Notice the position of the indent triangles in the ruler. The same two paragraphs follow; however, this hanging indent was created with a space and the Indent Here character.

Space Before and Space After

When you need to add space between body paragraphs, before subheads, or after headlines, you may be tempted to insert paragraph returns. Don't. If you use paragraph returns for spacing, the amount of space between paragraphs depends on the size of the invisible return character, which varies from font to font. And when text reflows in columns, you might end up with a spare paragraph return at the top of a column.

The precise method for adding space between paragraphs is to specify an exact amount of space in the **Space Before** and/or **Space After** fields. The **Space After** value is added to the **Space Before** value in consecutive paragraphs. **Space After** is not applied to paragraphs that fall at the bottom of a column, and **Space Before** is not applied to paragraphs that fall at the top of a column. Using the measurement system you prefer, you can enter values from 0 to 15" in increments as fine as .001.

Since the **Space Before** and **Space After** values are added together, you need to anticipate all the different types of paragraphs that might follow each other before creating paragraph style sheets. For example, say you intend for your Headline style sheet with its **Space After** to be followed by your Tag Line style sheet with no **Space Before**. That might be the perfect amount of space you want after a headline. However, if there is no tag line, and you launch right into a Subhead style sheet with a nonzero **Space Before** value, you'll get additional space. To prevent this, most template producers try to accomplish all their spacing needs using one or the other, but never both. Try specifying **Space After** only; you may need to create a few additional style sheets for paragraphs that fall immediately before a subhead or paragraph.

H&J

The **H&J** pop-up menu allows you to select a set of hyphenation and justification rules for a paragraph. If you're wondering how to make a paragraph hyphenate automatically, this is the place—just select an H&J that has **Automatic Hyphenation** checked. QuarkXPress includes one H&J called Standard, but you can create your own H&J settings. Selecting an H&J is the last step in implementing well-planned specifications for hyphenating and justifying text.

SEE ALSO

➤ *To create and edit H&J settings, see page 268*

Drop Caps

A drop cap in QuarkXPress is a fairly limited form of an initial cap, which designers use to draw your eye to a paragraph. Essentially, a few characters at the beginning of a paragraph are enlarged and dropped down into the paragraph. Although the text flows around drop caps nicely, you don't get any additional formatting such as color or typeface. (The characters aren't even capitalized as "caps" might suggest.)

Anyway, to have QuarkXPress automatically do this for you, check **Drop Caps**. Then, enter the number of characters—from

1 to 127—you want as drop caps in the **Character Count** field. To specify how many lines the characters drop, enter a number from 2 to 16 in the **Line Count** field. If you specify more drop caps than can fit on the first line of a paragraph, only those that fit become drop caps. The remaining characters drop to the next line, but their spacing is confused and they may overprint the first line.

You have to store all the rest of your drop cap formatting in a character style sheet, which you apply to the text separately. You can highlight your boring, little black Stone Serif four-line drop cap and apply a character style sheet that specifies bold, red Medici Script. While it's highlighted, you might notice that the size is reported as 100%. The **Drop Caps** setting overrides any other sizes specified; drop caps can be further enlarged up to 400% and reduced down to 16.7%.

SEE ALSO

➤ *To create and edit character style sheets, see page 299*

Keep Lines Together

Keep Lines Together is a glue that makes lines in a paragraph stick to each other. When a paragraph reaches the end of a column, it checks its **Keep Lines Together** setting to see what to do. If it's not checked, the paragraph places lines at the bottom of the column until it runs out of space; then it carries the rest of the lines to the top of the next column. The split between the number of lines left at the bottom and those carried to the top might be anything from 2/2, 3/5, 4/6 to 1/7, 5/1, 2/9. When **Keep Lines Together** is checked, you decide how many lines stay and how many lines go (see Figure 9.16).

Clicking **All Lines in ¶** glues the entire paragraph together. If it doesn't fit at the bottom of a column, the whole paragraph hops up to the top of the next column. If you don't want to go to that extreme, you can use the **Start** and **End** options. Click **Start** and then enter the minimum number of lines you want at the bottom of the column in the field. Enter the minimum number of lines you want at the top of a column in the **End** field. The defaults, 2 and 2, prevent orphans nicely. If the number of lines in the paragraph don't add up to the **Start** and **End** numbers (for example, if you enter 3 and 3 and you have a five-line paragraph), the whole paragraph gets glued together.

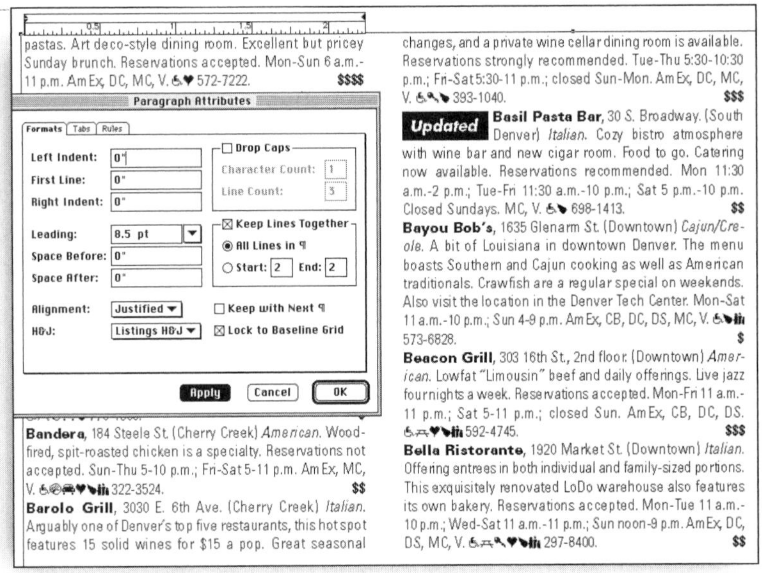

FIGURE 9.16

The last paragraph in the left column is a prime candidate for **Keep Lines Together**. Since **All Lines in ¶** is selected and **Apply** is clicked, the entire paragraph is about to jump up to the next column.

Keep with Next ¶

Keep with Next ¶ is another form of glue. When checked, it sticks a paragraph to the one following it. No matter how the text flows between columns, the two paragraphs will be inseparable. Usually, you use **Keep with Next ¶** on subheads so they stay with their associated body paragraph (see Figure 9.17). You need to be careful about overusing **Keep with Next ¶**, though. If you glue more paragraphs together than can fit in a column, you end up with text overflow.

Lock to Baseline Grid

Checking **Lock to Baseline Grid** snaps selected paragraphs to the grid you set up in Document Preferences. To see the grid, choose **Show Baseline Grid** from the **View** menu. If you lock all the paragraphs on a page to the baseline grid, all the lines of text align horizontally across column. Don't check **Lock to Baseline Grid** lightly; it's merely the last step involved in implementing a baseline grid.

Day 2

Against the far wall just beyond the stove, a simple wooden table fitted with odd chairs houses an essential resource for first-time visitors: a notebook promising instruction on everything a hut rookie needs to know. Topics of note range from hut etiquette – "Leave the woodpile higher than you found it," – to such basics as, "How to: fix the commode, light a fire, and, most importantly, turn on the hut." The latter is a lesson in the gauges and pumps that monitor the electricity-delivering solar panels, fueling the hut's sole nods to modern living.

Despite my eagerness for the peace and solitude of a back-country experience, I immediately wonder how we will fill so many hours. But I soon learn that the hours have a way of taking care of themselves, filled with the random detail and necessity of basic existence. With no telephone, no television, not even a radio, thoughts of the real world with all its inherent problems drift light years away. There is only time for cooking, cleaning, reading, skiing, and basking in the sun rays that slant through the many windows.

Day 3

Mornings begin at sunrise with the restocking and stoking of the potbelly stove downstairs. An old, cushy chair – the kind that has surely seen better days but may never be so old as to

stove, then crack eggs in the heavy skillet and lay bread on the cast-iron top to toast. We heat water on the stove for dish washing and try to hide food from our only other company, the mice.

The rest of the day passes in a mix of practical and play. Although Strawberry Creek Trail leads to Lake Granby, some eight miles away, we choose instead to carve circles in the meadow, wandering in and out of stands of pine, fir, and spruce, shooting down small slopes, exploring the forest.

At night, we make one last run, gliding in and out of the moonlit glade, listening for the sounds of the wildlife I know must be watching from the shadowy woods.

Day 4

In the morning I fix one last breakfast on the old white stove, check to ensure that all the coals have cooled, and stack our gear by the doorway for the Millers to retrieve.

We make our way back to the trailhead over untraveled snow, creating our own path through the woods, and already I am scheming how to make time for another trip. Next winter seems much too far away to wait for another visit, but summer is just around the corner.

As I glide over the wet snow, I imagine the forest some months from now when the trip in will be over a dusty trail surrounded by the green of aspen leaves, and the purples of the

FIGURE 9.17

Keep with Next ¶ is applied to the subheads in this article, so even through the "Day 3" subhead is starting to approach the bottom of the first column, there's no concern that it will break off from its paragraph if more text is added above it.

SEE ALSO

➤ *To set up a design using a baseline grid, see page 264*

Tabs

When you select the **Tabs** command from the **Style** menu or press ⌘+Shift+T (Ctrl+Shift+T), you jump into the **Tabs** part of Paragraph Attributes (see Figure 9.18). This area allows you to specify unlimited tab stops for the paragraph. The weird thing about tabs is that there's an invisible default tab stop at every half inch. When you create a new tab stop, all the invisible tab stops to the left are removed while the ones to the right remain.

QuarkXPress allows you to "style" your tab stops by choosing an alignment or a fill character. To create a tab stop, start by clicking one of the alignment buttons across the top: **Left**, **Center**, **Right**, **Decimal**, **Comma**, or **Align On**. The tab stop alignments work as follows:

- **Left** aligns text to the left of the tab stop.
- **Center** distributes text evenly on either side of the tab stop.
- **Right** aligns text to the right of the tab stop.

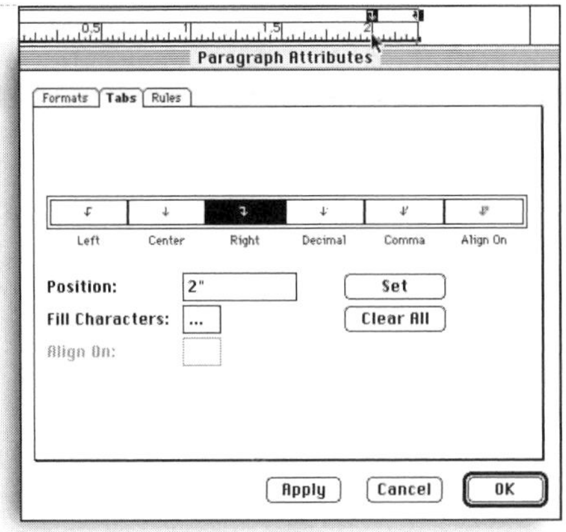

FIGURE 9.18

The Paragraph Attributes dialog box's **Tabs** tab allows you to create several kinds of tabs.

- **Decimal** aligns periods in the text with the tab stop. (Use this for a list of prices with decimal points so numbers such as $10.50, $230.75, and $36 align properly.)

- **Comma** aligns commas in text with the tab stop. (Use this for a list of numbers in the thousands and up so numbers such as 1,000; 10,000; and 30,000.05 align properly.)

- **Align On** aligns any printing character in text with the tab stop; you specify the character in the Align On field.

- If text should align on a decimal, comma, or other specified character, and the text does not contain that character, the last character in the text aligns on the tab stop. For example, in a list of numbers that should align on a comma, the number 100 would align to the left of the commas in the column.

Once you decide on alignment, you can specify the position of a tab stop using the tab ruler or the **Position** field.

If you're the numeric type, enter a value in the **Position** field and click **Set**. You can enter values in any measurement system in increments as fine as .001; the range of values you can enter depends on the column width. To create a series of tabs that are the same distance apart, you can have QuarkXPress calculate the numbers for you. Select the first tab, and then add the distance for the next tab to the value in the **Position** field. Click **Set** and

QuarkXPress does the math for you. For example, if your tab is at 2p3, and you want your next tab to be 9 picas from it, enter 2p3+p9 in the field. Click **Set** and you'll get a tab at 3p. Continue selecting tabs and adding values to create a series of tabs.

If you're the visual type, click an alignment button, and then drag that tab icon up onto the tab ruler. When you drag the tab icon around, the **Position** field updates so you can see precisely where the tab will be set. Click **Set** when you finish positioning the tab on the ruler. The tab ruler also provides triangles for setting **Left Indent**, **First Line Indent**, and **Right Indent**.

If you use dot leaders between table of contents entries and page numbers, or if you fill the white space between tabs for another reason, you can specify fill characters for tab stop. Click a tab icon on the ruler to select it; then enter one or two characters in the **Fill Characters** field. You can enter any printing characters and/or any type of space; if you enter two characters, they alternate. For example, you can enter a period and an en space for a loose dot leader, or you can enter an ellipses for a tight dot leader (see Figure 9.19). To create lines for an order form, some people use an underscore as a fill character. When you decide on the fill characters for the selected tab stop, click **Set**.

You can change any and all tab stops for a paragraph at any time. To change one tab stop, click its icon on the ruler to select it. To move it, drag it to a new position. To get rid of it, drag it off the ruler and let go. While a tab is selected, you can change its alignment by clicking one of the buttons, and you can enter new fill characters. To delete all your tab stops and revert to the invisible default tab stops at every half inch, click **Clear All**. If you're used to the old method of Option+clicking (Alt+clicking) the ruler to delete all tabs, it still works as well.

Rules

The **Rules** tab in Paragraph Attributes allows you to specify horizontal lines that flow with text. Paragraph rules are handy for creating tables and reverse type, but they are mostly used for graphic effects.

SEE ALSO

➤ *To use paragraph rules, see page 411*

A special kind of tab

QuarkXPress provides a right-indent tab that automatically aligns characters with the right indent of text. Just press Option+Tab (Alt+Tab) in text to hop right over to the edge. Right-indent tabs can't be edited so you can't change the alignment or add fill characters.

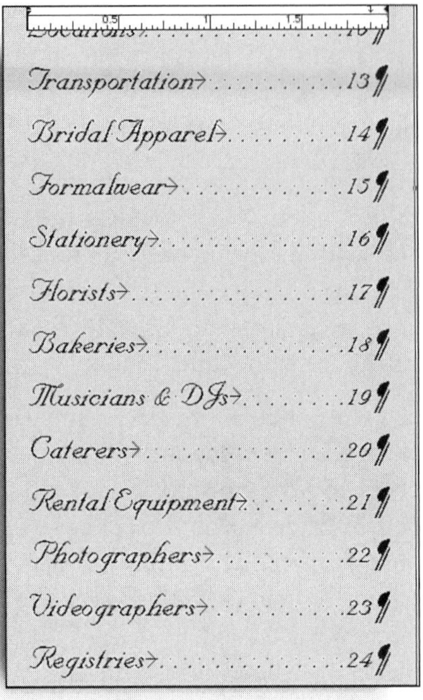

FIGURE **9.19**

To create a dot leader in a table of contents, you specify fill characters, such as a period and a space, for a tab.

Documents→ .... 10¶

Transportation→ .... 13¶

Bridal Apparel→ .... 14¶

Formalwear→ .... 15¶

Stationery→ .... 16¶

Florists→ .... 17¶

Bakeries→ .... 18¶

Musicians & DJs→ .... 19¶

Caterers→ .... 20¶

Rental Equipment→ .... 21¶

Photographers→ .... 22¶

Videographers→ .... 23¶

Registries→ .... 24¶

Implementing a Baseline Grid

When paragraphs of text are locked to baseline grid, lines of text align from column to column and from box to box. Check out various newsletters and magazines: Sometimes text aligns across columns, sometimes it doesn't. That's the difference between paragraphs that are locked to baseline grid and those that are not. Locking text to a baseline grid is purely a design choice. Some designers feel that rigid alignment isn't necessary to a successful layout—others believe symmetry is crucial. It's completely up to you, your design department, your audience, and the feel of your piece.

The Basics

To view the baseline grid, select **Show Baseline Grid** from the **View** menu or press Option+F7 (Alt+F7). If that hot pink brings back visions of '80s pop-singer hair, change it in the **Display** tab of Application Preferences. To lock a selected paragraph to the grid, check **Lock to Baseline Grid** in the Paragraph Formats dialog box (choose **Formats** from the **Style** menu). You can include **Lock to Baseline Grid** in paragraph style sheets so you don't have to apply it manually.

SEE ALSO

➤ *To change the color of the baseline grid, see page 75*

➤ *To set paragraph format attributes, see page 251*

Setting Up the Grid

Just like everything else in QuarkXPress, you can set detailed preferences for your baseline grid. In the **Paragraph** tab of Document Preferences, the Baseline Grid area contains two fields: **Start** and **Increment**. To determine where the grid starts at the top of a page, enter a value in the **Start** field. This value should be the same as the first baseline of your body copy. (In other words, don't lock your headline to the baseline grid—just the body text.) Enter a value in the **Increment** field to specify the vertical distance between the gridlines. The default **Start** value is 0.5 "; **Increment** is 12 points. To snap items to the baseline grid guides, turn on **Snap to Guides** in the **View** menu.

SEE ALSO

➤ *To set whether baseline grid guides are in front of document objects or behind them, see page 158*

Interacting with Leading

Line spacing in paragraphs locked to baseline grid is determined by a combination of the paragraph's vertical alignment (as specified in the Modify dialog box), its leading value, and the **Increment** value specified in the **Baseline Grid** area of the Document Preferences.

If a paragraph has **Vertical Alignment** that's **Justified** (set this in the Modify dialog box), the justified alignment overrides all leading values and the **Lock to Baseline Grid** setting. Only the first and last lines are locked to baseline grid; all other lines are spaced evenly between.

When paragraphs are locked to baseline grid, leading values are overridden because lines are automatically spaced in multiples of the grid's increment value. If the leading is less than or equal to the grid increment (for example 12 points of leading on a 12-point grid), lines of text lock to every gridline. If the leading is greater than the grid increment (for example 13 points of leading on a 12-point grid), a line of text locks to the next available gridline; in this case, every other gridline (effectively making your leading 24 points).

To lock paragraphs to the grid without disturbing the line spacing in your document, specify a grid **Increment** value equal to (or a multiple of) an absolute leading value.

Fine-Tuning Typography

Create and edit custom hyphenation and justification settings

Apply manual hyphenation

Specify custom hyphenation for individual words

Create and edit custom tracking and kerning tables

Copyfit with tracking, scaling, and vertical spacing

Eliminate widows and orphans

Create attractive ragged-justified text

Apply manual kerning

Once you finish flowing and formatting text, you'll probably see a few weak spots you need to clean up. Maybe a column of justified text has rivers, or one paragraph of left-aligned text looks particularly jagged. Maybe you have a couple letters sitting alone on a line or a subhead separated from its paragraph. Or maybe the text just flat out doesn't fit in the space you made for it. No matter what the problem is, you need a solution. With a combination of QuarkXPress features, you can solve most typographic dilemmas.

Controlling Hyphenation and Justification

QuarkXPress combines the settings for controlling hyphenation and for controlling text spacing into H&J settings. Although the combined settings affect the overall look of text in a column, the hyphenation process and justifying text are two different things. First, you'll look at all the hyphenation controls and then come back to *justification*.

To hyphenate text in QuarkXPress, first you create an H&J with automatic hyphenation turned on. Then you apply that H&J to paragraphs you want to hyphenate (through the Paragraph Attributes dialog box or through a *paragraph style sheet*). The way QuarkXPress automatically hyphenates that text is based on the **Hyphenation Method** setting in Document Preferences. You can customize the way words hyphenate by creating a list of hyphenation exceptions. Then you can fine-tune hyphenation manually using keyboard commands.

All automatic hyphenation in QuarkXPress follows a neat little hierarchy, whether QuarkXPress is actually hyphenating a word or just showing you its suggested hyphenation. From a word's point of view, here's how it knows whether or not to hyphenate:

1. Does my paragraph's H&J have hyphenation on? Do the **Smallest Word**, **Minimum Before**, **Minimum After**, and **Break Capitalized** settings allow me to hyphenate? If both are so, proceed to number 2.

2. Does the **Hyphens in a Row** or **Hyphenation Zone** prevent me from hyphenating? If not, I check with number 3.

3. Okay, I get to hyphenate, but now where? First, I look in the Hyphenation Exceptions. If I'm in it, I hyphenate the way it says to. If I'm not in there, I keep going to number 4.

4. So, this means QuarkXPress is going to figure out how to hyphenate me. First, it looks at the **Hyphenation Method** selected in Document Preferences. If it's **Expanded**, QuarkXPress looks in its little internal hyphenation dictionary. If I'm in there, that's the winner. If I'm not in there, or if **Enhanced** or **Standard** is selected for the **Hyphenation Method**, I go on to number 5.

5. Now, the algorithm appropriate to the hyphenation method kicks in and hyphenates the word. It tries to do a good job, but sometimes it gives crummy hyphenation. Those instances need to be corrected manually or through **Hyphenation Exceptions**.

Setting Hyphenation Preferences

When QuarkXPress hyphenates words automatically, it uses an algorithm. The algorithm looks at the length of words, at letter pairs, and so on to determine where it can insert hyphens. Quark has improved the algorithm in each major release of QuarkXPress. The problem with changing the algorithm is that it can change the way text hyphenates and therefore the way text flows. Fortunately, the hyphenation method is saved with documents, so documents will never reflow unless you change the setting. If you want to match the hyphenation of an older document, or if you prefer a previous hyphenation method, you can select one of the older hyphenation methods for a document.

The **Method** menu in the **Paragraph** tab of Document Preferences supplies the options for hyphenation: **Standard**, **Enhanced**, and **Expanded**. These options represent the hyphenation algorithm used by successive versions of

QuarkXPress—3.0 and earlier used Standard, 3.1–3.3 used Enhanced, and version 4 uses Expanded. The Expanded method also includes a small hyphenation dictionary, which it checks before inserting hyphens. You may find that you don't like the hyphenation specified in the dictionary used by this method and revert to the Enhanced method.

You can change the hyphenation method for the active document, or when no documents are open, you can change the hyphenation method for all new documents. (By default, **Expanded** is selected for all new QuarkXPress 4 documents.)

SEE ALSO

➤ *To change the hyphenation method, see page 57*

Working in the H&Js Dialog Box

When you first select **H&Js** from the **Edit** menu, the H&Js dialog box displays. This dialog box allows you to edit the list of H&Js associated with the current document, whose name appears in the title of the dialog box. If no documents are open, the name of the dialog box changes to Default H&Js. The default list of H&Js is automatically included in all new documents. If this dialog box looks familiar, it's because it looks just like the front end dialog box for creating and editing colors, style sheets, *list* definitions, *Dashes & Stripes*, and print styles. For the most part, these dialog boxes all look and work alike (see Figure 10.2).

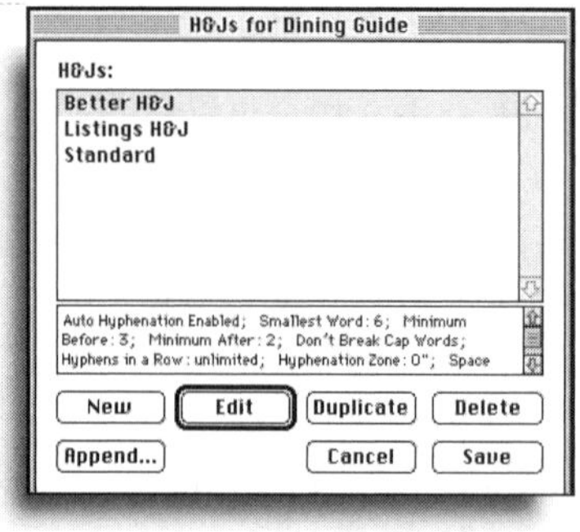

FIGURE 10.1

The H&Js dialog box lists the existing H&J settings.

The scroll list at the top of the dialog box allows you to select an H&J for editing or for viewing its characteristics in the field below. The H&J definition shown in the field is handy for refreshing your memory about an H&J without going all the way into the Edit H&J dialog box. You can multiple-select H&Js in this list by ⌘+clicking (Ctrl+clicking) to select noncontiguous H&Js or Shift+clicking to select a range of H&Js. However, the only thing you can do to multiple-selected H&Js is delete them.

All documents contain the default H&J called Standard, which you can edit but not delete. Standard is the default H&J selected for the Normal paragraph style sheet and for any new paragraph styles for which you don't specify a custom H&J. Standard is defined as follows: **Auto Hyphenation**, checked; **Smallest Word**, 6; **Minimum Before**, 3; **Minimum After**, 2; **Break Capitalized Words**, not checked; **Hyphens in a Row**, unlimited; **Hyphenation Zone**, 0"; **Space**, 85% **Min.**, 110% **Opt.**, 250% **Max.**; **Char**, 0% **Min.**, 0% **Opt.**, 4% **Max.**; **Flush Zone**, 0"; **Single Word Justify**, checked. You might want to edit Standard to reflect your most-used hyphenation settings (like the ones you use in body text).

SEE ALSO

➤ *To create and edit style sheets, see page 297*

➤ *To create and edit hyphenation and justification settings (H&Js), see page 268*

➤ *To create lists for generating tables of contents, see page 593*

➤ *To create and edit Dashes & Stripes frame styles, see page 120*

➤ *To create and edit print styles, see page 515*

New

New opens the Edit H&J dialog box so you can create a new H&J. You can create up to 1,000 H&Js for a document.

Edit

Edit opens the Edit H&J dialog box for the style sheet selected in the list. Although most dialog boxes link the **OK** or **Save** button to the Return (Enter) key, in this case, it's linked to the **Edit** button.

Duplicate

Duplicate is straightforward; it creates a copy of the selected H&J. The Edit H&J dialog box opens right up with the copied style sheet waiting to be edited.

Delete

Delete seems simple, but it's not. Before it deletes the selected H&Js, it looks through the document to see if they're used anywhere. And not just in formatted text—if they're selected in paragraph style sheets, they're considered to be "used" in the document. If an H&J is not in use, it gets quietly deleted. If an H&J is in use, a dialog box gives you the option to replace it with another H&J. The replacement H&J you choose will be applied to text and/or used in the appropriate paragraph style sheets.

Append

Append allows you to selectively add H&Js from other documents to this list of H&Js.

SEE ALSO
➤ *To append H&J settings from other documents, see page 146*

Compare

You can't see the **Compare** button, but it's there. ⌘+click (Ctrl+click) to select two H&Js in the list. Then press the Option key (Alt key) to change the **Append** button to **Compare** and click it. The Compare dialog box shows you both H&J definitions with the differences in bold. Use **Compare** any time you need to know the difference between two similar H&Js.

Cancel

The **Cancel** button is straightforward; it exits the H&Js dialog box without saving any changes.

Save

The **Save** button closes the H&Js dialog box, saving all your changes.

Hyphenation Rules in an H&J

Beyond simple decisions such as whether you want text to hyphenate or not, hyphenation rules should be set with the help of an editor. Although hyphenation does affect text flow, and therefore design, it can have a severe effect on legibility. For example, if you allow words to hyphenate after only one character, it may produce the best spacing, but it will cause readers to stumble. Nobody expects to see a single letter at the end of a line with a hyphen unless it's in "T-shirt." Style guides and dictionaries provide different hyphenation rules, so the key is to be consistent within a publication and within an organization.

To specify the hyphenation rules within an H&J:

1. Select **H&Js** from the **Edit** menu.

2. Click the **New** button or select an existing H&J, and click **Edit** to open the Edit H&J dialog box (see Figure 10.2).

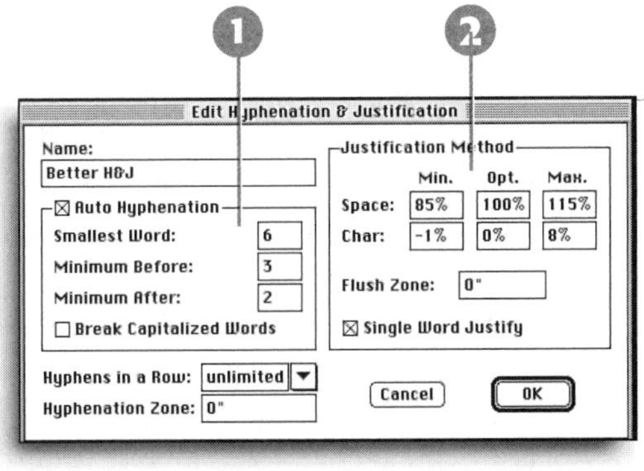

FIGURE 10.2

The Edit H&J dialog box contains controls for both hyphenation and justification.

1 Hyphenation controls

2 Justification controls

3. To turn hyphenation on, check **Auto Hyphenation**. To create an H&J for text that shouldn't hyphenate, such as headlines, don't check this box and disregard the remaining controls in the left side of the dialog box.

4. To specify how many characters a word must have in order to hyphenate automatically, use the **Smallest Word** field. The default is 6, which means that a word such as "older" cannot hyphenate, but "oldest" can. Enter a value between 3 and 20.

5. To specify the minimum number of characters that must precede a hyphen, use the **Minimum Before** field. The default is 3, which means that "nothing" cannot break like this "no-thing," but "nonexistent" can break like this "non-existent." Enter a value between 1 and 6 (although, editorially speaking, a 1 would be silly).

6. To specify the minimum number of characters that must follow a hyphen, use the **Minimum After** field. The default is 2, which means that "silly" can break like this: "sil-ly." Enter a value between 2 and 8. Although 2 seems small, it's probably the best choice for narrow columns since it allows words ending with "ly," "er," and "ed" to hyphenate. For longer columns, as in this book, use 3.

7. To allow words that start with capital letters to hyphenate, check **Break Capitalized Words**. The default is not checked so that proper names and the first words of sentences will not hyphenate. However, if the text contains a lot of names in narrow columns, and capitalized words aren't hyphenated, the *rag* in left-aligned text will be rough and justified text will have wacky spacing.

8. The **Hyphens in a Row** field specifies how many lines in a row can end in a hyphen. This includes automatic hyphens and any hyphens you enter manually. The value can range from 0 to 7. Because 0 is such a nonintuitive symbol for "unlimited," an alternative is to choose **Unlimited** from the menu attached to the field.

9. To specify how close a word must get to the edge of its column before it should think about hyphenating, use the **Hyphenation Zone** field. The **Hyphenation Zone** value is added to any other settings that bump the text in from the side of the column or box, including the right indent and the text inset. The default is 0", which means that a word can go all the way to the edge; if it doesn't fit, it checks other hyphenation criteria to see if it should hyphenate. With another value, the word can only get that close to the edge before it thinks about hyphenating.

For example, if the **Hyphenation Zone** value is 1 point, the text has a right indent of 1 point, and the one-column text box has a text inset of 1 point. In this case, when a word gets within 3 points of the side of the text box, it has to start thinking about hyphenating.

The **Hyphenation Zone** setting applies to all but justified text.

10. Click **OK**. Click **Save** to close the H&Js dialog box and save the changes.

SEE ALSO
➤ *To set the justification settings in the Edit H&J dialog box, see page 279*

Text Hyphenation

The final hyphenation in a document usually results from careful use of automatic features combined with a little manual fine-tuning.

Automatic Hyphenation

To specify hyphenation for a paragraph, all you do is select that paragraph and choose **Formats** from the **Style** menu or press ⌘+Shift+F (Ctrl+Shift+F). In the **Formats** tab, which is displayed by default, there's an **H&J** menu. Select the H&J you want to use for that paragraph. For body text, you'll probably choose one with automatic hyphenation turned on and a lot of attention put into its settings. However, for a headline, if hyphenation even comes into play, you might choose one with hyphenation off. Click **OK** to implement the new hyphenation settings.

Ideally, you'll include the appropriate H&J with your paragraph style sheets and rarely set it manually.

SEE ALSO
➤ *To format paragraphs of text, see page 251*
➤ *To specify an H&J setting for a paragraph style sheet, see page 298*

Manual Hyphenation

However, no matter how careful you are about setting up hyphenation, you'll probably still change some of it manually. You may be cleaning up rags or you may see a word with ugly hyphenation caused by the QuarkXPress algorithm. Or maybe you'd prefer a word hyphenate a different way, but you don't think you'll ever use it again so you don't want to put it in Hyphenation Exceptions.

What you need to do is insert *discretionary hyphens* in words. Discretionary hyphens pop themselves into words as needed. When text *reflows*, they go away if they're not needed. To enter discretionary hyphens, press ⌘+hyphen (Ctrl+hyphen) at opportune spots within words. The unfortunate thing about discretionary hyphens is that, even with invisibles on, they don't show up in QuarkXPress. Unless the word actually hyphenates, there's no evidence that you actually did anything. You can use discretionary hyphens to prevent words from hyphenating, to tell words where you prefer that they hyphenate, and to tell words where you absolutely want them to hyphenate.

- To prevent a word from hyphenating, place the text insertion bar immediately before it and enter a discretionary hyphen. By doing this, you're telling the word that it can only hyphenate the way you say it can. If you enter no other discretionary hyphens in the word, the word cannot hyphenate.

- To tell a word where you prefer it to hyphenate, place the text insertion bar between those two characters and enter a discretionary hyphen. The word will try to hyphenate there if spacing permits. However, the word may hyphenate differently depending on other hyphenation variables.

- To tell a word where you absolutely want it to hyphenate, first enter a discretionary hyphen before the word. Then, enter the discretionary hyphens throughout the word to specify where you want the word to hyphenate. Usually, that's just one spot, but it can be many.

- While you're fine-tuning, you can ask QuarkXPress for hyphenation advice by selecting **Suggested Hyphenation** from the **Utilities** menu.

For example, say you're writing an article and you mention the product name BeyondPress. You would prefer that BeyondPress break as "Beyond-Press," not "Be-yondPress." Since it's an isolated instance, you don't want to bother with Hyphenation Exceptions. So, you enter a discretionary hyphen between "Beyond" and "Press" to specify where you prefer the word to hyphenate. Then, to turn your preference into a mandate, enter a discretionary hyphen before the "B" in "Beyond." The word will never hyphenate any other way.

Hyphenation Exceptions

If there are words that you never want to hyphenate, or that you only want to hyphenate in particular spots, you can create a list of hyphenation exceptions. For example, most companies prefer not to hyphenate trademarked words, so you can enter frequently used trademarked words in hyphenation exceptions. QuarkXPress consults this list during automatic hyphenation and while providing suggested hyphenation.

Any time you find yourself correcting hyphenation manually, consider adding the word to Hyphenation Exceptions. You're extremely unlikely to "fill up" the Hyphenation Exceptions list, so don't worry about adding too many words and maxing it out. However, don't add words if you're changing their hyphenation for aesthetic reasons in a particular document rather than global editorial reasons. You may not want to be limited to specific hyphenation everywhere because it looks best in one spot.

To create and add to the list of hyphenation exceptions:

1. Select **Hyphenation Exceptions** from the **Utilities** menu (see Figure 10.3).

2. Type a word in the field with hyphens inserted. To keep the word from hyphenating at all, type the word in without hyphens. Unlike previous versions of QuarkXPress, accented and other special characters can be used in Hyphenation Exceptions.

Hunting down discretionary hyphens

Since discretionary hyphens are invisible, they're hard to get rid of. To eliminate them, place the text insertion bar right next to the first character in the word and press Delete (Backspace). If a discretionary hyphen was there, it's gone. If not, and a letter or space was deleted, undo the action with ⌘+Z (Ctrl+Z).

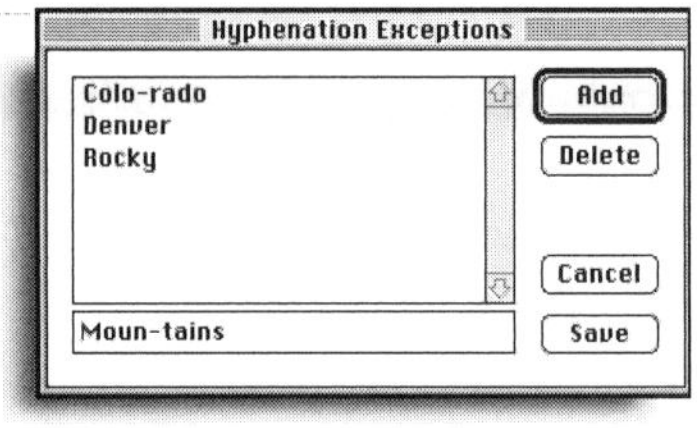

FIGURE 10.3

The Hyphenation Exceptions dialog box is where you specify custom hyphenations.

3. Click **Add**. To change a word in the list, simply enter it in the field with different hyphenation. The **Add** button changes to **Replace**.

4. Click **Save**.

If you create hyphenation exceptions with no documents open, they're saved in the XPress Preferences file and apply to all new documents. However, if a document is open, the hyphenation exceptions are saved with the document, but they fall into a weird category of settings that might be stored in the XPress Preferences file as well. If you see the Nonmatching Preferences alert when you open the document, and you click **Keep Document Settings**, changes you make to hyphenation exceptions are relegated to that document. If you didn't get the alert, or you clicked **Use XPress Preferences**, changes you make to hyphenation exceptions are saved in the document and in the XPress Preferences file. The other time hyphenation exceptions are saved in the XPress Preferences file is when you save a brand new document with edited hyphenation exceptions.

Why do you care about all this? Because hyphenation exceptions are one of the things that trigger the annoying Nonmatching Preferences alert. If you can get away with using one list of default hyphenation exceptions, you can kill one of the causes of the alert. But more importantly, you need to know how hyphenation exceptions are saved so you can be sure you're adding words consistently. If you never want a word to hyphenate a specific way, add it to individual documents and the default hyphenation exceptions. If specific clients have specific hyphenation requirements, make sure the hyphenation exceptions are stored with the document only.

SEE ALSO

➤ *To decide how to deal with the Nonmatching Preferences alert, see page 79*

Justification Rules in an H&J

Unlike hyphenation rules, which are editorial decisions, justification rules are purely design decisions. The controls specify how much flexibility QuarkXPress has in adding and removing space within paragraphs that are justified or force justified. (Some of the controls also affect the spacing of nonjustified text.) Although hyphenation and justification rules are discussed separately, the two do work together to produced legible, well-spaced text.

To specify the justification rules in an H&J:

1. Select **H&Js** from the **Edit** menu.

2. Click the **New** button or select an existing H&J, and click **Edit** to open the Edit H&J dialog box.

3. To specify the amount of space that can be added or removed between words to justify text, enter values in the **Space** fields. The values represent a percentage of the spacing that would normally be used between words in the current font and *point size*.

   QuarkXPress always spaces characters and words in nonjustified lines of text according to the **Optimum** value. QuarkXPress tries to space justified text according to the **Optimum** value as well. If it just won't work, QuarkXPress spaces text according to the **Minimum** and **Maximum** values. If that doesn't work, QuarkXPress rebels against the **Maximum** value to force text to justify.

4. To specify the amount of space that can be added or removed between individual characters to justify text, enter values in the **Character** fields. The values represent a percentage of the *en space* for the font and size in use.

5. To control when the last line of text in a justified paragraph is justified, enter a value in the **Flush Zone** field. Basically, the **Flush Zone** value tells the last line of text how close it has to get to the edge of the column before it can go ahead and spread out. If the last line of text doesn't reach the flush zone, it's left-aligned.

Similar to **Hyphenation Zone**, the **Flush Zone** value is added to any **Right Indent** or **Text Inset** values affecting the paragraph.

6. When the last line in a justified paragraph consists of a single word, you can control whether that word should spread out and justify. Checking **Single Word Justify** alone won't force a one-word line to justify; the word still has to reach the flush zone. To have paragraphs justify, forget about the **Flush Zone** and **Single Word Justify** settings and just choose **Force Justify** for the paragraph alignment.

7. Click **OK**. Click **Save** to close the H&Js dialog box and save the changes.

SEE ALSO

➤ *To control the width of en and em spaces, see page 65*

Using the Kern/Track Editor

QuarkXPress includes an XTension called the Kern/Track Editor that lets you modify the default *kerning* and *tracking* of individual fonts. If the XTension is running, the end of your **Utilities** menu provides two options: **Tracking Edit** and **Kerning Table Edit**. If you don't see those options, use the XTensions Manager, also in the **Utilities** menu, to enable the *XTension*; then restart QuarkXPress. Although the interface of the Kern/Track Editor has been slightly redesigned and improved in QuarkXPress 4, it works the same way it did in version 3.x and provides no additional functionality.

Whether you edit a font's kerning or tracking table, the effects on the fonts, the document, and QuarkXPress are generally the same:

- You need to have **Auto Kern Above** checked in the **Character** tab of Document Preferences. If you don't, your changes won't be applied.

- Realize that manual kerning and tracking is applied in addition to changes made to kerning and tracking tables. Until you apply kerning or tracking manually, the **Kern** and **Track** fields in QuarkXPress report "O."

■ Know that these changes are saved with open documents; when no documents are open, kerning and tracking modifications are saved in the XPress Preferences file for use with new documents.

■ Remember that you are not modifying the actual font. Changes made through the Kern/Track Editor are used only by QuarkXPress.

■ You don't need to keep the Kern/Track Editor XTension around to benefit from edited kerning and tracking tables. When you finish editing kerning or tracking, you can disable the XTension.

■ Because different weights and versions of a typeface may require different kerning and tracking, you must edit the tracking and kerning tables for each font in a family separately.

■ While using the Kern/Track Editor XTension can save you from making repetitive, laborious touch-ups to badly spaced text, it is no replacement for choosing a professional font with good kerning and tracking tables built-in.

■ You should proof modifications made to kerning and tracking tables on a 1200 dpi output device. What you see onscreen is not reliable enough for making final typographic decisions.

SEE ALSO

➤ *To enable and disable XTensions, see page 555*

Editing Tracking

Fonts have spacing information built into them, but they don't actually have tracking tables. When you use the Kern/Track Editor, you're actually creating a tracking table for a font. You do this by manipulating a curve on the graph. The slope of the curve represents increases and decreases in tracking in relation to different font sizes.

To create a tracking table for a font:

1. Select **Tracking Edit** from the **Utilities** menu. Select a font and double-click or click **Edit**.

    In the Edit Tracking dialog box, a flat line of zero indicates that the font has no tracking table. Text in this font, at any given point size, is not tracked. Tracking values can range from –100/200 to 100/200 em space for font sizes from 2 to 250. (Font sizes over 250 use the tracking specified for 250.)

2. To manipulate the curve, click to create points on it (see Figure 10.4). The distance between points represents a point size range. For example, to change the tracking for text from 24 to 36 points, click at 24 points and again at 36 points on the line.

FIGURE 10.4

The **Size** and **Track** fields in the upper-right corner describe the position of points on the curve. The current point location specifies that 9-point text be tracked –2.

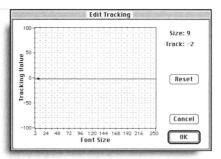

3. To specify the tracking for the point size range, drag one of the handles up or down. For example, dragging the point at 36 down to –20 on the **Tracking Value** axis, forces text at 36 points to be tracked –20. Text below 24 points is still tracked at zero, whereas text above 36 points is always tracked –20. Text between 24 and 36 points is tracked between 0 and –20 according to the intersection of the curve and graph.

    The curve can have up to four points, each representing ranges of point sizes. For example, the tracking range for body text might be 2 to 12 points, with another range for headline text from 12 to 36 points and a final range for display type of 48 points and up.

4. To delete a point on the curve, press the Option (Alt) key while clicking the point. To edit a point's location on the

curve, drag it to a new location. To return the curve to its original position, click **Reset** to revert it to zero.

5. Click **OK** and then click **Save**.

Editing Kerning Tables

Fonts have built-in kerning tables that consist of various character pairs and their kerning values. Using the Kern/Track Editor, you can change the built-in kerning values and add additional character pairs.

To edit a kerning table for a font:

1. Select **Kerning Table Edit** from the **Utilities** menu. Select a font and double-click or click **Edit**.

2. In the Edit Kerning Table dialog box, select an existing character pair from the **Kerning Pairs** list, or enter a new character pair in the **Pair** field. The character pair can include a space. The list shows all the character pairs in the font's kerning table and any you have previously added with the Kern/Track Editor. Kerning values can range from –500 to +500 in 1/200-em increments.

3. To specify a new kerning value, enter the number in the **Value** field. Or experiment with kerning using the arrows next to the field. Click the up or down arrow to increase or decrease kerning in increments of 10; press the Option (Alt) key while clicking the arrows to change the increment to 1. The **Preview** area updates as the kerning value changes (see Figure 10.5).

4. Click **Add**. You can have up to 8,000 kerning pairs in a font.

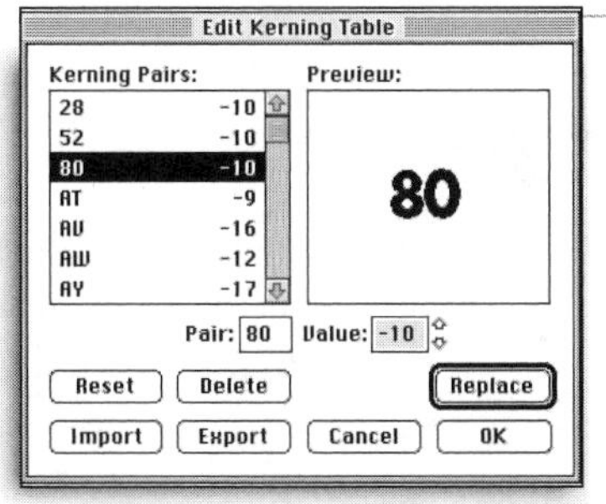

FIGURE 10.5

In the magazine 5280, kerning pairs are created for the logo font. The "52" and "28" pairs have been added with a –10 kerning value. The remaining character pair "80" is in the process of being added with the same –10 kerning value.

5. To delete a pair, select it in the list and click **Delete**. To edit a pair, select it in the list, enter a new value, and click **Replace**. To return the kerning table to its original values, click **Reset** to revert it to the font's built-in kerning table.

6. Click **OK**; then click **Save**.

Importing and Exporting Kerning Tables

The **Export** button in the Edit Kerning Table dialog box allows you to export a font's kerning table as an ASCII text file. You can edit a kerning table by editing its ASCII text file, and you can merge multiple kerning tables by combining their ASCII text files. The **Import** button in the Edit Kerning Table dialog box allows you to replace the kerning table for a font with one saved as an ASCII text file. You can use this technique to share edited kerning tables among similar fonts.

Copyfitting

Whether the copy a designer receives fits in the intended space depends entirely on the workflow. Many publications give writers a range for a story, like 800–1000 words. They compensate for long and short stories with graphics, runaround, ad placement, and so on. Others publications tell you to cover the topic in full, no matter how long or short the story ends up to be. They get all the stories in, and then plan the publication around them. The stories always "fit" because space is provided for them. Some publishers are exact; they know how many words they want and where it will go. The stories always fit because they are tailor-made to fit. No matter what the workflow is, you end up doing some copyfitting at some point. Here are a few places to start.

Tighten and Stretch

If the copy is just slightly off, you can usually adjust the typographic specifications to make it fit. With minimal adjustments, you can often fit a headline that's a few characters long, spread out a story that's a few paragraphs short, or pull in a story that's a couple paragraphs over. Try these on for size.

Tracking

Track body text in or out by as much as 3–5 units. To experiment with an article, save it, and then highlight all the text. Although the heads, subheads, and so on are highlighted, tracking them in and out is unlikely to add or remove lines of text. Try out different tracking values on all the text to see if it solves the spacing problem; then choose **Revert to Saved** from the **File** menu. If tracking isn't the solution, you have the previous formatting back. If tracking is the solution, apply the new tracking value to body text only, or edit the appropriate style sheets. (Edit the style sheets only if you're sure the new tracking value is appropriate for all the body text in the document.) Note: The amount of tracking you can apply while retaining legibility is entirely dependent on typeface, point size, column width, and so on. Although you'll hear the 3–5 range quoted often, it may not work with your particular typographic specifications.

For headlines, just highlight them and track in or out to see what you get. Since different headlines will probably have different tracking, leave the style sheets alone.

Scaling

Change the horizontal or vertical scale of body text. You can barely see a 5% change in scale, but you'll be surprised how much space you'll gain. Experiment the same as you do with tracking body text—save, then highlight the text, and scale it all. If it looks promising, revert to saved and apply the new scale to body text only.

Leading

Change the space between lines. If you're trying to force something to fill a specific text box, try turning on **Vertical Justify** (Modify dialog box, **Text** tab). If you're working with a whole article, try changing options in the **Formats** tab of Paragraph Attributes. Take advantage of the **Apply** button and the ability to perform math in fields. For example, say you highlight all the text and the **Leading** field reports 12 point. You can drop the leading 5% by entering 12 pt*95% in the field and clicking **Apply**. If the copy fits and the spacing looks okay, click **OK**. Otherwise, you can cancel out of the dialog box without harming the formatting. Another thing to try is altering the **Space Before** and **Space After** values for heads and subheads.

If altering the typographic specifications is not an option, or if the alterations get you close but not all the way there, you may need to do some light text editing. You can gain and lose inches by adding or removing subheads. Pop in a pull quote to add space, or hack off the second line in a headline to gain space. Look for paragraphs with a short last line and see if you can edit a couple words out to gain a line. To add a line, look for a paragraph with a long last line and pop a few extra words in until the text flows to the next line.

SEE ALSO

➤ *To track text, see page 248*

➤ *To scale text, see page 247*

➤ *To change Space Before and Space After values, see page 257*

➤ *To change leading, see page 253*

➤ *To edit style sheets, see page 302*

Fixing Widows and Orphans

A *widow* is a few characters alone on the last line of a paragraph. Generally, they look funny and should be fixed. Sometimes, they look fine. If the design and publication style are prejudiced against widows, you can usually fix them with QuarkXPress. Try tracking in slightly. Usually, the widow hops right up with the rest of the paragraph (see Figure 10.6). If not, try tracking out slightly. Another word may jump down and marry the widow. If tracking doesn't work, try tinkering with line endings. You can insert manual line breaks by pressing Shift+Return or experiment with the hyphenation. In desperate cases, get an editor to edit the widow out or ask a designer if the widow can stay.

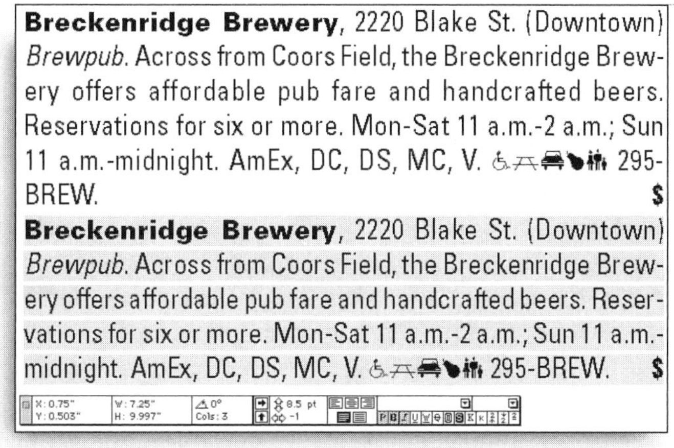

Breckenridge Brewery, 2220 Blake St. (Downtown) Brewpub. Across from Coors Field, the Breckenridge Brewery offers affordable pub fare and handcrafted beers. Reservations for six or more. Mon-Sat 11 a.m.-2 a.m.; Sun 11 a.m.-midnight. AmEx, DC, DS, MC, V. 295-BREW. $

Breckenridge Brewery, 2220 Blake St. (Downtown) Brewpub. Across from Coors Field, the Breckenridge Brewery offers affordable pub fare and handcrafted beers. Reservations for six or more. Mon-Sat 11 a.m.-2 a.m.; Sun 11 a.m.-midnight. AmEx, DC, DS, MC, V. 295-BREW. $

FIGURE 10.6

The last line of the first, untracked, paragraph is awkward. By simply tracking –1, as in the second paragraph, the lines even out.

An *orphan* is the first line of a paragraph that's left at the bottom of a column. Some publication styles have no problem with orphans, whereas others shun them. It's simple to prevent if you want to; just check **Keep Lines Together** in the **Formats** tab of Paragraph Attributes. Enter the minimum number of lines you want at the bottom of a column in the **Start** field and the minimum number of lines you want at the top of a column in the **End** field. This glues lines in a paragraph together so you can't get orphans. QuarkXPress also has a **Keep With Next** ¶ feature that lets you glue subheads to their paragraphs. Both **Keep Lines Together** and **Keep With Next** ¶ can and should be specified appropriately within paragraph style sheets.

Reducing Ugliness

Some typographic taboos, such as widows, jump right out at you. Others are more subtle. Try looking at a document upside down. Your inability to read the text forces you to concentrate on line endings and spacing. You no doubt notice a few spots that are simply formatted wrong: a lead paragraph that looks like a body paragraph or a subhead with the wrong space before. Those are simply mistakes and should be corrected through style sheets. Even if the document meets typographic specifications to the letter, it may not look perfect. Maybe the spacing in the headline looks awkward or you spot an em dash at the beginning of a line (and you hate that). These fall into the category of fine-tuning and can be carefully repaired in QuarkXPress.

Eliminating Rivers

Notice any columns that seem to have lines of white space running through them vertically. These are *rivers* and they usually result from poor hyphenation and justification settings. If rivers exist in the entire publication, it's time to edit the H&J. This can reflow the entire publication and cause lots of rework, but it will result in more legible text. If rivers are confined to a specific area, you might be able to track or fudge the line endings to dam the river. Otherwise, create a new H&J for the problem paragraphs. Apply it and then edit it a little at a time until the text looks better.

Fine-tuning Rags

If your document is ragged-right, look at the right side of each paragraph. The line endings should undulate in and out softly. If your paragraphs are severely jagged (and you didn't do it on purpose), you may need to reconsider the column width or the H&J. For example, if your H&J says don't **Break Capitalized Words**, and you're writing a society column full of names and places, you might get some hideous rag. If the rag is rough here and there, you can probably fix it with tracking. First, try tracking the whole paragraph in and out slightly. If that fails, try tracking the short lines to see if you can redistribute words. If you're opposed to tracking, you can try kerning around individual characters to add and remove space. The kerning method usually takes forever. Adjusting hyphenation and inserting manual line breaks (Shift+Return) may even out the lines as well (see Figure 10.7).

FIGURE 10.7

To create a smooth rag for this table of contents blurb, the designer inserted manual line breaks, an acceptable technique for one-time use text.

1 Tab symbol

2 Paragraph return symbol

3 Manual line break symbol

Cleaning up the Beginnings and Ends of Lines

Make one pass through your documents looking at nothing but the first character in each line. Occasionally, punctuation will get separated from text by an infiltrating space and you'll find a period or comma at the beginning of a line. Or you might find an em dash at the beginning of a line. If you prefer em dashes at the end of lines, replace the space before the em dash with a nonbreaking space by typing Ctrl+Space (Ctrl+5). You can also use a nonbreaking space to glue together terms such as Mac OS so they don't split at the end of a line. Make another pass through your document to look at line endings. Look for bizarre hyphenation, for example, if you did allow QuarkXPress to **Break Capitalized Words**, you still might not want to hyphenate last names such as "An-ton."

Adjusting Kerning

Glance at all the headlines in the document, looking for poor spacing within words. For example, in the sports section of the Denver papers, you see the abbreviation for the Colorado Avalanche hockey team almost every day in headlines like "AVs win!" The capital "AV" pair, notorious for poor spacing, can need a little kerning. Place the text insertion bar between the two characters and use keyboard commands to kern characters in: ⌘+Option+Shift+{ (Ctrl+Alt+Shift+{). On Mac OS, if a headline looks awkward due to ligatures, increase the **Break Above** point size in the **Character** tab of Document Preferences.

If you see recurring problems in your text that can be solved by editing style sheets, kerning and tracking tables, H&Js, and hyphenation exceptions, make these changes to the original template. Ideally, a well-structured template requires little fine-tuning within a document.

SEE ALSO

➤ *To change the **Break Above** value for ligatures in preferences, see page* 57

Setting Type with Style Sheets and Tags

Create and edit paragraph style sheets

Create and edit character style sheets

Delete style sheets

Apply style sheets to text

Plan and name style sheets for maximum efficiency

Once you're happy with all your typographic specifications, you can start applying them automatically. Nobody intends for you to sit there highlighting text and manually choosing options from the Attributes dialog boxes. You need to create *style sheets*, which can be applied with the click of a button and edited to make global formatting changes.

Planning Style Sheets

The best way to create style sheets is to format a bunch of sample text manually first. Set up your headlines, bylines, subheads, lead paragraphs, body paragraphs, bulleted lists, pull quotes, and so on. Remember to create and specify all the *H&Js* and colors you want to use in the text. Try to anticipate the need for tabs and set those up, too. When you're happy with the formatted sample text, you can create style sheets directly from it.

Next, take a good look at the text and plan your style sheets. It might even be worthwhile to print out the sample text and mark it up, indicating all the style sheets you'll need and how you'll set them up.

To start, identify all the different formats and how they differ from each other. Is the only difference between your lead paragraph and your body paragraphs a drop cap in the lead and a first line indent in the body? If so, you can use one style sheet as the basis for another. (When you edit a style sheet used as the basis for other style sheets, those edits ricochet through all the other style sheets.)

Then look for style sheets that almost always follow each other. For example, a body paragraph probably always follows the lead paragraph and the byline might always follow the headline. If you type text into QuarkXPress, you can set up a "next style" for style sheets; when you press the Return (Enter) key, a new style sheet kicks in automatically. (Don't get too excited though—**Next Style** only works when you type in QuarkXPress. It doesn't automatically format imported text.)

Look for character style sheet opportunities such as decorative *drop caps*, *dingbats* used for bullets, and numbers in lists. These *character style sheets* will be used as local formatting in addition to *paragraph style sheets*. However, you can also create character style sheets that are embedded in paragraph style sheets. If all your lead paragraphs, body paragraphs, and bulleted lists are in the same font, size, type style, and color, you can create one character style sheet that reflects those formats. When you embed the character style sheet in paragraph style sheets and then edit the character style sheet, all the paragraph style sheets update automatically.

Once you identify all the style sheets you need, establish naming conventions for your style sheets. Some users begin style names with numbers so they'll show up in a logical order; others include the name of the master page to which the style belongs. Whatever conventions you use, the idea is to make applying style sheets as efficient as possible for you.

Finally, after you establish naming conventions for the style sheets, you can plan keyboard commands for applying them. In general, you want to use modifier keys in combination with the numbers on the keypad and the function keys across the top of the keyboard. You can use the keypad keys without modifier keys for applying style sheets, but don't do it. The last thing you want to do is have users think they're typing in a phone number on the keypad and find out that instead they changed the style sheet seven times.

Finally, you're ready to create style sheets.

SEE ALSO

➤ *To create hyphenation and justification settings (H&Js), see page 268*

➤ *To define colors, see page 425*

➤ *To set tab stops, see page 256*

Using the Style Sheets Dialog Box

When you first select **Style Sheets** from the **Edit** menu, the Style Sheets list dialog box displays. This dialog box allows you to edit the list of style sheets associated with the current document, whose name appears in the title of the dialog box. If no documents are open, the name of the dialog box changes to Default Style Sheets. The default list of style sheets is automatically included in all new documents. If this dialog box looks familiar, it's because it looks just like the front end dialog box for creating and editing colors, *H&Js*, *list* definitions, *Dashes & Stripes*, and *print styles*. For the most part, these dialog boxes all look and work alike.

SEE ALSO

➤ *To define and edit colors, see page 431*

➤ *To create and edit hyphenation and justification settings (H&Js), see page 268*

➤ *To create lists for generating tables of contents, see page 593*

➤ *To create and edit Dashes & Stripes frame styles, see page 120*

➤ *To create and edit print styles, see page 515*

The Show Menu

The **Show** pop-up menu at the top enables you to control which style sheets display in the list (see Figure 11.1). Since the list of style sheets is alphabetical, paragraph and character style sheets appear mixed in the list. Sometimes it's easier to see what you're working with when you display only character or only paragraph style sheets. The **Style Sheets Not Used** menu choice is handy for "cleaning out a document." You can see which style sheets are not in use and delete them all.

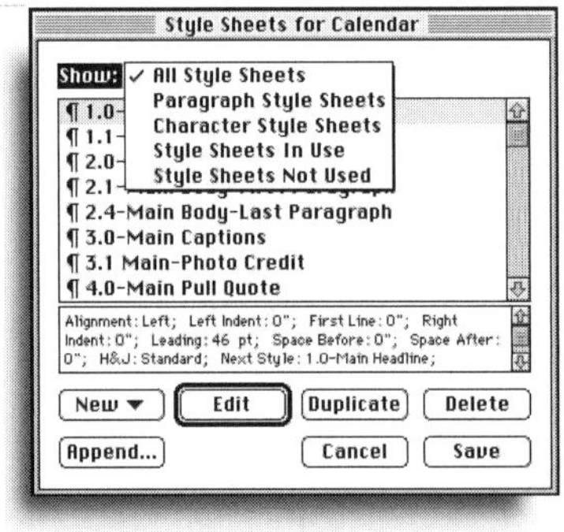

FIGURE 11.1

The Style Sheets dialog box gives you the option of viewing various groups of style sheets.

The List

The scroll list below the **Show** menu allows you to select a style sheet for editing, or for viewing its characteristics in the field below. The style sheet definition shown in the field is handy for refreshing your memory about a style sheet without going all the way into the Edit Style Sheet dialog box. You can multiple-select style sheets in this list by ⌘+clicking (Ctrl+clicking) to select noncontiguous styles or Shift+clicking to select a range of styles. However, the only thing you can do to multiple-selected style sheets is delete them.

The Buttons

The buttons in the lower portion of the Style Sheets dialog box do pretty much what they say, with a few anomalies.

New

Unlike any interface you've likely seen, the **New** button is really a little menu. Click and hold to display the ¶ **Paragraph** or **A Character** options. Select one to open the Edit Paragraph Style Sheet dialog box or the Edit Character Style Sheet dialog box. Lucky for Mac OS users, they can get around this by just clicking the **New** button.

Edit

Edit opens the Edit Paragraph Style Sheet or Edit Character Style Sheet dialog box for the style sheet selected in the list. Although most dialog boxes link the **OK** or **Save** button to the Return (Enter) key, in this case it's linked to the **Edit** button.

Duplicate

Duplicate is straightforward—it creates a copy of the selected style sheet. The Edit Paragraph/Character Style Sheet dialog box opens right up with the copied style sheet waiting to be edited.

Delete

Delete seems simple, but it's not. Before it deletes the selected style sheets, it looks through the document to see if they're used anywhere. And not just in text; if they're used as the basis for other style sheets, they're considered to be "used" in the document. If a style sheet is not in use, it gets quietly deleted. If a style sheet is in use, a dialog box gives you the option to replace it with another style sheet. The replacement style sheet you choose will be applied to text and/or used as the basis for other style sheets.

Normal and 3.x Style Sheets

While checking out the Style Sheets dialog box, you no doubt noticed the Normal paragraph style sheet and Normal character style sheet. These are the two default style sheets included with QuarkXPress, and they can't be deleted. The Normal paragraph style sheet is used when you start typing in a new text box or text path (unless you choose another style sheet before you start typing). The Normal character style sheet is—and must remain— embedded in the Normal character style sheet. If you intend to use the Normal paragraph style sheet, you should edit it to reflect your most commonly used paragraph attributes. You can edit the Normal character style sheet separately or click **Edit** inside the Normal paragraph style sheet to edit it. Either way, the Normal character style sheet specifies the character attributes for the Normal paragraph style sheet.

The fact is, you should format text with logically named style sheets that relate to the template and the content. Because you can't rename Normal, you're leaving people guessing about what text to apply it to. The best use of Normal is exactly what it does; it lets you start typing with some sort of formatting. Edit it to be something easy for you to read onscreen when entering rough text, but always replace Normal with the appropriate style sheet.

If you open a QuarkXPress 3.x document, all the paragraph style sheets come along and are added to the Normal paragraph style sheet and the Normal character style sheet in the list. Crack open one of your paragraph style sheets and notice the Character Attributes area. The **Style** menu says Default, which means that the character attributes belong specifically to this paragraph style sheet. When you click **Edit**, all you're doing is editing those character attributes (just like clicking the Character button in 3.x).

To update your style sheets to QuarkXPress 4, you should look through your document for tedious character formatting and create character style sheets. If you need the added flexibility of embedding character style sheets in paragraph style sheets, identify similar character attributes in paragraphs. Then, create that character style sheet and embed it in the appropriate paragraph style sheets. Because designers tend to use a limited number of fonts in a document, you might end up embedding three character style sheets in 20 paragraph style sheets. For example, the paragraph style sheets in a newsletter template for First Body, Body, First Bullet, Bullet, Last Bullet, and Last Paragraph probably might have different paragraph, but share the same character style sheets.

Creating Style Sheets

With careful planning behind you, creating the actual style sheets is easy. First make sure all the ingredients are ready by creating all the colors, H&Js, and Dashes & Stripes that you want to specify in style sheets. If you plan to embed character style sheets in paragraph style sheets, create your character style sheets first. And if you want to use some style sheets as the basis for others, obviously you'll need to create the "basis" style sheets first. Before jumping into the Style Sheets dialog box, you can "prespecify" the text formatting for the style sheet. All you do is highlight text for a character style sheet or click in a paragraph for a paragraph style sheet. Then go ahead and start.

SEE ALSO
➤ *To format text, see page 238*

Creating a Paragraph Style Sheet

To create a new paragraph style sheet:

1. Select **Style Sheets** from the **Edit** menu.

2. Click the **New** button to see the little menu that says ¶ **Paragraph** and **A Character**. Select ¶ **Paragraph** to open the Edit Paragraph Style Sheet dialog box (see Figure 11.2). (On Mac OS, bypass all this by just clicking **New**. On Windows, stick to the goofy button/menu.)

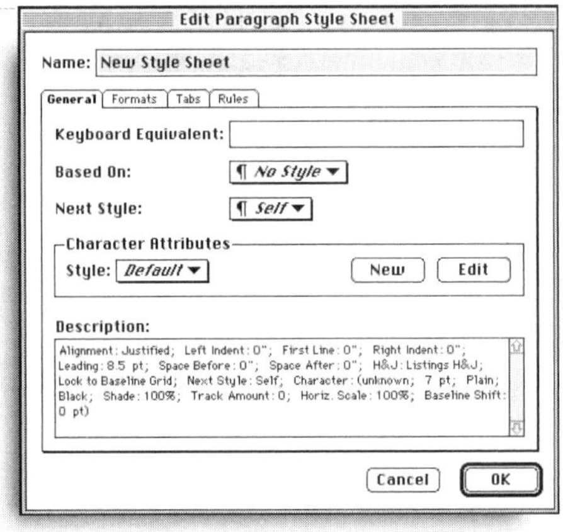

FIGURE 11.2

The Edit Paragraph Style Sheet dialog box has **Formats**, **Tabs**, and **Rules** tabs like the Paragraph Attributes dialog box.

3. Enter a name in the **Name** field.

4. To specify a keyboard command, click in the **Keyboard Equivalent** field. Then press the modifier keys; they'll be automatically spelled out in the field.

5. To base the paragraph style sheet on another paragraph style sheet, select one from the **Based On** menu. Remember that any changes to that paragraph style sheet affects this paragraph style sheet. For style sheets that aren't based on any other styles, leave the setting at **Self**.

6. To specify a paragraph style sheet for text that typically follows text in this paragraph style sheet, select one from the **Next Style** menu. When you type and press the Return (Enter) key, the **Next Style** automatically kicks in.

7. There are three options for specifying the character attributes of text in this paragraph style sheet: specifying character attributes specifically for this style sheet, embedding an existing character style sheet in it, or creating a new character style sheet to embed in it.

- The **Character Attributes** area provides a **Style** pop-up menu that lists a **Default** option and all your character style sheets. When you select **Default**, the character attributes belong exclusively to this paragraph style sheet. If text is highlighted, those attributes are preselected. Click **Edit** to change those attributes.

- To embed an existing character style sheet, select it from the **Style** menu.

- To create a new character style sheet to embed, click **New**. Use the **Formats**, **Tabs**, and **Rules** tabs (the same ones you're familiar with from the Paragraph Attributes dialog box) to specify paragraph attributes for the text. If you have text highlighted, those attributes are preselected.

8. When the style sheet is complete, click **OK**. Click **Save** to get back to the document, or continue creating new style sheets and click **Save** when they are complete.

Creating a Character Style Sheet

To create a new character style sheet:

1. Select **Style Sheets** from the **Edit** menu.

2. Click the **New** button to see the little menu that says ¶ **Paragraph** and **A Character**. Select **A Character** (see Figure 11.3).

3. Enter a name in the **Name** field.

4. To specify a keyboard command, click in the **Keyboard Equivalent** field. Then press the modifier keys; they'll be automatically spelled out in the field.

Be careful!

If you select a character style sheet and then click **Edit**, you're making a global edit to the character style sheet.

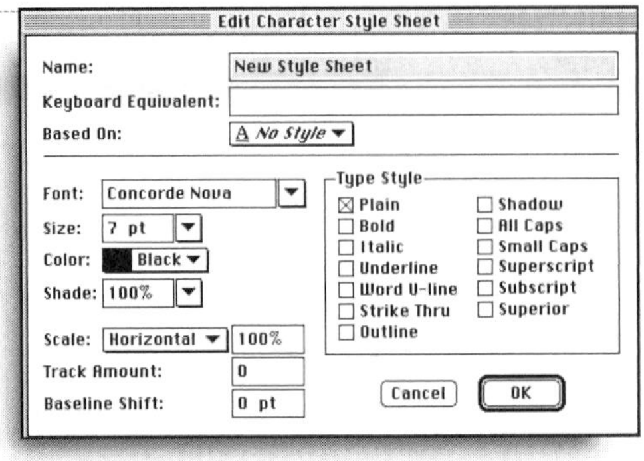

FIGURE 11.3

The Edit Character Style Sheet dialog box contains controls just like the ones in the Character Attributes dialog box.

5. To base the character style sheet on another character style sheet, select one from the **Based On** menu. Remember that any changes to that character style sheet affect this character style sheet. For style sheets that aren't based on any other styles, leave the setting at **Self**.

6. To create a character style sheet from scratch, use the **Character Attributes** controls shown in the dialog box to set up the style sheet. If text is highlighted, its attributes are preselected.

7. Click **OK**. Click **Save** to get back to the document, or continue creating new style sheets and click **Save** when they're finished.

Using the Style Sheets Palette

Speeding up style sheet creation

Use Shift+F11 to open the Style Sheets dialog box to help speed things up. Or Ctrl+click (right-click) in the Style Sheets palette to display a context-sensitive menu offering the New command. Make sure the Style Sheets palette is open (F11) and positioned so you can see it while the Style Sheets dialog box is open. Using the Style Sheets palette, you can see which style sheets you still need to create and which keyboard commands you've already assigned.

The Style Sheets palette is the quickest method for applying style sheets, so you'll probably have it open most of the time. To open it, select **Show Style Sheets** from the **View** menu or press F11 (see Figure 11.4). You can resize the palette by dragging the resize box in the lower right corner. And you can drag the divider bar between the paragraph style sheets list (at the top) and the character style sheets list (at the bottom). To get the palette out of your way, windowshade it, resize it, or close it by pressing F11 again or selecting **Hide Style Sheets** from the **View** menu.

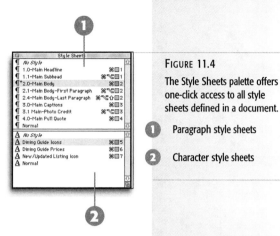

You can do four things with the Style Sheets palette:

- See which style sheets are applied
- Apply paragraph style sheets.
- Apply character style sheets.
- Edit the list of style sheets.

Feedback: Which Style Sheet Is Applied

Whenever it can, the Style Sheets palette tells you which style sheets are currently applied. To get feedback from the Style Sheets palette, do the following:

- To see the paragraph style sheet applied to a paragraph, click in it. The current paragraph style sheet is highlighted (see Figure 11.5).

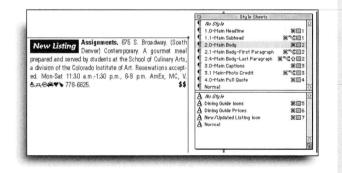

FIGURE 11.5
The Style Sheets palette highlights the paragraph style sheet applied to selected text.

- To see the character style sheet applied to a paragraph, click in it. If no character style sheet is embedded in the paragraph style sheet, and no character style sheet is applied at the text insertion point, nothing is highlighted in the character style sheet list. If a character style sheet is embedded or applied at the text insertion point, that character sheet is highlighted (see Figure 11.6).

FIGURE 11.6

The Style Sheets palette highlights any character style sheets applied to selected text, in addition to the paragraph style sheet.

1 Highlighted text

2 Paragraph style sheet

3 Character style sheet

- To see the character sheet applied to a word, double-click to highlight the word. The character style sheet is highlighted. If more than one character style sheet is applied, nothing is highlighted in the character style sheet list.

- To see the style sheets applied at the text insertion point, click in text and see what's highlighted in the paragraph style sheet and character style sheet lists.

The Style Sheets palette cannot highlight multiple styles. If you highlight text with multiple paragraph and character style sheets applied, nothing is highlighted in the palette.

Editing the Style Sheets List

When you're in the Style Sheets palette, ⌘+clicking (Ctrl+clicking) on a style sheet name opens the Style Sheets dialog box with that style sheet highlighted. Press Return to jump into Edit Style Sheet from there. Ctrl+click (right-click) a style sheet name to

Identifying keypad keys

Most style sheets are set up with a combination of modifier keys and numbers on the keypad. On Mac OS, keypad keys are indicated by a little square key icon in the Style Sheets palette. On Windows, keypad keys have a "KP" in front of the number.

display a menu that allows you to edit, duplicate, or delete that style sheet, or create a new style sheet (see Figure 11.7). Choosing **Duplicate** or **New** takes you right into the appropriate Edit Paragraph Style Sheet or Edit Character Style Sheet dialog box.

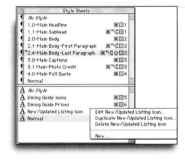

FIGURE 11.7

Ctrl+clicking (right-clicking) the Style Sheets palette displays a mini-menu for creating, editing, duplicating, and deleting style sheets.

Make your changes and click **OK**, then **Save**. Any text formatted with the changed style will be updated to match the new specifications, as long as you haven't overridden the changed attributes with local formatting.

Applying Style Sheets

To apply a style sheet, first indicate what you're applying it to. When it comes to paragraph style sheets, you don't need to be that careful—just click in a paragraph and it's selected. If you want to select a range of paragraphs, highlight at least a portion of all the paragraphs—there's no need to highlight from the first character of the first paragraph to the last character of the last paragraph. Character style sheets are another story. Select only the characters you want to apply the character style sheet to, considering whether to include spaces and punctuation following characters.

Once you indicate the paragraphs or characters, you have four options for selecting a style sheet.

SEE ALSO
➤ *To select text, see page 206*

The Style Menu

To use this painstakingly slow method, select an option from the **Paragraph Style Sheet** submenu or the **Character Style Sheet** submenu of the **Style** menu.

The Style Sheets Palette

If you're formatting more than one paragraph, get this palette open and keep it handy. (To open it, select **Show Style Sheets** from the **View** menu or press F11. You'll probably want to resize it so more paragraph style sheets and fewer character style sheets are showing.) Then, all you do is click the name of the paragraph style sheet or character style sheet you want to apply.

Keyboard Commands

When you create style sheets, you have the option to assign a keyboard equivalent. If you were smart when you made them, the most-used style sheets have the least demanding keyboard commands (fewer modifier keys requiring less contortion). And if your style sheets are numbered to indicate the hierarchy (1 Headline, 2 First Paragraph Text, and so on), maybe you incorporated those numbers into the keyboard commands (⌘+1 for Headline, ⌘+2 for First Paragraph, and so on). The keyboard commands appear right next to the style sheet names in the Style Sheets palette and the **Style Sheet** submenus. Press the command to apply the appropriate style sheet.

"Grabbing" a Paragraph Style Sheet

There's one more way to apply a paragraph style sheet, but it's fairly uncommon. What you do is "grab" the paragraph style sheet from another paragraph. Click in the paragraph you want to change (the target), and then Option+Shift+click (Alt+Shift+click) on a paragraph formatted with the desired paragraph style sheet (the source). When you do this, local overrides to paragraph attributes in the source text come along with the paragraph style sheet. However, local overrides to character attributes do not. (For example, if you changed the tabs in the source text from those specified in the style sheet, the new tabs will be applied to the target text. If you changed the color of the source text, the new color will not be applied to the target text.)

What Is No Style?

Although No Style is listed with other style sheets, it's actually the antistyle sheet. You apply it to text when you want it to completely lose its current formatting when you apply a style sheet. When you initially apply No Style to text, the text retains the paragraph formatting and character formatting applied to it, whether locally or via a style sheet. It's when you apply another style sheet that you can tell No Style was applied. All the current formatting is lost and the style sheet attributes are strictly applied.

Many people call this a "clean apply" and use it to clean up formatting mistakes made by other users. For example, if you can tell that someone has gone nuts changing kerning and tracking in a line, plus they've applied all kinds of inappropriate type styles to a paragraph, you might apply No Style and then reapply the paragraph style sheet.

"Clean-applying" is so common that it has a shortcut. All you do is click in the paragraph or select a range of paragraphs, then Option+click (Alt+click) the style sheet name in the Style Sheets palette. Unfortunately, there's no way to clean apply an instance of a style sheet using keyboard commands or menus. If a whole document is messed up beyond belief, select all the text, click No Style, and reapply all the style sheets.

The Mechanics of Applying Style Sheets

You might think that applying a style sheet will result in perfectly formatted text. Not so. QuarkXPress carefully maintains any manual formatting you did to the text before you applied the style sheet. That is, unless you tell it not to by first applying No

Style to the text. It takes a little playing around to figure out what's going on.

Say your text is in the default Normal paragraph style sheet, and you highlight all the text and change it to 14-point Stone Serif so you can see it easier onscreen. Then you try to apply the nice Body Text paragraph style sheet provided with the template. All the attributes of Normal that you didn't touch are replaced by Body Text, but the attributes you did touch are not. So your text is still in 14-point Stone Serif. You need to clean-apply in this case. However, say you're typing along in the default Normal style sheet, formatting a few words here and there with bold and italics as appropriate. Then, when you apply the Body Text paragraph style sheet, your bold and italics are maintained. In this case, that's probably what you wanted.

Be careful about formatting text too heavily before applying style sheets. You might get in a situation where your only choice is to clean-apply the style sheet, and you'll lose all the formatting you put in on purpose.

Changing Your Mind

What's that plus sign?

The plus sign that sometimes displays to the left of style sheet names in the Style Sheets palette indicates local formatting. When you click the text insertion bar in text, the Style Sheets palette highlights the paragraph style sheet applied to that text. If the text at the location of the text insertion bar contains any formatting not specified in the style sheet, the plus sign appears. The plus sign means that additional character attributes, paragraph attributes, and/or character style sheets are applied at that point.

What happens when you hate your text formatting? Even if your feelings about it are not as passionate as "hate," you'll need to change text formatting fairly often. You have several options for making global changes and special-case changes.

To make a global change, you can edit paragraph and character style sheets. If you use **Based On**, start by changing that style sheet. If you use embedded character style sheets, sometimes you can just change one of those. When you edit a style sheet, text is automatically reformatted according to the new specifications. Another way to make a global change is to delete a style sheet and replace it with another.

To make changes here and there, you can simply select text and apply a different style sheet. Or you can selectively find and change instances of the style sheet. (If you want to **Change All** in **Find/Change**, you might as well delete and replace the style sheet.) You can find/change text attributes also, applying different character attributes or a different style sheet. As a last resort, change paragraph and character attributes manually.

Adding Graphics

Illustrating with Boxes and Lines

Understand illustration terminology

Create Bézier objects

Edit Bézier points and segments

Combine simple shapes to build complex objects

Create repeating (tiled) designs

Create radially symmetrical designs

Although some die-hard users have been illustrating in QuarkXPress for years, they've struggled thus far with an application not really created for that purpose. With version 4, all this has changed. Not only has Quark added illustration tools to QuarkXPress, but it has done so on a sophisticated level that will make professional illustrators quite at home.

So if you don't yet own an illustration package but were planning to buy one, STOP! Everything you need is in QuarkXPress 4, not to mention ease-of-use aplenty.

Illustration Terminology

Illustration tools represent an entire branch of graphic arts by themselves. So some of the terminology used in this chapter might seem unfamiliar unless you read this section. Even if you're already familiar with Bézier jargon, pay special attention to the new terms offered here—Quark has made its own unique contribution to this lumpy pool of esoteri-speak.

- "Illustration" refers to a scalable page element or group of elements serving a pictorial or artistic purpose without photorealism. You don't use illustration tools to draw a rectangle or to modify a picture of Mom. You use them to draw filigrees, logos, clip art, custom type, diagrams of carburetors, and so on (see Figure 12.1).

FIGURE 12.1

Illustration tools let you draw smooth, scalable pictures as simple as this, or as complex as a diagram of a six-valve car engine.

- Vector-based and scalable describe objects that can be resized without bitmapping. Illustrations are vector-based, as are fonts. Graphics created using painting or photo-editing programs are just the opposite.

- *Bézier* technology, named after its inventor, is a way of defining vector curves in software. It relies on two control points that extend from each vertex. In QuarkXPress, these control points are called curve handles, and the vertices are called points.

- *Points* (often called anchor points or vertices in other applications) mark the locations where a curve shifts direction in a certain manner (see Figure 12.2).

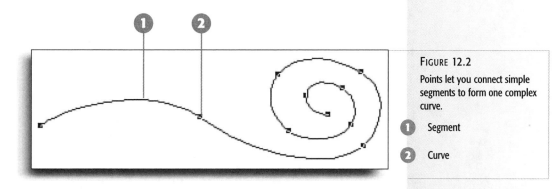

FIGURE 12.2

Points let you connect simple segments to form one complex curve.

❶ Segment

❷ Curve

- *Corner points* are used to create sharp transitions in Bézier curve items. When a point is designated as a corner point, its two curve handles move with total independence, allowing you to break the smoothness of the curve (see Figure 12.3).

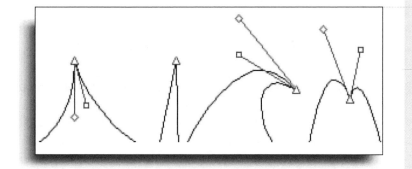

FIGURE 12.3

Corner points create transitions from one curve to the next.

■ *Smooth points* are used to preserve the smoothness of a curve.
When a point is designated as a smooth point, its two curve
handles revolve together around the point to help prevent
an overly sharp juncture (see Figure 12.4).

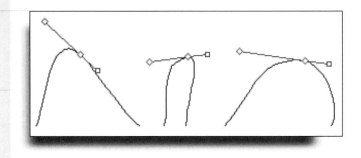

■ *Symmetrical points* are like smooth points that go a step further in preserving the smoothness of a curve. When a point
is designated as a symmetrical point, its two curve handles
revolve together around the point, and they remain equidistant from the point as well (see Figure 12.5). You will seldom use this type of point, because smooth points almost
always do the job just as well.

FIGURE 12.5

Symmetrical points are
smooth points whose curve
handles are symmetrical.

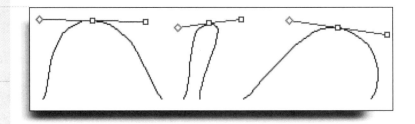

■ *Curve handles* (often called control points or direction points
in other applications) extend from points and become visible
when one or more points are selected. Each point owns
two curve handles. A curve handle's position in relation
to its point helps determine the shape of a segment (see
Figure 12.6).

FIGURE 12.6
Curve handles–the hallmark of Bézier technology–are the little doodads that stick out from a point whenever a segment or point is selected. Move them and your curve changes shape. (Here, all the points are shown selected.)

1 Curve handles

2 Segment

3 Point

- A *segment* is the part of a line or curve that resides between two adjacent points. Segments combine to form paths.

- *Curved segments* are standard Bézier segments. A segment that has been designated as a curved segment can be "bent" at any time.

- *Straight segments* are segments that cannot be bent. You get straight segments when you click to create new Bézier points without dragging to expose their curve handles. If you drag on a completed straight segment, it remains straight, and it moves with its adjoining points.

- A *path* or contour is one continuous Bézier curve. In QuarkXPress, some items in QuarkXPress—for example, a donut-shaped *picture box*—consist of two or more paths.

- *Line* is the QuarkXPress term for an open path. In other words, its endpoints always remain separate (see Figure 12.7).

FIGURE 12.7
A line is an open path.

- *Box* is the QuarkXPress term for a closed path or collection of closed paths. A box has no starting and ending points, but it does have various points with which you can resize and reshape it (see Figure 12.8). A box can contain pictures, text, a color, or a two-color blend. Its borders can be stroked using a frame.

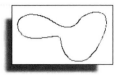

- *Freehand* is a quick-and-dirty method of drawing Bézier shapes. You simply drag the mouse according to your envisioned shape, and QuarkXPress plots the Bézier points and curve handles for you. In contrast, the traditional Bézier tools in QuarkXPress 4 (the tools with a paintbrush) let you draw a shape point by point for the highest possible accuracy. But if you're more interested in completing a shape as quickly as possible, the Freehand tools (☒ ☒ ☒ ☒) are a better choice.

Basic Bézier Editing

Even if you shun the traditional Bézier tools, you should learn how to edit all the merged shapes and freehand shapes you'll be creating. By the way, plenty of Quark's Bézier jargon is used in this section, so if you need to review the terminology at the beginning of this chapter, please do so!

First things first: After you complete an item that you want to reshape, choose **Edit** from the **Item** menu and make sure that the **Shape** option is checked. If it's checked, you'll see Bézier points instead of bounding box handles on your item.

You'll also need to select either the Item tool ⊕ or the Content tool ☜ . All Bézier editing in QuarkXPress is performed with one of these tools. For Bézier editing, it doesn't really matter which of the two you choose, so feel free to pick at random.

Bending Segments

The easiest way to edit Bézier curves in QuarkXPress is by simply clicking and dragging directly on segments to bend them. Unlike most illustration programs, QuarkXPress actually senses which part of a segment you drag, and in which direction you drag it. This lets you intuitively bend a segment just as if it were a piece of wire.

If you want a more accurate method of bending, click and drag curve handles to accomplish the same task. This might not seem quite as intuitive at first, but the method does have its rewards, especially when you add the modifier keys described later in this section.

There are some things to be aware of when bending segments:

- A segment is active whenever its two points are active. If you select all the points in your shape, you effectively select all the segments as well. This can be useful if you want to quickly change all straight segments to curved segments or vice versa.

- You can't bend a segment in its "straight" state. A straight segment is indicated by a depressed button in the Measurements palette when the segment is selected. If you want to change it to a curved segment, press the _ button while the segment is selected.

- Bending one segment might cause connected segments to bend as well, preventing you from creating a sharp transition in the path. This happens when the points attached to your segment are in a smooth or symmetrical state (which brings us to the next topic…).

Determining the State of a Bézier Point

To determine whether a Bézier point is in its corner, smooth, or symmetrical state, first select the point in question by clicking on it. On color monitors, the point turns blue. If the point serves as a juncture for two curved segments, its curve handles display as well. Most important, when a point is selected, its appearance tells you about its state:

- A blue diamond indicates a smooth point. If you drag a curve handle connected to a smooth point, its partner curve handle also moves, thereby preserving a smooth transition between segments.

- A blue triangle indicates a corner point. If you drag a curve handle connected to a corner point, it moves with total independence, allowing you to create a sharp transition between segments.

- A blue rectangle indicates a symmetrical point. The automatic features of QuarkXPress will never generate a symmetrical point, so don't count on seeing one unless you create it yourself. When a point is designated as a symmetrical point, its two curve handles revolve together around the point, and they remain equidistant from the point as well. Because smooth points offer similar benefits, you will seldom, if ever, use symmetrical points.

You can also tell the state of a selected point by looking at the Measurements palette, which you'll read about next.

Using the Measurements Palette in Bézier Editing

Measurements palette controls will aid you in editing Bézier items when one or more points or segments are selected. To familiarize yourself with the palette, make sure that Tool Tips are turned on, and then point at each field or icon.

-  makes the active points symmetrical.
-  makes the active points smooth.
-  makes the active points a corner.
-  makes the active segments straight.
-  makes the active segments curved.
- The **XP** field indicates the horizontal page position of the active point.
- The **YP** field indicates the vertical page position of the active point.
- The two rotation fields in the upper-right portion of the Measurements palette indicate the angles (in degrees) of the curve handles in relation to the active point.
- The field next to the diamond icon indicates the distance of the diamond-symbol curve handle from the active point. The field next to the square icon indicates the distance of the square-symbol curve handle from the active point.

All the preceding values can be edited directly from the palette, so feel free to change them any time while a Bézier point or segment is active.

SEE ALSO

➤ *To turn on Tool Tips, see page 31*

Using Keyboard Commands for Bézier Editing

To become very efficient at Bézier editing, you need to memorize at least a few of the keyboard commands in Table 12.1.

TABLE 12.1 Keyboard commands for Bézier editing

Function	Command
Add a Bézier point	Option+click (Alt+click) a segment
Delete a single Bézier point	Option+click (Alt+click) a point
Delete all active Bézier points	Choose the Item tool and press Delete (Backspace)
Change a smooth point to a corner point or vice versa	Control+drag (Ctrl+Shift+drag) a curve handle
Constrain a curve handle or a point to 45-degree movement	Shift+drag
Edit a Bézier shape or its components while drawing it	Press the ⌘ (Ctrl) key while you edit
Select all points in a single-path item	Double-click a point
Select all points in a multiple-path item	Triple-click a point
Retract curve handles	Control+click (Ctrl+Shift+click) a point
Expose curve handles	Control+drag (Ctrl+Shift+drag) from a point

Illustrating the Traditional Way

The **Merge** commands and Freehand tools offer definite advantages for certain tasks, but if you need real hands-on accuracy and smoothness, there's no substitute for the traditional Bézier tools. These tools work by allowing you to create each Bézier-point one at a time.

Using Traditional Bézier Tools

To create a point while simultaneously exposing its curve handles, drag the mouse, and then move on to do the same for the next point. (You can also create polygons composed of straight lines by simply clicking to create points.)

To complete a shape when using one of the Bézier box tools (⬛ ⬛), click on the start point. To complete a shape when using one of the other two Bézier tools (the line ⬛ or text path ⬛ tools), select a new tool.

Placing Points

Now, before you rely too heavily on the traditional Bézier tools, it might be helpful for you to understand a little Bézier point theory so that you know where to place points and where not to place points. Why? Because if you create too many points, your shape won't look smooth. On the other hand, if you have too few points, you will lack control over your shape.

There are basically four kinds of locations in a Bézier shape that require a point:

- Create a point wherever you envision a sharp transition (see Figure 12.9). As you create a point of this kind, drag the mouse to expose the point's curve handles; then ⌘+Ctrl+drag one of the curve handles to designate the point as a corner before you move on to create the next point. (To accomplish this in Windows, Ctrl+click a point and then press Ctrl+F1.) Also, when positioning curve handles, remember that segments embark from their points in the general direction of their associated curve handles.

FIGURE 12.9
Points delineate sharp transitions in a shape.

- Create points where you envision straight segments—one point at each end of every straight segment (see Figure 12.10). A simple click will suffice to create a point like this.

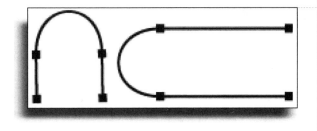

FIGURE 12.10
You need points at both ends of a straight segment.

- Create a point where you envision a curve shifting direction, as in the center of a letter S (see Figure 12.11). Drag the mouse to expose the curve handles when creating these points. Again, the curve handles should point in the direction you want your segments to go.

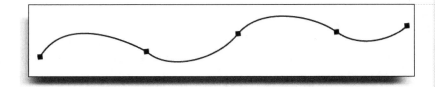

FIGURE 12.11
Create a point where a curve should shift direction.

- Create a point where you envision a curve continuing around beyond what you'd think of as a half-ellipse or half-circle (see Figure 12.12). For example, although an egg shape can be thought of as one continuous curve that never shifts direction, it still requires at least two points—one on each side of the egg. Drag the mouse to expose the curve handles when creating these points.

FIGURE 12.12

Create points on either side of an oval shape.

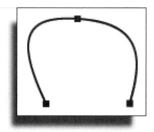

And there you have it—everything you need to know to draw perfectly accurate Béziers using the traditional tools. These methods do take some getting used to, but when you get the hang of them, you'll be thankful you learned.

Illustrating the Quick Way

Some people simply hate drawing with point-by-point Bézier tools, no matter what application they're built into. If you're one of those people, you'll be relieved to know that you can accomplish most illustration tasks in QuarkXPress 4 without ever touching the traditional Bézier tools. Even for those who are experienced with the more technical tools, knowledge of the **Merge** commands and Freehand tools in QuarkXPress cannot be ignored. They are the keys to saving time with illustration tasks of a simpler nature.

Merging Items

The **Merge** submenu under QuarkXPress's **Item** menu contains a set of commands that synthesize a new item based on the combined shapes of whatever items you have selected. Multiple items are replaced with a single item whenever a **Merge** command takes place.

Although the original items might include lines mixed with boxes, all the **Merge** commands produce a single Bézier box with one set of contents as their end result. (The only exception to this rule is the **Join Endpoints** command, which is designed exclusively for use with lines.)

Because the **Merge** commands work with standard-shape rectangles, ovals, and lines, they can be extremely useful when your envisioned box shape must be smooth, but simple. For example, if you wanted a *text box* shaped like a half-circle, it would be unwise to draw it using the Bézier Text Box tool; this tool would provide little assurance of achieving a perfect half circle, and it would also take a long time. Instead, you would perform the **Difference** command on a circle that is halfway covered by a rectangle. You'll take a closer look at the Difference command in the following list of **Merge** commands.

There are seven **Merge** commands in all:

Intersection

The **Intersection** command is like an "overlap finder." It locates any areas that overlap the item in back, retains these areas, and cuts out the rest (see Figure 12.13).

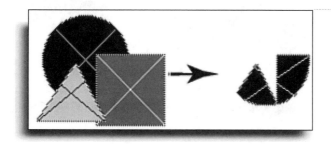

FIGURE 12.13
Intersection keeps overlaps and deletes areas that don't overlap.

Union

Union is arguably the most useful of all the **Merge** commands, although **Difference** is a close runner-up. The **Union** command simply combines all the item shapes into one shape (see Figure

12.14). All overlapped areas and non-overlapped areas are retained. This command is helpful even when the selected items don't overlap. For example, you can create a box made of two closed paths separated in space, but sharing one set of contents.

FIGURE 12.14

Union combines shapes into one larger shape.

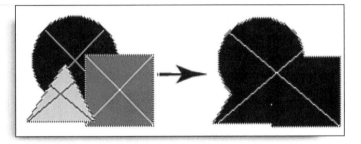

Difference

Difference is your QuarkXPress cookie cutter. It removes all the selected item shapes except for the shape at the back of the stack. Any portions that overlap the backmost shape get cut out. You can imagine the backmost shape as the dough, with the shapes in front of it acting as the cookie cutter. Difference is useful for punching holes in items to create donuts and Swiss cheese, but you will most often use it to "crop" or "erase" parts of a Bézier item (see Figure 12.15).

FIGURE 12.15

Difference restricts shapes to an area defined by the back-most object.

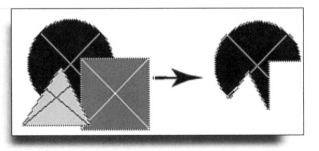

Reverse Difference

You won't use **Reverse Difference** very often, but it can occasionally be helpful when you need to "cookie cut" two or more items simultaneously. It works the same as Difference, with the shape at the back acting as your cookie cutter again, except what's left is everything outside that shape (see Figure 12.16).

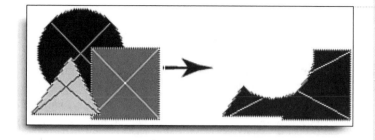

FIGURE 12.16
Reverse Difference deletes everything inside the area of the backmost object.

Exclusive Or and Combine

Exclusive Or and **Combine** are similar. Both commands retain all selected item shapes, but they cut out any areas that overlap. These commands are useful when you want to create a checkerboard effect, in which a shape reverses color at the point where it begins overlapping another shape (see Figure 12.17).

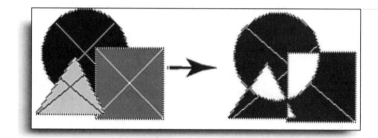

FIGURE 12.17
Exclusive Or and **Combine** remove overlaps.

The differences between **Exclusive Or** and **Combine** become apparent only when you reshape. If segments from one item cross over segments from another item in your original selection, **Exclusive Or** adds two Bézier points at each "crossroad." In contrast, the **Combine** command adds no such points—all existing points and paths are preserved as-is. Despite this, the result for both commands looks pretty similar at first.

Use **Exclusive Or** if you anticipate needing corner points where two items overlap (for example, where a circle meets a square). Use Combine if you anticipate needing to manipulate existing curves, even after they're merged with other shapes (for example, to edit the curve of a circle even if it's now part of a square). Don't worry about the choice you make though—you can always add, delete, and change points after performing the **Merge** command.

Join Endpoints

Join Endpoints is designed exclusively for use with Bézier lines. If you have two Bézier lines and you want to fuse them, use this command. Just make sure that an endpoint from one active line overlaps (or falls within the snap distance of) an endpoint from the other active line. **Join Endpoints** creates a single Bézier corner point to replace the two overlapping endpoints, and the result is a single Bézier line (see Figure 12.18). **Join Endpoints** produces its most accurate results when you start by snapping both endpoints to a horizontal and vertical *guide* pair. This technique ensures that the points are perfectly overlapped, and QuarkXPress is not forced to interpolate between their positions.

FIGURE 12.18
Join Endpoints creates one line from two.

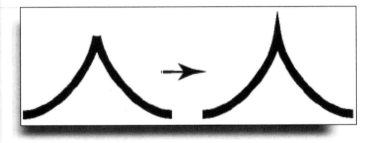

SEE ALSO

➤ *To draw text boxes, see page 103*

➤ *To draw picture boxes, see page 103*

Splitting Items

The **Split** commands in the **Item** menu are just the opposite of the **Merge** commands. Rather than creating one item from several, they create several items from one. The **Split** commands are available in two instances: (1) when the active item is a Bézier box consisting of two or more closed paths and (2) when the active item is a box with a border that "crosses over itself" like a figure eight.

How can **Split** commands help you illustrate? Well, by themselves, the **Split** commands won't help you illustrate at all. But if used with the **Merge** commands and **Text to Box**, the **Split** commands are immensely helpful for various tasks, which the following text describes.

There are two **Split** commands: **Outside Paths** and **All Paths**.

Outside Paths

Outside Paths is the first of the two Split commands. It creates a separate box for every path within the original box, but it does not do so for paths enclosed by other paths. In other words, it preserves "donut holes."

The **Outside Paths** command is especially useful after you've performed a **Text to Box** command. The Text to Box command creates a single, multiple-path Bézier box to collectively represent all the converted characters. To fill each character with a separate picture, make each character a separate box. The **Outside Paths** command can accomplish this job instantly, and it preserves the "donut holes" in your d's, o's, a's, and so on (see Figure 12.19).

FIGURE 12.19
Outside Paths is useful after you've performed a **Text to Box** command.

All Paths

The second **Split** command is **All Paths. All Paths** creates a separate box for every path within the original box, bar none (see Figure 12.20). Even "donut holes" are transformed into separate boxes. The **All Paths** command can sometimes be useful for "undoing" an earlier **Difference** command or an **Exclusive Or** command.

Finally, there are instances in which both **Split** commands act as a boon—especially when they are combined with the **Difference** command. Take a look at the following example.

FIGURE 12.20

All Paths creates as many separate boxes as possible.

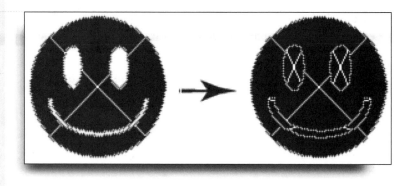

You want to draw a multicolored basketball. Each rubber panel in the basketball must have a different color applied. So the basketball must be composed of several boxes, but they must all fit together perfectly to form a circle. Is this possible? Yes—you just need to combine a few steps leading up to a **Split** command.

To draw a circle containing several independent boxes:

1. Draw a circular box using the Oval Picture Box tool ⊗ , and crisscross it with hairlines using the Bézier Line tool ✒ (see Figure 12.21).

FIGURE 12.21

Straight and Bézier lines overlap this circular box.

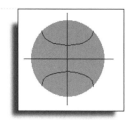

2. Marquee-select all the items, and choose **Merge** from the **Item** menu, then **Difference** from the submenu. The result is a single circular box made of multiple paths (see Figure 12.22).

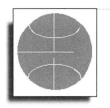

FIGURE 12.22
The **Difference** command converts the box and lines to one box.

3. Choose **Split** from the **Item** menu, then **All Paths** (or **Outside Paths**—it doesn't matter here) from the submenu. Now the basketball is composed of separate boxes, each of which can be filled with its own unique color or contents (see Figure 12.23). If you find the narrow white space between panels annoying, you can eliminate it by placing a colored circle behind the basketball, or by applying frames to outset the panels. (By the way, to outset a shape using a frame, you need to make sure that your framing preference is set to **Outside**.)

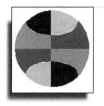

FIGURE 12.23
After you split all paths, the box breaks into several individual boxes.

Using steps very similar to those just described, the pattern in Figure 12.24 was drawn—all entirely within QuarkXPress. Each curved diamond shape is a separate QuarkXPress picture box.

SEE ALSO
➤ *To draw text boxes, see page 103*
➤ *To draw picture boxes, see page 103*

Drawing Freehand

The Freehand tools in QuarkXPress represent yet another quick way to create a Bézier item. You won't need much help learning to use these tools—they're designed to be as brainless as possible.

FIGURE 12.24

Creating this illustration with traditional drawing tools would take days; with **Merge** and **Split** commands, the time was condensed to several hours.

To use a Freehand tool, you merely select it in the Tool palette and then drag your mouse as though it were a pencil. (Option+click [Alt+click] to select the tool in the Tool palette if you want to create multiple shapes rapidly! This temporarily prevents QuarkXPress from switching back to Item-tool or Content-tool mode as it usually would.)

QuarkXPress displays your shape in progress as you drag. Keep the mouse button held down until you're ready to call the item complete, and then let go. Instantly, QuarkXPress builds a Bézier item based on your "mouse tracks." It plots all the points and curve handles for you.

All four Freehand tools are implemented in the same way. The only differences are in the type of item they create. To see the names of the tools, make sure that **Tool Tips** is turned on, and point at each tool:

- The Freehand Text Box tool 🄰 creates a Bézier text box.
- The Freehand Picture Box tool ⊗ creates a Bézier picture box.

- The Freehand Line tool ![icon] creates a Bézier line.
- The Freehand Text-Path tool ![icon] creates a Bézier text path.

SEE ALSO

➤ *To turn on Tool Tips, see page 31*

Adding Symmetry

Have you ever seen a symmetrical illustration like the row of horse heads shown in Figure 12.25 and asked yourself, "How did they do that?" Basically, symmetry is a simple matter of relying on the **Duplicate** command, some snapping to guides, the **Merge** commands, and some flipping. You've already read about most of these concepts in other parts of this book.

FIGURE 12.25
Achieving symmetry basically involves the **Duplicate** command, some snapping to guides, the **Merge** commands, and some occasional flipping.

By the way, if you're planning to draw a symmetrical design in QuarkXPress, I recommend that you work mainly with boxes and not lines. Boxes offer a far greater number of choices for merging, splitting, color, and alignment. They are also more intuitive. Besides, if you want to change your box into a line at the end of the process, all you have to do is select the box and choose **Shape** from the **Item** menu and then the straight line icon. (You can also change a Bézier line into a box by pressing the Option [Alt] key while choosing **Shape** from the **Item** menu and then the squiggly line icon.)

There's really only one thing that makes adding symmetry semi-complicated: if the repeating shape in your design must flow seamlessly into its duplicate, you'll have to make sure that this shape can be tiled smoothly.

SEE ALSO

➤ *To duplicate an object, see page 103*

➤ *To create ruler guides, see page 103*

➤ *To draw text boxes, see page 31*

➤ *To draw picture boxes, see page 31*

Preparing Tiles

Take a look again at the row of horse heads shown in Figure 12.25. This row—all one box—was built by merging several duplicates of the building-block horse head shown in Figure 12.26. Before this repeating horse head was duplicated, it was prepared for *tiling*. Tiling is the process of aligning duplicates of a design element so that their edges abut each other like the squares on a checkerboard.

FIGURE 12.26

This Bézier box has been prepared as a tile, to flow seamlessly into a horizontally aligned duplicate of itself.

Tiling preparation for a Bézier box can be performed in various ways, so it might be easiest to simply describe how the example in Figure 12.26 was prepared. Notice that the bottom four corner points of the shape in Figure 12.26 form a perfect rectangle. This is an easy and effective way to prepare for tiling. Here's how it's done.

To create a tiled pattern from a Bézier shape:

1. Create some extra points on the bottom of the shape.

2. Drag out two horizontal guides and two vertical guides from the *rulers*. The guides form an enclosed rectangle (see Figure 12.27).

3. Snap each of the four points on the bottom of the shape to the appropriate guide pair (see Figure 12.28).

FIGURE 12.27
Guides help you plot out symmetrical shapes.

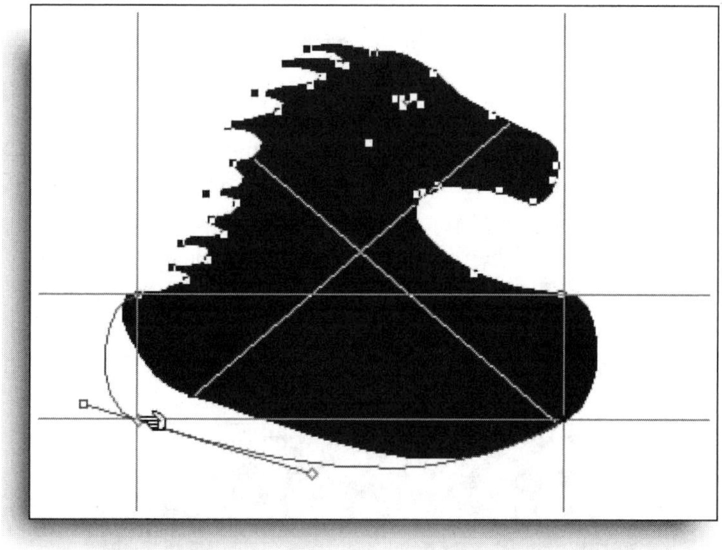

FIGURE 12.28
Use **Snap to Guides** (on the
View menu) to align points
with guides.

4. Shift+click all four points forming the bottom of the
shape to multiple-select them. Then click ⊟ in the
Measurements palette to make them all corner points, and
click ⬉ to make these four segments straight (see
Figure 12.29).

FIGURE 12.29

Shift+click to select all the points; then convert them all to corner points.

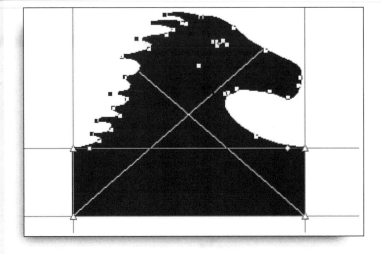

5. For a smooth curve to hide the juncture at the upper part of this new rectangular base, position the curve handles of the two upper corner points as 180-degree opposites (see Figure 12.30). When two curve handles are positioned as 180-degree opposites, they can be joined to form a smooth point. The fields in the Measurements palette make it easy to specify exact positions for the curve handles.

FIGURE 12.30

To place curve handles along the same horizontal access, rely on precise values displayed in the Measurements palette.

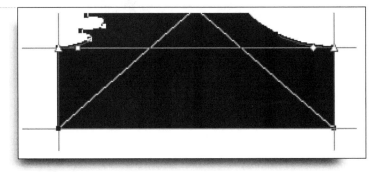

This is just one example of tile preparation, and you can surely think of others. After you get past this stage, the rest is fairly easy.

Tiling

After applying color and other attributes to your shape, you can usually create and align tiles by using the **Step and Repeat** command. Snapping to guides and the **Space/Align** command can also come in handy. You can then finish the whole process by performing a **Union** command to merge all the boxes into one.

But what if you're dealing with an odd shape and your intended "juncture" points lie somewhere inside the bounding box of your item? In such a case, the commands just mentioned won't help you align tiles. Instead, you'll need to go through the following procedure.

To snap your tiles to guides according to a specific Bézier point:

 1. Check **Snap to Guides** and **Show Guides** in the **View** menu.

 2. Create a crossed guide pair by dragging out a horizontal and vertical guide from the rulers.

 3. Select your box and make sure that its Bézier points are showing. (If not, choose **Edit** from the **Item** menu and check the **Shape** option.)

 4. Double-click a point to activate all the points in the box. (Triple-click a point if the box contains more than one path.)

 5. Decide which Bézier point will act as the juncture for aligning the first tile, and then drag this juncture point to the crossed guide pair. As long as a point is dragged, rather than a segment, the entire box will move without reshaping (see Figure 12.31).

 6. Snap a duplicate of this box to the same guide pair using all the preceding steps, and then perform a **Union** command on the two boxes to make them one. For a longer string of tiles, repeat all the steps using the new box.

SEE ALSO

➤ *To space or align objects, see page 131*

FIGURE 12.31

To snap a box to a guide according to any point you drag, first select all the points in the item, then drag a point.

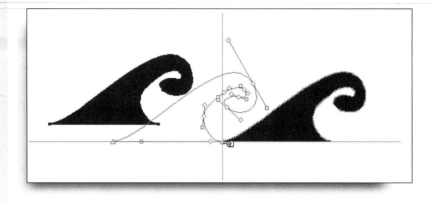

Flipping

In desktop publishing lingo, a "flipped" element is a mirror image of the original, either vertically or horizontally. Unfortunately, the QuarkXPress **Flip** command works only on box contents such as pictures or text. So what do you do if you want to flip a Bézier item? Basically, you just drag a resize handle in a certain way.

To flip a Bézier object:

1. Choose **Edit** from the **Item** menu, and then uncheck the **Shape** option for the active Bézier item so that its rectangular bounding box displays.

2. For a horizontal flip, highlight the **H** field in the Measurements palette. If you want a vertical flip, highlight the **W** field. Copy this value to the Clipboard.

3. Drag one of the middle-positioned resize handles (top- or bottom-middle handle for a vertical flip; left- or right-middle handle for a horizontal flip). Drag this handle until a mirror image appears on the opposite side (see Figure 12.32).

4. Paste the value on the Clipboard into the appropriate Measurements palette field (**W** or **H**).

FIGURE 12.32
You can flip an item by dragging a resize handle.

Creating Radial Symmetry

To create radial symmetry (like the kind you see in a drawing of the sun, for instance), you'll need to remember one or two of the techniques described previously in this section, but beyond that, there's only one additional technique you'll need: field math. QuarkXPress lets you insert math operators (+, −, /, and *) into the fields contained by palettes and dialog boxes.

How do these operators help you create radial symmetry? Well, let's say you're creating a logo for the Professional Dart Throwers Association. You have a box shaped like a dart, and now you want five identical darts radiating out from a common center.

To create a radially symmetrical design:

1. Divide 360 (the number of degrees in a circle) by the number of radial items in the design. For example, for five items radiating out, divide 360 by 5, giving a result of 72 degrees.

2. Duplicate the first box. With the new box selected, place the cursor after the existing value in the **Box Angle** field, and enter a + field math operator after the existing value. Follow this operator with the result from step 1. Press Return (Enter).

3. Perform step 2 again, but this time make sure that the newest box is selected when before performing the **Duplicate** command. Keep repeating this step to create the desired number of boxes, all of which should be angled differently.

4. Create a crossed guide pair, and snap the tips of each dart to the guide pair using the technique shown in Figure 12.31. This technique lets you snap an item to a guide according to any point you drag. Figure 12.33 shows the final result.

FIGURE 12.33

Radial symmetry is easy to achieve with a little math.

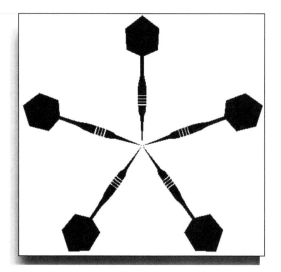

CHAPTER 13

Working with Images

A good proportion of your publications will probably contain images of one kind or another. In this chapter, you look at the various types of images, their relative strengths and weaknesses for your type of publishing, and in general, deal with images on your page.

Essentially, you place images the same way you place text, by filling a box with an image. And just like text, QuarkXPress allows you to perform a variety of manipulations to the image after it is in the box. But as always, there are better and quicker ways of doing some of these things to speed up your work and to make your life easier.

SEE ALSO

➤ *To import text into a document, see page 182*

Importing Picture Files

QuarkXPress 4 took a great leap forward in picture box handling by fixing one of those small, but aggravating, things that made life either nicer or more difficult. QuarkXPress now lets you *import* pictures into picture boxes with either the Item tool ⊕ or the Content tool 🖑 active. Pictures, like text, are imported by choosing **Get Picture** from the File menu or using the ⌘+E (Ctrl+E) keystroke. QuarkXPress supports quite a number of different file formats on both Mac OS and Windows platforms:

- EPS/DCS
- JPEG
- OS/2 BMP
- PAINT
- Photo CD
- PICT
- Scitex CT
- TIFF
- BMP
- PCX

Using Picture Boxes

New to QuarkXPress 4 are some new picture shapes and the menu used to pick them. QuarkXPress's new pop-out Tool palette menus now look a lot more like you-know-who's. Some of the new shapes and the way to use them are even useful. In fact, QuarkXPress now can even flow pictures inside type.

A new feature of the container box is that the box can now be easily changed from a *text box* to a *picture box*, and vice versa. When it's already a picture box, choosing **Content** from the **Item** menu and then choosing **Text** from the submenu changes it to a picture box. Converting a text box to a picture box is the same, only you'll want to choose **Picture** from the submenu instead. Unfortunately, there's no keyboard command to toggle between the two types of content for a box.

SEE ALSO

➤ *To create a picture box, see page 105*

➤ *To flow pictures inside type, see page 403*

Get Picture Dialog Box

Another new feature of QuarkXPress in version 4 is in the appearance and function of the Get Picture dialog box. When you select **Get Picture**, the specifications of the item you're going to import into the box appear in the dialog box—a real help in making sure you have the right version (and type) of the file you want to use. Clicking the **Preview** check box also shows you a visual representation of the image.

If it seems to take a long time to preview an image before importing it into a box, it's usually because the image is very large, it has a lot of layers, or the QuarkXPress document you're working on has gotten large also. Another reason might be a shortage of memory allocated to QuarkXPress.

A good way of speeding up the Get Picture process is to turn off the **Preview** button: QuarkXPress won't then spend a lot of time trying to draw the preview image in the little picture box in the Get Picture dialog box (see Figure 13.1).

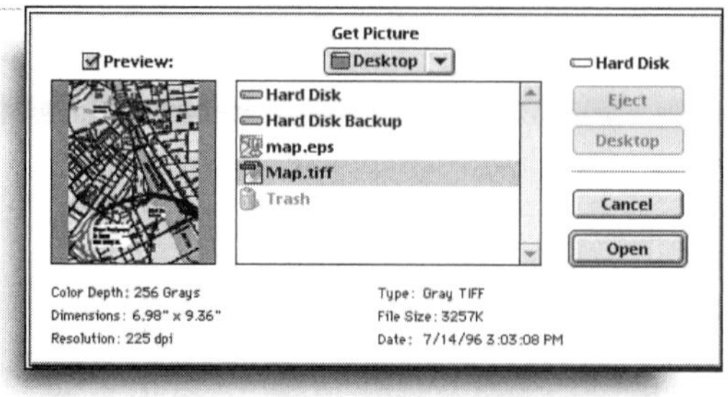

FIGURE 13.1

The Get Picture dialog box: note the new information box that shows the color depth, size, resolution, type, file size, and modification date of the items being brought into the picture box.

Lowering Picture Preview Resolution

A useful feature in QuarkXPress is the capability to bring the image onto the page at a lower *screen resolution* than normal. Large documents that use a lot of large photos for high-quality printing should probably use this trick: Hold the Shift key down while choosing the **Get Picture** command, and the image on your screen will automatically be *downsampled* to a 36 ppi (pixels per inch) image.

The image will be "rougher" but of sufficient resolution so you can check that you have the right one in the right box. For those who like to "work the keyboard" to keep your speed up, you can use ⌘+E (Ctrl+E) to open the Get Picture box, use the down arrow key to pick the file, and hold down the Shift key at the same time you hit the Enter key to flow the picture into its box. Keeping the images to the smaller preview size of 32ppi will significantly reduce the QuarkXPress file size, without affecting the quality of the printed images.

Picture Importing Problems

Do you have problems importing *JPEG*, *Photo CD*, or *PCX* images? QuarkXPress requires some *XTensions* to be loaded to correctly import those kinds of images—and even to just see them in the Get Picture dialog box. The XTensions you need are called JPEG Import, PCX Import, and Photo CD XTension. Like all extensions, they must be located in either the XTension folder that's inside the QuarkXPress application folder or loose in the QuarkXPress folder.

A default installation of QuarkXPress 4 should have installed these XTensions in the proper place at the time of installation. If you don't have them, or you suspect they might have become damaged, you can drag them from the XTension folder from the installation CD-ROM.

Sometimes a corrupt image preview can cause QuarkXPress to crash. To fix this problem, you can re-import all your picture previews at the same color depth when you open a document. Just hold the ⌘ (Ctrl) key when you click **Open** in the Open dialog box to open the QuarkXPress file.

SEE ALSO

➤ *To enable and disable XTensions, see page 555*

Modifying Images on Import

Two other functions of the **Get Picture** command are also available to convert one image type to another. Results can vary from platform to platform, and the file types can affect the final result, but some of these steps might be useful.

Converting Grayscale Images to Line Art

If you hold down the ⌘ (Ctrl) key while opening a *grayscale TIFF* file, the file imports as *line art* (black and white, with no grays). When QuarkXPress converts a grayscale image to line art, it takes everything lighter than the halfway point (50%, or a middle gray) and makes it white; everything darker than a 50% or a middle gray goes solid black. If you want to finesse an image to give it a mezzotint effect, you're probably better off trying some variations in an image editing application, rather than relying on this function. It's useful, but not too controllable.

Converting Color Images to Grayscale Images

Color TIFF images can be imported as grayscale TIFF images (stripping out the color) by holding down the ⌘ (Ctrl) key at the time you click **Open**.

QuarkXPress also allows you to print color images as though they were grayscale when you print. It does a pretty good job of converting color information to a usable grayscale equivalent. If you're constructing a document and you're not sure yet where the color positions are going to be located, you can do the whole publication with color images. Then do one of two things:

- Print the noncolor pages as grayscale, choosing **Grayscale** from the **Print Colors** pop-up menu in the **Output** tab of the Print dialog box.

- Re-import the color scans as grayscale images as described above.

If the quality of the grayscale image that's being created from a color image is an issue for you, you should probably run some tests to see which of the two ways produce a better image on your equipment or situation. You should probably also consider doing the entire conversion in Photoshop or another image editor, where you have control over the gray levels.

Pasting Images

The second method for importing pictures is the normal cut-and-paste. It can often be faster for things such as logos, dingbats, and other small items scattered throughout your publication. Keep in mind, though, that the image you pasted into the picture box is at the resolution you're going to see and to print it at: There is no higher *resolution* image for QuarkXPress to refer to when imaging. What you see is what you're going to get!

Cut-and-paste is also useful for *FPO* (For Position Only) images. In this scenario, you purposely do very *low resolution* scans and cut and paste them into picture boxes to "save the place" for the picture. Later on, a service bureau or printer rescans the images from the original copy into the proper resolution, does the proper color correction, and replaces your FPOs with the *high resolution* scans they've done.

If the resolution of the images is a problem, but you like the ease and usefulness of the cut-and-paste method, consider using a *library* to accomplish the same thing. A library image refers to the high resolution image just as though you brought the image into a picture box the regular way.

SEE ALSO

➤ *To store objects in a library, see page 143*

Getting Images Using Publish and Subscribe or OLE

The third most common way to place images into picture boxes is through *Publish and Subscribe* (for Mac OS) or *OLE* (Object Linking and Embedding, for Windows).

In Publish and Subscribe, applications such as Photoshop, FreeHand, and Illustrator can "publish" their output for QuarkXPress to "subscribe" to on the page. Why bother? Publish and Subscribe can be very useful if one work group is creating the images, which are constantly being updated, and another work group is designing the pages. The "Subscribed to" image on the QuarkXPress page can be automatically updated every time there is a new version of the illustration. This scenario is not for everybody, but useful, perhaps, in a newspaper, newsletter, or news magazine environment where the information is constantly changing and being updated.

Choose **Subscribe To** from the **Edit** menu and select a file in the dialog box that has .edition after its name (see Figure 13.2).

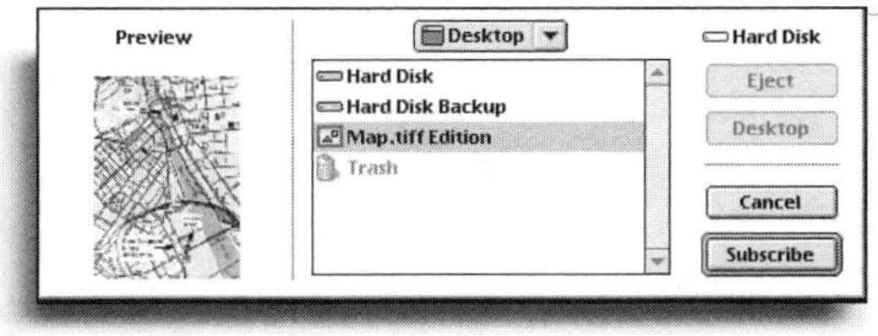

FIGURE 13.2

Publishing a document (in this case, from Photoshop) means the application will add the word ".edition" to the filename, something that's recommended to keep the file differentiated from the "parent" or original file.

After you place a picture using this method, the **Subscriber Options** menu item becomes available. Also available in the Subscriber Options dialog box box is information about the date and time of the latest edition and when it was last received. This is very useful as a tool to make sure you have the latest version, and that the latest has been "posted" to the right location for QuarkXPress to update (see Figure 13.3).

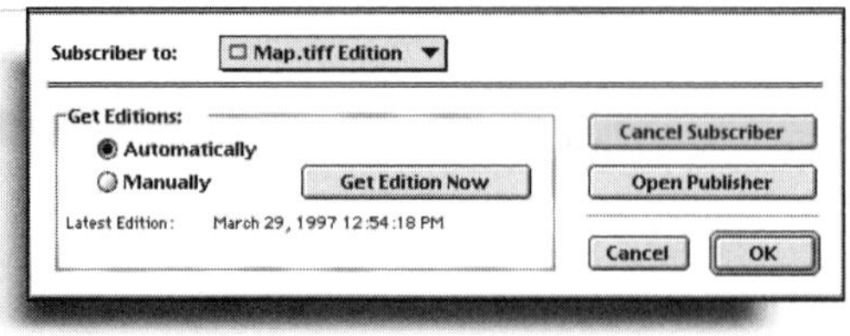

FIGURE 13.3

The **Subscriber Options** menu item allows you pick whether to have the image updated automatically every time the file is changed or the QuarkXPress document is opened up, or whether to "manually" update the image by choosing **Get Edition Now**.

Using Subscriber Options with any image

Double-clicking in an image box brings up the Subscriber Options dialog box even if you didn't place the image in the box using Publish and Subscribe. It's handy in checking the image name and version in any picture box, as well the location of the high-resolution source file. It also allows you to import the updated version of an image file that has been modified; however, if the image file has moved, you must update it through the Picture Usage dialog box.

The **Cancel Publisher** button that's part of the Subscriber Options dialog box does exactly that—releases the picture box for another image or another "Subscribe to" to be brought into the container. The **Open Publisher** button actually launches the application the original published item was created in, a handy way to make changes in the original and republish it.

Instead of Publish and Subscribe, Windows users have **Paste Special**, **Paste Link**, and **Links** commands in the **Edit** menu. These commands allow you to link graphics to their originating applications so that double-clicking on a graphic opens the program in which it was created. You can then edit the graphics and return to QuarkXPress, where your changes are reflected in the XPress document. The other feature of OLE is that it enables you to *embed* a graphic in an XPress document so that you don't need to keep the original file around. Check your Windows documentation for more information on using OLE.

Positioning Images

As in earlier versions of QuarkXPress, if a picture box is selected with the Item tool $\boxed{+\oplus+}$, the box moves if you grab it, or it moves in 1-point increments if you use the arrow keys to nudge it into location. (The Option+arrow (Alt+arrow) keys move the box one-tenth of a point at a time!) Moving the contents of the box works the same way, only you have to use the Content tool $\boxed{\text{🖑}}$.

SEE ALSO

➤ *To position boxes on a page, see page 123*

Positioning Images Manually

Images always start out flush with the top and left sides of the box, with the **Offset Across** and **Offset Down** values both set at 0. To reposition an image precisely, choose **Modify** from the **Item** menu or press ⌘+M (Ctrl+M), then click on the **Picture** tab and type in the precise location within the box using the **Offset Across** and the **Offset Down** fields (see Figure 13.4). As in most QuarkXPress dialog boxes, any measurement unit (picas, points, inches, millimeters, and so on) is okay, and you can do math in the boxes, mixing and matching measurements. (For instance, if the image's **Offset Down** position is at 1 inch and you want to move it down another 6 points, just type +p6 in the **Offset Down** field next to the 1 inch figure.)

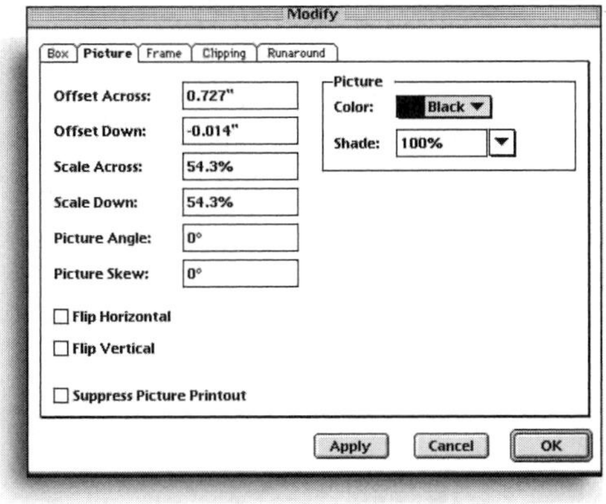

FIGURE 13.4

The Modify dialog box allows you to position images within picture boxes to one one-thousandths of an inch by typing in values in the **Offset Across** and **Offset Down** boxes. These are measured from the upper-left corner of the box.

Keep in mind that for any shape that is not a rectangle, the upper-left point is determined by a point that's formed by imaginary lines joined from the left-most point and the top-most point of the shape.

You can also type image coordinates into the **X+** and **Y+** fields on the right side of the Measurements palette; these fields work just like the **Offset Across** and **Offset Down** fields in the Modify dialog box (see Figure 13.5).

FIGURE 13.5

FIGURE 13.5

Here a 3.5" X 5.5" picture is placed in a 2" X 2" box. The upper-left corner of the picture is in the upper-left corner of the picture box. Note the Measurements palette: 100% image horizontally and vertically.

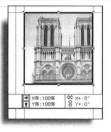

SEE ALSO

➤ *To create Bézier (non-rectangular) picture boxes, see page 318*

Centering Images in the Box

⌘+Shift+M (Ctrl+Shift+M) centers the image in the picture box after importing it. This function is useful to make sure the image is cropped by the box on all four sides, preventing any gaps between the image and the box border. Another situation when this command is useful is when you use the picture box to provide background color, with an image centered in the color block.

SEE ALSO

➤ *To apply a frame to a box, see page 114*

➤ *To apply color to a picture box, see page 443*

Resizing Images

Images always appear at full size (100%) in their boxes. Images can be resized within their boxes, or the boxes only can be resized, leaving the image the same size in a larger box. Or both the boxes and the images can be resized together as though they were one unit.

Scaling Images Numerically

Scaling images inside the picture box can be accomplished by choosing **Modify** from the **Item** menu or pressing ⌘+M (Ctrl+M). The **Picture** tab allows pretty much the same effects on the picture within the box as the **Box** tab does on the box itself.

Two additional check boxes exist in the **Picture** tab of the Modify dialog box: **Flip Horizontal** and **Flip Vertical**. They will do exactly as they say they will do: flip the image within the box. These controls exist in the Measurements palette as well; they're the arrow icons in the middle of the palette.

Sizing Images to the Box

To quickly see the whole image in the box, without distortion, use the ⌘+Option+Shift+F (Ctrl+Alt+Shift+F) key combination (see Figure 13.6 If you think of it as the ultimate fit-picture-to-box keystroke combination, the letter F actually makes some sense.)

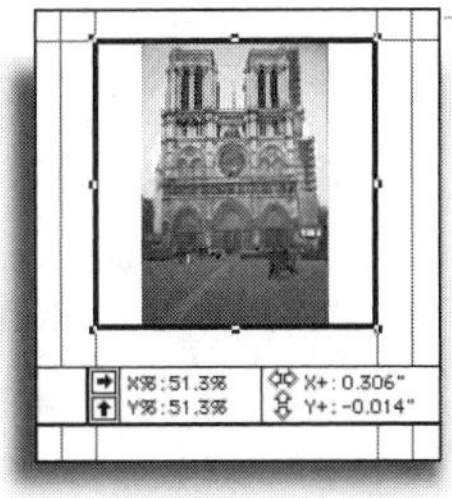

Keep image flipping to a minimum

Flipping images in QuarkXPress increases the printing time dramatically, because the computer has to look at all the image information in the original graphic file, and then recompute it to be flipped, before it can print. If you have a medium-to-large image that needs to be flipped, do it first in an image editor like Photoshop, and keep the flips to a minimum in QuarkXPress.

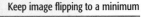

FIGURE 13.6

⌘+Option+Shift+F (Ctrl+Alt+Shift+F) makes the picture fill the box. Note that the longest dimension of the picture now fits in the box. The Measurements palette shows the picture is scaled proportionally to 51.3% to make the best fit in the box.

If you just use ⌘+Shift+F (Ctrl+Shift+F), the picture will fill the box, and distort itself to do it. So in a few cases, where the size and shape of the box is important in the layout, you can "amorphitize" a picture slightly to make it fit the box. Better yet, increase the picture size slightly within the box and move the picture around inside the frame with the Content tool [ ] to make the best crop for the shape (see Figure 13.7).

FIGURE 13.7

But ⌘+Shift+F (Ctrl+Shift+F) makes the whole picture fill all four sides of the box, even if it means distorting the picture to do it! The picture is now distorted to 75.9% horizontally and to 51.3% vertically to fill the picture box.

Resizing Images with Keyboard Shortcuts

You can also resize an image by using ⌘+Option+Shift+> (Ctrl+Alt+Shift+>)—the greater-than symbol above the period—to increase the size of the picture 5% at a time in the box. This is a great tool, because you can see the effects of the changes while not being distracted by boxes, mice, and other assorted clutter. And of course, ⌘+Option+Shift+< (Ctrl+Alt+Shift+<)—the less-than symbol above the comma—decreases the size of the picture in the box in the same 5% increments.

Resizing Boxes While Scaling Images

By far the most intuitive way of *cropping* and scaling an image is to bring it into a picture box larger than the image, crop the picture as you'd like to see it by moving the four sides in on the image, and then rescale both the box and its image to fit the layout. Like most QuarkXPress functions, you can save time and energy by learning which keystroke combinations do what you need to do. Scaling pictures and their boxes is easy when you know the trick.

For instance, you finally have the picture cropped just right, at the right size, and now the editor (art director, or insert the villain of your choice) wants it bigger (see Figure 13.8)!

FIGURE **13.8**

The perfectly cropped picture, one column wide. But now you want to make it bigger!

No problem, you say. Grabbing and moving the lower-right corner, though, will only make the box bigger, not the picture. All that resizing and cropping to do all over again.

Or if you make the mistake of holding down the Option (Alt) key while dragging the picture box bigger, the picture enlarges with the box, but it's all warped now because the proportion of the box changes as you drag the corner (see Figure 13.9).

FIGURE **13.9**

Dragging the lower-right corner with the Option (Alt) key held down allows the picture to be distorted to keep the same cropping, even when the proportions of the box change. Not a good thing!

But holding down ⌘+Option+Shift (Ctrl+Alt+Shift) while enlarging (or reducing) a picture box does the two things you want to accomplish: changes the size of the picture at the same time as it changes the size of the box, and it keeps the box and picture in the same proportions as the original, preventing the picture in the box from being distorted (see Figure 13.10).

FIGURE **13.10**

⌘+Option+Shift (Ctrl+Alt+Shift) held down as you drag any corner keeps the crop and keeps the picture box in proportion at the same time.

Don't enlarge pictures too much...

Making a picture smaller or slightly larger (by 10% or so) will have no effect on your final output. But if your image has been scanned to be used at a certain size for a particular halftone screen, enlarging it more than 10% or so will begin to seriously affect the quality of the image. You might have to go back and rescan or fix the image in your image application.

SEE ALSO

➤ *To resize picture boxes, see page 106*

Cropping Images

Cropping images in QuarkXPress is the same as in most DTP applications: just make the box smaller than the image, and the part of the image that doesn't fit in the box is cropped out. Dragging the middle handles of a box moves that side of the box. Dragging a corner changes the two sides attached to that corner.

But there's a drawback to cropping too much—the printer or other output device still has to rasterize (RIP, or compute the location of all the pixels) the entire image, even though some of it's not going to show up on the page. If you're cropping more than a little bit, it's much better to go back and make the crop in the image application, and reimport the image into QuarkXPress.

Similarly, if you have a scan that contains more than one image ("ganged," as they say in the prepress trade) but you only intend to use one image in each picture box, you're also asking for trouble. Say, for instance, you have six images on one sheet of paper that you scanned with your trusty flatbed scanner, and you're going to place each of the six images into six different boxes, leaving the other five not showing. When your printer goes to work, those six images will have to be processed six times each! Even though you don't see them on the page, the *RIP* does and will spend a lot of time computing things that you won't see, increasing the chances of crashes, bad images, and those wonderful Type 11 error messages.

You will actually save time "cutting apart" those six images from the single scan and making six individual files, to be imported into their own individual QuarkXPress picture boxes.

Exporting EPS Images

Sometimes, you might want to turn an entire QuarkXPress page, or document, into a graphic. You might want to show the cover of your magazine on another page of the same magazine, or you might need to grab a picture of a page for posting on your web site.

QuarkXPress makes it easy to save a page of your document as a standard *EPS* file. The file you save won't show any page boundaries, guidelines, or box containers. It's essentially a "dump" of what the page will look like when it's printed on paper or to film.

To create an EPS image of a page:

1. Make sure the finished document is opened to the page to be exported. Check the page number at the bottom-left corner of the window. It doesn't matter what the *view percentage* is or if guides or other invisibles are showing; the final EPS will be only the whole page, without invisibles.

2. Choose **Save Page as EPS** from the **File** menu, and the dialog box will pop up, offering a host of choices (see Figure 13.11).

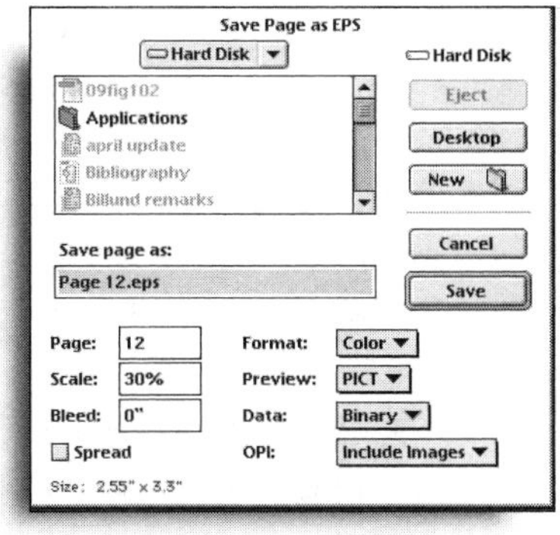

3. Type in a name for the EPS file.

4. In the **Page** field, enter the number of the page that's being exported—it defaults to the page currently showing. To save a spread (two facing pages in a normal document), check the **Spread** box.

Capturing a screen image

There are also times when you might want to export parts of a page, or dialog boxes and pop-up menus, if you're working on an in-house manual for staff members about how to do software tasks. Or you might want to include on your image files things such as *guides, baseline grid* lines, and so on. In that case, you need a screen shot utility such as Capture, FlashIt, or Snapz Pro for the Mac, and HyperSnap for Windows.

FIGURE 13.11

The Save Page as EPS dialog box includes many options to make the image work better with your final use for it.

Scaling EPS files

The **Size** setting shows what size the EPS file will have when it's first imported into another document, but since vector EPS files are scalable, you'll be able to resize the image as much as you want with no loss of printing quality.

5. To change the page size of the EPS file that's to be saved, change the percentage under **Scale**. The default setting of 50% reduces the page to half of its original size. When the **Scale** setting is changed, the **Size** field below it changes to show the exact size of the bounding box of the EPS.

6. Select a format from the **Format** pop-up menu. There are options for Macs and PCs (for more detailed information on these options, see "Selecting EPS File Formats" later in this section):

- **Color**—Standard full-color EPS file with color preview.

- **B&W**—Black-and-white EPS, with all the color items changed to grayscale.

- **DCS**—The Desktop Color Separation version of EPS, used when outputting negatives for four-color printing. Check with a service bureau or printer before using *DCS* formats.

- **DCS 2.0**—A new version of the DCS format that handles spot color plates as well as CMYK.

7. The **Data** field should be set to **Binary** unless the service bureau or printer has specifically requested otherwise.

8. If the printer or *service bureau* is using *OPI* (Open Prepress Interface) to separate full-color pages that include color bitmapped images, use the **OPI** pop-up menu to choose how pictures and comments are included. For more details on these options, see "Using Data and OPI Settings" later in this section. If the final output won't use OPI, don't worry about this step.

9. Click **Save** to create the file. This EPS file can be imported into QuarkXPress (or other applications) or used in slide shows, on the web, or just about any other place an EPS image can be used.

Hey, we're almost done, but one thing you must remember is that EPS images, no matter where they originated from, must have the fonts installed in the computer system that sends the job to the printer. They don't necessarily have to be on the RIP, but it's better if they are located there, too.

If you use *TrueType* fonts, we wish you a lot of luck. A joint technology effort some years ago by both Apple and Microsoft, it was supposed to solve the problems of hunger, the population explosion, and civil disobedience. Too bad nobody adopted it, and from everything we hear at service bureaus and printers we deal with, TrueType fonts are their biggest source of font headaches. If you're confined to a Windows machine to do this work, we also wish you well on that score.

SEE ALSO
➤ *To learn more about font formats, see page 228*

Selecting EPS File Formats

In special situations, you might need to know more about the format options in the Save Page as EPS dialog box, so here are more details.

Mac Color and Mac B&W

These two options give you a normal EPS file. As it turns out, choosing between **Color** and **B&W** doesn't just affect the screen preview image. The choice also affects the way that QuarkXPress writes the *PostScript* code. If you choose **B&W**, color items are actually changed into grayscale items, and the file is a lot smaller in file size. If you use only grayscale pages, it's a better deal for your hard disk space to save those images in grayscale only.

DCS and DCS 2.0

Choosing **DCS** makes QuarkXPress save five (yes, five) files to your disk: one master file containing a preview image, and four process color (CMYK) files containing the actual image data.

DCS 2.0, the new version of the Desktop Color Separation format, handles cyan, magenta, yellow, black, and as many spot colors as you want. The good part about this is that all your spot colors get put on their own plates, which can make production, and hence reproduction, quite a bit easier. The not-so-good part is that RGB images might not get separated correctly. Another solution is simply to use preseparated CMYK images (TIFF or DCS) instead of RGB.

EPS files and suppressed graphics

Creating an EPS file of a page with a graphic that has been suppressed does not suppress the screen image of that graphic (although it still suppresses the printing of the picture). If you don't want to see the screen preview in the EPS file, you can cover it with another picture box (a rectangle or a polygon perhaps) with its background color set to 0% black (or white) before creating the EPS file.

Also note that using DCS 2.0 results in only one file on your hard drive, not five or more. However, I don't know anybody who uses DCS. Most commercial printers and service bureaus prefer TIFF files for photo images, and Illustrator or FreeHand EPS files for drawn images.

PC Formats

PC formats are becoming more and more relevant in the new era of cross-platform compatibility. On the Mac, preview images are low-resolution images placed in the resource fork of the picture's file. PC files don't have resource forks, so this method doesn't work. Instead, the preview image is placed as a header in the beginning of the EPS file. In other words, it's kind of like putting a low-resolution TIFF at the beginning of the EPS file. A Mac will be able to read the PC preview, so these are safe options for use on either platform.

Stick to 8.3 for filenames

When saving a PC EPS file, it's best to give your image a name that's not longer than eight letters, followed by .EPS. Even though Windows 95 allows long filenames, you never know where your file will be headed and what operating system is going to try and read it, so it's best to be on the safe side.

Using Data and OPI Settings

One thing to remember about the **Data** and **OPI** options is that they affect only *bitmapped* image data in TIFF and EPS file formats. If you're not using either, you can ignore these settings.

You'll almost always use **Binary** as your **Data** setting, mostly because images saved in binary format are about half the size of those that use **ASCII**. However, *ASCII* data can be much easier for service bureaus or printers to work with if there are errors when printing. ASCII data is also necessary if the image will ever be printed over a serial connection (from a DOS or UNIX box, for instance). Binary images won't print over a serial connection.

The **OPI** method is based on post-separating full-color pages that include color bitmapped images—especially scanned images. For example, you can import a low-resolution *RGB* TIFF file into a QuarkXPress document, save that page as EPS, and separate it on either a high-end color system (such as Hell or Crosfield) or on your imagesetter using a program such as Imation PrePrint Pro. Instead of QuarkXPress including the whole TIFF image in the PostScript file, it just throws in OPI comments that say what the name of the scanned image file is, and where the separation program can find it.

This is nice for a couple of reasons. First and foremost is the file size. An EPS file with the image data included can be enormous. Sometimes, it's nicer to leave the image data on disk somewhere else and just manipulate a minimal EPS file (one that just includes OPI comments about where to find the image data). Another good reason is to work with the file on a system such as Kodak's Prophecy.

The trick to building a PostScript file with OPI comments is the OPI pop-up menu. You have three choices:

- **Include Images**—Used most often. With this option selected, QuarkXPress works as it normally does, printing all the TIFF and EPS pictures (or including them in an EPS). It includes pictures in TIFF and EPS formats and substitutes the low-resolution TIFF if the higher-resolution printing file for the pictures cannot be found.

- **Omit TIFF**—The basic setting for OPI comments. QuarkXPress replaces all TIFF pictures in the file with OPI comments that can be read by an OPI reader such as Imation PrePrint Pro.

- **Omit TIFF & EPS**—A setting for EPS substitution as well as TIFF substitution. Apparently the OPI specs talk about this, but no software currently recognizes this setting. So, as far as I can tell, this selection is useless for now. Well, I guess it's always nice to have the option.

Preparing Images for Output

QuarkXPress links pictures in its picture boxes to the original file and expects the original file to be in the same place it was when you placed it on the page. If you moved the files, perhaps off a hard disk onto a removable disk to take it to a service bureau, QuarkXPress will ask you to locate the files before printing. While you can bypass this step and elect to print using the preview images that the program does store in each file, imported images will then look "jaggy" on the output. At any time, you can check to make sure QuarkXPress can locate all the pictures with the Usage dialog box.

Confirming Picture Status Before Output

Choose **Usage** from the **Utilities** menu to see the new Usage dialog box, with tabs for **Fonts** and **Pictures**. The **Pictures** tab allows you to update and locate all your pictures (see Figure 13.12).

FIGURE 13.12

Clicking on the **More Information** box brings up useful information to make sure you have the right file.

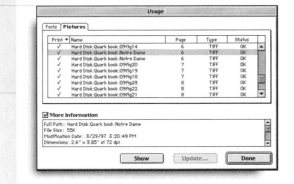

Saving pictures where they won't slow you down

It's generally not a good idea to leave pictures (or anything else, for that matter) on the *pasteboard* area. It makes the file larger and slows printing because the RIP has to process that information just as though it were on the page, even though it won't print. If you feel you must have those items handy, consider building them into the *template* for your publication(s) or placing them in a library, to be dragged onto the page only when you need them.

One nice new feature is the **Print** check mark to the left of the picture name. If you want to really speed up proofing, for instance, and just print the QuarkXPress pages with text and some of the smaller images, you can deselect the printing of an individual picture or group of pictures by unchecking the **Print** check mark. Other columns of information in the **Pictures** tab contain the filename and the page the picture is on. If a dagger (‡) is in front of the page number, it means the picture is located on the pasteboard next to the page.

Reading right, the Usage dialog box continues with the type of picture it is, followed by **Status**. It's here that problems will show up: an **OK** means just that: the image is where QuarkXPress can find it, and you're ready to rip. (Sorry about that.)

But if an image's status shows as **Modified**, it means that QuarkXPress knows where the image is, but that the file has been changed to a different file type of the same date and time—possible when you export an EPS file from Illustrator or

FreeHand and save the drawing right afterward with the same name in a different location—or that the date it was last saved is different from the one that was imported on the page. A **Missing** message means QuarkXPress can't find it at all; in all probability, the file was moved or renamed.

The new dialog box also contains a lot more useful information, accessible by clicking on the **More Information** box. It shows information on the path of the picture as well as the file type, file size, modification date and time, dimensions—both width and height, as well as number of pixels per inch—and the type (color or black and white) and the number of levels of pixels, extremely useful in making sure you have the right files for your output.

You can still jump to the page to check on any questionable images by clicking on the **Show** button.

If an image is missing, clicking on the **Update** button brings up a Find dialog box (see Figure 13.13).

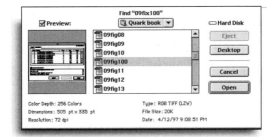

FIGURE 13.13

If one of your images is missing, clicking on the **Update** button brings up the Find dialog box to let you find the missing picture. After you find it, clicking on **Open** reestablishes the path.

A nice, or not so nice depending on what you're doing at the time, feature of the Find dialog box is that if you purposely want to replace a picture with one that has a new name, this allows you to. Keep in mind, though, that if your original picture has, for instance, been scaled at 82% in a 3 " X 5 " picture box, the new one will take its place in the same size box, also at 82%. So it had better be in the same size and proportions as the one it's replacing, or it won't fit the box correctly in either the height or the depth.

In other words, all modifications to a picture box such as offset, rotation, size, and shape apply to the re-importation of a modified image. But if you simply select a new picture to be placed in the box as a way to replace an image, QuarkXPress will always bring in the new image at 100%, and the image will have to be recropped and resized.

Preventing Missing-Modified Pictures Alert

You can set QuarkXPress to automatically update and look for missing pictures by changing the **Auto Picture Import** setting in Document Preferences. The pull-down menu has three settings: **Off**, **On**, and **On (Verify)**. **Off** means that modified pictures will not be re-imported until you take action by updating the modified pictures under the Usage dialog box's **Picture** tab or when you go to print and the dreaded "Some disk files for pictures in this document are missing or have been modified" message appears.

The **On** setting means that QuarkXPress will always update modified images if they are in the right location, and merely have a new creation date. And **On (Verify)** means that when you open a QuarkXPress document, QuarkXPress will bring up a list of images that have been modified, and will ask you to say **OK**, just like the Find dialog box does.

Under some circumstances, keeping the automatic picture updating on can slow down and momentarily make your machine pause—and can be a distraction. If you use images from a library, for instance, that are stored in an OPI or on a server someplace else on a network, the automatic picture updating will look all over the network for those images. Every situation is different, of course, but be suspicious of auto picture updating if your network seems hesitant or bogged down at seemingly random moments.

SEE ALSO

➤ *To change the Auto Picture Import Setting in Document Preferences, see page 52*

Storing Pictures Consistently

The secret of success in working with QuarkXPress is due in large part to having an organized work flow, and making sure everybody else in your work group understands what that work flow is. There is no single plan or scenario that's better than another. Some scenarios are the following:

- If you do your own scanning and *color correction*, you can set up the images to be anyplace at all that QuarkXPress can find: on your hard drive, a file server, an OPI server, or even a SyQuest, Zip, or Jaz removable drive.

- If you do your own scanning, but somebody else does the color correction, you'll probably have to tell QuarkXPress to replace the files because any images that you imported onto the page before the color correction was done will now have a new date.

- If you do low-resolution FPO (For Position Only) scans to do the design with, while the slides or other originals are out to service bureau for high-resolution scanning, then you (or the printer) are definitely going to have to tell QuarkXPress where the high-resolution images are and substitute them for the FPOs.

- If you have a service bureau do the scans and the color correction, and then have them give you those images to place on the page, you just need to make sure all the images are with the QuarkXPress file when you send it to the printer.

- In many cases, the printer or the service bureau will give you the low-resolution images for you to use to design the job with, but hang onto the high-resolution scans because they are planning to use an OPI scenario to image the pages. In that case, the "substitution" is automatic, as long as nobody has changed the name, size, or date of either file. (In the "early" days of this process, Scitex used the same scenario and called it APR, or Automatic Picture Replacement. But in such a "closed" system where it was likely only one or two operators worked on the files, the problems were far fewer.)

- And if you are in a "closed" shop, where you do all your own scanning, color, and black-and-white correction, and your own imaging corrections, you can set it up any way you want. Just make sure the images you put on the page don't change name, date, or location.

The point is, whatever work flow you use, QuarkXPress is still going to be "looking" for the images to send to the printer/imagesetter in the same location it was in when you brought it onto the QuarkXPress page, with the same modification date and the same name.

Modifying Images

Images brought into QuarkXPress *picture boxes* can be modified in QuarkXPress by having *borders*, colors, and *tints* added, as well as having *contrast* attributes changed. Like all picture modifications in QuarkXPress, these changes don't affect the original file. The changes and enhancements are actually applied to the *PostScript* description of the picture box, to be added to the print file when the file is printed.

Coloring Images

Lots of times you'd maybe like to add a *spot color* to an image, or add a tint in a second color to some photos. QuarkXPress allows you to add a second color, or even a blend of colors, to your images. But it's important to understand what will happen with the color for each type of image you have.

Working with Eligible File Formats

QuarkXPress allows a lot of manipulation with images in color and the color of the container box. Even though the examples used here are rectangular, the same principles apply for pictures used in other shapes, too. The file formats whose color you can manipulate include the following:

- JPEG
- WMF
- PAINT
- PICT
- Scitex CT
- TIFF
- PCX

The image file formats whose color you can't manipulate are EPS and its sister *DCS*, a pre-color-separated version of EPS.

SEE ALSO

➤ *To import pictures, see page 338*

Applying Colors and Shades

You can add color to the image by choosing **Color** from the
Style menu and then picking a color from the submenu, by
using ⌘+M (Ctrl+M) and the **Picture** tab, or by using the
Colors palette (see Figure 14.1); the ⊠ icon at the top of the
palette refers to picture box contents. Both ways allow you to
change the color of the image. Don't forget: the only colors
available to be applied to your image are the basic nine-color
menu QuarkXPress provides, plus any that you create and add to
the menu.

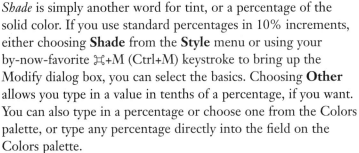

FIGURE 14.1

The Colors palette contains
both color and shade controls
for images.

1 Frame Color button

2 Picture Color button

3 Background Color button

4 Shade field

5 Colors

Shade is simply another word for tint, or a percentage of the
solid color. If you use standard percentages in 10% increments,
either choosing **Shade** from the **Style** menu or using your
by-now-favorite ⌘+M (Ctrl+M) keystroke to bring up the
Modify dialog box, you can select the basics. Choosing **Other**
allows you type in a value in tenths of a percentage, if you want.
You can also type in a percentage or choose one from the Colors
palette, or type any percentage directly into the field on the
Colors palette.

An image that has to have type dropped over a dark area might
benefit from a lighter version of the halftone applied underneath
the type, using the **Shade** command. In this case, we duplicated
the original picture, changed the tone of the new picture on the
top to a 40% tone of the original, made it smaller, and added the
type on top (see Figures 14.2 and 14.3).

1. Duplicate a picture by selecting it and choosing **Step and Repeat** from the **Item** menu, and make 1 copy with 0 in both the **Horizontal** and **Vertical Offset** fields. This will create an exact copy of the photo on top of the original.

FIGURE 14.2

Changing the offset to 0 will place the duplicate right over the original.

Step and Repeat

Repeat Count:	1
Horizontal Offset:	0"
Vertical Offset:	0"

Cancel   OK

2. Select the new picture with the Content tool 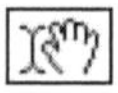  , and apply a lighter shade. The better the printing, the more subtle this can be. (In this example, the top photo was toned to 40%.)

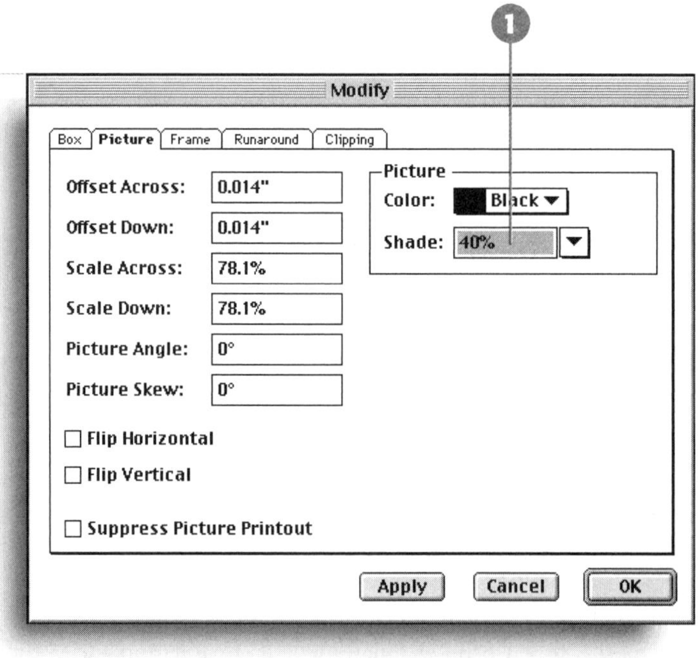

❶

FIGURE 14.3

Setting the **Shade** percentage to a lower number adjusts the tonality of the selected picture.

❶ Change the Shade percentage

Modify

Box | **Picture** | Frame | Runaround | Clipping

		┌─Picture─		
Offset Across:	0.014"	Color:	■ Black ▼	
Offset Down:	0.014"	Shade:	40%	▼
Scale Across:	78.1%			
Scale Down:	78.1%			
Picture Angle:	0°			
Picture Skew:	0°			

☐ Flip Horizontal

☐ Flip Vertical

☐ Suppress Picture Printout

Apply   Cancel   OK

3. Now make the top picture smaller by moving the middle handles of each side of the picture box so that the lighter image is the size of the text block that will be placed over it, being careful not to nudge it out of position.

4. Add the text box and text on top of the screened image.

SEE ALSO

➤ *To define and apply colors, see page 431*

Making Negative Images

Negative is the third option in the **Style** menu when a picture is selected; its keyboard alternative is ⌘+Shift+hyphen (Ctrl+Shift+hyphen). It has no equivalent in the Modify dialog box. It does what it says: translates the image to its negative values, so it looks just like a film negative would look in black and white. The **Negative** command applied to a color image makes it look like a color negative would look, not necessarily useful unless you're doing a publication about photography!

Modifying Image Contrast

It's probably better to think about modifying an image you're going to use in QuarkXPress with an image editor such as Photoshop or Live Picture. Their controls over preview, *highlight* and *shadow* values, *color management*, and so on are far better implemented and have more variety than you'll find in QuarkXPress.

What QuarkXPress's controls are good for is controlling color backgrounds, duotones (or multiple tones), and text *runarounds* of paths you've made. And sometimes, time being what it is, it's easier to *silhouette* a photo at the last minute in QuarkXPress as the design changes, rather than go back to the imaging application to play with channels, paths, and outlines there. Because the controls in QuarkXPress don't affect the original image itself, the QuarkXPress controls are useful if, after imaging a page the first time, you want to "bump up" the midtones. Working on the image in QuarkXPress is the fastest way to accomplish it, especially when you don't have the original image application!

Another factor is what kind of imaging machine you use. If you just print to a laser printer, what you specify using the **Contrast** and **Halftone** commands has a big impact on the printed copy. But if you're in a prepress environment with proprietary *RIP*, *OPI* servers, print servers, or any scenario even slightly more complex than a desktop printer, many of the settings you try in this section will be overridden by the more sophisticated RIP that's in use. Many of the values described here, such as dot shape, highlight and shadow values, midtone values, and so on are definable in most RIPs and should be set up to match the negative, plate, paper, and press characteristics of the job. It's best to check with somebody knowledgeable in your prepress situation to find out what's possible, and what's desirable, with some of the features in the rest of this chapter.

SEE ALSO

➤ *To run text around an image, see page 388*

➤ *To print documents, see page 495*

➤ *To prepare a document for high-resolution output, see page 517*

Working with Eligible File Formats

The file formats whose contrast you can manipulate include the following:

- JPEG
- BMP
- PhotoCD
- PICT
- Scitex CT
- TIFF

The only image file formats whose contrast can't be manipulated are EPS and DCS.

Remember that on most platforms using QuarkXPress, the *grayscale* pictures are likely to have only 254 tones of gray plus a solid black and a pure white (no black at all). It was found many years ago that the human eye only needs that many shades of gray for the brain to see a "continuous" tone image that looks like it has an infinite number of gray tones.

Using the Picture Contrast Specifications Dialog Box

The **Contrast** menu item is found under the **View** menu. But it's a lot faster if you learn that it's ⌘+Shift+C (Ctrl+Shift+C): the keyboard equivalent takes you to the Picture Contrast Specifications dialog box a lot quicker (see Figure 14.4). The picture contrast control manipulates those 256 shades of gray in a black and white picture, or the color shades, which can number in the millions.

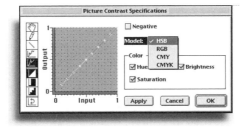

FIGURE 14.4

The Picture Contrast Specifications dialog box allows you to manipulate the contrast of the picture.

Color pictures in bitmapped format (TIFF and *PICT*, for example) can be edited in *HSB* (hue, saturation, and brightness), RGB (red, green and blue—what your screen uses to show the image), CMY (cyan, magenta, and yellow—three of the *process colors* used in four-color printing), and CMYK (cyan, magenta, yellow, and black—the four process ink colors used in most color printing).

The various controls affect the picture in different ways, detailed in the following sections. The best way to create truly unique images for your page is to spend some time playing with the controls to see the effect they have on the specific images you're working on. If the picture is grayscale, only one curve is available. If the picture is in color, you can edit one or more curves at the same time: three for HSB and CMY; four for CMYK.

A good trick to get used to, in the Picture Contrast Specifications dialog box or anywhere you see it, is to use the **Apply** button. This shows you the changes you're considering without applying them permanently. Using ⌘+A (Ctrl+A) from the keyboard is the same as using the **Apply** button (but only when you're in a dialog box; the rest of the time it's **Select All**).

Why is black called "K"?

The reason the black is referred to as "K" rather than "B" is that the black color plate, when printed first as it often is, is also called the "key:" the colors to which the others have to "register" or line up on. Also, since many people think of cyan as "blue," "B" could mean either black or cyan.

An even better trick if you're not sure about what you're doing or want to see the effects of your changes quickly is to do the following: Hold down the Option (Alt) key and press the **Apply** button, or use ⌘+Option+A (Ctrl+Alt+A) from the keyboard. Any changes from now on to the picture using the contrast box will be applied to the picture as you make the changes. Instant preview! The **Apply** button stays in the Instant Preview mode even when you close the dialog box and open it up later for another picture. To "un-stick" the key, just use Option+Apply or ⌘+Option+A (Ctrl+Alt+A) again. The Apply button will return to its normal state.

The Picture Contrast Controls

The nine picture contrast boxes work pretty much the way you'd expect them to. Grouped in three major areas separated by light gray bars, the first five at the top of the bar allow you to manipulate the curves. The next group of three boxes reshape the curves into one of three basic starting curves. And the last tool inverts changes made on the curve (see Figure 14.5).

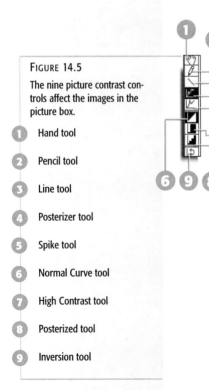

FIGURE 14.5

The nine picture contrast controls affect the images in the picture box.

1. Hand tool

2. Pencil tool

3. Line tool

4. Posterizer tool

5. Spike tool

6. Normal Curve tool

7. High Contrast tool

8. Posterized tool

9. Inversion tool

1. The **Hand** tool moves the entire curve shape within the contrast box. Holding down the Shift key while using it confines the reshaping to either the horizontal or vertical. And when you move a curve to the edge of the box and release the mouse, the curve flattens out where it meets the side of the box (see Figure 14.6).

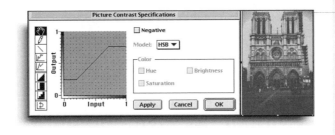

FIGURE 14.6

The diagonal contrast curve was moved left until the diagonal curve was clipped on the top and left sides, and then dragged back to the middle. The effect of these moves was to "clip" the highlight and shadow detail and leave just the midtones in the image.

2. The **Pencil** tool allows you to draw your own tonal curve. Although QuarkXPress is to be considered admirable in offering this choice, the actual use of the tool is awkward at best. It's virtually impossible to draw a smooth, accurate curve with this tool (although using a graphics tablet and stylus helps). Again, you're probably better off making subtle changes such as lightening or darkening the midtones in your image manipulation software before bringing the image onto the page (see Figure 14.7).

FIGURE 14.7

A shallow "S" shape was attempted to lighten up the midtones, usually a good thing to do with scans that are done on desktop equipment.

3. The **Line** tool allows you make linear adjustments to the curve. Purely for special effects, it's another of these tools that's too hard to control for useful production work but has some interesting effects if you play with it long enough. Holding down the Shift key moves the modifications horizontally and/or vertically. Keep in mind that as you move portions of the curve on top of each other or next to each other, you are "clipping" again the number of gray (or color) shades that are being used to display, and ultimately be output, the image (see Figure 14.8).

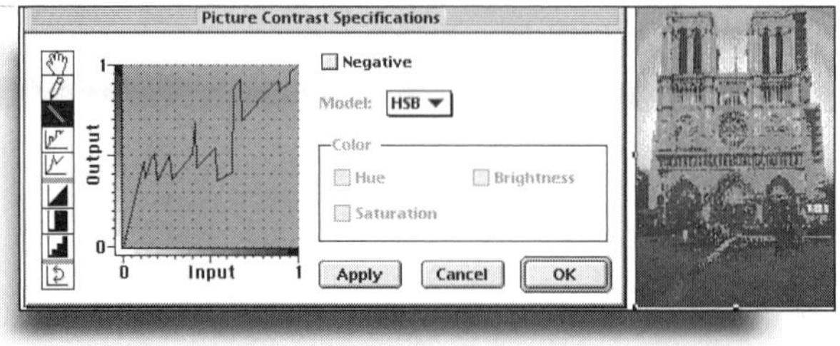

FIGURE 14.8

The **Line** tool's main purpose seems to be to make the picture "chunky" by throwing away some of the levels of 256 tones in each of the colors in the original.

4. The tool that QuarkXPress calls the **Posterizer** might be the best one to use within QuarkXPress. When you understand what it does, and combining it with QuarkXPress's color palette for the image or for the background, you can get some very interesting effects using this tool. Essentially, it purposely "throws away" a lot of the 256 shades of color (see Figure 14.9). A color image manipulated this way, each color having a slightly different curve or posterization effect applied to it, can really stretch the capability of a printer to reproduce it like you saw on the screen. Definitely something to play with on a long winter's afternoon!

FIGURE 14.9

The **Posterizer** tool was used, and some of its points moved, to accomplish this effect. It's basically a picture that has only pure white, a 25% gray, a 50% gray, a 75% gray, and a solid black.

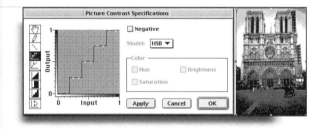

5. Quark calls the next tool the **Spike** tool, but you can also consider it a fine-tuning version of the **Posterizer** tool. It puts points along the curve at 10% intervals so you can grab them and move them a little more conveniently. If you play long enough with the five manipulation tools with a good, full scale photo, you'll begin to discover the infinite variations that can be made to a photo for effect (see Figure 14.10).

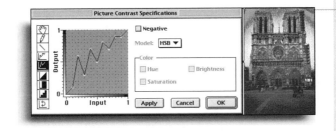

FIGURE 14.10

The **Spike** tool allows you grab points and move them in 10% increments. Here, the 20% tone has been changed to a 60% tone, the 40% tones has been changed to a 70% tone, and the 60% tone has been changed to an 80% tone, effectively making "bands" in the normally light sky.

6. The next three tools set or reset the curves back to their default positions so you can play again with the five manipulation tools. Called, in order, the **Normal Curve** tool, the **High Contrast** tool, and the **Posterized** tool, they are the basic starting points for manipulating the contrast of the image (see Figures 14.11 through 14.13).

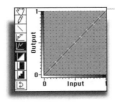

FIGURE 14.11

The **Normal Curve** tool's default is a 45° straight line, based on the assumption that a 10% tone in the original will be a 10% tone when you output it to a printer, an 80% tone in the original will be an 80% on output, and so on.

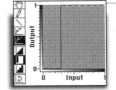

FIGURE 14.12

The **High Contrast** tool eliminates some of the tones, in effect making the output just black and white. In this curve, pure white and everything up to a 30% tone of gray will be output at 0% (white). Everything in the original photo from 30% gray up to solid black (100%) will be output at solid black.

FIGURE 14.13

The **Posterized** tool is nothing more than the **High Contrast** tool with a few more "output" points added. This default curve says, in essence, to take everything in the original picture that's between 0% (white) and 10% gray, and make it white. Then take everything between 10% and 30% gray in the original and make it 20% at output. And so on.

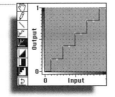

The bottom group of tools in the dialog box consists of just one tool, the **Inversion** tool. It flips the curves currently selected on the graph portion of the picture contrast box, inverting the changes you've made to the image.

Last, but not least, the Picture Contrast Specifications dialog box has a **Negative** check box to convert the image to a reverse of the picture's current contrast. Clicking in the box applies any changes being considered in the contrast curves: it's like saying **OK**. (Of course, ⌘+Z (Ctrl+Z) will reverse the last change and bring you back to where you were.)

Creating Custom Halftone Screens for Images

QuarkXPress also has the capability to create special screens and effects right within QuarkXPress itself. You can't preview them; printing them is the only way to preview the effects each of the commands will have. As in other image manipulation features of QuarkXPress, it's best to ask the local tech guru where you're going to be printing the final job (in-house or out-of-house) the effect that the RIP is going to have on any of these settings. Some RIPs are set up to override settings coming from a file to produce consistent output.

SEE ALSO

➤ To print documents, see page 495
➤ To prepare a document for high-resolution output, see page 517

Working with Eligible File Formats

The file formats whose *halftone* screen can be manipulated include the following:

- JPEG
- BMP
- PAINT
- PICT
- TIFF

Image file formats whose halftone screen can't be manipulated are *EPS*, *DCS*, and Scitex CT.

Using the Picture Halftone Specifications Dialog Box

Choose **Halftone** from the **Style** menu—⌘+Shift+H (Ctrl+Shift+H)—to modify the halftone screening of images for special effects. Don't go here to set your printer's halftone specifications or to set up images for *high-resolution* output. It's pretty much for special effects only, and they're pretty crude at that, with very few choices.

Any modifications made to a picture using this box will override the settings you make in the **Output** tab of the **Print** dialog box when you print. Caution: This might or might not be true when you're in a prepress environment with proprietary RIPs. The best way to use these special effects is, as always, to try them out when you're not on deadline or otherwise busy, so you'll know what happens ahead of time (see Figure 14.14).

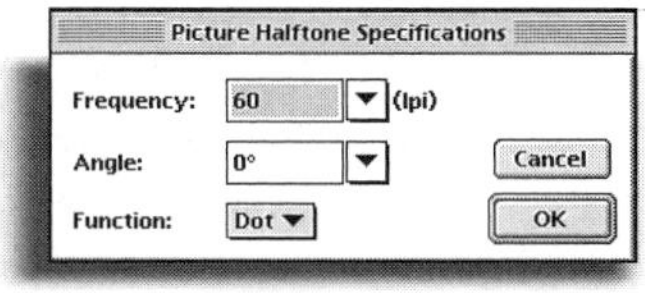

FIGURE 14.14

The Picture Halftone Specifications dialog box is for special effects that you can't preview on the screen.

Clipping Paths and Alpha Channels

There are two major methods in QuarkXPress for doing special functions like *silhouetting* pictures and wrapping type around objects. You can create *clipping paths* and *channels* in an image editing application such as Photoshop, and QuarkXPress will recognize them and use them to clip or to make *runarounds*. Or you can create both the clipping paths and the runaround paths in QuarkXPress.

Clipping paths are closed shapes (in *Bézier* format) that define what will print and what will not print. You usually tell the software to print the items inside the Bézier shape and not to print the image outside the Bézier shape, but that's not always the case. A single picture can also have many clipping paths.

A channel, or alpha channel, is usually just another way of describing which areas are to print and which areas are not to print.

A runaround path is created in QuarkXPress and tells QuarkXPress where to run the type. The path doesn't have to be the same size or shape of the clipping path, although usually it's better to have QuarkXPress generate the runaround from the clipping path and then modify it to make the type flow around the shape better.

SEE ALSO

➤ *To run text around an image, see page 388*

Working with Eligible File Formats

QuarkXPress can create its own clipping paths for image files in any format. The program can also use embedded alpha channels or clipping paths from the following formats:

- TIFFs can have embedded paths and alpha channels.
- EPS, BMP, JPEG, PCX, PICT, and Scitex CT file formats can only contain embedded paths.
- Any Photoshop image that QuarkXPress can read will also let QuarkXPress read the embedded paths in that file.

Using Existing Clipping Paths and Alpha Channels

QuarkXPress allows you to choose from paths and channels already embedded in Photoshop images. The advantages are that you only have to do the work of creating the masks (*paths* and *channels*) once in a file to use it, not only with QuarkXPress, but also for other uses such as web pages. The choice is yours: The tools QuarkXPress provides are easier to use than the Photoshop tools, if you're not a frequent Photoshop user. Keep in mind that these sets of tools are for how the picture will be reproduced: what will get silhouetted and what will not. Text runaround is another set of commands in the Item>Modify>Runaround menu.

Creating Clipping Paths

Choose **Clipping** from the **Item** menu to fine-tune the silhouetting of images. ⌘+Option+T (Ctrl+Alt+T) works as well; either method brings up the **Clipping** tab in the Modify dialog box, where you can choose the clipping path method from the **Type** pop-up menu (see Figure 14.15). QuarkXPress's clipping paths don't affect your original picture files: They simply use the high resolution files to draw a path around the selection and then store that information as part of the picture box's attributes in the QuarkXPress file for later output.

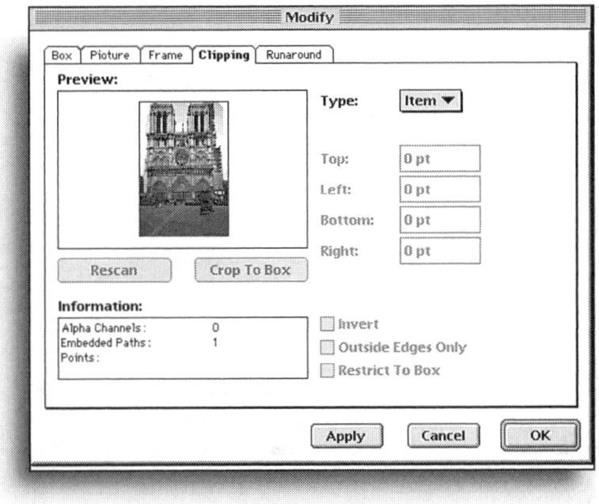

FIGURE 14.15
The **Clipping** tab in the Modify dialog box, with the information box that contains statistics about the choices.

Unfortunately, there is no way to "preview" the results of the clipping except for the little window view in the Clipping tab. You can, however, edit the paths after they are all done.

Clipping the Image to the Box

Choosing **Item** crops the image to the picture box, whatever shape the picture box is in. It doesn't actually create a clipping path. The **Picture Bounds** function, described next, actually clips the image to the box shape.

Clipping Using Picture Bounds

The **Picture Bounds** choice clips a picture to its original shape. The values in the **Top**, **Left**, **Bottom**, and **Right** fields are the outset (or inset) of the clipping path from the picture box's present boundary. A positive value outsets (adds to) the clipping path: negative numbers in the values fields inset (subtract from) the clipping path.

Clipping Using Embedded Paths

The **Embedded Path** choice changes your choices somewhat. It looks for a path (or more than one if more than one is present) in the image, and you can use the pop-up menu to the right to select the specific path you want the image clipped to (see Figure 14.16).

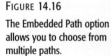

FIGURE **14.16**

The Embedded Path option allows you to choose from multiple paths.

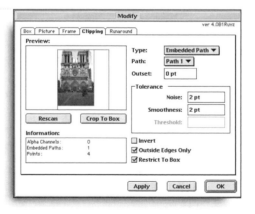

Clipping Using Alpha Channels

The **Alpha Channel** choice is used for those images that have been imported with an alpha channel included. An alpha channel differs from a Bézier clipping path in that it is a selection created with an 8-bit mask. An 8-bit mask is a grayscale image used to indicate which parts of the image are going to be visible and which parts will be transparent, and because it's 8-bits it can contain a lot more information about toning, feathering, and so on than a path.

Clipping Using Non-White Areas

The **Non-White Areas** choice is very useful if your picture has a strong white or black background behind the basic subject. The best results are obtained when there is a lot of contrast between the foreground and the background. Product and table-top photography is a good choice for this kind of silhouetting; you can save a lot of time (and money) by not having to create the channels or paths in an image editing program first. It can also be useful for images produced by scanning objects directly on a flatbed scanner.

Modifying the Generated Path: the Tolerance Menu

The secret to a successful clipping path lies in understanding how big your image is, how big it's going to be used, the number of *pixels* per inch in the original image, and what the final output is going to be. Generally speaking, the higher the resolution of the original picture, and the higher the resolution of the output, the better the results will look. (But that's true of all desktop technology, anyway!)

Above all, don't click on the **Apply** button under the assumption you'll get a quick preview of the clipping path: QuarkXPress has to sit there and calculate the clipping path from the high-resolution file anyway. And if you wait all that time for the Apply button, and click on the OK button, Quark does it all over again. That's great if you're looking to take a long break for lunch. (And maybe a jog around the park, and maybe get the car washed.)

Here's how to fine-tune the clipping paths you generate within QuarkXPress. Keep in mind these tools only work with the **Embedded Path**, **Alpha Channel**, or **Non-White Areas** commands in the **Clipping** tab of the Modify dialog box (⌘+M (Ctrl+M)).

The Outset Field

The **Outset** field changes the size of the clipping area to make it larger, smaller, or the same size as the image you clipped. A positive number in the outset field makes the clipping path further from the object: A negative number in the field decreases the amount of image included in the clipping path (see Figures 14.17 and 14.18).

Noise Field

The **Noise** field deletes "stray" pixels from the clipping path that are smaller than the value you set. For instance, if you set the value in **Noise** to 5 points, any paths QuarkXPress sees that are 5 points or less in diameter are eliminated from the path.

The noise filter works on all the paths in the same image as though they were one path. The implications are that if you had an image with many small pieces scattered around some large objects, the value you give the **Noise** level will affect them all. So if the small pieces are 6 points in size, a **Noise** value of 6 will eliminate all the small pieces from the clipping path.

The Smoothness Field

The **Smoothness** field looks at all the pixels along the edge of the clipping path to determine how many points to create. At a setting of 0, it places a point at every pixel and makes the clipping path very complicated—and will probably cause some problems at printing time. A setting of 2 points creates a clipping mask with far fewer points in it and yet still fairly accurately renders outline of the image faithfully. A value as high as 18 will be almost useless, as it will create an outline 18 points away from where you really want it. But it will be smooth and contain very few points!

Again, experimentation off-deadline will pay many benefits, and you'll need to make many prints to test the various settings. The **Information** box displays the number of points after you created the clipping path. Keep an eye on the total number of clipping paths you create for the whole document: There's probably a ceiling you shouldn't get near to prevent crashes and PostScript errors.

The Threshold Field

The **Threshold** field (available only for the **Non-White Areas** and **Alpha Channels** types of clipping paths) looks at the level of gray you want to start throwing away to create the clipping path. If the background is very white, with few shadows, a number of 10 or 15 would work fine. The number you set in the field is the gray value that will become white, and of course, every gray value below that number also becomes white.

Rescan Button

The **Rescan** button rebuilds the clipping path based on whatever changes you made since the last clipping values were entered in the value boxes. Don't use the **Apply** button; there's no advantage to trying to look at a preview because it takes just as long to do the preview as it does to click on **Apply**, and if you do click on **Apply**, it does it all over again.

Three More Commands for Some Interesting Effects

Creative effects can be made by combining clipping paths inside and outside picture boxes. These effects can be combined with how you color the box, the object, and the page. With the addition of **XTensions** such as ShadowCaster to create soft shadow effects, a lot of the things that previously had to be done in drawing programs can now be done in QuarkXPress.

Making an Image Outside of the Clipping Path

If you click **Invert** in the **Clipping** tab, the background color of the picture box fills the clipped shape where the clipping took place, and the "outside" of the image will be the printing part. Think of it as the reverse of everything you've done with clipping up to now.

Making Paths Inside Paths

Checking **Restrict to Box** means the clipping path stops where it encounters an edge of a picture box, so the net effect is to make a silhouette contained within the picture box. Not checking **Outside Edges Only** causes QuarkXPress to make as many clipping paths as needed to match your settings of **Outset**, **Noise**, **Smoothness**, and **Threshold**. If the image contains "holes," they'll be clipped too—so an image of a doughnut would have a path along its outside edge and along its inner hole.

Making an Image "Pop Out" of a Picture Box

The **Restrict to Box** check box does just that: if the image is larger than the box, the clipping paths are created with the edges of the picture box as the outermost boundary. But if the **Restrict to Box** box is not checked, QuarkXPress will silhouette the entire object and lay the entire silhouette on top of the picture box, which means that you can get some nice effects with a colored box seemingly having some portions of the image fly out of some portions of the box.

Editing Clipping Paths

QuarkXPress does allow you edit the shape(s) of clipping paths. Simply choose **Item** from the **Edit** menu, then **Clipping Path** from the submenu, or press Option+Shift+F4 (Alt+Shift+F4), and you'll be presented with a bunch of green points that are, in fact, Bézier *points* (see Figure 14.19). This is very useful for making better curves and reducing the number of points and, in general, cleaning up the outline before printing.

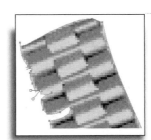

FIGURE 14.19

QuarkXPress allows you to edit the Bézier paths that it has created.

Just don't move the image inside its picture box when you're all done: you'll "mis-register" the image with its clipped path. The image that lies underneath the clipping path is only QuarkXPress's low resolution "screen image" of your higher resolution image file, so the editing requires a little bit of guesswork about where some pixels begin and end. If you're really critical, it's better to go back to Photoshop and make the better curves on an image that can display more pixels.

SEE ALSO

➤ *To edit Bézier paths, see page 314*

Clipping paths aren't backward-compatible

If you're saving your file as a 3.x-format file, which version 4 now allows you to do, users of QuarkXPress 3.x won't see your QuarkXPress-generated clipping paths when they print or view the file. There's just too much difference in the way QuarkXPress handles these clipping paths for 3.x to successfully work with them.

Enhancing Type
with Graphics

In this chapter, we look at combining graphics with text as well as using text, or type, itself as a graphic element. Always remember that you have an extensive selection of graphics quickly available, literally at your fingertips, from any keyboard.

Typography is an art and type itself is art; used effectively they can enhance your document just as much as or even more than imported graphic images. With the addition of more sophisticated *runarounds* and the capability to turn text into *paths* or *boxes*, QuarkXPress 4 has become a more self-sufficient application for achieving many graphic effects. You can accomplish a lot without having to use another application.

Text Wraps

Layering is a core concept when it comes to wrapping text around a graphic element or other item. The runaround is applied to the top item and affects the items underneath it. If you have trouble getting runarounds to work, it often means you don't have items stacked in the proper order.

SEE ALSO

➤ *To understand how QuarkXPress layers objects, see page 6*

Wrapping Text Around Items

Text can be wrapped around any item—a text box, picture box, *no-content box*, or line. This is different from wrapping text around the content of a box, but keep reading and you'll find out about that, too.

SEE ALSO

➤ *To create a text box, see page 105*

➤ *To create a picture box, see page 105*

➤ *To create a no-content box, see page 111*

➤ *To create a line, see page 106*

Item Runaround

To run text around an item:

1. Select the front item using either the Content [icon] or Item [icon] tool.

2. Select **Modify** from the **Item** menu, then click on the **Runaround** tab. Pressing ⌘+T (Ctrl+T) goes directly to the **Runaround** tab (see Figures 15.1 through 15.3)

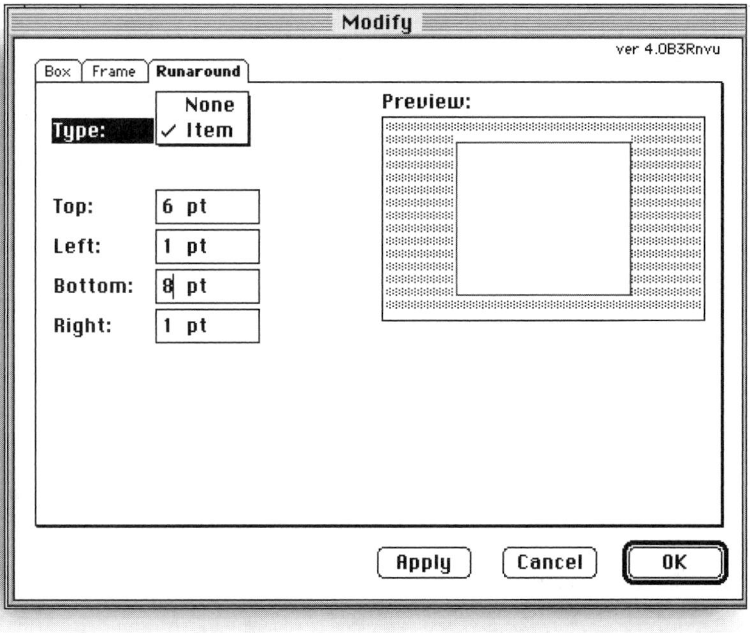

FIGURE 15.1

The **Runaround** tab of the Modify dialog box includes a preview of how the runaround will look.

3. Pick the type of runaround desired. If the item is a text or no-content box, there are only two choices: **None** or **Item**.

4. Type in the amount of runaround needed on each side of the item. The amounts do not all have to be the same.

If you select **None** as the type of runaround, none of the text sitting behind the runaround item is shifted; it continues to flow as if there is no obstructing item at all. The small preview window gives you a bit of a hint about how your choices will take effect. Use the **Apply** button to update the preview after you have made changes.

All-Sided Runaround

New in QuarkXPress 4 is the capability to have text run around all the sides of an obstructing item (see Figure 15.4). To accomplish this, you need to take an extra step before determining the runarounds.

Lorem ipsum dolor sit amet, consectetuer adipiscing elit, sed diam nonummy nibh euismod tincidunt ut laoreet dolore magna aliquam erat volutpat. Ut wisi enim ad minim veniam, quis nostrud exerci tation ullamcorper suscipit lobortis nisl ut aliquip ex ea commodo consequat. Duis autem vel eum iriure dolor in hendrerit in vulputate velit esse molestie consequat, vel illum dolore eu feugiat nulla facilisis at vero eros et accumsan et iusto odio dignissim qui blandit praesent luptatum zzril delenit augue duis dolore te feugait nulla facilisi. Lorem ipsum dolor sit amet, consectetuer adipiscing elit, sed diam nonummy nibh euismod tincidunt ut laoreet dolore magna aliquam erat volutpat. Ut wisi enim ad minim veniam, quis nostrud exerci tation ullamcorper suscipit lobortis nisl ut aliquip ex ea commodo

Lorem ipsum dolor sit amet, consectetuer adipiscing elit, sed diam nonummy nibh euismod tincidunt ut laoreet dolore magna aliquam erat volutpat. Ut wisi enim ad minim veniam, quis nostrud exerci tation ullamcorper suscipit lobortis nisl ut aliquip ex ea commodo consequat. Duis autem vel eum iriure dolor in hendrerit in vulputate velit esse molestie consequat, vel illum dolore eu feugiat nulla facilisis at vero eros et accumsan et iusto odio dignissim qui blandit praesent luptatum zzril delenit augue duis dolore te feugait nulla facilisi. Lorem ipsum dolor sit amet, consectetuer adipiscing elit, sed diam nonummy nibh euismod tincidunt ut laoreet dolore magna aliquam erat volutpat. Ut wisi enim ad minim veniam, quis nostrud exerci tation ullamcorper suscipit lobortis nisl ut aliquip ex ea commodo consequat.
Duis autem vel eum iriure dolor in her

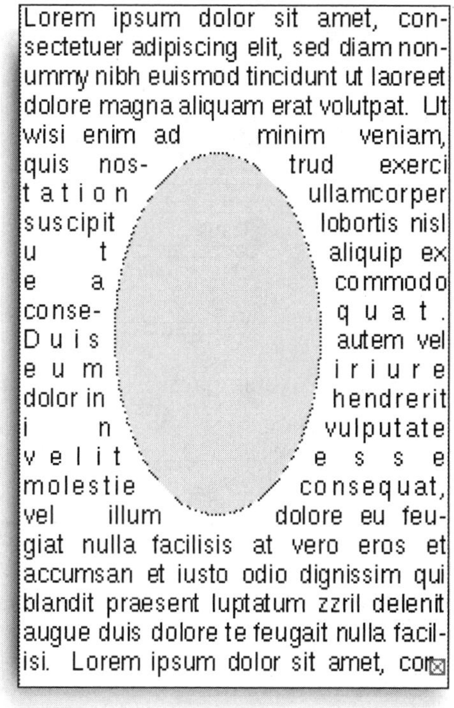

Lorem ipsum dolor sit amet, consectetuer adipiscing elit, sed diam nonummy nibh euismod tincidunt ut laoreet
dolore magna aliquam erat volutpat. Ut
wisi enim ad   minim   veniam,
quis nos-   trud   exerci
t a t i o n   ullamcorper
suscipit   lobortis nisl
u   t   aliquip ex
e   a   commodo
conse-   q u a t .
D u i s   autem vel
e u m   i r i u r e
dolor in   hendrerit
i   n   vulputate
v e l i t   e   s   s   e
molestie   consequat,
vel   illum   dolore eu feugiat nulla facilisis at vero eros et
accumsan et iusto odio dignissim qui
blandit praesent luptatum zzril delenit
augue duis dolore te feugait nulla facilisi. Lorem ipsum dolor sit amet, con

FIGURE 15.4

Text can run around all sides of
an item.

1. Select the text box that is being obstructed, using either the
   Item or Content tool.

2. Choose **Modify** from the **Item** menu and click on the **Text**
   tab. Click the box next to **Run Text Around All Sides** (see
   Figure 15.5).

3. Click **OK**.

4. Select the obstructing box and set the runaround as noted
   above.

It is fine to modify the text box after setting the runaround
rather than before. The preview in the Runaround dialog, however, will be accurate only if you select **Run Text Around All
Sides** first.

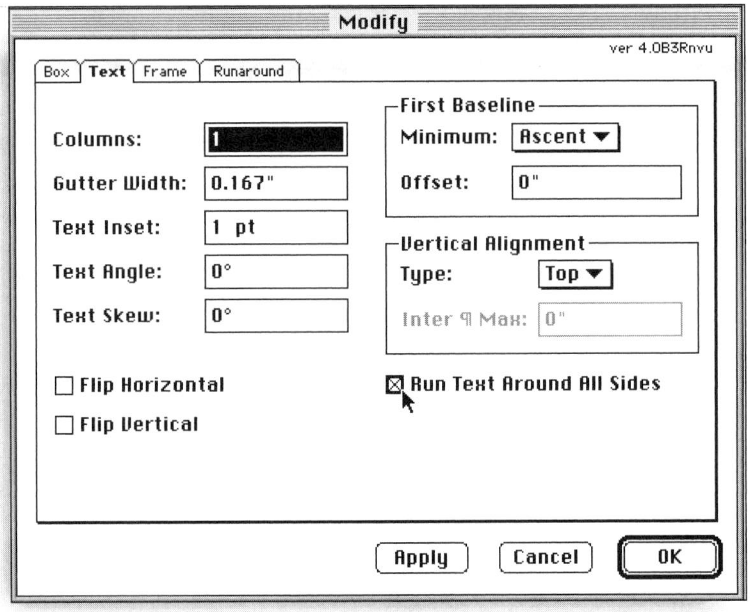

FIGURE 15.5

The Text tab of the Modify dialog box contains just one runaround control.

Maintain Leading

This preference setting affects your runarounds to some degree. If turned on, the runaround along the bottom of an item or image might change from what you specified. The **Maintain Leading** setting pushes the text in the underlying box to the next *baseline* on the baseline grid instead of letting it continue at the offset you selected. The purpose of this is to keep text aligned horizontally in side-by-side columns. If you don't care about the horizontal alignment of text across columns, and maintaining precise measurements on runarounds is more important, **Maintain Leading** should be turned off.

SEE ALSO

➤ *To turn on **Maintain Leading**, see page 59*

Wrapping Text Around Images

When wrapping text around graphic images instead of around the box containing the image, you have many more choices to make and more options for how your runaround will work.

Some options require knowledge of embedded *clipping paths* and *channels*, as well as clipping paths generated in QuarkXPress.

SEE ALSO

➤ *To use embedded clipping paths, see page 374*

➤ *To create clipping paths, see page 375*

➤ *To edit clipping paths, see page 381*

Custom Text Wraps

When you have a picture box with something in it, you have many more choices about how your runaround will work. Highlight your picture box with either the Content or Item tool, then select **Modify** from the **Item** menu, then click on the **Runaround** tab, or press ⌘+T (Ctrl+T) to go directly to the **Runaround** tab (see Figure 15.6).

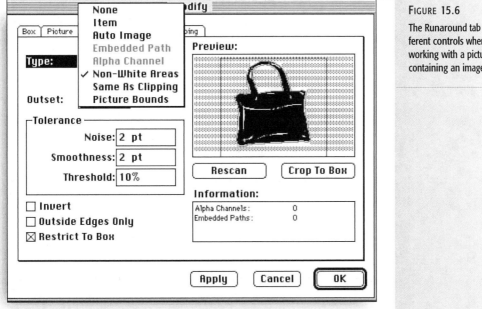

FIGURE 15.6

The Runaround tab shows different controls when you're working with a picture box containing an image.

Now instead of just two types of runarounds, you may have up to eight, depending on the content of the box:

- **None** does not change text flow; the background box acts as if there is no obstructing image in front of it.
- **Item** forces text to flow around the outside edges of the box.
- **Auto Image** forces text in the background box to flow around the non-white portions of the image. This runaround path cannot be edited.
- **Embedded Path** uses a clipping path already existing in the imported graphic to determine the runaround. Text reflows around the image.
- **Alpha Channel** uses an alpha channel already existing in the imported graphic to determine the runaround. Text reflows around the image.
- **Non-White Areas** creates a runaround path similar to that created by **Auto Image**, except that it can be edited.
- **Same As Clipping** uses the path specified in the **Clipping** tab of the Modify dialog box, either embedded or created by QuarkXPress.
- **Picture Bounds** creates a runaround path that follows the shape of the graphic, including any white area. This results in a rectangular runaround._

Additional choices in this dialog box depend on what type of runaround you select. They are not all available for every type of runaround.

- **Outset** determines how far away from the image your text will flow.
- **Noise** deals with small non-white areas within your image. A higher number masks out small bits of noise surrounded by white by determining the smallest allowable closed path. Notice in Figure 15.7 that the area inside the purse handle has no text running inside it. The **Noise** value is set so high that QuarkXPress has masked off the entire area.

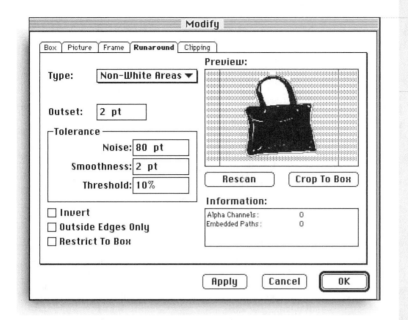

FIGURE 15.7

A high **Noise** value excludes areas of the image from the runaround path.

- **Smoothness** determines how many points are used to create the runaround path. Higher numbers produce more angular runarounds and are less accurate in following the shape of the image (see Figure 15.8).

- **Threshold**: Higher numbers mean QuarkXPress sees more of the image as being white. The higher the number, the darker the areas QuarkXPress "sees" as white. If **Threshold** is set to 100%, QuarkXPress sees the entire image as white (see Figure 15.9).

- **Invert** forces text to flow inside the shape of your image instead of around and outside the image (see Figure 15.10).

- **Outside Edges Only** makes the runaround path follow only the outside edge of the image. If **Outside Edges Only** were not checked in Figure 15.11, text would run inside the purse handle.

- **Restrict To Box** keeps the runaround effect inside the box containing the image, even if the outset or other selections would naturally take the runaround path outside the edges of the box (see Figure 15.12).

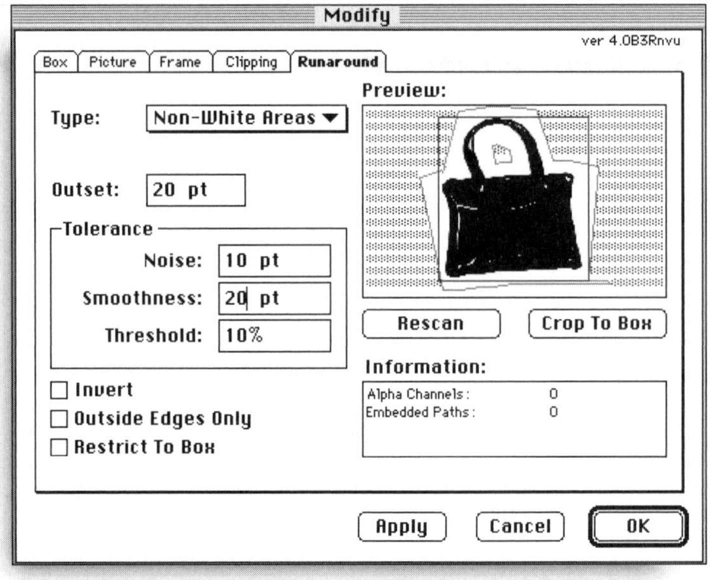

FIGURE 15.8

The higher the **Smoothness** value, the less accurate the runaround path.

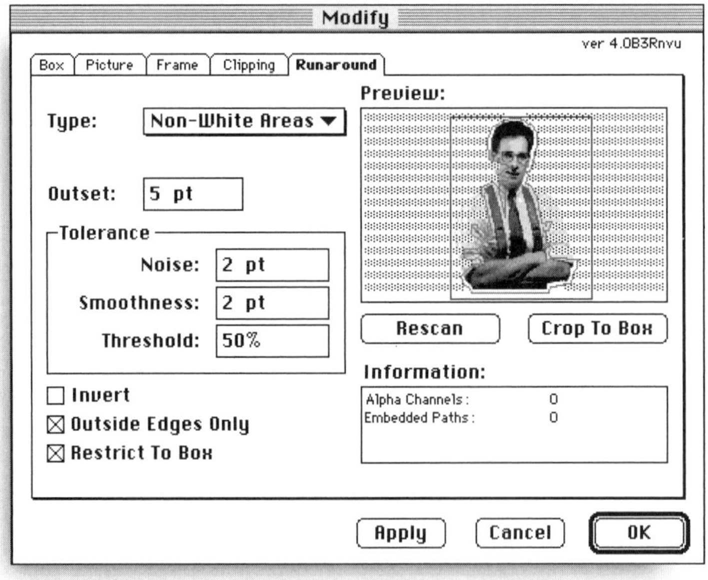

FIGURE 15.9

High **Threshold** values place white areas of the image outside the runaround path.

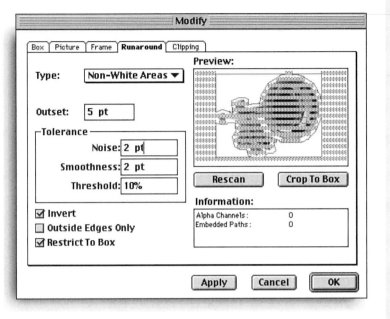

FIGURE 15.10

An inverted runaround path
places text over the image.

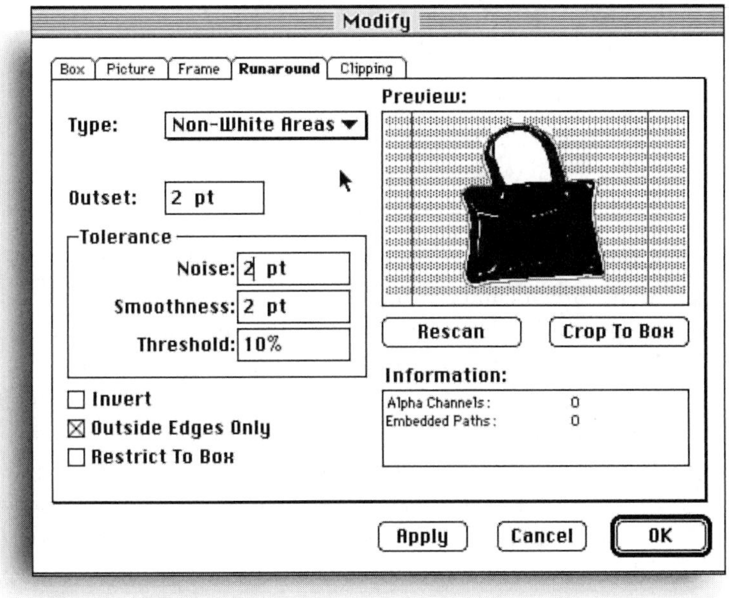

Modify

Box | Picture | Frame | **Runaround** | Clipping

Type: Non-White Areas ▼

Outset: 5 pt

Tolerance

Noise: 2 pt
Smoothness: 2 pt
Threshold: 10%

☑ Invert
☐ Outside Edges Only
☑ Restrict To Box

Preview:

Rescan | Crop To Box

Information:

Alpha Channels: 0
Embedded Paths: 0

Apply | Cancel | OK

FIGURE 15.11

Outside Edges Only forces
text to stay outside the purse
handle.

Modify

Box | Picture | Frame | **Runaround** | Clipping

Type: Non-White Areas ▼

Outset: 2 pt

Tolerance

Noise: 2 pt
Smoothness: 2 pt
Threshold: 10%

☐ Invert
☒ Outside Edges Only
☐ Restrict To Box

Preview:

Rescan | Crop To Box

Information:

Alpha Channels: 0
Embedded Paths: 0

Apply | Cancel | OK

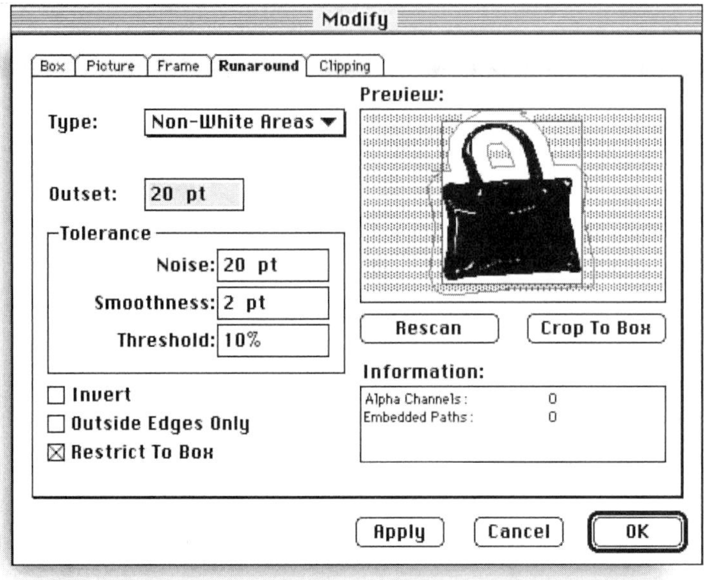

FIGURE 15.12

Restrict To Box keeps the runaround path outside the box from taking effect.

- **Information** reports how many alpha channels or embedded paths an imported graphic image contains.

- **Rescan image** updates the preview.

- **Crop To Box** acts much the same as **Restrict To Box**, but it actually alters the runaround path to stay within the boundaries of the picture box.

After you have created a custom runaround path, it can be edited in the same manner as *Bézier* curves. Select the box containing the graphic with a runaround and then choose **Edit** from the **Item** menu and **Runaround** from the submenu, or press Option+F4 (Alt+F4), which acts as a toggle switch to turn display of the path on and off (see Figure 15.13). The path appears around the image. Move any of the points or adjust the *control handles* on the *points*. To add a new point, hold down the Option (Alt) key and click the path. Use the same key combination to delete a point by Option+clicking (Alt+clicking) it.

SEE ALSO

➤ *To edit Bézier curves, see page 314*

Lorem ipsum dolor sit amet, consectetuer adipiscing elit, sed diam nonummy nibh euismod tincidunt ut laoreet dolore magna aliquam erat volutpat. Ut wisi enim ad minim veniam, quis nostrud exerci tation ullamcorper suscipit lobortis nisl ut aliquip ex ea commodo consequat. Duis autem vel eum iriure dolor in hendrerit in vulputate velit esse molestie consequat, vel illum dolore eu feugiat nulla facilisis at vero eros et accumsan et iusto odio dignissim qui blandit praesent luptatum zzril delenit augue duis dolore te feugait nulla facilisi. Lorem ipsum dolor sit amet, consectetuer adipiscing elit, sed diam nonummy nibh euismod tincidunt ut laoreet dolore magna aliquam erat volutpat. Ut wisi enim ad minim veniam, quis nostrud exerci tation ullamcorper nostrud exerci suscipit lobortis nisl ut aliquip ex ea commodo consequat. Duis autem vel hendrerit in eum iriure dolor in esse molestie vulputate velit illum dolore eu consequat, vel sis at vero eros et feugiat nulla facili- accumsan et iusto odio dignissim qui blandit praesent luptatum zzril delenit augue duis dolore te feugait nulla facilisi.

Existing Paths and Channels for Text Wraps

QuarkXPress 4 recognizes clipping paths and alpha channels created in other applications. If you import a graphic with any of these features, you can use this built-in information to create a runaround path in QuarkXPress. Not only is this a time-saving feature, but it helps ensure accuracy in the way the graphic is displayed in relationship to surrounding text. Upon importing a graphic containing this information, the **Embedded Path** and **Alpha Channel** types are available in the **Runaround** tab in the **Modify** dialog box.

SEE ALSO

➤ *To import a picture, see page 339*

Clipping Tab Settings for Text Wraps

If you use QuarkXPress to create a clipping path, you can use that same path for a text runaround. Remember that every imported graphic has a clipping path of some sort—if you haven't specified one, then the default is **Item**, which is the same as the boundaries of the picture box. So if you haven't actually gone to the **Clipping** tab and created a new path, selecting the **Same As Clipping** option in the **Runaround** tab simply flows the text around the box.

SEE ALSO

➤ *To set clipping path options, see page 375*

Text Along a Path

QuarkXPress 4 can flow text along almost any path you can create. You can even link a text path from or to a text box.

Creating the Path

Text paths don't print

By default, the paths created by the text path tools have a width of 0 points, so they show on-screen as gray lines but they don't print.

Text paths are created using tools similar to those you would use to create a line. The pop-out Tool palette contains a selection of four text path tools.

Straight Paths

To create a straight text path, select the Line Text-Path tool ⬙ or the Orthogonal Text-Path tool ⬙ . Click and drag to create a path. The resulting path appears gray on your monitor but does not print (see Figure 15.14). The Line Text-Path tool draws text paths at any angle; the Orthogonal Text-Path tool draws text paths only at 90° angles.

Curved Paths

There are also two tools for creating curved text paths. The only difference between them is how they are used.

The Freehand Text-Path tool ⬙ creates a free-flowing line. To use it, click the tool and then click and drag to the shape you want the path to take. Bézier points are automatically placed on the path as you drag the mouse; you can adjust the path using standard Bézier editing techniques.

The Bézier Text-Path tool also creates Bézier lines (see Figure 15.15), but you must place the points and angle the curves yourself as you draw the path. To draw angled lines, select the tool and then click everywhere you want a point on the path. To draw curved lines, select the tool, then click and drag everywhere you want a control point.

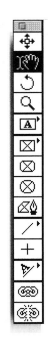

FIGURE 15.14
The Line and Orthogonal Text-Path tools create straight lines.

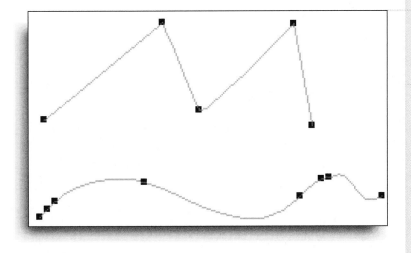

FIGURE 15.15
The Bézier and Freehand Text-Path tools create curved and angled lines.

SEE ALSO

➤ *To draw Bézier lines, see page 317*

Entering and Formatting Text

For the most part, entering and formatting text along a text path works just as it does in a *text box*—just click and start typing, or click and import a text file. Any formatting that you can apply to text in a box can also be applied to text along a path, including color and formatting styles like baseline shift.

Typed or Imported Text

Text paths act like regular text boxes. Most of the time when using a text path, you'll probably just type a line of text. To type along the path, select the path with the Content tool 🖑 and begin typing. To import text, select the path with the same tool, and then choose **Get Text** from the **File** menu or press ⌘+E (Ctrl+E) to select the text file you want to import. If the text is too long for the path, the text overflow symbol ⊠ appears at the end of the path. You can lengthen the path to accommodate the text or link to another path or text box using the regular Linking tool ⊗ .

SEE ALSO

➤ *To import text, see page 182*

➤ *To edit text, see page 204*

➤ *To link text boxes or text paths, see page 191*

Formatted Text

Standard type formatting commands or style sheets are used with text paths. Highlight any text you want to format by dragging your cursor through it. The Measurements palette looks just like a palette for a regular text box except that there is a different type of **Flip** button in the center of the palette (see Figure 15.16).

SEE ALSO

➤ *To format characters, see page 240*

➤ *To format paragraphs, see page 251*

➤ *To create paragraph style sheets, see page 298*

➤ *To create paragraph style sheets, see page 299*

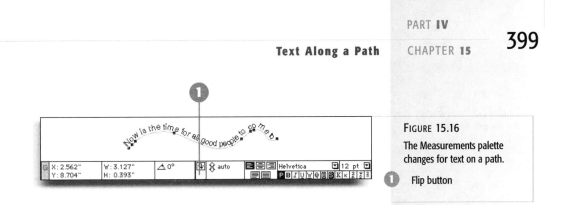

FIGURE **15.16**

The Measurements palette changes for text on a path.

❶ Flip button

Positioning Text on the Path

Some additional controls for text on a path are not used for the plain vanilla variety of text boxes. They are accessed through the Modify dialog box, where you discover a **Text Path** tab along with **Line** and **Runaround** tabs. The **Runaround** tab works just as it would for any other item. However, there are some important choices to be made in the **Line** and **Text Path** tabs.

Although the default mode for the line when putting text on a path is a color of None and a *hairline* width, you can make the line any width you want and give it a color so it shows when you print. The **Line** tab is where you select any styling you want to give the path itself. It uses the same controls as you would use when styling a line without text (see Figure 15.17). You can select any width, any style, or color and even put an arrowhead on it.

Once you have styled the path line, you can move to the **Text Path** tab to further refine your text on a path (see Figure 15.18).

SEE ALSO

➤ *To apply styling attributes to a line, see page 116*

Orientation

Text Orientation determines how the text angles along the path (see Figure 15.19). The two choices on the left allow the vertical strokes of type to rotate along the curve, keeping type perpendicular to the curve. The top-left choice keeps the letterform intact (a rainbow arc effect), while the bottom-left option allows distortion of the letterform, creating a bit of a three-dimensional effect (think of it as skewed).

FIGURE 15.17

The **Line** tab allows you to alter the path itself in a text path.

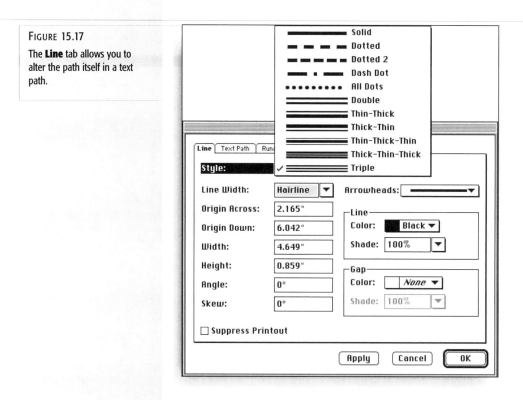

FIGURE 15.18

The **Text Path** tab lets you position text along the path.

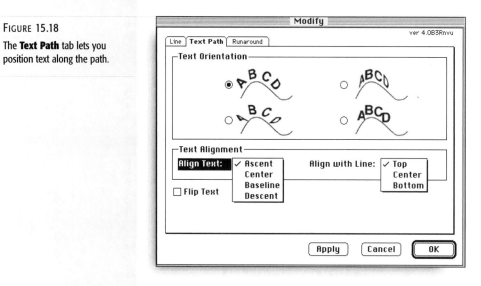

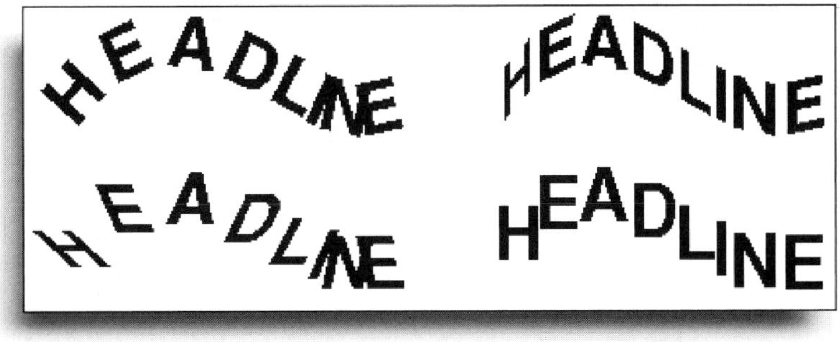

FIGURE 15.19

These four versions of the word "Headline" are the result of choosing each of the four **Text Orientation** options.

Over on the right side, the choices keep vertical strokes of type perpendicular to the page edge (or the rotation angle if the path is rotated). The top right option allows letterforms to conform to the shape of the path (ribbon style), while the bottom right choice keeps the letterform intact (a stair-step rendering).

Alignment

When working with a text path, alignment does not mean centered, justified, right-aligned, or left-aligned along the line. Instead, the **Text Alignment** controls deal with how text relates vertically to the line of the path itself. Even if you have opted to keep the line invisible, these controls make a difference in how the text flows along the path. If you selected a weight and color for the line so it shows when the document is printed, the controls are even more critical.

The **Align Text** and **Align with Line** choices read like a sentence; if you choose **Ascent** from the **Align Text** pop-up menu and **Bottom** from the **Align with Line** pop-up menu, you're telling QuarkXPress to align the *ascenders* of the text with the bottom of the line (see Figure 15.20). The small squares in the center of the path are the points on the line. You actually have 12 different choices about how your text aligns in relation to the path. To flow text inside the line used for the path, you would choose **Center** from the **Align with Line** pop-up menu. Figure 15.21 shows this type of treatment on a path that makes the text look as if it is flowing along a ribbon.

FIGURE 15.20

Here, the text's ascenders are aligned along the bottom of the line.

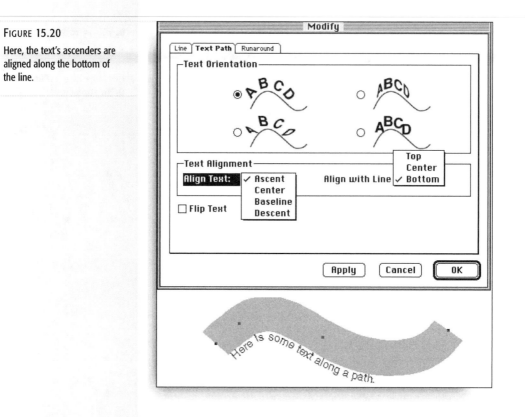

FIGURE 15.21

Here, the text is centered vertically on the line.

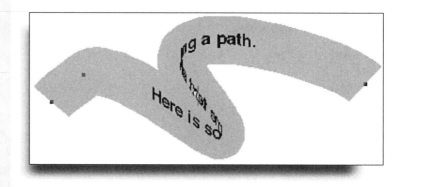

Flipping Text

The final control in the **Text Path** tab flips the text. Invoking **Flip Text** turns the text upside down and starts it at the other end of the path (see Figure 15.22). The same results are achieved when you use the **Flip** buttons in the middle of the Measurements palette.

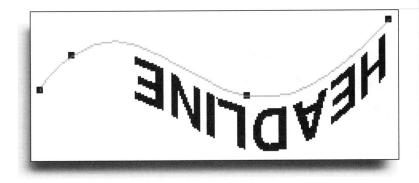

FIGURE 15.22
Here text along a path is flipped.

Text-Shaped Boxes

Although you could draw boxes that look like type, it is much easier (and a whole lot faster) to simply convert a selected piece of text to a picture or text box. Either conversion allows you to place information inside the newly created box, such as more text or a graphic image of some sort. You can also convert a single character at a time. One caveat—you can convert only a single line of text at a time to a box.

Converting Text to a Picture Box

To convert a single letter or line of text into a picture box:

1. Highlight the text by dragging your cursor through it.

2. Select **Text to Box** from the **Style** drop-down menu. This creates a new *compound picture box* shaped like the text, without disturbing the text. To delete the text and create a compound picture box that's *anchored* in the text box, hold down Option (Alt) while choosing **Text to Box**.

It really can't get much easier than this (see Figure 15.23). The new picture box has an X through it just like other picture boxes so you can tell what it is. Import a texture, picture, or any other graphic element into the box, and it fills the shape of the letters.

You also can put a frame on the letters, fill them with a color, skew them, or do anything else you normally do to a picture box. Notice that the letters are treated as a single box. A quick design note—make sure an imported graphic image fills the box enough to define the shape of the letters or they will be hard to read.

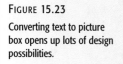

FIGURE 15.23

Converting text to picture box opens up lots of design possibilities.

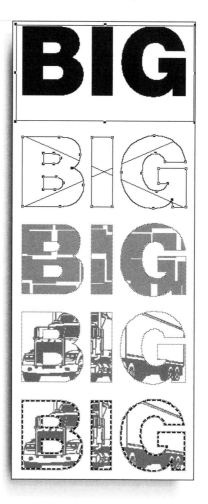

Converting a Picture Box to a Text Box

After making the initial conversion of text to a picture box, you then can turn the picture box into a text box and actually type

inside it. With the text-shaped picture box selected, choose
Content from the **Item** menu and select **Text** from the submenu.

Notice that the X through the box disappears and it now
assumes the attributes of a text box (see Figure 15.24). The letters are combined in one compound text box; to split them into
separate boxes, select the box and choose **Split** from the **Item**
menu, then **Outside Paths** from the submenu.

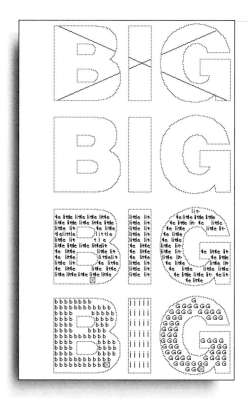

FIGURE 15.24
Text-shaped text boxes can
contain text in several
configurations.

If you split a line of text into its separate letter shapes, you can
have both picture and text boxes in the same word, or keep them
all as text boxes and put different text in each shape. You could
also keep them all as picture boxes and put a different graphic
element in each shape. There are myriad creative possibilities.

Editing Text-Shaped Boxes

A text-shaped picture or text box is a Bézier box and has control points that you can use to change its shape (see Figure 15.25). Click and drag on the point you want to move; click and drag the control handles to change the angle of a curve.

SEE ALSO

➤ *To edit Bézier shapes, see page 314*

Anchoring Objects in Text

Anchoring items within text ensures that they continue to flow with the text if you edit the text or change the size of boxes. New in QuarkXPress 4 is the capability to anchor lines (a real treat for those who often make forms) and the option of anchoring non-rectangular items. You also can create *paragraph rules*, which flow above or below a paragraph. These often are used for making reversed text or charts.

Anchoring Boxes and Lines

Anchoring an item (box or line) is a six-step process that, once understood, is easily and quickly done.

To anchor an object in text:

1. Create the item you want to anchor.
2. With the Item tool ⊕ active, select it.
3. Cut the item using ⌘+X (Ctrl+X).
4. Select the Content tool 🖑.
5. Place the cursor in your text where you want the item anchored.
6. Paste the item into position using ⌘+V (Ctrl+V).

Select an anchored box using either the Content or Item tool, and some new controls appear at the extreme left edge of the Measurements palette (see Figure 15.26). Click the top one and the anchored box aligns to the ascender height of the surrounding text. The bottom icon aligns the box with the baseline of the surrounding text.

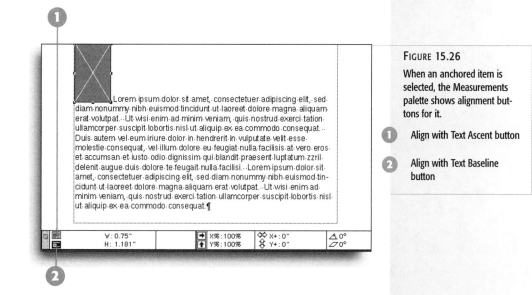

FIGURE 15.26

When an anchored item is selected, the Measurements palette shows alignment buttons for it.

① Align with Text Ascent button

② Align with Text Baseline button

Anchored lines always align to the baseline of the text by default. To change them, choose **Modify** from the **Item** menu and click the **Line** or **Box** tab (depending on which the item is), then click **Ascent** or adjust the **Offset** in the **Align with Text** area (see Figures 15.27 and 15.28).

Editing Anchored Items

Once the item has been anchored, it is edited much like text. To delete or copy it, select it by dragging the cursor across it. You can copy and paste an anchored item into another location and it retains its anchored characteristics.

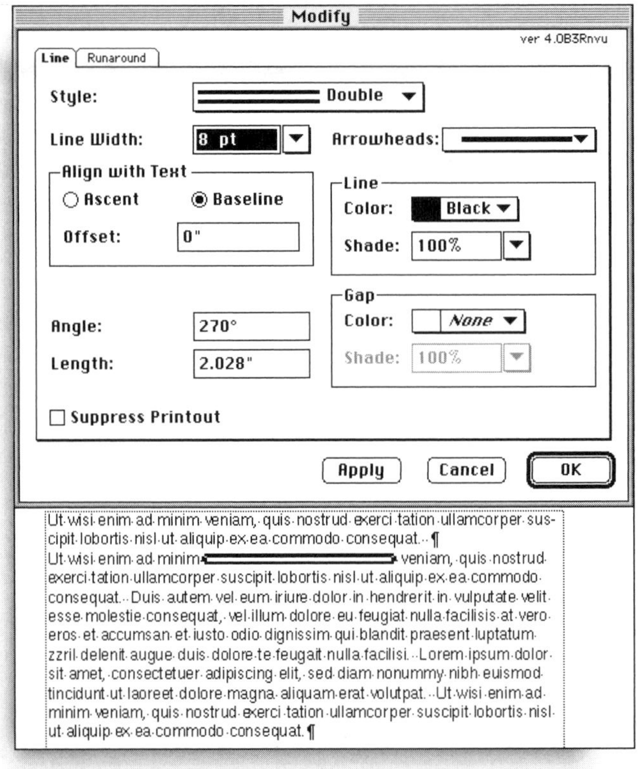

FIGURE 15.27

The **Line** tab shows up when an anchored item is a line.

Anchored items also can be resized. Boxes have eight handles and straight lines have one at each end. Resizing a text or picture box does not resize its contents. Bézier lines have eight handles, just like boxes. Dragging those handles reshapes the line.

SEE ALSO

➤ *To resize standard boxes and lines, see page 106*

➤ *To reshape Bézier objects, see page 314*

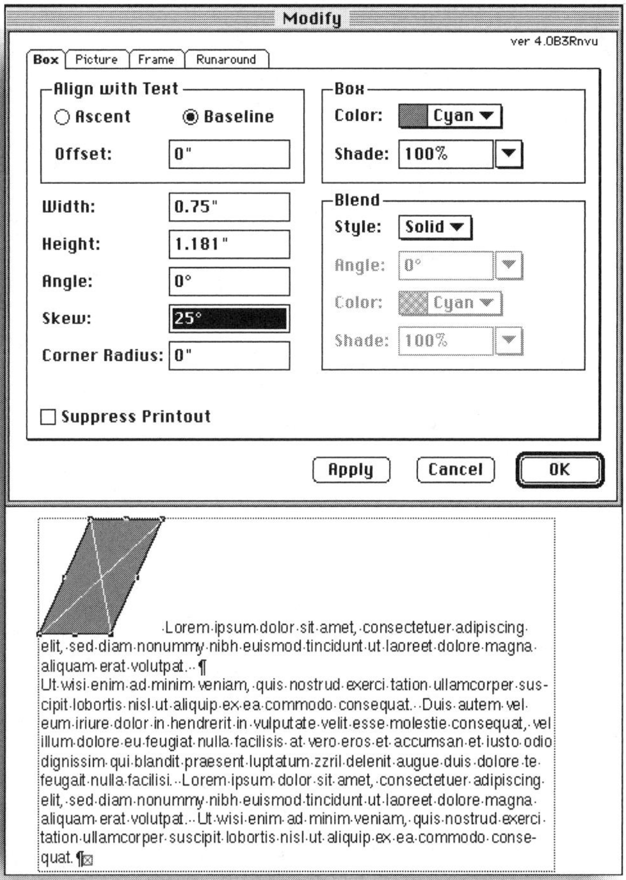

FIGURE 15.28
Anchored boxes produce a
Box tab.

Positioning Anchored Items

You can shift the position of your anchored item, whether it is a
box or line, by using the same commands you would use for text:
baseline shift or leading. To invoke these options, highlight the
anchored item by dragging the cursor through it, just like you
would highlight text (make sure you are not highlighting the
content of the item). Use keyboard commands or go to the **Style**
menu to select the appropriate choices.

SEE ALSO

➤ *To apply baseline shift, see page 250*

➤ *To adjust leading, see page 58*

Tips About Anchored Items

Here are some tips and hints about working with anchored items.

- Anchored items must be at least two points smaller than the box in which they are being anchored, both horizontally and vertically. If they are too big, you'll see a text overflow icon ☒ in the target box. The only way to recover from this is to make your target text box bigger. The anchored item then reappears and you can resize it.

- If you want an anchored box to sit right at the edge of your target text box, the anchored box must have a runaround of 0. Even if you select a runaround of **None** before you anchor the box, it switches to an **Item** runaround once anchored.

- Items can be anchored right next to each other. For example, anchoring an empty box next to another is a way of creating the effect of an asymmetrical runaround.

- The runaround of Bézier lines is harder to control than the runaround of boxes. Even with a runaround applied, lines may overlap the surrounding text.

- Text on a path can be anchored just like a box or line.

- Anchored text boxes cannot be linked in a text chain.

- Text converted to a box can be anchored, but once anchored, it cannot be split.

Creating Rules that Flow with Paragraphs

Rules that flow with paragraphs are used for a whole variety of purposes, from being purely decorative, to being visual section dividers, to organizing chart information, to creating reversed type.

Specifying Paragraph Rules

Whatever purpose you have for your paragraph rule, the process always starts exactly the same way. Select a paragraph or several paragraphs of text and then choose **Rules** from the **Style** menu, or press ⌘+Shift+N (Ctrl+Shift+N). The **Rules** tab of the Paragraph Attributes dialog box appears (see Figure 15.29).

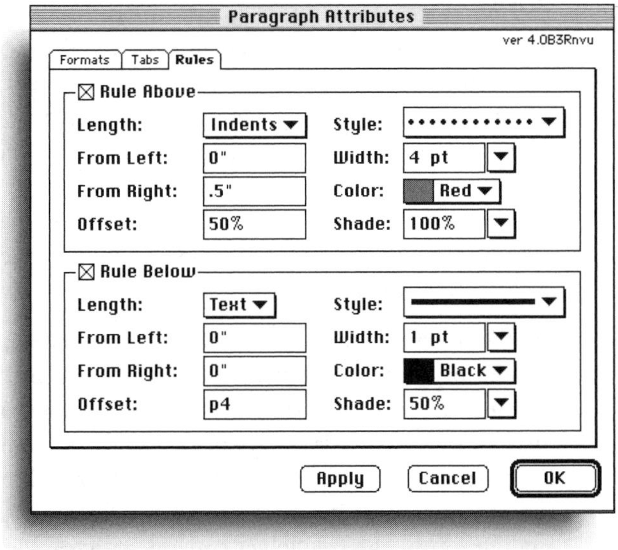

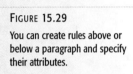

FIGURE 15.29

You can create rules above or below a paragraph and specify their attributes.

First, select **Rule Above** or **Rule Below**, or both. The look and positioning of the rule is determined by the choices you make in the dialog box.

Length

Text means the rule will be the length of the adjacent line of text (either the first or last line of the paragraph depending on whether you are using **Rule Above** or **Rule Below**). Indent means the rule will be the width of your text box, less any **Text Inset** value and any **Left**, **Right**, or **First Indent** values.

SEE ALSO

➤ *To apply left, right, and first line indents to text, see page 256*

From Left/Right

Entering positive numbers here will move the ends of the rule in toward the center of the box by the value entered in these boxes. If there's a left or right indent applied to the selected text, you can enter a negative value here to extend the paragraph rule out closer to the sides of the text box than the text itself extends.

Offset

If you enter values here in percentages, the rule's offset from the text relates to the amount of space between paragraphs. For example, entering 50% puts a rule exactly halfway between your selected paragraph and the adjacent one. Even if you change the space between the paragraphs, the rule always stays halfway between them. You never have to worry about a paragraph rule running into nearby text. Only positive percentages can be used in the **Offset** field.

On the other hand, you can specify a non-relative, specific amount of offset by entering measurements in inches, points, centimeters, and so on in this box. When you use a fixed measurement, the offset is always measured from the baseline. For a **Rule Above**, a positive amount moves the rule higher; a negative amount makes it lower. For a **Rule Below**, a positive amount moves the rule lower and a negative amount moves the rule higher in relation to the line of type. The amount of negative fixed offset allowed is limited to half the width of the rule.

These are important constraints to remember, particularly when you want to use paragraph rules to make reversed type. Also, the only way to have a **Rule Above** display and print properly if it is used on a paragraph at the top of a text box or column is to use a fixed measurement.

Other Attributes and Options

The other options are similar to those for any rule.

- **Style** includes any dash or stripe defined in your document.
- **Width** is selected as you would for any line used in your document.

- **Color** can be any document color.
- **Shade** allows you to tint your rule.
- **Apply** lets you check the effect of your choices as you work.

SEE ALSO

➤ *To understand formatting attributes for rules, see page 116*

Uses for Paragraph Rules

Paragraph rules offer many options for design. And because they can be applied automatically via a *paragraph style sheet*, they're ideal for ensuring consistency in text elements like subheads and tables.

Rules for Reverse Type

Use a **Rule Above** with a fixed offset to create reversed type (see Figure 15.30). Select a rule width greater than the point size of your type. It will probably need a small amount of negative off-set to position your type in the middle of the rule. Make the rule any color you want and select white for your type. You can also make the rule and type contrasting colors, but remember that you cannot *trap* this type of two color set-up unless you apply the trapping via the Trap Specifications dialog box; these trapping settings will apply throughout the document. Use the **Apply** button to fine-tune your adjustments.

Rules for Tables and Charts

Paragraph rules are a convenient way of setting off information in tables and charts (see Figure 15.31). One style is to use a light tint of a color behind some lines and not behind others (using the technique described above for reverse type). Another style would be to use a rule between lines of the chart (using the percentage method so the positioning stays consistent no matter what you do to leading or space above/below). Be creative and explore a variety of options—you'll be surprised at how easy it is to not only dress up a chart or table, but make it more readable and understandable at the same time.

FIGURE 15.30

Paragraph rules allow you to automate reversed type.

FIGURE 15.30

Paragraph rules allow you to automate reversed type.

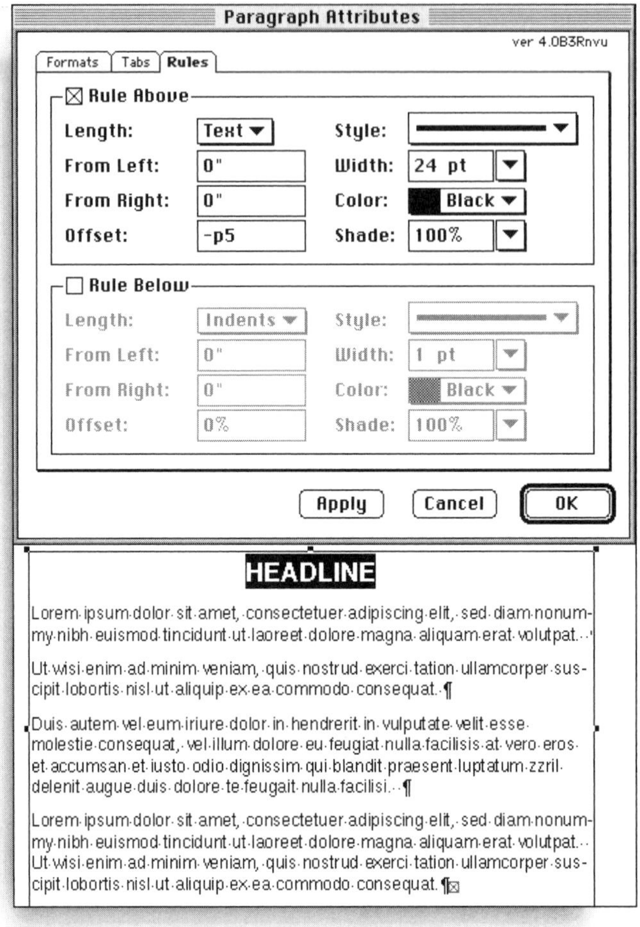

FIGURE 15.31

Tables can make good use of paragraph rules.

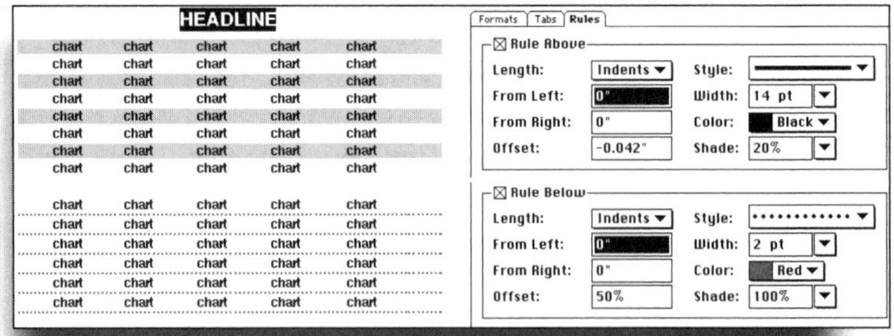

Paragraph Rule Tips

There are so many things you can do with this feature that it is difficult to limit the discussion. However, here are a few tips and tricks that might make your work easier or more finished looking.

- Need to simulate the writing lines on a legal pad? Define a rule above or below and then start entering paragraph returns.

- When making reversed text, it is nice to have the text indented a bit from the ends of the rule (see Figure 15.32). There are a couple of steps required to do this. First, in the Paragraph Attributes **Formats** tab, indent your text from both left and right. Then move to the **Rules** tab and select **Rule Above**. Choose **Text** for the **Length**. In both the left and right indent boxes, enter the same number(s) you just used in the **Formats** tab but place a minus (–) sign in front of it.

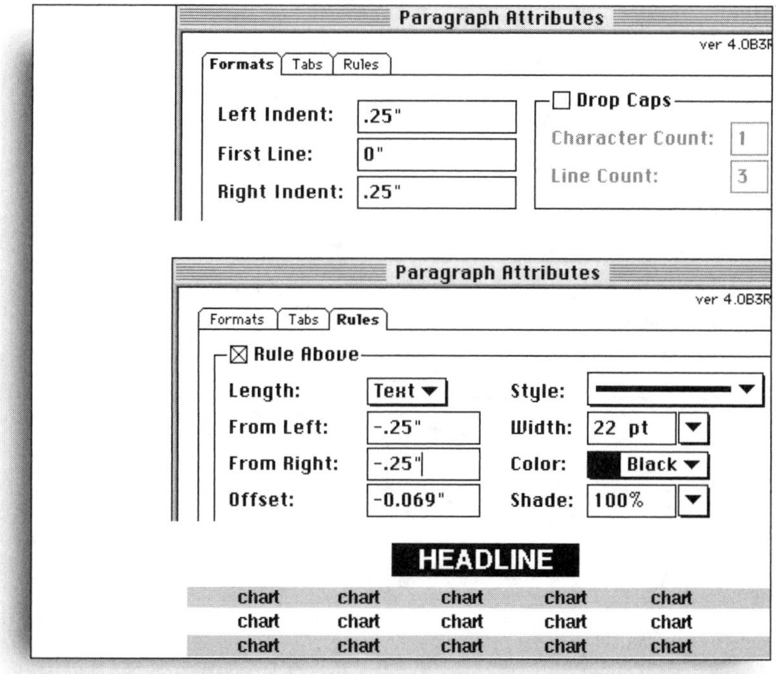

FIGURE 15.32

A text inset cleans up the look of a paragraph rule.

- If you have a *frame* around a text box and want the rules to meet the frame, make sure there's no text inset applied to the box. To indent text from the sides of the box, apply left and right indents instead. This way you can set up a negative indent for the rule so it meets the frame around the box. Use the technique described in the previous tip to achieve the effect you need.

- Instead of reversed text you can put a rule where the text isn't by combining **Rule Above** and **Rule Below** (see Figure 15.46). This usually takes a bit of fussing, but once you make it work, you can combine it with a style sheet and use it over and over. See the example for the appropriate setup. The white rule must always be the **Rule Below**. You may need to use some baseline shift on the text to get it to work just right. Remember the rule about negative offsets—just half the width of the rule.

FIGURE 15.33

Paragraph rules can create a line where there is no text.

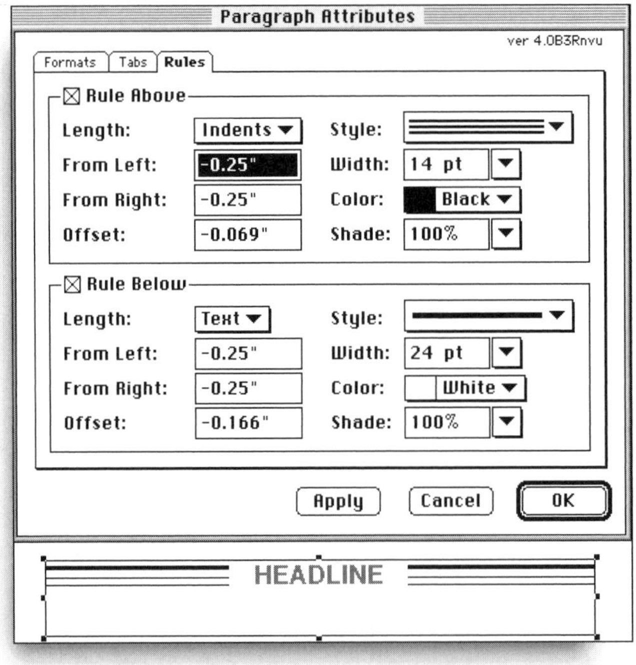

- Another way of combining **Rule Above** and **Rule Below** results in a box around the text (see Figure 15.34). This may take a bit of tweaking to set up correctly, but if you want to use it several times in a document, it's worth the effort once you turn it into a style sheet. Again, the white rule must always be the rule below.

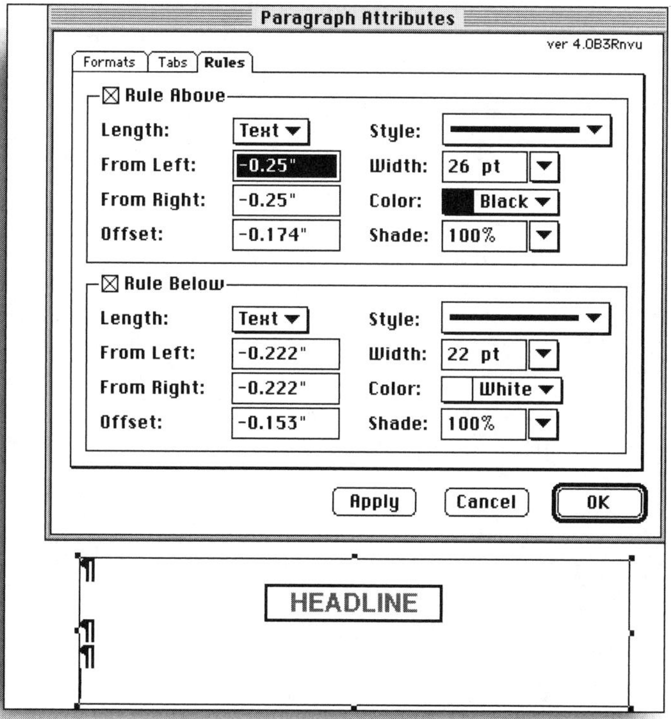

Paragraph Attributes
ver 4.0B3Rnvu

Formats | Tabs | **Rules**

☒ **Rule Above**

Length:	Text ▼	Style:	──────── ▼
From Left:	-0.25"	Width:	26 pt ▼
From Right:	-0.25"	Color:	Black ▼
Offset:	-0.174"	Shade:	100% ▼

☒ **Rule Below**

Length:	Text ▼	Style:	──────── ▼
From Left:	-0.222"	Width:	22 pt ▼
From Right:	-0.222"	Color:	White ▼
Offset:	-0.153"	Shade:	100% ▼

(Apply) (Cancel) [OK]

HEADLINE

FIGURE 15.34
You can use paragraph rules to create a box around text.

SEE ALSO

➤ *To apply left, right, and first line indents to text, see page 256*

Initial Caps

Since the days when people first applied some sort of carbon to papyrus, decorative *initial caps* have been used to dress up and call attention to text. Medieval illuminated manuscripts made the decorative capital an art form unto itself. You can do the same for your documents, with a lot less work and in a lot less time.

Using Images

Spell checking with initial caps

When you use either of these techniques for creating a decorative initial cap, be alert to the fact that when you check the spelling in your document, all the instances where you replaced the first letter of a word with an anchored box show up as incorrect. Do a good spellcheck before you replace text with a box of any type to help eliminate confusion. Of course, if the initial cap in the anchored box is wrong, you are on your own for checking (and it does happen).

There are a couple of different ways to use imported images as initial decorative caps. When using either of these methods, be aware that they affect spellchecking in your document.

Imported Initial Cap Graphics

An anchored picture box at the start of a paragraph and a collection of initial caps graphics is one way to form decorative caps. Replace the first letter in a paragraph with an anchored picture box and import the appropriate graphic image (see Figure 15.48).

Many vendors have collections of decorative caps in all sorts of styles. Often these are editable *EPS* files so you can change colors (in a drawing application) to match the color palette of your document, or turn them into one-color art by using tints or shades of the base color.

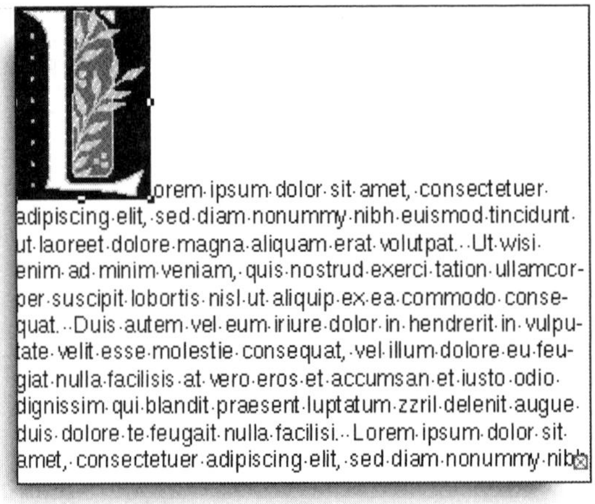

FIGURE 15.35

This is just one example of an imported initial cap.

Lorem·ipsum·dolor·sit·amet,·consectetuer·adipiscing·elit,·sed·diam·nonummy·nibh·euismod·tincidunt·ut·laoreet·dolore·magna·aliquam·erat·volutpat.··Ut·wisi·enim·ad·minim·veniam,·quis·nostrud·exerci·tation·ullamcorper·suscipit·lobortis·nisl·ut·aliquip·ex·ea·commodo·consequat.··Duis·autem·vel·eum·iriure·dolor·in·hendrerit·in·vulputate·velit·esse·molestie·consequat,·vel·illum·dolore·eu·feugiat·nulla·facilisis·at·vero·eros·et·accumsan·et·iusto·odio·dignissim·qui·blandit·praesent·luptatum·zzril·delenit·augue·duis·dolore·te·feugait·nulla·facilisi.··Lorem·ipsum·dolor·sit·amet,·consectetuer·adipiscing·elit,·sed·diam·nonummy·nibh

When using an anchored box, remember to set the runaround before you anchor the box and that the runaround is the same for all sides of the box. Create a second, empty anchored box if you need a little extra space between an anchored box and the surrounding text.

QuarkXPress lets you anchor a nonrectangular box (either for importing an initial cap or text turned into a box). The text surrounding the box, however, wraps around an imaginary rectangular shape based on the outside horizontal and vertical widths of the non-rectangular shape (see Figure 15.36). If you want your text to wrap and follow the shape of a letter (such as along the angled stroke of a V), you have to do some manual work involving *kerning*, *soft returns*, and perhaps some non-breaking spaces. Then remember as soon as you edit any of the text, change the shape/size of the text box, or change the size of the type, everything has to be done again.

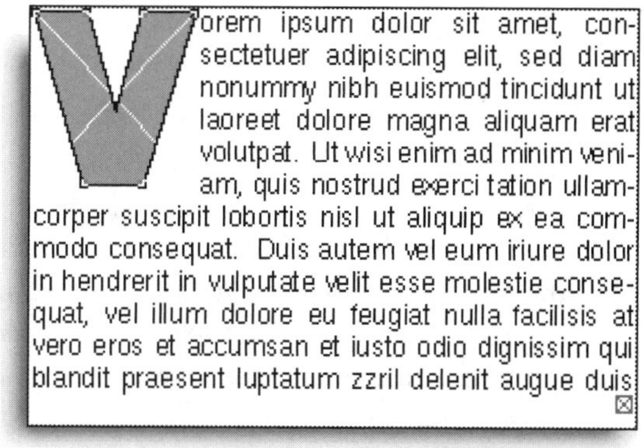

FIGURE 15.36

A non-rectangular anchored box presents some text wrap challenges.

Imported Pictures in Text-Shaped Boxes

A second method of using imported graphics is to create a text-shaped picture box and import an image or texture into the box (see Figure 15.37).

SEE ALSO

➤ *To import pictures, see page 339*

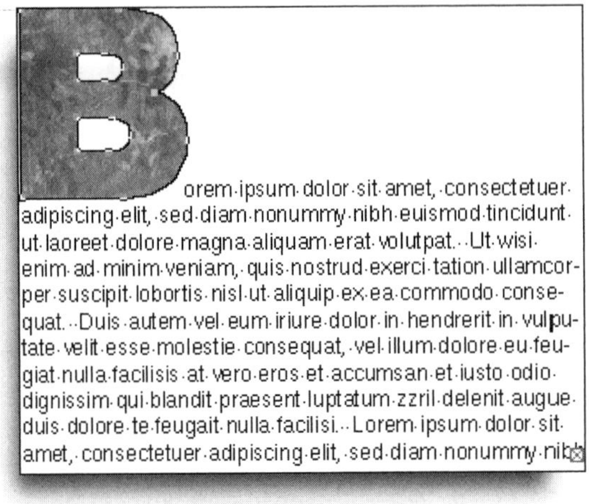

FIGURE 15.37

A picture imported into a text-shaped picture box can produce a striking initial cap.

Embellishing Characters

Another way of creating decorative caps is to simply embellish the type without turning it into a text or picture box. Here, at least, spell checking works as expected, because letters are not being replaced with something else.

Applying styling characteristics to the first letter (or letters) in a paragraph is quick and easy. Simply highlight the text you want to work with and style it any way you desire. You might make the first letter larger, you might change the typeface, you might change from a *roman* font to an *italic* or *oblique* font, or perhaps you might just change the color. The list of things to do is as long as your imagination. The one thing you cannot do is skew the text, because skewing always applies to all the text in a text box. If you want to skew the initial cap, you'll have to use an anchored text box containing just that letter. After you have created something you like for an initial cap, you can save it as a *character style sheet.*

SEE ALSO

➤ *To format characters, see page 240*

➤ *To create a character style sheet, see page 299*

Creating Automatic Drop Caps

Saving the easiest for last, the absolute quickest way to create a decorative initial cap is to choose **Formats** from the **Style** menu to create a *drop cap*. Pressing ⌘+Shift+F (Ctrl+Shift+F) takes you to the right spot right away. They are called drop caps for a reason. Unlike text that you might style manually where the initial cap is enlarged and sits on the baseline, drop caps hang from the cap height of your text and drop down into the rest of the text in the paragraph that then runs around the drop cap. This is the only method in QuarkXPress to make an initial cap part of a paragraph style sheet.

In the **Formats** tab of the Paragraph Attributes dialog box, click **Drop Cap**. Decide how many letters you want to include and how many lines deep into the paragraph you want the drop cap to fall. This method makes the size of the drop cap relative to the size of the type in the paragraph and uses the same font as the rest of the type in the paragraph. (If you want a fixed size drop cap, use the manual method described above and adjust the baseline shift.)

These attributes also can become part of a paragraph style sheet by either editing the **Formats** tab of an existing paragraph style sheet or creating a new one.

After you set up an automatic drop cap paragraph style, you can make further enhancements to the drop cap by creating a character style for it. Because the automatic drop cap uses the same font as the rest of the text in the paragraph, you may want to change it to a contrasting font, change the color, or alter it in some other fashion. Everywhere you use the drop cap paragraph style, highlight the drop cap character and apply the character style manually. You'll have consistency throughout your document for the treatment of all your drop caps.

Although the creation of decorative initial caps and drop caps may be limited only by your imagination, a few hints and tips might make your work easier:

- Watch kerning around these characters. Depending on the size and shape of the letterform, you may need to do some manual adjusting between the cap and the next letter. This is true whether you use an anchored box, an automatic drop cap, or style an initial cap manually.

- Although initial and drop caps line up mathematically with the left edge of your text, that may not always be visually correct or appealing. As in other uses of these characters, it depends a great deal on the shape of the letter form. In these instances you might want move the character a bit to the left so that it balances better with the following text. Enter a space before the initial or drop cap or anchored box. (If you are using automatic drop caps, you also need to change the number of characters in the drop cap.) Place the cursor between the cap or box and the space before it and decrease the kerning. This may even move the cap or anchored box outside the text box, but don't worry, it will still print. Since you can't see it, you should print some quick proofs to make sure your adjustments are correct.

- A paragraph style in QuarkXPress can have only one character style associated with it. If you create an automatic drop cap paragraph style and want it to be in any way different from the character style associated with the paragraph, you need to manually apply a different character style to the drop cap.

SEE ALSO

➤ *To create paragraph style sheets, see page 298*

➤ *To create character style sheets, see page 299*

PART

V

Color and Output

CHAPTER

16

Creating and Applying Color

Create new colors

Edit existing colors

Apply colors to text, boxes, and lines

Apply color tints to objects

Create color blends

Specify default colors for newly created objects

Incorporate color in style sheets

Apply color to imported grayscale images

If you're not using color now in your QuarkXPress pages, you probably will be soon! On-demand short-run color printing is the fastest growing area of the graphic arts industry. It's only a question of time before you create color pages for print. If you create your web work in QuarkXPress, you already use color. And if you use color in your documents that go to a printer, there are ways to make the process less painful for both you and the printer.

QuarkXPress allows you to use common standardized *color matching systems* (such as PANTONE), create your own colors, or convert from one set of color values (such as PANTONE *spot colors*) to another (such as *four-color process*).

SEE ALSO

➤ *To learn about color matching systems, see page 461*

Creating Colors

QuarkXPress allows you to use the *color model* that's most appropriate for the kind of work you're doing, or the model you're most familiar with. Artists are usually more at home in *HSB*; prepress houses and printers are more comfortable with *CMYK*; and high-end printers are becoming more at home with *Hexachrome*. If you do Web work, get comfortable with working in RGB: that's going to be your "final" output.

Color models are kept in the Color folder inside your QuarkXPress folder, just as *XTensions* are kept in the XTensions folder. If you think you (or your coworkers who obviously don't understand color the way you do) have too many choices, just drag the color models you don't want to see into another folder. You can, if you want, drag them to the Unused XTensions folder or create an Unused Colors folder. In either case, the color models that are not in the Color folder will not load when QuarkXPress starts up again.

Each QuarkXPress document starts out with several colors available in its color list: white, black, red, green, blue, cyan, magenta, yellow, and Registration. Colors you can't delete, for obvious

---

Don't use Registration for rich blacks

Registration prints 100% on each of the four color plates–very useful for creating printable registration, fold, or trim marks if you need to. Do not use Registration to create a *rich black* in large areas. A rich black is usually 100% black with some magenta and cyan in it to make the black seem even blacker than it is. But most press people shudder when the accumulated values of all four ink colors begin to approach more than 250% at any given point on the paper. The paper gets tacky, and the inks begin to stick to each other instead of to the paper.

reasons, are black, white, magenta, cyan, yellow, and Registration. Up to 1,000 colors can be defined in a single QuarkXPress document.

To see the colors defined in a document and define new ones, you have to use the Colors dialog box (see Figure 16.1). This dialog box displays all the colors in the document and shows how they're defined (what type of color model was used to create them, whether they're spot or process colors, and so on). A new feature in QuarkXPress 4 allows you to display various color types (such as spot, process, and so on) in your document in the Colors dialog box by choosing what kind of colors you want to see from the **Show** pop-up menu.

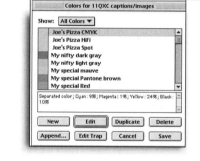

FIGURE 16.1

In the Colors dialog box, the **Show** menu lets you display different kinds of colors, and clicking on a color shows what color model was used to create the color.

- **All Colors** displays—you guessed it—all the colors in your document, or all the colors that are in your current XPress Preferences file if there is no document open at the time. This can be useful to figure out if you described the same color two or even three different ways.

- **Spot Colors** displays only those colors you created specifically to be used as *spot colors*, regardless of the color model used to create them.

- **Process Colors** displays only the CMYK colors and the *HiFi* colors, even though you may use them in your document.

- **Multi-Ink Colors** displays only those colors you created by combining color from other models.

- **Colors In Use** is very useful; obviously, it displays only those colors that are in use in the current document. It's a way to check and make sure the great color you created is actually in use, rather than having to jump to the page, select the item, and check out the color.

- **Colors Not Used** is even a bigger deal: your printer or service provider (or your own in-house imaging department) will be elated if you remove all the unused colors in your document before you try and print it. You save a lot of printing time and reduce the size of your document a lot by eliminating the colors you're not using. To do this, choose **Colors Not Used**; then click on each color (or click at one end of the list and Shift+click at the other to select all the colors) and click **Delete** to remove it from the list.

To create a color, first you need to decide what kind of color you want to create: CMYK process, spot, Hexachrome, or *multi-ink*. The process for specifying the attributes of each kind of color is slightly different, but in general, creating a color consists of just a few steps:

To create a new color:

1. Choose **Colors** from the **Edit** menu (Shift+F12) and click **New**.

2. Choose a color model from the **Model** pop-up menu and click **Spot Color** on or off, depending on whether this color should print on one plate (on) or be separated into process colors (off).

3. Choose a color from the swatches (if using a color matching systems, such as PANTONE) or the color picker (if using a color model: RGB, HSB, or CMYK) (see Figure 16.2).

4. To create an HSB, *RGB*, *LAB*, or CMYK color, use the sliders or type in new values to modify the choice.

5. Enter a name for the color in the **Name** field and click **OK** to add it to the document's color list. Then **Save** to save the changes to the color list.

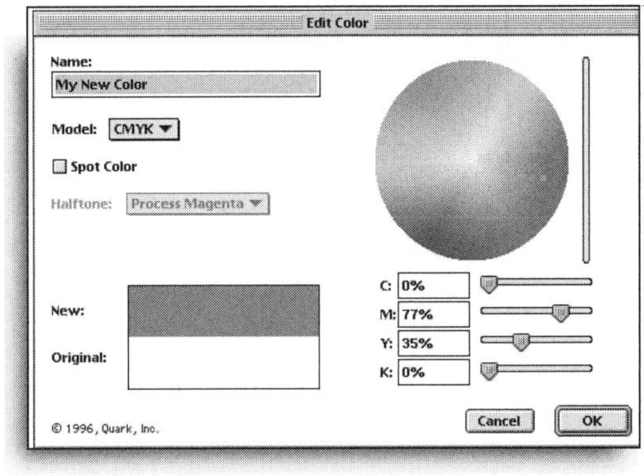

FIGURE 16.2
Creating new colors without
the use of the color models
provided uses the color wheel
in the operating system.

If you choose **HSB**, **RGB**, **LAB**, or **CMYK** from the **Model** pop-up menu, you see a color wheel that you can click on to choose a color; the color wheel is the same for all three models. The difference between the three models is in the sliders below the color wheel. In the case of **CMYK**, you see four sliders, one each for cyan, magenta, yellow, and black. You can create or modify a color by moving the sliders or typing values in the entry fields next to them.

In most cases, you want to create colors in CMYK; that's what your printer is going to use. If you really love a color in RGB, for instance, you can convert that to a CMYK equivalent by following these steps.

To convert RGB colors to CMYK:

1. Open the existing color by choosing **Colors** from the **Edit** menu, clicking on the name of the color to convert, and clicking **Edit**.

2. In the **Model** pop-up menu, change the color from the model in which you created the color (in this case, **RGB**) to **CMYK**. Items that can be modified in this window are **Name**, **Model**, and **Spot Color**, as well as the *halftone* screen. You can also use the color wheel to modify the values for HSB, RGB, LAB, and CMYK values. The sliders work okay, but if you have a specific color you want to create and know the CMYK values in percentages, you can type in the values for CMYK.

In all probability, the color on the top of the swatch box next to the **New** label will be slightly different than the bottom half of the swatch box next to the word **Original** (see Figure 16.3). That's because two different color models may not produce identical colors. And besides, who color-corrected your screen, and to what model did they color-correct it? In most cases, ignore the differences unless you really know what you're doing.

FIGURE 16.3

Changing from one color model to another creates two boxes (**Original** and **New**) to allow swatch matching.

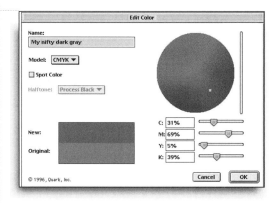

Matching CMYK colors on press

If you always output to the same RIP and print on the same press, the best thing to do is to set up a swatch page with known percentages of CMYK in your samples and print it. Then pick the colors you like and copy their percentages of CMYK into a new color palette for your publications. Then it won't make any difference what a color looks like on your screen; you know that you'll like it when it comes off the press, which is what counts.

3. Either choose a new name or save the new CMYK specification with the old name, thereby automatically replacing all the colors in the document that were named "My Favorite Blue" in RGB with the same color in CMYK.

Existing colors that are close to what you want to create can be copied by using the **Duplicate** command in the Colors dialog box. The Edit Color dialog box automatically opens and allows you to tweak the existing color into a new one. QuarkXPress adds "Copy of" to the original color's name for the new color.

The **Delete** button in the Colors dialog box does just that: deletes a color from the menu. Accidentally deleting a color used in the document brings up an alert, a feature for which we should all thank Quark.

SEE ALSO

➤ *To create multimedia and web projects, see page 536*

➤ *To prepare files for high-resolution output, see page 517*

➤ *To print files, see page 495*

➤ *To create multi-ink or Hexachrome colors, see page 466*

Editing a Document's Colors List

Editing colors is similar to creating colors. Call up the dialog box by choosing **Colors** from the **Edit** menu or pressing Shift+F12, choose a color to edit, and click on **Edit**. Double-clicking (Ctrl+clicking) on the color name also brings up the Edit Colors dialog box.

Editing Colors

Any of the tools used to create a color can be used to modify the color. The only difference is that you see the new color compared with the color you started with. Clicking **OK** brings you back to the Colors dialog box. Clicking **Save** replaces the old color with the new one without any warning; it's very easy to overwrite a new color with an old color name. Make sure you change the name in the **Name** field before clicking **OK** if you want a new color in addition to the old color.

Deleting and Replacing Colors

If you're not sure you're going to like the new color any better, you might want to create a backup copy of the old color by clicking the **Duplicate** button, then make the changes to the original color. Your changes will happen throughout the document, so you can look at them and maybe even proof them.

If you later decide to go back to the original color, delete the original color and a dialog box pops up asking if it's okay to delete the color and to replace it with another. Then simply replace the color with the backup copy you made, and all the uses of that color change back to your first choice. Anywhere the color was used (*lines*, *boxes*, *borders*, pictures, and so on) will change. Any use of that color in blends will also change (see Figure 16.4).

Quick access to the Edit Colors dialog box

Holding down the ⌘ (Ctrl) key as you click on a color in the color palettes brings up the Edit Colors dialog box. This is a real time-saver from having to drag down the menus.

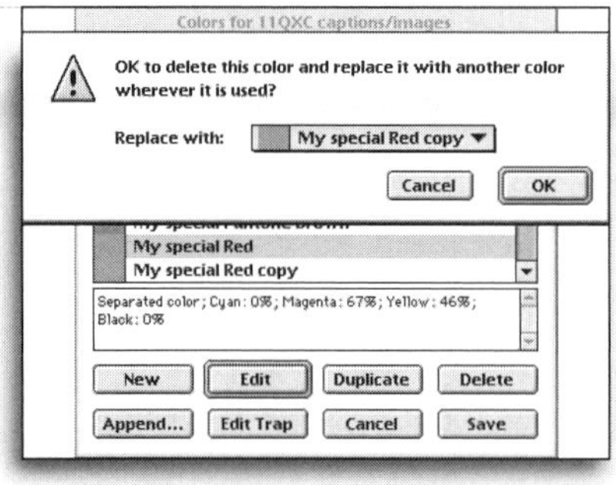

Applying Colors

You can apply colors to text and objects from the Modify dialog box (choose ⌘+M (Ctrl+M)). However, if you apply a lot of colors and screen territory is not a problem, it's far easier to have the Colors palette up on the screen, where you can just pick and drag a color to the box or *frame*. F12 brings up the Colors palette. Click on the **Background Color** icon or **Frame Color** icon as appropriate (see Figure 16.5).

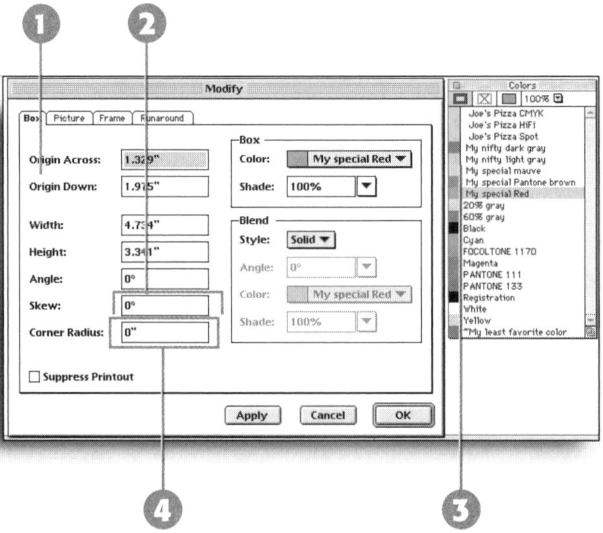

FIGURE 16.5

These are the two most common ways to apply color to objects: the Modify dialog box and the Colors palette.

① Frame Color

② Picture color

③ Background Color

④ Colors

Using the Colors Palette

If more than one object is selected, clicking on a color in the Colors palette colors all the objects you selected with that color.

If you have multiple items selected, clicking in a color changes all the selected objects. Dragging the color from the palette to an object, even if it's not selected, also changes the color of the object. Oddly enough, if you're working with a *group* of objects, dragging a color swatch to an object within the group affects only that object, not the group. And it doesn't make any difference if the items are selected (see Figure 16.6).

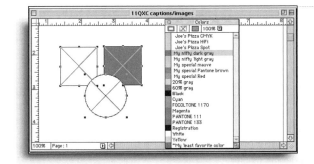

FIGURE 16.6
You can color grouped objects all at once by clicking on a color, or one at a time by dragging a swatch from the Colors palette.

Across the top of the Colors palette are icons for applying color to various objects.

- The **Frame Color** icon applies the color you selected to the border of a *text* or *picture box*. Just select the box, set the frame width, and click once in the Colors palette for the color you want (see Figure 16.7), or drag a color swatch to the box border.

FIGURE 16.7
The **Frame Color** icon in the Colors palette applies colors to any borders on content boxes.

- The **Text Color** icon, when selected in conjunction with selected text, applies the color to the selected type only. Just click once on the color sample. Dragging color swatches from the Colors palette doesn't work to color type, but a single click does fine (see Figure 16.8).

FIGURE 16.8

The **Text Color** icon in the Colors palette applies colors to any type that has been high-lighted.

- When you've drawn a rule, the box in the second position changes to a rule and allows you to apply a color to rules only. Select the color with a single click (see Figure 16.9), or drag a color swatch to the rule.

FIGURE 16.9

When a rule is selected, the only icon at the top of the Colors palette is the **Line Color** icon.

1 Line Color icon

- The third box over is the **Background Color** icon, for the "fill" function. Notice that when you click on this icon, the palette holds a few new menus. More on those in a minute. When selected, the object you apply color to fills with the color. This is true for picture boxes, text boxes, and *no-content boxes* (see Figure 16.10).

FIGURE 16.10

The **Background Color** icon in the Colors palette applies colors to any content boxes.

But where's the color?

If you choose a new color for an object in the Colors palette, yet it doesn't change color, check the shade percentage of the object. A 0% shade of any color looks like white.

To apply a solid color from the Colors palette, bring the palette to the screen (if it isn't already) by pressing F12. Make sure you select either the **Line** icon or the **Frame** icon from the icons across the top of the Colors palette. Select the object (or objects by Shift+clicking on the objects one at a time) and click once on the color in the Colors palette you want to apply to the object(s). That's it. You're done.

SEE ALSO

➤ *To group objects, see page 133*

Using the Shade Menu

To the right of the Colors palette's three icons is a pop-up menu with a percentage displayed next to it. The menu applies shades of the color(s) selected in 10% increments. Sometimes, it's just easier to highlight the 100% and type in a number. You don't need to type the % mark: QuarkXPress assumes the number you type will be a percentage. The percentages can be expressed in tenths also: 12.2% is allowed. And in a typical QuarkXPress nicety, if you type 12.237% in the field, QuarkXPress drops that back to 12.3%: 12.376 becomes 12.4% (see Figure 16.11).

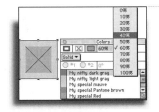

FIGURE 16.11

Percentages of the color can be specified in 10% increments with the pull-down menu, or in tenths of a percentage by typing the number.

Creating Blends with the Colors Palette

Blends are the combination of any two colors in a box, text, or object. You cannot apply blends to lines or frames, although you do have a way to get around this. The blends can be any tone (percentage) of any color, including black and white. And, as you'll see, the blends can be one of six types and can run at any angle you want within the box. Quark's blends options includes the basic set and the Cool Blends from the Cool Blend XTension. Make sure the Cool Blends XTension is in your XTension folder so you can use some of these tricks.

The Colors palette allows you to see the effect of blend choices on your objects immediately, something that's sometimes difficult to do with the Modify dialog box because it takes so much of the screen's real estate.

The options for blend type are shown in a pop-up menu below the three icons at the top of the palette. If the currently selected object doesn't have a blend, the menu setting is **Solid**. Below the menu are radio buttons labeled 1 and 2, used to indicate which of the two blend colors, as well as their percentages (tints), you're currently editing. Doing blends is easy if you follow the process step by step.

To create a blend with the Colors palette:

1. Select a picture or text box (or Shift+click to select more than one box). Click the Background icon on the Colors palette, then select a blend type, something other than **Solid** in the pop-up menu.

2. The menu should show two buttons labeled 1 and 2, and the 1 should be selected. The first color chosen for a box will always be number 1. Select a color by clicking once on the color in the palette or by dragging the color to the box (see Figure 16.12).

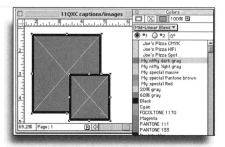

FIGURE 16.12

Here, the first of two colors for a blend has been selected.

3. Now click the number 2 button, and select the second color with a single click on the color square in the Colors palette (see Figure 16.13).

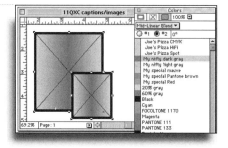

FIGURE 16.13

A second, lighter color has been applied to two selected boxes with a Mid-Linear blend.

4. To change the angle of the blend, type a new number in the box to the right of the number 2 button. Don't get too subtle here; increments of 90° seem to work the best. Keep in mind that QuarkXPress rotates blends, like everything else, counterclockwise, so color 1 will start out at the left side of the box and move to the bottom with a rotation of 90°. The box takes negative values, too; a value of 270° is equal to a value of –90° (see Figure 16.14).

Dragging a swatch colors only one box

If you drag a color to a grouped set of boxes, the color will apply only to the box you drag the swatch to. To apply the first or second color to all of the boxes in the group you selected, you must use the single-click-on-the-swatch method.

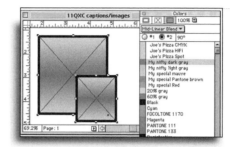

FIGURE 16.14

The same two boxes are shown here with the Mid-Level blend rotated 90 degrees.

5. Now try the other five blend types in the menu to see what they do to your box (see Figure 16.15).

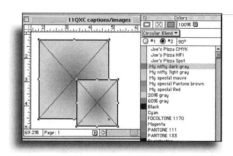

FIGURE 16.15

Here are the same two boxes with a 2-point back border and a circular blend applied with the same two colors, showing the versatility and variety offered with blends.

Get familiar with the way you can use blends and the look they take on. Blends can be very effective in black and white or one-color newsletters, menus, and a variety of other designs. They are quick and effective ways to add tones and levels to otherwise straightforward text and picture boxes.

Displaying accurate blends

Make sure **Accurate Blends** is turned on in your preferences to display the best possible version of the blends you create. If you know that you will never, under any circumstances, create a blend (and that's very hard to do after you've made your first one), you can turn off **Accurate Blends** and speed up your screen refresh rate a little.

Colored type on a colored background—made easy

Many folks think they have to create two objects and fiddle forever to make colored type on a colored background. Don't. Create the text in a box, and color the box background one color; then color the type another color. Centering the type in the box both horizontally and vertically creates a nice little reverse bar subhead, and you won't have to worry about leaving the background behind when you move the text. And if you're really brave, you can apply a frame in yet another color and it will still all be in one piece.

Using the Modify Dialog Box

Choosing **Modify** from the **Item** menu brings up the Modify dialog box, where you can click on the **Box**, **Line**, or **Group** tab, depending on what's currently selected—a single box, a single line, or multiple objects (see Figure 16.16). If a box is selected, the Modify dialog box also contains a **Frame** tab (see Figure 16.17). For boxes and lines, choosing a color is a simple operation: pick one from the **Color** pop-up menu in the **Box** or **Line** area, respectively.

FIGURE 16.16

Grouping boxes before coloring them can save time.

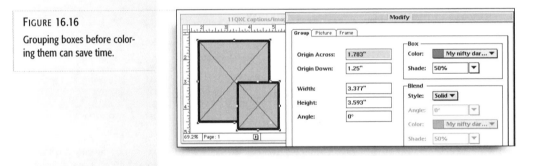

FIGURE 16.17

The **Frame** tab allows you to choose a frame color as well as a style.

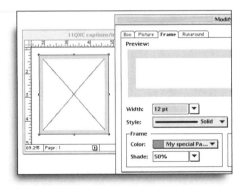

Frame colors are a bit more complicated. A new feature in QuarkXPress allows you to color frames that formerly had only white backgrounds in two colors: one color for the black part of the frame, and another for the white areas of the frame. For this operation, you need to use the Modify dialog box; the Colors palette only affects the black portions of the frame.

To color a box frame with the Modify dialog box:

1. Create the box and pick a frame. Choosing **Frame** from the **Item** menu ⌘+B (Ctrl+B) brings up the **Frame** tab of the Modify dialog box. Usually, the frames that work best in color are the ones that are a little ornate and that are used wider than 6 points or so (see Figure 16.18).

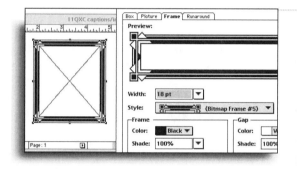

FIGURE 16.18

Coloring the more ornate frames offers more choices of interesting things to do with both foreground and background color.

2. Pick a color from the **Color** pop-up menu in the **Frame** area. This color replaces the black in the original frame (see Figure 16.19).

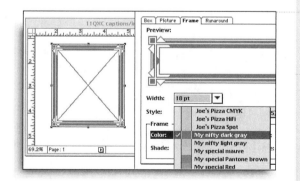

FIGURE 16.19

First select the frame's primary color.

3. Now pick a color in the **Gap** area. Whatever color you pick here replaces the background white color, or fills in the "gaps" behind the frame (see Figure 16.20).

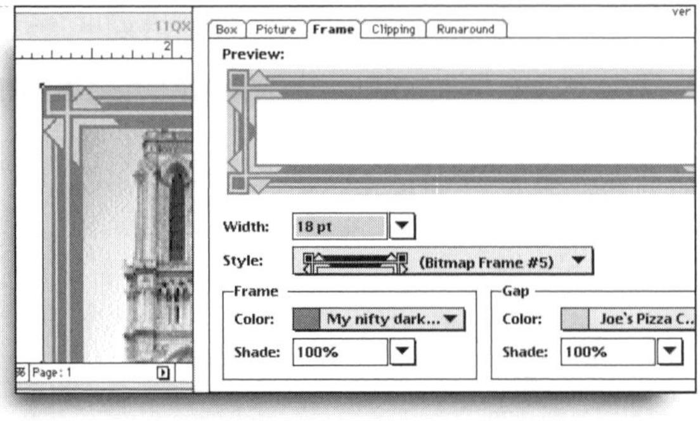

FIGURE 16.20

Selecting the second color in the **Gap** area fills the background with that color, replacing what was white.

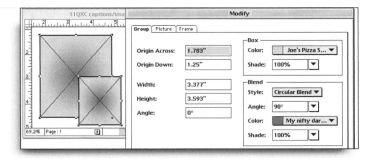

Transparent gaps in frames

If you pick **None** as a **Gap** color, you might expect the background color of the box, or an *imported* image contained in the box, to show through where the white was. Forget it; it doesn't work. The gap will allow whatever's behind the box to show instead.

4. Now make sure to select a width for the frame. Most times, if it looks as though nothing happened, it's because no value was entered for the width, or the size of the frame was specified as being too small.

Creating Blends with the Modify Dialog Box

You can generate blend effects from the **Box** tab in the Modify dialog box (⌘+M/Ctrl+M) as well as from the Colors palette. A few things are slightly different, however. The color in the top area (labeled **Box**) is the "primary" color, equivalent to the color picked in the number 1 button in the Colors palette. The color chosen in the **Blend** area is equivalent to the color chosen in the number 2 button. You select the type of blend in the **Style** pop-up menu (see Figure 16.21).

FIGURE 16.21

You can also apply blends within the Modify dialog box.

The dialog box has the added feature of having an **Apply** button. The **Apply** button is useful on a big screen to see in a hurry the effects you made, without having to bring up the dialog box repeatedly. On smaller screens, (17 inches or less) I prefer using the palette. It's faster and takes up less screen real estate.

If you select more than one object to apply a blend to, the **Box** tab changes to a **Group** tab, but the functions are the same.

Using the Color Submenu

Type (but not boxes or lines) can also be colored by using the **Color** submenu in the **Style** menu (see Figure 16.22).

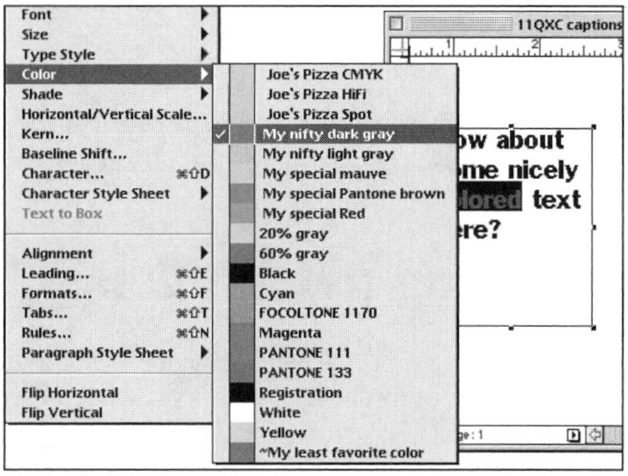

FIGURE 16.22

Choosing **Color** from the **Style** menu and making a choice from the submenu colors previously selected text.

Specifying Color in Style Sheets

Any attribute that can be applied to text while it's onscreen can also be applied to *style sheets*, both paragraph and character. So if you have a color *initial cap* or a color boldface lead-in on certain paragraphs, the color of the type can become just as much a part of the style sheets as the font, the size, and so on.

In the Edit Style Sheets dialog box, there's a color pop-up menu that matches your Colors palette. Simply apply the color of your choice to the character (or paragraph) style sheet you're creating. Don't forget, if you later change the color within the color name, or change the name of the color by deleting it and replacing it with another, the type as well as all the objects built from that color will also change (see Figure 16.23).

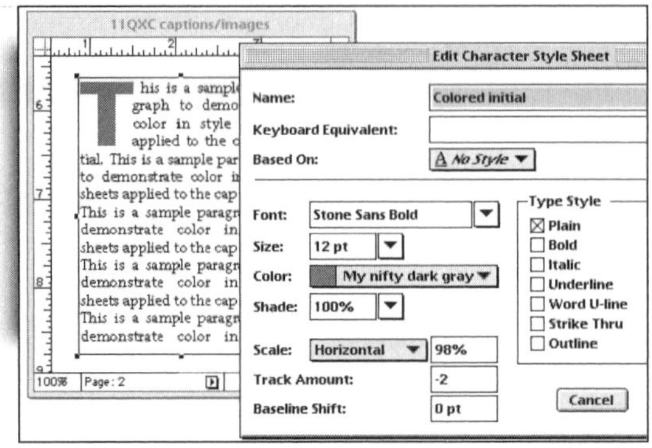

FIGURE 16.23

Colors can be made part of style sheets for both character and paragraph style sheets.

SEE ALSO

➤ *To create and edit paragraph style sheets, see page 298*

➤ *To create and edit character style sheets, see page 299*

Specifying Default Colors for Items

If you want all your text boxes to be 0% black (which some pre-press houses prefer), or if you want all your picture boxes to come with a 12-point frame in your favorite shade of mauve, you can modify the defaults in the toolbox so that these things happen automatically every time you create the box.

If you do these things with no document open, the changes you make to the defaults in the Tool preferences apply to all new documents you create in the future. If you make these changes with a document open on the screen, the changes apply only to that document.

To change default colors for tools:

1. Double-click on the item to change in the Tool palette. The Document Preferences dialog box opens, open to the Tool tab (see Figure 16.24).

2. Before clicking **Modify**, look for a minute at the other choices—they're a new feature in QuarkXPress 4. For all picture boxes, regardless of shape, to have 12-point mauve frames, click **Select Similar Types**. All the picture box tools

will be selected, and all their defaults will be changed. This feature is a real time-saver (see Figure 16.25).

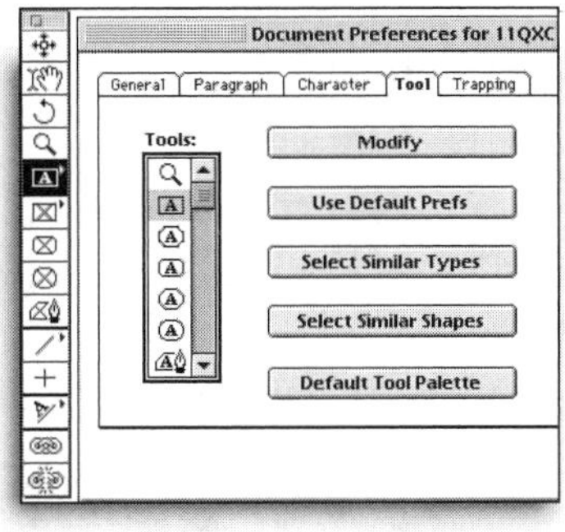

FIGURE 16.24
Changing the default colors is an easy click away for all boxes, frames, and rules.

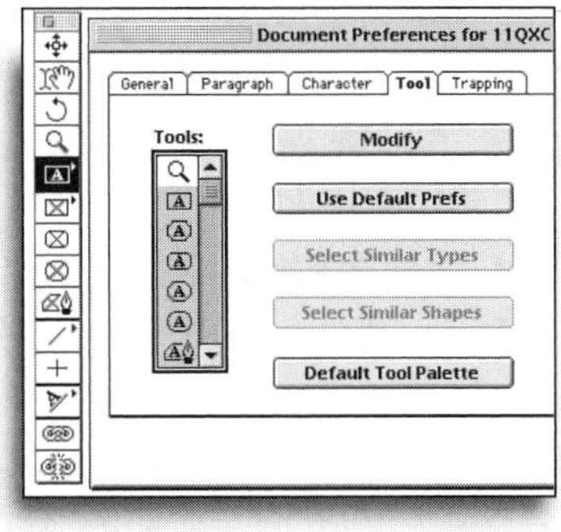

FIGURE 16.25
Selecting **Similar Shapes** or **Similar Types** can save lots of time if you want all the preferences to be the same.

3. Now click **Modify** to bring up the Modify dialog box. Its tabs will vary depending on the type of tools being modified. Defaults can be set for the color of boxes in the **Box** tab, the color of lines in the **Line** tab, or frame attributes in the **Frame** tab. Go to the **Frame** tab, and select a color ("My Special Mauve," in this case) and change the width of the frame from 0 (the preset default that essentially produces no frame at all) to 12 points (see Figure 16.26).

Creating Special Effects

You're not restricted to coloring box background and leaving it at that. Try spicing up your designs by coloring text, frames, and lines with blends, or applying color to imported grayscale or black and white images.

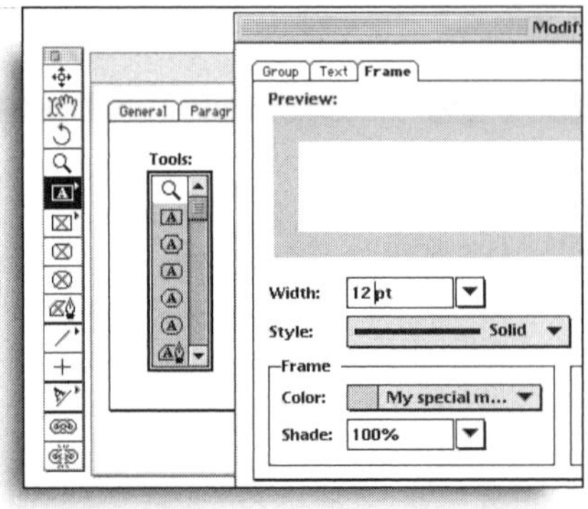

FIGURE 16.26

Changing default frame attributes is an option in the Document Preferences dialog box.

Coloring Text with Blends

Although text can take colors and shades of colors, they can't take blends. But with the new *Bézier* capability of XPress, you can easily create blends in text.

To apply a colored blend to text:

1. Create your text. Bold sans serif type works best in a situation such as this: blends can be very subtle, and the largest possible area helps the reader to see the effects you created. This example uses Franklin Gothic No 2.

2. Convert the type to a compound picture box by choosing **Text to Box** from the **Style** menu (see Figure 16.27).

FIGURE 16.27

To make type hold blends, first convert the type to boxes with the **Text to Box** command.

3. The type is now no longer type; it's a picture box, and as such, can take the blend across the whole line of type. From the Colors palette, click on the **Background Color** icon and select color 1.

4. Then select color 2 to complete the blend (see Figure 16.28).

5. If you want to apply a blend to each letter in the line, choose **Split** from the **Item** menu and then choose **Outside Paths** from the submenu to break the line into individual letters. The blend will be applied to each letter individually, and the open spaces in the middle of the letters will allow the background color to show through (see Figure 16.29).

FIGURE 16.29
To apply the blend in step 3 to each letter, split the box using the **Outside Paths** option.

Coloring Lines and Frames with Blends

Although frames and lines can take colors and shades of colors, they can't take blends. But with the new Bézier capability of XPress, you can easily create the equivalent of blended lines and frames.

To create a line or frame with a blend:

1. Draw a box (an ellipse in the example) on the page.

2. Make a copy exactly on top of the image at the same size by choosing **Step and Repeat** from the **Item** menu or pressing ⌘+Option+D (Ctrl+Alt+D)and setting both **Horizontal** and **Vertical Offsets** to 0 (see Figure 16.30).

3. Scale what will be the inside edge of the shape. An easy way to do that is to use the Measurements palette and subtract equal amounts from both the horizontal measure and the vertical measure. Remember that you can "do the math" in the Measurements palette. In this sample, 14 points (0p14) was subtracted from the height and the width of the top ellipse created with the **Step and Repeat** command (see Figure 16.31).

FIGURE 16.30

Step one in making a frame that can be filled with a blend is to draw the shape and copy it on top of itself.

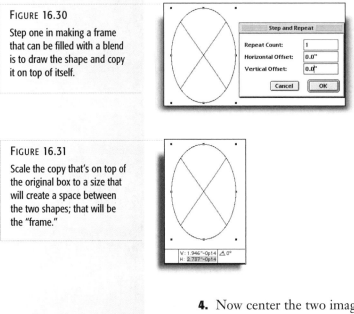

FIGURE 16.31

Scale the copy that's on top of the original box to a size that will create a space between the two shapes; that will be the "frame."

4. Now center the two images on each other, to make the frame equally sized all around. Select both shapes, and choose **Space/Align** from the **Item** menu or get to it by pressing ⌘+comma (Ctrl+comma). Select **Center** for both the **Horizontal** and **Vertical** alignment functions (see Figure 16.32).

FIGURE 16.32

Align the two shapes centered on each other with the Space/Align Items dialog box.

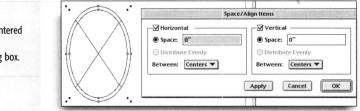

5. Making sure that both shapes are still selected, choose **Merge** from the **Item** menu, then **Difference** from the submenu, and the two objects become one frame, with a hole in the center (see Figure 16.33).

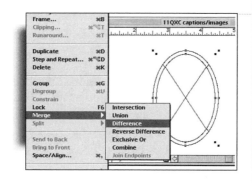

FIGURE 16.33

The final step is to make an object out of the two boxes with the **Difference** option of the **Merge** command.

6. Now the two objects are one, with a hole in it, that can be colored, shaded, and blended—or filled with a picture or text. To place another color or picture within the frame, create another box and center it behind the frame. Here, the new frame is filled with a blend and a favorite Paris picture is in the middle (see Figure 16.34).

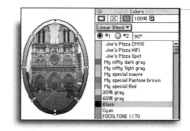

FIGURE 16.34

A linear blend applied to the new frame created from two box shapes, converted to Bèzier shapes and filled. The picture was inserted in another picture box that lies behind the frame.

You can handle a line or rule the same way, but even more simply. Just make a picture box that's long and narrow and fill it with your favorite blends and colors. Just keep in mind that the smaller the pseudo-rule gets, the less likely it is that people will even see the blend (see Figure 16.35).

SEE ALSO

➤ *To use the Merge and Split commands, see page 320*

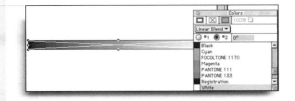

Coloring Images

Grayscale images inside picture boxes can also be colored, if the image is of the right file type. The box itself can be colored a second color, and if your use of colors knows no boundaries of taste or extravagance, you can use a third and fourth color on a frame for the box. The eligible file types are as follows:

- *TIFF*
- *PICT*
- *JPEG*
- *EPS* (raster only)—actually, you can only color the box background with EPS files, but Photoshop's EPS format allows transparent whites, so that the box color shows through in white and light areas. You can't color the black areas.

Coloring the images inside a box is the same as coloring text in a box, or any other object. The tools are the same, but results may vary depending on the file type and the quality and content of the image.

To assign a color to an image:

1. Select the picture box with the Content tool ![icon].

2. Choose a color for the picture itself (the black areas, in other words) in either of two ways:
   - Choose a color from the **Color** submenu of the **Style** menu.
   - Click on ![icon] at the top of the Colors palette, and choose a color in the list.

3. Click on ![icon] at the top of the Colors palette and choose a color for the box background; this color shows through in the white areas of the image.

4. Adjust the shade of either or both colors in either of two ways:

- Choose a percentage from the **Shade** submenu of the **Style** menu.
- Choose a shade from the Colors palette **Shade** menu or type in a percentage.

The Modify dialog box allows you to change picture colors, as well; the controls are located in the **Picture** area of the **Box** tab and are only available when the selected box contains a picture.

SEE ALSO

➤ *To import a picture, see page 339*

CHAPTER 17

Matching and Managing Color

Use RGB and HSB color for Web and multimedia projects

Use CMYK and Hexachrome color for print projects

Specify colors from color matching systems

Define Hexachrome and multi-ink colors

Improve color fidelity with color management

Color is a mysterious thing—it may seem simple, but making colors on your computer monitor match the colors you'll see in print is near-impossible. What you need to know up front are some basics:

1. You can never reproduce the range of colors that exist in nature.

   Even the finest grain, lowest ASA film only records a small fraction of the colors in nature. Scanning the slide (or print) reduces the range of colors even more, and printing ink-on-paper reduces the number further. And the lower the quality of the paper and the scan resolution, the further away you are from the original. Each step in the process reduces the amount of information in the image.

   For example, a *24-bit* color monitor can reproduce more than 16.7 million colors, and although the human eye can theoretically perceive even more, the differences are so minute as to be practically irrelevant. However, those two ranges of colors don't entirely intersect. Four-color process printing can reproduce approximately 5,000 colors, whereas the PANTONE Process Color Matching system contains approximately 3,000. Using *HiFi* printing increases the number of colors available somewhat; PANTONE's *Hexachrome* six-color printing system can reproduce almost all the colors visible on a computer monitor.

2. What you see on the screen bears no relationship to what will be seen on paper because the way the color is reproduced is totally different.

3. Not all colors you see on the screen can be reproduced on paper.

4. Not all colors that can be reproduced on paper can be seen on the screen.

   What this means is that the *gamut* (or range) of colors that you can see varies from model to model. The cruder the printing (65 line screen on newsprint, for instance), the smaller the gamut that is reproduced (see Figure 17.1).

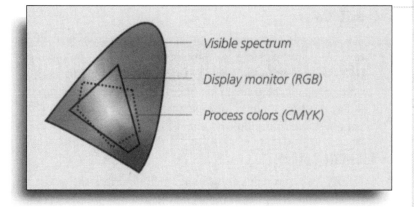

FIGURE 17.1

Just a small portion of the visible gamut from monitors and process color demonstrates that you can't see the full range of colors in any case.

Seeing Color

You see colors in nature because sunlight contains all the colors of the rainbow, and objects in nature reflect and absorb those colors in varying degrees. Obviously, you see a green leaf because the leaf reflects back to your eyes the color green, while absorbing all the other colors in the rainbow.

Color Models

Over the years, various "models" have evolved in an effort to describe what color is, and to put a handle on explaining how it works and how to reproduce it on paper, on TV, and on computer screens, as well as by other methods.

HSB Color

HSB stands for hue, saturation, and brightness. It's a way of describing color that artists are familiar with because that's the way paint colors are generally mixed. Hue is the color of an object: yellow, green, blue, or any other color. Saturation measures the amount of the color present in the object you're looking at: is it a pure, bright yellow with a lot of pigment in it, or is it more gray than color? Brightness is a way of describing how much black is present in a color: is it dark or light?

RGB Color

RGB is an additive color system in which each color is made up of three primary colors: red, green, and blue. Used in monitors (both computer and television), this is where Sony got its tricolored logo and the trade name of Trinitron ("tri" means three). There are three "guns" (one each for red, green, and blue) that paint colored light onto the screen.

CMYK Color

CMYK is a subtractive color model that describes the colors used in four-color (or process color) printing. The letters stand for the names of the colors: C for cyan, M for magenta, Y for yellow, and K for black. Black is often called the "key" color, the one to which all the others had to register (or align with), hence its designation as K, not B. The use of B would have also been confusing with RGB and the use of B for blue.

LAB (or CIELAB) Color

The CIELAB (Commission Internationale de L'Eclairage— International Commission for Color) or *LAB* color model was created in an attempt to define color regardless of the source, hardware, or printing methods used. QuarkXPress uses a variation of this model called D50 Illuminant, which is the version of LAB color that's used most commonly.

HiFi Color

HiFi (High Fidelity) printing defines color printing with more than four colors, usually six colors (or more.) In addition to slightly different, "cleaner" CMYK colors, HiFi uses added colors (mostly orange and green) to extend the gamut (range) of colors that can be reproduced, sometimes up to 20% or more. Traditionally, four-color printing has problems reproducing subtle shades of green and orange, and by adding these to the press, it requires less "work" on the part of CMYK to reproduce these tones. With more than 7,000 six-color presses in the U.S. alone, this is an area of printing technology that is rapidly growing more popular. HiFi color is usually used in combination with *stochastic screening* and waterless offset printing.

Spot Color

Spot color is just another way of saying you want to add another ink color, and therefore another printing plate, to a job. Traditional uses for spot color have been letterheads, envelopes, and business cards (often called a two-color job), but you see a lot more creative use of two colors (or more) in lieu of black on colored papers for flyers, brochures, pamphlets, and so on. Theoretically, you have no limit to the number of spot colors on a job: it's limited only by your budget, time, and the goodwill of your printer. (Each color has to have its own printing plate, and the press has to be cleaned of all ink after running each color.)

Additive and Subtractive Color

Colors on a video screen are seen and created exactly the opposite of color on paper. Red, green, and blue "guns" excite phosphors on a cathode ray tube (your television screen or computer monitor). The color white is created when all three color guns excite the same or adjacent pixels on the screen, creating red, green, and blue light simultaneously. The three colors of light combine to create white light, so this kind of color reproduction is called *additive* color. This is exactly the opposite of ink on paper, in which all three (or four) colors added together make black (see Figure 17.2).

Subtractive color systems require that you take away all color to achieve white, and they're reflective color. Inks on paper, just like natural objects such as an apple or an orange, are seen as the color they are because the different rainbow colors of light contained in sunlight are absorbed in varying degrees by the object, and the remaining colors are reflected back to the eye. An orange is orange because it absorbs all the colors in the rainbow except orange.

FIGURE 17.2

The three "guns" on TV or computer monitor tubes create white where they merge.

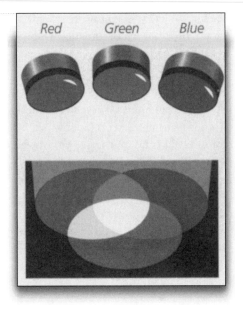

Full-color images on paper are reproduced using at least three colors: cyan, magenta, and yellow, the respective opposites of red, green, and blue. Usually, black is also added to sharpen up the results and to make the shadow details crisper, and it's also usually needed because there's type on the page, too. Black type can be created using cyan, magenta, and yellow, but registering the three colors during printing would be more trouble than it's worth, so black ink is used. Also, cyan, magenta, and yellow don't produce a true solid black when combined because the colored inks you use don't perfectly match the theoretical colors—you actually get a muddy brown when you combine them. These four colors are commonly called *process colors* (see Figure 17.3).

More and more, additional colors are added to the basic process colors to make the print job match the original copy more closely by extending the color gamut available on a printing press. Printing processes that use extra process colors are called HiFi color; the best-known HiFi process is PANTONE's Hexachrome, which adds orange and green inks to the basic four color process inks. Using these two new colors aids in reproducing colors that are troublesome in normal process color printing.

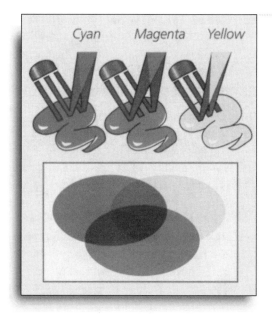

FIGURE 17.3

In theory, cyan, magenta, and yellow should produce a good black. In practice, it doesn't.

Matching Color

Despite the best efforts of many vendors to make a match between your scanner or other input, your screen, and your printer or proofer, there are some basic reasons that you may never be satisfied with the results.

Reflective flatbed scanners usually see color as RGB and, at least on the desktop, are fairly limited in the range of tones they can capture. This characteristic of scanners is called *dynamic range* or D^{Max}, and most flatbed scanners don't score much higher than 3.0 or 3.2 on a 4.0 scale.

Transparency scanners are usually a little bit better, and it's also easier to make a transparency look good on the first pass as opposed to a print scanned on a *flatbed scanner*. These scanners, in the $1,000–$2,000 price range, give satisfactory results for good quality offset printing, and they're usually overkill for web or presentation work in which all you need to do is drive the screen.

Drum scanners, ranging from $20,000 desktop drums to high-end, $200,000-plus scanners, still have one basic problem: their output is often "interpreted" by fairly inexperienced desktop operators with little color correction knowledge or experience. And these users generally try and "correct" color by tweaking the image until it looks good on the screen. Wrong!

What you see on the screen, and on a color proof from a desktop printer, bears little resemblance to what may be produced on a good quality offset press. It's understanding the range of colors that each device is capable of producing that makes the difference. There are colors on the screen that no printing press can ever hope to reproduce. And there are colors on press that can't display on a screen. And that's not even taking into consideration the fact that the scanner may not have captured even half of the colors present in the original copy.

Despite these fundamental problems, today's *color management* software attempts to bridge the gap between the colors designers see onscreen and the colors they get in final printed pieces. How successful color management is remains a matter of opinion. Another answer is to stick to using colors chosen from a *color matching* system such as *PANTONE* or *TruMatch*; colors are chosen from a printed swatchbook and what they look like onscreen is irrelevant.

SEE ALSO

➤ *To turn on QuarkXPress's color management system, see page 467*

Choosing a Color Model

You usually want to specify only two types of color in documents that you're preparing for print reproduction: process color or spot color, or in some cases a combination of the two. You can use both types of colors in one document (such as a four-color bank advertisement that also uses a PANTONE spot color for the bank's logo), or you can create colors that combine spot and process inks (multi-ink colors). Finally, you can use Pantone Hexachrome (HiFi) color—the four process colors plus orange and green.

When you output to a proofing device such as a desktop color printer, the color processor in the printer will try to simulate spot colors using its three or four inks or toners. Just keep in mind that your final goal in prepress is to output one piece of film per page per color. So if you have a one-page, four-color job that also uses one Pantone color (such as that bank advertisement), you produce five pieces of film (or *plates*): one for each of the four process colors, plus one for the spot color.

Specifying spot colors is generally a lot easier if you stick with the PANTONE Matching System, at least in the United States. All U.S. printers use it; it's been around for a long time, and everybody understands it. All offset and letterpress ink manufacturers in the U.S. mix their inks in compliance with the Pantone standard. Use the PANTONE Color Formula Guide for accurate, solid, specific colors you use as a separate printing plate: true spot colors. You should also know beforehand what kind of paper stock your job is going to be printed on, so you'll know whether to use uncoated samples or coated samples from the Pantone books and specifications. The glossier the paper, the more it reflects; and remember, you see colors because of how they reflect from the paper (or substrate) (see Figure 17.4).

Because designers are used to using Pantone colors, they often choose Pantone colors even for process color jobs and specify that these colors should be converted to their process color equivalents when the job is output. A glance at the PANTONE Process Color Imaging Guide swatchbook, though, will show that most Pantone colors can't be accurately simulated with process colors. Pantone has created the Pro-Sim color matching system for these designers; this system contains only Pantone colors that can be closely matched with process colors, and it specifies the process color mix that should be used with each color.

Pantone's newest color matching system, the PANTONE Hexachrome Color System, containing more than 2,000 colors, can be used to choose HiFi colors. While many more than 2,000 colors can be printed with the Hexachrome process, these are representative colors that are shown in a printed swatchbook.

There are some Pantone colors that do not translate to the four-

Choosing Web colors

Colors for the Web should be limited to the 216 that are common to the Mac OS and Windows system palettes. Pantone sells ColorWeb, a version of this color palette that can be used with QuarkXPress and other programs; see the Pantone Web site at www. pantone.com.

FIGURE 17.4

The PANTONE Process color guide describes to designers and printers alike how to reproduce over 3,000 colors using just cyan, magenta, yellow, and black.

color process. If you select a Pantone color that does not have a four-color equivalent, the **Separation** box in the Document tab of the **Print** dialog box will be dimmed and unavailable.

Pantone color guides can be purchased from many sources: sometimes prepress magazines and graphic design magazines offer special deals: three or four of the guides at a special package price. Pantone offers a Color Survival Kit that contains the Solid to Process guide, the Process Guide, and the Formula Guide. Everybody should have this as a starter kit. Other guides are available for High Fidelity Color, Tints, Color plus Blacks, Foils, Metallics, Solid Colors, Pastels, and so on. Pantone also makes books of PMS colors that have tear-out swatches you can send to the printer with your job, just in case the printer needs something to match. And the company makes plug-ins and XTensions for most computer software.

Stay away from DIC and Toyo unless you're preparing a job to be printed in the Far East, and then check with your printer as to what standard will be used for your job.

TruMatch (about 2,000 colors) and Focoltone (763 colors) sell *swatchbooks* showing colors that can be built from the basic four-color printing inks. Check with your printer or service bureau first before building your document. Swatchbooks for those standards are available, just like the swatch books from Pantone.

Using Color Matching Systems

You can pick colors from any model (PANTONE, Focoltone, and so on); the important thing is to know why you use a particular color model and what the final output of that color will be. There is no other hint in this book that's worth more than this one: Check with your printer first before creating a bunch of colors in a color matching system.

To create a new color, choose **Colors** from the **Edit** menu and click **New**. From there, you can access any one of the color models previously discussed. Pick your color, name it, and save it. Any of these colors can be spot colors—an ink mixed to that specific color and run on the press as a single plate—or process-separated colors. It's generally best to stick with the default setting for the color model you're using; for example, TruMatch colors are four-color process colors by design, but Pantone colors are spot colors designed to be used with a custom-mixed ink. If you convert from spot to process or vice versa, don't expect an exact match. To make a spot color into a process color, make sure you do not check the **Spot Color** box, and make sure **CMYK** is chosen from the **Model** pop-up menu.

TruMatch and Focoltone

Choose either **TruMatch** or **Focoltone** from the **Model** menu. Pick a color either by typing in the alphanumeric designation of the color, if you know what it is (probably from a swatchbook), or scroll through the colors until you find the one you want. Remember, though, that your monitor does not accurately show how the colors will look when they're printed.

Because the TruMatch and Focoltone color definitions are based on four-color separations, you see when you select the color in the Colors dialog box that it's a separated color. To tweak it a little, you can switch to CMYK mode and change the values (see Figure 17.5).

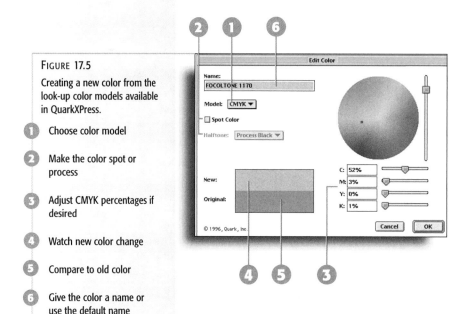

FIGURE 17.5

Creating a new color from the look-up color models available in QuarkXPress.

1. Choose color model

2. Make the color spot or process

3. Adjust CMYK percentages if desired

4. Watch new color change

5. Compare to old color

6. Give the color a name or use the default name

In the **Name** field, QuarkXPress automatically inserts the name of the color from the color model being used. You might want to take this opportunity to rename it in the Name field to something more useful, such as "Joe's Pizza corporate color" for instance (see Figure 17.6).

Once you save that color, you can edit it just as any other color can be edited. You might want to think about "converting" all your spot colors to process colors. It's probable that "Joe's Pizza" corporate color can be used in one job as a spot color, and in another job be reproduced using four colors. Naming the colors appropriately ("Joe's Pizza CMYK" and "Joe's Pizza Spot" might be good choices) can help you sort through this mess later as you find out the four-color job you spent three weeks on for Joe's Pizza was changed, at the last minute, to a spot color job for budgetary reasons.

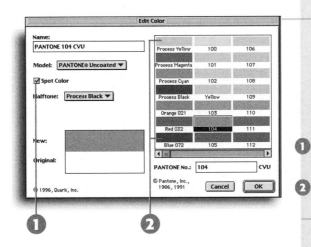

SEE ALSO

➤ *To define a color, see page 426*

Pantone

The same principles apply to Pantone colors as apply to any other color definition. You just have to know if the color is going be created on press with four-color (or more) process inks, or if the job will be run with spot color.

Spot (Premixed) Colors

For Pantone spot colors, choose from the **PANTONE** or **PANTONE Uncoated** options in the **Model** menu. These colors are automatically assumed to be a spot color, as evidenced by the fact the **Spot Color** box will be checked and the information box in the color selector shows it's a spot color (see Figure 17.7).

Process Colors

For Pantone process colors, choose either the **PANTONE Process** or the **PANTONE ProSim** options. The **PANTONE Process** model matches colors from the PANTONE Process Color System Guides mentioned earlier. If you own one of these guides, hold it up to the monitor you're working on. No matter what the room light conditions or the monitor quality, you're still trying to compare subtractive with additive color models, and they'll never match! The real point of all this is that if you specify Pantone 1111-1 because that's what you liked when you saw it in the swatchbook, then that's what the printer should deliver on press (see Figures 17.8 and 17.9).

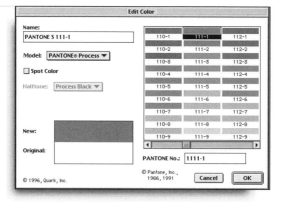

FIGURE 17.8

What you see is not what you get. Pick colors from printed samples, not from what they look like on the screen.

The **PANTONE ProSim** (Process Simulator) model delivers process colors (CMYK) that match Pantone's spot colors. Here's where you go when you want to provide the same color menu items in your QuarkXPress documents in both four-color and spot color: Joe's Pizza will be happy that you picked a corporate identity color that can be reproduced in both spot and process printing. (See Figure 17.20.)

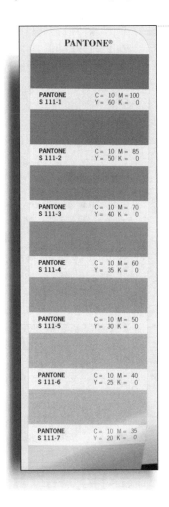

FIGURE 17.9
What's important is what the ink on the paper is going to look like; this is shown in the printed swatchbook.

Hexachrome Colors

Hexachrome colors are also assumed to be process (separated) colors based on PANTONE's Hexachrome Color System, which uses the four process colors plus green and orange. Think of it as a specific type of HiFi color. If your job runs in this specific color model, you should specify all your colors as Hexachrome to get the best results from the additional two inks used. Because the cyan, magenta, and yellow inks used in Hexachrome are slightly different than regular CMYK inks, you'll be surprised if you don't specify all your colors in Hexachrome. And this also applies to *EPS* files you import into QuarkXPress: the colors in your FreeHand and Illustrator files should have been built with the Hexachrome model also. If they're not, don't be surprised if the EPS files produce colors that look a lot different than the QuarkXPress colors.

SEE ALSO

➤ *To define a color, see page 426*

DIC and Toyo

The **DIC** and **Toyo** color models, commonly used in Japan, are spot colors only. They have no process (four-color) equivalents, which may be a limiting factor for you. With the increasing number of jobs designed and sent to Asia (Hong Kong and Singapore) for printing, this may be a factor in some of the work you do. Don't use either of these color models without checking first with your printer as to whether they even have access to inks that use these models to mix their colors. As previously mentioned, if you don't even want to see these in the **Model** menu, quit QuarkXPress, drag the files you don't need from the Color folder within the XPress folder to some other folder, and restart QuarkXPress.

SEE ALSO

➤ *To define a color, see page 426*

Multi-Ink and High-Fidelity (HiFi) Colors

Because the whole area of multi-ink colors is fairly new, there are no handy reference guides to help you build multi-ink colors.

To build multi-ink or HiFi colors, start by building the basic colors you use to make your finished colors. Start with the printer and ask what inks they're going to use. If you know that one of the additional colors will be a bright red that will be used to "bump" the color of that nice foreign sports car you always wanted, for instance, that color can be created as a new color and added to the menu of spot colors. All spot colors appear on the menu and can then be used to build multiple colors. Think of the process colors as just four "spot" colors that are mixed on the page: all you do is add more "spot" colors to play with in building new colors.

After the colors that will be used on the press have been added to the document (check this using the **Spot Colors** option from the **Show** menu in the Colors dialog box), you can then proceed to build your special color(s), one color at a time, by manually adding color percentages one at a time to the new color you build (see Figure 17.10).

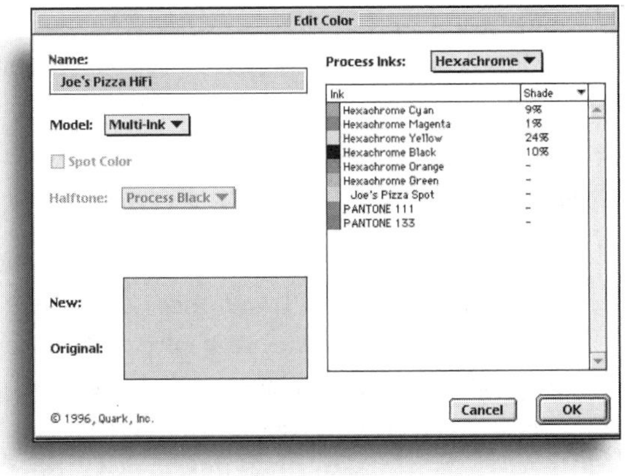

FIGURE 17.10
Building a multi-ink color is not as easy as building regular Pantone and process colors.

Color Management with the CMS XTension

If you've read a single issue of any DTP trade magazine in the last year, you've probably seen an article about color management. It's a hot topic these days, mainly because this technology has finally gotten to the point where it's almost useful. Today's color management software—including that used in QuarkXPress 4—modifies color information based on device profiles that detail how different monitors, scanners, and printers distort color. Using this system, a color monitor can be coaxed to display color that's closer to what you'll actually get when you print a document, and a printer can be fiddled around to produce images that are closer to what you saw onscreen when you created them.

To accomplish this magic, you need to give QuarkXPress three pieces of information for each color element or image you use:

- What scanner or digital camera was used to capture the image, or what monitor was used when the image was color-corrected
- What monitor you're viewing the image on right now
- What printer you'll use to output the document

Using this information, QuarkXPress attempts to reconcile the final output of the document with what it thinks you're expecting. You can also choose to have the display on your monitor adjusted to more closely reflect what that final output will look like.

Choosing Default Device Profiles

The initial setup for using color management is done in the Color Management Preferences dialog box, where you specify the default preferences to be used when importing, creating, and printing color images and elements. These settings are application-level, meaning that they'll be used for every document you create or open in QuarkXPress, rather than just the currently open document. Don't worry, though; there are plenty of chances to change the profile used for a specific image, as you import it, while you're editing the XPress document and when you print the document.

To set default profiles:

1. Choose **Preferences** from the **Edit** menu, then **Color Management** from the submenu to bring up the Color Management Preferences dialog box (see Figure 17.11).

2. Click on **Color Management Active** to turn on color management.

Color Management Preferences for Color Management

☒ Color Management Active

┌─Destination Profiles────────────────────
Monitor: [Apple 13" RGB Standard ▼]
Composite Printer: [Hewlett-Packard DeskJet 1200C/PS ▼]
Separation Printer: [3M Matchprint ▼]

┌─Default Source Profiles─────────────────
[RGB] [CMYK] [Hexachrome]
Color: [Apple 13" RGB Standard ▼]
Image: [EPSON Expression636 ▼]

Display Correction: [Composite Printer Color Space ▼]

Correction ▼	Color Model
√	RGB
√	CMYK
√	Hexachrome
√	TRUMATCH

[Cancel]   [OK]

3. Choose **Destination Profiles** from the three pop-up menus. These profiles include those installed by QuarkXPress and any previously installed in your system. Most color-capable devices these days come with *device profiles*, and you can obtain them from most manufacturer's web sites if you don't have the ones you need.

- **Monitor** should be the monitor on which the document will be viewed.

- **Composite Printer** should be the color printer or proofer on which composite (color) proofs will be printed.

- **Separation Printer** should be the imagesetter on which film separations will be produced.

4. Choose **Default Source Profiles** for each of the three color models shown: **RGB**, **CMYK**, and **Hexachrome**. These are the profiles that will be applied to images in these color models. For example, when a CMYK file is imported, QuarkXPress applies the source profile from the **Image** pop-up menu under the **CMYK** tab here.

- The **Color** setting determines the profile used for color elements created in QuarkXPress—colored boxes or lines. This will generally be the monitor profile, because most people choose colors based on how they look onscreen.

- The **Image** setting determines the profile used for imported color images, no matter what their format. This will generally be the profile for your scanner or digital camera. If you have images scanned by a service bureau, ask the staff for a copy of the appropriate profile.

5. Click **OK** to set color management in motion.

Choosing Profiles for Individual Images

Profiles can be assigned when images are imported and changed at any time using the Profile Information palette. A Profile Usage dialog box lets you keep track of what profiles are assigned to what images.

To assign a device profile to an image as you import it:

1. In the Get Picture dialog box, click on the name of an image file and wait a second. QuarkXPress takes a little time to evaluate the image, about as along as it takes to show the image preview, and it grays out the **Profile** pop-up menu until it's done with this process.

2. When the **Profile** menu is available, choose a profile for the image's source—usually the scanner or digital camera used to capture the image. The profiles listed in the menu are those that match the color space of the image, not necessarily those that are appropriate, so the list may include printer profiles.

3. Click on **Color Correction** to turn color management off or on for this particular image. If **Color Correction** is off, no adjustments will be made to this image when it's printed.

4. Click **Open** to finish importing the image.

The specified profile is assigned to the image, and that's the source profile that's used for display and printing unless you change it. You can see the profiles that have been assigned to

various images in the document by choosing **Usage** from the
Utilities menu and clicking on the **Profiles** tab (see Figure
17.12). Choose a profile from the **Profiles** tab; any images or
preference settings using that profile will be listed in the dialog
box. Click on **More Information** to display information such
as the profile's manufacturer and its type (printer, scanner, or
monitor).

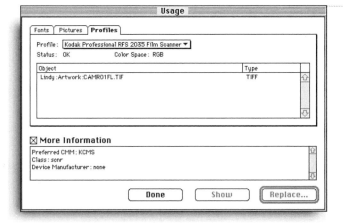

FIGURE 17.12

The **Profiles** tab of the Usage
dialog box tells you what
images use what device
profiles.

To display an image, click on its filename in the **Object** list and
click **Show**. To change the profile for an image, click on an
image name in the **Object** list and click **Replace** to bring up the
Replace Profile dialog (see Figure 17.13). Choose a replacement
profile and click **OK**. When you finish examining the profile
usage for your document, click **Done**.

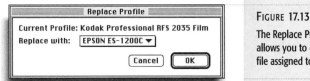

FIGURE 17.13

The Replace Profile dialog box
allows you to change the profile assigned to images.

You can also change source profiles and turn color correction off
and on for individual graphics using the Profile Information
palette (choose **Profile Information** from the **View** menu).
Click on a *picture box*, then choose a profile from the palette's

menu and click **Color Correction** off or on (see Figure 17.14). You'll notice a brief delay in redrawing the image when you change a profile; XPress actually re-imports the image based on the new information you just provided.

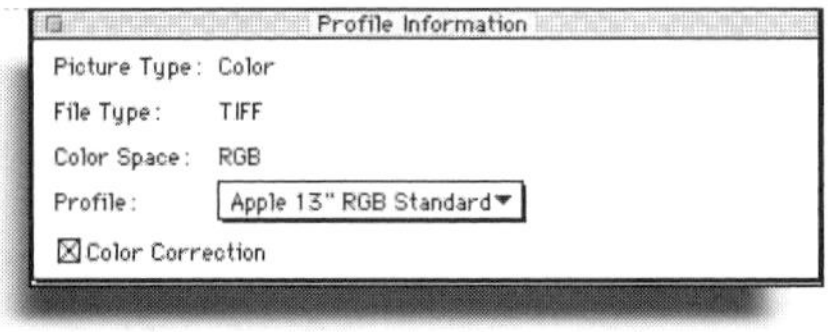

FIGURE 17.14

The Profile Information palette gives you profile information on individual images.

Choosing Profiles When Printing

You can change your mind again about destination profiles when you're printing a document.

To change color management settings when printing:

1. In the Print dialog box, click on the **Color Management** tab to see the color management options (see Figure 17.15).

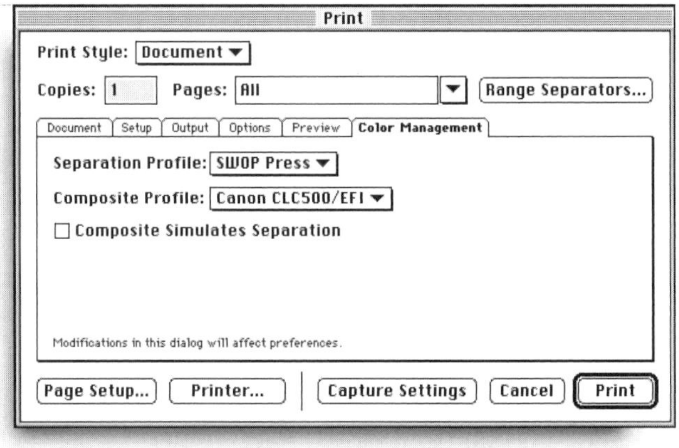

FIGURE 17.15

The **Color Management** tab of the Print dialog box gives you one last chance to change your mind about device profiles.

2. Choose a profile from the **Composite Profile** menu if you're printing color proofs.

3. Choose a profile from the **Separation Profile** menu if you're printing film separations.

4. Click on **Composite Simulates Separation** to print a color proof that will be color-corrected to match the results of printing separations with the **Separation Profile** option you chose.

5. Click **Print** to print using the profiles you chose.

Viewing Color Onscreen

The Color Management Preferences dialog box also includes controls for how color appears onscreen. You can have QuarkXPress adjust the monitor display to correspond to the expected results using the output device you specified. Be warned: The results can be startling, especially when those vivid RGB colors suddenly turn all muddy.

To activate onscreen color correction:

1. Choose **Preferences** from the **Edit** menu, then **Color Management** to bring up the Color Management Preferences dialog box (see Figure 17.72).

2. From the **Display Correction** pop-up menu, choose an option:

   • **Off** keeps the display as it always has been, without correction.

   • **Monitor Color Space** displays colors as they look on the monitor shown in the Destination Profiles area.

   • **Composite Printer Color Space** uses the destination profile you specified for a composite color printer to correct the color display.

   • **Separation Printer Color Space** corrects the monitor display based on the profile selected for Separation Printer.

3. Click under **Correction** next to each color model listed to add or remove the check mark, or click on the name of the color model. Then click on **Correction** to display a pop-up menu with the options **Off** and **On**. For example, it might be a waste of processing time to have **Pantone** and **TruMatch** colors corrected, because they're generally chosen based on the printed swatchbooks so it doesn't matter what they look like onscreen.

4. Click **OK** to apply the changes.

CHAPTER

18

Trapping

Trapping in QuarkXPress, or for printing in general, does not involve the use of large steel devices with loaded springs. Rather, trapping in prepress is often like walking through forest brush that's filled with such devices. To trap or not to trap—the answer often lies in talking to your printer, service bureau, or in-house prepress maven. There are as many opinions about QuarkXPress trapping as there are furry critters still living in the forests.

What Is Trapping?

Trapping is needed when you print two colors adjacent to each other that vary a great deal in hue. Any light color next to any dark color, for instance, is a candidate for trapping. Trapping compensates for the fact that, no matter how good the printer or the press is, colors do not always appear on the sheet where they're supposed to. If you see little areas of the paper color showing through between adjacent colors, the color is out of register. (And that's register, not registration. Registration is when you sign up for a course or seminar in QuarkXPress. Register is what happens on a press when the colors are printed on a sheet.)

The way two overlapping colors are printed on top of each other without changing either color is through the use of a *knockout*—an unprinted area of the background color that allows the fore-ground color to be printed directly on the paper. When two colors are out of register, you get a knockout error (see Figure 18.1).

Trapping is nothing more than expanding the lighter of the two colors so that it overlaps the darker, adjacent area of color. Think about that for a minute: if you expand the darker of the two, then you'd have a larger area of darker color than the designer intends. By expanding the lighter of the two colors, however, the darker, more noticeable areas stay the same size and shape, while the lighter, expanded colors tend to get "absorbed" by the darker color.

FIGURE **18.1**
Printing type over a lighter color using a knockout can allow the paper to show through when the colors are not in register.

There are only a few simple rules regarding trapping.

1. All colors should *spread* underneath (or be *overprinted* totally by) black. Black, being the most noticeable of the four (or more) *process colors* in printing, should always be printed "on top of" any other colors (see Figure 18.2).

FIGURE **18.2**
Overprinting a solid black on lighter colors produces no chance of knockout errors.

2. Yellow should always spread under cyan, magenta, or black. Mistakes in the yellow printing are the least noticeable because the color is the lightest hue being used. By running the yellow under darker colors along the edge, it also makes the color change caused by having two colors overprint each other far less noticeable.

3. Pure cyan (100%) and pure magenta (100%) should always spread under each other equally. Both colors are pretty dominant and are about the same intensity.

4. Lighter backgrounds should *choke* the darker overprint. This process is called choking because the lighter color's knock-out is reduced in size (choked) so it slips underneath the darker, more dominant color (see Figure 18.3).

FIGURE **18.3**

Traditional choking reduces the knockout area (or looked at another way, it enlarges the area under the overprint).

5. Lighter overprints should "spread" over the darker backgrounds; the lighter color will extend into the dark background area. (see Figure 18.4).

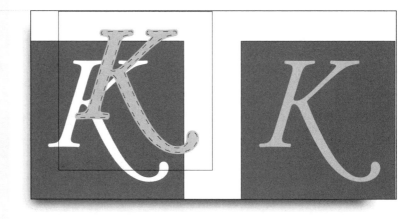

FIGURE **18.4**

Traditional spreading expands the lighter color over the darker color's knockout.

Trapping in QuarkXPress

QuarkXPress doesn't always look at trapping the way prepress professionals do. It treats chokes and spreads by defining an *object color* as being against a *background color*, which is probably more intuitive for users but not the stuff that printing plates are made of. Sometimes the object needs to be spread; sometimes the background needs to be spread. QuarkXPress determines whether a color chokes or spreads based on its luminance (a fancy word for lightness or brightness) compared to the other adjacent colors.

QuarkXPress Overprints

Chokes and spreads are not always necessary: QuarkXPress can define any color to be an overprint color. Overprinted colors do not use knockouts, so there is no choking or spreading to be done. Depending on the colors you use, this can either cause problems or provide an opportunity, however you want to look at it.

If you print a solid cyan block of type that's been specified to overprint over a yellow field, your type comes out green! (Yellow plus blue equals green in *subtractive* colors; remember your Crayola box?) The shade of green depends on the density and transparency of the inks, the whiteness of the paper, and so on. So if you want to keep two colors the same as you've specified on your file and onscreen, you don't want to overprint.

Overprinting, however, can provide an opportunity. If your background is 20% magenta, for instance, and your overprinted type is 20% magenta and 50% black, then you're in great shape. You don't want to use a knockout because all you're really doing (as far as the output for negatives and plates is concerned) is adding a 50% black on top of the background.

Check with an expert before trapping

Before messing with any of this stuff, you should check with your service bureau, printer, or in-house imaging center. Many *RIPs* these days are more sophisticated than QuarkXPress's model for trapping and many RIPs also overwrite QuarkXPress's values, making any changes and work you do here for naught.

QuarkXPress Knockouts

Any color that QuarkXPress calls an object color can be specified to knock out another (background) color so that the background color won't print behind the object color, regardless of what QuarkXPress's trapping brain would ordinarily do for those two colors. The overlapping area that would normally be the trap is eliminated. In other words, applying a knockout to a color eliminates trapping for that color and the object(s) over it. I can't think of a reason why anyone would want to do this, but you can.

Setting Traps

Trapping in QuarkXPress can be set at four levels. Each higher level overwrites all the settings in any of the previous levels.

1. Default trapping: Trapping values that are set in the Document Preferences without a document open on the screen are used for all new documents created from then on. Any changes here are saved in the XPress Preferences file that's found in your QuarkXPress folder.

2. Document default trapping: If you set trapping in the Document Preferences with a document open, the new settings override the defaults in the XPress Preferences file for that document only. The new values are stored as part of the document.

3. Color-specific trapping: If you set a trapping value for a specific color in a document, the new values override both Document and XPress Preferences values for that color. The new values are stored as part of the document.

4. Item-specific trapping: If you set trapping specifically for an item or items, those settings override the specific color values, the document setting, and the XPress Preferences setting. The new values are stored as part of the document. More on that is covered in the following section.

Setting Trapping Preferences

Quark's defaults are to trap colors .144 of a point, a truly small amount. It's equal to only one-tenth of one-72nd of an inch; it's about 1/100th of an inch. Although it may seem small, it's not bad for good quality offset printing. If you're working at a newspaper, using coarse screens and coarser paper, setting trapping to a half-point or more is not unrealistic. Like all these values, check first with the guys in the back room to see what they'll have!

Let's take a look at the defaults and what they mean. Remember, doing this with no document open changes the XPress Preferences file and makes those changes available to every document you create in the future. Doing these steps with a file open changes only the settings for that document.

To set trapping preferences:

1. Choose **Preferences** from the **Edit** menu and then **Document** from the submenu; click on the **Trapping** tab (see Figure 18.5).

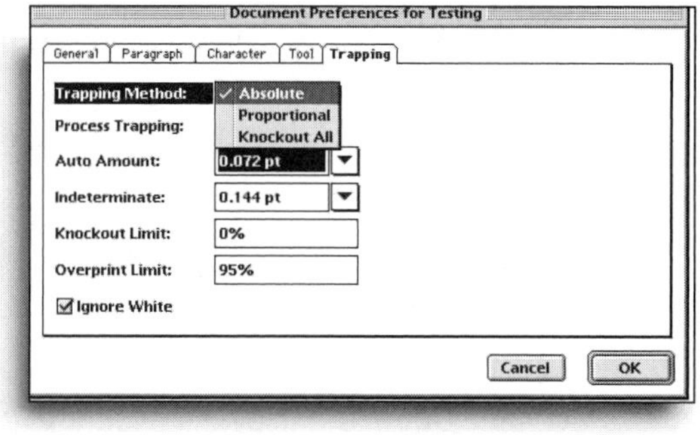

FIGURE 18.5
Default trapping values are determined in the preferences.

2. Make a choice from the first pop-up menu.
   - **Absolute** uses the values in the **Auto Amount** and **Indeterminate** fields to make traps. If the object color is darker than the background, then the object is choked by the background in the amount set by the **Auto Amount** field. If the object color is lighter than the background, the object is spread by the amount in

the **Auto Amount** field. The poorer quality the printing is and the coarser the printing screen, the larger this number should be.

- Using **Proportional** trapping is a little more complex. QuarkXPress looks at the two colors in question, compares the difference in their luminance, or brightness, and uses this value to calculate how much to trap those two colors. Two colors that have equal or almost equal luminance would have a trapping value close to zero. Colors that have a big difference in their luminance would have a trapping value set at or near the value in the box.

- **Knockout All** turns off all trapping, printing all objects with a zero trap amount. Turning off trapping of all kinds is also useful for proofing to a lot of PostScript color laser printers and other desktop color printers. It may also be required in your prepress situation.

3. The **Process Trapping** pop-up menu has two choices: **On** or **Off**. When it's on, QuarkXPress traps each plate of a process color separately to make traps more subtle-looking; when it's off, QuarkXPress traps objects the same on all color plates. Using **Process Trapping** increases RIP times and requires greater processing power.

4. **Auto Amount** determines how much trapping is applied—in other words, how big an overlap is used. The values in this box should only be set in consultation with a printer or service bureau.

   Auto Amount also has an **Overprint** choice in the pop-up menu. Choosing **Overprint** overrides trapping values set elsewhere in QuarkXPress.

5. Enter a value in the **Indeterminate** field for QuarkXPress to figure the amount of trap to calculate and apply to items that have "indeterminate" colors. That's a fancy way of saying that when confronted with an imported photo, or an EPS files with a complicated blend in it, QuarkXPress would go crazy trying to figure a different trapping value for every combination of an overlaid object and every pixel it

touches in the picture file. So QuarkXPress uses an absolute value from this field. **Indeterminate** also has a value of **Overprint** in its pop-up menu. This is preferable if you know your indeterminate objects are darker than anything in the background.

6. **Knockout Limit** controls the point at which the object color knocks out a background color. It's best left at the default of zero, meaning it always knocks out the background whenever knockout is specified. The better the quality of printing, the more the lack of a knockout will be apparent.

7. **Overprint Limit** sets the point at which a black object or type overprints in the trap specifications; leave this one alone. The default of 95% means that any black used at 95.1% or more up to a 100% will indeed overprint. It's kind of a fail-safe method for making sure only pure, almost solid or solid colors overprint rather than trapping. Setting the value to 100% creates a knockout and traps all "solid" colors.

8. Last and most certainly not least is the checkbox for **Ignore White**. Leave it alone; in other words, leave it checked. It tells QuarkXPress to ignore the fact that there might be white as a background. Since white isn't an ink color (usually), there can be no trap calculation. If **Ignore White** is unchecked, the trapping takes place at the setting for Indeterminate trapping and you might not like the results.

Specifying Trapping for Specific Colors

Settings in the Edit Trap dialog box override the Trapping preferences. Unlike most QuarkXPress preferences and choices, you can't make changes to trapping for specific colors with no documents open. When you do make these changes with a document open (which also means you can get access to all those nifty colors you've created, something you can't do when no file is open), then the changes apply only to the document.

There may be a color you've created that you want to trap differently than all the rest. Maybe it's a *Hexachrome* color or a fifth color in *PMS* ink or metallic inks, and you want to make sure it won't knock out underlying colors or create traps. Here's where to go to get that done—although it's not really recommended. QuarkXPress, if left to its own devices, produces adequate trapping with the default values. If you're in a closed environment where all the work done is going to a given set of *imagesetters* through a known RIP, and that never changes, special trapping values for your press and paper may be better set at the RIP, so that they can apply to all files in a consistent manner.

To specify trapping values for a specific color:

1. Choose **Colors** from the **Edit** menu or press Shift+F12.

2. Choose the color to change the trapping for. Click the **Edit Trap** button. In the Edit Trap dialog box, all the document's colors except the one chosen are listed (see Figure 18.6). This is because these settings change the actions of the background colors that the color may sit on, not the object color itself.

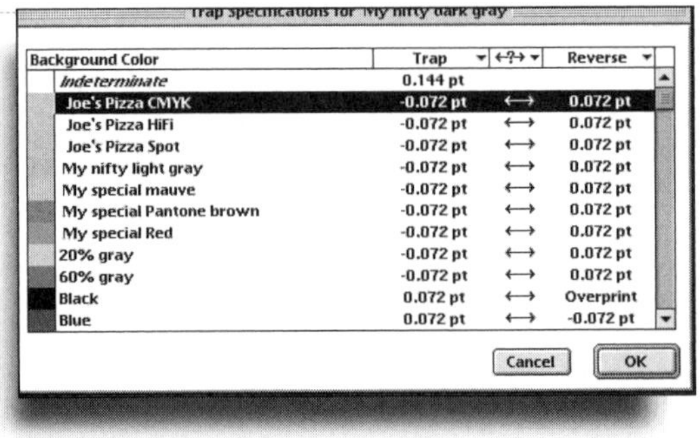

FIGURE 18.6

Changing the trapping settings for a specific color changes all the uses of that color in the document.

3. Click on a color from the **Background Color** list and choose a trapping type from the pop-up menu under the **Trap** column.

- **Overprint** will overprint the named color on top of the selected **Background Color**. Don't forget, if the **Overprint Limit** is set to 95% (the default), then the top object color must be used at 95.1% or higher for the overprint to take effect. This is a useful approach to take if there is a particular color that will normally trap in the usual way, but should overprint a specific background color.

- **Knockout** is used to create a knockout in the background when your object color lies on top of the background.
- Choose **Auto Amount (+)** to spread the color by the value specified in the **Auto Amount** field in the Trapping preferences.
- Choose **Auto Amount (-)** to choke the color by the value specified in the **Auto Amount** field in the Trapping preferences.
- Choose **Custom** to specify a specific choke or spread for the named color. A dialog box pops up, asking for a value. Any number will work in any measurement system.

5. In between **Trap** and **Reverse** in the Trap Specifications dialog box is a pop-up menu QuarkXPress calls **Trap Relationship** that has two choices: to make dependent or independent traps. The value displayed is the current relationship between the two colors and it's assumed that the settings will be applied symmetrically.

- Choose dependent traps (represented by a double-headed arrow) to trust QuarkXPress to calculate reverse traps—the trapping values to be used when the color being edited is the background and the currently selected color in the **Background Color** column is the foreground.
- Choose independent traps to use different overlap amounts when the two colors are reversed.

6. The **Reverse** pop-up menu shows the reverse trapping values for the selected object color and background color. The values in **Reverse** apply when the selected **Background Color** is the object color and the color whose trap is being edited is the background. The **Reverse** value is calculated automatically when using dependent traps. If a **Reverse** value for a color that uses dependent traps is changed, the corresponding value in the **Trap** column changes with it.

7. Click **OK** to finish changing trapping values and **Save** to save the changes.

SEE ALSO

➤ *To define colors, see page 426*

➤ *To apply colors to objects, see page 432*

Overriding Trapping for Specific Items

QuarkXPress also allows you to tweak trapping values for specific objects. If you do this, then the changes apply only to that one object and its background. If you delete either one later, the special trapping values disappear also. Values you change here change all the previous settings you may have made in the preferences or via color-specific trapping. The only exception to this is that the **Knockout All** settings remain the same (see Figure 18.7).

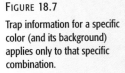

FIGURE 18.7

Trap information for a specific color (and its background) applies only to that specific combination.

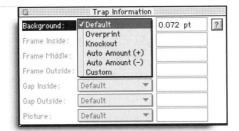

Lines, boxes, and text that lie over pictures can be set to overprint in one of three different ways: to knock out, overprint, or trap to the background picture using the Trap Information palette (press Option+F12 (Ctrl+F12) or choose Show Trap Information from the **View** menu). The options in the palette change depending on the selected item.

One exception is that the picture content of a box (imported pictures) is not affected by any of these changes. *EPS* files with layers of colors need to contain their own trapping information, as does any type over photo images that have been created elsewhere.

Trapping Text

To change trapping settings for a text box:

1. Select the text and choose **Show Trap Information** from the **View** menu or press Option+F12 (Ctrl+F12). Here you can make changes for the box's text, its frame, and its background color (see Figure 18.8).

2. Choose a color for which to adjust settings.

   - If the box has a background color and no frame, then **Background** is available.

   - If the box has a frame, then **Frame** is available, but Background is not.

   - If text is selected, then **Text** is available.

   - All these settings start out at **Default**, which uses the current preference settings and those defined in the Edit Trap dialog box.

3. Choose a setting from each pop-up menu.

   - **Overprint** will overprint the item.

   - **Knockout** does just that; the active item knocks out from the background.

   - **Auto Amount (+)** and **Auto Amount (-)** apply the **Auto Amount** value from the Trapping preferences as a spread or a choke, respectively.

   - **Custom** brings up a dialog box where a trapping value can be entered.

Trapping Frames and Lines

Frame colors always traps to the box background color first; then to the second color in the frame, if it uses two; and then to other backgrounds. A line always traps to its own second color, if one is used, then to any background behind it. QuarkXPress does not apply trapping to imported pictures, but you can apply trapping to the frame on the *picture box* to accomplish a fairly good trap to a picture in a box that has a frame.

To trap a frame:

1. Select a box whose frame contains both frame and gap colors. Choose **Show Trap Information** from the **View** menu or press Option+F12 (Ctrl+F12).

2. Choose a part of the frame to trap.

- If the frame is a single color, **Frame Inside** and **Frame Outside** are available.
- If the frame uses two colors, **Frame Inside**, **Frame Middle**, and **Frame Outside** are available.
- **Frame Inside** applies trapping between the inside of the frame and the background color of the box; **Frame Outside** applies trapping between the outside color of the frame and any background colors behind the object box; and **Frame Middle**, if present, applies trapping between the two colors used in the frame wherever they meet.

3. Choose a setting from each pop-up menu.

- **Overprint** will overprint the item.
- **Knockout** does just that; the active item knocks out from the background.
- **Auto Amount (+)** and **Auto Amount (-)** apply the **Auto Amount** value from the Trapping preferences as a spread or a choke, respectively.
- **Custom** brings up a dialog box where a trapping value can be entered.

Trapping lines works similarly to trapping frames.

To trap a line:

1. Select a line and choose **Show Trap Information** from the **View** menu or press Option+F12 (Ctrl+F12).

2. Choose a part of the line to trap.

- If the line is a simple solid line, **Line** is available.
- If the line is dashed, dotted, or otherwise has a second color, then **Line Middle** and **Gap** are available. **Line Middle** traps colors within the line to each other and **Gap** colors the second color.

3. Choose a setting from each pop-up menu.

- **Overprint** will overprint the item.
- **Knockout** does just that; the active item knocks out from the background.

- **Auto Amount (+)** and **Auto Amount (-)** apply the **Auto Amount** value from the Trapping preferences as a spread or a choke, respectively.
- **Custom** brings up a dialog box where a trapping value can be entered.

SEE ALSO

➤ *To create text boxes, see page 104*

➤ *To create lines, see page 106*

➤ *To apply frame styles to boxes, see page 114*

Printing

There will always be people who insist that word processors are perfectly good programs for desktop publishing. But when it comes to professional final output—four-color printing, or even tweaking laser printouts so they're just right—QuarkXPress really puts those other programs in their place. Printing is a complex subject, but this chapter will guide you in your quest for the best possible output.

Planning for Printing

Color, fonts, images, and page size affect your printed output, as well as your work flow and how you describe these items to QuarkXPress.

Working with Printer Description Files

Earlier versions of QuarkXPress used special files called PDFs—Printer Description Files—to take advantage of the capabilities of various printers. In version 4, QuarkXPress uses only industry-standard *PPDs—PostScript* Printer Descriptions—which come with your system software.

Every time you do a software install, update the system software, or add a new utility, there's a very good chance that the installer also added a whole host of printer descriptions to your system. Not only are they taking up hard disk space, you probably also have multiple descriptions for the same printer if your computer has been around for a while. All these descriptions are "available" to QuarkXPress for use, but you really want to have only those you need. You can always copy the unused PPDs to a floppy or other disk if you need one later.

Eliminate all the PPDs from the folder for printers that you don't have access to, and make sure you have a PPD for any printer you have access to. All printers and *imagesetters* these days come with PostScript printer drivers for both Mac OS and Windows systems, and you can usually find updates at the vendor's web site. If you work in a relatively closed system and send QuarkXPress files to a *RIP* (raster image processor) from some vendor such as EFI, Harlequin, or Autologic, you also need the

PPD file for those devices. If you're doing work at home or in the office that will eventually be printed on some other device that is not on your present network, you'll need the PPD file for that device also so that you can *preflight* your file for the device it will eventually be printed on.

QuarkXPress's PPD Manager allows you to control which of the installed PPDs loads when you start QuarkXPress. Choose **PPD Manager** from the **Utilities** menu, and a dialog box appears that shows all the PPDs stored on your system. You can choose to turn off and on various PPDs instead of having to plow through the various system folders and files. You can access PPDs in only one folder at a time, but you can place them wherever you want on your hard drive and still allow QuarkXPress access to them— just change the **System PPD Folder** setting by clicking the **Select** button (see Figure 19.1).

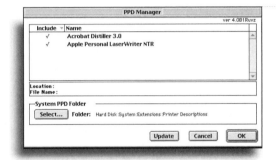

FIGURE 19.1

QuarkXPress's new PPD Manager makes dealing with printer drivers a little easier.

Click on **Update** for the changes to be made in the Print dialog box's **Setup** tab.

Starting With the Right Size

Printing a job to a printer that isn't set up like the final film or plates will be set up can be a troublesome exercise. If your printer uses only letter-sized paper, and your page size is A4 or 9" X 12", what to do? You can print your job in a reduced size to fit the paper, or you can print the job full-size and *tile* it, forcing you to cut and paste pieces of paper together to the final size.

In either case, make sure your page size, as you've set it up in the document, is the way you want to see the final job. Printing and proofing can change the image size, but all service bureaus and in-house output devices assume you want the job imaged at 100%; they won't change the image size unless you request it.

SEE ALSO

➤ *To create a new document, see page 84*

Using Appropriate Colors, Images, and Fonts

Although it's easy just to press ⌘+P (Ctrl+P) and print, you'll get better results and decrease the time it takes to print if you take care of business first.

To prepare a document for efficient printing:

1. First, eliminate the bold, italic, and bold italic styles applied to text. Replace them, using the **Fonts** tab of the Usage dialog box, with the true bold, italic, or bold italic version of each font. Many service bureaus still complain about text reflowing when these attributes are accessed through text styles rather than by using the correct bold and italic fonts.

2. Make sure all the necessary fonts are installed properly— *PostScript Type 1* fonts have two components, a screen font and a printer font, and both are needed. *TrueType* fonts have only one part. Also, make sure there's only one version of each font installed—having both TrueType and PostScript version of a font loaded at the same time is bound to cause problems.

3. Delete all images, text blocks, and other "leftovers" from the pasteboard area of the file. Even though they don't image, they take up processing time, and they make the file larger than it needs to be.

4. Eliminate all unused colors. QuarkXPress now makes that much easier to do with the **Not Used** option in the **Show** pop-up menu of the Colors dialog box.

5. Make sure images are in usable formats, preferably *TIFF* and *EPS*.

6. Define all colors in *CMYK* for print and *RGB* for web work, unless told otherwise by a printer, a service bureau, or an in-house prepress department.

Once these steps are taken, you'll have fewer printing problems and your files will print faster.

SEE ALSO

➤ *To change font styles to the correct bold and italic fonts, see page 517*

➤ *To define colors, see page 426*

➤ *To import images, see page 338*

➤ *To delete colors, see page 431*

Using the Print Dialog Box

Although the Print dialog box (see Figure 19.2) is the same for all users of QuarkXPress 4, some subordinate dialogs will vary depending on your system software and printer drivers. The samples shown here were captured on a Mac with System 7.6.1 and LaserWriter 8.4.2.

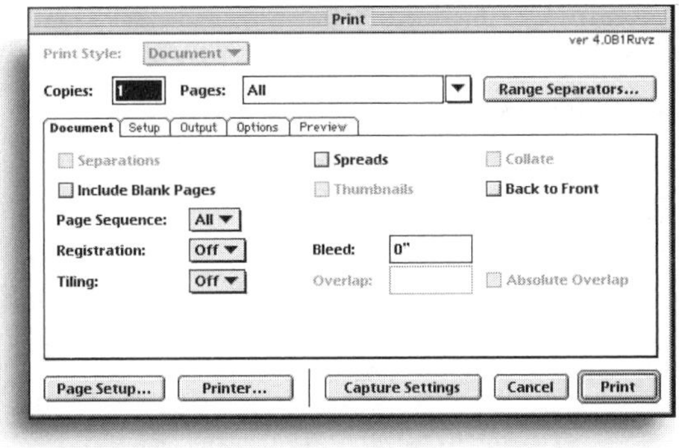

FIGURE 19.2

The basic Print dialog box will be the same no matter what system you're using.

QuarkXPress no longer allows you direct access to the Page Setup (Printer Setup) dialog box; although you can choose **Page Setup (Printer Setup)** from the **File** menu, QuarkXPress displays the Print dialog box. The settings that used to be in the Page Setup (Printer Setup) dialog box are now accessible through the Print dialog box, with its five different tabs.

Color management adds a tab to the Print dialog

A sixth tab, **Color Management**, appears if you run the Quark CMS *XTension*. More information on *color management* is given in Chapter 17, "Matching and Managing Color."

Setting Print Options

Although the Print dialog box contains a bewildering number of choices, most of the time you can accept the default settings. If you're doing this, the only things you'll need to worry about are the main settings, those outside the tabs.

To set the main print controls:

1. First, enter the number of copies to print. The default is 1, but the number can be as high as 999.

2. Choose which pages to print. By default, the **Pages** field says **All**, but it will accept the page numbers of any pages in the document. Typing a range of numbers separated by a hyphen, such as 3–7, in the **Pages** field will force QuarkXPress to print pages 3 through 7 in the document (see Figure 19.3). These commands can be combined in any order and any fashion: typing 1,4–6,9,11–13 prints pages 1, 4, 5, 6, 9, 11, 12, and 13 of the document.

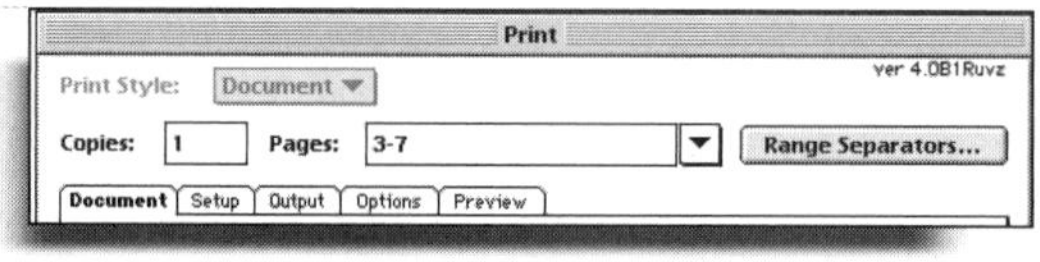

FIGURE 19.3

The dash in a range of numbers means to print those pages and all the pages in between those numbers.

Using a plus sign in front of the page number prints the absolute page in the document; in other words, type +6 to print the sixth page in the document, regardless of its actual page number.

3. Choose a *print style*, if any have been defined, from the **Print Styles** menu.

4. The **Page Setup** button brings up a dialog box that is somewhat familiar (see Figure 19.4). It allows some basic printing choices. They may vary from the screen shot shown here, depending on the system version and printer driver.

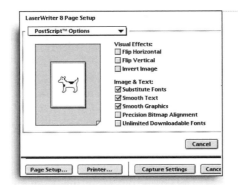

FIGURE 19.4
Certain choices in the Page Setup dialog box depend on version, printer driver, and operating system.

5. The **Printer** button brings up a new dialog box that is also primarily the function of the printer driver. The options shown here are provided by LaserWriter version 8.4.2 and will probably be different with other printer drivers.

6. The remaining buttons in the dialog box are fairly simple in function. **Capture Settings** saves all the present settings to memory and closes the dialog box. **Cancel** does just that: cancels the printing. **Print** sends the file off to the printer specified.

Document Tab

The **Document** tab (see Figure 19.5) offers the following choices:

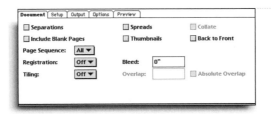

FIGURE 19.5
The **Document** tab offers basic choices.

Separations

Separations prints a printing *plate* for each of the colors specified in your document. A file with process colors produces four printouts of each page: one each for the yellow, cyan, magenta, and black colors in *process* printing. If you have *spot colors* in your file, a separate plate prints for each spot color you specified.

Spreads

Spreads prints facing pages from your document. If you're lucky enough to have access to a tabloid-sized printer (11 " X 17 ") and you're printing proofs for a booklet with a page size of 8 1/2 " X 11 ", use **Spreads** to print (sideways) pages facing each other on the 11 " X 17 " sheet.

Collate

Collate, available when you print more than one copy, prints the document one at a time. If you want to print two copies of a four-page document, it prints pages 1, 2, 3, and 4 the first time, and then pages 1, 2, 3, and 4 a second time. This can be useful if you don't want to collate the pages yourself, but it takes a lot longer, because the printer's RIP processes each page twice.

Back to Front

Back to Front prints the last page first, the next to the last page second, and so on. This feature is very useful if your printer Include Blank Pages.

Include Blank Pages

Include Blank Pages prints all pages in the document, whether they have any type or graphics on them or not. If your design includes purposely blank pages, leave this on; if you don't want blank pages and prefer to save paper by never printing any that accidentally show up, click it off.

Thumbnails

Thumbnails prints small images of the pages on your piece of paper. Using it for an 8 1/2 " X 11 " page, printing to an 8 1/2 " X 11 " sheet of paper, reduces the page image so that you get five pages across by five pages deep, or 25 very small pages per sheet of paper. This feature can be useful for looking at the flow of a particular document, but be warned that printing one page of 25 thumbnails takes as long as printing the 25 pages. (**Thumbnails** is not available when you chose **Separations**: some software gurus decided that would probably never be used, and they're probably right!)

Page Sequence

The **Page Sequence** pop-up menu contains an **All** option that you can change to **Odd** or **Even**. This is a very useful menu choice to print the final proof copy to be submitted to the printer, the client, or the boss. You can print all the even pages first, put the printed pages back into the printer, and then print the back sides of the same sheets using the **Odd** pages choice.

Registration

The **Registration** menu has three options: the default is **Off**, with two additional options of **Centered** and **Off Center**. **Centered** places the *registration marks* (those things that look like the crosshairs of a sniper's rifle) exactly on the center of the page vertically and horizontally. The **Off Center** option staggers the pairs (horizontally and vertically) somewhat, which some printers and strippers prefer. When you print with registration marks on, the file prints out with the name of the file, the date and time, and the page number in the margin. This can be very useful for keeping track of revisions and versions of a file as it wends its way through the editing process.

Tiling

Tiling allows you to print your pages on printers with smaller-sized paper than your document, with enough of an overlap so that you can paste together the pieces later to make a full-sized replica of the finished piece. The **Preview** tab button can help you to visualize your way through tiling options (see Figure 19.6).

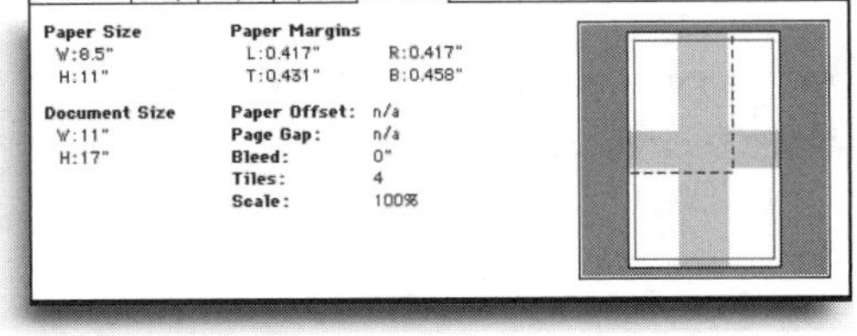

FIGURE 19.6

You can preview the various **Tiling** options in the **Preview** tab.

Manual tiling allows you to determine where each tile begins by dragging a new zero point for your document onto the page from the upper-left corner of the rulers. **Automatic** tiling makes QuarkXPress compute how many tiles are needed based on all the factors involved: document page size, printer page size, the amount of overlap wanted, and the fact that QuarkXPress is going to put those *crop marks* and marginal data on each and every page.

Absolute Overlap, when checked, calculates the amount of overlap needed on each page, starting with the upper-left corner of the document. If **Absolute Overlap** is not checked, your document, when finally pasted back together, will appear centered on the overall assembled sheets of paper (or film).

Bleed

In the **Bleed** field, you can specify how much of a printed area you want to extend outside of the page margins. In order for an image or color to run off the edge of the page (to *bleed* in printer parlance), it must be printed on the paper beyond the edge of what will be the final trim size (usually a quarter-inch or so). Check with your printer before setting this.

Setup Tab

The second tab in the Print dialog box is labeled **Setup** and contains the following settings (see Figure 19.7).

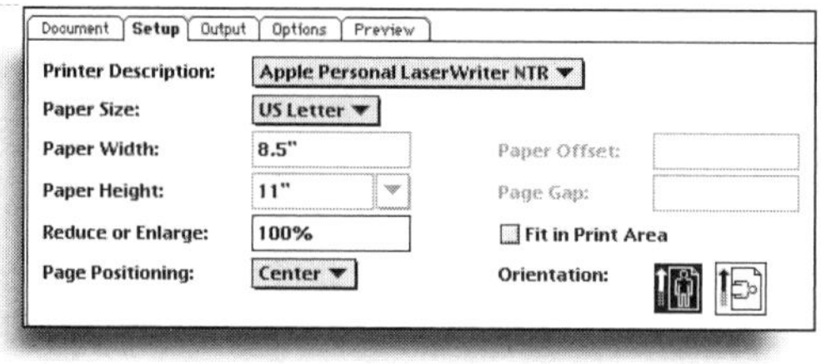

FIGURE 19.7

The **Setup** tab provides many options formerly available in the Page Setup (Printer Setup) dialog box.

Printer Description

The **Printer Description** pop-up menu contains all the printer descriptions (PPD files) set to load in the PPD Manager. This is where you pick the printer that, hopefully, matches the printer you plan to print to. In addition, QuarkXPress also adds three generic descriptions built into QuarkXPress itself: **Generic B&W**, **Generic Color**, and **Generic Imagesetter**; you can use these if you don't have a PPD file for the printer you plan to use.

Paper Size, Paper Width, and Paper Height

The values in the **Paper Size**, **Paper Width**, and **Paper Height** fields change based on the PPD you select.

If you pick an imagesetter in the **Printer Descriptions** menu, additional choices are also available. The **Paper Offset** and the **Page Gap** fields become available. Check with your in-house administrator for the proper settings for imagesetter values. Whatever you specify may be automatically overwritten by the imagesetter's RIP, or the settings you establish here might disrupt other jobs going through the same RIP.

Reduce and Enlarge

Reduce and **Enlarge** are for doing exactly that.

Page Positioning

In most cases, leave **Page Positioning** set to **Left Edge**, unless you know you want to add extra film or paper in various ways around the outside of the page image. **Left** puts the page image in the upper-left corner of the output media: right to the upper-right corner. **Center** centers the image on the media left and right, as well as vertically. **Center Horizontally** and **Center Vertically** do exactly as they say: center the page image as chosen on the imagesetter's media.

Fit in Print Area

Fit in Print Area calculates how much of a reduction (or enlargement) is needed to make your page fit on the printer page and enters in the value for you.

Orientation

QuarkXPress automatically calculates **Orientation** and will always default to portrait (vertical) if your page width is smaller than your page depth. Conversely, it picks the **Landscape** orientation of your page width if it is wider than your page depth.

Output Tab: Black and White

The third tab, **Output**, contains the specific information related to the printer driver you chose and contains the information you need to print color as well as black and white. Take a look at the black and white options first (see Figure 19.8).

Print Colors

Assuming you chose a black and white printer in the **Setup** tab, your choices in the **Print Colors** menu will be **Black & White** and **Grayscale**. Choose **Black & White** to print everything in either black or white with no grays. Choose **Grayscale** for smoother printing; colors will be converted to gray values.

Halftoning

Picking **Conventional** or **Printer** in the **Halftoning** pop-up menu affects how the photos and screens print. If all you're doing is proofing to laser printer, keep the selection on **Printer**. Then whatever printer you send it to will use the best values that printer has to reproduce the tones, and you won't have to worry about it. (Notice, too, that the **Frequency** window, which determines the number of halftone dots per inch, grays out and becomes unavailable when you select the **Printer** option.

But if you print to an imagesetter, the **Conventional** setting uses the printer description file's calculated values for the halftone screen. Check first with your in-house administrators for their recommendation.

Resolution

Resolution changes depending on the printer driver selected. Simple laser printers offer few choices: the more sophisticated the printer, the more options for *dpi* (dots per inch: the number of dots per inch the imagesetter or printer lays down) and *lpi* (lines per inch: the number of halftone dots per inch the halftone screen uses).

Output Tab: Color

Here's your last chance, and a good one at that, to make sure you don't have spot colors print on a process print job. Your choices in the **Output** tab change if you pick a printer or image-setter that handles color pages (see Figure 19.9). First, go to the **Document** tab and check the **Separations** box; then travel to the **Setup** tab and make sure a color printer or RIP set to handle color is selected in the **Printer Description** menu.

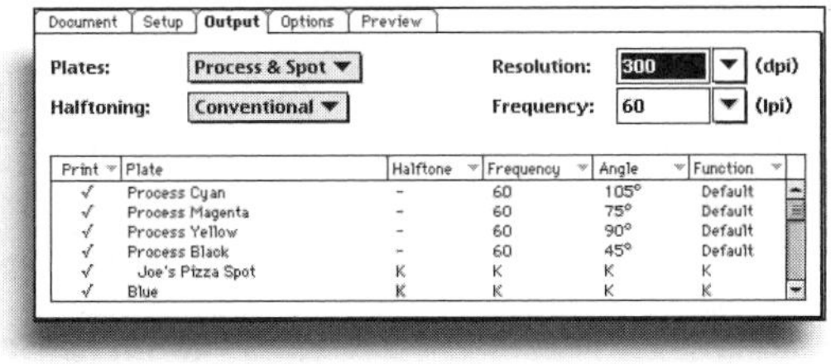

FIGURE 19.9

The **Output** tab's settings change when you choose a color printer in the **Setup** tab.

Plates

The **Plates** menu has two choices: **Process & Spot** and **Convert to Process**. With the **Process & Spot** option chosen, you can see at a glance in the plates list what color plates QuarkXPress will output. Choose **Convert to Process** to have all spot colors converted to four-color equivalents when printing, resulting in only four plates. The color definitions in the file aren't changed.

Plates List

You can deselect individual colors by clicking on the check mark in the left column of the plates list. This can be extremely useful at final output time when some changes have been made to text, for instance, and you want to output just the black plate, the only plate that has changes.

Printing duotones correctly

Here's where you can make sure that *duotones* print correctly without a moiré pattern. Changing the angle of the second spot color to an angle that won't interfere without the black (or other color) screen angle can be set here. Blends that consist of two spot colors (including black in this case) should not have the same screen angles.

When using **Process & Spot**, you can edit the **Frequency** (number of halftone dots per inch), the **Angle** (degree angle of that particular color), and the **Function** (dot shape of the halftone color: round, elliptical, and so on) of any spot color in the plates list. Any option with a line through it is not editable.

Resolution

The default value in the **Resolution** field is the default resolution of the printer. To change the setting, choose from the pop-up menu or type in the values you want to use.

Frequency

The **Frequency** menu allows you to change all the frequencies at once, as opposed to changing them individually in the plates list. Choosing **Other** brings up a box that you can use to specify a new frequency.

Options Tab

The **Options** tab is used primarily for PostScript-related items related to outputting files, as shown in Figure 19.10. As mentioned before, many times (and repeated here because you may be browsing for information and not reading this book as you read a novel), use these settings only if you fully understand the impact your choices will have on the whole organization, the work flow, and the final output device. With QuarkXPress's new print styles and the fact that the final RIP you send the file to may have overrides set for many of these features, you can optimize printing for proof purposes and printing for final output. If you have a multitude of printer brands, types, and ages on your network, it will be worth somebody's time to set up definitive print setting configurations for each printer, save them as printer styles, and import them into your organization's templates.

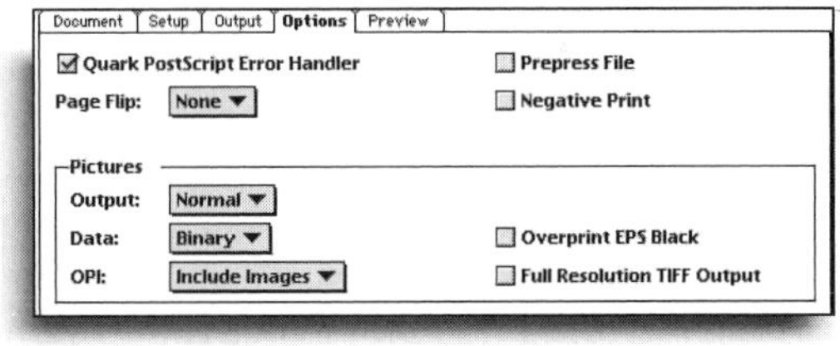

FIGURE 19.10
The **Options** tab contains PostScript printer options.

Quark PostScript Error Handler

Checking **Quark PostScript Error Handler** provides some good tools for figuring out which elements in a file are causing output errors. If your document has something in it that can't be imaged (a bad font, image, a badly constructed trap or clipping path, or perhaps something caused by an XTension), QuarkXPress prints out all it can up to the point where it encounters the problem. Then it prints an error report that contains the box outline in black and a background in 50% black tone. A message also prints in the upper-left corner of the error report that tells you the type of item that caused the error. Now if you lay the error report over the last page that printed (use a light table or hold the two sheets up to window), you see immediately where the problem occurred on the page.

If you use another vendor's PostScript error reporting utility, QuarkXPress appends its comments to the end of the other vendor's report. This reporting function is available only when you print to a PostScript printer; printing to a non-PostScript printer will not produce the error report. Error handling can also be made part of any print style, described later in this chapter.

Negative Print

The **Negative Print** check box will do just that: print a negative version of your page. If your RIP is already set up to do that, leave this box alone. The **Negative** button, used in conjunction with the **Page Flip** options, allows you to image the page with the emulsion side of the film where your printer wants it. Check here, also, for the proper output type for your printer or service bureau.

Page Flip

The **Page Flip** pop-up menu offers four choices that in conjunction with the **Negative** button can produce any type of film your printer prefers. One of the most common combinations in the U.S. is to produce film with the image reading right (that means left to right, the same way you'd read the finished product) and the film emulsion in the "down" position, meaning the emulsion will be on the opposite side of the film as you read the page right; this configuration is referred to as RRED. The combination for producing that result is to choose **Horizontal** (or **Vertical**) in the **Page Flip** menu and clicking on the **Negative Print** check box.

Output

The **Output** pop-up menu offers you the choice of **Normal**, **Low Resolution**, and **Rough** for the output of pictures. **Normal**, of course, produces the end result you want and images the pictures at the full resolution you specified in the various setup boxes, using the full information available in the original picture. The **Low Resolution** choice images the page with the pictures represented by the screen resolution, saving a lot of time to proof pages if all you're doing is proofing the page for someone to check copy and captions, for instance. And the **Rough** choice prints the page with no pictures at all in picture boxes.

Data

The **Data** option also has three choices: **Binary** (the default), **ASCII**, and **Clean 8-Bit**. **Binary** is the default because that's what works best, is the fastest, and causes the fewest problems. The **ASCII** option produces a "more portable" file format that can be read, for instance, by word processing programs and is often a little more friendly for print server programs. The third choice, **Clean 8-Bit**, combines ASCII and binary elements in a single file that's the most versatile and portable of the three. When printing or creating a PostScript file, start with **Binary** and only try the other two options if you get errors; this is only likely to happen with older printers.

OPI

The **OPI** options are to **Include Images**, **Omit TIFF**, and **Omit TIFF & EPS**. Use the **Include Images** option if you're not working with an *OPI* server and you want your images to print normally to laser printers as well as to the imagesetter RIP. **Omit TIFF** replaces all TIFF files in the document with OPI comments but images the EPS files. The **Omit TIFF & EPS** option substitutes OPI comments for both TIFF and EPS files.

Overprint EPS Black

The **Overprint EPS Black** check box does exactly that: It makes any solid black in an EPS file in your document overprint any other colors in the EPS file, and overrides any parameters that may have been set in the original drawing program. Generally, if your EPS files are graphics with type, let QuarkXPress overprint the EPS black.

Full Resolution TIFF Output

The **Full Resolution TIFF Output** setting is also self-explanatory. Checking it always downloads the full resolution information from any TIFF file to the resolution that the printer can handle. Although it gives the best results, it slows down printing, especially on a busy network with many people doing a lot of proofing on a variety of printers. If you're in that kind of a situation, with shared printers over a network, you might consider setting up a print style sheet in which this value, and some others, are set to print proofs to certain printers with reduced TIFF information. If **Full Resolution TIFF Output** is not checked, only the amount of information needed to match the lpi settings you made for the document is sent to the printer.

Preview Tab

The **Preview** tab is another new feature in QuarkXPress 4 that not only allows you to preview how the page will fit on the sheet but also provides some very useful statistics that may prevent an improperly setup job from wasting time, money, film, and paper (see Figure 19.11). A wealth of information is available here that reflects the choices made elsewhere in the Print dialog box and shows the results of those choices.

The **Paper Size** and **Paper Margins** values refer to the media in the printer, whether it's paper or film. The **Paper Offset**, **Page Gaps**, **Bleed**, **Tile**, and **Scale** information is also extremely valuable prepress information. Looking here first can save many problems of trying to print oversized documents to undersized paper. The **Document Size** refers, of course, to the document you're trying to print.

The visual preview window to the right can be very useful also, especially in understanding tiling, and for a spot check to see if the page is landscape or portrait. You can see at a glance (in blue) how your page is oriented to the way it will actually print from the printer. This is useful to spot check things such as whether bleeds or crop marks are on or off, and other relationships between the page and the printer.

Printing Spreads and Imposing Pages

You can print spreads (facing pages) using QuarkXPress, assuming that the paper in the printer is large enough to handle two pages. A pamphlet that has a page size of 5 1/2 " by 8 1/2 " is a perfect candidate to be printed as spreads on a letter-sized printer. And a printer with tabloid-sized paper (11 " X 17 ") is a perfect candidate to print spreads from a letter-sized (8 1/2 " X 11 ") document.

Experienced QuarkXPress users know that this works only if the document uses facing-page master pages. If you use *templates* to create newsletters, and so on, make sure the template uses facing pages.

However, this option only prints page 2 facing page 3, page 4 facing page 5, and so on; this configuration is called *reader's spreads*. Although that's useful for editorial people to check how two pages are going to look facing each other, or to show clients and other people, it doesn't help in creating a dummy to see the whole "book." In such a dummy, in an eight-page document for instance, you want page 8 on the same sheet of paper with page 1 to its right: page 2 on the same sheet of paper with page 7 to its right, and so on. This configuration is called *printer's spreads*.

In proofing pages to a laser printer, you can move pages around to "fool" QuarkXPress into thinking certain pages are spreads when they are not. In the hypothetical eight-page document, here's how to do it.

To create printer's spreads manually:

1. Make a copy of the document first and work on the copy.

2. Change the page numbers to absolute numbers, which lock in the real number to that page. In other words, replace the automatic page number character on each page (⌘+3 or Ctrl+3) with the real page number.

3. If the document was not created with facing pages, go to the Document Layout palette (choose **Show Document Layout** from the **View** menu or press F10), click on the first page, and make it a section starting with that page number by clicking on the page name in the bottom of the Document Layout palette and entering the number of the page as the page number in the Section dialog box (see Figure 19.12).

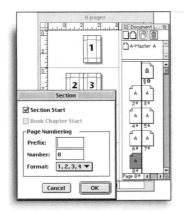

FIGURE 19.12

Changing the page numbers to be absolute is the first step in reordering the pages for spread output.

3. In the Document Layout palette, drag each right page down to create a blank space next to each page (see Figure 19.13).

FIGURE 19.13
Dragging down pages to stagger them in the Document Layout window provides room to eventually move the pages to their opposite positions in the next step.

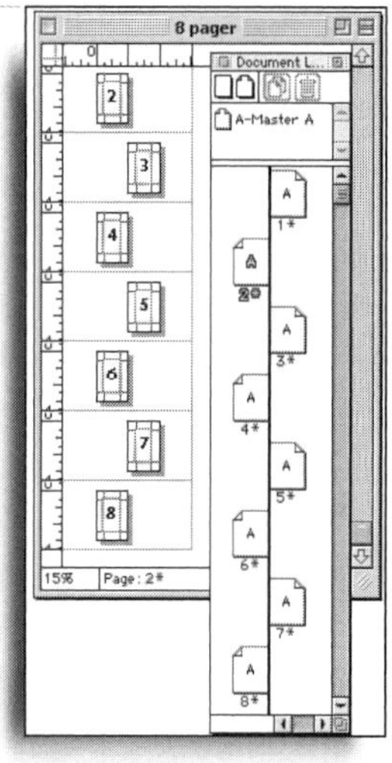

4. Then drag (while still in the Document Layout palette) page 8 above page 1, and it appears on the left side of the Document Layout palette. Now drag page 1 up next to it. That's just where it should print on a spread that can be made into a folding dummy of the final job (see Figure 19.14).

FIGURE 19.14
Dragging page 8 on top of page 1 and then moving page 1 alongside 8 starts the shift of pages.

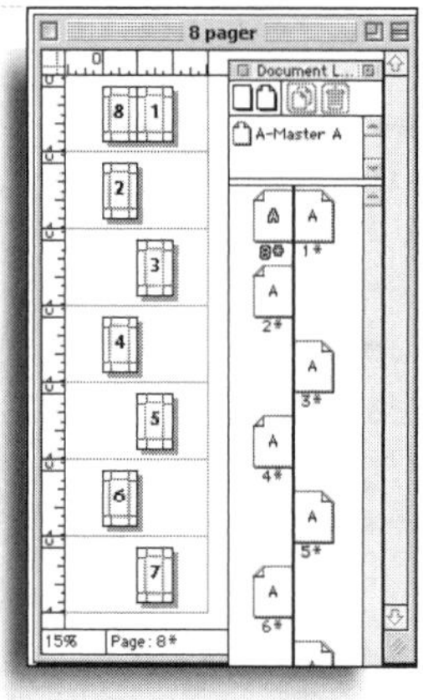

5. Follow the same procedure for the other pages, dragging 7 straight up next to 2, 6 up next to 3, and 5 up next to 4 (see Figure 19.15).

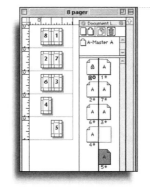

FIGURE 19.15

Dragging the appropriate page up next to its proper neighbor (for spread printing purposes) finishes the setup for printing pages as a printer would.

6. Now just print, choosing **Spreads** in the Print dialog box and choosing which pages to print. All four spreads can be printed at once (eight pages) and the paper run back through the printer again to print a second time, producing two complete books, ready to fold and staple. Or use the same trick described earlier to print pages 1 and 8 on the back of pages 2 and 7, and so on, which produces a perfect imitation of the finished booklet.

Printers have a different problem. Although they want the same results (page 1 next to page 8, in the example), they want to do it with the specifications of their RIP in mind—and in a production environment. There are XTensions, as well as stand-alone software, that impose the pages for printers and allow the printer (or service bureau) to specify such esoteric parameters as *creep*. (Creep is the printer's name for the fact that the image in the gutter is less viewable on the outer pages of a signature because of the bulk-up of the signature; a creep function compensates for that by pushing out slightly the images from the gutter on those pages that need it.) This *imposition* software usually works by creating an EPS image of each page on-the-fly and then rearranging those pages based on the parameters for page size, how many pages "up" are going to be printed at one time on a sheet (4, 8 16, and so on), whether the job is a "work and turn," and so on.

Many printers, however, still do this imposition work by hand, using conventional strippers to strip individual pages onto a page form for proofing and platemaking. In a relatively closed environment such as a magazine, or a catalog house when all the pages are always going to be the same size, using imposition software makes good sense. It's fairly easy to set up the parameters for a 48-page book, a 56-page book, and so on, and have the RIP output the pages late at night when there are no other competing pages headed for the RIP. In environments in print shops where every job is different, it can take as long to set up a job in the imposition software as it takes to just let a stripper strip up the film on platemaking sheets.

SEE ALSO

➤ *To create a facing-page document, see page 84*

➤ *To convert an existing single-sided document to facing pages, see page 167*

➤ *To convert documents to templates, see page 90*

➤ *To move pages with the Document Layout palette, see page 156*

Imagesetters and Color Separations

Primarily, if you're the creator of QuarkXPress documents, you'll be mostly interested in printing to laser printers, color inkjets, and other desktop printers, to see what your document will look like when you deliver it to the printer, convert it to the web, and so on. But if you're a printer or prepress house in the business of receiving files from others to be output for purposes of putting plates on a press, your needs and output parameters are going to be different. In this section, you learn about the special needs of the prepress folks.

Setting Up for Imagesetters

Imagesetters are PostScript devices and are different from the desktop printers others use in that the paper (and they can be loaded with photosensitive papers as well as with photosensitive film) is usually 14 inches or wider and comes on a roll, so that it can have a page depth of 20 inches or more.

Most RIPs of this kind can be set up with print server software that will determine the resolution, *screen angles*, right-reading characteristics, page width and length, and everything else that's needed to produce film (or paper) with the proper characteristics. And the print server software can be configured to produce many settings that can be broadcast over a network. The users, however, need a copy of the printer driver in their Printer Descriptions folder. The choices the users have will match the characteristics of the RIP.

In the same way the RIP is set up through the print server to broadcast specific settings with unique file names, the user can build (or you can build for the user to import) matching print styles, characteristic for characteristic, to make sure images and settings are consistent. Or if the software allows, set up your RIP settings to override any inconsistent settings from the users.

The Print dialog box's **Setup** tab allows you to select the PPD for your imagesetter. If it isn't in the list, its PPD has not been placed in the Printer Descriptions folder. Items to match in the print settings and the RIP are the following:

- **Paper Width** should match the media width.
- **Paper Height** defaults to Automatic, so the cut-off matches the actual length of the document. Any values you do enter in the field to save film should not be greater than the length the imagesetter actually supports. Continuous feed or non-drum imagesetters work best with the depth set to **Automatic**.
- **Page Positioning** is entirely up to you and your operation: If you routinely image pages two-up on 20-inch-wide film, a setting of **Left Edge** or **Center Horizontal** is probably appropriate. Other operations that image a variety of jobs with no consistency might prefer to center all pages on the media. And if you image only the same size pages all day (as, for instance, in a newspaper or magazine environment), you can play with **Page Width**, **Page Height**, and the **Positioning** settings to get the maximum use of your film.

- **Paper Offset** is the distance from the left edge of the media to where the imaging begins. Each and every RIP and accompanying hardware has different characteristics, and if you feel the edges of your images are not as sharp as the centers, you might want to purposely set this value rather high to make sure your image is sharp across the whole field. But if you're confident that your imagesetter is crystal sharp across its entire width, you can set this number as low as you feel comfortable with—and maybe save a little film in the process.

- **Page Gap** is extra space between pages as they roll out of the imagesetter. Plan on the proper amount for bleeds, registration, and crop marks.

- The **Reduce** or **Enlarge** field in production environments should always be set to 100%. (There is no reason I can think of to image a page at something other than what the customer provides. Unless, of course, the customer delivered the job to you at 6" X 9" when they meant the page size to be 7" X 10 1/2".)

- **Orientation** can save paper or film: The same rules apply as do for printing to desktop printers; if the **Orientation** icon is vertical (**Portrait**), and the width is less than the depth, it will print "right side up." And if the width is more than the depth (as might be the case with imposed spreads), the **Landscape** icon will appear highlighted.

Setting Up for Color Separations

Making sure that the colors print as *color separations* is perhaps the most obvious job a printer or prepress house can have. It's not always sure what the customer's intent was just by looking at the file. Colors meant to be printed as process colors might be specified as spot colors, and some colors that are specified as process might be unprintable unless they are converted to a spot color. Obviously, close cooperation with the sales representative and the in-house staff is critical. Some things to look for are the following:

1. Check to make sure the **Separations** box is checked in the **Document** tab.

2. Check to make sure that the **Plates** pop-up menu in the **Output** tab is set correctly for the job being done. QuarkXPress's capability to convert spot color to its equivalent process combinations at this stage can save a lot of time and prevent work in going back to redefine the color. Assuming the spot color is even possible to achieve using the process colors, this might indeed be a real boon to printers and service bureaus.

Combining Settings into Reusable Print Styles

Print styles, another new feature of QuarkXPress, also promise to save time and resources if used with a plan of document management in your situation. Used correctly, saving a series of print styles, one for each type of printer, will save money, time, and frustration when printing proofs and printing final output.

To create a print style:

1. Choose **Print Styles** from the **Edit** menu, and click on **New** (see Figure 19.16).

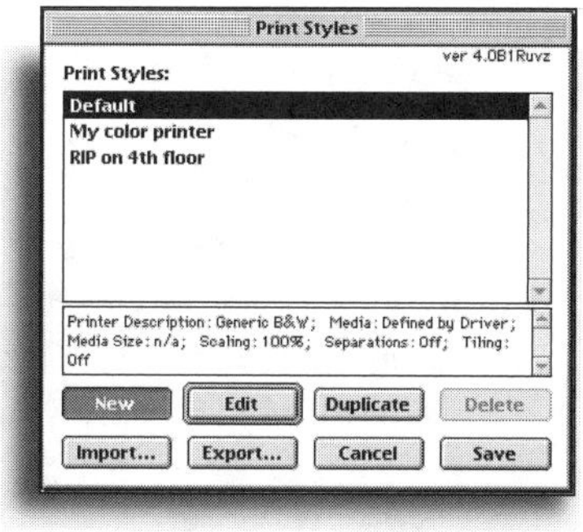

FIGURE 19.16

Create a new print style in the Print Styles dialog box.

2. Clicking on **New** brings up an Edit Print Style dialog box that looks just like the Print dialog box. Carefully choose the proper settings in the **Document, Setup, Output,** and **Options** tabs, as described in the previous sections (see Figure 19.17). It's a good idea to set up a practice document with typical TIFF and EPS images, in a common page size,

and write down the options as they're set and tested. After the options are set for a particular printer, transfer them to the Edit Print Style dialog box.

3. When all the options are set, click **OK** and give the print style a new name that everyone on the network will understand: "Color Printer" is not too descriptive (unless there's only one), but "Mike's QMS Color" might make sense, especially if the printer has been renamed "Mike's QMS Color" and that's what people see on the network when they pick the printer.

Unfortunately, you can't set up a document to print just the way you want to and then define the style with those parameters. You have to create a new print style for each and every set of printing options you want to use. The proper use of the **Duplicate** and **Import** buttons, though, could save some work. As you're working in the Print Styles dialog box, clicking on a print style shows its basic characteristics at the bottom of the dialog box. This is useful for making sure you duplicate or edit the proper file.

All new QuarkXPress documents use the default print style, called Document. The first time you print, the Document print style will be used, based on the default. The best way to save time and mistakes is to alter the Document print style to match the most commonly used printer in your group.

Any new print styles you create become part of that workstation's XPress Preferences file. So in order to share those with others, you can either export the print styles and have others import them as needed, or just give the other workstations your XPress Preferences file. But keep in mind that if you do that, they'll also inherit your H&Js, colors, and other preferences, something you may not want to have happen. In terms of planning workflow, it might be better to incorporate print styles in all your templates, as well as save them in a place that's accessible to all (such as a server) so others can import them into their documents as needed.

To export a printer style so that it can be incorporated into templates or shared with others, select a print style in the Print Styles dialog box and click **Export**, choose your storage location/disk, give it a new name (or the old name if that's what you want, and click on **Export**.

To import a print style (or a number of them individually), click on **Import** in the Print Styles dialog box. Locate the file you need, and click on the **Open** button. That description is now shown in the Print Styles dialog box and will appear in the Print dialog's **Print Style** pop-up menu.

Print styles can be deleted by selecting the setting and clicking the **Delete** button. Don't forget to save the new list.

Preparing Documents for Service Bureaus

At some point, most QuarkXPress users will need to hand files off to someone else for output, whether that's color proofs, camera-ready paper, or film. Some helpful features have been added in QuarkXPress to make this process easier, but it's still important to double-check certain document parameters and use a checklist to make sure all the necessary components are going along with the files.

Confirming Document Statistics

On one level, users can preflight their own files by following some simple rules. Whether the designer, copy editor, some sort of technical guru, or the owner of the company does it (and it's possible all of those people will do it, or that all of the people are a one-person shop!), somebody should do it. If you don't do it before the job goes out to the printer or service bureau, then you'll pay somebody to do it for you there. Either way, you pay.

To perform a preflight check:

1. Check for images. Choose **Usage** from the **Utilities** menu and click on the Pictures tab to check whether QuarkXPress knows the path to the images in the file. If some images are marked as missing, locate the files on the hard drive and drag them into the same folder that the other images reside in (see Figure 19.18). Then double-click each "missing" file and locate it for QuarkXPress. If the software sees additional missing files in the same place, it will ask for permission to update them all at once.

Avoid missing pictures altogether

QuarkXPress automatically finds images that are moved into the same folder that the file itself resides in. Hint: Keep all your files (at least initially when you work on a document) in the same folder as your QuarkXPress file.

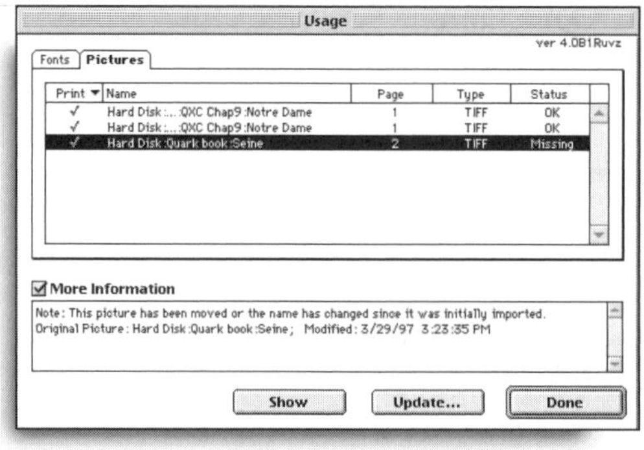

FIGURE 19.18

Missing and modified pictures can be flagged, shown, and updated from the Usage dialog box.

If a picture is shown as having been modified, the date or file type or some aspect of the file has changed since it was brought onto the QuarkXPress page. Double-click on the picture, and QuarkXPress will ask if you want to update the file. If it's definitely the same image, click **OK**, and QuarkXPress will update the file (see Figure 19.19).

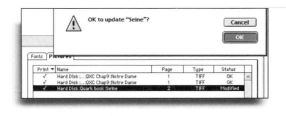

FIGURE 19.19
Modified pictures can be updated via the **Update** button.

2. Check the fonts. This is not as easy to do as checking the images because the font names themselves can be confusing. (If it's any consolation, a well-designed publication will make use of the weights and varieties of just a few font families.)

It's too bad QuarkXPress doesn't allow these two windows (Picture Usage and Font Usage) to be printed; it certainly would help a lot.

Fonts, ideally, should all be in one place, but with the use of font utilities such as Suitcase and Adobe Type Manager, they can be anywhere on a hard drive. The best bet is stay organized enough so that fonts reside in either one of two places: with the system software and then also maybe in a folder labeled "Other Fonts," or some such thing, on the base level of the hard disk.

Remember: Fonts used in EPS files should also be included. EPS files still need "access" to the font outline information in the font that was used to create the file. This issue can get difficult sometimes when the illustration was provided by somebody else and the software that created the file isn't available. Preflight software such as FlightCheck can look at EPS files and report the fonts used in them, and the Collect for Output report also reports them.

3. If the document has color, and some new colors were defined in it, check them to make sure they are the "right" colors. If printing to a four-color press in four colors, make sure all the colors in the document are made up of process colors. Do this by choosing **Colors** from the **Edit** menu (or pressing Shift+F12) and selecting **Colors Not Used** in the Edit Colors dialog box and checking the list of colors shown. First eliminate all colors that aren't being used (see Figure 19.20).

FIGURE 19.20

Deleting unused colors is as easy as selecting them with the **Colors Not Used** menu choice in the Edit Colors dialog box and clicking on **Delete**.

FIGURE 19.20

Deleting unused colors is as easy as selecting them with the **Colors Not Used** menu choice in the Edit Colors dialog box and clicking on **Delete**.

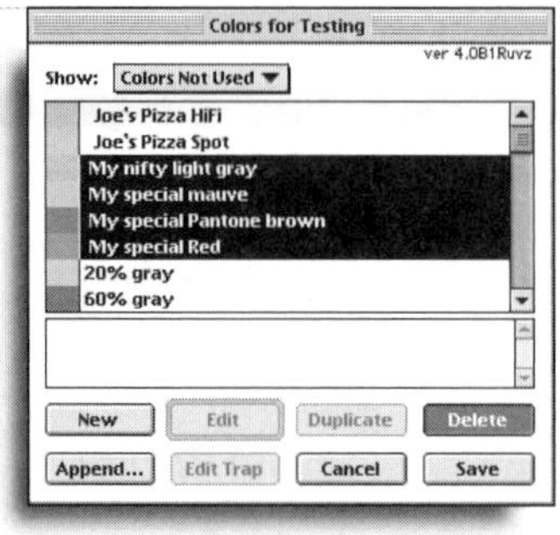

Then change the **Show** option to **Colors In Use**, and make sure the colors shown are all the right kind. If the document uses a spot color and black only, make sure that's what appears in the window, and that the spot color is not made up of process inks. Clicking in the color name will display the attributes of that color (spot, process, and so on) in the window under the list of colors (see Figure 19.21).

FIGURE 19.21

Checking the status of colors used in a document is as easy as clicking on a color in the Edit Colors dialog box and seeing in the information box what the color is composed of.

4. Check the files for material in the pasteboard area. Remove them. "But wait," you say. "I'm going to need them again in the next issue." Items such as these make files hard to output, and it's never a good idea to use an "old" document to do a "new" document anyway. The basic document without body type and specific images should be made into a template so all the fonts, colors, style sheets, and so on are built in. Then build each issue from scratch from that template.

The items on the pasteboard area should be dragged into a library for that client and then deleted from the file that is sent out to be printed.

5. Were any XTensions used that are needed by the service bureau? If the final printing is done with a RIP or other device, and no changes have been made to the QuarkXPress folder, this shouldn't be a problem. Most XTensions are well behaved, in that once they have done their work, they won't be needed again just to output a file to a printer.

There are exceptions: A few years ago Markzware came out with an XTension to alter the pasteboard area of QuarkXPress files, called PasteboardXT. Nobody thought it was necessary (and it usually isn't) to send along the XTensions used to create a document just to print it. Well, people all over the world were getting messages that the PasteboardXT XTension was missing and they couldn't use their files. Markzware had to quickly rewrite the XTension so that files on which it had been used could be opened without the XTension installed, and much to their credit, posted a free XTension called Pasteboard XTerminator to kill the effects of the original Pasteboard XTension. So be careful: Check it out first just in case an XTension was used that turns out to have been written by Uncle Freddie's nephew in the garage, who doesn't follow QuarkXPress's guidelines.

SEE ALSO

➤ *To define colors, see page 426*

➤ *To import images, see page 338*

➤ *To enable and disable XTensions, see page 555*

Collecting Files for Output

Quark took a mighty leap forward some years ago when it invented the Collect for Output concept. This command allows the user to save a copy of the QuarkXPress file, copies of all its images, and a report about the QuarkXPress file in a new folder and location. With the newer, faster SCSI drives, you can even save this information to removable media such as SyQuest, Zip, or Jaz drives, and not worry about having enough space on the hard drive—just about having enough space in the removable drive.

To collect files for output:

1. Choose **Collect for Output** from the **File** menu, and either create a new folder on the hard drive (caution: not creating or specifying a folder will dump the nine gazillion files loose on the desktop) or go to an attached removable drive. For a 5MB QuarkXPress file and 60MB of images, then the disk will need 65MB free (plus a small amount for the report) of space on the disk space to store the generated copies (see Figure 19.22).

FIGURE 19.22

When executing a **Collect for Output** command, make sure to either create or designate a folder for all the file to go into, and that you have enough disk space.

If this isn't the final Collect for Output, just a test run, click on **Report Only** and generate only the text report about the QuarkXPress file.

2. The report that is generated uses *XPress Tags* coding to format its text. To open it, first open the "Output Report Template" file in the QuarkXPress application folder and then click in the text box at the bottom of the page and import the report, making sure that **Include Styles** is checked. The report itself is quite detailed and full of information about the file, the copy of QuarkXPress, and the fonts, colors, XTensions, style sheets, and trapping in the file (see Figure 19.23).

I always print it out, make two copies, and include the printed version of the file and a copy of the document report on
the disk with the QuarkXPress file(s) and the images and
fonts.

Delivering Documents to Service Bureaus

This brings you to the issue of delivering jobs to the outside
world: people who are going to get your QuarkXPress file(s) to
the press and put ink on paper. You have read some of this
before, but for those of you who jumped to this section first,
here's what you need to know.

Basic operating premise: The service bureau or printer needs
everything you had on your desktop and in your system when
you created the file to print the file. Even in-house, if somebody
else is going to output the files you created and that person is
going to do it from a different work station, you must act as
though you're sending the files to a service bureau that is not in-
house. (That's a good argument to make sure everybody on the
network has the same versions of system and application software, access to the same fonts, and can share other things such
as templates, preference files, and so on.)

Saving the File as PostScript

For files you're sending to a printer or service bureau, you can create a PostScript print file instead of sending the QuarkXPress files, along with fonts and graphics. PostScript files can be sent to the imaging device directly, and they are guaranteed to contain all the images and color information (and the fonts as well, if you choose that option when creating the file).

Make sure your file is run through a preflight check to clean it up before sending it out for output. The more you do, the less the service bureau has to do, and the cheaper the job will be to image. And you might save significant time that you could lose if the service bureau has to call the next day and tell you it couldn't do the job because it was missing a file, a file was in the wrong format, or a font was missing that it didn't have.

Creating a PostScript file is easily done in most programs, including QuarkXPress, as part of the printing process: instead of printing to a printer, you print to a file. It takes a lot of space on your hard disk, because you're capturing, in PostScript code, all the font information and all the image information, in addition to the page layout information. The other big disadvantage is that if changes need to be made to the file, it is, for all practical purposes, not editable. You have to go back to the original file, make the change(s), and generate another PostScript file.

The proper way to create a single file in QuarkXPress that can be sent to a printer or service bureau is to choose **Print** from the **File** menu (or press ⌘+P (Ctrl+P)) and click on the **Printer** button at the bottom of the dialog box. That brings up an additional Print dialog box that looks like the one you see in other applications. Here you can choose the **File** option, as opposed to the Printer option; this choice may appear as a pop-up menu at the top of the dialog box, or as radio buttons or check boxes. Every PostScript printer driver has a **File** option, but it will be in a different place depending on which one you use and what platform you work on.

After choosing **File**, click **Save**; you're then presented with a dialog box offering PostScript file options (see Figure 19.24). Choose a name for the file; choose a Format (**PostScript Job**);

choose **ASCII** or **Binary** (**Binary** is preferable but **ASCII** may be more compatible); choose PostScript level compatibility; and choose which fonts to include (preferably **All**).

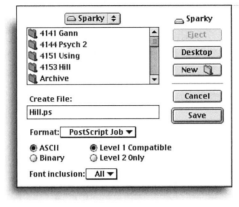

FIGURE 19.24
When saving PostScript files, you have the option of including no fonts, some fonts, or all fonts.

Again, check with your printer first before delivering this kind of a file to them. It's been my experience that most printers and service bureaus want a "native" QuarkXPress file because when you call the next day because you spotted another typo after giving the job to the printer, they can just open the file and make the change themselves, without having to send the files back and forth and waste time in the process. The advantage to sending a PostScript file is that you don't have to also send the graphics, and if you choose the **Include Fonts** option in the printer driver's Print dialog box, you don't have to send the fonts. But if there may be changes to be made on the file later, sending PostScript files is not a good option.

Delivering the Images

Delivering the images is a lot like delivering pizza: make sure it's timely and full of everything you can think of. And that includes images of all kinds. For example, if you're unsure of whether the image you cut and pasted needs to be on the same disk, put it there anyway. Another reason to do that is that if the file became corrupted somewhere in the process (a not unlikely occurrence in the Mac world, and even more so in the Mac to

Windows, Windows to Mac world), the service bureau may fix the original, native file and rescue the job at 11:00 at night when you'd prefer not to be awakened. When in doubt, include it!

The basics (and realities) of prepress publishing of ink on paper is that there are standards that most service bureaus can deal with daily on a production basis. The following files and formats will not cause them as many problems as others:

- TIFF for photos.
- EPS for illustrations created in the drawing programs Adobe Illustrator and Macromedia FreeHand. Don't use CorelDRAW unless you check first with the printer; earlier versions of this program can create bad PostScript that won't necessarily print correctly or at all.
- EPS for photos only if they have a mask, path, or channel to perform some kind of special effect.

But there are exceptions: When working in certain OPI environments, you may have to save the original high-resolution images in a special version of EPS or a special version of TIFF. Check with your in-house administrator.

Delivering the Fonts

Although we would certainly not advise anyone at any time to break the law, it is being broken on a daily basis in the prepress world. Depending on when and where you bought your fonts, and who the font foundry was, you promised to use that font for only one printer, or lots of workstations and one or two printers, or one workstation and many printers (and the number varies), or any combination of the above.

To make it work in the real world, however, what generally happens is that you provide the printer or service bureau all the fonts you used in your document (and don't forget the true bold, italic, and bold italic versions, too), they load them and use them to output your job, and then, when your job is done, they throw them away and don't use them for anybody else's job. Or at least that's what they tell me they do. While illegal (mostly), it is accepted common practice to provide your fonts at the same time you provide the job. It's necessary, in fact, because even two copies of a font from the same foundry may actually be different versions with different character widths.

Too bad Quark doesn't provide a Collect for Output function for fonts. But wait: A QuarkXTension called FontSneak is available and will copy the outline and bitmapped files from your system (or anywhere else you have them on your hard disk) to a folder you can copy to your media you use to deliver the job.

Make sure you include both the bitmapped screen and the outline (printer) files for each PostScript Type 1 font you deliver. You can strip out all the sizes except 12 or 14 point from the bitmap version if you want: Assume, unless told otherwise, that everybody uses Adobe Type Manager, which allows you to do that. But you must include the outline (printer) file for each version of the face you use: the regular, the bold, the italic, the bold italic, the black, and so on (see Figure 19.25).

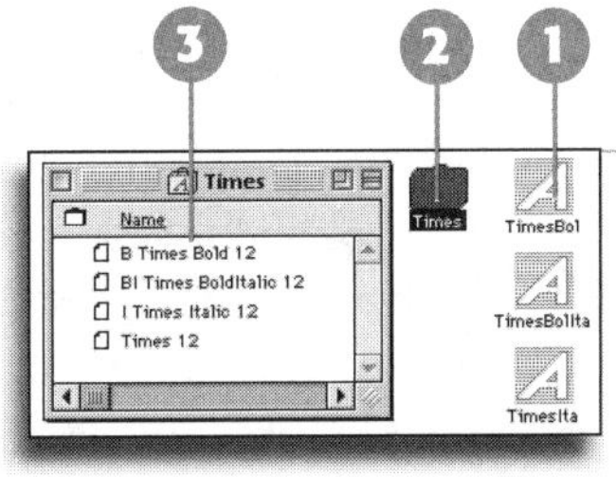

FIGURE 19.25

Here a Mac OS screen (bitmap) font has been stripped of extraneous sizes, with its corresponding printer (outline) fonts.

1 Screen fonts

2 Suitcase file containing screen fonts

3 Printer fonts

As previously stated, make sure the Font Usage dialog box shows only <<Plain>> next to the font name. You'll get fewer surprises when the file is RIPed elsewhere if your Helvetica <<Bold>> is converted to B Helvetica Bold <<Plain>> in the menu. Then QuarkXPress will be forced to use the true bold, italic, and so on fonts that you provided in the previous step (see Figure 19.26).

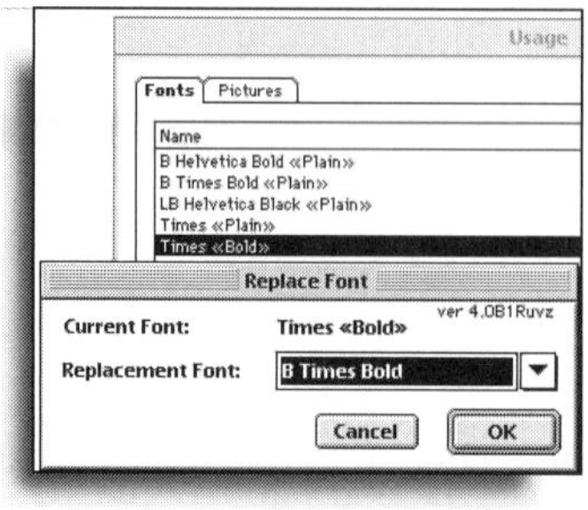

FIGURE **19.26**

The new font substitution function is nowhere near as useful as the version in 3.x, and the font substitution dialog box is extremely nonintuitive.

A tougher font issue to handle is the continuing saga of TrueType fonts versus PostScript Type 1 fonts. Most service bureaus don't like TrueType fonts. (You can tell a TrueType font by the logo on its suitcase (Mac) or next to its name in the **Font** submenu (Windows) and the fact that it doesn't have a printer or outline file to go with it. The bitmapped screen fonts and printer outline information are all in one file.) Check with your printer or service bureau first. "Fonts for free" downloaded from the Internet are always suspect. Try them first, and maybe even send a test file to the printer or service bureau first before using them in your document. Many printers and service bureaus use their RIP to send information to laser printers, bypassing the printer's built-in PostScript RIP, and can effectively "proof" the job on paper at low (or no) cost to you, and know if the RIP will image the film okay.

TrueType fonts are all self-contained, without a separate printer (or outline) file(s) to go with the screen font file, as do the Type 1 fonts (see Figure 19.27).

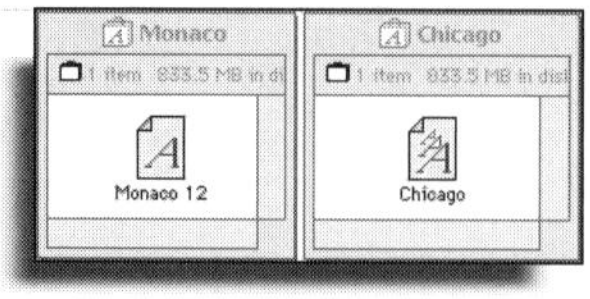

FIGURE **19.27**

The difference at a glance between Type 1 fonts (left) and a TrueType font (right) on a Mac.

Don't assume that the printer has the basics such as Helvetica and Zapf Dingbats on their machines and that they match your versions perfectly. There are many versions of Helvetica, even those distributed by Apple and Adobe, and they might behave differently from machine to machine. In fact, if you upgraded or installed software lately, check the basic fonts in your system folder, such as Courier, Chicago, Monaco: The suitcases are probably made up of a mixture of Type 1 and TrueType versions of the same font. (Fonts with city names such as Monaco and New York are not meant to be used in your files for printing: They were designed to be used for the system menus and to be displayed only on your screen. That's why they don't usually have an outline version included.)

Other fonts, such as Zapf Dingbats, have also changed over the years, and I've had characters in Dingbats do a baseline shift on me from my machine to the printer's machine. So include the basics too, if they're in your document.

You may also have some weird fonts in the font list that you know you didn't use and that aren't even loaded on your machine. In all probability, if the original was provided by some-body else, or it came from a template made by somebody else or at another time, there are fonts in style sheets you're not using. Or there are blank spaces in the document that are "leftovers" from an earlier version or from an earlier file that you made this new file from. It's worth the time to search these out and elimi-nate them. The slightest shift of even a blank space because it changed from "Harvey's weird font" to Courier (a fixed-width font that has equal widths for all its characters) might cause a whole paragraph to reflow, and also affect the flow of copy from page to page.

Use the **Fonts** tab in the Usage dialog box to select the font in question, click on **Show First**, and QuarkXPress jumps to the page with the font in question and highlights it. If you choose to replace it with something you already use, click on **Replace** and choose a new font from the pop-up menu (see Figure 19.28).

Replacing fonts with care

When you use the **Replace** function in the **Fonts** tab of the Usage dialog box, QuarkXPress replaces all uses of that font with your new choice and doesn't let you pick and choose which ones to change. That can lead to a disaster in its own right, so use it with caution. Use Find/Change instead if you're not sure you want to replace all instances of the problem font.

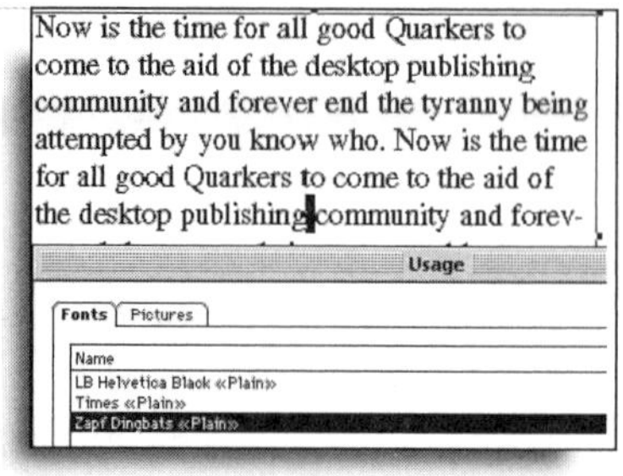

FIGURE 19.28

Use the Usage dialog box's search and replace function to ferret out strange fonts that might affect H&J and text flow when they get to a service bureau.

Delivering the Files

So now you have a perfect document: the extra images and junk have been deleted, the fonts and images have been collected, and now it's time to deliver the job.

First, check with the printers to see what kind of media they prefer. Most good-sized printers and service bureaus take just about anything, and many run out and buy the right drive if they need to, for a good customer. Some of the more commonly accepted media are the following:

- SyQuest disks. Even though they've been around for a while, they're still in use and I would predict that every printer or service bureau can take these ubiquitous disks. They're available in sizes now that range from the original 44MB to the newer 270 MB and the 1.5GB SyJet.

- Zip disks, with 100MB of storage, quickly became a standard for printers. Quick, small removable disks and the drives themselves are cheap and readily available.

- Jaz drives have also quickly taken over for the larger files (with images) that have to be transported back and forth. Their 1GB of storage can take, on one disk, the entire contents of most jobs that you produce, even the 48-page annual report in back-to-back color. Jaz drives run less than $350 and are a good alternative for larger jobs (and for backups of workstation and servers, too, for that matter).

- Simple jobs such as four-page black and white flyers and so on can still be delivered on floppy disks if they fit on one or two. I put the QuarkXPress files and images on one, usually, and the fonts on another.

- Stay away from DAT tape—or all tape of any kind for that matter. The bureaus and printers I deal with don't want to deal with it: too many formats and too slow a process reading the files onto their disks. With SyQuest, Zip, and Jaz, the printer can work directly from your disks and not have to copy files.

- Magneto-optical disks (1.3GB of storage) and CD-ROMS are other possibilities, but less commonly used. Check first before investing in these drives and methods.

Whatever the choice (and you'll probably end up using two or even three of the above media to get files to the printer), perform some routine housekeeping on the disks from time to time. Reformatting and reinitializing the disks from time to time keeps their drivers up to date, as well as cleans up the drive and locks out sectors that may become bad. And don't assume you'll use these forever: They do go bad over time and with use.

In addition to the files on the disk, deliver a laser proof (if that's all you have access to) and or a color proof from a desktop color printer of all the pages so that the printer knows, for instance, that you meant to have that picture on page 23 be upside down. It's also helpful to the printer/service bureau to see what your type looks like, where line breaks occur, and in general, to see what your intent is. Color pages can be proofed in color if you have a color printer of one kind or another available, but I'm sure you will both understand it's for informational purposes only and not to be matched. The colors you get from the printed final job should be the colors you specify in QuarkXPress.

And while you're printing out the final version, make two copies and keep one for yourself. Sounds basic, but many printers have told me many customers don't do that. And of course, you want to keep a copy of the QuarkXPress file itself on your hard disk, at least until the job is printed, bound, and delivered. Many problems of output can be resolved on the phone with the printer or service bureau after you delivered the job if you both have copies of the QuarkXPress file and your laser proofs.

Include something in writing that explains the job. Usually, most big-company purchase orders are not designed to take the kind of detail you need to deliver information to a printer, so if the printers don't supply their form, you need to devise a form that you can "fill out" for each and every print job that goes out the door. Include the following on that form, as a minimum:

- The name of the job: You and the printer can easily know which job you're talking about if they have three or four jobs from you in the shop at the same time.

- The number of copies.

- The number of pages (48-page booklet including cover—44 plus cover).

- The trim size (9" X 12").

- The paper stock(s) with brand name, weight, type, and any special handling (10 point "Joe's paper" cover, white, with 70# "Joe's" Ivory text).

- The ink(s) and any special information pertaining to the inks. (This is a five-color job, process inks plus PMS 243. All five colors are on all 48 pages. The outside covers and all inside pages contain bleeds.)

- Bindery considerations (saddle stitch versus wire bound, versus simple bound, and so on).

- What's included on the disk. I always tell them how many files in QuarkXPress and how many TIFF and EPS images there are and in what applications they were created in, and the names and numbers of the fonts if there aren't too many. The process of writing this out also is a good double-check for you to make sure all the files you need to send them are actually on the media you're sending. And their knowing what applications the TIFF and EPS files were created in may save some time if they have a problem with one or two of the files.

- Any special considerations, delivery schedules, and so on. (Naturally, you want the job yesterday: if you'd wanted the job next week, you would have given it to them next week!)

It often gets overlooked, but the Output Request Template that Quark provides for use with the Collect for Output report has a form at the top of the first page with most of this information. Take a look—it might just suit your needs perfectly.

Making Overheads

One trick I learned a while back was to send the QuarkXPress file directly to a laser printer loaded with clear plastic film designed for use in copy machines. It makes a decent overhead transparency, a medium I prefer for presentations because you can leave the room lights on, and allows you to draw arrows, circles, and diagrams as you display the transparency. When printing overheads, don't send a lot of pages at the same time, because the heat build-up of the laser printer may crinkle the plastic. Wait a few minutes for the printer to cool down in between sending pages to the printer.

If you have access to a film recorder (imagesetter), you can also make terrific overhead transparencies that are as good as the resolution of the imagesetter, with perfect shades of gray, by sending the image as a negative image. In the Print dialog box, click **Page Setup** and choose **Invert Image** in the **Page Setup** dialog box. This sends a negative image of your pages to a machine that has been set up to produce negatives. Two negatives make a positive in prepress, too. You'll have a terrific positive to be used as an overhead transparency, or for other purposes, too, such as rear-lighted photo displays, signs, and so on (see Figure 19.29).

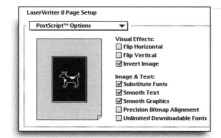

FIGURE 19.29

Printing a reverse image to an imagesetter that's already set up to print negatives can make nifty overhead transparencies, as well as rear-lighted signs, photos, and so on.

Creating Multimedia Projects

Create QuarkImmedia presentations

Create Acrobat PDF documents

Export HTML text from QuarkXPress documents

Create complete Web sites from QuarkXPress documents

Convert QuarkXPress documents to Web images

Not all documents are destined for print, or solely for print. These days, it's not uncommon to be asked to convert an existing document to some electronic format, whether it's Adobe's Acrobat *PDF*, *HTML*, or an onscreen presentation. And with the introduction of *QuarkImmedia*, a multimedia design *XTension*, Quark has attempted to position QuarkXPress as a platform for creating original presentations, not just converting print documents.

Converting Documents into QuarkImmedia

More than just an XTension

Just because it's an XTension, don't be fooled into thinking Immedia isn't a major investment. It's a full-featured presentation program in the form of a QuarkXTension, so it doesn't come cheap. It retails for as much as QuarkXPress, although you can sometimes find the two bundled for a significant savings. You can download a free Immedia demo for Mac OS at www. quark.com/demo002.htm.

One of the reasons Quark took so many years to release QuarkXPress 4 is that the company was concentrating on the development of QuarkImmedia, an XTension that lets you create multimedia presentations within QuarkXPress. Using Immedia, you can distribute and display QuarkXPress documents on the web in their original forms, complete with graphics, fonts, and pixel-perfect layout—as well as multimedia bells and whistles such as sound, video, hyperlinked buttons, and impressive video transitions between pages. Immedia presentations can also be distributed on disk as standalone documents.

You can start from scratch to create an Immedia presentation (see Figure 20.1) or you can start with an existing QuarkXPress document. Unlike other multimedia applications such as Director, Immedia is intended to cater to designers, especially those who are already used to the fine design control that QuarkXPress offers.

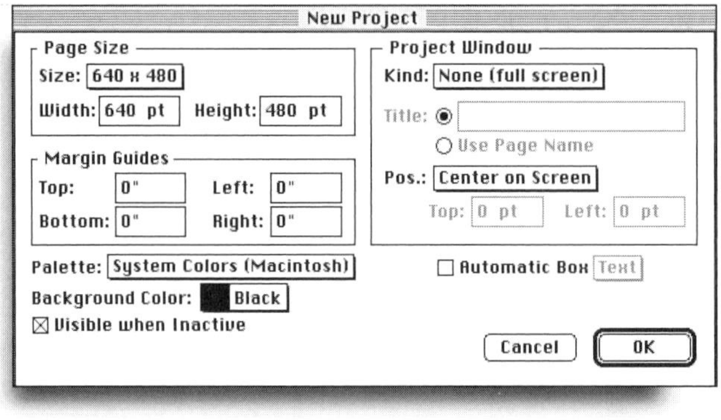

FIGURE 20.1

Immedia's New Project dialog box lets you set options at the beginning of a project.

Most of Immedia's functions are contained in a floating palette with six tabs.

In the **Page** tab, you can control the aspects of each page in the project; you can give a page a name, assign it an action, and control the transition effect used when a viewer reaches that page (see Figure 20.2). Actions such as playing a sound can be performed when the viewer leaves the page, as well. The **Page** tab also lets you determine how long the page is displayed—until the viewer chooses to leave it or for a specified amount of time, after which another page appears.

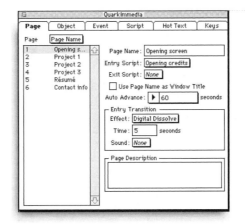

FIGURE 20.2
The **Page** tab controls attributes of each page in a project.

The **Object** controls, obviously, affect objects on a page. To work with an object so that you can use Immedia's features with it—to turn it into a button or a hotlink, for example—you first have to specify it as an Immedia object. For example, you can specify that a picture box is actually a movie box and then import a QuickTime movie into the box (see Figure 20.3).

When users click on objects in an Immedia presentation, any of dozens of things can happen, from printing to opening a Web page in the user's browser software. The **Event** tab lets you assign these events to objects, as well as choose to play sounds and display special cursors when an object is clicked (see Figure 20.4).

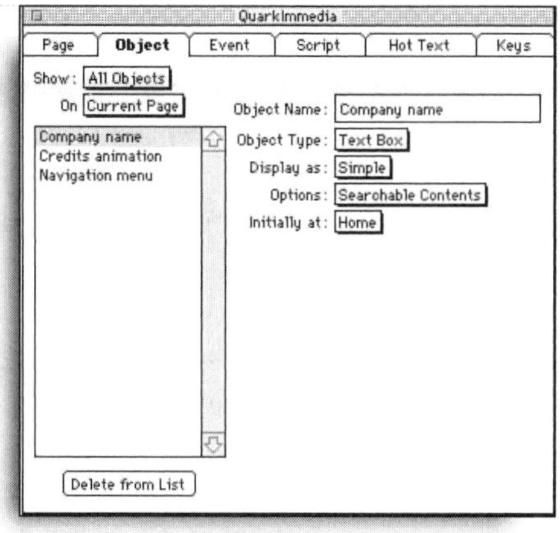

FIGURE 20.3

The **Object** tab controls attributes of each object on a page.

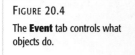

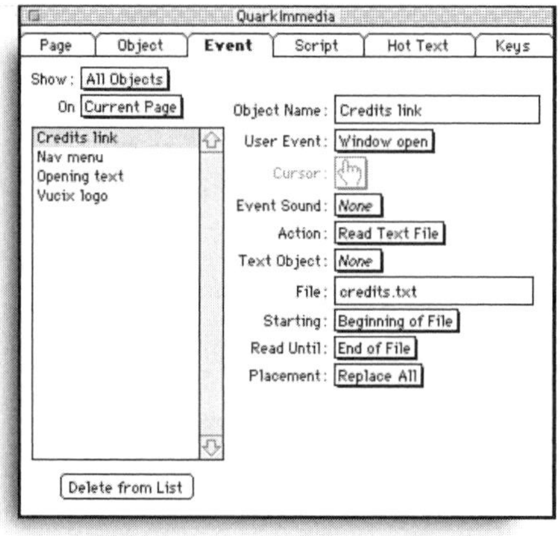

FIGURE 20.4

The **Event** tab controls what objects do.

To perform more than one action consecutively, you can create scripts that contain series of actions using the **Script** tab. A script can be assigned to an object or a page, so that multiple actions take place when the page is viewed or the object is clicked. No coding is required; to create a script, choose actions from a menu and rearrange them by dragging (see Figure 20.5).

Like boxes and other discrete objects, sections of text—from one character to an entire pageful—can trigger actions. When the viewer clicks on this "hot text," the page changes, a sound plays, or a *URL* is opened. As with other objects that can trigger actions, using the **Hot Text** tab you can control factors such as transitions and which page is opened (see Figure 20.6).

FIGURE 20.5

The **Script** tab lets you create series of actions that can be assigned to pages or objects.

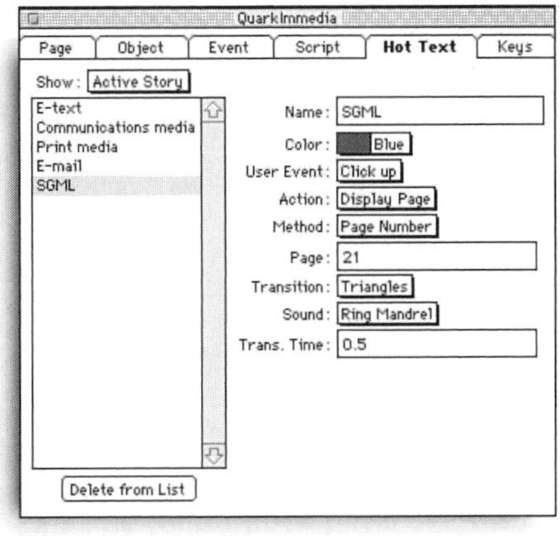

FIGURE 20.6

The **Hot Text** tab allows you to create hyperlinks.

You can trigger actions using keyboard shortcuts, and the **Keys** tab is where you can assign those shortcuts (see Figure 20.7).

In addition to the Immedia palette, Immedia adds a **QuarkImmedia** menu to the right of XPress's **Utilities** menu, containing a group of more administrative functions (see Figure 20.8):

- **Engage** runs the project, just as though you had encountered it on a Web page or double-clicked it as a standalone document.

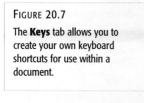

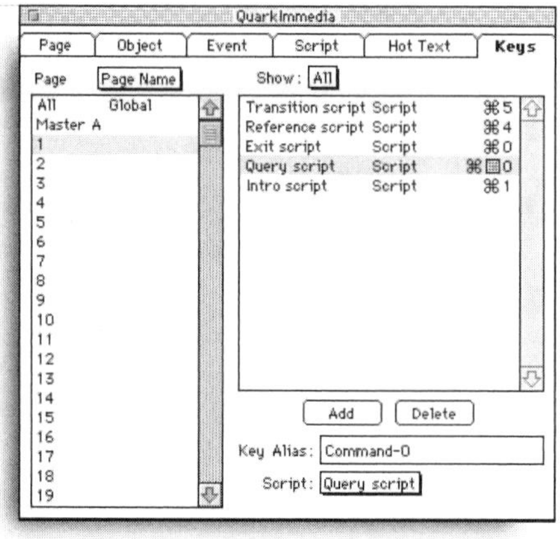

FIGURE 20.7

The **Keys** tab allows you to create your own keyboard shortcuts for use within a document.

FIGURE 20.8

The **QuarkImmedia** menu controls programming and playing Immedia projects.

- **Use Debugger** displays a window while the project is running that documents the commands and actions used in the project and lets you know where the problem is if something doesn't work as it should.

- **MenuMaker** lets you create pop-up menus and add menus to the menu bar at the top of the screen. From the MenuMaker dialog box, you can also load and save sets of menu commands for use in other projects.

- **Custom Transitions** brings up a dialog box in which you can create custom variations on Immedia's standard transition effects, which govern how the change from one page to another looks. These are similar to the transition effects used on television between scenes. You can edit the duration, color, direction, orientation, and size of each transition.

- **Make Index** creates an HTML-formatted list of all the text used in a project. This enables an Immedia project to be searched by the Internet's many search engines, which can't read Immedia files but can read and index HTML files. Index files are generally never seen by projects' viewers because there aren't links to them anywhere.

- **Export Settings** determines how Immedia objects are handled when files are exported, including how sound and video should be resampled and whether a copyright notice should be embedded in projects.

- **Export** allows you to save Immedia files in different ways depending on their destination—the Internet, a CD-ROM, or another storage and distribution method. You can control attributes of files exported from Immedia: compression levels, how filenames are assigned when one document is exported to more than one file, and whether the Immedia viewer application is embedded in the presentation. If the viewer isn't embedded, the reader must have the viewer software to read the Immedia file.

- **Convert to QuarkImmedia** changes a QuarkXPress file into an Immedia file, after you specify Immedia—only attributes such as the screen's background color (which shows around the edges of the project if it doesn't fill the screen), the project's color palette, and the kind of window in which the project should appear when it's viewed.

- **QuarkImmedia Usage** lists the Immedia objects in the file and gives information about them. It works just like the QuarkXPress Usage dialog box, displaying the pathname to each imported movie, picture, or sound file and letting you know whether that file has been moved or changed. These elements aren't embedded in the Immedia project until it's exported, so if you try to export the file after moving some of the support files, you need to relink the files in this dialog box just as you relink picture files in the **Picture** tab of the Usage dialog box before printing a QuarkXPress document.

Changing from QuarkXPress to QuarkImmedia

When you start with an existing QuarkXPress document, use the **Convert to QuarkImmedia** command before doing anything else. Until the document has been converted, the other commands in the Immedia menu aren't available.

- **About QuarkImmedia** shows a splash screen with development credits for the software.

After you create an Immedia project, you have two choices. You can export it as a standalone file, with an embedded copy of the Immedia Viewer application; this file can be viewed by anyone. Or you can export the project without the embedded viewer (this is what you'd do if you were adding the project to your web site) and require users to download the free Immedia Viewer application. The viewer is a standalone application that needs to be specified as your web browser's helper application for Immedia files before you can view Immedia projects on the Web.

Converting Documents into Acrobat PDF

Though Adobe keeps adding more presentation-type features to its Acrobat software so that you can create interactive Acrobat documents and even games, Acrobat's real strength is the capability to preserve typography and design when a document is distributed and even printed across multiple computer platforms.

Acrobat's PDF (Portable Document Format) is the equivalent of pre-RIPed PostScript code, so a PDF document can be printed on any printer and look just as good as the original document did when printed on a PostScript printer. Any time you need to distribute a document to people who need to view and print it but who don't have the software and fonts with which the document was created, Acrobat is your best bet.

QuarkXPress users have two ways to create PDF documents from XPress documents. If you're not working in a PostScript environment (not likely if you're a QuarkXPress user), the PDF Writer printer driver lets you "print" an Acrobat document directly to disk, just as you would print a file to the printer or create a PostScript disk file (see Figure 20.9). First, you have to target the PDF Writer driver, either in the Chooser (Mac OS) or in the Printer pop-up menu in the Print dialog box (Windows). PDF Writer doesn't handle PostScript-only features, so if you use *EPS* artwork, you'll want to avoid PDF Writer.

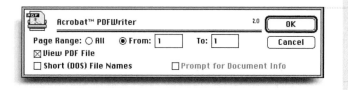

FIGURE 20.9

If PDF Writer is targeted, the Print dialog box turns into a Create PDF dialog box.

For more control over the conversion process, you can use Acrobat Distiller (see Figure 20.10). This application "distills" a *PostScript file* to convert it to a PDF file (see Figure 20.11).

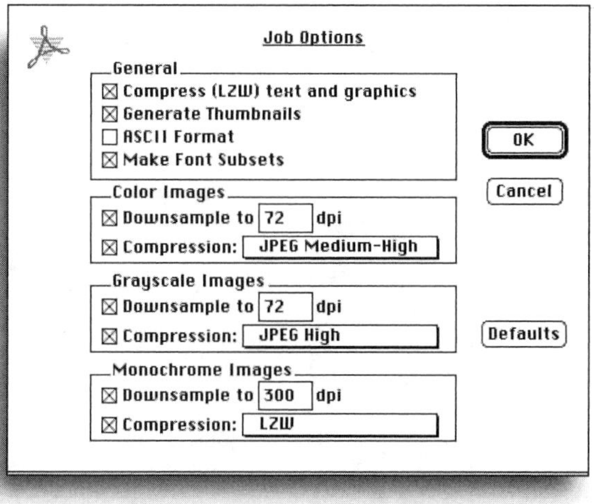

FIGURE 20.10

The Job Options dialog box gives you more control over how Distiller creates PDF files—once options are set.

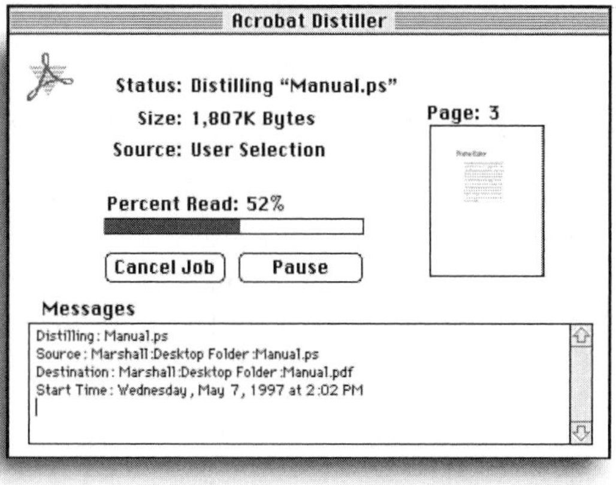

FIGURE 20.11

Creating a PDF file is just one step.

The results are the same, whichever method you use. A third product, Acrobat Exchange, allows you to add notes, hyperlinks, and other features to PDF files (see Figure 20.12). Acrobat Reader is available free from Adobe in Mac OS, Windows, and UNIX versions; Adobe allows you to distribute it on-disk with Acrobat files, or you can link to it on your web site so that surfers can download it before downloading your Acrobat files. An Acrobat plug-in that allows Acrobat documents to be read within Netscape Navigator or Microsoft Internet Explorer is also free.

FIGURE 20.12

Acrobat Exchange lets you edit some attributes of PDF documents and add special features.

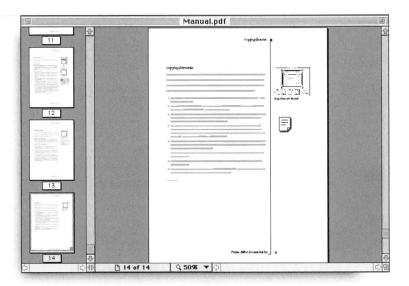

Converting Documents into HTML

Sometimes, the content of a document is more important than a beautiful design. When that's the case, HTML is the way to get information on the Web. It's a text-based coding system that's interpreted by Web browser software to display text in different sizes, alignments, and (a few) fonts. Although future revisions of

HTML will allow more control over design elements, the current version allows only very limited formatting: basal text, five heading levels, a few kinds of lists, and so on.

Don't be deceived, though—HTML has many advantages over other methods of presenting content on the web. (Although its design limitations cause many designers to view it with an extremely jaundiced eye.) HTML files are small, saving on upload and download time, and they're searchable by Internet search engines such as AltaVista. HTML is a cross-platform, accessible to anyone with an Internet connection, whether it's on a Windows, Mac OS, UNIX, or other system. And, although HTML coding can be confusing at first if you try to create it "by hand," it's easy to generate HTML documents directly from QuarkXPress with XTensions such as HexWeb and BeyondPress.

Exporting Text and Applying Tags

If you already know HTML, you may prefer to export text from QuarkXPress and add your own HTML coding. Or if you're just learning HTML, starting with a structured document in QuarkXPress can eliminate some design decisions, allowing you to focus on learning the codes that make the HTML version of your document match the QuarkXPress version as closely as possible.

SEE ALSO

➤ *To export text, see page 184*

Using the BeyondPress XTension

The nice thing about BeyondPress is that it allows you to map QuarkXPress styles to HTML styles, so you can be very specific about what style different text elements should use.

To create an HTML document with BeyondPress:

1. Choose **Show Document Content** from the **View** menu to see BeyondPress's Document Content palette (see Figure 20.13). For text or a graphic to be included in the resulting HTML files, it has be listed here.

Moving to the next level with HTML

You can use tables and other tricks to format HTML text more precisely; for more information, consult an HTML guide such as *HTML Studio Skills* (Hayden Books, 1997).

Getting all the text out of a QuarkXPress document

The TeXTractor XTension can be helpful when you export text from QuarkXPress; it can export all the text in the document to one or several text files. It's from Vision's Edge (www.visionsedge.com).

FIGURE 20.13

The Document Content palette can list all the elements in a QuarkXPress document.

2. Click the **Add All Items** button to add all items in the QuarkXPress document to the palette.

3. All the text and graphics in the document are listed in the palette, under a folder representing the HTML document that will be created. To divide the elements into more HTML documents, click the **Add Folder** button, rename the new folder (at the bottom of the palette), and drag items into it.

4. To reorder items, drag them up or down in the palette.

5. To change the attributes of an item, click on the entry next to it in the **HTML** column. Some items have menus, indicated by small triangles, that show up if you click and hold. Here the type of item, for example, can be specified, as well as what head level it should use or whether it should be converted to a graphic. Other items (graphics) have **Modify** buttons; clicking on these takes you to a Modify dialog box where the picture can be scaled and otherwise edited.

6. To export a document, click to select its folder and choose **Export** from the pop-up menu in the **HTML** column next to it.

If you want to get more precise, BeyondPress lets you do that. As previously mentioned, you can map paragraph styles to HTML styles to more tightly control what HTML styles are used; you can add hyperlinks and other HTML elements such as line breaks; and you can specify the destination platform so that BeyondPress gets the filenames and text attributes right when it converts files.

Using the HexWeb XTension

HexWeb can build an entire hierarchical web site, and its HexScape XT lets you use Netscape plug-ins as you create pages.

To create an HTML document from QuarkXPress with HexWeb:

1. In the HexWeb preferences dialog box, indicate the **Main Path**—the root folder that will contain all the graphics and other files for the Web site (see Figure 20.14).

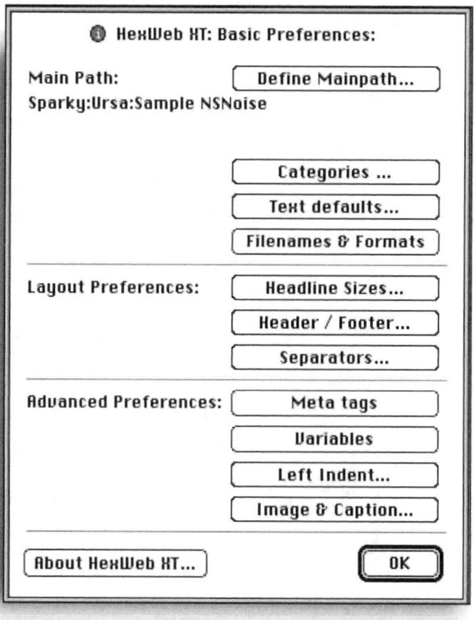

FIGURE 20.14
HexWeb's preferences dialog box is the starting point.

2. Set the other HexWeb preferences, such as what size of QuarkXPress type should be mapped to what heading level. Other preferences allow you to specify header and footer text to be added to each HTML file, choose a format for converted graphics, and use more advanced HTML tags like META.

3. Choose **Show HexWeb Export** from the **Utilities** menu to bring up the HexWeb Export palette (see Figure 20.15).

FIGURE 20.15

The HexWeb Export palette controls the directory structure for the resulting Web site.

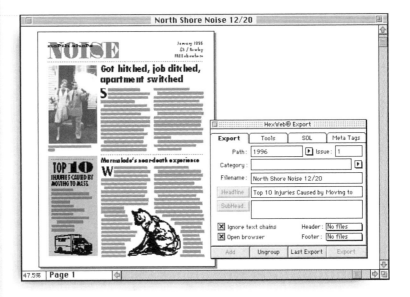

4. Fill in the **Path**, **Issue**, **Category**, and **Filename** fields in the HexWeb Export palette. These determine the directory structure that will be used for the files HexWeb creates. In Figure 20.15, the **Path** is 1996, the **Issue** is 1, the **Filename** is North Shore Noise 12/20, and there isn't a **Category**. When this file is exported, it's named North Shore Noise 1220.html, and it's in a folder called 1, which is in another folder called 1997.

5. Select the headline text and click the **Headline** button to fill it in; then do the same with the subhead text, if there is any.

6. Using the **Item** tool ⊕ , Shift+click on each text box, in order, that you want to include in the exported HTML file.

7. Click **Export**.

Of course, many other options are available; you can specify how an object should be treated, for one thing, so that a text name-plate can be converted to a graphic, preserving its look. HexWeb is a German product and could use a little interface clean-up (the translators weren't too clear on English capitalization rules) but it works quickly and cleanly.

Putting Documents on the Web as Images

Much of the time, there's no need to go through the complex process of converting a QuarkXPress document to HTML using a program such as BeyondPress. This may be required if the QuarkXPress document (and especially the text) is the focus of the web page, and if users need to click on text that is within the QuarkXPress document. But if, for example, you're merely exporting book covers you've done in QuarkXPress for use on a Web page used to sell that book on-line, you can simply treat that book cover as a graphic.

The easiest way to create this graphic is to save the QuarkXPress page as an EPS file. You can then open it in Photoshop (or another graphics application that can handle various file formats). There, you can resize the image, play with the color palette to make the eventual file size smaller, perhaps sharpen the image a bit, and so on. Save it as a GIF or JPEG file, and it's ready to be linked to a Web page by whomever needs it. Simple. And you don't need to buy yet another application to do it, either.

SEE ALSO

➤ To export pages as EPS files, see page 351

PART

VI

Advanced Features

CHAPTER

21

Using XTensions

XTensions are software modules that add custom publishing features to QuarkXPress. Some XTensions have stand-alone components, but most run exclusively with QuarkXPress. XTensions have the capability to add menu commands, dialog box controls, palettes, and tools to QuarkXPress.

You can purchase XTensions to do everything from converting QuarkXPress documents to HTML and creating custom drop shadows to adding words to your Hyphenation Exceptions and checking documents to ensure correct output. QuarkXPress ships with a variety of XTensions, including import/export *filters* for word processors, Cool Blends for creating fancy *gradients*, and the Index XTension. Additional Freebies XTensions from Quark are available on the company's Web site at www.quark.com.

Purchasing XTensions

XTensions are available for both Mac OS and Windows versions of QuarkXPress from Quark, distributors, and third-party XTensions developers. When it comes to XTensions, Windows users are at a disadvantage. Most XTensions are developed exclusively—or at least first—for Mac OS. The best way to get information about and purchase an XTension is through the Web, although you can call for information if you're not online.

Quark

Quark sells special purpose XTensions, such as QuarkImmedia, for multimedia publishing and the editorial management XTensions that make up the Quark Publishing System. To account for features that didn't make it into version 4, Quark has begun producing Freebies XTensions and posting them online. In fact, the Tables XTension might be out by the time you read this. For more information, visit Quark's Web site at www.quark.com or call 1-800-676-4575.

Distributors

Several distribution companies have been created because of the XTensions industry. Some sell XTensions exclusively, whereas others also provide various publishing add-ons. Give the following a try:

- XPresso Bar: www.xpressobar.com (They don't actually sell XTensions, they just point you to people who do.)
- XT-now: www.xt-now.com or 415-283-1811
- World Wide Power Company: www2.thepowerco.com/twwpc/ or 1-800-940-USER

Developers

Some developers sell their XTensions directly in addition to selling them through distributors. Try the following for reliable XTensions and service:

- Extensis: www.extensis.com or 1-800-796-9798
- A Lowly Apprentice Production: www.alap.com or 1-888-818-5790
- Markzware: www.markzware.com or 1-800-3000-3532
- Vision's Edge: www.xtender.com or 1-800-XTENDER

Enabling and Disabling XTensions

QuarkXPress 4 actually snags a feature away from its XTensions developers: the XTensions Manager. In previous versions of QuarkXPress, you had to enable XTensions by manually placing them loose in the QuarkXPress folder or in the XTension folder. To disable XTensions, you had to make your own folder called something such as Unused XTensions and place them there. Less informed users got around this hassle by simply running all their XTensions at once—not realizing that all these XTensions were needlessly gobbling memory that could be used by QuarkXPress.

QuarkXPress 4 includes an XTensions Manager dialog box for enabling and disabling XTensions, creating sets of XTensions, and troubleshooting XTensions. You can display the XTensions Manager and confirm which XTensions are running when you launch QuarkXPress. To do this, press the Spacebar while QuarkXPress is starting up. You can also set an Application Preference to have the XTensions Manager display every time you launch QuarkXPress.

To open the XTensions Manager while QuarkXPress is running, select **XTensions Manager** from the **Utilities** menu. If you make changes while QuarkXPress is running, you have to quit and relaunch for the changes to take affect. XTensions are integrated into QuarkXPress and memory is allocated to them when the program is launched. There is no way for QuarkXPress to integrate XTension features on-the-fly.

No matter how you open the dialog box, once you're in, it works the same. First, you notice that it lists all your XTensions. These are all the XTensions in your XTension folder and your XTension Disabled folder. (If you don't have an XTension Disabled folder yet, don't worry. QuarkXPress will make it for you as soon as you disable an XTension.) The dialog box gives you more information about the XTension, such as whether it was rewritten for QuarkXPress 4. You can select an XTension and click **About** to learn about the developer, and so on.

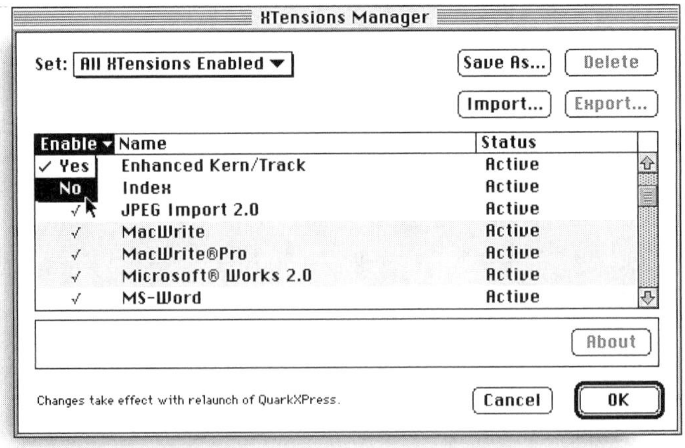

FIGURE 21.1

The XTensions Manager dialog box enables you to control which XTensions load with QuarkXPress without physically moving files.

- To enable an individual XTension, click to select it. Select **Yes** from the **Enable** menu or click in the column to add a check mark.

- To enable several XTensions, select them. Press Shift to select several XTensions in a row; press ⌘ (Ctrl) to select noncontiguous XTensions. Select **Yes** from the **Enable** menu or click in the column to add a check mark.

- If you want to save this group of XTensions to use later, you can create an XTensions set. While the XTensions are selected, click **Set**. Enter a name for the set and click OK. Any time you want to use that set, you can select it from the **Set** menu.

Installing New XTensions

The XTensions Manager doesn't really help with installing new XTensions. To install an XTension, drag its icon to the XTension folder or XTension Disabled folder inside your QuarkXPress folder. (Of course, if the XTension comes with an installer, follow its instructions.) If you place the XTension in the XTension folder, it will load the next time you launch QuarkXPress; you don't have to enable it in the XTensions Manager. In fact, if you can't get used to using the XTensions Manager, you can enable and disable XTensions all day long by moving them between the XTension and XTension Disabled folders.

Be aware that the evaluation copies of most XTensions temporarily turn QuarkXPress into a demo version. You won't be able to save or print from QuarkXPress. Remove evaluation XTensions as soon as you finish checking them out.

Troubleshooting XTensions

There will be no XTension trouble in QuarkXPress 4, so forget we mentioned it. Wait, did you say your document won't open? QuarkXPress crashes when you double-click the document? If you use any third-party XTensions, especially third-party XTensions from different vendors, you might have an XTension problem.

XTension loading isn't guaranteed

While no might always mean no, yes doesn't always mean yes. When you select Yes from the Enable menu, all it means is that QuarkXPress will attempt to load the XTension. If QuarkXPress encounters a problem with the XTension, it might not load. If this happens, you will receive an alert.

Why not an XTensions folder?

Why is that folder called XTension when it most likely contains more than one XTension? In version 3.3 when the XTension folder was introduced, the folder name was singular to limit the folder name to eight characters. This allowed for the same name on both Mac OS and Windows. With Windows 95, you'd think Quark could loosen up and be more accurate. But no, although the name was temporarily pluralized during development, it reverted to singular for no apparent reason.

Forget anything you ever knew about troubleshooting by moving things in and out of folders. You have the XTensions Manager now. The first thing to try is disabling all XTensions, relaunching QuarkXPress, and reopening the document. One of three things happens:

- The document opens just fine. This is an indication that an XTension was in fact causing a problem. Now you have to figure out which one.

- The document refuses to open without certain XTensions present. For example, if you create blends using Cool Blends in a document, you need the Cool Blends XTension to even open the document.

- The document still crashes, which means that XTensions are probably not the problem here.

If the document refused to open for lack of XTensions, enable the XTensions the document wants and then relaunch QuarkXPress. At this point, if the document won't open, it's probably one of those XTensions causing the problem.

If the document opens fine, you're in the same situation as the document that opened fine with no XTensions running; you need to figure out who the bad guy is. If there's a new XTension in town, it's probably introducing the problem. This is not to say it's causing the problem; maybe it's just conflicting with another XTension.

See what happens when you disable the new XTension. Then see what happens if you enable the new XTension and disable all other XTensions. If all is fine both times, you have a conflict between the new guy and one or more of the old guys. Even if you don't have a new XTension, you might have two XTensions that started conflicting because of how they were used in a document.

To find out which XTensions are conflicting, use the divide-and-conquer method. Enable half your XTensions and see if everything is fine. If so, you know those XTensions work fine together. If not, break the group containing the bad XTensions in half and test them separately. Eventually, you'll find one little

XTension that's not playing well with others. (We hope! It's conceivable that more than one XTension is fighting with others.)

Once you isolate your problem to a specific XTension, you can start solving the problem. First, contact the XTension's developers. They might know about the conflict and have updates all ready for you. Second, consider whether you even use all those XTensions and whether you need to use them in combination. If not, create XTensions sets containing XTensions that like each other and are necessary for specific documents.

SEE ALSO

➤ *To create blends with Cool Blends, see page 435*

Using XPress Tags

The XPress Tags *filter* is an *XTension* that allows you to *export* and *import* formatted text from a QuarkXPress document. Exporting and importing in XPress Tags format works just like exporting and importing in Microsoft Word format or WordPerfect format. The main difference is that unlike an exported Microsoft Word document, which can't be viewed without Microsoft Word, an XPress Tags file can be viewed and edited in any word processing application that can open a plain *ASCII* text file.

When you open an XPress Tags file, you see that all your typographical formatting has been translated into ASCII codes such as, for example, `<B>bold<B>` or `<I>italic<I>`. If you know how to edit these codes, you can do some very handy things with them. For example, you can Find/Change attributes that you can't find/change in QuarkXPress. You can strip local attributes from a text flow without having to reapply all your intentional local formatting. You can even create an XPress Tags files from scratch in a word processor, if you're so inclined. But before we go into all that, let's explain the exporting, editing, and importing process.

SEE ALSO

➤ *To import text, see page 183*

➤ *To export text, see page 184*

➤ *To format text, see page 238*

XPress Tags can't do it all

XPress Tags describe typographical formatting, but they do not describe page geometry. You can export a story in XPress Tags format, but you can't save an entire layout in XPress Tags format.

How XPress Tags Work

QuarkXPress has an arsenal of typographical features. Consequently, XPress Tags needs an arsenal of codes to represent all those features. It's unnecessary to list all these codes—they're all covered in the QuarkXPress documentation. Plus, any time you need one, you can get it by formatting text and exporting it to look at its tags. However, we can at least give you the basics.

With the exception of style sheet definitions and applications, all XPress Tags must be enclosed by greater-than and less-than brackets, `<like so>`. You can have a single tag between a pair of these brackets, or you can have a whole series of them.

Many tags work in pairs. You use such a tag once to turn a feature on, and then again to turn it off. For example, you can use the following two codes to make a word bold:

```
This is a <B>bold<B> word.
```

Other tags require parameters, just like their corresponding QuarkXPress features. For example, if you use the horizontal scale feature, you have to specify how much you want to scale the text:

```
This text is <h200>horizontally scaled<h100>.
```

XPress Tags work in reverse

The <B> example shown assumes that the paragraph containing it is not bold. If the paragraph in which this pair of tags occurred was bold, the word "bold" would be plain.

Some tags require a whole series of parameters. For example, to specify that a line has a left tab at .5" and a right tab with a dot leader at 6", the tag reads:

```
<*t(36,0,"1 ",434,2,"2..");>
```

The specifications for the two tab stops this paragraph uses are organized into sets of three values within the parentheses. In this example, the first tab begins 36 points from the left margin, uses alignment number zero (left), and uses a space as a fill character (the 1 means the leader was specified as a single-character leader, even though it's followed by two spaces). The second tab begins 434 points (6") from the left margin, uses alignment number two (right), and uses two dots as a fill character.

You can use XPress Tags both to define and to apply *style sheets*. To define a style sheet, you simply begin a line with an @ character followed immediately by the style sheet name and an equals sign. Next, you use a series of tags enclosed by less than and greater than signs to specify the style sheet's attributes. We won't go into what each specific tag means (that's what your QuarkXPress manuals are for), but a typical style sheet definition might look something like this:

```
@TextStyle=<*L*h"Standard"*kn0*kt0*ra0*rb0*d0*p(0,0,0,0,0,6,
g,"U.S. English")*t(0,0,"1 ")
:Ps100t0h100z12k0b0c"Black"f"Palatino-Roman">
```

To apply a style sheet to a line of text in an XPress Tags file, simply begin the line with an @ followed immediately by the name of the style sheet and a colon, like this:

```
@TextStyle:This text will use the TextStyle style sheet.
```

XPress Tags version numbers

A version tag appears at the beginning of each exported XPress Tags file:

`<v1.70><e0>`

This tag shows which version of the XPress Tags filter was used to export the file (here, 1.7) and the character set code (here, Mac OS). The version tag isn't mandatory (an XPress Tags file will import fine without it) but if a file already has this tag at the beginning, you should leave it there. Newer versions of the XPress Tags filter include fixes to bugs that existed in older versions, but this tag must be present for these fixes to work properly with files exported by older versions of the filter.

As with other XPress Tags, we highly recommend that you format text with paragraph and character style sheets, and then export it so you can view the XPress Tags. This gives you the most accurate XPress Tags definition and saves a lot of time.

What if your text includes one of the special characters used by XPress tags (@, \, <, and >)? Just put the character between a pair of XPress Tags brackets and precede it with a \. For example, "Send e-mail to <talyn@nilenet.com>" translates into XPress Tags like this:

```
Send e-mail to <\<>talyn<\@>nilenet.com<\>>
```

SEE ALSO

➤ *To create style sheets, see page 297*
➤ *To apply style sheets to text, see page 303*

Reading XPress Tags

If you don't have your QuarkXPress manuals handy, you can figure out the code for an attribute by applying that attribute to some text, exporting the text in XPress Tags format, and then looking at the resulting file. For example, say you want to find out what the XPress Tag for baseline shift is. Just type a few words, baseline shift a word in the middle, and then select the words and export them in XPress Tags format. The resulting file should look something like this:

```
<v1.70><e0>
@Normal=[S"","Normal"]<*L*h"Standard"*kn0*kt(2,2)*ra0*rb0*d0*
p(0,0,0,12,0,12,g,"U.S. English")*t(0,0,"2 "):
Ps100t0h100z9k0b0c"Black"f"Palatino-Roman">
@Normal:<$>baseline <$b4>shifted<$b$> text
```

Before you scream, remember you can pretty much ignore all but the last line. The first line simply contains the version and character set codes; the series of lines that begins with `@Normal=` is the definition of the Normal style sheet.

The last line begins with `@Normal:` to show that this paragraph uses the Normal style sheet. The initial `<$>` means to use the style sheet's specifications. The next `$` is just to make sure you're still using the style sheet's specifications; it isn't really necessary, but it doesn't hurt to have it there.

Now, finally, what you've been waiting for: the tag for baseline shift. This is a lowercase b, followed by a number indicating how much to shift the text. At the end of the shifted text, another lower case b is followed by a $ to indicate the text should be set back to the baseline shift specified by the style sheet.

Exporting and Importing XPress Tags

To export or import in XPress Tags format, you must have the XPress Tags Filter installed. The filter is an XTension, so you enable it through the XTensions Manager.

To export text as XPress Tags when the filter is enabled:

1. Open a document and select the Content tool [icon].

2. Click in the text box that contains the text you want to export.

3. Select **Save Text** from the **File** menu or press ⌘+Option+E (Ctrl+Alt+E) to open the Save Text dialog box.

4. Click **Selected Text** or **Entire Story** (if you choose **Selected Text**, only the currently selected text will be exported).

5. Select **XPress Tags** from the **Format** pop-up menu.

6. Specify a name and location for the file; then click **Save**.

You can view and edit the resulting file in any word processing application that supports plain ASCII text files. Or if you want, you can view and edit the file in QuarkXPress. To do so, first create a new document with an automatic text box. Then click in the automatic text box with the Content tool and select **Get Text** from the **File** menu or press ⌘+E (Ctrl+E) to display the Get Text dialog box. Choose the exported file in the scrolling list, and make sure **Convert Quotes** and **Include Style Sheets** are not checked. (You'll see why in a minute.)

Click **OK** to import the text. If you're normal, you may scream at this point; it's a little scary the first time you see it. Before we start explaining, though, two very important points about XPress Tags:

One text box at a time

When you export in XPress Tags format, you aren't necessarily exporting all the text in the document; you're only exporting text from the selected text box or chain of text boxes. If your document has more than one text chain, you may need to export several separate files to get all the text in your document.

Choosing which part of the text to export

If text is selected when you open the Save Text dialog box, the **Selected Text** radio button is selected by default. If you want to export all the text in the current box or chain, make sure **Entire Story** is selected.

Anchored boxes not included

If you export text containing anchored boxes in XPress Tags format, the anchored boxes are not exported. If you need to do XPress Tags work on a story that includes anchored boxes, export only the portions of the story that do not contain anchored boxes–or realize that you will be losing information.

1. Many XPress Tag codes use straight quotes ("‚'). If you import an XPress Tags file with Convert Quotes checked, these straight quotes are converted to curly quotes ("‚"‚'‚'). If you try to import an XPress Tags file containing straight quotes that have been converted to curly quotes, it won't work and you won't be happy. So if you want to edit XPress Tags files in QuarkXPress, make sure the **Convert Quotes** box is not checked.

2. You can control whether QuarkXPress interprets XPress Tags by checking or not checking the **Include Style Sheets** box. If this box is not checked, the tags are simply read into the box as plain ASCII text, allowing you to edit them. If this box is checked, though, QuarkXPress reads the tags and converts them into formatting. If you want to edit the tags in an XPress Tags file using QuarkXPress, you must make sure that **Include Style Sheets** is not checked.

Now import that same XPress Tags file again, this time with **Include Style Sheets** checked. The text should look exactly the same in the new document as it did in the document from which it was exported (with the obvious difference that the boxes in this document may be shaped differently).

SEE ALSO

➤ *To import text, see page 183*

➤ *To export text, see page 184*

Working with Tagged Text

At this point—if you're still reading—you're probably wondering what you can do with all this information. Well, let us tell you.

The main thing XPress Tags files are good for is find/change operations. The QuarkXPress Find/Change feature is powerful, but sometimes it just isn't powerful enough. For example, say you get a file from a friend who likes to use the right indent tab character (Option+Tab [Shift+tab]). This infuriates you because you prefer to set your tabs up manually. How can you convert all those ridiculous right indent tab characters to regular tab characters?

Simple: export the text in XPress Tags format, open the file in a text editor (or import it into a QuarkXPress document with **Include Style Sheets** not checked), and use a search-and-replace feature to replace all occurrences of <\t> with plain old tabs.

Other characters that can't be accessed through the QuarkXPress Find/Change feature include the nonbreaking standard space (<\f> in XPress Tags) and the nonbreaking standard hyphen (<\!-> in XPress Tags).

As if things weren't already complicated enough—if you use the QuarkXPress Find/Change feature on these tags, remember that the backslash is a special character in the Find/Change dialog box. To get QuarkXPress to find a backslash, you must enter \\. Thus, to get QuarkXPress to find <\h>, you must enter <\\h>.

XPress Tags also lets you run search-and-replace operations on attributes such as tab settings, rule settings, horizontal/vertical scale, tracking, kerning, and baseline shift. This lets you perform some very useful and unorthodox operations.

As you begin working with XPress Tags, you will find dozens of tasks that you can accomplish much more quickly and easily with XPress Tags. For example, assume you have a bulleted list of commands or features for a project, and you want to alphabetize the list without losing any formatting. Simply export the list in XPress Tags format, open up the exported file in a word processor that lets you sort text, sort the list, and then reimport it into QuarkXPress.

For another example, say you have a long document with lots of local formatting, and some of the paragraphs have been tracked in or out to get rid of widows and orphans. You want to get rid of the local tracking, but you don't want to get rid of any of the other local formatting. It would be easy if you could just select all the text and set the tracking to zero, but you can't because different style sheets use different amounts of tracking. How can you do it without giving yourself numb fingers? You've probably already guessed that the solution is to export the document in XPress Tags format, then use Find/Change to find tags like <$t3> and <$t-1> and change them to <$>.

XPress Tags don't do nonbreaking em dashes

There currently is no way to distinguish a breaking em dash from a nonbreaking em dash in XPress Tags. If you export a text flow that contains nonbreaking em dashes, they will turn into breaking em dashes when you import the file.

Getting text from QPS to QuarkXPress

If you use QPS, you may have run into a situation where you need to move formatted text from QuarkXPress to QuarkCopyDesk, or vice versa. If you try to do this using cut and paste, you lose all your formatting. However, if you export the text in XPress Tags format from one application and then import it into the other, the formatting remains intact. Even if you don't use QPS, you might want to look into QuarkCopyDesk SE. It doesn't let you draw boxes or work with pictures, but it lets you use all the typographical features of QuarkXPress, and you can use XPress Tags to move QuarkCopyDesk text into a QuarkXPress document after it has been written. QuarkCopyDesk SE is available from Quark for approximately $300, which makes it an attractive alternative if not everyone in your company uses the layout features of QuarkXPress. (And no, you don't have to have QPS to use it.)

SEE ALSO

➤ *To search and replace text, see page 212*

The $ Tag

You can specify any kind of formatting you want in an XPress Tags file without ever using the $ tag. We're going to devote a whole subsection to it anyway, though, because it's used extensively in files that have been exported in XPress Tags format.

When the $ tag appears without a code before it, it means, "reset all type style attributes to the style sheet's specifications." So for example, in a plain-text paragraph, `This is <BIOSU>bold italic outlined underlined shadowed<$>` text is functionally equivalent to `This is <BIOSU>bold italic outlined underlined shadowed<BIOSU>` text.

When the $ tag appears after a code, it means, "reset this attribute to the style sheet's specifications." So, for example, in a plain text paragraph, `this is <B>bold<B$>` text is functionally equivalent to `this is <B>bold<B>` text.

The $ tag serves two purposes. First, it lets you reset all the text style attributes of a paragraph to the style sheet's specifications with a single tag (as in the preceding first example). Secondly, it makes sure that text reverts to the right format after a local formatting change, even if the style sheet definitions in a target document are different from those in the source document.

One last note about the $ tag. When it appears without a code before it, the $ tag resets all the type style attributes to the paragraph style sheet's specifications. "Type style attributes" includes everything on the **Type Style** submenu of the **Style** menu: bold, italic, outline, shadow, strike thru, underline, word underline, small caps, all caps, superscript, subscript, and superior. It does not include any of the other text attributes on the **Style** menu, such as baseline shift, tracking, horizontal/vertical scale, and so forth. These attributes must be manually reset to the style sheet's attributes by giving their code followed by a $ tag.

Using XPress Tags for Template Changes

The Find/Change opportunities provided by an XPress Tags file can be a real boon if you're creating documents in a *template* that is occasionally updated by a designer. For example, say you're documenting a program, and the template dictates that any word that appears in the program interface should be 75% Pantone 541. You've been working in this template for several months when the designer changes his mind and decides he wants all interface words to be 90% Pantone 371. You might be able to fix the color problem by changing the definition of Pantone 541—provided the color isn't used for anything else—but how do you run a find/change on the shade?

The non-XPress-Tags-savvy answer to this dilemma is to go through all the documentation and manually change each instance of the color/shade pair. The XPress-Tags-savvy answer, though, is much simpler. First, you export the file in XPress Tags format (the results might look something like this):

```
@Text 01:<$>Choose <$s75c"PANTONE 541 CV">Image -<\>>
Mutilate <$s100c$>to display the <$s75c"PANTONE 541
CV">Mutilate Image <$s100c$>dialog box.
```

Then you run a search-and-replace, replacing all occurrences of `s75c"PANTONE 541 CV"` with `s90c"PANTONE 371 CV"`, to get:

```
@Text 01:<$>Choose <$s90c"PANTONE 371 CV">Image -<\>>
Mutilate <$s100c$>to display the <$s90c"PANTONE 371
CV">Mutilate Image <$s100c$>dialog box.
```

Then you save the resulting text file, and import it into the template with **Import Style Sheets** on.

SEE ALSO

➤ *To save a file as a template, see page 90*

Using Book Files

Create files to build into a book

Create a book file to organize files as chapters

Add, remove, and reorder chapters in a book

Use a book to open or print chapters

Automate page numbering within a book

Synchronize styles in chapters within a book

Don't let the name fool you—*books* are not just for publishing books. A book is a collection of QuarkXPress documents that multiple users can access through a palette (see Figure 23.1). The Book palette provides options for tracking multiple documents, ensuring consistency among documents, and controlling page numbering. Whenever you work on a multiple-document publication, you can manage the files by collecting them into a book. Magazines and catalogs are great candidates for the Book feature. Although the Book feature is intended for multiple users working on the same publication, it works even better for a single user managing a long document.

FIGURE 23.1

A book contains links to all the documents that make up a publication. The Book palette lets you open the associated documents (called chapters), rearrange chapters, and print chapters.

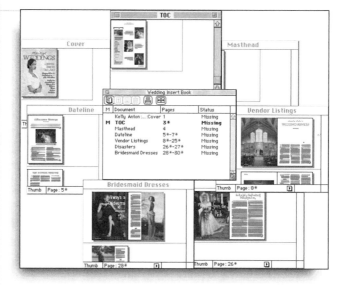

The advantages to using the Book feature include automatic page numbering across documents, consistency among styles throughout a book, and easy file tracking. You can also create tables of contents and indexes for all the documents in a book. The one big disadvantage of the Book feature is that it's set up to force multiple users to open and edit documents over a network.

(Network traffic can make opening and saving documents extremely slow, and it can make documents susceptible to corruption. Depending on the type of network, you may not be able to save over the network at all.) There are workarounds for editing over the network, but they almost negate the benefits of using the Book feature in the first place. After you understand the Book feature in full, and take a look at your workflow, you can decide whether you can work across a network or if you can tolerate the workarounds.

SEE ALSO

➤ *To create tables of contents, see page 592*

➤ *To create indexes, see page 600*

Creating a Template for Book Chapters

Before you jump right in and create your book, you need a good *template* for the documents (called chapters) that will be part of the book. The template should be the starting point for most chapters in the book (with the exception of maybe the cover and divider pages).

Include Everything You Need

To reap all the benefits of using the Book feature, it's especially important that you start with a strong template. The template should include all the *master pages* necessary for the book, with *automatic page numbering* specified on the appropriate master pages (see Figure 23.2). If your book has continuous page numbering, automatic page numbers update all by themselves when you rearrange chapters in a book. In addition, the template should include any *paragraph style sheets*, *character style sheets*, colors, *H&Js*, *lists*, and *Dashes & Stripes* patterns that might be used in the book. Eventually, if you need to update any of those settings, you can modify them in one chapter and have the changes affect all other chapters.

Use automatic page numbering

Whether your book will have continuous page numbering or be divided into sections of page numbers, you should use automatic page numbering for chapters. To create an automatic page number within chapters, type ⌘+3 (Ctrl+3) on a master page. If you opt for the alternative of simply typing a big number on each page in your document, QuarkXPress has no idea that those characters are page numbers and you'll gain none of the page numbering benefits of the Book feature.

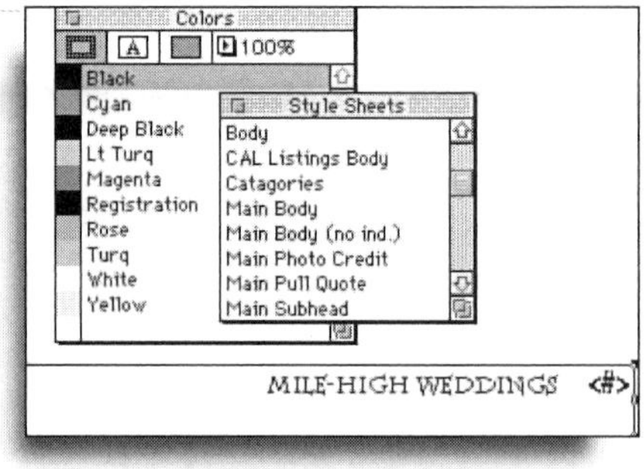

FIGURE 23.2

Create all the colors, style sheets, and master pages used in the publication, and make sure to specify automatic page numbers on the master pages.

SEE ALSO

➤ *To create master pages, see page 155*

➤ *To create paragraph style sheets, see page 298*

➤ *To create character style sheets, see page 299*

➤ *To create colors, see page 426*

➤ *To create hyphenation and justification settings (H&Js) , see page 270*

➤ *To create lists for generating tables of contents, see page 593*

➤ *To create Dashes & Stripes, see page 117*

➤ *To design an efficient template, see page 200*

➤ *To create automatic page numbers, see page 172*

➤ *To view master pages, see page 151*

Delete Everything You Don't Need

Although it's important that your template include everything that might be used throughout a book, be sure to strip out extraneous information. Get rid of the default red, green, and blue colors, and make sure the colors list contains only colors that are intended for output of the document. For example, if you know it's a *process color* job, don't include *spot colors*. If you have multiple users working on the book, you'll want to make the template as foolproof as possible, so don't give them options they shouldn't be touching. In addition to deleting unused colors, be sure to delete any and all master pages, style sheets, H&Js, and Dashes & Stripes that should not be used in the publication.

SEE ALSO

➤ *To delete colors, see page 431*
➤ *To delete master pages, see page 163*
➤ *To delete style sheets, see page 295*
➤ *To delete H&J settings, see page 277*
➤ *To delete Dashes & Stripes, see page 122*

The Completed Template

When you're happy with the template formatting, be sure to actually save the document as a template in the Save As dialog box. You can then use the template to start creating documents for the book.

One of the documents in the book will eventually become the book's *master chapter*, which defines the style sheets, colors, H&Js, lists, and Dashes & Stripes that the designer intended for use throughout the book. After you start working on chapters in a book, you may find that you need to update a style throughout the book. The Book palette allows you to *synchronize* all the styles in the other chapters to match the master chapter. Synchronizing is also handy when you suspect that users have been rebelliously modifying styles in individual chapters. The capability to synchronize styles and update automatic page numbers—and the simple fact that long documents usually have consistent formatting throughout—rely on a solid template.

All that said, the reality is that you don't need to prepare a template for a book. You can wing it and place any old documents you want in a book. If you have a publication with an original design for each and every page, and all you want is to keep track of files, you can skip the template preparation.

SEE ALSO
➤ *To save a document as a template, see page 90*
➤ *To synchronize chapters in a book, see page 588*

Creating Documents for Use in a Book

Because chapters in a book are just documents, all you do is create documents from your template, or even just placeholder documents. Because you can add and remove chapters from a book at any time, if you're in a workgroup, you need to start out with a document for each chapter. For example, if you split out all the articles in a magazine into different documents, create a document for each one.

SEE ALSO

➤ *To create new documents, see page 84*

Names

Give your documents short, logical names; there's not a ton of room in the palette for displaying chapter names. The chapters sort any way you want them to in a book, so you don't need to worry about having the file names in alphabetic or numeric order. Remember that you have another level of hierarchy using books—if your book is called "Frogs," there's no reason to put the word "Frogs" in each chapter name. As with any other document, you can change the name of a chapter in a book any time. However, it can't hurt to establish naming conventions up front.

SEE ALSO

➤ *To save new documents, see page 88*

Storage

Keep it all together

Store all the supplies for the book—libraries, graphics, site-licensed fonts, auxiliary dictionaries, XPress Preferences, and so on—in the same folder as the book so everyone has access to them.

Next you have to decide where to put those documents. If it's just you working on a book, put all the documents in one folder (see Figure 23.3). In a workgroup, it's a whole other story. What you do is have multiple users open copies of the book file, which you have stored on a shared drive or network server (much like QuarkXPress libraries have always worked). The users open the chapters they're working on through the palette. This is where file sharing takes over. To open chapters, users need access to the location of the documents. You can put the book file and all the chapters in one shared location for access by all users, or you can divide up the chapters into limited access folders. Users may have access to all the chapters or only to the chapters assigned to them. (But, of course, users must have file-sharing access to the book file.) You can move your documents any time and update their location through the Book palette. All this file storage and sharing happens at the operating system level, not through QuarkXPress.

FIGURE 23.3

You can store all the chapters of a book, and the book file itself, in one folder. However, if you have multiple users accessing the book, you might want to set up limited access folders for different chapters.

Creating a Book File

This is the easiest part of working with books. Choose **Book** from the **New** submenu of the **File** menu. In the New Book dialog box, choose a location for the book file. If multiple users will be accessing the book, store it in an appropriately shared location (or move it later). Enter a name for the book and click **Create**. Your new book is a palette that displays in front of all open documents. The book stays open until you close it; it even reopens automatically when you restart QuarkXPress.

The buttons at the top of the palette let you add and manipulate chapters in the book (see Figure 23.4). The buttons, described from left to right across the top of the palette, do the following: the **Add Chapter** button ▦ adds chapters, the **Move Chapter Up** button ⬆ moves chapters up in the list, the **Move Chapter Down** ⬇ button moves chapters down in the list, the **Remove Chapter** ▦ button deletes chapters, the **Print Chapters** ▦ button prints selected chapters, and the **Synchronize Book** button ▦ synchronizes styles in chapters.

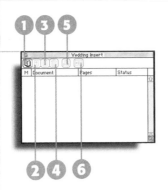

FIGURE 23.4

Buttons across the top of the
Book palette let you add,
rearrange, remove, print, and
synchronize chapters.

1. Add Chapter button

2. Move Chapter Up button

3. Move Chapter Down button

4. Remove Chapter button

5. Print Chapters button

6. Synchronize Book button

Don't worry, be happy

Don't worry if you accidentally add
the wrong document to a book. You
can remove it from the book without affecting the document.

Adding Chapters to a Book

The first chapter you add to the book is, by default, the master
chapter. Because the master chapter is the basis for all styles
used in the book, make sure to add a chapter based on the book's
template (not, for example, the book's cover). Click the **Add
Chapter** button 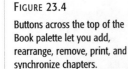 on the palette and use the Add New
Chapter dialog box to select the first chapter. Click **Add**. (If the
document was created in a previous version of QuarkXPress, a
warning lets you know that the document will be updated to the
QuarkXPress 4 file format. This is necessary and harmless, so
click **OK**.) Although this automatically becomes the master
chapter (indicated by the bold **M** to the left of the chapter
name), you can change the master chapter later.

Once you add your master chapter, use the **Add Chapter** button
and Add New Chapter dialog box to add all the chapters that are
ready for the book. You can add up to 1,000 chapters to an individual book, but if you try to put the same chapter in two different books, QuarkXPress warns you that this may not be a good
idea. New chapters are added after the selected chapter in the
Book palette. If no chapter is selected, new chapters are added to
the end of the list. You can reorder chapters quickly, so the initial order doesn't matter that much. As you continue to work on
the book, you can add chapters in this manner any time you
want.

The chapter list portion of the Book palette, shown in Figure
23.4, provides the following information:

- The **M** column displays an M next to the book's master chapter.

- The **Document** column displays the name of the QuarkXPress document.

- The **Pages** column displays either continuous page numbering or individual sections (indicated by asterisks).

- The **Status** column indicates whether the chapter is Available, Open, Modified, or Missing.

If you're familiar with the picture file status notations in the **Picture** tab of the Usage dialog box, you'll understand the possible messages for chapter status pretty quickly.

- **Available** means the chapter is sitting there in its folder waiting to be opened by someone.

- **Open** means that you have the chapter open on your machine.

- **A user name** (actually the name of that person's computer) indicates that someone else has the chapter open.

- **Modified** means someone opened the chapter through the **Open** command in the **File** menu, edited it, and closed it. The changes will not be recorded to the book until the chapter is opened through the Book palette.

- **Missing** means that the document file for the chapter was moved from its original location. You can locate a missing chapter by attempting to open it through the Book palette.

To open, print, and synchronize chapters, they need to be **Available**. You can reorder chapters regardless of their status.

Saving Books

The only way to save changes to a book is to close it. Once you add your initial chapters, close the book and reopen it before continuing to work. Then, while you're working on the book, close it periodically to save changes. (If you quit QuarkXPress every night before going home, that may be enough saving for you.) Saving a book does not save changes to the documents within the book.

Opening Books and Chapters

There's no mystery to opening books—it's just like opening a document or library. You can locate the file icon and double-click it, or choose **Open** from the **File** menu and locate the book file. Select the book file and click **Open**. (As with other shared files, the book must be in a location you have access to.) A copy of the Book palette opens on your machine. As with libraries, multiple users can open the same book file. Any changes made to the book are reflected in all open copies of the book. You can open up to 25 books at a time, in addition to the combined 25 documents and libraries you may have open.

There are two ways to open chapters. The first is obvious—through the Book palette. The other method, through the **Open** command in the **File** menu, allows you to edit chapters offline when you don't have access to the entire book.

Opening Chapters Through Books

In most cases, you'll open a chapter through its Book palette. All you do is double-click its name. If the status is **Available**, the chapter will open right up. If the status is **Modified** or **Missing**, the Locate Chapter dialog box allows you to find the chapter and update its link to the book (see Figure 23.5).

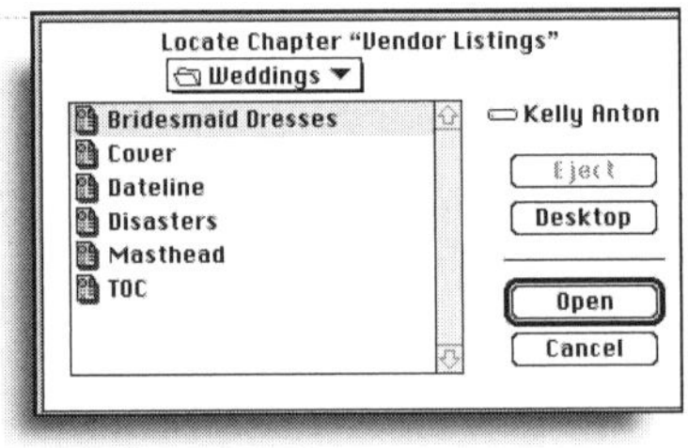

FIGURE 23.5

The Locate Chapter dialog box is similar to the Missing/Modified Picture dialog box; it lets you find and select the file.

Unfortunately, this chapter opening operation doesn't save a copy of the chapter on your hard drive while you're working. You're just working over the network, with the document still on the server. If the files are small enough and the network fast enough, this may be manageable. But if your files are huge, working over the network probably isn't realistic. And depending on the type of network, you may not be able to perform saves at all. You may have to resort to copying the picture to your hard drive and using the **Open** command.

Opening Chapters Via the Open Command

The second method for opening chapters is using the **Open** command in the **File** menu. In this case, you're opening the chapter outside of its book. This is okay, except the Book palette won't report to other users that you have the chapter open. And depending on your page numbering scheme, the page numbers may not be correct while you're working on the chapter offline. The chapter can't see the other chapters to know where its page numbering should start.

There's not much reason to open a chapter this way over the network. If you're going to do this, you'll want to drag a copy of the chapter to your own hard drive to edit. To make sure that nobody else starts editing your precious chapter in the meantime, move the chapter to another folder so it's reported as **Missing** in the Book palette. After you edit the chapter, you can drag the updated chapter back into the correct location. Whenever you edit a chapter offline and then return it to its original location, its status changes to **Modified** in the Book palette. To update it, all you need to do is double-click it. Locate the chapter and click **Open**.

SEE ALSO

➤ *To open documents, see page 88*

Assigning and Updating Page Numbers in a Book

The way page numbering works in a book depends on how it's set up in the chapters. Your chapters might have continuous page numbers only, *section page numbers* only, or a combination of the two. A section is a group of individually numbered pages within a document that you create using the Section dialog box. Sections, for example, allow you to divide up the page

---

Networks may hinder working with books

If it's just you working on a book on your hard drive, there are no drawbacks to the Book feature. It's a great way to keep track of your files, update your page numbers, and ensure consistency among documents. While these characteristics also apply to books used in a workgroup, the matter of working over the network may outweigh the benefits. It's worth experimenting with opening books through the Book palette and copying them to your hard drive to see if either method—or a combination of both—works for your projects. You might even try making your books later; produce draft chapters from the book's template on local machines and then combine the files into a book for minor edits and page numbering later.

numbering of introductory material (with lowercase Roman numerals i, ii, iii, and so on) from the remainder of a book (with standard numerals 1, 2, 3, and so on). Section page numbers can also contain a prefix such as "A.4" or "3.2."

Continuous Page Numbers

If all your chapters have continuous page numbers (from 1 to end with no sections), when you add the chapters to a book, the page numbers become sequential throughout the book. This means that if the first chapter ends on page 16, the second chapter starts on page 17. When you rearrange chapters in the book, the page numbers update accordingly.

In books with facing-page chapters, the Book feature assigns odd page numbers to right-facing pages and even page numbers to left-facing pages, regardless of the number of actual pages (see Figure 23.6). It also assumes that all chapters start on a right-facing page. For example, if the first chapter contains pages 1–5 (ending on a right-facing page), the first page of the second chapter is page 7. The Book feature assumes you'll add a blank left-facing page 6 to the end of the first chapter.

FIGURE 23.6

In books made up of facing-page chapters, QuarkXPress assumes that the first page of a chapter begins on the right.

Section Page Numbers

If all your chapters have *section starts* on the first page, when you add the chapters to a book, the page numbering does not change. The Book feature respects your page numbering scheme; even if you rearrange chapters, the page numbers stay the same (see Figure 23.7).

SEE ALSO

➤ *To start section page numbering, see page 173*

FIGURE 23.7

Section page numbers are maintained within the book even if you reorder the chapters.

Combining Continuous and Section Page Numbers

If you have a combination of chapters with continuous page numbers and section page numbers, the page numbering depends on chapter order. If a chapter contains a section start on its first page, the book assigns section page numbers to that chapter. If a chapter does not contain a section start on the first page, it starts up where the last page of the previous chapter left off. If the last page of the previous chapter is section page number 3.12, the first page of the next chapter is page 3.13. If the last page of the previous chapter is continuous page number 172, the first page of the next chapter is page 173.

Whenever the book encounters a section start in a chapter, that section start remains in effect throughout the following chapters until the book finds the next section start (see Figure 23.8). If a section starts in the middle of one chapter, and the next chapter does not contain a section start, the midchapter section start is still in power. The **Pages** column in the Book palette displays asterisks next to section page numbers (similar to the Document Layout palette).

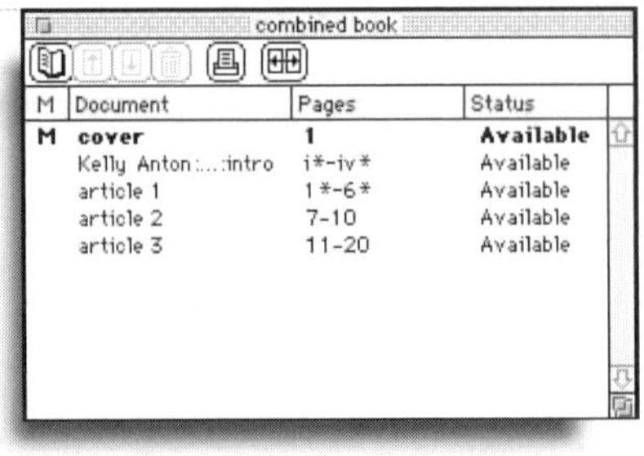

FIGURE 23.8

If you start a section in one chapter, its page numbering continues through other chapters until the book encounters another section start.

When you rearrange chapters with continuous page numbers and section page numbers, chapters without section starts continue the page numbering from the previous chapter. Chapters with section starts maintain their section starts.

Removing "Old" Section Starts

You may have used section starts in QuarkXPress 3.3 documents to mimic continuous page numbering in a publication. For example, say the first document in your publication contains pages 1–4. To start the page numbering in the second document on page 5, you create a section start. If you add these documents to a book, you no longer need the section starts. You can remove them and use the continuous page numbering implemented by the book. With continuous page numbering in effect, you can add pages, rearrange chapters, and be assured of correct page numbering.

To remove a section start, open the chapter. Press F10 to open the Document Layout palette and click the page containing the section start (indicated by an asterisk next to its page number). Click the page number field in the lower-left corner of the Document Layout palette to display the Section dialog box. Remove the check mark from **Section Start** and click **OK**. When you close the chapter, the page numbers in the book update (see Figure 23.9)

FIGURE 23.9

If you remove all the sections from a book's chapters, the pages are renumbered sequentially.

But wait a minute. What about that **Book Chapter Start** option that appears in the Section dialog box? When you removed the check mark from **Section Start**, **Book Chapter Start** appeared checked automatically. A **Book Chapter Start** essentially tells the chapter to grab its page numbering from the chapter before it. Oddly enough, when you open a chapter through its book, **Book Chapter Start** is always gray. You can never check it or remove the check mark. And while it is checked when you remove the check mark from **Section Start**, it isn't checked for chapters that never did contain a section start. The **Book Chapter Start** check box is only available when you open a chapter while its book is closed. In that case, you can remove the check mark so the document starts its page numbering at 1 rather than where the last chapter left off (see Figure 23.10).

Lefthand starting pages and books don't mix

In facing-page documents, the only way to start a document on a left-facing page is to put a section start on the first left-facing page and then delete the first right-facing page. This rule is still true of chapters in books. If you need documents to start on a left-facing page, do not remove the section starts. Unfortunately, in this scenario you can't use the automatic page numbering provided by the Book feature.

FIGURE 23.10

When you check **Book Chapter Start**, it indicates that the chapter starts its page numbering where the previous chapter left off.

Rearranging Chapters

The two arrow buttons [↑] [↓] at the top of the Book palette let you move chapters up and down in the list. The list order determines the continuous page numbering of a book. If you decide midstream to move one article in front of another, you can do so by simply moving it up in the list. To move a chapter, click to select and click the arrow to move it up or down once. Continue to click until the chapter is where you want it. You can also Option+drag (Alt+drag) chapters up and down in the list.

If the chapter has a section start on the first page, the chapter's page numbering does not change regardless of its order in the list (see Figure 23.11). If the chapter doesn't have a section start, its page numbering changes as you move it up and down in the list.

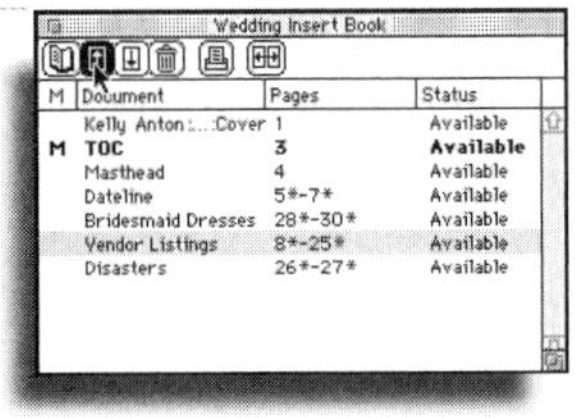

FIGURE 23.11

Chapters with section page numbering, indicated by asterisks in the **Pages** column, do not change when the chapters are reordered.

Anyone with an open copy of a book can rearrange the chapters. The chapters don't even have to be **Available**; you can have the rearranging take effect once the chapters are **Available** (closed, found, and so on). This might be a bad thing, but there's no way to stop it.

Removing Chapters from a Book

QPS works with the Book feature

If you're familiar with the Quark Publishing System, you may be concerned that you need to remove the chapters from the book to deliver them for high-resolution output. With books, that's not the case. (It's not even the case with QPS if the output provider is in-house and set up on QPS.) Book files do not require special XTensions or setup. You can and should send them off to a service bureau with their documents for output. If you don't send the book, you run the risk of altering continuous page numbering.

The reason to remove a chapter from a book is simple: The chapter is no longer appropriate for the book. Removing the chapter doesn't delete the document or anything. All it does is remove the document's links to the book; the chapter is no longer listed in the Book palette and the document can become a chapter in another book. (If the document's page numbering was based on continuous page numbering across the book, the document's page numbering will restart at page 1.)

To remove a chapter, click to select it and click the **Remove Chapter** button on the Book palette. To remove multiple chapters, Shift+click to select a range or ⌘+click (Ctrl+click) to select discontiguous chapters; then click the **Remove Chapter** button (see Figure 23.12). An alert asks you to confirm the deletion; click **OK**.

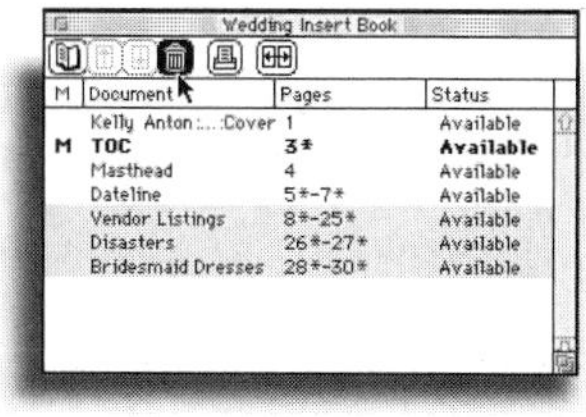

FIGURE 23.12

You can multiple-select chapters and remove them all from the book by clicking the **Remove Chapter** button.

Synchronizing Chapters

Synchronizing attempts to ensure consistent formatting among all the chapters in a book. When you synchronize a book, all the styles in each chapter are compared to a standard set of master styles defined by the master chapter. ("Styles" refers to the collection of style sheets, colors, H&Js, lists, and dashes and stripes in each chapter.) Although it doesn't go to the extent of letting you know about changes to master pages or rampant local formatting, it goes a long way toward achieving consistency.

How Synchronizing Works

Obviously, synchronizing is intended for documents that are all based on the same template. If your book consists of six articles that all have a Headline paragraph style sheet, but the style sheet is customized to each article, then synchronizing would be a bad thing. However, if the Headlines are supposed to be the same in all the articles, synchronizing helps ensure that. The **Synchronize Book** button works like this:

- Any master styles missing from a chapter are added to it.

- Any modifications to master styles are implemented in chapter styles.

- Any modifications in chapter styles are overridden by the master styles.

- Any additional styles in chapters are maintained.

The goal is to make sure the same set of style sheets, colors, H&Js, lists, and Dashes & Stripes exists in each document, while allowing each document to have some individual characteristics.

Realize that when you do synchronize, you can cause serious reflow and other changes in chapters. For example, if one user modified a table style sheet to allow for additional tabs, when you synchronize, you'll strip out those tabs. The key is to make sure your master chapter has adequate styles and that users don't modify those styles. If they need special formatting, they should format the text locally (without style sheets) or create additional style sheets. If the situation merits, they might even have their changes implemented in the master chapter.

How to Synchronize

First, notify all the book users that you'll be synchronizing. At the least, they'll have to close their chapters so synchronize can access them. At this point, the style rebels should come forward and let you know that they've been tinkering with style sheets, colors, and so on. You'll have the chance to decide whether the tinkering is OK and whether the changes should be implemented globally. If the tinkering is OK, but you don't want it to be global, the user will have to redo the formatting with additional style sheets or local formatting.

Next, confirm all the styles in your current master chapter. (The master chapter is indicated by the bold **M** in the first column of the Book palette.) If the list is complete and the definitions are correct, you're ready to synchronize. If not, modify and add styles until the master chapter is perfect (you may need to append styles from other chapters). Or make a different chapter the master chapter by selecting the chapter and clicking in the blank **M** column in the Book palette next to its name.

Then click **Synchronize Book** on the Book palette 🔳 . Click **OK** to the wordy warning so the synchronizing can start (see Figure 23.13). QuarkXPress invisibly opens, modifies, saves, and closes each chapter. If a chapter is missing or modified, the Locate Chapter dialog box asks you to find it. If QuarkXPress can't find all the chapters, you can't synchronize them.

This will modify the Style Sheets, Colors, H&Js, Lists, and Dashes & Stripes in chapters as necessary to match those in the master chapter.

`Cancel`

`OK`

FIGURE 23.13

When you click **Synchronize Book**, this alert describes precisely what will happen.

Printing Chapters

For consistent printing, you can select multiple chapters in a book and send them to the printer with the same settings. The chapters must be **Available** or **Open** on your machine. First, select all the chapters you want to print, Shift+click to select a range of chapters, and ⌘+click (Ctrl+click) to select discontiguous chapters. Then click the **Print Chapters** button 🖨 at the top of the palette (see Figure 23.14). In the Print dialog box, set up the printing specifications for all the selected chapters and click **Print**. QuarkXPress opens each chapter invisibly and sends it off to print. (You may encounter the standard Missing/Modified pictures alert for individual chapters. Deal with it as usual.) If you work with large chapters across a network, be prepared for printing to take some time.

FIGURE 23.14

You can select multiple chapters and print them with the same specifications from the Book palette.

If you deliver a book to a service bureau for printing, be sure to bring the book file. The service bureau can open and print the chapters through the Book palette; opening the chapters independent of the book file risks altering continuous page numbers.

Creating print styles for draft printing

If you print a lot of drafts, create a print style for the book. For example, if the drafts are primarily for proofing text, the print style might specify **Rough** printing (no pictures) and **Black & White** output (for sharp type). You can export the print style and share it with everyone who's working on the book. When you're ready to output color proofs and film, you or your service bureau can create print styles for those as well.

Creating Indexes and Lists

Define lists based on document style sheets

Build list contents in the Lists palette

Place formatted lists in documents

Tag text for inclusion in an index

Place formatted indexes in documents

Prior to QuarkXPress 4, working with multidocument publications such as magazines, catalogs, and books was largely a manual process. First, you had to keep track of all the files and page numbering across files. Then you had to create a table of contents by hand. And if you needed an index, that had to be created by hand or with an *XTension*. QuarkXPress 4 strives to solve long-document publishing challenges with its *Book*, *Lists*, and indexing features. Unfortunately, these first generation features could use some serious fine-tuning before they become powerful enough to meet all your long-document needs. But with some careful planning, you can make them work to your advantage. Chapter 23 introduced the Book feature; this chapter explores lists and indexes.

Tables of Contents and Other Lists

A list is a table of contents, figures list, list of dates, and so on that is pulled from a document or book and reformatted automatically. The text in the list is pulled out of documents according to *paragraph style sheets*. For example, to create a table of contents for a book, you might extract all the text in your chapter and section head style sheets, and then format it with the table of contents style sheets. You can generate an updated list any time the text in your document or book changes.

The contents of a list are an in-between state most of the time; the information has been extracted from the documents but it's not formatted as a list yet. During this time, the list content hangs around in the Lists palette. The palette allows you to view a list for a document or book, jump to the location of listed text in a document or book, update a list when text changes, and build a formatted list in a text box.

To get the most out of the Lists feature, don't limit its use to creating tables of contents. And don't limit it to long documents or lists that include page numbers. Any time you want to be sure you have the right contents and, if applicable, the right page numbers, use the Lists feature. You can build a list of contributing writers to a magazine by pulling all the text in your byline style sheet. Or you can summarize a long outline by extracting the heads and listing them at the top of a document. You may have to create more paragraph style sheets and apply them more conscientiously than before, but it's worth it.

Creating Style Sheets for Lists

Before you even think of creating a list, make all your paragraph style sheets (lists do not work with *character style sheets*). You need style sheets for the finished list (the actual table of contents) and you need style sheets for the text in the document that makes up the list.

You can start by making a mock-up of your list; your list can include up to eight levels of hierarchy. The mock-up ensures that you'll create all the necessary paragraph style sheets for the list, and it forces you to identify the text in the document that corresponds to the text in the list. Once you have identified the needs of your list, create all your paragraph style sheets. Keep your style sheet names short because the area that displays them in the Edit List dialog box is, unfortunately, tiny. If you create a list for an entire book, make sure the appropriate style sheets are used in each chapter.

In a book TOC scenario, you might make four style sheets: Chapter Name, Section Head, TOCChapter Name, and TOCSection Head. The Chapter Name and Section Head style sheets will be applied to text throughout the document; the TOCChapter Name and TOCSection Head style sheets are used by the Lists feature to automatically format your list.

SEE ALSO
➤ *To create paragraph style sheets, see page 298*

Defining a List

To use the Lists feature, the first thing you have to do is define a list. The definition specifies which paragraph style sheets contain the relevant text and how that text should be formatted when it appears in the list. If you want your list to be included with all new documents, create the list when no documents are open. If your list will be used with a book, create the list in the book's original template or its master chapter. If the list is just for one document, open that document.

To define a list:

1. Select **Lists** from the **Edit** menu.

2. In the Lists dialog box, click **New**.

3. In the Edit List dialog box, type a name in the **Name** field. For the book TOCscenario, enter "Book TOC."

4. The **Available Styles** area lists all the paragraph style sheets in the document. Identify the style sheets used throughout your documents to format text that makes up the list, and don't choose style sheets used to format body text; each paragraph in a list is limited to 256 characters.

   Select each style sheet. Click to select one style sheet, Shift+click to select a range of style sheets, and ⌘+click (Ctrl+click) to select discontiguous style sheets. To put the selected style sheet(s) in the **Styles in List** area, double-click or click the arrow. A list can include up to 32 style sheets. For the Book TOC, enter the Chapter Name and Section Head style sheets.

5. The **Styles in List** area is where the list styles are assigned functions. Choose a **Level** to assign a hierarchy to text in the list; the hierarchy is indicated by indents in the Lists palette. Make the Chapter Name style sheet **Level 1** and the Section Head style sheet **Level 2**. There can be as many as eight different levels.

6. Some parts of a list will include page numbers and other parts will not. In fact, some lists won't have page numbers at all. The **Numbering Options** are fairly self-evident: **Text Only** suppresses page number, **Text Page #** places the page number after the list text, and **Page # Text** places the page number before list text. For a list with page numbers, a tab separates the text and the page number in the final list. In the Book TOC, don't include page numbers for the Chapter

Name style sheet, but do include page numbers for the Section Head style sheet.

7. When QuarkXPress builds a formatted list, it finds all the text in the appropriate paragraph style sheet, places the text hierarchically in the list, and then transforms the text by applying the paragraph style sheet used in the actual list (the table of contents and so on).

The **Format As** menu shows all the paragraph style sheets in the document; each of the styles included in the list can have a corresponding formatting style sheet. In the Book TOC, text in the Chapter Name style sheet gets formatted as TOCChapter Name and the Section Head text gets formatted as TOCSection Head (see Figure 24.1).

8. By default, QuarkXPress creates lists according to text box creation order. To make the list to be alphabetical within each level, check **Alphabetical**. A table of contents wouldn't make sense in alphabetical order, so don't check it in the Book TOC.

9. Click **OK** and the new list shows at the top of the Lists dialog box. Click **Save** to start using the list.

Creating Lists in the Lists Palette

The Lists palette is the holding place for lists in flux. You can use the Lists palette to choose which list you want to display and work with, whether that list is for a document or an entire book, and to update the active list if text in the documents has changed.

To display and update a list in the Lists palette:

1. Open the Lists palette by choosing **Show Lists** from near the bottom of the **View** menu. The Lists palette is large and empty.

2. The **Show List For** menu can create a list for any open book or for the active document. To create a table of contents for a whole book, make sure that book is open and all the chapters are **Available**. To create a list for the current document only, choose **Current Document**.

3. If **Current Document** is selected, the **List Name** menu contains all the lists defined in the active document. If a book is selected in the **Show List For** menu, the **List Name** menu shows all the lists defined for the book's master chapter. Select the list to display.

4. Click **Update**. QuarkXPress builds the list by looking at the active document or all the book chapters, finding all the relevant text, and sorting it hierarchically at the bottom of the Lists palette (see Figure 24.2).

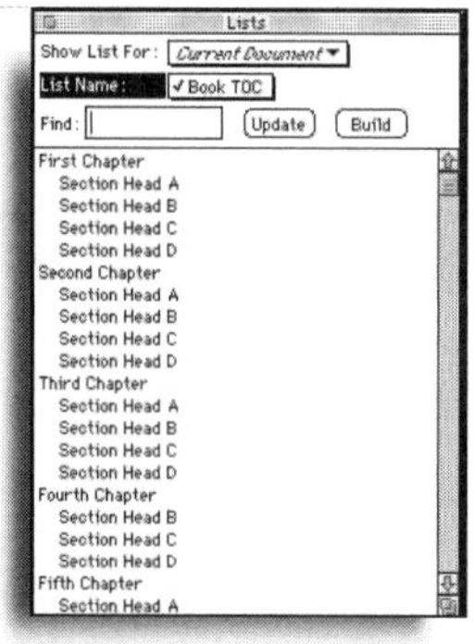

FIGURE 24.2

The **Update** button regenerates the contents of the list shown in the lower portion of the Lists palette.

5. Any time the text changes, click **Update** to generate a new list.

You can keep this list around while you work, or you can build it right away, close the Lists palette, and move on.

Navigating with the Lists Palette

The Lists palette allows you to navigate through a document or book by double-clicking any entry in the list. If the entry is in the active document, QuarkXPress automatically jumps to that location in the document. If the entry is in a book chapter, QuarkXPress opens the chapter (if it's Available) and jumps to that location in the document. This can be handy if you scroll through a list and notice that one of the headings is lacking parallel construction. You can double-click the heading to jump to the text, edit the text, and then update the list.

If your list is long and you don't feel like scrolling through it to find a particular entry, you can type an entry in the **Find** field. QuarkXPress jumps to the location of that text in the list. Unlike Find/Change, the **Find** field has no concept of "Find First" or "Find Next"; all it can do is find the first reference of text you type in.

Placing Formatted Lists in Documents

Although lists that are hanging around in the Lists palette are handy for navigation, that's probably not why you created them. You want to use that list somewhere in the publication and you want it to be correctly formatted.

First, open the QuarkXPress document or book chapter that will contain the formatted list (for example, the document containing the table of contents). This document does not need to contain any of the text the list is generated from, but it does need to contain the list definition. If for some reason it does not, use the **Append** command in the **File** menu to import the list definition from another document. The correct paragraph style sheets will come right along with it. If you work on a book, you can add the list definition to the chapter by *synchronizing*.

To add the list definition to the chapter:

1. Open the Lists palette by choosing **Show Lists** from the **View** menu.

2. Use the **Show List For** and **List Name** menus to display the list to be inserted into the document.

Don't make lists part of an existing text flow

If your list will contain page numbers, do not put the list in a text box containing text from which the list was built. If you do, the text will reflow, but the list won't know it and it will show incorrect page numbers.

3. Make sure all the chapters of a book are Available so QuarkXPress can create the most up-to-date list.

4. Select the *text box* that will contain the formatted list. If the list is long, select an automatic text box or a box that's already linked to an adequate number of boxes.

5. Click **Build**. The list text is flowed into the text box and the **Format As** paragraph style sheets specified for the list are applied automatically. Page numbers are inserted according to the specifications (see Figure 24.3).

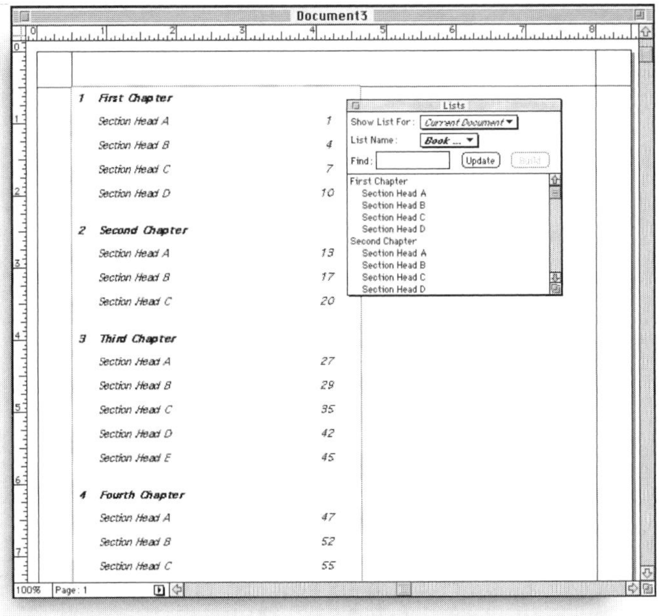

FIGURE 24.3

When you build a list, the text in the palette is flowed into the active text box and formatted.

If the list is just a placeholder to get an idea how long the final list will be, you can save the document and move on.

If this is the final list, you might want to apply additional formatting in the document. For example, if the list contains page numbers, you can apply a character style sheet to change the color and type style of the numbers. Or maybe you didn't anticipate the tab between the text and page number and forgot to specify *tab leaders*; you can edit the style sheet to refine the tab.

Sometimes, you have to delete text from a built list. If you pull a list of contributors from a magazine's byline paragraph style sheet, each line in the list might look like "By Robert Writer." The "By" is extraneous so you need to delete it from each line in the list.

Remember, for the list to be "final," you need to be sure you're finished editing the text. Once the list is in a document, it's just text. There are no links between a list and the text it was extracted from. If you edit the text, you have to build the list again. If you edit or apply additional formatting to the built list, you have to do that each time you recreate it. Even if you took precautions in making your final list, you may not have much luck convincing a copy editor that there's no need to check the list against the contents of a document or book.

SEE ALSO

➤ *To append lists from other documents, see page 146*

➤ *To synchronize chapters in a book, see page 588*

Updating and Replacing Lists

When you create a list in the Lists palette, all you're doing is capturing a moment in time. There are no dynamic links between the text that is formatted with list style sheets, the text displayed in the Lists palette, and the formatted list placed in a document. As you continue to work on documents or books that contain lists, you need to update the lists. All you do is click the **Update** button on the palette. If you're updating a list for a book, all the book chapters need to be **Available**.

One nice thing does happen when you try to build a list that already exists in a document. When you click **Build**, QuarkXPress checks out the current document to see if you've already placed the list in it somewhere. If so, it gives you an alert. You can choose whether to keep the old list and place the current list somewhere else, or you can replace the existing list.

When you get a text overflow symbol instead of a list

What if you build a list and you don't see anything but an overflow symbol ⊠ in the text box? Is it because your **Format As** style sheets are trying to squeeze 120-point type in a 2″ text box? Possibly, but probably not. Sometimes, it's overuse of **Keep with Next** ¶ causing the problem. If you have **Keep with Next** ¶ specified for most or all of the style sheets used to format the list, the paragraphs are all stuck together so they can't fit in the box. To confirm this diagnosis, press ⌘+A (Ctrl+A) to select all the text in the box. Choose **Paragraph Attributes** from the **Style** menu. If the **Keep with Next** ¶ check box is gray or checked, don't check it, and then click **Apply**. If your text displays now, you've located the problem. But don't solve the problem in this sloppy way. Click **Cancel** and then edit the paragraph style sheets used in the list appropriately.

Hints for Working with Lists

When you work with lists in QuarkXPress:

- Apply the correct paragraph style sheet to any text that will be included in a list. This is the only way to get text into a list.

- Don't include special characters in list text if you can help it. Although the characters will translate properly into the final list, they won't display properly in the Lists palette.

- Don't apply paragraph style sheets used in lists to non-text items (for example, a paragraph return or next box character). This results in "holes" in your built list.

- Don't delete any of the paragraph style sheets used in lists.

- Test your list definition on an early draft of the publication. Edit the list definition and style sheets as necessary.

- Update your lists every time you open the Lists palette.

- Build the final list only when you're sure the text in the publication is frozen.

- Perform final edits on your final list.

- Have faith in lists. Don't drive yourself crazy checking over lists if you're confident that you carefully formatted all your text and built the most up-to-date list.

Indexes

The QuarkXPress Index XTension allows you to tag text for the index; assign hierarchy and styles to the text; build the index with the appropriate formatting and punctuation; and generate an updated index when the text changes. However, if you know anything about indexing, you know that QuarkXPress is not doing the indexing for you. The features in QuarkXPress are intended for a thoughtful indexer—that means a person—to create a detailed, conceptual index. The indexing features do not lend themselves to indexes compiled from a word list or indexes that are lists of things on a page rather than concepts on a page.

The feature is intended for one person to go through each page in a document, evaluate it, and tag its contents for the index. Basically, the task of deciding what goes in the index and how it's listed is still manual. What's automated is the laborious task of typing the index, formatting it, and then updating it if the text changes. Beware of calling it automatic indexing; the Index XTension doesn't make good indexers any more than design software makes good designers.

Selecting Your Index Process

The hard thing about indexing is not the actual task in QuarkXPress. It's the strategy. You need answers to a whole lot of questions before you even touch QuarkXPress:

- What type of index does the document require? A simple index like one you might find in a cookbook? Or a complex, multileveled, cross-referenced index you might find in a how-to-take-care-of-a-baby book?

- Will the index be nested (with up to four levels of hierarchy usually indicated by deeper indents) or run-in (with two levels of hierarchy in paragraph form)?

- How long will the indexing process take for each chapter? Do you need to schedule time to make one indexing pass while the documents are in flux and then another pass for the final index? Or will the indexing all be post-production?

- Who will create the index? If your writers are working in QuarkXPress, do you expect them to tag words as they write? For more complex indexes, will you use professional indexers in the organization or hire a freelance indexer?

- How will the indexer ensure consistency across multiple documents? Is there a word/concept list for the indexer to start from?

The answers to these questions determine who will use the QuarkXPress Index XTension and how they will use it. When you have the answers to these questions, you can start to prepare your QuarkXPress documents.

Preparing to Index

You might want to dive right in and start tagging words for an index, figuring you'll clean up any problems later. Don't. You'll be sorry. Your tags may not make sense within the final index and you'll have to do a whole bunch of editing. For example, what if you're halfway through the index for a manual and you decide you want to italicize all the cross-references? First, you have to create a character style sheet that specifies italic type style or an oblique font. Then, you have to go back and find each cross-reference you created and choose that character style sheet for it. Or it might be something more disastrous such as tagging text for a four-level nested index while the book calls for a run-in index (which is inherently two levels).

A few short steps at the beginning can save you lots of time later.

Creating a Mock-Up of the Final Index

What you need to do is work backward. First create a mock-up of the finished index design. The mock-up needs to include the index *master page*, paragraph style sheets for alphabetic dividers (A, B, C, and so on), paragraph style sheets for all the levels in the index, character style sheets for any special formatting within the index, and the punctuation used throughout the index. Obviously, the mock-up will indicate whether the index is nested or run-in and have appropriate style sheets for the respective format.

In a nested index (with multiple levels), each level is usually indicated by a deeper indent. You should include these indents (or another provision for indicating levels) in the paragraph style sheet. QuarkXPress will not insert these indents in the built index for you. Name the style sheets like this: Letter Headings, First Level, Second Level, Third Level, and Fourth Level. These are the names of menus that you choose style sheets from in the Build Index dialog box. When you build the index, you'll have no question about which style sheet to choose.

The index master page should also contain an *automatic text box*. You'll refer to the mock-up as you set index preferences, tag text for the index, and build the index, so keep it on hand (see Figure 24.4).

Copy from a standard format

Most large publishing houses have standard index formats that have been tested by readers for legibility and ease of use. If you're unsure of how to format an index, check the index of a similar book from a well-known publisher.

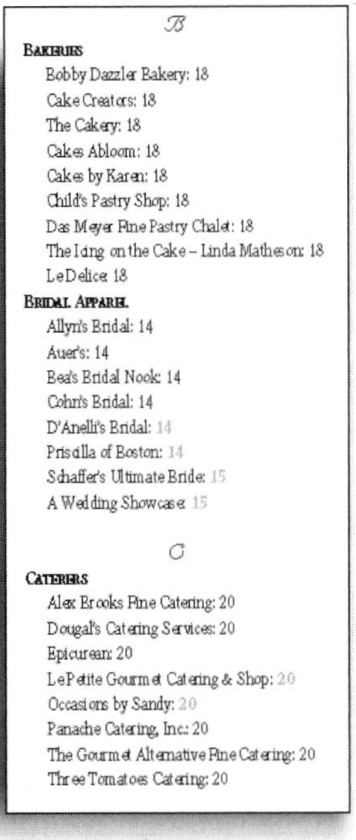

B

BAKERIES
Bobby Dazzler Bakery: 18
Cake Creators: 18
The Cakery: 18
Cakes Abloom: 18
Cakes by Karen: 18
Child's Pastry Shop: 18
Das Meyer Fine Pastry Chalet: 18
The Icing on the Cake – Linda Matheson: 18
LeDelice: 18
BRIDAL APPAREL
Allyn's Bridal: 14
Auer's: 14
Bea's Bridal Nook: 14
Cohn's Bridal: 14
D'Anelli's Bridal: 14
Priscilla of Boston: 14
Schaffer's Ultimate Bride: 15
A Wedding Showcase: 15

C

CATERERS
Alex Brooks Fine Catering: 20
Dougal's Catering Services: 20
Epicurean: 20
LePetite Gourmet Catering & Shop: 20
Occasions by Sandy: 20
Panache Catering, Inc.: 20
The Gourmet Alternative Fine Catering: 20
Three Tomatoes Catering: 20

FIGURE 24.4

Your index mock-up should reflect the hierarchy, formatting, and punctuation of your final index.

SEE ALSO

- *To create master pages, see page 155*
- *To create paragraph style sheets, see page 298*
- *To create character style sheets, see page 299*
- *To create an automatic text box, see page 190*

Preparing Documents and Books

You can build an index for either a document or a book. If you're indexing one document, make sure the index style sheets and master pages from the index mock-up are included in the document. If you're indexing a book, use the synchronize feature to add all the index style sheets to all the chapters in the book. You only need the index master pages in the chapter that will actually contain the index.

SEE ALSO

- *To append style sheets from a document, see page 146*
- *To synchronize chapters in a book, see page 588*

Alternative ways to index multiple documents

The only way to create one index for multiple documents is through the Book feature. But, this doesn't mean you actually have to use a book in your workflow. If books don't work for you, you can tag the documents individually for the index and then pop them in a book to build the index. (Make sure the page numbering in the documents isn't changed by the Book feature.) When the index is final, you can pull the documents out of the book. When you tag text, it doesn't make any difference whether the documents are part of a book or not. The Index palette can display only the index for the current document, not for the whole book. An alternative to using books for multiple-document indexing is to merge the documents into one document via thumbnail drag. If you're going to do this, it had better be a fairly small book.

Creating a Word List

The Index XTension won't let you import a word list or existing index to start indexing from, and you can't build an index by searching for and listing all instances of a word. People who have no idea how to index will therefore maintain that the indexing features in QuarkXPress are "useless." That is not the case. In fact, QuarkXPress may help produce better indexes by forcing indexers to take a good look at the contents of a page and decide what goes in the index. What if, for example, the index for this book listed every page that contains the word "preference" under the "Preferences" entry. The word "preference" probably appears every five or ten pages. The reader would have a terrible time identifying the pages where preferences are covered in full.

That said, a word list or existing index is extremely useful for creating a consistent and thorough index. For one thing, it lays out all the possibilities. If you see "preference" in the word list, it reminds you to look at each page to see if that word appears and to then determine if its use is significant enough for the index. A word list also helps you keep language consistent; you don't want to end up with three different headings such as "pre-ferred settings," "preference," and "preferences" for the same concept.

The key here is to not let QuarkXPress handicap you. There's no reason not to create a word list or start from an existing index just because you can't import it into QuarkXPress. Just print out a copy and refer to it as you tag index text onscreen.

SEE ALSO

➤ *To print documents, see page 495*

Installing the Index XTension

The Index XTension is installed by default, but it's disabled because most people don't index. To enable it choose **XTensions Manager** from the **Utilities** menu. Choose an XTensions set that includes the Index XTension or select the Index XTension in the list and choose **Yes** from the **Enable** menu. If you can't find the Index XTension in the list, you probably didn't install it. You need to copy the XTension from the QuarkXPress CD, place it in your XTension folder, and make sure it's enabled in the XTensions Manager. After enabling the Index XTension, restart QuarkXPress.

SEE ALSO

➤ *To install XTensions, see page 557*

➤ *To enable and disable XTensions, see page 555*

Index Palette Overview

To tag words for an index, you need to be familiar with the Index palette. The palette is divided into three sections: the **Entry** area, which is where you specify the text of an index entry; the **Reference** area, where you describe the page numbers that should be listed for the entry; and the **Entries** area, which shows everything you tagged for the index (see Figure 24.5). To open the Index palette, choose **Show Index** from the **View** menu or press ⌘+Option+I (Ctrl+Alt+I).

Index tags don't require the Index XTension

Opening and editing documents that contain index tags does not require the Index XTension. If you are not indexing or generating indexes, you can disable the Index XTension to free up more RAM for other QuarkXPress operations.

FIGURE 24.5

The Index palette lets you add entries to the index for the current document.

Entry Section

The **Entry** section at the top of the Index palette is where you define the text that is listed in the index.

Text Field

The **Text** field is where you enter the text that actually appears in the index. If you highlight text in the document, it's automatically placed in the **Text** field. You can use this text as your index entry, edit it, or replace it. The highlighted text still marks the start of the index entry. If text is not highlighted in the document, you can "mark" a place for the index entry by placing the text insertion bar in text. Then you can type an entry in the **Text** field.

Most of the time, the **Text** field contains an instance of a word or a phrase that summarizes some text on the page. Although the **Text** field can contain up to 255 characters, it's doubtful that you'll ever bump into that limit.

Sort As Field

The **Sort As** field allows you to change the alphabetic sorting of a word. QuarkXPress normally sorts index entries according to the *ASCII* table: first spaces, then symbols, then punctuation, then numbers, then the alphabet. You can copy the text in the **Text** field, paste it in the **Sort As** field, and then edit it.

The **Sort As** field is useful for listing numbers according to their spelling ("21st" under "Twenty-first"), listing abbreviations according to their full spelling ("St." as "Saint" or "Street"), and removing articles from phrases ("The Bible" under "Bible") (see Figure 24.6).

Level Menu

The **Level** menu allows you to specify the hierarchy of an index entry. A run-in index can have two levels and a nested index can have four levels, but watch out because QuarkXPress has no idea what kind of index you're trying to make. It makes levels available to you that you should not be using. Once you create a **First Level** index entry, you can start creating **Second Level** entries. After you create a **Second Level** entry, you can start creating **Third Level** entries, and so on.

FIGURE 24.6

The **Sort As** field lets you specify a different alphabetical sorting for an index entry.

When you create a **First Level** entry, it's sorted alphabetically within the other **First Level** entries. When you create a **Second Level** entry, it's placed under the **First Level** entry that has the arrow next to it. The **Second Level** entry is sorted alphabetically inside its **First Level** entry. This placement continues with **Third Level** and **Fourth Level** entries.

Reference Section

The **Reference** area is where you specify what an index entry refers to, such as a page number, a range of page numbers, or another entry (as in a cross reference). You can also use this area to apply a character style sheet to the page number(s) or cross-reference text.

If you want the page number(s) or cross reference text for an entry to look different from the index entry (for example, index entries that refer to definitions in a glossary might be italicized), you can select one of your character style sheets from the **Style** menu. The paragraph style sheet on the index entry and the character style sheet on a page number will not cancel each other out. For example, if the text in the index entry is bold, and the character style sheet also applies bold, this doesn't result in plain face text. You still get what you wanted—bold.

To specify how much text an index entry covers, you use the **Scope** menu, which offers the following choices:

- **Selection Start** specifies the page numbers that contain the index marker's open bracket. This option is useful for indexing one instance of a word or phrase.

- **Selection Text** specifies the page numbers that contain currently highlighted text. This option is useful for indexing text that is contained on more than one page (or that might eventually flow to more than one page). As a rule, **Selection Text** is a better choice than **Selection Start**, because you never know when text might break across two pages.

- **To Style** specifies the page numbers from the index marker's open bracket, through its close bracket, continuing to the point that a new (**Next**) or selected paragraph style sheet is applied. This option is useful for templates that call for style sheet changes with topic changes. (For example, in a cookbook, you might index each recipe until the next heading style sheet.)

- **Specified # of ¶** specifies the page numbers from the index marker's open bracket, through its close bracket, continuing through a specified number of paragraphs. This option is only useful if you're positive the text is frozen. If you know that the next three paragraphs cover a topic, you can enter 3 in the field. However, if you add or delete text in that area, the three paragraphs referenced by the index entry may change.

- **To End Of** specifies the page numbers from the index marker's open bracket to the end of the current **Story** or **Document**. This option is useful for indexing a broad range of text, such as a whole chapter, without highlighting it all.

- **Suppress Page #** specifies no page numbers for an index entry. This option is useful for creating headings in indexes.

- **X-Ref** specifies no page numbers; a reference to another index entry is given instead.

The **Add** button allows you to add a new index entry, or another page number/cross-reference for an existing index entry, to the Entries list.

The **Find Next** button allows you to find the next occurrence of an indexed word in a story. (Don't get excited. You can't find words in the text or specific indexed words. Basically, you get to find the next index marker.)

The **Delete** button allows you to remove an entry from an index. The entry, its page numbers, its cross-references, and all entries nested under it are removed from the index as well. You can Option+click (Alt+click) the **Delete** button to delete all index entries for an entire document.

The **Edit** button allows you to modify a selected index entry or a selected reference (a page number or cross-reference). When an index entry is selected, the **Text**, **Sort As**, and **Level** controls are available. When a reference is selected, the **Style** and **Scope** controls are available.

Entries Section

The **Entries** list displays all the entries you added to the index and all their page numbers and cross-references.

The arrow in the left column specifies which entry to place a new second level, third level, or fourth level index entry under. You can click in the column to move the arrow.

The triangle next to index entries allows you to open up an entry to display the entries nested inside it, its page numbers, and its cross-references.

The **Entries** column shows all the index entries. You can select index entries and edit or delete them. The number next to the **Entries** heading is the total number of different entries you added to the index. This number corresponds approximately to the number of paragraphs in the finished index for this document.

The **Occurrences** column lists the number of page number references and cross-references you specified for each index entry.

Tagging Text for an Index

First, you can have some fun by picking a nifty color for your index markers. Index markers are brackets around words and phrases or little flags in words that indicate indexed text. You only see index markers when the Index palette is open. The default color for index markers, red, can be a little school-teacherish, but it's easy to pick a color you like better in the Index preferences. If you're going to be passing the documents around to other indexers, take the different monitor settings into account. No need to make the perfect shade of purple on a monitor with millions of colors if it's going to display as blue everywhere it goes.

On to more serious pursuits: tagging text for the index. Before anyone starts tagging, set up the indexer with the following:

- The word list, topic list, or existing index to start from.
- Access to a copy of QuarkXPress with the Index XTension installed and running.
- The largest monitor available; it's best if the indexer can see the whole page so he can get an idea of what's on it.
- Access to all the chapters if the index is for a book.
- Greek pictures in the documents to speed up screen redraw.

The instructions for tagging text include examples from a simple two-level index. The index is actually a listing of vendors that appears in a magazine—something you commonly see in the back of a fashion magazine, for example. Once you understand the basics of tagging text through a simple example, you can easily apply those concepts to a more complex index.

SEE ALSO

➤ *To greek pictures, see page* 77

First Level Entries

First Level entries are the primary topics that make up an index. If your index is nothing but a list of words that appears in a document, those are all **First Level** entries. Depending on your indexing process, you might skim over a document once and add all the **First Level** entries, and then go back and add the necessary subentries. You need the Content tool [⌖] and the Index palette showing to start.

To tag first-level entries:

1. First, tell QuarkXPress where the text to index starts by clicking the *text insertion bar* at that location. All references to this index entry start at this location in text.

   To include more text at this point, highlight it. However, stay away from highlighting more than a word, short phrase, or paragraph. There are other methods for indicating long ranges of text than highlighting it.

2. Now define the index entry, which is the text that actually shows up in the index. To do this, click the **Text** field in the Index palette. If text was highlighted, it's already in the field and can be used as the index entry. Otherwise, type the entry in the **Text** field. In the final index, all index entries are capitalized automatically, so don't worry about the capitalization.

   If a whole bunch of text in the document is highlighted, the first 255 characters are in the **Text** field. While those 255 characters probably contain the words that should appear in the entry, it's probably faster to just delete it all and type the entry in. To get rid of the text, drag to highlight it all and hit the Delete (Backspace) key.

3. To change the way this word sorts in the index, enter the correct sorting in the **Sort As** field. This doesn't change the entry, just where it appears alphabetically in the index. Text can be cut and pasted from the **Text** field as necessary to complete the **Sort As** field. In most cases, this field won't be used.

4. Make sure the **Level** menu says **First Level**. At this point, the text for the entry, how it sorts alphabetically, and where it goes in the index hierarchy have all be defined. Next, the page numbers that will be listed for this occurrence of the index entry must be specified.

5. If the template or index formatting calls for a different style on page numbers, choose a character style sheet from the **Style** menu (see Figure 24.7).

DENVER MUSEUM OF NATURAL HISTORY, *2001 Colorado Blvd., Denver.* Rehearsal dinners, receptions. May sound strange, but the glassed atriums provide a beautiful, unique spot for large parties, with access to exhibits available. 6 p.m.-11 p.m. only; Sun-Tue only through Mar 16, 1997. Five rooms, capacities 60, 80, 200, 250, and 500. Reserve one month in advance. In-house catering only; $18-$40/person, all inclusive. Call for appointment. 370-6479 phone, 331-6492 fax.

"What a terrific location. The event coordinator will get involved to the extent you wish, the food was excellent, and the large atriums with high ceilings and marble pillars are a great setting." – Laynie, Denver

Creating entries that include an entire chapter

Often, a **First Level** entry lists all the page numbers in a chapter and then the subentries supply a breakdown of what's on all those pages. To create an entry that covers all the text in a chapter, click the text insertion bar somewhere on the first page of the chapter and choose **To End Of: Document** for the **Scope**. Even if the chapter has only one continuous text chain, don't highlight all the text and use the **Selection Text Scope**. If you add more text and pages to the end of the chapter, that text won't be included in the index entry. Plus, when you highlight all the text, a bunch of it ends up in the **Text** field and you have to delete it.

6. Tell QuarkXPress how many pages this index entry should cover using the **Scope** menu (see Figure 27.8). These are the page numbers listed in the index. Most of the time this will be something simple such as **Selection Text**, but the other scopes are useful in special situations. **Suppress Page #** is often used for headings in indexes, and **X-Ref** is used strictly for creating cross references.

7. Finally, click **Add** on the Index palette (see Figure 24.9). You have a keyboard command for this—⌘+Option+Shift+I (Ctrl+Alt+Shift+I)—but it's not that useful for indexing because so many other options require you to use the mouse anyway.

FIGURE 24.8

The **Scope** tells QuarkXPress which pages to list for the index entry. For example, an index entry might simply list the page a word is on. Or an entry might continue until the end of a section.

FIGURE 24.9

Before you click **Add**, confirm all the settings in the **Entry** and **Reference** areas.

When you add an index entry, index markers (in your color of choice) flag that text so you know it's part of the index. If text is highlighted, the indexed text is enclosed in brackets. Otherwise, a little box is placed at the location of the text insertion bar.

Subentries

Once you have some **First Level** index entries, you can start creating subentries. Now's the time to consult your index mock-up. If you create a run-in index, you can place **Second Level** entries under the **First Level** entries, but you have to stop there. When you build a run-in index, the **Second Level** entries follow the **First Level** entry in paragraph form. If you create a nested index, your mock-up should show how many levels you can use. Although QuarkXPress allows up to four levels, you rarely see an index with more than three levels. When you build a nested index, the entries are placed hierarchically according to their level. (Usually each level is indicated by a deeper indent, but this depends on the design.)

Creating a subentry is almost the same as creating a **First Level** entry. You just need to pay special attention to where the entry will be placed.

To tag index subentries:

1. Specify which entry to place the new entry under. An arrow in the left column of the **Entries** area shows which index entry is selected. Click in the column to move the arrow to another entry (see Figure 24.10).

FIGURE 24.10

Click the arrow on the left side of the Entries area to indicate a location for a new subentry.

2. Assign a hierarchy to the entry by selecting an option from the **Level** menu in the **Entry** area (see Figure 24.11). The contents of the **Level** menu depend on the hierarchy of the selected index entry. For example, if the arrow is next to a **First Level** entry, only **First Level** and **Second Level** are available. (Therefore, the only way to create a **Fourth Level** index entry is to place the arrow next to a **Third Level** entry.)

FIGURE 24.11

Options in the **Level** menu become available according to the selected index entry. If a second level entry is available, **Third Level** is available, but not **Fourth Level**.

3. Use the **Text**, **Sort As**, **Style**, and **Scope** controls as for a **First Level** entry and then click **Add**.

The new entry is flagged with index markers in text and sorted alphabetically within its level in the Index palette.

Additional References to Entries

Once an entry is in the Index palette, you can build on it, adding more page number references as they occur in the document. One way you can do this is by creating and adding an entry the way you always do; QuarkXPress automatically combines the new entry with the existing entry. This works best for indexing individual highlighted words. The other way to do this is to set up a new entry, but ignore the contents of the **Text** field (even if highlighted text is in the field). Scroll through your index entries to find the entry you're adding this reference to and click on it. The text for that entry is automatically placed in the **Text** field. Click **Add**. This method ensures consistency among entries and saves you from typing in entries all the time.

When you add references to existing entries, pay special attention to the level setting and the location of the arrow. QuarkXPress won't (and shouldn't) combine references to entries from different levels. For example, if you tag another reference to the **First Level** entry "Bakeries," and the **Level** menu is set to **Second Level**, QuarkXPress creates a new **Second Level** entry called "Bakeries." If you do make a mistake, select the new entry and click the **Delete** button on the palette. You can't edit an entry's level.

Same Text Under Different Entries

QuarkXPress won't let you create two different index entries from the same selected text. For example, if you select the word "cake" and try to index it under the "Bakeries" and "Caterers" index entries, you can't do it. At least it seems that way.

You can index that text again, you just can't select it in exactly the same way. You can either select a smaller range of text within the brackets (in "cake" you can select "ak") or place the text insertion bar in the text. When you create a second entry from the same text, you may need to be more judicious about the **Scope**. If you were using **Selection Text**, you no longer have the same text selection, so if the text ends up breaking across two pages, your index entry won't pick that up. Normally, you'll only be indexing a few words this way so it's not a big concern.

Cross-References

Think of cross-references as just any other page number; all they do is link you to another entry that gives you a page number. For example, if you look up "Bakeries" and it says "See Caterers," you can expect (in a good index) to find a page number under "Caterers."

When you think of cross-references as a roundabout method for finding a page number, it makes sense that you make a cross-reference using the **Scope** menu in the Index palette. The **Scope** usually defines the range of text (and therefore pages) an entry covers. You can create new entries that are nothing but cross-references and you can create cross-references for existing entries. These steps include an example that cross-references the "Bakeries" entry to the "Caterers" entry in an existing index. The final index says "Bakeries. See also "Caterers."

To tag index cross-references:

1. Click anywhere in text. The location is meaningless because the entry sends readers somewhere else rather than providing page numbers.

2. Specify the index entry the cross-reference will be listed under by entering a new entry in the **Text** field or by clicking an existing entry. In this example, click "Bakeries" in the **Entries** list.

3. If creating a new entry to cross-reference, make sure the **Level** menu is set correctly.

4. In the **Reference** area, choose **X-Ref** from the **Scope** menu. A little menu appears next to it with the options **See**, **See also**, or **See herein**. **See** means "no information here, look at that other entry." **See also** means "here's some information, but you might find more under this other entry." **See herein** means "you're in the right entry, but look under this subentry." (If you need **See also herein**, just type "herein" in the field along with the cross-reference text.) In this example, choose **See also** because there is information under both entries.

5. Specify where this cross-reference is sending the reader by typing text in the small field next to the **X-Ref** menus or by clicking an existing entry. Clicking an existing entry is far safer because it guarantees that the entry the reader is being sent to actually exists. However, if the entry is in another chapter of a book, there's no choice but to type the entry. In the example, click the "Caterers" entry.

6. For punctuation after the cross-reference text in the index, enter it after the text in the field. (The punctuation preceding the cross-reference is specified in Index Preferences and added when you build the index.) For the example, type a period after the word "Caterers" in the field.

7. If the cross-reference text in this index is in a different style from the rest of the index text, apply one of your character style sheets to it. Choose an option from the **Style** menu.

The style applies to the text you enter in the field, not to the **See**, **See also**, or **See herein**. In the example, cross-references are formatted the same as the rest of the entry, so leave the setting at **Entry's Style**.

8. Click **Add**.

After you add a cross-reference, the text displays under the index entry. If necessary, click the triangle next to the entry to see the page numbers and cross-references (see Figure 24.12). To check which type of cross-reference it is (**See**, **See also**, **See herein**), select the reference text and consult the **Scope** menu. When you generate the formatted index, cross-references are placed after the page numbers listed for an entry.

FIGURE 24.12

A pop-up menu and field in the **Scope** area let you specify the text for a cross-reference.

Making "See," "See also," and "See herein" italic

In many indexes, the **See**, **See also**, or **See herein** part of a cross-reference sentence is in italics, whereas the referenced text is plain ("*See also* Caterers"). This is the exact opposite of what QuarkXPress would do if you chose an italic **Style** for the cross-reference ("See also *Caterers*"). If your index formatting calls for a different type style on **See**, **See also**, and **See herein**, use Find/Change in the final index to apply a character style sheet to those words to make them consistent.

Editing Index Entries

The **Edit** button, which looks like a pencil, on the Index palette allows you to edit the selected index entry or reference (page number or cross-reference). Select an entry or reference and click **Edit**; the icon is reversed to show that you're in edit mode. You can also double-click an entry or reference to activate edit mode.

You can edit the **Text** or **Sort As** information for an entry, but you can't edit the **Level**. (QuarkXPress lets you select another **Level**, but when you finish editing the entry, the **Level** menu snaps back to its previous setting.) For a reference, you can edit the **Style** or **Scope**. When you finish editing the entry or reference, click the **Edit** button again or press Return (Enter).

When you edit indexed text, it's a good idea to display the Index palette so you can see all the index markers. You'll want to be sure you're not indiscriminately deleting or changing indexed text. Keep in mind that index markers simply mark a location in text to provide a page number for the built index. Index markers have no idea what text is between them, so if you edit the text, you may need to edit the entry.

Say you select the word "Wedding" and index it as a **First Level** entry. Then you edit the text inside the index markers to say "Marriage." The entry in the Index palette still says "Wedding." If you have only one reference to the "Wedding" index entry, you can go ahead and edit the entry to say "Marriage." However, if there were more references to "Wedding," you might need to think about how to fix the situation. Does changing the index entry make sense for all the references? Or should you create two different index entries? That's why QuarkXPress doesn't link text in the document to index entries, and that's why you need to be careful about editing indexed text.

Deleting Index Entries

There are four options for deleting index entries: deleting text in the document, deleting individual references to index entries, deleting entire index entries, and deleting the contents of the Index palette.

- If you delete text in the document that contains index markers, that reference to the entry is removed from the Index palette. If you get down to the last occurrence of the entry in the text, and you delete that text, the entry is deleted entirely from the Index palette.

- If you want to delete an individual reference to an entry, select it and click the **Delete** button. (Click the triangle next to an entry to see the references.) The index markers are removed from that reference to the index entry. If that was the last reference to the index entry, the entry is removed as well.

- If you want to delete an entire index entry, including all its references, cross-references, and page numbers, select it and click **Delete**. Because this has the potential to delete a lot of your work, an alert asks you to confirm the deletion. All index markers associated with the deleted entries are removed.

- To get rid of existing index markers so you can start over, Option+Shift+click (Alt+Shift+click) the **Delete** button. This cleans out the Index palette and removes all index markers from text. This potentially dangerous action tosses up an alert so you can change your mind and cancel.

Indexing Tips and Tricks

Indexing can be tedious, but as you start working you'll find shortcuts that make it easy for you. Try these for starters:

- Give yourself space—on your desk and onscreen. If you refer to a hard copy word list, make room to spread it out. You might even want a hard copy of the entire publication to refer to while indexing each chapter electronically. In QuarkXPress, select the Content tool 🖑 and then hide all palettes except the Index palette. You won't need any other tools or controls. You can even gain a little space by hiding the rulers. Make room for your coffee cup, too—indexing can get more than a little boring.

- If you really want to index all instances of a word, or even variations of the word, you can use the Find/Change palette along with the Index palette. Set up the **Find** criteria, but don't settle for finding a simple word. Take advantage of the **Whole Word** and **Ignore Case** options, the wild card character, and even character attributes if possible. Click the **Find** button; text that matches the **Find** criteria is highlighted in the document. Set up the index entry correctly and click **Add**.

Now you're set to continue with a faster method. Press **Find** again. When you find an instance of the text you want to index, just press ⌘+Option+Shift+I (Ctrl+Alt+Shift+I) to add it to the index. If the index entry is defined the same way for the whole document, you can zip right through the index.

- When you index a name, you may want it to be listed last name first. For example, you'd index "Robert Andrew" as "Andrew, Robert." The only way to reverse the names in QuarkXPress is by cutting and pasting. When you do your cutting and pasting, make sure you don't leave any spaces before or after the index entry text. If you do, they'll appear in the index.

- Use keyboard commands for indexing: ⌘+Option+I (Ctrl+Alt+I) opens the Index palette or highlights the **Text** field (if it's already open). ⌘+Option+Shift+I (Ctrl+Alt+Shift+I) clicks the **Add** button. You can double-click to edit an index entry rather than clicking the **Edit** button. And, finally, you can Option+Shift+click (Alt+Shift+click) the **Delete** button to delete an entire index rather than deleting entries one by one.

- If you start from an existing index or a word list, you can bring that text into the Index palette. By importing it? No. It's pretty manual. Import or paste the text into a text box on the document's pasteboard. Create index entries from that text by highlighting the text and choosing the appropriate level. Use the **Suppress Page # Scope** for all the entries. Then, when you go through the document, add the new entries to the ones existing in the palette. When you finish, you can delete the text box on the pasteboard. Any entries that you didn't find in the document are deleted from the Index palette.

SEE ALSO

➤ *To find and change text, see page 212*

Generating a Formatted Index

Generating an index is relatively quick and painless, so you'll probably want to create several drafts throughout the indexing process. You might create one as soon as you have some text tagged just to confirm that your master page, style sheets, and punctuation all work together to produce the desired results. Later, you might start checking for inconsistencies, repetition, and so on. (One thing you can be assured of is that you don't need to check page numbering; QuarkXPress is not going to pull the wrong automatic page numbers for an index entry.)

When you do build the index, QuarkXPress takes the master page you select and flows the text into it while applying the correct paragraph and character style sheets. The result is just text on a page; the index is not linked to the document so it will not update automatically if you update the text in the indexed documents.

Setting Preferences for Index Punctuation

When you build an index, QuarkXPress automatically inserts punctuation according to your Index preferences (for example, it can insert commas in a list of page numbers). Index preferences are saved with each document. When you build an index, QuarkXPress uses the Index preferences from the active document (see Figure 24.13).

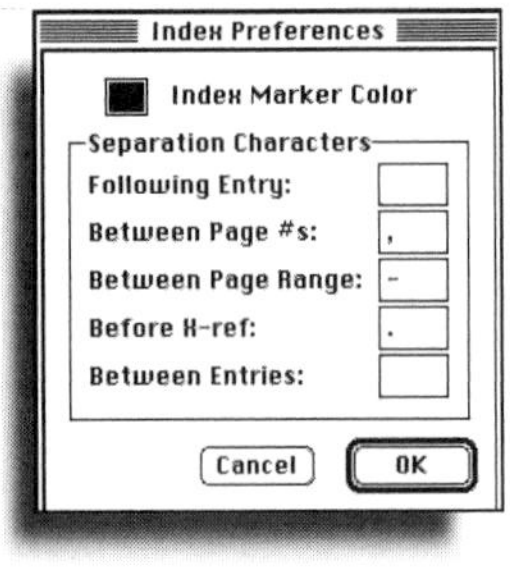

FIGURE 24.13

Use the Index Preferences dialog box to specify the punctuation used in your index.

Use the fields in the **Separation Characters** area to specify the punctuation. As the area name indicates, you're not limited to punctuation. You can use words and phrases, for example, you might use the word "to" between a range of page numbers rather than an en dash.

The **Separation Characters** fields also accept special characters, including en dashes, nonbreaking dashes, and nonbreaking spaces. Speaking of spaces, you must enter any spaces preceding or following characters in the fields along with the punctuation or text. (Don't get too carried away with nonbreaking spaces and dashes; if you glue all the text together none of it will display.) You can even enter invisible characters such as tabs or paragraph returns in the fields. Just use the same symbol that displays in the Find/Change palette for the symbol (for example, \t for tab or \p for paragraph return).

This is the time to consult your index mock-up; it should show you how to set up the punctuation for the index. You have the following options for **Separation Characters**:

- **Following Entry** defines the characters after an individual index entry, usually a comma or a colon followed by a space (Weddings: 16).

- **Between Page #s** defines the characters that separate a list of page numbers, usually a comma followed by a space (Weddings: 16, 23, 30).

- **Between Page Range** defines the characters that indicate a range of page numbers, usually a hyphen or en dash (Weddings: 16–30).

- **Before X-Ref** defines the characters that precede a cross reference, usually a period followed by a space (Weddings:16, 23, 30. See also Ceremonies). If no page numbers follow an index entry, the **Before X-Ref** punctuation is used in place of the **Following Entry** punctuation (Weddings. See also Ceremonies).

    Remember that the punctuation following a cross-reference should be entered in the **X-Ref** field of the Index palette.

- **Between Entries** defines the characters between index entries in a run-in index, usually a semicolon or period followed by a space. If you specify **Between Entries** characters for a nested index, those characters are placed at the end of every paragraph in the index (which will amount to almost every line).

SEE ALSO

➤ *To change Index preferences, see page 72*

Building the Index

If you prepared an index mock-up, including its style sheets and master pages, building an index is a breeze. If you didn't, once you take a look at the Build Index dialog box, you'll probably cancel out and go do that. Without the proper style sheets, you can't even build a draft index that makes sense. Have your index mock-up on hand when you build the index.

If you're going to build an index for a book, open the book and make sure all the chapters are **Available**. Make sure the book's master chapter includes all the index style sheets (append them from your mock-up index if necessary) and then synchronize the book. Open the chapter that will include the index.

To build a formatted index:

1. Confirm the Index preferences for the active document. The index will be placed in this document.

2. Select **Build Index** from the **Utilities** menu (see Figure 24.14).

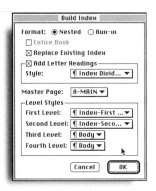

FIGURE 24.14

The Build Index dialog box is where you choose a master page and paragraph style sheets for your index.

3. Select the **Format** of your index: **Nested** or **Run-in**. If your index includes more than two levels of information, click **Nested**.

4. To create an index for the entire book, check **Entire Book**.

5. If you already created a version of the index in this document, check **Replace Existing Index**. There's not much

reason to remove the check mark from this; perhaps you might be comparing two versions of the same index.

6. To insert alphabetic dividers in the index (A, B, C, and so on), check **Add Letter Headings** and select the appropriate paragraph style sheet.

7. Select the **Master Page** created for the index. The **Master Page** menu lists only master pages that include automatic text boxes.

8. Select paragraph style sheets from the **Level Styles** menus to specify how the text for each level of the index is formatted. When you create a run-in index, all the levels under each entry are flowed into the same paragraph. Therefore, you can select only a **First Level** style.

9. Click **OK**.

QuarkXPress extracts all the index information from the current document or all the chapters in the open book. All the index information is combined and sorted. Then, QuarkXPress inserts pages, beginning with a right-facing page, at the end of the active document. The pages are not linked to the current text chain; the index is always in its own text chain. Finally, QuarkXPress capitalizes the first word of each index entry, formats each entry according to the specified paragraph style sheets, applies character style sheets to references as specified in the Index palette, and inserts separation characters defined in the Index Preferences dialog box. Once the index is complete, save the document (see Figure 24.15).

SEE ALSO

➤ *To append styles from a document, see page 146*

Reviewing Your Final Index

The great thing about indexing electronically is you can change the content of your documents any time and create a new index with updated entries and page numbers. The fact that the page numbers will always be correct doesn't mean you don't have to review the index. You have two important areas to check: content and style.

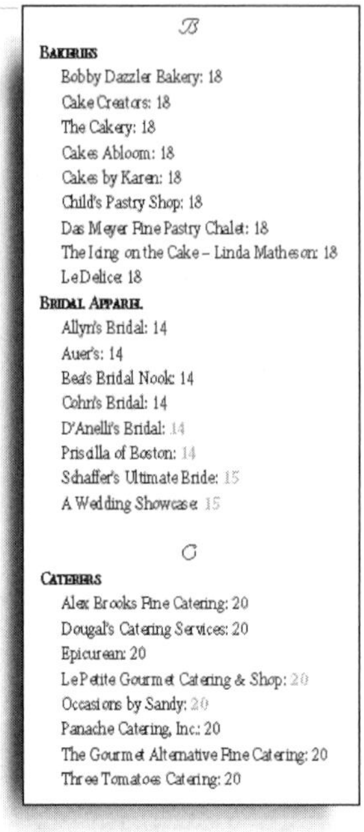

FIGURE 24.15

If you created a mock-up of your index, prepared a master page and paragraph style sheets, and set up the punctuation in the Index Preferences dialog box, your final index should look very similar to your mock-up.

B

BAKERIES
  Bobby Dazzler Bakery: 18
  Cake Creators: 18
  The Cakery: 18
  Cakes Abloom: 18
  Cakes by Karen: 18
  Child's Pastry Shop: 18
  Das Meyer Fine Pastry Chalet: 18
  The Icing on the Cake – Linda Matheson: 18
  Le Delice: 18
BRIDAL APPAREL
  Allyn's Bridal: 14
  Auer's: 14
  Bea's Bridal Nook: 14
  Cohn's Bridal: 14
  D'Anelli's Bridal: 14
  Priscilla of Boston: 14
  Schaffer's Ultimate Bride: 15
  A Wedding Showcase: 15

C

CATERERS
  Alex Brooks Fine Catering: 20
  Dougal's Catering Services: 20
  Epicurean: 20
  Le Petite Gourmet Catering & Shop: 20
  Occasions by Sandy: 20
  Panache Catering, Inc.: 20
  The Gourmet Alternative Fine Catering: 20
  Three Tomatoes Catering: 20

Index Content

As soon as you have an entire document or all the chapters in a book tagged for the index, you should build a draft to review. Give it good overview—is it way too long or obviously too short? Are any topics completely missing from the index? Look for long lists of references under individual entries; you don't want to send readers to 30 places in a book. Then start reviewing the index line by line. Make sure all the cross-references actually go somewhere and that subentries aren't too repetitive. Check the way entries sort: Look for names that should have been last name first, punctuation that's interfering with sorting, and entries that start with articles. Mark any problems on a hard copy of the index.

If you see any dagger (Mac OS) or **PB** (Windows) symbols instead of page numbers in the index, you have indexed text that will not print. The text may be on the pasteboard, overflowing its box, or obscured by another item. Mark these instances in the index and see if the problems need to be solved in the document.

In the unlikely case that the hidden indexed text is intentional, you can delete the daggers or **PB**s from the index. You can use Find/Change to make sure you resolved all instances of hidden indexed text. (On Mac OS, press Option+T to enter the dagger in the **Find** field. On Windows, just enter the text "PB" in the **Find** field.)

After you review the index content, don't edit the built index. Go back to each chapter or the document and change the way it's indexed. Rebuild and review the index as often as you need to.

Style

If you worked from an index mock-up while using the Index XTension, your built index is likely to be perfectly formatted and easy to read. If it's not, experiment with editing the paragraph and character style sheets in the built index. If you index a book and change the style sheets, be sure to synchronize the book. If the index pages are crowded looking, you might need to revise the index master page or create a new one. If the punctuation is a problem, change it in Index Preferences. Some style issues, such as the style of page numbers, require changes to the indexing in the document. Rebuild the index each time you want to see the results of your changes.

After the content and style of the index are final, you can get to fine-tuning. This means local formatting, applying special case type styles, changing line breaks, changing column breaks, combining letter headings with only a few entries, and so on. In a long index, this work is tedious, so make sure you're working on the final index. If you build the index again, all your local formatting will be lost.

Glossary

8-bit Video that uses 8 binary characters to represent each color on a computer monitor; allows for 256 different colors.

16-bit Video that uses 16 binary characters to represent each color on a computer monitor; allows for 65,536 different colors.

24-bit Video that uses 24 binary characters to represent each color on a computer monitor; allows for 16,777,216 different colors.

absolute page numbers Numbers representing each page's position in a document; the fifth page in a document has an absolute page number of 5, regardless of its *section page number*.

additive color Colors created by combining different colors of light; if all possible colors are added together, they make white light.

agates Measurement unit used by in advertising; an agate line is 1/14th of an inch.

alpha channel Non-printing *grayscale channel* stored in a raster image file that can be used to mask parts of the image.

anchored Attached to a text flow; anchored frames are boxes pasted into a text flow like text characters.

append Import from another document.

ascenders The parts of letterforms that rise above the *x-height*, such as the tall stems of "h" and "k."

ascent The height of the ascenders in text, which is often slightly higher than *cap height*.

ASCII American Standard Code for Information Interchange; a file format that can contain only plain text, with no formatting.

auto leading Line spacing determined automatically by the *point size* of the text being spaced.

Auto Page Insertion QuarkXPress feature that adds pages automatically when text becomes too long to fit in the existing text boxes.

automatic page number Special character that displays and prints as the appropriate *section page number* when used on a *document page*.

automatic text box   Text box placed on a master page that allows *Auto Page Insertion* to take place when the length of the document's text exceeds the size of the available text boxes.

auxiliary dictionary   Spell checking dictionary that can be added to and edited by the user.

background color   The color of a box, as opposed to the color of its contents or border.

banding   Bands of color seen in blends when printed on low-resolution printers.

banner   The flag or nameplate of a publication, showing its name in a distinctive type.

baseline   The invisible line on which the bottoms of letters sit and below which *descenders* fall.

baseline grid   Regular series of non-printing horizontal guides that can be used to place elements on a page

Bézier   Method of describing curves mathematically; in practice, Bézier curves are manipulated by moving their endpoints and moving *control points* that aren't on the curve at all.

bitmap   Graphic composed of a grid of dots, each of which can be only one color. Enlarging a bitmap graphic makes the dots larger and more apparent.

bitmap frames   Custom *frames* created using the Frame Editor application.

bleed   Extend off the edge of a page.

blend   Background composed of one color fading into another.

bold   Letterforms that are heavier and thicker than normal (*roman*) letters.

book   File containing references to multiple component files, called chapters, that allows users to print and renumber pages in the chapters without opening the individual files.

border   See *frame*.

box   A shape that can contain a picture (*picture box*), text (*text box*), or nothing (*no-content box*).

cap height   The height of capital letters.

channel   Grayscale image that makes up one component of a color image; each color (red, green, and blue, or cyan, magenta, yellow, and black) is represented by a channel, and other channels are called *alpha channels*.

character style sheet   Named set of type specifications (such as color, size, and font) that can be applied to selected text on a character level.

choke   Extend surrounding color into a surrounded area of another color to avoid paper show-through during printing.

cicero   A unit of measurement equal to about 13 points or 2/11ths of an inch.

Clipboard   A location within the system software where information copied or cut from a document is temporarily stored.

clipping path A *Bézier* path that can determine what parts of an image are printed and what parts are suppressed.

CMYK Cyan, magenta, yellow, and black, the four *process colors*.

color correction Alteration of color as it's being displayed or printed to more closely match a given standard.

color depth The number of bits used to define the color of each pixel in a displayed image.

color management Software system to improve display and output of color.

color matching system Combination of pre-defined colors and a printed swatchbook showing those colors, used to choose predictable colors for use in a design.

color model Method of defining color, such as *CMYK*, *RGB*, or *HSB*.

color proof Color printout that is close enough to the final on-press outcome that it can be used to decide on which colors will be used.

color separation The conversion of a color image into four grayscale images, each representing one of the four process colors, which will be printed with the four process inks to recreate the color image.

compound picture box A picture box composed of multiple component boxes.

constrain Force to remain symmetrical; holding down the Shift key while resizing a rectangular box, for example, forces the box to become a square.

contrast The difference between light and dark areas of an image.

control point The end of an imaginary "lever" that can be moved to adjust a curved segment in a *Bézier* shape.

corner point Point on a *Bézier* shape with straight segments on one or both sides of it.

creep The fact that when pages are folded together and trimmed, the inner pages will appear to have smaller outside margins than the outer pages—the text area of the page appears to "creep" outward.

crop Delete or suppress printing of areas of an image.

crop marks Lines outside the trim area of a page indicating where that trim area falls; also called trim marks.

cross-reference Index entry that refers to another entry rather than to document page numbers.

curve handle See *control point*.

curved segment A section of a *Bézier* shape that curves, so that the points on either side of it have *control points* that can be used to adjust the curve.

Dashes & Stripes Named custom line and frame styles.

DCS Desktop Color Separation, a pre-*color-separated* image file format related to *EPS*.

device profile File containing information about how a particular device (such as a scanner, monitor, or printer) represents color.

dingbat   Decorative type character, such as a square or round bullet, as opposed to a text character.

discretionary hyphen   Special character that, depending on its position within a word, keeps the word from hyphenating or forces it to hyphenate at a particular spot; if the word doesn't fall at the end of a line, the discretionary hyphen character doesn't show.

document page   Page contained in the body of a document, as opposed to a non-printing *master page*.

dots per inch   A measure of *resolution*; the higher the number of dots per inch (dpi), the higher the resolution of an image and the larger its file.

downsample   Reduce the number of *pixels* in an image so that its *resolution* is lower.

dpi   see *dots per inch*.

drop cap   A large capital letter whose *baseline* sits on the second or a subsequent line of the text it introduces.

drum scanner   A device used to transfer image information from an original attached to a rotating drum inside the scanner to a digital format.

duotone   Grayscale image whose midtones (medium gray tones) are replaced by a color, making it a two-color image.

dynamic range   The range of brightness levels contained in an image or discernible by a scanner.

em dash   A dash the same width as an *em space*.

em space   Space equal, in theory, to the width of a capital "M"; the size of an em space in QuarkXPress is either the width of a two zeroes or a number of points equal to the *point size*.

embed   Copy into a document; text is embedded in QuarkXPress documents, but pictures are not.

en dash   A dash the same width as an *en space*, wider than a hyphen but narrower than an *em dash*.

en space   Space equal, in theory, to the width of a capital "N"; the size of an en space in QuarkXPress is either the width of a zero or a number of points equal to half the *point size*.

endcap   Shape used for the ends of a line, such as an arrow.

endpoints   Points indicating the ends of a line or curve.

EPS   Encapsulated PostScript image, consisting of PostScript data in a form that can be referenced by other programs than the originating one, thus allowing the image to be imported by other programs.

export   Transfer data from one document to another, generally in a different format.

facing-page document   One that contains pages specified as left and right.

filter   Software designed to convert data from one type, such as a Microsoft Word text file, to another, such as QuarkXPress text.

flatbed scanner   A device similar to a photocopier used to transfer image information from an original laid on the scanner's bed to a digital format.

flex space   A user-defined space character of any width from 1% to 400% of a word space.

fold lines   Dashed rules indicating where printed output should be folded by the printer or bindery.

folio   Page number.

footer   information placed at the bottom of each page in a design, often including a title and a folio.

four-color process   Printing process using four colors of ink—cyan, magenta, yellow, and black.

FPO   For position only; generally, a low-resolution image is marked FPO to indicate that it should be replaced during the production process by a high-resolution image.

frame   A rule, whether simple or complex, around the edge of a *box*.

gamut   The range of colors a particular device can reproduce.

gap color   Color displayed between *rules* or dashes in a complex *frame*.

gradient   See *blend*.

gray levels   Shades of gray in an image.

grayscale   An image type that contains black, white, and shades of gray.

greek   Display text or pictures as gray boxes to speed up screen redraw.

grid   Geometric plan for a design that includes a specified number of columns and horizontal areas on a page.

group   Multiple objects that can be moved and resized as one.

guide   Non-printing colored line on a page or on the pasteboard that can be used to place objects.

gutter   In reference to columns, the space between them; in reference to facing pages, the inner margin.

H&Js   Named groups of settings controlling hyphenation and justification.

hairline   A thin rule, traditionally set as the thinnest rule a particular output device can print.

halftone   A printed image formed of thousands or even millions of tiny dots.

hanging indent   Indent applied to the second and subsequent lines of a paragraph, so that the first line projects to the left of the other lines.

header   Information placed at the top of each page in a design, often including a title and a folio.

Hexachrome   Pantone's HiFi color system, which uses intensified versions of the four process ink colors and adds green and orange for a greater range of achievable colors.

HiFi color   Various methods of printing more true-to-life color images, including improved screening methods and added color inks, such as Pantone's Hexachrome system.

High Fidelity color   See *HiFi color*.

high resolution   Image containing a large number of *dots per inch*.

highlight   Light areas of an image.

HSB   Hue, Saturation, Brightness; a system of defining colors based on their hue, the intensity of the hue, and the amount of white in the color.

HTML   HyperText Markup Language, the coding system used to format text for the World Wide Web.

hyphenation   Automatic addition of hyphens to words broken at the end of a line of text.

hyphenation exceptions   A user-specified list of words that should be hyphenated a particular way or not hyphenated at all.

imagesetter   High-resolution output device that can print on film or paper.

import   Copy into another file; imported text in a QuarkXPress document is *embedded* in the document, while only a low-resolution preview of imported images is *embedded.*

imposition   The arrangement of pages on printing plates such that when printed, folded, and bound, the pages will appear in the correct order.

indeterminate   Term used to describe objects whose color QuarkXPress can't determine, such as imported photographs.

index marker   Non-printing indicator applied to text that will be referenced in an index.

initial cap   Large or decorative capital letter used to at the beginning of a document, chapter, or section.

interlinear spacing   See *leading*.

italic   Letterforms that are slightly cursive in form and tilted to the right.

JPEG   Joint Photographic Experts Group, an image file format that can be highly compressed to yield extremely small files, but that removes data from the image to do so.

jumpline   A line of text referring the reader to another page.

justification   The automatic addition of small amounts of space between letters and words to align the text with both left and right margins.

kerning   Manual addition or reduction of space between characters to produce optimal visual spacing.

kerning table   Set of values indicating how individual letter pairs should be kerned.

knockout   Colored area that isn't printed because another colored object is in front of it in the document.

LAB   Method of describing colors that uses one brightness value and two different, interacting hue values.

landscape   The horizontal orientation of a page, such that it's wider than it is tall.

leading   The distance from the baseline of one line of text to the baseline of the line above it.

letterform   The shape of a text character.

library   A file containing QuarkXPress objects that can be copied or dragged into document files without affecting the originals.

ligature   Text character made by combining two or more other characters, such as "ff" or "ffi."

line   Curved or straight shape defined by two *endpoints*.

line art   *Imported* picture containing only black and white, with no color or gray shades.

line color   Color of the *rules* or dashes in a complex *frame*.

list   Text extracted from a document or documents because it has a specified *paragraph style sheet* applied to it; tables of contents can be created by generating lists of all the text that uses chapter number and chapter title *style sheets*.

local items   Objects created and placed on a document page, as opposed to *master page items*.

low resolution   Image containing a small number of *dots per inch*.

lpi   Lines per inch; the frequency of the dots used to make a *halftone*.

luminosity   The brightness of a color.

mailing indicia   The symbols and text required by the postal service to be placed on bulk mail.

margin guides   Non-printing, stationary guides indicating the margin measurements entered when a document was created.

marquee   To select objects by clicking outside the group and dragging with the mouse until the visible rectangle (marquee) indicating the selected area encompasses all the objects.

master chapter   The chapter from which all others take their *master pages, style sheets*, and so on when a *book* is *synchronized*; by default, the first chapter added to a *book*.

master document   See *master chapter*.

master page   Non-printing pages in a document whose design is reproduced on any *document pages* to which they're applied.

master page items   Objects placed on a document page by virtue of the master page applied to that page.

multi-ink color   A color that combines process and spot inks, or multiple spot inks.

nested index   Index in which subentries follow main entries on subsequent lines rather than on the same line.

no-content box   A box that can't contain text or pictures; used only as a graphic element in itself.

nonbreaking space   A space character that cannot be separated from the words on either side of it.

Nonmatching Preferences alert   Dialog box that appears when a document's preferences don't match the application preferences associated with a particular copy of QuarkXPress.

object color   The frontmost of two or more colors to be *trapped*.

oblique   Letterforms that are tilted to the right without being *italic*.

old-style numerals   Number characters that sit at different levels, rather than all on the baseline.

OLE   Object Linking and Embedding; Windows-native method of linking imported images to their originating files so that when the original is altered, the imported image updates automatically.

OPI   Open Prepress Interface; a system that allows *low-resolution* images to be replaced with *high-resolution* versions of the same images as the document is printed.

orientation   Direction of the long axis of a page; see also *landscape* and *portrait*.

orphan   The first line of a paragraph falling at the bottom of a page.

overprint   To print one ink color on top of a second ink color.

page guides   *Guides* that run across one page on a *spread* and not across the *pasteboard* or the other page.

Pantone   Company that produces *color matching systems* for choosing colors.

paragraph rule   Rule automatically placed above or below a paragraph that flows with the text.

paragraph style sheet   Named set of type specifications (such as font, leading, and tab stops) that can be applied to selected text on a paragraph level.

pasteboard   The area surrounding document or master pages; objects on the pasteboard will not be printed.

path   *Bézier* line.

PCX   Image file format used by the PC Paintbrush program.

PDF   Portable Document Format, the format used by Adobe Acrobat documents.

perforation lines   Dashed rules indicating where printed output should be perforated by the printer or bindery.

Photo CD   Image file format created by Kodak for use with its proprietary scanning and compact disc storage system.

pica   Unit of measurement equal to 72 points or 1/6th of an inch.

PICT   Image file format used by Mac OS computers; the native format of the Mac OS.

picture box   *Box* of any shape that contains an imported picture.

pixel   Picture element; a single dot of colored light on a computer monitor.

placed   A file that is referred to in but not copied into another document, as opposed to *embedded* files.

plate   Sheet of metal, polyester, or other material that determines what areas of a sheet of paper are inked and what areas are not during the printing process.

PMS   Pantone Matching System, a color matching system for spot colors.

point   A unit of measurement equal to 1/72nd of an inch; also, a handle by which a *Bézier* shape can be altered.

point size   The size of type measured in points; generally, the type actually measures less than the nominal point size, because the point size is based on the size of blocks of old-style metal type rather than the height of the letters themselves.

portrait   The vertical orientation of a page, such that it's taller than it is wide.

PostScript   A page description language used by printers and *imagesetters*.

PostScript file   A file that can be transmitted to a printer and output regardless of whether the user has the original application or fonts used to create the document printed.

PostScript Type 1   Font format in which screen and printer versions are contained in separate files.

PPD   File that describes the characteristics and features of a particular printer model.

preflight   Make sure a file is optimized for printing, with all fonts and imported graphics present, all colors correctly defined, and so on.

print style   Named group of printer settings within QuarkXPress.

printer's spreads   Page spreads set up such that the correct pages will face each other after a document is printed, folded, and bound.

process color   Color created from a combination of the four process ink colors cyan, magenta, yellow, and black.

profile   See *device profile*.

Publish and Subscribe   Mac OS-native method of linking imported images to their originating files so that when the original is altered, the imported image updates automatically.

pull quotes   Short sections of an article or other text used as a graphic element, generally in larger type than the body text.

QuarkImmedia   Multimedia design XTension.

rag   Pattern formed by the non-straight edge of left-justified or right-justified text.

reader's spreads   Page spreads set up such that the correct pages face each other within a document.

reflow   See *text reflow*.

register   Alignment of multiple colors printed on the same page.

registration   See *register*.

registration marks   Symbols printed outside the trim area of a page and used to align the multiple color plates needed in color printing.

resolution   The frequency of dots used to represent an image; a 300 *dpi* image is composed of tiny dots placed on a grid at the rate of 300 per inch in each direction.

RGB Red, green, and blue, the colors of light used to display color images on-screen.

rich black A black made up of black ink combined with another ink color such as magenta or cyan to give it added richness.

right-indent tab A character that pushes any text following it on a line over to the right margin.

RIP Raster image processor, the software and hardware combination that converts PostScript printing data into dots placed on a page by a printer or imagesetter.

river A lengthy vertical or diagonal area of white space produced by the position of works in a text flow.

roman Not *italic* or *bold*.

RTF Rich Text Format, a text coding system invented by Microsoft and used to translate text from format to another.

rule See *line*.

ruler guides Movable non-printing guides placed on a page by clicking and dragging on the *rulers*.

rulers A measurement scale along the top and left sides of a document window; rulers can be displayed or hidden as the user prefers.

run-in head Heading followed by body text on the same line.

run-in index Index in which subentries follow main entries on the same line rather than on subsequent lines.

runaround Text forced to flow around, instead of over, an obstructing object.

runaround path *Bézier* path used to indicate where text should flow around an image.

screen angle Angle at which a grid of *halftone* dots is placed; different colors printed on the same page need to be printed at different angles to avoid unattractive patterns.

screen resolution Number of *pixels* per inch on a monitor.

section page number Number assigned to a page via a *section start* rather than by virtue of its position in the document.

section start Page on which page numbering is started at different number than the page would ordinarily page.

segment Section of a *Bézier* shape between two points.

serif Type that has small crosspieces at the ends of strokes; each crosspiece is called a serif.

service bureau Company that specializes in printing and scanning files for others.

shade Color used at less than 100% intensity.

shadow Dark areas of an image.

silhouette Outline an object in an image so that the rest of the image does not display or print.

single-sided Document that does not use *facing pages*.

skew   Tilt the top of a shape to the left or right without moving the bottom.

small caps   Letters shaped like capital letters but sized like lower-case letters.

smart space   Space inserted by QuarkXPress after a word if you paste it into existing text.

smooth point   Point on a *Bézier* shape with curves on either side of it.

snap to   "Gravity" effect in which objects moved within a specified distance of a guide are pulled to the guide.

soft return   Key combination that forces text to a new line without creating a new paragraph.

spine   The edge of a book or magazine formed from the edges of the bound pages.

spot color   Color which, when printed, will be produced by one color of ink instead of a combination of inks.

spread   Two or more *facing pages*.

spread guides   *Guides* that run across both pages on a *spread* and across the *pasteboard*.

stacking   Layering order of objects on a page, based on the order in which they were created.

stochastic screening   Method of creating a halftone screen with randomly placed dots, rather than ones on a grid.

story   Text contained in one *text box* or a series of linked text boxes.

straight segments   Non-curved portions of a *Bézier* shape.

style sheet   Named set of type settings, for either character or paragraph attributes, that can be applied to text all at once by choosing the style sheet.

subscript   Character placed below the baseline and generally smaller than surrounding text.

subtractive color   Colors created by combining different colors of pigment; to get white, all color must be removed, or subtracted.

superior   Small character raised above the baseline such that its cap height aligns with the cap height of the larger text surrounding it.

superscript   Character placed above the baseline and generally smaller than surrounding text.

swatchbook   Printed sample book of colors in a *color matching system*.

symmetrical point   Point on a *Bézier* shape with symmetrical curves on either side of it.

synchronize   Adjust master pages, style sheets, and other attributes of individual chapters in a book to match those in the *master chapter*.

tab leader   Multiples of the same character displayed along the width of a tab character, such as the dots that often run from a chapter title to its page number in a table of contents.

template   QuarkXPress file that creates an identical unnamed file when opened.

text box   *Box* of any shape that contains text.

text chain   Text contained in a series of linked *text boxes*.

text insertion bar   Cursor indicating that letters typed on the keyboard will be inserted at the cursor's location.

text path   Curved or straight line along which text can be placed.

text reflow   Change in the length of a section of text due to a change in its attributes, such as its *point size* or font.

thumbnail drag   Copy pages from one document to another by placing both in thumbnail view and dragging pages between document windows.

thumbnail view   View percentage of a document equivalent to about 10 percent, at which individual objects can't be selected, only pages.

TIFF   Tag Image File Format, a bitmap image format.

tiling   Printing a large page on multiple smaller sheets of paper so that a full-size proof can be assembled by attaching the individual "tiles."

tint   See *shade*.

tracking   Spacing between letters; tracking can be applied on a case-by-case basis or globally via tracking tables.

tracking table   Set of values indicating how type should be spaced at various sizes.

trapping   Adjusting the shapes of colored objects on a page where they touch each other so that the paper will not show through if the colors don't align correctly during printing.

trim lines   Rules indicating where printed output should be cut by the printer or bindery.

trim size   The final size of a document once it is printed and trimmed according to the crop marks.

TrueType   Font format containing both screen and printer versions of a font in a single file.

TruMatch   Color matching system containing colors that can be created from the four *process* inks.

typographers' quotes   Properly shaped and oriented quotation marks, as opposed to *straight quotes*.

URL   Uniform resource locator—the "address" of a page on the World Wide Web.

view percentage   Size of a document viewed on-screen relative to the document's actual size, 100 percent.

widow   The last line of a paragraph falling at the top of a page.

x coordinate   Position relative to the zero point on the horizontal ruler.

x,y coordinates   Position relative to both the horizontal and vertical rulers, with the *x coordinate* always given first.

x-height   The height of lower-case letters, about halfway between the *baseline* and *cap height*.

XPress Tags   Coding language that can be used to represent text style attributes in text imported into or exported from QuarkXPress.

XTension   Software that adds features to QuarkXPress

y coordinate   Position relative to the zero point on the vertical ruler.

Index